THEY SAY IF I KEEP SINNIN' THAT I'M A DIE 'CAUSE I'M RIDING. AND THEM THINGS KEEP SPINNIN'.
I'M DRESSED IN THE BEST LINEN. AFTER THE CASH. THE POWER AND WOMEN. FEEL ME.
THAT'S THE ONLY LIFE I KNOW. ONCE AGAIN HUSTLING. WATCH ME BLOW. THAT THUG LIFE DEEP IN MY BONES
FROM A LITTLE HUSTLER TO GANGSTER FULL BLOWN.
SO NOW THAT I'M GROWN. I CALL THE STREETS MY HOME. THEY'RE THE ONLY ONES
THAT SHOW ME LOVE TILL I'M GONE.
IF SOMETHING GOES DOWN. THEN IT'S ON. MY NEIGHBORHOOD SAYIN' I'M BAD TO THE BONE.
I REALLY DON'T WANNA DIE. BUT I THINK THAT IT'S COMIN'.
I'D RATHER BE GUNNIN' INSTEAD OF RUNNIN'.
SOMEBODY PLEASE PRAY FOR ME. THIS MIGHT BE THE LAST DAY FOR ME. AND THAT'S REAL.

I WON'T HIDE BEHIND DANCERS OR FAKE IMAGE ENHANCERS.
ALL I WANTED WAS A CHANCE TO BE ME. AN MC.
'CAUSE THIS RAP THING IS GRIMY. BORDERLINE HAZARDOUS. I'M BRINGING IT BACK TO LIFE LIKE CHRIST DID LAZARUS.
HAVE YOU HAD A NAZARITE BRING YOU BACK FROM A TRAGIC DEATH?
AND ROCK SHALOM WHILE OTHERS ROCK THE CHROME?
I'M TIRED OF SEEING INTELLECT OOZE OUT YOUR DOME. STREET BRILLIANCE ALWAYS CHASING STREET MILLIONS
BUT PLANS GET THWARTED 'CAUSE DEATH IS REWARDED. THE PRICE IS YOUR LIFE. AHHH COULDN'T AFFORD IT.
THE LAMB'S BOOK OF LIFE. AHH. WASN'T RECORDED. JUDGMENT'S COMING AFTER RIGOR MORTIS.
CAN'T KEEP TREATING THIS LIFE LIKE A TOILET.
HERE COMES THE FLUSH. WATCH YOUR SOUL GET CRUSHED.
NOW YOU'RE NUMB LIKE YOUR COCAINE FROM ALL OF YOUR PAIN.
BUT HE'LL FREE YOU FROM YOUR SHAME AND THE SIN WITHIN.
SO YOU GO FROM HAVING NO NAME TO CHRIST KNOWING YOUR NAME.
AND YOU AND MY GOD CAN BE FRIENDS AGAIN. WHOA!

IT'S REAL SON. REAL ONES. REAL GUNS. REAL NIGHTS. REAL FIGHTS. REAL LIFE.
TAKEN WITH THAT STEEL.
REAL LIVES. REAL HIGHS. REAL NINES. REAL CRIMES. REALIZE LIL HOMEY AND TELL ME WHAT'S REAL.

IT'S REAL SON. REAL ONES. REAL GUNS. REAL NIGHTS. REAL FIGHTS. REAL LIFE.
TAKEN WITH THAT STEEL. REAL LIVES. REAL HIGHS. REAL NINES. REAL CRIMES.
REALIZE LIL HOMEY AND TELL ME WHAT'S REAL.

real

The Complete New Testament

NCV
NEW CENTURY VERSION®

NELSON BIBLES
A Division of Thomas Nelson Publishers
Since 1798

www.thomasnelson.com

REAL: THE NEW TESTAMENT

The preliminary research and development of the New Century Version was done by the World Bible Translation Center, Inc., Fort Worth, TX 76182.

Managing Company: Soul Publishing, Inc.
Managing Editors: Michele Clark Jenkins and Stephanie Perry Moore
Project Manager: Brenda Noel
Cover Models: Josh Alston, Gomeyz Givens, Shanika Mitchell, John Moorer, Jonathan Rainey, and Joanna Robinson
Cover Stylist: Tanya Chavis
Cover Photo: Albert B. Cooper
Cover Design: Marc Whitaker

Interior Photography: Andrew Brezinski, Albert Cooper and Roger Cannon
Interior Layout and Design: Heather Dryden
Interior Design Manager: Brecca Theele
Line and Copy Editors: Joyce Dinkins, Joan Guest and Linda Taylor

Content Review: Bishop Kenneth C. Ulmer, Pastor Tommy Kyllonen, John W. Moorer and Dean Heath.

Contributors: Josh Alston, Daven Baptiste, Winnie Clark-Jenkins, John F. Dilworth II, Deljah Dixon, Donna I. Douglas, John Fichtner, Quisa Foster, Derwin Gray, Rachelle Guillory, James Guitard, Dean Heath, Keren Heath, Phil Jackson, Terrance Johnson, Tommy Kyllonen, G. Craige Lewis, Fred Lynch, Markesha McWilliams, Derrick Moore, John W. Moorer, Victoria Christopher Murray, Kendra Norman-Bellamy, Mike Parker, Paula Parker, Cedric Perry, Joannna Robinson, Naomi Shedd, Catina Slade, Dr. Kenneth C. Ulmer, Michael Woodard, Platinum Souls and Jonathan Rainey.

God Unit & Jail's No Joke writers have been concealed.

We are grateful to Bishop Joseph Garlington and Bishop Kenneth C. Ulmer for their advice and guidance.

Special thanks to Mel Banks Jr., Randall Barrett, Andrew Brezinski, Jenell Clark, Nichole Duncan, Wayne Hastings, Jessie Hightower, Kym Jenkins, Jack Lyons, Adria Miller, Sheldyn Moore, Brandy Murray, Cynthia Peace, Amandi Rhett, Randy Roberts, Yolanda Robinson, Ulysses Salett, Pierre Salmon, Bob Sanford and Laurie Whaley.

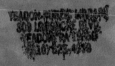

Note From the Co-Editor
Starting out real

Starting out real, let me tell you what this is and why we put it out there. Real is the entire New Testament Bible in a format that is meant to be familiar to you. The articles that surround the Bible text were written for the playa who may be familiar with the Bible and probably spent some time up in church, but who wants to get a better hold on what the point of it all is.

Real is meant to get you thinking about eternity in terms of the here and now. It's meant to answer the question, "What's in it for me?" and there is no better "how to" book on living a jammin' life. It's about you and how you live and what happens when you die.

Straight up, when we are in heaven, we will look around and there will be more folks than anyone can count. But be clear that this mass of people will have come from every nation, tribe, people, and language of the earth. (Rev. 7:9) That means that there will be people there who look like me and people there who will look like you. The point is that we will all be people who have, during our life on earth, accepted the culture of Christ.

Revelation 7:9 is also very clear that we will have our individual stripes, otherwise we'd all look alike when we got up there. That tells me that it's okay to be into whatever earthly thing I'm into musically, artistically, culturally, communally, socially, economically, politically, and even sexually as long as it pleases God. This book is a good place to start figuring out what pleases God because it's his word and it never changes.

Why'd we do it? Because I know that I will be up in heaven and I am praying that I will see you up in there too. It is because of that prayer, that all of us—the editors, contributors and publishers have brought you "Real." But in the meantime, there's a successful and rich life to be had before we get to heaven. So we want you to see that the Word of God is for you, at this time, and in this place. And, just for you, we've given it some different packaging...but the Word is the same as it's always been.

The features presented in Real were created so that you could look for answers to immediate issues in your life. So, if you want to resolve some issues of right and wrong, you should check out Deep Issues, Think Straight, and the quick checks and balances of The World Says/The Word Says.

We've also included some lines to answer your basic questions about what it means to live like a follower of Christ. Reading He's Got Answers, Bible 411, and How Ya Travelin' should help give some good intros to basic Bible understandings.

But, what is most unique about this Bible, besides the breakthrough BibleZine format, are the features that talk about the urban cultural and music scene as it relates to a Christian lifestyle in Real Rhymes and Music Reviews. We've also done some artistic renditions of Scripture in The Script.

We know that there are issues that we've got to address for you head on about where the line is drawn between the "anything goes" life on earth and our accountability to Christ. We hope that the positions put out there in Music Reviews and the article Hip Hop and Christian? will cause you to consider who and what you stand for. We hope that both features will stimulate a dialogue among you and your crew.

In most of our articles you will find Scripture references. We urge you not take what we wrote as true but to go to the source of what we've written and dig out the truth for yourself. The Bible is the living Word of God and it is supposed to be studied and gnawed on and rapped about and wrestled through. But it all starts and ends with seeking God. If you ask the questions, God will answer them and that's for REAL.

Michele Clark Jenkins
Co-Editor

TABLE OF CONTENTS

TABLE OF CONTENTS

TABLE OF CONTENTS

HEART CRY
DILEMMAS, PRAYERS AND ANSWERS

ARTICLES
THOUGHT PROVOKING PIECES

URBAN TRILOGY
FICTIONAL STORIES

OTHER FEATURES
Viewpoint
Personal Answers to Big Questions

HE'S GOT ANSWERS
WORD RESPONSES TO FAQ

PEEP THIS
FACTS YOU NEED TO KNOW

THE REAL TRUTH ABOUT LIFE

NEW CENTURY VERSION INFORMATION:

God never intended the Bible to be too difficult to understand. The writers of the Bible recorded God's Word in familiar, everyday language. God wanted to make sure his Word was clear and that people would not have to struggle to understand what he said to them.

Language has changed since back in the day, but the New Century Version captures the clear and simple message the very first readers understood, using the language of today. This version presents the Bible as God intended it: clear and dynamic.

A team of scholars from the World Bible Translation Center worked together with twenty-one other experienced Bible scholars from all over the world to translate the text directly from the best available Greek and Hebrew texts. The writers of the New Century Version avoided outdated words and phrases and kept the sentences short and simple, making this version much easier to comprehend. However, you can trust that this Bible accurately and clearly presents God's Word as it came to us in the original languages.

We acknowledge the infallibility of God's Word and yet our own frailty. We pray that God will use this Bible to help you grow closer to him and to understand his rich truth for yourself. To God be the Glory.

THE NEW TESTAMENT

MATTHEW

WHAT'S maTTHEW'S aNGLE ON JESUS?

Did he only come for the rich folks in the sub-urbs or does he identify with folks on the street? Well, just look at his ancestors. He had a prosti-tute, a two-timing thug, and a player in his family tree. His mom and stepdad were exiles in Africa. He was misunderstood by society. Yes, Jesus could identify and keep it real with regular folks. As an adult, he had no home of his own, but slept and ate on the road as he traveled around teach-ing and helping folks. Yet he didn't let that bring him down or make him bitter. He kept his head up when the haters and pretenders took their best shots at him, because he knew his identity . . . he is the King of Kings and Lord of Lords.

Matthew recorded over two dozen prophecies from the Old Testament about this King of Kings that were fulfilled by Jesus during his lifetime! If you do your homework, you'll find historical facts back up the truth found in scripture... Matthew's Jesus is for *real*.

THE FAMILY HISTORY OF JESUS

1 This is the family history of Jesus Christ. He came from the family of David, and David came from the family of Abraham.

2 Abraham was the father[n] of Isaac. Isaac was the father of Jacob. Jacob was the father of Judah and his brothers. 3 Judah was the father of Perez and Zerah. (Their mother was Tamar.) Perez was the father of Hezron. Hezron was the father of Ram. 4 Ram was the father of Amminadab. Amminadab was the father of Nahshon. Nahshon was the father of Salmon. 5 Salmon was the father of Boaz. (Boaz's mother was Rahab.) Boaz was the father of Obed. (Obed's mother was Ruth.) Obed was the father of Jesse.

6 Jesse was the father of King David. David was the father of Solomon. (Solomon's mother had been Uriah's wife.) 7 Solomon was the father of Rehoboam. Rehoboam was the father of Abijah. Abijah was the father of Asa.[n] 8 Asa was the father of Jehoshaphat. Jehoshaphat was the father of Jehoram. Jehoram was the ancestor of Uzziah.

9 Uzziah was the father of Jotham. Jotham was the father of Ahaz. Ahaz was the father of Hezekiah. 10 Hezekiah was the father of Manasseh. Manasseh was the father of Amon. Amon was the father of Josiah. 11 Josiah was the grandfather of Jehoiachin[n] and his brothers. (This was at the time that the people were taken to Babylon.) 12 After they were taken to Babylon: Jehoiachin was the father of Shealtiel. Shealtiel was the grandfather of Zerubbabel. 13 Zerubbabel was the father of Abiud. Abiud was the father of Eliakim. Eliakim was the father of Azor. 14 Azor was the father of Zadok. Zadok was the father of Akim. Akim was the father of Eliud. 15 Eliud was the father of Eleazar. Eleazar was the father of Matthan.

Matthan was the father of Jacob. 16 Jacob was the father of Joseph. Joseph was the husband of Mary, and Mary was the mother of Jesus. Jesus is called the Christ.

17 So there were fourteen generations from Abraham to David. And there were fourteen generations from David until the people were taken to Babylon. And there were fourteen generations from the time when the people were taken to Babylon until Christ was born.

Jesus

Jesus, meaning "God Saves," is what Joseph named the son his wife gave birth to in Bethlehem about 2000 years ago. Another name given this son was Immanuel, which means "God is with us" (Matthew 1:23). Jesus is the singly most significant person in all of the past, present and future. The impact of this one life on our world is undeniable. As an adult, Jesus taught about God, performed miracles, challenged the religious system of the day, and mixed with the poor and the sinners. But he didn't do all this just because he was a good person. Jesus was unique among all who have ever lived or ever will live – he was at the same time truly God and truly a man, fully Deity and fully human. Some have called him the "second Adam" because he was the first of a completely new race of people. In Romans 5:12, Paul tells us that sin came into the world through the first Adam. By the second Adam, people are made right with God and have true life (Romans 5:17-19) – a life infused with the character of God. By his life, death and resurrection from the dead, Jesus truly lived up to his name – God is with us!

DOES HE IDENTIFY WITH FOLKS ON THE STREET?

 1:2 father "Father" in Jewish lists of ancestors can sometimes mean grandfather or more distant relative. **1:7 Asa** Some Greek copies read "Asaph," another name for Asa (see 1 Chronicles 3:10). **1:11 Jehoiachin** The Greek reads "Jeconiah," another name for Jehoiachin (see 2 Kings 24:6 and 1 Chronicles 3:16).

365

1   HOLIDAY—New Year's Day   Morris Chestnut's birthday

2   Pray for a friend that has lost a loved one

3

4   **Think outside
the box:**
New Year,
New Attitude:
What am I going
to do differently?

5

6

7

8

9

10

11

12

"It hurts but you pick
yourself up
and move on like nothing
happened."
–Aaliyah

13 Attend or host a Martin Luther King, Jr. event to commemorate his life

14 It's your birthday, LL Cool J!

15 HOLIDAY—Martin Luther King's Birthday

16

17 HOLIDAY—Martin Luther King's Birthday observed

18

19 **Get a friend, hit the gym**

20

21

22

23 On This Day In History 1977—ABC TV premiered *Roots*—The Mini Series

24 It's your birthday, Will Smith!

25 Happy Birthday Alicia Keys!

26

27 **Buy a "Thinking of You"**
card for a special friend

28

29

30 Super Bowl Sunday,

31 **Whose house?**

MUSIC REVIEWS

ARTIST: JOHN THE BAPTIST   ALBUM: BAPTIZING THE GAME

Playing *Baptizing the Game*, the latest album by John the Baptist, is guaranteed to be a hype listening experience. The album samples reggae, R&B, and rap sounds, all of which John performs well. The tracks are deep with a lot of heart and emotion behind the music. This CD is one that you can and should turn up really loud in the car. You don't have to be a Christian to dig this album because John speaks street truth. He talks about the thoughts and struggles that rise up out of our everyday lives just living on this earth. This album is one that you can listen to over and over and not get sick. Every time I listen to *Baptizing the Game*, I hear something new that I didn't hear before.

"ACCEPTED"

THE BIRTH OF JESUS CHRIST

[18]This is how the birth of Jesus Christ came about. His mother Mary was engaged[n] to marry Joseph, but before they married, she learned she was pregnant by the power of the Holy Spirit. [19]Because Mary's husband, Joseph, was a good man, he did not want to disgrace her in public, so he planned to divorce her secretly.

[20]While Joseph thought about these things, an angel of the Lord came to him in a dream. The angel said, "Joseph, descendant of David, don't be afraid to take Mary as your wife, because the baby in her is from the Holy Spirit. [21]She will give birth to a son, and you will name him Jesus,[n] because he will save his people from their sins."

[22]All this happened to bring about what the Lord had said through the prophet: [23]"The virgin will be pregnant. She will have a son, and they will name him Immanuel,"[n] which means "God is with us."

[24]When Joseph woke up, he did what the Lord's angel had told him to do. Joseph took Mary as his wife, [25]but he did not have sexual relations with her until she gave birth to the son. And Joseph named him Jesus.

WISE MEN COME TO VISIT JESUS

2 Jesus was born in the town of Bethlehem in Judea during the time when Herod was king. When Jesus was born, some wise men from the east came to Jerusalem. [2]They asked, "Where is the baby who was born to be the king of the Jews? We saw his star in the east and have come to worship him."

[3]When King Herod heard this, he was troubled, as were all the people in Jerusalem. [4]Herod called a meeting of all the leading priests and teachers of the law and asked them where the Christ would be born. [5]They answered, "In the town of Bethlehem in Judea. The prophet wrote about this in the Scriptures:

[6]'But you, Bethlehem, in the land of Judah,
are not just an insignificant village in Judah.
A ruler will come from you who who will be like a shepherd for my people Israel.' "   *Micah 5:2*

[7]Then Herod had a secret meeting with the wise men and learned from them the exact time they first saw the star. [8]He sent the wise men to Bethlehem, saying, "Look carefully for the child. When you find him, come tell me so I can worship him too."

[9]After the wise men heard the king, they left. The star that they had seen in the east went before them until it stopped above the place where the child was. [10]When the wise men saw the star, they were filled with joy. [11]They came to the house where the child was and saw him with his mother, Mary, and they bowed down and worshiped him. They opened their gifts and gave him treasures of gold, frankincense, and myrrh. [12]But God warned the wise men in a dream not to go back to Herod, so they returned to their own country by a different way.

 1:18 engaged For the Jewish people an engagement was a lasting agreement, which could only be broken by a divorce. If a bride-to-be was unfaithful, it was considered adultery, and she could be put to death.   **1:21 Jesus** The name "Jesus" means "salvation."   **1:23 "The virgin . . . Immanuel"** Quotation from Isaiah 7:14.

▶ **5**

JESUS' PARENTS TAKE HIM TO EGYPT

13After they left, an angel of the Lord came to Joseph in a dream and said, "Get up! Take the child and his mother and escape to Egypt, because Herod is starting to look for the child so he can kill him. Stay in Egypt until I tell you to return."

14So Joseph got up and left for Egypt during the night with the child and his mother. 15And Joseph stayed in Egypt until Herod died. This happened to bring about what the Lord had said through the prophet: "I called my son out of Egypt."n

HEROD KILLS THE BABY BOYS

16When Herod saw that the wise men had tricked him, he was furious. So he gave an order to kill all the baby boys in Bethlehem and in the surrounding area who were two years old or younger. This was in keeping with the time he learned from the wise men. 17So what God had said through the prophet Jeremiah came true:

18"A voice was heard in Ramah
    of painful crying and deep
        sadness:
    Rachel crying for her children.
    She refused to be comforted,
        because her children are dead."
                        Jeremiah 31:15

JOSEPH AND MARY RETURN

19After Herod died, an angel of the Lord spoke to Joseph in a dream while he was in Egypt. 20The angel said, "Get up! Take the child and his mother and go to the land of Israel, because the people who were trying to kill the child are now dead."

21So Joseph took the child and his mother and went to Israel. 22But he heard that Archelaus was now king in Judea since his father Herod had died. So Joseph was afraid to go there. After being warned in a dream, he went to the area of Galilee, 23to a town called Nazareth, and lived there. And so what God had said through the prophets came true: "He will be called a Nazarene."n

THE WORK OF JOHN THE BAPTIST

3 About that time John the Baptist began preaching in the desert area of Judea. 2John said, "Change your hearts and lives because the kingdom of heaven is near." 3John the Baptist is the one Isaiah the prophet was talking about when he said:

"This is a voice of one
    who calls out in the desert:
'Prepare the way for the Lord.
    Make the road straight for him.'"
                        Isaiah 40:3

4John's clothes were made from camel's hair, and he wore a leather belt around his waist. For food, he ate locusts and wild honey. 5Many people came from Jerusalem and Judea and all the area around the Jordan River to hear John. 6They confessed their sins, and he baptized them in the Jordan River.

7Many of the Pharisees and Sadducees came to the place where John was baptizing people. When John saw them, he said, "You are snakes! Who warned you to run away from God's coming punishment? 8Do the things that show you really have changed your hearts and lives. 9And don't think you can say to yourselves, 'Abraham is our father.' I tell you that God could make children for Abraham from these rocks. 10The ax is now ready to cut down the trees, and every tree that does not produce good fruit will be cut down and thrown into the fire.n

11"I baptize you with water to show that your hearts and lives have changed. But there is one coming after me who is greater than I am, whose sandals I am not good enough to carry. He will baptize you with the Holy Spirit and fire. 12He will come ready to clean the grain, separating the good grain from the chaff. He will put the good part of the grain into his barn, but he will burn the chaff with a fire that cannot be put out."n

JESUS IS BAPTIZED BY JOHN

13At that time Jesus came from Galilee to the Jordan River and wanted John to baptize him. 14But John tried to stop him, saying, "Why do you come to me to be baptized? I need to be baptized by you!"

15Jesus answered, "Let it be this way for now. We should do all things that are God's will." So John agreed to baptize Jesus.

16As soon as Jesus was baptized, he came up out of the water. Then heaven opened, and he saw God's Spirit coming down on him like a dove. 17And a voice from heaven said, "This is my Son, whom I love, and I am very pleased with him."

THE TEMPTATION OF JESUS

4 Then the Spirit led Jesus into the desert to be tempted by the devil. 2Jesus fasted for forty days and nights. After this, he was very hungry. 3The devil came to Jesus to tempt him, saying, "If you are the Son of God, tell these rocks to become bread."

4Jesus answered, "It is written in the Scriptures, 'A person lives not on bread alone, but by everything God says.'"n

5Then the devil led Jesus to the holy city of Jerusalem and put him on a high place of the Temple. 6The devil said, "If you are the Son of God, jump down, because it is written in the Scriptures:

'He has put his angels in charge of
        you.
    They will catch you in their hands
    so that you will not hit your foot on
        a rock.'"   *Psalm 91:11-12*

7Jesus answered him, "It also says in the Scriptures, 'Do not test the Lord your God.'"n

8Then the devil led Jesus to the top of a very high mountain and showed him all the kingdoms of the world and all their splendor. 9The devil said, "If you will bow down and worship me, I will give you all these things."

2:15 "I called . . . Egypt." Quotation from Hosea 11:1. **2:23** Nazarene A person from the town of Nazareth. Matthew may be referring to Isaiah 11:1, where the Hebrew word translated "branch" sounds like "Nazarene." **3:10** The ax . . . fire. This means that God is ready to punish his people who do not obey him. **3:12** He will . . . out. This means that Jesus will come to separate good people from bad people, saving the good and punishing the bad. **4:4** 'A person . . . says.' Quotation from Deuteronomy 8:3. **4:7** 'Do . . . God.' Quotation from Deuteronomy 6:16.

GOD UNIT

OVERCOMING THUG LIFE

My dad had been in an alcoholic coma for years and my mother was sickly, in and out of the hospital. I had an older sister but she lived outside my world. I needed people in my life to relate to, so I turned to the ones I called my "bruhs." I knew I could count on my boys on the street. We were thick as thieves. We actually *were* thieves, sometimes. We'd been a little of everything: playas, thugs, rappers, dealers, and users. We did it all just trying to be somebody. We didn't belong to a big-name gang; we had our own "set." Our set ran tight, and we rarely opened our circle to outsiders.

I had promised myself that, although my other friends used drugs and abused alcohol continuously, I would be different. I guarded myself; I really did. Anytime I went out, I was the designated driver. While my bruhs were drunk, high, slurring their words and throwing up, I was big brother, taking care of each one of them. And then one night, I thought, "One drink won't hurt." Then, in time, it was one puff-puff-give from a blunt. Before I knew it, I was drinking, smoking weed and using cocaine.

I lost it all. My father and mother died. My friends had their own problems with drugs and the law and began to disappear. I spent time locked up and was left alone with the worst person possible – me. I had broken my own rules. I could trust no one, not even myself.

I thought I was alone till I went to visit my grandmother's church one day. I hadn't been in a church since my mom's funeral, but God knew just where to find me. The minister talked that day about how God forgave Paul for all he had done, and how he had turned his life around. There was a young lady who sang a song about God being able to heal and use anyone. I needed that. My life began to change that day. I am beginning to learn that having Jesus in my set gives me true significance. I'm recovering from all the hurt I've experienced and I know that when I stand before God, he will recognize me as a part of his set. Now I know that, in God's eyes, I am somebody and I can always count on him.

Luke 19:10 — The Son of Man came to find lost people and save them.

---

[10]Jesus said to the devil, "Go away from me, Satan! It is written in the Scriptures, 'You must worship the Lord your God and serve only him.'"[n]

[11]So the devil left Jesus, and angels came and took care of him.

JESUS BEGINS WORK IN GALILEE

[12]When Jesus heard that John had been put in prison, he went back to Galilee. [13]He left Nazareth and went to live in Capernaum, a town near Lake Galilee, in the area near Zebulun and Naphtali. [14]Jesus did this to bring about what the prophet Isaiah had said:

[15]"Land of Zebulun and land of
   Naphtali

along the sea,
beyond the Jordan River.
This is Galilee where the
   non-Jewish people live.
[16]These people who live in darkness
   will see a great light.
They live in a place covered with the
   shadows of death,
but a light will shine on them."
        Isaiah 9:1-2

JESUS CHOOSES SOME FOLLOWERS

[17]From that time Jesus began to preach, saying, "Change your hearts and lives, because the kingdom of heaven is near."

[18]As Jesus was walking by Lake Galilee, he saw two brothers, Simon (called Peter) and his brother Andrew. They were throwing a net into the lake because they were fishermen. [19]Jesus said, "Come follow me, and I will make you fish for people." [20]So Simon and Andrew immediately left their nets and followed him.

[21]As Jesus continued walking by Lake Galilee, he saw two other brothers, James and John, the sons of Zebedee. They were in a boat with their father Zebedee, mending their nets. Jesus told them to come with him. [22]Immediately they left the boat and their father, and they followed Jesus.

4:10 'You . . . him.' Quotation from Deuteronomy 6:13.

JESUS TEACHES AND HEALS PEOPLE

[23]Jesus went everywhere in Galilee, teaching in the synagogues, preaching the Good News about the kingdom of heaven, and healing all the people's diseases and sicknesses. [24]The news about Jesus spread all over Syria, and people brought all the sick to him. They were suffering from different kinds of diseases. Some were in great pain, some had demons, some were epileptics,[n] and some were paralyzed. Jesus healed all of them. [25]Many people from Galilee, the Ten Towns,[n] Jerusalem, Judea, and the land across the Jordan River followed him.

JESUS TEACHES THE PEOPLE

5 When Jesus saw the crowds, he went up on a hill and sat down. His followers came to him, [2]and he began to teach them, saying:

[3]"They are blessed who realize their
   spiritual poverty,
   for the kingdom of heaven belongs
   to them.
[4]They are blessed who grieve,
   for God will comfort them.
[5]They are blessed who are humble,
   for the whole earth will be theirs.
[6]They are blessed who hunger and
   thirst after justice,
   for they will be satisfied.
[7]They are blessed who show mercy to
   others,
   for God will show mercy to them.
[8]They are blessed whose thoughts
   are pure,
   for they will see God.
[9]They are blessed who work for peace,
   for they will be called God's
   children.
[10]They are blessed who are persecuted
   for doing good,
   for the kingdom of heaven belongs
   to them.
[11]"People will insult you and hurt you. They will lie and say all kinds of evil

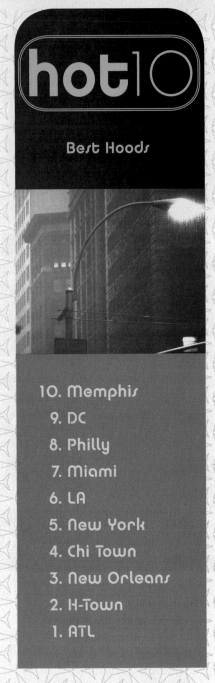

hot 10

Best Hoods

10. Memphis
9. DC
8. Philly
7. Miami
6. LA
5. New York
4. Chi Town
3. New Orleans
2. H-Town
1. ATL

things about you because you follow me. But when they do, you will be blessed. [12]Rejoice and be glad, because you have a great reward waiting for you in heaven. People did the same evil things to the prophets who lived before you.

YOU ARE LIKE SALT AND LIGHT

[13]"You are the salt of the earth. But if the salt loses its salty taste, it cannot be made salty again. It is good for nothing, except to be thrown out and walked on.

[14]"You are the light that gives light to the world. A city that is built on a hill cannot be hidden. [15]And people don't hide a light under a bowl. They put it on a lampstand so the light shines for all the people in the house. [16]In the same way, you should be a light for other people. Live so that they will see the good things you do and will praise your Father in heaven.

THE IMPORTANCE OF THE LAW

[17]"Don't think that I have come to destroy the law of Moses or the teaching of the prophets. I have not come to destroy them but to bring about what they said. [18]I tell you the truth, nothing will disappear from the law until heaven and earth are gone. Not even the smallest letter or the smallest part of a letter will be lost until everything has happened. [19]Whoever refuses to obey any command and teaches other people not to obey that command will be the least important in the kingdom of heaven. But whoever obeys the commands and teaches other people to obey them will be great in the kingdom of heaven. [20]I tell you that if you are no more obedient than the teachers of the law and the Pharisees, you will never enter the kingdom of heaven.

JESUS TEACHES ABOUT ANGER

[21]"You have heard that it was said to our people long ago, 'You must not murder anyone.[n] Anyone who murders another will be judged.' [22]But I tell you, if you are angry with a brother or sister,[n] you will be judged. If you say bad things to a brother or sister, you will be judged by the council. And if you call someone a fool, you will be in danger of the fire of hell.

[23]"So when you offer your gift to God at the altar, and you remember that your brother or sister has something against you, [24]leave your gift there at the altar. Go and make peace with that person, and then come and offer your gift.

4:24 epileptics People with a disease that causes them sometimes to lose control of their bodies and maybe faint, shake strongly, or not be able to move.   **4:25 Ten Towns** In Greek, called "Decapolis." It was an area east of Lake Galilee that once had ten main towns.   **5:21 'You . . . anyone.'** Quotation from Exodus 20:13; Deuteronomy 5:17.   **5:22 sister** Some Greek copies continue, "without a reason."

25"If your enemy is taking you to court, become friends quickly, before you go to court. Otherwise, your enemy might turn you over to the judge, and the judge might give you to a guard to put you in jail. 26I tell you the truth, you will not leave there until you have paid everything you owe.

JESUS TEACHES ABOUT SEXUAL SIN

27"You have heard that it was said, 'You must not be guilty of adultery.'[n] 28But I tell you that if anyone looks at a woman and wants to sin sexually with her, in his mind he has already done that sin with the woman. 29If your right eye causes you to sin, take it out and throw it away. It is better to lose one part of your body than to have your whole body thrown into hell. 30If your right hand causes you to sin, cut it off and throw it away. It is better to lose one part of your body than for your whole body to go into hell.

JESUS TEACHES ABOUT DIVORCE

31"It was also said, 'Anyone who divorces his wife must give her a written divorce paper.'[n] 32But I tell you that anyone who divorces his wife forces her to be guilty of adultery. The only reason for a man to divorce his wife is if she has sexual relations with another man. And anyone who marries that divorced woman is guilty of adultery.

MAKE PROMISES CAREFULLY

33"You have heard that it was said to our people long ago, 'Don't break your promises, but keep the promises you make to the Lord.'[n] 34But I tell you, never swear an oath. Don't swear an oath using the name of heaven, because heaven is God's throne. 35Don't swear an oath using the name of the earth, because the earth belongs to God. Don't swear an oath using the name of Jerusalem, because that is the city of the great King. 36Don't even swear by your own head, because you cannot make one hair on your head become white or black.

37Say only yes if you mean yes, and no if you mean no. If you say more than yes or no, it is from the Evil One.

DON'T FIGHT BACK

38"You have heard that it was said, 'An eye for an eye, and a tooth for a tooth.'[n] 39But I tell you, don't stand up against an evil person. If someone slaps you on the right cheek, turn to him the other cheek also. 40If someone wants to sue you in court and take your shirt, let him have your coat also. 41If someone forces you to go with him one mile, go with him two miles. 42If a person asks you for something, give it to him. Don't refuse to give to someone who wants to borrow from you.

LOVE ALL PEOPLE

43"You have heard that it was said, 'Love your neighbor[n] and hate your enemies.' 44But I say to you, love your enemies. Pray for those who hurt you.[n] 45If you do this, you will be true children of your Father in heaven. He causes the sun to rise on good people and on evil people, and he sends rain to those who do right and to those who do wrong. 46If you love only the people who love you, you will get no reward. Even the tax collectors do that. 47And if you are nice only to your friends, you are no better than other people. Even those who don't know God are nice to their friends. 48So you must be perfect, just as your Father in heaven is perfect.

JESUS TEACHES ABOUT GIVING

6 "Be careful! When you do good things, don't do them in front of people to be seen by them. If you do that, you will have no reward from your Father in heaven.

2"When you give to the poor, don't be like the hypocrites. They blow trumpets in the synagogues and on the streets so that people will see them and honor them. I tell you the truth, those hypocrites already have their full reward.

3So when you give to the poor, don't let anyone know what you are doing. 4Your giving should be done in secret. Your Father can see what is done in secret, and he will reward you.

JESUS TEACHES ABOUT PRAYER

5"When you pray, don't be like the hypocrites. They love to stand in the synagogues and on the street corners and pray so people will see them. I tell you the truth, they already have their full reward. 6When you pray, you should go into your room and close the door and pray to your Father who cannot be seen. Your Father can see what is done in secret, and he will reward you.

7"And when you pray, don't be like those people who don't know God. They continue saying things that mean nothing, thinking that God will hear them because of their many words. 8Don't be like them, because your Father knows the things you need before you ask him. 9So when you pray, you should pray like this:

'Our Father in heaven,
  may your name always be kept holy.
10May your kingdom come
  and what you want be done,
  here on earth as it is in heaven.
11Give us the food we need for each
  day.
12Forgive us for our sins,
  just as we have forgiven those
  who sinned against us.
13And do not cause us to be tempted,
  but save us from the Evil One.'
    [The kingdom, the power, and
    the glory are yours forever.
    Amen.][n]

14Yes, if you forgive others for their sins, your Father in heaven will also forgive you for your sins. 15But if you don't forgive others, your Father in heaven will not forgive your sins.

JESUS TEACHES ABOUT WORSHIP

16"When you fast,[n] don't put on a sad face like the hypocrites. They make their faces look sad to show people they are fasting. I tell you the truth, those hypocrites already have their full reward. [17]So when you fast, comb your hair and wash your face. [18]Then people will not know that you are fasting, but your Father, whom you cannot see, will see you. Your Father sees what is done in secret, and he will reward you.

GOD IS MORE IMPORTANT THAN MONEY

[19]"Don't store treasures for yourselves here on earth where moths and rust will destroy them and thieves can break in and steal them. [20]But store your treasures in heaven where they cannot be destroyed by moths or rust and where thieves cannot break in and steal them. [21]Your heart will be where your treasure is.

[22]"The eye is a light for the body. If your eyes are good, your whole body will be full of light. [23]But if your eyes are evil, your whole body will be full of darkness. And if the only light you have is really darkness, then you have the worst darkness.

[24]"No one can serve two masters. The person will hate one master and love the

He's got answers

IF you go to church, will you go to heaven? If you don't go to church, will you not go to heaven?

Two things need to be discussed in response to your question.

First, church is not a place, although many Christians meet in buildings set aside for that purpose. Church is whenever God's family gathers together to worship and to learn more about him. Jesus said, "...if two or three people come together in my name, I am there with them" (Matthew 18:20). That is church; the location is not important. Churches meet in a wide variety of places besides church buildings; they meet in living rooms, in school gyms, in tents, on the beach.

Second, entrance into heaven — salvation — is not based upon where you go, what you eat, how you dress, or anything that you do; it is based solely upon your relationship with God. You get a relationship with God through his Son, Jesus Christ. Heaven is the eternal home for God's children; if you are his child, then you will go to Heaven.

Read on: Luke 23:43; Romans 10:9-10; John 3:16; Ephesians 2:8-9

PEEP THIS:

People aged 18 to 24 are the most racially and ethnically diverse generation in American history. One in three is not White.

other, or will follow one master and refuse to follow the other. You cannot serve both God and worldly riches.

DON'T WORRY

[25]"So I tell you, don't worry about the food or drink you need to live, or about the clothes you need for your body. Life is more than food, and the body is more than clothes. [26]Look at the birds in the air. They don't plant or harvest or store food in barns, but your heavenly Father feeds them. And you know that you are worth much more than the birds. [27]You cannot add any time to your life by worrying about it.

[28]"And why do you worry about clothes? Look at how the lilies in the field grow. They don't work or make clothes for themselves. [29]But I tell you that even Solomon with his riches was not dressed as beautifully as one of these flowers. [30]God clothes the grass in the field, which is alive today but tomorrow is thrown into the fire. So you can be even more sure that God will clothe you. Don't have so little faith! [31]Don't worry and say, 'What will we eat?' or 'What will we drink?' or 'What will we wear?' [32]The people who don't know God keep trying to get these things, and your Father in heaven knows you need them. [33]Seek first God's kingdom and what God wants. Then all your other needs will be met as well. [34]So don't worry about tomorrow, because tomorrow will have its own worries. Each day has enough trouble of its own.

BE CAREFUL ABOUT JUDGING OTHERS

7 "Don't judge others, or you will be judged. ²You will be judged in the same way that you judge others, and the amount you give to others will be given to you.

³"Why do you notice the little piece of dust in your friend's eye, but you don't notice the big piece of wood in your own eye? ⁴How can you say to your friend, 'Let me take that little piece of dust out of your eye'? Look at yourself! You still have that big piece of wood in your own eye. ⁵You hypocrite! First, take the wood out of your own eye. Then you will see clearly to take the dust out of your friend's eye.

⁶"Don't give holy things to dogs, and don't throw your pearls before pigs. Pigs will only trample on them, and dogs will turn to attack you.

ASK GOD FOR WHAT YOU NEED

⁷"Ask, and God will give to you. Search, and you will find. Knock, and the door will open for you. ⁸Yes, everyone who asks will receive. Everyone who searches will find. And everyone who knocks will have the door opened.

⁹"If your children ask for bread, which of you would give them a stone? ¹⁰Or if your children ask for a fish, would you give them a snake? ¹¹Even though you are bad, you know how to give good gifts to your children. How much more your heavenly Father will give good things to those who ask him!

THE MOST IMPORTANT RULE

¹²"Do to others what you want them to do to you. This is the meaning of the law of Moses and the teaching of the prophets.

THE WAY TO HEAVEN IS HARD

¹³"Enter through the narrow gate. The gate is wide and the road is wide that leads to hell, and many people enter through that gate. ¹⁴But the gate is small and the road is narrow that leads to true life. Only a few people find that road.

PEOPLE KNOW YOU BY YOUR ACTIONS

¹⁵"Be careful of false prophets. They come to you looking gentle like sheep, but they are really dangerous like wolves. ¹⁶You will know these people by

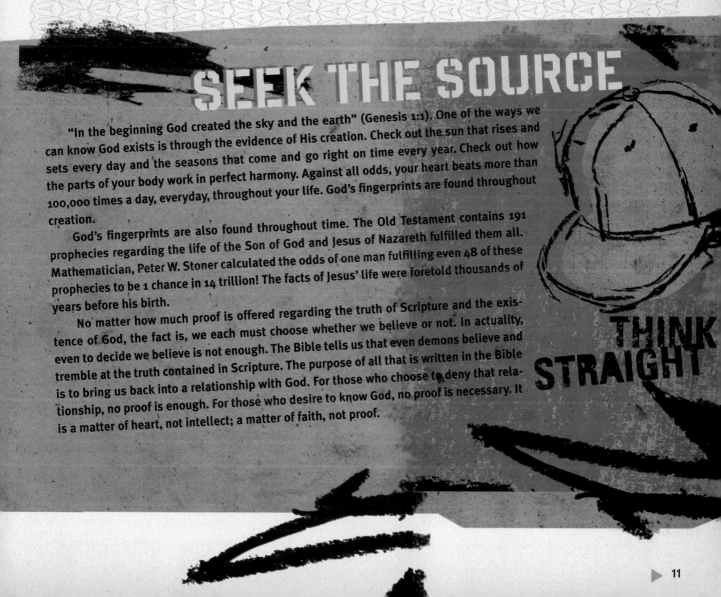

SEEK THE SOURCE

"In the beginning God created the sky and the earth" (Genesis 1:1). One of the ways we can know God exists is through the evidence of His creation. Check out the sun that rises and sets every day and the seasons that come and go right on time every year. Check out how the parts of your body work in perfect harmony. Against all odds, your heart beats more than 100,000 times a day, everyday, throughout your life. God's fingerprints are found throughout creation.

God's fingerprints are also found throughout time. The Old Testament contains 191 prophecies regarding the life of the Son of God and Jesus of Nazareth fulfilled them all. Mathematician, Peter W. Stoner calculated the odds of one man fulfilling even 48 of these prophecies to be 1 chance in 14 trillion! The facts of Jesus' life were foretold thousands of years before his birth.

No matter how much proof is offered regarding the truth of Scripture and the existence of God, the fact is, we each must choose whether we believe or not. In actuality, even to decide we believe is not enough. The Bible tells us that even demons believe and tremble at the truth contained in Scripture. The purpose of all that is written in the Bible is to bring us back into a relationship with God. For those who choose to deny that relationship, no proof is enough. For those who desire to know God, no proof is necessary. It is a matter of heart, not intellect; a matter of faith, not proof.

THINK STRAIGHT

OVERCOMING

▶ PRIDE

Pride should be called the silent killer. It will sneak up on you if you're not careful. A lot of people deal with this issue. They can't handle criticism, or they have to be right all the time. Pride is tasteless, colorless, and sizeless, yet it is the hardest thing to swallow.

The Bible sends out many warnings about pride. Proverbs 16:18 says, "Pride will destroy a person; a proud attitude leads to ruin." Philippians 2:3 states, "When you do things, do not let selfishness or pride be your guide. Instead, be humble and give more honor to others than to yourselves." Check your heart. Be honest with yourself. Do you tend to think that your way is always the right way? Your pride may be preventing you from really listening to others. Maybe somebody else does have a valid point of view. It's time you found out.

what they do. Grapes don't come from thornbushes, and figs don't come from thorny weeds. [17]In the same way, every good tree produces good fruit, but a bad tree produces bad fruit. [18]A good tree cannot produce bad fruit, and a bad tree cannot produce good fruit. [19]Every tree that does not produce good fruit is cut down and thrown into the fire. [20]In the same way, you will know these false prophets by what they do.

[21]"Not all those who say 'You are our Lord' will enter the kingdom of heaven. The only people who will enter the kingdom of heaven are those who do what my Father in heaven wants. [22]On the last day many people will say to me, 'Lord, Lord, we spoke for you, and through you we forced out demons and did many miracles.' [23]Then I will tell them clearly, 'Get away from me, you who do evil. I never knew you.'

TWO KINDS OF PEOPLE

[24]"Everyone who hears my words and obeys them is like a wise man who built his house on rock. [25]It rained hard, the floods came, and the winds blew and hit that house. But it did not fall, because it was built on rock. [26]Everyone who hears my words and does not obey them is like a foolish man who built his house on sand. [27]It rained hard, the floods came, and the winds blew and hit that house, and it fell with a big crash."

[28]When Jesus finished saying these things, the people were amazed at his teaching, [29]because he did not teach like their teachers of the law. He taught like a person who had authority.

JESUS HEALS A SICK MAN

8 When Jesus came down from the hill, great crowds followed him. [2]Then a man with a skin disease came to Jesus. The man bowed down before him and said, "Lord, you can heal me if you will."

[3]Jesus reached out his hand and touched the man and said, "I will. Be healed!" And immediately the man was healed from his disease. [4]Then Jesus said to him, "Don't tell anyone about this. But go and show yourself to the priest[n] and offer the gift Moses commanded[n] for people who are made well. This will show the people what I have done."

JESUS HEALS A SOLDIER'S SERVANT

[5]When Jesus entered the city of Capernaum, an army officer came to him, begging for help. [6]The officer said, "Lord, my servant is at home in bed. He can't move his body and is in much pain."

[7]Jesus said to the officer, "I will go and heal him."

[8]The officer answered, "Lord, I am not worthy for you to come into my house. You only need to command it, and my servant will be healed. [9]I, too, am a man under the authority of others, and I have soldiers under my command. I tell one soldier, 'Go,' and he goes. I tell another soldier, 'Come,' and he comes. I say to my servant, 'Do this,' and my servant does it.

[10]When Jesus heard this, he was amazed. He said to those who were following him, "I tell you the truth, this is the greatest faith I have found, even in Israel. [11]Many people will come from the east and from the west and will sit and eat with Abraham, Isaac, and Jacob in the kingdom of heaven. [12]But those people who should be in the kingdom will be thrown outside into the darkness, where people will cry and grind their teeth with pain."

[13]Then Jesus said to the officer, "Go home. Your servant will be healed just as you believed he would." And his servant was healed that same hour.

8:4 show . . . priest The Law of Moses said a priest must say when a Jewish person with a skin disease was well. **8:4 Moses commanded** Read about this in Leviticus 14:1-32.

JESUS HEALS MANY PEOPLE

[14]When Jesus went to Peter's house, he saw that Peter's mother-in-law was sick in bed with a fever. [15]Jesus touched her hand, and the fever left her. Then she stood up and began to serve Jesus.

[16]That evening people brought to Jesus many who had demons. Jesus spoke and the demons left them, and he healed all the sick. [17]He did these things to bring about what Isaiah the prophet had said:

"He took our suffering on him
and carried our diseases."

Isaiah 53:4

PEOPLE WANT TO FOLLOW JESUS

[18]When Jesus saw the crowd around him, he told his followers to go to the other side of the lake. [19]Then a teacher of the law came to Jesus and said, "Teacher, I will follow you any place you go."

[20]Jesus said to him, "The foxes have holes to live in, and the birds have nests, but the Son of Man has no place to rest his head."

[21]Another man, one of Jesus' followers, said to him, "Lord, first let me go and bury my father."

[22]But Jesus told him, "Follow me, and let the people who are dead bury their own dead."

JESUS CALMS A STORM

[23]Jesus got into a boat, and his followers went with him. [24]A great storm arose on the lake so that waves covered the boat, but Jesus was sleeping. [25]His followers went to him and woke him, saying, "Lord, save us! We will drown!"

[26]Jesus answered, "Why are you afraid? You don't have enough faith." Then Jesus got up and gave a command to the wind and the waves, and it became completely calm.

[27]The men were amazed and said, "What kind of man is this? Even the wind and the waves obey him!"

JESUS HEALS TWO MEN WITH DEMONS

[28]When Jesus arrived at the other side of the lake in the area of the Gadarene[n] people, two men who had demons in them met him. These men lived in the burial caves and were so dangerous that people could not use the road by those caves. [29]They shouted, "What do you want with us, Son of God? Did you come here to torture us before the right time?"

[30]Near that place there was a large herd of pigs feeding. [31]The demons begged Jesus, "If you make us leave these men, please send us into that herd of pigs."

[32]Jesus said to them, "Go!" So the demons left the men and went into the pigs. Then the whole herd rushed down the hill into the lake and were drowned. [33]The herdsmen ran away and went into town, where they told about all of this and what had happened to the men who had demons. [34]Then the whole town went out to see Jesus. When they saw him, they begged him to leave their area.

JESUS HEALS A PARALYZED MAN

9 Jesus got into a boat and went back across the lake to his own town. [2]Some people brought to Jesus a man who was paralyzed and lying on a mat. When Jesus saw the faith of these people, he said to the paralyzed man, "Be encouraged, young man. Your sins are forgiven."

[3]Some of the teachers of the law said to themselves, "This man speaks as if he were God. That is blasphemy!"[n]

[4]Knowing their thoughts, Jesus said, "Why are you thinking evil thoughts? [5]Which is easier: to say, 'Your sins are forgiven,' or to tell him, 'Stand up and walk'? [6]But I will prove to you that the Son of Man has authority on earth to forgive sins." Then Jesus said to the paralyzed man, "Stand up, take your mat, and go home." [7]And the man stood up and went home. [8]When the people saw this, they were amazed and praised God for giving power like this to human beings.

JESUS CHOOSES MATTHEW

[9]When Jesus was leaving, he saw a man named Matthew sitting in the tax collector's booth. Jesus said to him, "Follow me," and he stood up and followed Jesus.

[10]As Jesus was having dinner at Matthew's house, many tax collectors and "sinners" came and ate with Jesus and his followers. [11]When the Pharisees saw this, they asked Jesus' followers, "Why

8:28 Gadarene From Gadara, an area southeast of Lake Galilee. The exact location is uncertain and some Greek copies read "Gergesene"; others read "Gerasene."
9:3 blasphemy Saying things against God or not showing respect for God.

does your teacher eat with tax collectors and sinners?"

[12]When Jesus heard them, he said, "It is not the healthy people who need a doctor, but the sick. [13]Go and learn what this means: 'I want kindness more than I want animal sacrifices.'[n] I did not come to invite good people but to invite sinners."

JESUS' FOLLOWERS ARE CRITICIZED

[14]Then the followers of John[n] came to Jesus and said, "Why do we and the Pharisees often fast[n] for a certain time, but your followers don't?"

[15]Jesus answered, "The friends of the bridegroom are not sad while he is with them. But the time will come when the bridegroom will be taken from them, and then they will fast.

[16]"No one sews a patch of unshrunk cloth over a hole in an old coat. If he does, the patch will shrink and pull away from the coat, making the hole worse. [17]Also, people never pour new wine into old leather bags. Otherwise, the bags will break, the wine will spill, and the wine bags will be ruined. But people always pour new wine into new wine bags. Then both will continue to be good."

JESUS GIVES LIFE TO A DEAD GIRL AND HEALS A SICK WOMAN

[18]While Jesus was saying these things, a leader of the synagogue came to him. He bowed down before Jesus and said, "My daughter has just died. But if you come and lay your hand on her, she will live again." [19]So Jesus and his followers stood up and went with the leader.

[20]Then a woman who had been bleeding for twelve years came behind Jesus and touched the edge of his coat. [21]She was thinking, "If I can just touch his clothes, I will be healed."

[22]Jesus turned and saw the woman and said, "Be encouraged, dear woman. You are made well because you believed." And the woman was healed from that moment on.

[23]Jesus continued along with the leader and went into his house. There he saw the funeral musicians and many people crying. [24]Jesus said, "Go away. The girl is not dead, only asleep." But the people laughed at him. [25]After the crowd had been thrown out of the house, Jesus went into the girl's room and took hold of her hand, and she stood up. [26]The news about this spread all around the area.

JESUS HEALS MORE PEOPLE

[27]When Jesus was leaving there, two blind men followed him. They cried out, "Have mercy on us, Son of David!"

[28]After Jesus went inside, the blind men went with him. He asked the men, "Do you believe that I can make you see again?"

They answered, "Yes, Lord."

[29]Then Jesus touched their eyes and said, "Because you believe I can make you see again, it will happen." [30]Then the men were able to see. But Jesus warned them strongly, saying, "Don't tell anyone about this." [31]But the blind men left and spread the news about Jesus all around that area.

[32]When the two men were leaving, some people brought another man to Jesus. This man could not talk because he had a demon in him. [33]After Jesus forced the demon to leave the man, he was able to speak. The crowd was amazed and said, "We have never seen anything like this in Israel."

[34]But the Pharisees said, "The prince of demons is the one that gives him power to force demons out."

[35]Jesus traveled through all the towns and villages, teaching in their synagogues, preaching the Good News about the kingdom, and healing all kinds of diseases and sicknesses. [36]When he saw the crowds, he felt sorry for them because they were hurting and helpless, like sheep without a shepherd. [37]Jesus said to his followers, "There are many people to harvest but only a few workers to help harvest them. [38]Pray to the Lord, who owns the harvest, that he will send more workers to gather his harvest."[n]

JESUS SENDS OUT HIS APOSTLES

10 Jesus called his twelve followers together and gave them authority to drive out evil spirits and to heal every kind of disease and sickness. [2]These are the names of the twelve apostles: Simon (also called Peter) and his brother Andrew; James son of Zebedee, and his brother John; [3]Philip and Bartholomew; Thomas and Matthew, the tax collector; James son of Alphaeus, and Thaddaeus; [4]Simon the Zealot and Judas Iscariot, who turned against Jesus.

[5]Jesus sent out these twelve men with the following order: "Don't go to the non-Jewish people or to any town where the Samaritans live. [6]But go to the people of Israel, who are like lost sheep. [7]When you go, preach this: 'The kingdom of heaven is near.' [8]Heal the sick, raise the dead to life again, heal those who have skin diseases, and force demons out of people. I give you these powers freely, so help other people freely. [9]Don't carry any money with you—gold or silver or copper. [10]Don't carry a bag or extra clothes or sandals or a walking stick. Workers should be given what they need.

[11]"When you enter a city or town, find some worthy person there and stay in that home until you leave. [12]When you enter that home, say, 'Peace be with you.' [13]If the people there welcome you, let your peace stay there. But if they don't welcome you, take back the peace you wished for them. [14]And if a home or town refuses to welcome you or listen to you, leave that place and shake its dust off your feet.[n] [15]I tell you the truth, on the Judgment Day it will be better for the towns of Sodom and Gomorrah[n] than for the people of that town.

JESUS WARNS HIS APOSTLES

[16]"Listen, I am sending you out like sheep among wolves. So be as clever as

9:13 'I want . . . sacrifices.' Quotation from Hosea 6:6. 9:14 John John the Baptist, who preached to people about Christ's coming (Matthew 3, Luke 3). 9:14 fast The people would give up eating for a special time of prayer and worship to God. It was also done to show sadness and disappointment. 9:37-38 "There are . . . harvest." As a farmer sends workers to harvest the grain, Jesus sends his followers to bring people to God. 10:14 shake . . . feet A warning. It showed that they had rejected these people. 10:15 Sodom and Gomorrah Two cities that God destroyed because the people were so evil.

IMPACT!

100 Black Men of America

Mentoring, education, health and wellness, and economic development are the major program components of 100 Black Men of America (100). This distinguished organization of professional brothers consists of 102 chapters in the U.S., England, Africa, and the Caribbean. Their mission is to improve the quality of life of African-Americans, particularly young males. The 100 leads by example, teaching empowerment and self-reliance. They also host some of the hottest black college football games and golf tournaments. To learn about the programs and events that support 100 Black Men initiatives in your area, visit their Web site at www.100BlackMen.org or call their national headquarters at 1-800-598-3411 for more information.

snakes and as innocent as doves. [17]Be careful of people, because they will arrest you and take you to court and whip you in their synagogues. [18]Because of me you will be taken to stand before governors and kings, and you will tell them and the non-Jewish people about me. [19]When you are arrested, don't worry about what to say or how to say it. At that time you will be given the things to say. [20]It will not really be you speaking but the Spirit of your Father speaking through you.

[21]"Brothers will give their own brothers to be killed, and fathers will give their own children to be killed. Children will fight against their own parents and have them put to death. [22]All people will hate you because you follow me, but those people who keep their faith until the end will be saved. [23]When you are treated badly in one city, run to another city. I tell you the truth, you will not fin-ish going through all the cities of Israel before the Son of Man comes.

[24]"A student is not better than his teacher, and a servant is not better than his master. [25]A student should be satisfied to become like his teacher; a servant should be satisfied to become like his master. If the head of the family is called Beelzebul, then the other members of the family will be called worse names!

FEAR GOD, NOT PEOPLE

[26]"So don't be afraid of those people, because everything that is hidden will be shown. Everything that is secret will be made known. [27]I tell you these things in the dark, but I want you to tell them in the light. What you hear whispered in your ear you should shout from the housetops. [28]Don't be afraid of people, who can kill the body but cannot kill the soul. The only one you should fear is the one who can destroy the soul and the body in hell. [29]Two sparrows cost only a penny, but not even one of them can die without your Father's knowing it. [30]God even knows how many hairs are on your head. [31]So don't be afraid. You are worth much more than many sparrows.

TELL PEOPLE ABOUT YOUR FAITH

[32]"All those who stand before others and say they believe in me, I will say before my Father in heaven that they belong to me. [33]But all who stand before others and say they do not believe in me, I will say before my Father in heaven that they do not belong to me.

[34]"Don't think that I came to bring peace to the earth. I did not come to bring peace, but a sword. [35]I have come so that

'a son will be against his father,
  a daughter will be against her
    mother,

a daughter-in-law will be against her mother-in-law.

36 A person's enemies will be members of his own family.'

Micah 7:6

37"Those who love their father or mother more than they love me are not worthy to be my followers. Those who love their son or daughter more than they love me are not worthy to be my followers. 38Whoever is not willing to carry the cross and follow me is not worthy of me. 39Those who try to hold on to their lives will give up true life. Those who give up their lives for me will hold on to true life. 40Whoever accepts you also accepts me, and whoever accepts me also accepts the One who sent me. 41Whoever meets a prophet and accepts him will receive the reward of a prophet. And whoever accepts a good person because that person is good will receive the reward of a good person. 42Those who give one of these little ones a cup of cold water because they are my followers will truly get their reward."

PEEP THIS:

JESUS AND JOHN THE BAPTIST

11 After Jesus finished telling these things to his twelve followers, he left there and went to the towns in Galilee to teach and preach.

2John the Baptist was in prison, but he heard about what the Christ was doing. So John sent some of his followers to Jesus. 3They asked him, "Are you the One who is to come, or should we wait for someone else?"

4Jesus answered them, "Go tell John what you hear and see: 5The blind can see, the crippled can walk, and people with skin diseases are healed. The deaf can hear, the dead are raised to life, and the Good News is preached to the poor. 6Those who do not stumble in their faith because of me are blessed."

7As John's followers were leaving, Jesus began talking to the people about John. Jesus said, "What did you go out into the desert to see? A reed[n] blown by the wind? 8What did you go out to see? A man dressed in fine clothes? No, those who wear fine clothes live in kings' palaces. 9So why did you go out? To see a prophet? Yes, and I tell you, John is more than a prophet. 10This was written about him:

'I will send my messenger ahead of you,
who will prepare the way for you.'

Malachi 3:1

11I tell you the truth, John the Baptist is greater than any other person ever born, but even the least important person in the kingdom of heaven is greater than John. 12Since the time John the Baptist came until now, the kingdom of heaven has been going forward in strength, and people have been trying to take it by force. 13All the prophets and the law of Moses told about what would happen until the time John came. 14And if you will believe what they said, you will believe that John is Elijah, whom they said would come. 15Let those with ears use them and listen!

16"What can I say about the people of this time? What are they like? They are like children sitting in the marketplace, who call out to each other,

17'We played music for you, but you did not dance;
we sang a sad song, but you did not cry.'

18John came and did not eat or drink like other people. So people say, 'He has a demon.' 19The Son of Man came, eating and drinking, and people say, 'Look at him! He eats too much and drinks too much wine, and he is a friend of tax collectors and sinners.' But wisdom is proved to be right by what she does."

JESUS WARNS UNBELIEVERS

20Then Jesus criticized the cities where he did most of his miracles, because the people did not change their lives and stop sinning. 21He said, "How terrible for you, Korazin! How terrible for you, Bethsaida! If the same miracles I did in you had happened in Tyre and Sidon,[n] those people would have changed their lives a long time ago. They would have worn rough cloth and put ashes on themselves to show they had changed. 22But I tell you, on the Judgment Day it will be better for Tyre and Sidon than for you. 23And you, Capernaum,[n] will you be lifted up to heaven? No, you will be thrown down to the depths. If the miracles I did in you had happened in Sodom,[n] its people would have stopped sinning, and it would still be a city today. 24But I tell you, on the Judgment Day it will be better for Sodom than for you."

JESUS OFFERS REST TO PEOPLE

25At that time Jesus said, "I praise you, Father, Lord of heaven and earth, because you have hidden these things from the people who are wise and smart. But you have shown them to those who are like little children. 26Yes, Father, this is what you really wanted.

27"My Father has given me all things. No one knows the Son, except the Father. And no one knows the Father, except the Son and those whom the Son chooses to tell.

28"Come to me, all of you who are tired and have heavy loads, and I will give you rest. 29Accept my teachings and learn from me, because I am gentle and humble in spirit, and you will find rest for your lives. 30The burden that I ask you to accept is easy; the load I give you to carry is light."

11:7 reed It means that John was not ordinary or weak like grass blown by the wind. **11:21 Tyre and Sidon** Towns where wicked people lived. **11:21, 23 Korazin . . . Bethsaida . . . Capernaum** Towns by Lake Galilee where Jesus preached to the people. **11:23 Sodom** A city that God destroyed because the people were so evil.

CONNECTED

CONNECTED TO THE FATHER:

COMPLETE YOUR ASSIGNMENT

A college student took a course in which the entire grade depended upon a single paper. The student cut class most of the semester, so a few days before the paper was due he had to spend hours at the library. He stayed up late each evening working on the paper and did not sleep at all the night before it was due. The next morning he walked proudly into class and submitted his assignment. With a smile to himself, he thought how crafty he was to have missed most of the semester's classes and still have every reason to anticipate an excellent grade. The professor returned his paper a few days later with a note on the cover page, "Good content. Good research. Grade: F." The student read the comments with confusion and frustration. Then a further comment from the professor caught his attention, "THIS WAS NOT THE CORRECT ASSIGNMENT."

Jesus, God's only Son, was entrusted with the most crucial assignment ever received. His was the task of making salvation available to all people for all time. Jesus' death paid the price for our sin, and his resurrection assures us of eternal life. Just before his death on the cross, Jesus prayed to his Father, "I have glorified you on earth. I have finished the work which you have given me to do." Jesus accomplished all that God had assigned to him. His last words before he died were, "It is finished." His obedience to God brought understanding and enlightenment to others of the nature and heart of God. In this way, he glorified his Father.

We all have an assignment from God, a purpose to fulfill. What is your assignment? Whatever it is, God has given you all you need to accomplish and excel. Obey the voice within that spurs you on toward the completion of your assignment and you, too, will glorify God with your life *(1 Corinthians 10:31).*

JESUS IS LORD OF THE SABBATH

12 At that time Jesus was walking through some fields of grain on a Sabbath day. His followers were hungry, so they began to pick the grain and eat it. [2]When the Pharisees saw this, they said to Jesus, "Look! Your followers are doing what is unlawful to do on the Sabbath day."

[3]Jesus answered, "Have you not read what David did when he and the people with him were hungry? [4]He went into God's house, and he and those with him ate the holy bread, which was lawful only for priests to eat. [5]And have you not read in the law of Moses that on every Sabbath day the priests in the Temple break this law about the Sabbath day? But the priests are not wrong for doing that. [6]I tell you that there is something here that is greater than the Temple. [7]The Scripture says, 'I want kindness more than I want animal sacrifices.'[n] You don't really know what those words mean. If you understood them, you would not judge those who have done nothing wrong.

[8]"So the Son of Man is Lord of the Sabbath day."

JESUS HEALS A MAN'S HAND

[9]Jesus left there and went into their synagogue, [10]where there was a man with a crippled hand. They were looking for a reason to accuse Jesus, so they asked him, "Is it right to heal on the Sabbath day?"[n]

[11]Jesus answered, "If any of you has a sheep, and it falls into a ditch on the Sabbath day, you will help it out of the ditch. [12]Surely a human being is more important than a sheep. So it is lawful to do good things on the Sabbath day."

[13]Then Jesus said to the man with the crippled hand, "Hold out your hand." The man held out his hand, and it became well again, like the other hand. [14]But the Pharisees left and made plans to kill Jesus.

 12:7 'I . . . sacrifices.' Quotation from Hosea 6:6. 12:10 Is it right . . . day? It was against Jewish Law to work on the Sabbath day.

WORLD SAYS, WORD SAYS,

DO WHATCHA LIKE

If you must put others down to make yourself feel good – do it. If you like to smoke, if you like to drink, if you like having sex outside of marriage – do it. Do what makes you feel good; if you like it, it must be okay. Just *do it!*

"So I tell you: Live by following the Spirit. Then you will not do what your sinful selves want. Our sinful selves want what is against the Spirit, and the Spirit wants what is against our sinful selves. The two are against each other, so you cannot do just what you please" (Galatians 5:16-17).

"Those who belong to Christ Jesus have crucified their own sinful selves. They have given up their old selfish feelings and the evil things they wanted to do" (Galatians 5:24).

JESUS IS GOD'S CHOSEN SERVANT

[15]Jesus knew what the Pharisees were doing, so he left that place. Many people followed him, and he healed all who were sick. [16]But Jesus warned the people not to tell who he was. [17]He did these things to bring about what Isaiah the prophet had said:

[18]"Here is my servant whom I have chosen.
I love him, and I am pleased with him.
I will put my Spirit upon him,
and he will tell of my justice to all people.
[19]He will not argue or cry out;
no one will hear his voice in the streets.
[20]He will not break a crushed blade of grass
or put out even a weak flame
until he makes justice win the victory.
[21] In him will the non-Jewish people find hope." *Isaiah 42:1-4*

JESUS' POWER IS FROM GOD

[22]Then some people brought to Jesus a man who was blind and could not talk, because he had a demon. Jesus healed the man so that he could talk and see. [23]All the people were amazed and said, "Perhaps this man is the Son of David!" [24]When the Pharisees heard this, they said, "Jesus uses the power of Beelzebul, the ruler of demons, to force demons out of people."

[25]Jesus knew what the Pharisees were thinking, so he said to them, "Every kingdom that is divided against itself will be destroyed. And any city or family that is divided against itself will not continue. [26]And if Satan forces out himself, then Satan is divided against himself, and his kingdom will not continue. [27]You say that I use the power of Beelzebul to force out demons. If that is true, then what power do your people use to force out demons? So they will be your judges. [28]But if I use the power of God's Spirit to force out demons, then the kingdom of God has come to you.

[29]"If anyone wants to enter a strong person's house and steal his things, he must first tie up the strong person. Then he can steal the things from the house.

[30]"Whoever is not with me is against me. Whoever does not work with me is working against me. [31]So I tell you, people can be forgiven for every sin and everything they say against God. But whoever speaks against the Holy Spirit will not be forgiven. [32]Anyone who speaks against the Son of Man can be forgiven, but anyone who speaks against the Holy Spirit will not be forgiven, now or in the future.

PEOPLE KNOW YOU BY YOUR WORDS

[33]"If you want good fruit, you must make the tree good. If your tree is not good, it will have bad fruit. A tree is known by the kind of fruit it produces. [34]You snakes! You are evil people, so how can you say anything good? The mouth speaks the things that are in the heart. [35]Good people have good things in their hearts, and so they say good things. But evil people have evil in their hearts, so they say evil things. [36]And I tell you that on the Judgment Day people will be responsible for every careless thing they have said. [37]The words you have said will be used to judge you. Some of your words will prove you right, but some of your words will prove you guilty."

THE PEOPLE ASK FOR A MIRACLE

[38]Then some of the Pharisees and teachers of the law answered Jesus, saying, "Teacher, we want to see you work a miracle as a sign."

[39]Jesus answered, "Evil and sinful people are the ones who want to see a miracle for a sign. But no sign will be given to them, except the sign of the prophet Jonah. [40]Jonah was in the stomach of the big fish for three days and three nights. In the same way, the Son of Man will be in the grave three days and three nights. [41]On the Judgment Day the

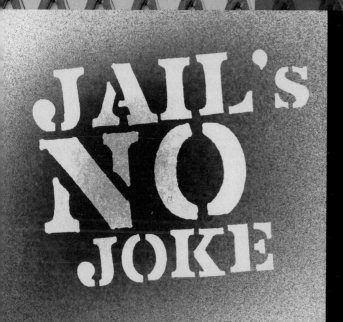

JAIL'S NO JOKE

The Lord gives me strength and makes me sing; he has saved me. Exodus 15:2

Open my eyes to see the miracles in your teachings. Psalm 119:18

I can do all things through Christ, because he gives me strength. Philippians 4:13

Jail Breaks Even the Toughest Man

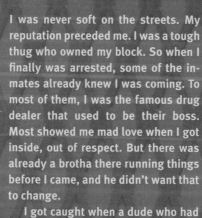

I was never soft on the streets. My reputation preceded me. I was a tough thug who owned my block. So when I finally was arrested, some of the inmates already knew I was coming. To most of them, I was the famous drug dealer that used to be their boss. Most showed me mad love when I got inside, out of respect. But there was already a brotha there running things before I came, and he didn't want that to change.

I got caught when a dude who had run my dope for years got busted. To minimize his time, he sold me out to the feds. I couldn't get bail, so we ended up in the same facility. I was supposed to be there until my trial, and he was there for a year. He and the brotha runnin' things got together and staged an ambush my first night there. Five guys tore me up and I ended up in the infirmary, hoping to make it through another day. I survived and from that day

on I had to watch my back. I lived the scared life, and I needed a protector. I couldn't sleep through the night. I felt immense anguish over my past, and I was weak.

In my cell was a Bible. I'd looked at the dingy, holy book for months before I opened it and began to read. I read the book of Matthew all night long and it forever changed my life. Since that night, not one day goes that I do not read God's Word. As I understood and accepted Jesus' love for me, I felt protected, comforted, and healed in a way that made me stronger than any fake power on the streets ever could. I'm now in a federal prison serving an eight-year sentence. I'll be up for parole in two years. When I get out, I know I'll use my influence to win people to Christ. I can't wait to share my life lesson. Only in him is there true strength.

people from Nineveh[n] will stand up with you people who live now, and they will show that you are guilty. When Jonah preached to them, they were sorry and changed their lives. And I tell you that someone greater than Jonah is here. [42]On the Judgment Day, the Queen of the South[n] will stand up with you people who live today. She will show that you are guilty, because she came from far away to listen to Solomon's wise teaching. And I tell you that someone greater than Solomon is here.

PEOPLE TODAY ARE FULL OF EVIL

[43]"When an evil spirit comes out of a person, it travels through dry places, looking for a place to rest, but it doesn't find it. [44]So the spirit says, 'I will go back to the house I left.' When the spirit comes back, it finds the house still empty, swept clean, and made neat. [45]Then the evil spirit goes out and brings seven other spirits even more evil than it is, and they go in and live there. So the person has even more trouble than before. It is the same way with the evil people who live today."

JESUS' TRUE FAMILY

[46]While Jesus was talking to the people, his mother and brothers stood outside, trying to find a way to talk to him. [47]Someone told Jesus, "Your mother and brothers are standing outside, and they want to talk to you."[n]

[48]He answered, "Who is my mother? Who are my brothers?" [49]Then he pointed to his followers and said, "Here are my mother and my brothers. [50]My true brother and sister and mother are those who do what my Father in heaven wants."

A STORY ABOUT PLANTING SEED

13 That same day Jesus went out of the house and sat by the lake. [2]Large crowds gathered around him, so he got into a boat and sat down, while the people stood on the shore. [3]Then Jesus used stories to teach them many things. He said: "A farmer went out to plant his seed. [4]While he was planting, some seed fell by the road, and the birds came and ate it all up. [5]Some seed fell on rocky ground, where there wasn't much dirt. That seed grew very fast, because the ground was not deep. [6]But when the sun rose, the plants dried up, because they did not have deep roots. [7]Some other seed fell among thorny weeds, which grew and choked the good plants. [8]Some other seed fell on good ground where it grew and produced a crop. Some plants made a hundred times more, some made sixty times more, and some made thirty times more. [9]Let those with ears use them and listen."

> THE DEAF CAN HEAR, THE DEAD ARE RAISED TO LIFE, AND THE GOOD NEWS IS PREACHED TO THE POOR.

WHY JESUS USED STORIES TO TEACH

[10]The followers came to Jesus and asked, "Why do you use stories to teach the people?"

[11]Jesus answered, "You have been chosen to know the secrets about the kingdom of heaven, but others cannot know these secrets. [12]Those who have understanding will be given more, and they will have all they need. But those who do not have understanding, even what they have will be taken away from them. [13]This is why I use stories to teach the people: They see, but they don't really see. They hear, but they don't really hear or understand. [14]So they show that the things Isaiah said about them are true:

'You will listen and listen, but you
    will not understand.
You will look and look, but you
    will not learn.
[15]For the minds of these people have
    become stubborn.
They do not hear with their ears,
    and they have closed their eyes.
Otherwise they might really
    understand
what they see with their eyes
and hear with their ears.
They might really understand in
    their minds
and come back to me and be
    healed.'   *Isaiah 6:9-10*

[16]But you are blessed, because you see with your eyes and hear with your ears. [17]I tell you the truth, many prophets and good people wanted to see the things that you now see, but they did not see them. And they wanted to hear the things that you now hear, but they did not hear them.

JESUS EXPLAINS THE SEED STORY

[18]"So listen to the meaning of that story about the farmer. [19]What is the seed that fell by the road? That seed is like the person who hears the message about the kingdom but does not understand it. The Evil One comes and takes away what was planted in that person's heart. [20]And what is the seed that fell on rocky ground? That seed is like the person who hears the teaching and quickly accepts it with joy. [21]But he does not let the teaching go deep into his life, so he keeps it only a short time. When trouble or persecution comes because of the teaching he accepted, he quickly gives up. [22]And what is the seed that fell among the thorny weeds? That seed is like the person who hears the teaching

12:41 Nineveh The city where Jonah preached to warn the people. Read Jonah 3.   **12:42 Queen of the South** The Queen of Sheba. She traveled a thousand miles to learn God's wisdom from Solomon. Read 1 Kings 10:1-13.   **12:47 Someone . . . you.** Some Greek copies do not have verse 47.

▶ 20

REAL RHYMES:

PULL DIS TRIGGA

BY JOHN MOORER (A/K/A JOHN THE BAPTIST)

I TRY MY BEST TO BE KIND, BUT SOMETIMES IN THE BACK OF MY MIND
I'M HAVIN' THOUGHTS OF A KILLA. BUT I'LL DO YEARS IF I PULL DIS TRIGGA.
FROM DELAWARE TO ATL, LOVE OR HATE ME WELL.
SOME WISH ME STRAIGHT TO JAIL OR TRY TO CURSE ME WITH FLAKEY SPELLS.
THEY DON'T KNOW, MAN, MY OLD MAN WAS COLDER THAN A SNOWMAN.
I WON SOME AND I LOST SOME, BUT TOO OFTEN
I WAS CLOSE TO GIVING UP THE GHOST IN MY COFFIN.
I'M TRYIN' TO SHINE LIGHT WITHIN 'CAUSE THIS CHRISTIAN IS IN TIMBS AND LOOKS LIKE THEM.
LORD WHAT ALL THIS JUNK BE 'BOUT? I TURNED THE OTHER CHEEK THEY THINK THEY PUNKED ME OUT.
I TELL 'EM THAT YOU LOVE 'EM BUT SOME COULD CARE LESS.
I'M AMONGST REAL KILLAS GORILLAS THAT'S FEARLESS
THEY DON'T FEAR DEATH, LIFE, OR HELL. THEY DON'T FEAR GLOCKS, COPS, OR JAIL.
I KNOW I'M FREE FROM THE SIN IN ME BUT IT'S ALMOST LIKE HIM OR ME
SOMEBODY GOTTA GO.

I TRY MY BEST TO BE KIND BUT SOMETIMES IN THE BACK OF MY MIND
I'M HAVIN' THOUGHTS OF A KILLA. BUT I'LL DO YEARS IF I PULL DIS TRIGGA.
AND SO I TRY TO UNWIND BUT SOMETIMES LIFE IS SO UNKIND.
I'M HAVIN' THOUGHTS OF A KILLA BUT I'LL DO YEARS IF A PULL DIS TRIGGA.

I THINK BACK ON MY SON, HE WOULDA BEEN 12.
I COULD A SNAPPED ON HIS KILLA, IT WOULDA BEEN HELL.
I COULDA BEEN JAILED, COULDA BEEN HELD WITH NO BOND,
BUT MY FAM WOULDA HAD TO LIVE LIFE WITH NO JOHN.
MY MIND'S ON THE LAW SAYING EYE FOR EYE.
DEMONIC INFLUENCES SAYIN' RIDE OR DIE.
LOAD THE CLIP, GRIP, CLUTCH AND BUST. ASHES TO ASHES AND DUST TO DUST.
ROUND FOR ROUND I CAN DOWN HIM WITH EASE SO I'M PRAYIN' TO GOD, I'M DOWN ON MY KNEES.
LORD I NEED YOU, MY SPIRIT WANTS TO PLEASE YOU BUT RIGHT NOW MY FLESH IS REAL DIESEL.
I KNOW WHERE HE LIVES, I KNOW WHERE HE GOES, I'M ALREADY SEEIN' HIS BODY FULL OF HOLES.
DELIVER ME BEFORE I GET TOO BITTER. BUT I'LL DO YEARS IF I PULL DIS TRIGGA.

I TRY MY BEST TO BE KIND BUT SOMETIMES IN THE BACK OF MY MIND
I'M HAVIN' THOUGHTS OF A KILLA. BUT I'LL DO YEARS IF I PULL DIS TRIGGA.
AND SO I TRY TO UNWIND BUT SOMETIMES LIFE IS SO UNKIND.
I'M HAVIN' THOUGHTS OF A KILLA BUT I'LL DO YEARS IF I PULL DIS TRIGGA.

but lets worries about this life and the temptation of wealth stop that teaching from growing. So the teaching does not produce fruit[n] in that person's life. [23]But what is the seed that fell on the good ground? That seed is like the person who hears the teaching and understands it. That person grows and produces fruit, sometimes a hundred times more, sometimes sixty times more, and sometimes thirty times more."

A STORY ABOUT WHEAT AND WEEDS

[24]Then Jesus told them another story: "The kingdom of heaven is like a man who planted good seed in his field. [25]That night, when everyone was asleep, his enemy came and planted weeds among the wheat and then left. [26]Later, the wheat sprouted and the heads of grain grew, but the weeds also grew. [27]Then the man's servants came to him and said, 'You planted good seed in your field. Where did the weeds come from?' [28]The man answered, 'An enemy planted

What does God think about music?

God loves music. Take a look in a Bible concordance and you'll find many references to music, songs, instruments, and singers. Besides worship of the Lord, some of the songs found in the Bible express the love between a husband and wife, a parent and child, friendship, even the beauty of nature; they tell stories, grieve, express frustration, and rejoice over victories.

Music — like all of the arts — is a gift from God, given to man as a means of expression. Instruments, rhythms, volume, are neither good nor bad. Whether someone likes jazz, rock, blues, classical, or reggae is entirely a matter of taste. The problem arises when the lyrics or the song's intended purpose — either by the songwriter or the performer — are opposed to what the Bible teaches.

Read on: James 1:17; Ephesians 5:19; I Corinthians 14:26; Matthew 21:16; James 5:13

PEEP THIS:

Twenty-five percent of college students are involved in activist activities (29 percent were involved in 1969).

weeds.' The servants asked, 'Do you want us to pull up the weeds?' [29]The man answered, 'No, because when you pull up the weeds, you might also pull up the wheat. [30]Let the weeds and the wheat grow together until the harvest time. At harvest time I will tell the workers, "First gather the weeds and tie them together to be burned. Then gather the wheat and bring it to my barn." ' "

STORIES OF MUSTARD SEED AND YEAST

[31]Then Jesus told another story: "The kingdom of heaven is like a mustard seed that a man planted in his field. [32]That seed is the smallest of all seeds, but when it grows, it is one of the largest garden plants. It becomes big enough for the wild birds to come and build nests in its branches."

[33]Then Jesus told another story: "The kingdom of heaven is like yeast that a woman took and hid in a large tub of flour until it made all the dough rise."

[34]Jesus used stories to tell all these things to the people; he always used stories to teach them. [35]This is as the prophet said:

"I will speak using stories;
I will tell things that have been
  secret since the world was
  made."
Psalm 78:2

JESUS EXPLAINS ABOUT THE WEEDS

[36]Then Jesus left the crowd and went into the house. His followers came to him and said, "Explain to us the meaning of the story about the weeds in the field."

[37]Jesus answered, "The man who planted the good seed in the field is the Son of Man. [38]The field is the world, and the good seed are all of God's children who belong to the kingdom. The weeds are those people who belong to the Evil One. [39]And the enemy who planted the bad seed is the devil. The harvest time is the end of the age, and the workers who gather are God's angels.

13:22 **produce fruit** To produce fruit means to have in your life the good things God wants.

40"Just as the weeds are pulled up and burned in the fire, so it will be at the end of the age. 41The Son of Man will send out his angels, and they will gather out of his kingdom all who cause sin and all who do evil. 42The angels will throw them into the blazing furnace, where the people will cry and grind their teeth with pain. 43Then the good people will shine like the sun in the kingdom of their Father. Let those with ears use them and listen.

STORIES OF A TREASURE AND A PEARL

44"The kingdom of heaven is like a treasure hidden in a field. One day a man found the treasure, and then he hid it in the field again. He was so happy that he went and sold everything he owned to buy that field.

45"Also, the kingdom of heaven is like a man looking for fine pearls. 46When he found a very valuable pearl, he went and sold everything he had and bought it.

A STORY OF A FISHING NET

47"Also, the kingdom of heaven is like a net that was put into the lake and caught many different kinds of fish. 48When it was full, the fishermen pulled the net to the shore. They sat down and put all the good fish in baskets and threw away the bad fish. 49It will be this way at the end of the age. The angels will come and separate the evil people from the good people. 50The angels will throw the evil people into the blazing furnace, where people will cry and grind their teeth with pain."

51Jesus asked his followers, "Do you understand all these things?"

They answered, "Yes, we understand."

52Then Jesus said to them, "So every teacher of the law who has been taught about the kingdom of heaven is like the owner of a house. He brings out both new things and old things he has saved."

THE SCRIPT

Jesus Calms the Storm
Matthew 8:23-27

Jesus caught a boat to cross the waters and to get remote.
The disciples followed him, as was the normal code.
And before they knew it, they got swallowed in a furious storm,
   right on the sea.
The kind known to hit with quick force on these waters of
   Galilee;
Especially when you're out on the lake trying to get across.
But the Lord wasn't even scared, of course.
He was finally free from the crowds, and below the ship's bow,
   asleep by now.
Just entering that deep stage of snoozing where nothin' was
   moving,
Then the disciples broke him outta his groove with
   cries and shrills and squeals!

Screaming, "Master, please save us 'cause right now our fates
   are sealed!"
Jesus awoke and asked them, "Are y'all doubters out here
   pouting for real?
What's the deal? Where's all that faith you always talking about
   when I'm not around?
How you gone' doubt right now? Check this out." And with that,
   Jesus stood up and spoke to the elements. "Yea that's it!
I'm talking to the waters and clouds.
Rain and wind, y'all both calm down."
Now you talk about tripping out!
All the men had open mouths, "What kind of man are
   we around . . .
Even the forces of nature bowing to his sound?"

Take this with you: When storms come into our lives we think
   that God must be "sleeping." But no storm can rage that
   one word from Jesus can't calm.

JESUS GOES TO HIS HOMETOWN

⁵³When Jesus finished teaching with these stories, he left there. ⁵⁴He went to his hometown and taught the people in the synagogue, and they were amazed. They said, "Where did this man get this wisdom and this power to do miracles? ⁵⁵He is just the son of a carpenter. His mother is Mary, and his brothers are James, Joseph, Simon, and Judas. ⁵⁶And all his sisters are here with us. Where then does this man get all these things?" ⁵⁷So the people were upset with Jesus.

But Jesus said to them, "A prophet is honored everywhere except in his hometown and in his own home."

⁵⁸So he did not do many miracles there because they had no faith.

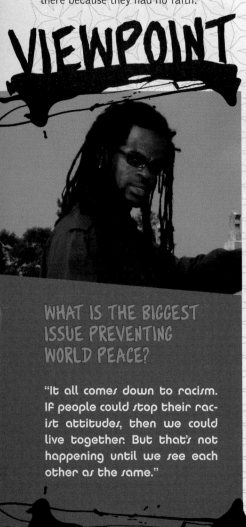

VIEWPOINT

WHAT IS THE BIGGEST ISSUE PREVENTING WORLD PEACE?

"It all comes down to racism. If people could stop their racist attitudes, then we could live together. But that's not happening until we see each other as the same."

HOW JOHN THE BAPTIST WAS KILLED

14 At that time Herod, the ruler of Galilee, heard the reports about Jesus. ²So he said to his servants, "Jesus is John the Baptist, who has risen from the dead. That is why he can work these miracles."

³Sometime before this, Herod had arrested John, tied him up, and put him into prison. Herod did this because of Herodias, who had been the wife of Philip, Herod's brother. ⁴John had been telling Herod, "It is not lawful for you to be married to Herodias." ⁵Herod wanted to kill John, but he was afraid of the people, because they believed John was a prophet.

⁶On Herod's birthday, the daughter of Herodias danced for Herod and his guests, and she pleased him. ⁷So he promised with an oath to give her anything she wanted. ⁸Herodias told her daughter what to ask for, so she said to Herod, "Give me the head of John the Baptist here on a platter." ⁹Although King Herod was very sad, he had made a promise, and his dinner guests had heard him. So Herod ordered that what she asked for be done. ¹⁰He sent soldiers to the prison to cut off John's head. ¹¹And they brought it on a platter and gave it to the girl, and she took it to her mother. ¹²John's followers came and got his body and buried it. Then they went and told Jesus.

MORE THAN FIVE THOUSAND FED

¹³When Jesus heard what had happened to John, he left in a boat and went to a lonely place by himself. But the crowds heard about it and followed him on foot from the towns. ¹⁴When he arrived, he saw a great crowd waiting. He felt sorry for them and healed those who were sick.

¹⁵When it was evening, his followers came to him and said, "No one lives in this place, and it is already late. Send the people away so they can go to the towns and buy food for themselves."

¹⁶But Jesus answered, "They don't need to go away. You give them something to eat."

¹⁷They said to him, "But we have only five loaves of bread and two fish."

¹⁸Jesus said, "Bring the bread and the fish to me." ¹⁹Then he told the people to sit down on the grass. He took the five loaves and the two fish and, looking to heaven, he thanked God for the food. Jesus divided the bread and gave it to his followers, who gave it to the people. ²⁰All the people ate and were satisfied. Then the followers filled twelve baskets with the leftover pieces of food. ²¹There were about five thousand men there who ate, not counting women and children.

JESUS WALKS ON THE WATER

²²Immediately Jesus told his followers to get into the boat and go ahead of him across the lake. He stayed there to send the people home. ²³After he had sent them away, he went by himself up into the hills to pray. It was late, and Jesus was there alone. ²⁴By this time, the boat was already far away from land. It was being hit by waves, because the wind was blowing against it.

²⁵Between three and six o'clock in the morning, Jesus came to them, walking on the water. ²⁶When his followers saw him walking on the water, they were afraid. They said, "It's a ghost!" and cried out in fear.

²⁷But Jesus quickly spoke to them, "Have courage! It is I. Do not be afraid."

²⁸Peter said, "Lord, if it is really you, then command me to come to you on the water."

²⁹Jesus said, "Come."

And Peter left the boat and walked on the water to Jesus. ³⁰But when Peter saw the wind and the waves, he became afraid and began to sink. He shouted, "Lord, save me!"

PASSING GOD'S TEST

Ⓘ was two weeks away from receiving my diploma in journalism, I was the editor for the university student newspaper, and I had a part-time job in the mailroom at the television station downtown. On top of this, a story I had written about my church's work with the homeless was being published in the local newspaper. I had applied for a job as newsroom assistant and I was sure I would bag the job.

I was shocked when I read the announcement on the employee bulletin board: "Please join us in welcoming our new newsroom assistant, George Jones from Columbus, Ohio, where he recently graduated from . . ." I couldn't read the rest because I was on fire. They hadn't even given me an interview!

Later, I phoned one of the men in my church, and he helped me to calm down. "You may think they dissed you, but God's got something special for you, young bruh." So I tried to thank God for what he had in my future. I remembered all of the homeless men and their families and, though my work in the mailroom could be discouraging, I was grateful to have a job. I could wait for God's special plan for me to unfold.

Months later, while delivering a package, I discovered one of the anchormen was putting together a program about the city's homeless. I told him about my article in the local paper and about the work my church was doing. He came down to the mailroom to read the article, then arranged to send a television crew to the homeless shelter my church had built.

As it turned out, *I* got to interview some of the homeless men on camera! When the story aired, the television station manager was blown away by how natural I came across on camera. He decided to make interviews with the homeless a regular part of the programming—and he made me an associate producer for public affairs! On top of that, the station agreed to pay for me to continue my education.

I now help produce television programs that focus on the needs of the poor and how the church and others in the community can work together to meet the needs. George Jones, who turned out to be a great news writer, comes alongside and we work together. Further, I'm getting a second degree in urban affairs and communications—and someone else is paying for it.

Romans 8:28: We know that in everything God works for the good of those who love him.

---

[31] Immediately Jesus reached out his hand and caught Peter. Jesus said, "Your faith is small. Why did you doubt?"

[32] After they got into the boat, the wind became calm. [33] Then those who were in the boat worshiped Jesus and said, "Truly you are the Son of God!"

[34] When they had crossed the lake, they came to shore at Gennesaret. [35] When the people there recognized Jesus, they told people all around there that Jesus had come, and they brought all their sick to him. [36] They begged Jesus to let them touch just the edge of his coat, and all who touched it were healed.

OBEY GOD'S LAW

15 Then some Pharisees and teachers of the law came to Jesus from Jerusalem. They asked him, [2] "Why don't your followers obey the unwritten laws which have been handed down to us? They don't wash their hands before they eat."

[3] Jesus answered, "And why do you refuse to obey God's command so that you can follow your own teachings? [4] God said, 'Honor your father and your mother,' and 'Anyone who says cruel things to his father or mother must be put to death.' [5] But you say a person can tell his father or mother, 'I have something I could use to help you, but I have given it to God already.' [6] You teach that person not to honor his father or his mother. You rejected what God said

---

 15:4 'Honor . . . mother.' Quotation from Exodus 20:12; Deuteronomy 5:16. 15:4 'Anyone . . . death.' Quotation from Exodus 21:17.

for the sake of your own rules. [7]You are hypocrites! Isaiah was right when he said about you:

[8]These people show honor to me
   with words,
   but their hearts are far from me.
[9]Their worship of me is worthless.
   The things they teach are nothing
   but human rules.' " *Isaiah 29:13*

[10]After Jesus called the crowd to him, he said, "Listen and understand what I am saying. [11]It is not what people put into their mouths that makes them unclean. It is what comes out of their mouths that makes them unclean."

[12]Then his followers came to him and asked, "Do you know that the Pharisees are angry because of what you said?"

[13]Jesus answered, "Every plant that my Father in heaven has not planted himself will be pulled up by the roots. [14]Stay away from the Pharisees; they are blind leaders.[n] And if a blind person leads a blind person, both will fall into a ditch."

[15]Peter said, "Explain the example to us."

[16]Jesus said, "Do you still not understand? [17]Surely you know that all the food that enters the mouth goes into the stomach and then goes out of the body. [18]But what people say with their mouths comes from the way they think; these are the things that make people unclean. [19]Out of the mind come evil thoughts, murder, adultery, sexual sins, stealing, lying, and speaking evil of others. [20]These things make people unclean; eating with unwashed hands does not make them unclean."

JESUS HELPS A NON-JEWISH WOMAN

[21]Jesus left that place and went to the area of Tyre and Sidon. [22]A Canaanite woman from that area came to Jesus

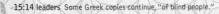
15:14 leaders Some Greek copies continue, "of blind people."

and cried out, "Lord, Son of David, have mercy on me! My daughter has a demon, and she is suffering very much."

[23]But Jesus did not answer the woman. So his followers came to Jesus and begged him, "Tell the woman to go away. She is following us and shouting."

[24]Jesus answered, "God sent me only to the lost sheep, the people of Israel."

[25]Then the woman came to Jesus again and bowed before him and said, "Lord, help me!"

[26]Jesus answered, "It is not right to take the children's bread and give it to the dogs."

[27]The woman said, "Yes, Lord, but even the dogs eat the crumbs that fall from their masters' table."

[28]Then Jesus answered, "Woman, you have great faith! I will do what you asked." And at that moment the woman's daughter was healed.

JESUS HEALS MANY PEOPLE

[29]After leaving there, Jesus went along the shore of Lake Galilee. He went up on a hill and sat there.

[30]Great crowds came to Jesus, bringing with them the lame, the blind, the crippled, those who could not speak, and many others. They put them at Jesus' feet, and he healed them. [31]The crowd was amazed when they saw that people who could not speak before were now able to speak. The crippled were made strong. The lame could walk, and the blind could see. And they praised the God of Israel for this.

MORE THAN FOUR THOUSAND FED

[32]Jesus called his followers to him and said, "I feel sorry for these people, because they have already been with me three days, and they have nothing to eat. I don't want to send them away hungry. They might faint while going home."

[33]His followers asked him, "How can we get enough bread to feed all these people? We are far away from any town."

[34]Jesus asked, "How many loaves of bread do you have?"

They answered, "Seven, and a few small fish."

[35]Jesus told the people to sit on the ground. [36]He took the seven loaves of bread and the fish and gave thanks to God. Then he divided the food and gave it to his followers, and they gave it to the people. [37]All the people ate and were satisfied. Then his followers filled seven baskets with the leftover pieces of food. [38]There were about four thousand men there who ate, besides women and children. [39]After sending the people home, Jesus got into the boat and went to the area of Magadan.

> THEIR WORSHIP OF ME IS WORTHLESS. THE THINGS THEY TEACH ARE NOTHING BUT HUMAN RULES.

THE LEADERS ASK FOR A MIRACLE

16 The Pharisees and Sadducees came to Jesus, wanting to trick him. So they asked him to show them a miracle from God.

[2]Jesus answered,[n] "At sunset you say we will have good weather, because the sky is red. [3]And in the morning you say that it will be a rainy day, because the sky is dark and red. You see these signs in the sky and know what they mean. In the same way, you see the things that I am doing now, but you don't know their meaning. [4]Evil and sinful people ask for a miracle as a sign, but they will not be given any sign, except the sign of Jonah."[n] Then Jesus left them and went away.

GUARD AGAINST WRONG TEACHINGS

[5]Jesus' followers went across the lake, but they had forgotten to bring bread. [6]Jesus said to them, "Be careful! Beware of the yeast of the Pharisees and the Sadducees."

[7]His followers discussed the meaning of this, saying, "He said this because we forgot to bring bread."

[8]Knowing what they were talking about, Jesus asked them, "Why are you talking about not having bread? Your faith is small. [9]Do you still not understand? Remember the five loaves of bread that fed the five thousand? And remember that you filled many baskets with the leftovers? [10]Or the seven loaves of bread that fed the four thousand and the many baskets you filled then also? [11]I was not talking to you about bread. Why don't you understand that? I am telling you to beware of the yeast of the Pharisees and the Sadducees." [12]Then the followers understood that Jesus was not telling them to beware of the yeast used in bread but to beware of the teaching of the Pharisees and the Sadducees.

PETER SAYS JESUS IS THE CHRIST

[13]When Jesus came to the area of Caesarea Philippi, he asked his followers, "Who do people say the Son of Man is?"

[14]They answered, "Some say you are John the Baptist. Others say you are Elijah, and still others say you are Jeremiah or one of the prophets."

[15]Then Jesus asked them, "And who do you say I am?"

[16]Simon Peter answered, "You are the Christ, the Son of the living God."

[17]Jesus answered, "You are blessed, Simon son of Jonah, because no person taught you that. My Father in heaven showed you who I am. [18]So I tell you, you are Peter.[n] On this rock I will build my church, and the power of death will not be able to defeat it. [19]I will give you the

keys of the kingdom of heaven; the things you don't allow on earth will be the things that God does not allow, and the things you allow on earth will be the things that God allows." [20]Then Jesus warned his followers not to tell anyone he was the Christ.

JESUS SAYS THAT HE MUST DIE

[21]From that time on Jesus began telling his followers that he must go to Jerusalem, where the Jewish elders, the leading priests, and the teachers of the law would make him suffer many things. He told them he must be killed and then be raised from the dead on the third day.

[22]Peter took Jesus aside and told him not to talk like that. He said, "God save you from those things, Lord! Those things will never happen to you!"

[23]Then Jesus said to Peter, "Go away from me, Satan![n] You are not helping me! You don't care about the things of God, but only about the things people think are important."

[24]Then Jesus said to his followers, "If people want to follow me, they must give up the things they want. They must be willing even to give up their lives to follow me. [25]Those who want to save their lives will give up true life, and those who

He's got answers

I worry all the time. How can I stop?

"Don't worry." That's a lot easier said than done. Worry can knot your stomach, rob your sleep, steal your concentration, even destroy your health. But worrying cannot help anything. The Bible says you cannot add any time to your life by worrying about it.

Behind worry is fear and insecurity. Fear of something happening that you are helpless to do anything about; and insecurity that no one cares about you, not even God. But God does care for you. When Jesus talked to his disciples about worry, he pointed out how God cares for the birds and then told them that they were worth much more than the birds.

What are you worried about; are there any practical steps you can take? Just doing something can loosen the grip worry can have on your life. If you feel like it is beyond your ability, find someone who can help you look at your situation, whether it is a good counselor, a doctor, or just someone who loves the Lord.

Sometimes dealing with worry goes beyond fixing a single situation; it takes dealing with thought patterns. "Think happy thoughts," might sound too simple, but there is truth in that statement. Find scriptures in the Bible that encourage you and when you feel worry coming on, repeat these scriptures to yourself. And remember, you are worth much more than the birds.

Read on: Matthew 6:25-34; Philippians 4:6-7; Philippians 4:19

PEEP THIS:

College students' objectives considered essential or very important: 73.2 percent—being well off financially; 73.6 percent—raising a family; 63.2 percent—helping others in difficulty.

give up their lives for me will have true life. [26]It is worthless to have the whole world if they lose their souls. They could never pay enough to buy back their souls. [27]The Son of Man will come again with his Father's glory and with his angels. At that time, he will reward them for what they have done. [28]I tell you the truth, some people standing here will see the Son of Man coming with his kingdom before they die."

JESUS TALKS WITH MOSES AND ELIJAH

17 Six days later, Jesus took Peter, James, and John, the brother of James, up on a high mountain by themselves. [2]While they watched, Jesus' appearance was changed; his face became bright like the sun, and his clothes became white as light. [3]Then Moses and Elijah[n] appeared to them, talking with Jesus.

[4]Peter said to Jesus, "Lord, it is good that we are here. If you want, I will put up three tents here—one for you, one for Moses, and one for Elijah."

[5]While Peter was talking, a bright cloud covered them. A voice came from the cloud and said, "This is my Son, whom I love, and I am very pleased with him. Listen to him!"

[6]When his followers heard the voice,

16:23 Satan Name for the devil, meaning "the enemy." Jesus means that Peter was talking like Satan. 17:3 Moses and Elijah Two of the most important Jewish leaders in the past. God had given Moses the Law, and Elijah was an important prophet.

they were so frightened they fell to the ground. [7]But Jesus went to them and touched them and said, "Stand up. Don't be afraid." [8]When they looked up, they saw Jesus was now alone.

[9]As they were coming down the mountain, Jesus commanded them not to tell anyone about what they had seen until the Son of Man had risen from the dead.

[10]Then his followers asked him, "Why do the teachers of the law say that Elijah must come first?"

[11]Jesus answered, "They are right to say that Elijah is coming and that he will make everything the way it should be. [12]But I tell you that Elijah has already come, and they did not recognize him. They did to him whatever they wanted to do. It will be the same with the Son of Man; those same people will make the Son of Man suffer." [13]Then the followers understood that Jesus was talking about John the Baptist.

JESUS HEALS A SICK BOY

[14]When Jesus and his followers came back to the crowd, a man came to Jesus and bowed before him. [15]The man said, "Lord, have mercy on my son. He has epilepsy[n] and is suffering very much, because he often falls into the fire or into the water. [16]I brought him to your followers, but they could not cure him."

[17]Jesus answered, "You people have no faith, and your lives are all wrong. How long must I put up with you? How long must I continue to be patient with you? Bring the boy here." [18]Jesus commanded the demon inside the boy. Then the demon came out, and the boy was healed from that time on.

[19]The followers came to Jesus when he was alone and asked, "Why couldn't we force the demon out?"

[20]Jesus answered, "Because your faith is too small. I tell you the truth, if your faith is as big as a mustard seed, you can say to this mountain, 'Move from here to there,' and it will move. All things will be possible for you. [[21]That kind of spirit comes out only if you use prayer and fasting.]"[n]

JESUS TALKS ABOUT HIS DEATH

[22]While Jesus' followers were gathering in Galilee, he said to them, "The Son of Man will be handed over to people, [23]and they will kill him. But on the third day he will be raised from the dead." And the followers were filled with sadness.

JESUS TALKS ABOUT PAYING TAXES

[24]When Jesus and his followers came to Capernaum, the men who collected the Temple tax came to Peter. They asked, "Does your teacher pay the Temple tax?"

[25]Peter answered, "Yes, Jesus pays the tax."

IF PEOPLE WANT TO FOLLOW ME, THEY MUST GIVE UP THE THINGS THEY WANT.

Peter went into the house, but before he could speak, Jesus said to him, "What do you think? The kings of the earth collect different kinds of taxes. But who pays the taxes—the king's children or others?"

[26]Peter answered, "Other people pay the taxes."

Jesus said to Peter, "Then the children of the king don't have to pay taxes. [27]But we don't want to upset these tax collectors. So go to the lake and fish. After you catch the first fish, open its mouth and you will find a coin. Take that coin and give it to the tax collectors for you and me."

WHO IS THE GREATEST?

18 At that time the followers came to Jesus and asked, "Who is greatest in the kingdom of heaven?"

[2]Jesus called a little child to him and stood the child before his followers. [3]Then he said, "I tell you the truth, you must change and become like little children. Otherwise, you will never enter the kingdom of heaven. [4]The greatest person in the kingdom of heaven is the one who makes himself humble like this child.

[5]"Whoever accepts a child in my name accepts me. [6]If one of these little children believes in me, and someone causes that child to sin, it would be better for that person to have a large stone tied around the neck and be drowned in the sea. [7]How terrible for the people of the world because of the things that cause them to sin. Such things will happen, but how terrible for the one who causes them to happen! [8]If your hand or your foot causes you to sin, cut it off and throw it away. It is better for you to lose part of your body and live forever than to have two hands and two feet and be thrown into the fire that burns forever. [9]If your eye causes you to sin, take it out and throw it away. It is better for you to have only one eye and live forever than to have two eyes and be thrown into the fire of hell.

A LOST SHEEP

[10]"Be careful. Don't think these little children are worth nothing. I tell you that they have angels in heaven who are always with my Father in heaven. [[11]The Son of Man came to save lost people.]"[n]

[12]"If a man has a hundred sheep but one of the sheep gets lost, he will leave the other ninety-nine on the hill and go to look for the lost sheep. [13]I tell you the truth, if he finds it he is happier about that one sheep than about the ninety-nine that were never lost. [14]In the same way,

---

 17:15 epilepsy A disease that causes a person sometimes to lose control of his body and maybe faint, shake strongly, or not be able to move. **17:21 That . . . fasting.** Some Greek copies do not contain the bracketed text. **18:11 The . . . people.** Some Greek copies do not contain the bracketed text.

your Father in heaven does not want any of these little children to be lost.

WHEN A PERSON SINS AGAINST YOU

15"If your fellow believer sins against you,[n] go and tell him in private what he did wrong. If he listens to you, you have helped that person to be your brother or sister again. 16But if he refuses to listen, go to him again and take one or two other people with you. 'Every case may be proved by two or three witnesses.'[n] 17If he refuses to listen to them, tell the church. If he refuses to listen to the church, then treat him like a person who does not believe in God or like a tax collector.

18"I tell you the truth, the things you don't allow on earth will be the things God does not allow. And the things you allow on earth will be the things that God allows.

19"Also, I tell you that if two of you on earth agree about something and pray for it, it will be done for you by my Father in heaven. 20This is true because if two or three people come together in my name, I am there with them."

AN UNFORGIVING SERVANT

21Then Peter came to Jesus and asked, "Lord, when my fellow believer sins against me, how many times must I forgive him? Should I forgive him as many as seven times?"

22Jesus answered, "I tell you, you must forgive him more than seven times. You must forgive him even if he wrongs you seventy times seven.

23"The kingdom of heaven is like a king who decided to collect the money his servants owed him. 24When the king began to collect his money, a servant who owed him several million dollars was brought to him. 25But the servant did not have enough money to pay his master, the king. So the master ordered that everything the servant owned should be sold, even the servant's wife and children. Then the money would be used to pay the king what the servant owed.

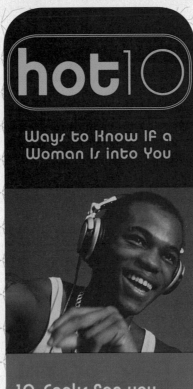

hot 10

Ways to Know If a Woman Is into You

10. Cooks for you
9. Spends quality time with you
8. Makes eye contact
7. Can't stop smiling
6. Listens to you
5. Introduces you to her friends
4. Laughs at your corny jokes
3. Late-night phone calls
2. Actually calls you
1. Gives you her real phone number

26"But the servant fell on his knees and begged, 'Be patient with me, and I will pay you everything I owe.' 27The master felt sorry for his servant and told him he did not have to pay it back. Then he let the servant go free.

28"Later, that same servant found another servant who owed him a few dollars. The servant grabbed him around the neck and said, 'Pay me the money you owe me!'

29"The other servant fell on his knees and begged him, 'Be patient with me, and I will pay you everything I owe.'

30"But the first servant refused to be patient. He threw the other servant into prison until he could pay everything he owed. 31When the other servants saw what had happened, they were very sorry. So they went and told their master all that had happened.

32"Then the master called his servant in and said, 'You evil servant! Because you begged me to forget what you owed, I told you that you did not have to pay anything. 33You should have showed mercy to that other servant, just as I showed mercy to you.' 34The master was very angry and put the servant in prison to be punished until he could pay everything he owed.

35"This king did what my heavenly Father will do to you if you do not forgive your brother or sister from your heart."

JESUS TEACHES ABOUT DIVORCE

19 After Jesus said all these things, he left Galilee and went into the area of Judea on the other side of the Jordan River. 2Large crowds followed him, and he healed them there.

3Some Pharisees came to Jesus and tried to trick him. They asked, "Is it right for a man to divorce his wife for any reason he chooses?"

4Jesus answered, "Surely you have read in the Scriptures: When God made

---

 18:15 against you Some Greek copies do not have "against you." **18:16 'Every . . . witnesses.'** Quotation from Deuteronomy 19:15.

the world, 'he made them male and female.'ⁿ ⁵And God said, 'So a man will leave his father and mother and be united with his wife, and the two will become one body.'ⁿ ⁶So there are not two, but one. God has joined the two together, so no one should separate them.''

⁷The Pharisees asked, ''Why then did Moses give a command for a man to divorce his wife by giving her divorce papers?''

⁸Jesus answered, ''Moses allowed you to divorce your wives because you refused to accept God's teaching, but divorce was not allowed in the beginning. ⁹I tell you that anyone who divorces his wife and marries another woman is guilty of adultery.ⁿ The only reason for a man to divorce his wife is if his wife has sexual relations with another man.''

¹⁰The followers said to him, ''If that is the only reason a man can divorce his wife, it is better not to marry.''

¹¹Jesus answered, ''Not everyone can accept this teaching, but God has made some able to accept it. ¹²There are different reasons why some men cannot marry. Some men were born without the ability to become fathers. Others were made that way later in life by other people. And some men have given up marriage because of the kingdom of heaven. But the person who can marry should accept this teaching about marriage.''ⁿ

JESUS WELCOMES CHILDREN

¹³Then the people brought their little children to Jesus so he could put his hands on themⁿ and pray for them. His followers told them to stop, ¹⁴but Jesus said, ''Let the little children come to me. Don't stop them, because the kingdom of heaven belongs to people who are like these children.'' ¹⁵After Jesus put his hands on the children, he left there.

A RICH YOUNG MAN'S QUESTION

¹⁶A man came to Jesus and asked, ''Teacher, what good thing must I do to have life forever?''

¹⁷Jesus answered, ''Why do you ask

me about what is good? Only God is good. But if you want to have life forever, obey the commands.''

¹⁸The man asked, ''Which commands?''

Jesus answered, '' 'You must not murder anyone; you must not be guilty of adultery; you must not steal; you must not tell lies about your neighbor; ¹⁹honor your father and mother;ⁿ and love your neighbor as you love yourself.' ''ⁿ

²⁰The young man said, ''I have obeyed all these things. What else do I need to do?''

²¹Jesus answered, ''If you want to be perfect, then go and sell your possessions and give the money to the poor. If you do this, you will have treasure in heaven. Then come and follow me.''

²²But when the young man heard this, he left sorrowfully, because he was rich.

²³Then Jesus said to his followers, ''I tell you the truth, it will be hard for a rich person to enter the kingdom of heaven. ²⁴Yes, I tell you that it is easier for a camel to go through the eye of a needle than for a rich person to enter the kingdom of God.''

²⁵When Jesus' followers heard this, they were very surprised and asked, ''Then who can be saved?''

²⁶Jesus looked at them and said, ''For people this is impossible, but for God all things are possible.''

²⁷Peter said to Jesus, ''Look, we have left everything and followed you. So what will we have?''

²⁸Jesus said to them, ''I tell you the truth, when the age to come has arrived, the Son of Man will sit on his great throne. All of you who followed me will also sit on twelve thrones, judging the twelve tribes of Israel. ²⁹And all those who have left houses, brothers, sisters, father, mother,ⁿ children, or farms to follow me will get much more than they left, and they will have life forever. ³⁰Many who are first now will be last in the future. And many who are last now will be first in the future.

VIEWPOINT

WHAT IS THE BIGGEST ISSUE PREVENTING WORLD PEACE?

''Peace is not a reality in the world because of man's arrogance. The fact that people believe in different gods has caused war in the world. If men would simply come down from their high horse, there would be more peace in the world today. If we could all agree to disagree about our religious differences, maybe we could live peacefully.''

A STORY ABOUT WORKERS

20 ''The kingdom of heaven is like a person who owned some land. One morning, he went out very early to hire some people to work in his vineyard. ²The man agreed to pay the workers

 19:4 'he made . . . female' Quotation from Genesis 1:27 or 5:2. 19:5 'So . . . body.' Quotation from Genesis 2:24. 19:9 adultery Some Greek copies continue, ''And anyone who marries a divorced woman is guilty of adultery.'' Compare Matthew 5:32. 19:12 But . . . marriage. This may also mean, ''The person who can accept this teaching about not marrying should accept it.'' 19:13 put his hands on them Showing that Jesus gave special blessings to these children. 19:19 'You . . . mother.' Quotation from Exodus 20:12-16; Deuteronomy 5:16-20. 19:19 'love . . . yourself.' Quotation from Leviticus 19:18. 19:29 mother Some Greek copies continue, ''or wife.''

▶ 31

one coin[n] for working that day. Then he sent them into the vineyard to work. [3]About nine o'clock the man went to the marketplace and saw some other people standing there, doing nothing. [4]So he said to them, 'If you go and work in my vineyard, I will pay you what your work is worth.' [5]So they went to work in the vineyard. The man went out again about twelve o'clock and three o'clock and did the same thing. [6]About five o'clock the man went to the marketplace again and saw others standing there. He asked them, 'Why did you stand here all day doing nothing?' [7]They answered, 'No one gave us a job.' The man said to them, 'Then you can go and work in my vineyard.'

[8]"At the end of the day, the owner of the vineyard said to the boss of all the workers, 'Call the workers and pay them. Start with the last people I hired and end with those I hired first.'

[9]"When the workers who were hired at five o'clock came to get their pay, each received one coin. [10]When the workers who were hired first came to get their pay, they thought they would be paid more than the others. But each one of them also received one coin. [11]When they got their coin, they complained to the man who owned the land. [12]They said, 'Those people were hired last and worked only one hour. But you paid them the same as you paid us who worked hard all day in the hot sun.' [13]But the man who owned the vineyard said to one of those workers, 'Friend, I am being fair to you. You agreed to work for one coin. [14]So take your pay and go. I want to give the man who was hired last the same pay that I gave you. [15]I can do what I want with my own money. Are you jealous because I am good to those people?'

[16]"So those who are last now will someday be first, and those who are first now will someday be last."

JESUS TALKS ABOUT HIS OWN DEATH

[17]While Jesus was going to Jerusalem, he took his twelve followers aside privately and said to them, [18]"Look, we are going to Jerusalem. The Son of Man will be turned over to the leading priests and the teachers of the law, and they will say that he must die. [19]They will give the Son of Man to the non-Jewish people to laugh at him and beat him with whips and crucify him. But on the third day, he will be raised to life again."

A MOTHER ASKS JESUS A FAVOR

[20]Then the wife of Zebedee came to Jesus with her sons. She bowed before him and asked him to do something for her.

[21]Jesus asked, "What do you want?"

She said, "Promise that one of my sons will sit at your right side and the other will sit at your left side in your kingdom."

[22]But Jesus said, "You don't understand what you are asking. Can you drink the cup that I am about to drink?"[n]

The sons answered, "Yes, we can."

[23]Jesus said to them, "You will drink from my cup. But I cannot choose who will sit at my right or my left; those places belong to those for whom my Father has prepared them."

[24]When the other ten followers heard this, they were angry with the two brothers.

[25]Jesus called all the followers together and said, "You know that the rulers of the non-Jewish people love to show their power over the people. And their important leaders love to use all their authority. [26]But it should not be that way among you. Whoever wants to become great among you must serve the rest of you like a servant. [27]Whoever wants to become first among you must serve the rest of you like a slave. [28]In the same way, the Son of Man did not come to be served. He came to serve others and to give his life as a ransom for many people."

JESUS HEALS TWO BLIND MEN

[29]When Jesus and his followers were leaving Jericho, a great many people followed him. [30]Two blind men sitting by the road heard that Jesus was going by, so they shouted, "Lord, Son of David, have mercy on us!"

[31]The people warned the blind men to be quiet, but they shouted even more, "Lord, Son of David, have mercy on us!"

[32]Jesus stopped and said to the blind men, "What do you want me to do for you?"

[33]They answered, "Lord, we want to see."

[34]Jesus felt sorry for the blind men and touched their eyes, and at once they could see. Then they followed Jesus.

JESUS ENTERS JERUSALEM AS A KING

21 As Jesus and his followers were coming closer to Jerusalem, they stopped at Bethphage at the hill called the Mount of Olives. From there Jesus sent two of his followers [2]and said to them, "Go to the town you can see there. When you enter it, you will quickly find a donkey tied there with its colt. Untie them and bring them to me. [3]If anyone asks you why you are taking the donkeys, say that the Master needs them, and he will send them at once."

[4]This was to bring about what the prophet had said:

[5]"Tell the people of Jerusalem,
    'Your king is coming to you.
    He is gentle and riding on a donkey,
    on the colt of a donkey.' "
                    Isaiah 62:11; Zechariah 9:9

[6]The followers went and did what Jesus told them to do. [7]They brought the donkey and the colt to Jesus and laid their coats on them, and Jesus sat on them. [8]Many people spread their coats on the road. Others cut branches from the trees and spread them on the road. [9]The people were walking ahead of Jesus and behind him, shouting,

"Praise[n] to the Son of David!

20:2 coin A Roman denarius. One coin was the average pay for one day's work. **20:22 drink . . . drink** Jesus used the idea of drinking from a cup to ask if they could accept the same terrible things that would happen to him. **21:9 Praise** Literally, "Hosanna," a Hebrew word used at first in praying to God for help. At this time it was probably a shout of joy used in praising God or his Messiah.

CONNECTED

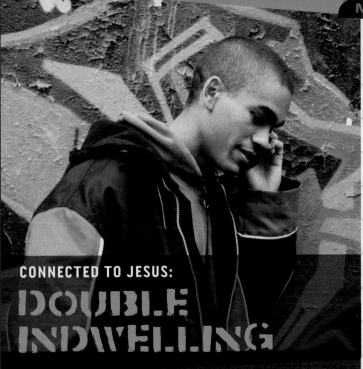

CONNECTED TO JESUS:

DOUBLE INDWELLING

One of the most amazing truths of the Word of God is that when we accept Jesus Christ as Lord and Savior, he comes to dwell in our lives as our Lord. The Apostle Paul describes this connection to Jesus as "Christ himself, who is in you. He is our only hope for glory" (Colossians 1:27). On the other hand, Paul also says that when we accept Christ, we are "all baptized into one body"—the body of Christ (1 Corinthians 12:13). Watch this now: Christ is in us; but we are also in Christ! It is a kind of double indwelling. We are never alone because Christ loves us enough to live *in* us. When we accept Christ, it is not just a religious ritual. We surrender our lives to him and he comes to live in us.

Remember also that he is omnipresent, which means he is everywhere: He is in you and in me at the same time. If he is in you and me at the same time, that gives each of us who accept him a connection to each other. We are all part of Christ's body. That's kinda deep.

But don't think that makes you just like everybody else to him. Although all of God's promises in the Bible apply to everyone, Jesus thought that you were so special that he died just for you. If you were the only person on earth, he still would have sacrificed himself on the cross for you. Jesus loves you so much that he welcomes you into himself as part of his body, the church. He loves you so much that he sets up residence in your life, bringing hope and joy and salvation. You are in Christ and Christ is in you. He's all you need.

God bless the One who comes in the name of the Lord! *Psalm 118:26* Praise to God in heaven!"

[10] When Jesus entered Jerusalem, all the city was filled with excitement. The people asked, "Who is this man?"

[11] The crowd said, "This man is Jesus, the prophet from the town of Nazareth in Galilee."

JESUS GOES TO THE TEMPLE

[12] Jesus went into the Temple and threw out all the people who were buying and selling there. He turned over the tables of those who were exchanging different kinds of money, and he upset the benches of those who were selling doves. [13] Jesus said to all the people there, "It is written in the Scriptures, 'My Temple will be called a house for prayer.'[n] But you are changing it into a 'hideout for robbers.'"[n]

[14] The blind and crippled people came to Jesus in the Temple, and he healed them. [15] The leading priests and the teachers of the law saw that Jesus was doing wonderful things and that the children were praising him in the Temple, saying, "Praise[n] to the Son of David." All these things made the priests and the teachers of the law very angry.

[16] They asked Jesus, "Do you hear the things these children are saying?"

Jesus answered, "Yes. Haven't you read in the Scriptures, 'You have taught children and babies to sing praises'?"[n]

[17] Then Jesus left and went out of the city to Bethany, where he spent the night.

THE POWER OF FAITH

[18] Early the next morning, as Jesus was going back to the city, he became hungry. [19] Seeing a fig tree beside the road, Jesus went to it, but there were no figs on the tree, only leaves. So Jesus said to the tree, "You will never again have fruit." The tree immediately dried up.

[20] When his followers saw this, they were amazed. They asked, "How did the fig tree dry up so quickly?"

[21] Jesus answered, "I tell you the truth,

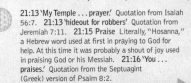

21:13 'My Temple . . . prayer.' Quotation from Isaiah 56:7. 21:13 'hideout for robbers' Quotation from Jeremiah 7:11. 21:15 Praise Literally, "Hosanna," a Hebrew word used at first in praying to God for help. At this time it was probably a shout of joy used in praising God or his Messiah. 21:16 'You . . . praises.' Quotation from the Septuagint (Greek) version of Psalm 8:2.

365

FEBRUARY

1 Invite a friend to church

2
3 **Think outside the box:** What don't I know about African American History?

4
5
6
7
8

> "I have failed over and over and over again in my life. And that's precisely why I succeed."
> - *Michael Jordan*

9
10

11 HOLIDAY—Ash Wednesday. It's your birthday, Kelly Rowland and Brandy!

12 On This Day In History 1909—the NAACP was founded.

13 Valentines Day. On This Day In History 1967—Aretha Franklin records the hit single "Respect."

14
15
16 Happy Birthday Michael Jordan!

17
18 **What are you wrapping for your Valentine?**

19
20 On This Day In History 1965—Malcolm X was assassinated.

21
22 **It's Black History Month, read the biography of a civil rights leader.**

23
24
25
26 It's your birthday Rozonda "Chili" Thomas!

27
28
29 **Become a mentor, contact a non-profit organization that's looking for volunteers.**

30
31

MUSIC REVIEWS

ARTIST: WU TANG   ALBUM: THE W   CUT: "JAH WORLD"

Wu Tang Clan is one of the most respected hip-hop groups in the business, and they have a very large urban following. But watch out! They are not talking about Christ. The Bible says "Many will come in my name, saying, 'I am the Christ,' and they will fool many people" (Matthew 24:5). Check these lyrics from the song "Jah World" by Wu Tang Clan: "I, jahova god, jah rastafari, Who is seated in zion and reigneth in the hearts of all flesh whoi." Their lyrics do not honor God, and they go so far as to refer to themselves as "I, jahova god." In one of the videos on their website, "To Da Road" they cut off the head of Christ and take his spirit to form the group. Just so you know . . .

"REJECTED"

---

if you have faith and do not doubt, you will be able to do what I did to this tree and even more. You will be able to say to this mountain, 'Go, fall into the sea.' And if you have faith, it will happen. ²²If you believe, you will get anything you ask for in prayer."

LEADERS DOUBT JESUS' AUTHORITY

²³Jesus went to the Temple, and while he was teaching there, the leading priests and the elders of the people came to him. They said, "What authority do you have to do these things? Who gave you this authority?"

²⁴Jesus answered, "I also will ask you a question. If you answer me, then I will tell you what authority I have to do these things. ²⁵Tell me: When John baptized people, did that come from God or just from other people?"

They argued about Jesus' question, saying, "If we answer, 'John's baptism was from God,' Jesus will say, 'Then why didn't you believe him?' ²⁶But if we say, 'It was from people,' we are afraid of what the crowd will do because they all believe that John was a prophet."

²⁷So they answered Jesus, "We don't know."

Jesus said to them, "Then I won't tell you what authority I have to do these things.

A STORY ABOUT TWO SONS

²⁸"Tell me what you think about this: A man had two sons. He went to the first son and said, 'Son, go and work today in my vineyard.' ²⁹The son answered, 'I will not go.' But later the son changed his mind and went. ³⁰Then the father went to the other son and said, 'Son, go and work today in my vineyard.' The son answered, 'Yes, sir, I will go and work,' but he did not go. ³¹Which of the two sons obeyed his father?"

The priests and leaders answered, "The first son."

Jesus said to them, "I tell you the truth, the tax collectors and the prostitutes will enter the kingdom of God before you do. ³²John came to show you the right way to live. You did not believe him, but the tax collectors and prostitutes believed him. Even after seeing

this, you still refused to change your ways and believe him.

A STORY ABOUT GOD'S SON

³³"Listen to this story: There was a man who owned a vineyard. He put a wall around it and dug a hole for a winepress and built a tower. Then he leased the land to some farmers and left for a trip. ³⁴When it was time for the grapes to be picked, he sent his servants to the farmers to get his share of the grapes. ³⁵But the farmers grabbed the servants, beat one, killed another, and then killed a third servant with stones. ³⁶So the man sent some other servants to the farmers, even more than he sent the first time. But the farmers did the same thing to the servants that they had done before. ³⁷So the man decided to send his son to the farmers. He said, 'They will respect my son.' ³⁸But when the farmers saw the son, they said to each other, 'This son will inherit the vineyard. If we kill him, it will be ours!' ³⁹Then the farmers grabbed the son, threw him out of the vineyard, and killed him. ⁴⁰So what will the owner of the vineyard do to these farmers when he comes?"

WORLD SAYS, WORD SAYS,

USING PROFANITY

Cursing isn't bad; it's an expression—a language that others understand. It's normal to cuss. Everyone does it; just look around. There is nothing wrong with it. Especially when you're mad, you must get the point across that you mean business. What's the big deal anyway? It's just words.

"You must not use the name of the LORD your God thoughtlessly; the LORD will punish anyone who misuses his name" (Exodus 20:7).

"But what people say with their mouths comes from the way they think; these are the things that make people unclean" (Matthew 15:18).

"The mouth speaks the things that are in the heart" (Matthew 12:34).

"When you talk, do not say harmful things, but say what people need—words that will help others become stronger. Then what you say will do good to those who listen to you" (Ephesians 4:29).

---

[41]The priests and leaders said, "He will surely kill those evil men. Then he will lease the vineyard to some other farmers who will give him his share of the crop at harvest time."

[42]Jesus said to them, "Surely you have read this in the Scriptures:

'The stone that the builders
  rejected
became the cornerstone.
The Lord did this,
  and it is wonderful to us.'
                    Psalm 118:22-23

[43]"So I tell you that the kingdom of God will be taken away from you and given to people who do the things God wants in his kingdom. [44]The person who falls on this stone will be broken, and on whomever that stone falls, that person will be crushed.'"

[45]When the leading priests and the Pharisees heard these stories, they knew Jesus was talking about them. [46]They wanted to arrest him, but they were afraid of the people, because the people believed that Jesus was a prophet.

A STORY ABOUT A WEDDING FEAST

22 Jesus again used stories to teach them. He said, [2]"The kingdom of heaven is like a king who prepared a wedding feast for his son. [3]The king invited some people to the feast. When the feast was ready, the king sent his servants to tell the people, but they refused to come.

[4]"Then the king sent other servants, saying, 'Tell those who have been invited that my feast is ready. I have killed my best bulls and calves for the dinner, and everything is ready. Come to the wedding feast.'

[5]"But the people refused to listen to the servants and left to do other things. One went to work in his field, and another went to his business. [6]Some of the other people grabbed the servants, beat them, and killed them. [7]The king was furious and sent his army to kill the murderers and burn their city.

[8]"After that, the king said to his servants, 'The wedding feast is ready. I invited those people, but they were not worthy to come. [9]So go to the street corners and invite everyone you find to come to my feast.' [10]So the servants went into the streets and gathered all the people they could find, both good and bad. And the wedding hall was filled with guests.

[11]"When the king came in to see the guests, he saw a man who was not dressed for a wedding. [12]The king said, 'Friend, how were you allowed to come in here? You are not dressed for a wedding.' But the man said nothing. [13]So the king told some servants, 'Tie this man's hands and feet. Throw him out into the darkness, where people will cry and grind their teeth with pain.'

[14]"Yes, many are invited, but only a few are chosen."

IS IT RIGHT TO PAY TAXES OR NOT?

[15]Then the Pharisees left that place and made plans to trap Jesus in saying

---

21:44 The . . . crushed. Some Greek copies do not have verse 44.

something wrong. [16]They sent some of their own followers and some people from the group called Herodians.[n] They said, "Teacher, we know that you are an honest man and that you teach the truth about God's way. You are not afraid of what other people think about you, because you pay no attention to who they are. [17]So tell us what you think. Is it right to pay taxes to Caesar or not?"

[18]But knowing that these leaders were trying to trick him, Jesus said, "You hypocrites! Why are you trying to trap me? [19]Show me a coin used for paying the tax." So the men showed him a coin.[n] [20]Then Jesus asked, "Whose image and name are on the coin?"

[21]The men answered, "Caesar's."

Then Jesus said to them, "Give to Caesar the things that are Caesar's, and give to God the things that are God's."

[22]When the men heard what Jesus said, they were amazed and left him and went away.

SOME SADDUCEES TRY TO TRICK JESUS

[23]That same day some Sadducees came to Jesus and asked him a question. (Sadducees believed that people would not rise from the dead.) [24]They said, "Teacher, Moses said if a married man dies without having children, his brother must marry the widow and have children for him. [25]Once there were seven brothers among us. The first one married and died. Since he had no children, his brother married the widow. [26]Then the second brother also died. The same thing happened to the third brother and all the other brothers. [27]Finally, the woman died. [28]Since all seven men had married her, when people rise from the dead, whose wife will she be?"

[29]Jesus answered, "You don't understand, because you don't know what the Scriptures say, and you don't know about the power of God. [30]When people rise from the dead, they will not marry, nor will they be given to someone to marry.

They will be like the angels in heaven. [31]Surely you have read what God said to you about rising from the dead. [32]God said, 'I am the God of Abraham, the God of Isaac, and the God of Jacob.'[n] God is the God of the living, not the dead."

[33]When the people heard this, they were amazed at Jesus' teaching.

THE MOST IMPORTANT COMMAND

[34]When the Pharisees learned that the Sadducees could not argue with Jesus' answers to them, the Pharisees met together. [35]One Pharisee, who was an expert on the law of Moses, asked Jesus this question to test him: [36]"Teacher, which command in the law is the most important?"

[37]Jesus answered, " 'Love the Lord your God with all your heart, all your soul, and all your mind.'[n] [38]This is the first and most important command. [39]And the second command is like the first: 'Love your neighbor as you love yourself.'[n] [40]All the law and the writings of the prophets depend on these two commands."

JESUS QUESTIONS THE PHARISEES

[41]While the Pharisees were together, Jesus asked them, [42]"What do you think about the Christ? Whose son is he?"

They answered, "The Christ is the Son of David."

[43]Then Jesus said to them, "Then why did David call him 'Lord'? David, speaking by the power of the Holy Spirit, said,

[44]'The Lord said to my Lord,
"Sit by me at my right side,
until I put your enemies under
    your control." '   Psalm 110:1

[45]David calls the Christ 'Lord,' so how can the Christ be his son?"

[46]None of the Pharisees could answer Jesus' question, and after that day no one was brave enough to ask him any more questions.

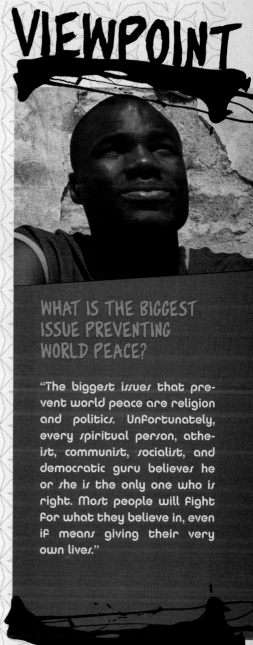

VIEWPOINT

WHAT IS THE BIGGEST ISSUE PREVENTING WORLD PEACE?

"The biggest issues that prevent world peace are religion and politics. Unfortunately, every spiritual person, atheist, communist, socialist, and democratic guru believes he or she is the only one who is right. Most people will fight for what they believe in, even if means giving their very own lives."

JESUS ACCUSES SOME LEADERS

23 Then Jesus said to the crowds and to his followers, [2]"The teachers of the law and the Pharisees have the authority to tell you what the law of Moses says. [3]So you should obey and follow what-

---

22:16 Herodians A political group that followed Herod and his family. **22:19 coin** A Roman denarius. One coin was the average pay for one day's work. **22:32 'I am . . . Jacob.'** Quotation from Exodus 3:6. **22:37 'Love . . . mind.'** Quotation from Deuteronomy 6:5. **22:39 'Love . . . yourself.'** Quotation from Leviticus 19:18.

ever they tell you, but their lives are not good examples for you to follow. They tell you to do things, but they themselves don't do them. [4]They make strict rules and try to force people to obey them, but they are unwilling to help those who struggle under the weight of their rules.

PEEP THIS:

By 2007, the female-to-male ratio is projected to be 57 to 43.

[5]"They do good things so that other people will see them. They enlarge the little boxes[n] holding Scriptures that they wear, and they make their special prayer clothes very long. [6]Those Pharisees and teachers of the law love to have the most important seats at feasts and in the synagogues. [7]They love people to greet them with respect in the marketplaces, and they love to have people call them 'Teacher.'

[8]"But you must not be called 'Teacher,' because you have only one Teacher, and you are all brothers and sisters together. [9]And don't call any person on earth 'Father,' because you have one Father, who is in heaven. [10]And you should not be called 'Master,' because you have only one Master, the Christ. [11]Whoever is your servant is the greatest among you. [12]Whoever makes himself great will be made humble. Whoever makes himself humble will be made great.

[13]"How terrible for you, teachers of the law and Pharisees! You are hypocrites! You close the door for people to enter the kingdom of heaven. You yourselves don't enter, and you stop others who are trying to enter. [[14]How terrible for you, teachers of the law and Pharisees. You are hypocrites. You take away widows' houses, and you say long prayers so that people will notice you. So you will have a worse punishment.][n]

[15]"How terrible for you, teachers of the law and Pharisees! You are hypocrites! You travel across land and sea to find one person who will change to your ways. When you find that person, you make him more fit for hell than you are.

[16]"How terrible for you! You guide the people, but you are blind. You say, 'If people swear by the Temple when they make a promise, that means nothing. But if they swear by the gold that is in the Temple, they must keep that promise.' [17]You are blind fools! Which is greater: the gold or the Temple that makes that gold holy? [18]And you say, 'If people swear by the altar when they make a promise, that means nothing. But if they swear by the gift on the altar, they must keep that promise.' [19]You are blind! Which is greater: the gift or the altar that makes the gift holy? [20]The person who swears by the altar is really using the altar and also everything on the altar. [21]And the person who swears by the Temple is really using the Temple and also everything in the Temple. [22]The person who swears by heaven is also using God's throne and the One who sits on that throne.

[23]"How terrible for you, teachers of the law and Pharisees! You are hypocrites! You give to God one-tenth of everything you earn—even your mint, dill, and cumin.[n] But you don't obey the really important teachings of the law—justice, mercy, and being loyal. These are the things you should do, as well as those other things. [24]You guide the people, but you are blind! You are like a person who picks a fly out of a drink and then swallows a camel![n]

[25]"How terrible for you, teachers of the law and Pharisees! You are hypocrites! You wash the outside of your cups and dishes, but inside they are full of things you got by cheating others and by pleasing only yourselves. [26]Pharisees, you are blind! First make the inside of the cup clean, and then the outside of the cup can be truly clean.

[27]"How terrible for you, teachers of the law and Pharisees! You are hypocrites! You are like tombs that are painted white. Outside, those tombs look fine, but inside, they are full of the bones of dead people and all kinds of unclean things. [28]It is the same with you. People look at you and think you are good, but on the inside you are full of hypocrisy and evil.

[29]"How terrible for you, teachers of the law and Pharisees! You are hypocrites! You build tombs for the prophets, and you show honor to the graves of those who lived good lives. [30]You say, 'If we had lived during the time of our ancestors, we would not have helped them kill the prophets.' [31]But you give proof that you are descendants of those who murdered the prophets. [32]And you will complete the sin that your ancestors started.

[33]"You are snakes! A family of poisonous snakes! How are you going to escape God's judgment? [34]So I tell you this: I am sending to you prophets and wise men and teachers. Some of them you will kill and crucify. Some of them you will beat in your synagogues and chase from town to town. [35]So you will be guilty for the death of all the good people who have been killed on earth—from the murder of that good man Abel to the murder of Zechariah[n] son of Berakiah, whom you murdered between the Temple and the altar. [36]I tell you the truth, all of these things will happen to you people who are living now.

JESUS FEELS SORRY FOR JERUSALEM

[37]"Jerusalem, Jerusalem! You kill the prophets and stone to death those who are sent to you. Many times I wanted

---

23:5 boxes Small leather boxes containing four important Scriptures. Some Jews tied these to their foreheads and left arms, probably to show they were very religious. **23:14 How . . . punishment.** Some Greek copies do not contain the bracketed text. **23:23 mint, dill, and cumin** Small plants grown in gardens and used for spices. Only very religious people would be careful enough to give a tenth of these plants. **23:24 You . . . camel!** Meaning, "You worry about the smallest mistakes but commit the biggest sin." **23:35 Abel . . . Zechariah** In the order of the books of the Hebrew Old Testament, the first and last men to be murdered.

to gather your people as a hen gathers her chicks under her wings, but you did not let me. [38]Now your house will be left completely empty. [39]I tell you, you will not see me again until that time when you will say, 'God bless the One who comes in the name of the Lord.' ""

THE TEMPLE WILL BE DESTROYED

24 As Jesus left the Temple and was walking away, his followers came up to show him the Temple's buildings. [2]Jesus asked, "Do you see all these buildings? I tell you the truth, not one stone will be left on another. Every stone will be thrown down to the ground."

[3]Later, as Jesus was sitting on the Mount of Olives, his followers came to be alone with him. They said, "Tell us, when will these things happen? And what will be the sign that it is time for you to come again and for this age to end?"

[4]Jesus answered, "Be careful that no one fools you. [5]Many will come in my name, saying, 'I am the Christ,' and they will fool many people. [6]You will hear about wars and stories of wars that are coming, but don't be afraid. These things must happen before the end comes. [7]Nations will fight against other nations; kingdoms will fight against other kingdoms. There will be times when there is no food for people to eat, and there will be earthquakes in different places. [8]These things are like the first pains when something new is about to be born.

[9]"Then people will arrest you, hand you over to be hurt, and kill you. They will hate you because you believe in me. [10]At that time, many will lose their faith, and they will turn against each other and hate each other. [11]Many false prophets will come and cause many people to believe lies. [12]There will be more and more evil in the world, so most people will stop showing their love for each other. [13]But those people who keep their faith until the end will be saved. [14]The Good News about God's kingdom will be preached in all the world, to every nation. Then the end will come.

23:39 'God . . . Lord.' Quotation from Psalm 118:26.

LIFE OR DEATH

Eternity is a concept that boggles the mind. It is time without beginning and without end – therefore it is not time, but the absence of it. God exists in eternity and is the only completely eternal being. He has no beginning and he will never cease to exist. Although we are created and, therefore, have a beginning, God created us to be like him. From the moment of our creation, our existence is everlasting, perpetual, forever. The essence of who we are (our spirits) did not begin when we were born and will not end when our body dies.

When God created the first man and woman (Adam and Eve), they were spiritually connected with God. They were created to live eternally with him. But God wanted his creation to enter into a love relationship with him. True love cannot be demanded; it must be a product of free choice, so God gave Adam and Eve the ability to choose. He had presented the entire created world to them as a gift. Only the fruit of one tree was forbidden. God told them that eating this fruit would result in death for them and all their children. Satan told them that God had lied and that they would not die but would be like God if they ate the fruit. They chose to believe Satan and disobey God. The death that came upon them was much more profound than just the fact that their bodies would eventually die. Their relationship with God was severed and they experienced spiritual death by being separated from the source of life. Although the essence of who they were would remain for eternity, it was an eternity to be spent outside the presence of God. An eternity in a place totally devoid of all that is good and holy, ruled by evil, darkness and pain. Had God not intervened, their destiny would have been an eternity in hell, the kingdom of their chosen master.

As the children of Adam and Eve, we have been born into this same spiritually dead state. We face an eternity outside the presence of God. But Jesus, the Son of God, came to reinstate our lost spiritual connection to God the Father. He came to provide a way for us to be "born again" and become spiritually alive. He took our death upon himself and was resurrected to new life. This new life is now made available to us. If we will simply accept that Jesus is the way God has provided for us to regain a relationship with him, we can be reconnected to God. By choosing to believe Jesus, we can enter into the kingdom of God and live in his presence for eternity.

Everlasting life or eternal death, heaven or hell, the choice is yours. (Read John 3:16)

THINK STRAIGHT

OVERCOMING

▶ LOW SELF-ESTEEM

To be unhappy with who you are can devastate your life. It can make you desperate to find validation and approval from others, regardless the cost. Or it can cause you to shut down and hide from the world. When your self image is negative, you are constantly either driven to find someone to believe in you or you give up on ever receiving the approval of another. If this is you, don't despair, there is an answer.

God believes in you. He made you just as you are, and he doesn't make mistakes. In Psalm 139 verses 13 through 16 it says, "You made my whole being; you formed me in my mother's body. I praise you because you made me in an amazing and wonderful way. What you have done is wonderful. I know this very well. You saw my bones being formed as I took shape in my mother's body. When I was put together there, you saw my body as it was formed." God thinks you're wonderful. As you dive into your relationship with God, you will begin to realize that his validation is all that you need.

---

[15]"Daniel the prophet spoke about 'a blasphemous object that brings destruction.'[n] You will see this standing in the holy place." (You who read this should understand what it means.) [16]"At that time, the people in Judea should run away to the mountains. [17]If people are on the roofs[n] of their houses, they must not go down to get anything out of their houses. [18]If people are in the fields, they must not go back to get their coats. [19]At that time, how terrible it will be for women who are pregnant or have nursing babies! [20]Pray that it will not be winter or a Sabbath day when these things happen and you have to run away, [21]because at that time there will be much trouble. There will be more trouble than there has ever been since the beginning of the world until now, and nothing as bad will ever happen again. [22]God has decided to make that terrible time short. Otherwise, no one would go on living. But God will make that time short to help the people he has chosen. [23]At that time, someone might say to you, 'Look, there is the Christ!' Or another person might say, 'There he is!' But don't believe them. [24]False Christs and false prophets will come and perform great wonders and miracles. They will try to fool even the people God has chosen, if that is possible. [25]Now I have warned you about this before it happens.

[26]"If people tell you, 'The Christ is in the desert,' don't go there. If they say, 'The Christ is in the inner room,' don't believe it. [27]When the Son of Man comes, he will be seen by everyone, like lightning flashing from the east to the west. [28]Wherever the dead body is, there the vultures will gather.

[29]"Soon after the trouble of those days,

'the sun will grow dark,
    and the moon will not give its
        light.
The stars will fall from the sky.
And the powers of the heavens
    will be shaken.' *Isaiah 13:10; 34:4*

[30]"At that time, the sign of the Son of Man will appear in the sky. Then all the peoples of the world will cry. They will see the Son of Man coming on clouds in the sky with great power and glory. [31]He will use a loud trumpet to send his angels all around the earth, and they will gather his chosen people from every part of the world.

[32]"Learn a lesson from the fig tree: When its branches become green and soft and new leaves appear, you know summer is near. [33]In the same way, when you see all these things happening, you will know that the time is near, ready to come. [34]I tell you the truth, all these things will happen while the people of this time are still living. [35]Earth and sky will be destroyed, but the words I have said will never be destroyed.

WHEN WILL JESUS COME AGAIN?

[36]"No one knows when that day or time will be, not the angels in heaven, not even the Son.[n] Only the Father knows. [37]When the Son of Man comes, it will be like what happened during Noah's time. [38]In those days before the flood, people were eating and drinking, marrying and giving their children to be married, until the day Noah entered the boat. [39]They knew nothing about what was happening until the flood came and destroyed them. It will be the same when the Son of Man comes. [40]Two men will be in the field. One will be taken, and the other will be left. [41]Two women will be grinding grain with a mill.[n] One will be taken, and the other will be left.

[42]"So always be ready, because you

24:15 'a blasphemous object that brings destruction' Mentioned in Daniel 9:27; 12:11 (see also Daniel 11:31). **24:17 roofs** In Bible times houses were built with flat roofs. The roof was used for drying things such as flax and fruit. And it was used as an extra room, as a place for worship, and as a cool place to sleep in the summer. **24:36 not even the Son** Some Greek copies do not have this phrase. **24:41 mill** Two large, round, flat rocks used for grinding grain to make flour.

don't know the day your Lord will come. [43]Remember this: If the owner of the house knew what time of night a thief was coming, the owner would watch and not let the thief break in. [44]So you also must be ready, because the Son of Man will come at a time you don't expect him.

[45]"Who is the wise and loyal servant that the master trusts to give the other servants their food at the right time? [46]When the master comes and finds the servant doing his work, the servant will be blessed. [47]I tell you the truth, the master will choose that servant to take care of everything he owns. [48]But suppose that evil servant thinks to himself, 'My master will not come back soon,' [49]and he begins to beat the other servants and eat and get drunk with others like him? [50]The master will come when that servant is not ready and is not expecting him. [51]Then the master will cut him in pieces and send him away to be with the hypocrites, where people will cry and grind their teeth with pain.

A STORY ABOUT TEN BRIDESMAIDS

25 "At that time the kingdom of heaven will be like ten bridesmaids who took their lamps and went to wait for the bridegroom. [2]Five of them were foolish and five were wise. [3]The five foolish bridesmaids took their lamps, but they did not take more oil for the lamps to burn. [4]The wise bridesmaids took their lamps and more oil in jars. [5]Because the bridegroom was late, they became sleepy and went to sleep.

[6]"At midnight someone cried out, 'The bridegroom is coming! Come and meet him!' [7]Then all the bridesmaids woke up and got their lamps ready. [8]But the foolish ones said to the wise, 'Give us some of your oil, because our lamps are going out.' [9]The wise bridesmaids answered, 'No, the oil we have might not be enough for all of us. Go to the people who sell oil and buy some for yourselves.'

[10]"So while the five foolish bridesmaids went to buy oil, the bridegroom came. The bridesmaids who were ready went in with the bridegroom to the wedding feast. Then the door was closed and locked.

[11]"Later the others came back and said, 'Sir, sir, open the door to let us in.' [12]But the bridegroom answered, 'I tell you the truth, I don't want to know you.'

[13]"So always be ready, because you don't know the day or the hour the Son of Man will come.

IMPACT!

Athletes in Action

Do you got game? Athletes in Action (AIA) is a ministry that uses sports to spread the gospel. Competing both nationally and internationally, they represent nine sports, including baseball, basketball, and track and field. Athletes and coaches are trained on how to use the sporting events as opportunities to minister with God's Word. AIA even has an ongoing ministry with professional teams including NFL, MLS, MLB, and NBA teams. You can get information about Athletes in Action teams by visiting their Web site, www.aia.com.

A STORY ABOUT THREE SERVANTS

14"The kingdom of heaven is like a man who was going to another place for a visit. Before he left, he called for his servants and told them to take care of his things while he was gone. 15He gave one servant five bags of gold, another servant two bags of gold, and a third servant one bag of gold, to each one as much as he could handle. Then he left. 16The servant who got five bags went quickly to invest the money and earned five more bags. 17In the same way, the servant who had two bags invested them and earned two more. 18But the servant who got one bag went out and dug a hole in the ground and hid the master's money.

19"After a long time the master came home and asked the servants what they did with his money. 20The servant who was given five bags of gold brought five more bags to the master and said, 'Master, you trusted me to care for five bags of gold, so I used your five bags to

He's got answers

Will God actually help me even when I have messed up so bad?

What do you mean by bad? Have you lied about someone you love? Have you threatened innocent people? Have you encouraged murder? If you have done any of these things, then you are in the same company as the Apostles Peter and Paul. Peter lied about knowing Jesus. Paul threatened to imprison and kill Christians. When Steven refused to denounce the Lord, Paul helped the people who killed Steven. Lying, violence, and murder are pretty bad, but these men would become leaders among Christians.

What changed Peter and Paul? They asked for forgiveness.

Forgiveness. That's it. The Bible is full of stories about people who messed up their lives and yet God forgave them. There is no life so messed up that God can't — or won't — help. Better still, once he forgives, he forgets our mess-ups and never brings them up again.

What could be better than that?

Read on: Romans 5:6-8; Luke 7:36-49; 2 Corinthians 5:17

PEEP THIS:

There are more women than men in high-level math and science courses, student government, and honor societies. Females read more books, outperform males in artistic and musical abilities, and study abroad in higher numbers.

earn five more.' 21The master answered, 'You did well. You are a good and loyal servant. Because you were loyal with small things, I will let you care for much greater things. Come and share my joy with me.'

22"Then the servant who had been given two bags of gold came to the master and said, 'Master, you gave me two bags of gold to care for, so I used your two bags to earn two more.' 23The master answered, 'You did well. You are a good and loyal servant. Because you were loyal with small things, I will let you care for much greater things. Come and share my joy with me.'

24"Then the servant who had been given one bag of gold came to the master and said, 'Master, I knew that you were a hard man. You harvest things you did not plant. You gather crops where you did not sow any seed. 25So I was afraid and went and hid your money in the ground. Here is your bag of gold.' 26The master answered, 'You are a wicked and lazy servant! You say you knew that I harvest things I did not plant and that I gather crops where I did not sow any seed. 27So you should have put my gold in the bank. Then, when I came home, I would have received my gold back with interest.'

28"So the master told his other servants, 'Take the bag of gold from that servant and give it to the servant who has ten bags of gold. 29Those who have much will get more, and they will have much more than they need. But those who do not have much will have everything taken away from them.' 30Then the master said, 'Throw that useless servant outside, into the darkness where people will cry and grind their teeth with pain.'

THE KING WILL JUDGE ALL PEOPLE

31"The Son of Man will come again in his great glory, with all his angels. He will be King and sit on his great throne. 32All the nations of the world will be gathered before him, and he will separate them into two groups as a shepherd separates the sheep from the goats. 33The Son of

Man will put the sheep on his right and the goats on his left.

34"Then the King will say to the people on his right, 'Come, my Father has given you his blessing. Receive the kingdom God has prepared for you since the world was made. 35I was hungry, and you gave me food. I was thirsty, and you gave me something to drink. I was alone and away from home, and you invited me into your house. 36I was without clothes, and you gave me something to wear. I was sick, and you cared for me. I was in prison, and you visited me.'

37"Then the good people will answer, 'Lord, when did we see you hungry and give you food, or thirsty and give you something to drink? 38When did we see you alone and away from home and invite you into our house? When did we see you without clothes and give you something to wear? 39When did we see you sick or in prison and care for you?'

40"Then the King will answer, 'I tell you the truth, anything you did for even the least of my people here, you also did for me.'

41"Then the King will say to those on his left, 'Go away from me. You will be punished. Go into the fire that burns forever that was prepared for the devil and his angels. 42I was hungry, and you gave me nothing to eat. I was thirsty, and you gave me nothing to drink. 43I was alone and away from home, and you did not invite me into your house. I was without clothes, and you gave me nothing to wear. I was sick and in prison, and you did not care for me.'

44"Then those people will answer, 'Lord, when did we see you hungry or thirsty or alone and away from home or without clothes or sick or in prison? When did we see these things and not help you?'

45"Then the King will answer, 'I tell you the truth, anything you refused to do for even the least of my people here, you refused to do for me.'

46"These people will go off to be punished forever, but the good people will go to live forever."

HOW YA TRAVELIN'?

WORK WELL, WORK GOOD

Are you just fronting, or are you really digging in and getting the work done right? You know the difference. You show up at work, but you don't do anything more than absolutely necessary. You drag through the day and whip out of there as soon as the clock strikes "go home time." And doing exactly what you're asked to do—no more, no less—doesn't necessarily make you a good worker either. Proverbs 14:23 says, "Those who work hard make a profit." The following are some lessons for working well:

When you *delay* starting work, do it poorly, or don't finish; it makes you feel lousy for a long time. Poor workers always wind up poor (Proverbs 10:4), depressed (Proverbs 19:15 and Proverbs 26:14-15), and fearful (Proverbs 26:13 and Proverbs 22:13). The life of poor workers is so hard and overwhelming that many spend their whole lives looking for an escape.

Work done well (finished with excellence) makes you feel *great* for a long time (Genesis 1:4, 10, 12, 18, 21, 25, 31). Several times after God finished creating something, the Bible says that he saw that it was "good." Ecclesiastes 5:12 says, "Those who work hard sleep in peace."

Complaining is the opposite of being a hard worker. Complaining drains your energy. "What you say can mean life or death. Those who speak with care will be rewarded" (Proverbs 18:21). Isaiah 53:7 tells us that even when Jesus was beaten down and punished, he did not say a word. "Do everything without complaining" (Philippians 2:14).

God wants to guide and bless your work because God loves you and God loves work. "Everything you do or say should be done to obey Jesus your Lord" (Colossians 3:17).

THE PLAN TO KILL JESUS

26 After Jesus finished saying all these things, he told his followers, [2]"You know that the day after tomorrow is the day of the Passover Feast. On that day the Son of Man will be given to his enemies to be crucified."

[3]Then the leading priests and the elders had a meeting at the palace of the high priest, named Caiaphas. [4]At the meeting, they planned to set a trap to arrest Jesus and kill him. [5]But they said, "We must not do it during the feast, because the people might cause a riot."

PERFUME FOR JESUS' BURIAL

[6]Jesus was in Bethany at the house of Simon, who had a skin disease. [7]While Jesus was there, a woman approached him with an alabaster jar filled with expensive perfume. She poured this perfume on Jesus' head while he was eating.

[8]His followers were upset when they saw the woman do this. They asked, "Why waste that perfume? [9]It could have been sold for a great deal of money and the money given to the poor."

[10]Knowing what had happened, Jesus said, "Why are you troubling this woman? She did an excellent thing for me. [11]You will always have the poor with you, but you will not always have me. [12]This woman poured perfume on my body to prepare me for burial. [13]I tell you the truth, wherever the Good News is preached in all the world, what this woman has done will be told, and people will remember her."

JUDAS BECOMES AN ENEMY OF JESUS

[14]Then one of the twelve apostles, Judas Iscariot, went to talk to the leading priests. [15]He said, "What will you pay me for giving Jesus to you?" And they gave him thirty silver coins. [16]After that, Judas watched for the best time to turn Jesus in.

JESUS EATS THE PASSOVER MEAL

[17]On the first day of the Feast of Unleavened Bread, the followers came to Jesus. They said, "Where do you want us to prepare for you to eat the Passover meal?"

[18]Jesus answered, "Go into the city to a certain man and tell him, 'The Teacher says: "The chosen time is near. I will have the Passover with my followers at your house." ' " [19]The followers did what Jesus told them to do, and they prepared the Passover meal.

[20]In the evening Jesus was sitting at the table with his twelve followers. [21]As they were eating, Jesus said, "I tell you the truth, one of you will turn against me."

[22]This made the followers very sad. Each one began to say to Jesus, "Surely, Lord, I am not the one who will turn against you, am I?"

[23]Jesus answered, "The man who has dipped his hand with me into the bowl is the one who will turn against me. [24]The Son of Man will die, just as the Scriptures say. But how terrible it will be for the person who hands the Son of Man over to be killed. It would be better for him if he had never been born."

[25]Then Judas, who would give Jesus to his enemies, said to Jesus, "Teacher, surely I am not the one, am I?"

Jesus answered, "Yes, it is you."

THE LORD'S SUPPER

[26]While they were eating, Jesus took some bread and thanked God for it and broke it. Then he gave it to his followers and said, "Take this bread and eat it; this is my body."

[27]Then Jesus took a cup and thanked God for it and gave it to the followers. He said, "Every one of you drink this. [28]This is my blood which is the new[n] agreement that God makes with his people. This blood is poured out for many to forgive their sins. [29]I tell you this: I will not drink of this fruit of the vine[n] again until that day when I drink it new with you in my Father's kingdom."

[30]After singing a hymn, they went out to the Mount of Olives.

JESUS' FOLLOWERS WILL LEAVE HIM

[31]Jesus told his followers, "Tonight you will all stumble in your faith on account of me, because it is written in the Scriptures:

'I will kill the shepherd,
and the sheep will scatter.'

Zechariah 13:7

[32]But after I rise from the dead, I will go ahead of you into Galilee."

[33]Peter said, "Everyone else may stumble in their faith because of you, but I will not."

[34]Jesus said, "I tell you the truth, tonight before the rooster crows you will say three times that you don't know me."

[35]But Peter said, "I will never say that I don't know you! I will even die with you!" And all the other followers said the same thing.

JESUS PRAYS ALONE

[36]Then Jesus went with his followers to a place called Gethsemane. He said to them, "Sit here while I go over there and pray." [37]He took Peter and the two sons of Zebedee with him, and he began to be very sad and troubled. [38]He said to them, "My heart is full of sorrow, to the point of death. Stay here and watch with me."

[39]After walking a little farther away from them, Jesus fell to the ground and prayed, "My Father, if it is possible, do not give me this cup[n] of suffering. But do what you want, not what I want."

[40]Then Jesus went back to his followers and found them asleep. He said to Peter, "You men could not stay awake with me for one hour? [41]Stay awake and pray for strength against temptation. The spirit wants to do what is right, but the body is weak."

[42]Then Jesus went away a second time and prayed, "My Father, if it is not pos-

---

26:28 new Some Greek copies do not have this word. Compare Luke 22:20. **26:29 fruit of the vine** Product of the grapevine; this may also be translated "wine." **26:39 cup** Jesus is talking about the terrible things that will happen to him. Accepting these things will be very hard, like drinking a cup of something bitter.

sible for this painful thing to be taken from me, and if I must do it, I pray that what you want will be done."

[43]Then he went back to his followers, and again he found them asleep, because their eyes were heavy. [44]So Jesus left them and went away and prayed a third time, saying the same thing.

[45]Then Jesus went back to his followers and said, "Are you still sleeping and resting? The time has come for the Son of Man to be handed over to sinful people. [46]Get up, we must go. Look, here comes the man who has turned against me."

JESUS IS ARRESTED

[47]While Jesus was still speaking, Judas, one of the twelve apostles, came up. With him were many people carrying swords and clubs who had been sent from the leading priests and the Jewish elders of the people. [48]Judas had planned to give them a signal, saying, "The man I kiss is Jesus. Arrest him." [49]At once Judas went to Jesus and said, "Greetings, Teacher!" and kissed him.

[50]Jesus answered, "Friend, do what you came to do."

Then the people came and grabbed Jesus and arrested him. [51]When that happened, one of Jesus' followers reached for his sword and pulled it out. He struck the servant of the high priest and cut off his ear.

[52]Jesus said to the man, "Put your sword back in its place. All who use swords will be killed with swords. [53]Surely you know I could ask my Father, and he would give me more than twelve armies of angels. [54]But it must happen this way to bring about what the Scriptures say."

[55]Then Jesus said to the crowd, "You came to get me with swords and clubs as if I were a criminal. Every day I sat in

THE SCRIPT

Jesus Feeds 5,000

Matthew 14:13-22

When Jesus heard that his cousin, John, was murdered,
It stirred him' till he could no longer avert it. He went out to the desert
Trying to find a brief, secluded moment.
He trekked to the outback but soon the crowds were up on it.
They discovered his location and passed word to all the villages.
Before you knew it, multitudes came out like a pilgrimage!
Including deaf, dumb, and blind, all approached the great physician.
Jesus saw them all and had deep feelings for them and began healing.
This experience was extremely delirious as, nonstop, Jesus ministered deliverance.
'Til it was the evening and the disciples asked him to take a break.
They said, "We're out here in the boondocks, and it's getting mad late.
Maybe we should let the people make it to the village by the lake
So they can get some food ('cause it's been hours since they ate)."
But Jesus said, "Wait. Don't send them away because they'll faint.

We'll give them food to eat, in fact, we'll give em' a banquet!"
Once again the disciples couldn't figure out his statements.
"All we have are these five loaves of bread and two baked fish."
Jesus said, "That's enough, let me take it.
You all just make the people sit and be patient."
So they went and did as the master had said.
Jesus took the fish and bread and lifted up his head
Smiling, he blessed the provisions,
Broke them up and began to give them to the men, women, and children
Via the disciples; and you know they were trippin'.
Because as much as Jesus passed to them, they passed to the people.
The food seemed unending! It was enough for everyone to get full.
They even collected the leftovers and had twelve baskets full to pull!
The miracle was hysterical! Mind blowin'! Five thousand young and old men,
Plus the ladies and the babies, you have to throw in.
A huge crowd of folk that day got blessed
And word about Jesus spread from Bethsaida to Gennesaret.

Take this with you: When the needs in your life are great, trust in the Lord. He will supply far more than you could ever ask or imagine.

VIEWPOINT

WHAT IS THE BIGGEST ISSUE PREVENTING WORLD PEACE?

"It's all about respect. People ain't respecting each other. I'm not having you come in my house and take over without a fight. It's like this: I'm a black man and I want my respect. If somebody comes at me wrong, I ain't having it. It's on."

the Temple teaching, and you did not arrest me there. ⁵⁶But all these things have happened so that it will come about as the prophets wrote." Then all of Jesus' followers left him and ran away.

JESUS BEFORE THE LEADERS

⁵⁷Those people who arrested Jesus led him to the house of Caiaphas, the high priest, where the teachers of the law and the elders were gathered. ⁵⁸Peter followed far behind to the courtyard of the high priest's house, and he sat down with the guards to see what would happen to Jesus.

⁵⁹The leading priests and the whole Jewish council tried to find something false against Jesus so they could kill him. ⁶⁰Many people came and told lies about him, but the council could find no real reason to kill him. Then two people came and said, ⁶¹"This man said, 'I can destroy the Temple of God and build it again in three days.'"

⁶²Then the high priest stood up and said to Jesus, "Aren't you going to answer? Don't you have something to say about their charges against you?" ⁶³But Jesus said nothing.

Again the high priest said to Jesus, "I command you by the power of the living God: Tell us if you are the Christ, the Son of God."

⁶⁴Jesus answered, "Those are your words. But I tell you, in the future you will see the Son of Man sitting at the right hand of God, the Powerful One, and coming on clouds in the sky."

⁶⁵When the high priest heard this, he tore his clothes and said, "This man has said things that are against God! We don't need any more witnesses; you all heard him say these things against God. ⁶⁶What do you think?"

The people answered, "He should die."

⁶⁷Then the people there spat in Jesus' face and beat him with their fists. Others slapped him. ⁶⁸They said, "Prove to us that you are a prophet, you Christ! Tell us who hit you!"

PETER SAYS HE DOESN'T KNOW JESUS

⁶⁹At that time, as Peter was sitting in the courtyard, a servant girl came to him and said, "You also were with Jesus of Galilee."

⁷⁰But Peter said to all the people there that he was never with Jesus. He said, "I don't know what you are talking about."

⁷¹When he left the courtyard and was at the gate, another girl saw him. She said to the people there, "This man was with Jesus of Nazareth."

⁷²Again, Peter said he was never with him, saying, "I swear I don't know this man Jesus!"

⁷³A short time later, some people standing there went to Peter and said, "Surely you are one of those who followed Jesus. The way you talk shows it."

⁷⁴Then Peter began to place a curse on himself and swear, "I don't know the man." At once, a rooster crowed. ⁷⁵And Peter remembered what Jesus had told him: "Before the rooster crows, you will say three times that you don't know me." Then Peter went outside and cried painfully.

JESUS IS TAKEN TO PILATE

27 Early the next morning, all the leading priests and elders of the people decided that Jesus should die. ²They tied him, led him away, and turned him over to Pilate, the governor.

JUDAS KILLS HIMSELF

³Judas, the one who had given Jesus to his enemies, saw that they had decided to kill Jesus. Then he was very sorry for what he had done. So he took the thirty silver coins back to the priests and the leaders, ⁴saying, "I sinned; I handed over to you an innocent man."

The leaders answered, "What is that to us? That's your problem, not ours."

⁵So Judas threw the money into the Temple. Then he went off and hanged himself.

⁶The leading priests picked up the silver coins in the Temple and said, "Our law does not allow us to keep this money with the Temple money, because it has paid for a man's death." ⁷So they decided to use the coins to buy Potter's Field as a place to bury strangers who died in Jerusalem. ⁸That is why that field is still called the Field of Blood. ⁹So what Jeremiah the prophet had said

came true: "They took thirty silver coins. That is how little the Israelites thought he was worth. [10]They used those thirty silver coins to buy the potter's field, as the Lord commanded me."[n]

PILATE QUESTIONS JESUS

[11]Jesus stood before Pilate the governor, and Pilate asked him, "Are you the king of the Jews?"

Jesus answered, "Those are your words."

[12]When the leading priests and the elders accused Jesus, he said nothing.

[13]So Pilate said to Jesus, "Don't you hear them accusing you of all these things?"

[14]But Jesus said nothing in answer to Pilate, and Pilate was very surprised at this.

PILATE TRIES TO FREE JESUS

[15]Every year at the time of Passover the governor would free one prisoner whom the people chose. [16]At that time there was a man in prison, named Barabbas,[n] who was known to be very bad. [17]When the people gathered at Pilate's house, Pilate said, "Whom do you want me to set free: Barabbas[n] or Jesus who is called the Christ?" [18]Pilate knew that they turned Jesus in to him because they were jealous.

[19]While Pilate was sitting there on the judge's seat, his wife sent this message to him: "Don't do

27:9-10 "They . . . commanded me." See Zechariah 11:12-13 and Jeremiah 32:6-9. 27:16-17 Barabbas Some Greek copies read "Jesus Barabbas."

DEEP ISSUES

Guns and Violence

Our culture continually glorifies violence. You can hear it in our music, see it in our movies, and even watch it play out in everyday real life. Many people turn to violence and guns to solve their problems. That only adds to their problems. It doesn't solve anything.

Several hip-hop artists continually promote this violent lifestyle in their music. Also, several of those same artists are now six-feet-underground or doing time behind bars. It's been a wake-up call for some, but others just continue with the madness.

When will we learn? When we get angry, we sometimes want to resort to violence, including maybe even using a gun. We think this will handle a situation and make us feel better. It never does. It always equals even more drama. We've all been done dirty before. People have broken promises, disrespected us, and stolen from us. We've all wanted to get revenge. We feel like they deserve it, right? Even though we know it's not right, we feel this should justify it. The old saying still applies, "Two wrongs don't make a right." If we assault someone or use a gun, the judge isn't going to care about why. The fact is that we did it.

Prisons are filling up as the government makes stricter laws regarding guns being used in crimes. There are many other ways that we can deal with our frustrations and our enemies. Anyone can get loud and pull out a gat and start busting shots, but someone who is smart and has self-control will think it through. A real man or real woman knows how to stay cool and controlled.

Self-control is a characteristic of God's Spirit. When we have a real relationship with our Creator, we also learn to trust that he's got our back. He'll handle it for us. It might not be right away, but that's where the trust part comes in. Make no mistake. God will deal with them, but in his time and in his own way. Check out Romans 12:17-21. These verses tell us not to take revenge, but let God repay. We should pray for our enemies and not boast when we see them falling.

If we open our eyes and really look at the people who use violence and guns, we'll see some weak, confused, insecure people with no future—unless they change. Most of us have probably known someone killed by senseless violence. If we know what is true and live that truth, we know violence and guns should never be our options.

anything to that man, because he is innocent. Today I had a dream about him, and it troubled me very much."

20But the leading priests and elders convinced the crowd to ask for Barabbas to be freed and for Jesus to be killed.

21Pilate said, "I have Barabbas and Jesus. Which do you want me to set free for you?"

The people answered, "Barabbas."

22Pilate asked, "So what should I do with Jesus, the one called the Christ?"

They all answered, "Crucify him!"

23Pilate asked, "Why? What wrong has he done?"

But they shouted louder, "Crucify him!"

24When Pilate saw that he could do nothing about this and that a riot was starting, he took some water and washed his hands[n] in front of the crowd. Then he said, "I am not guilty of this man's death. You are the ones who are causing it!"

25All the people answered, "We and our children will be responsible for his death."

26Then he set Barabbas free. But Jesus was beaten with whips and handed over to the soldiers to be crucified.

27The governor's soldiers took Jesus into the governor's palace, and they all gathered around him. 28They took off his clothes and put a red robe on him. 29Using thorny branches, they made a crown, put it on his head, and put a stick in his right hand. Then the soldiers bowed before Jesus and made fun of him, saying, "Hail, King of the Jews!" 30They spat on Jesus. Then they took his stick and began to beat him on the head. 31After they finished, the soldiers took off the robe and put his own clothes on him again. Then they led him away to be crucified.

JESUS IS CRUCIFIED

32As the soldiers were going out of the city with Jesus, they forced a man from Cyrene, named Simon, to carry the cross for Jesus. 33They all came to the place called Golgotha, which means the Place of the Skull. 34The soldiers gave Jesus wine mixed with gall[n] to drink. He tasted the wine but refused to drink it. 35When the soldiers had crucified him, they threw lots to decide who would get his clothes.[n] 36The soldiers sat there and continued watching him. 37They put a sign above Jesus' head with a charge against him. It said: THIS IS JESUS, THE KING OF THE JEWS. 38Two robbers were crucified beside Jesus, one on the right and the other on the left. 39People walked by and insulted Jesus and shook their heads, 40saying, "You said you could destroy the Temple and build it again in three days. So save yourself! Come down from that cross if you are really the Son of God!"

41The leading priests, the teachers of the law, and the Jewish elders were also making fun of Jesus. 42They said, "He saved others, but he can't save himself! He says he is the king of Israel! If he is the king, let him come down now from the cross. Then we will believe in him. 43He trusts in God, so let God save him now, if God really wants him. He himself said, 'I am the Son of God.' " 44And in the same way, the robbers who were being crucified beside Jesus also insulted him.

JESUS DIES

45At noon the whole country became dark, and the darkness lasted for three hours. 46About three o'clock Jesus cried out in a loud voice, "Eli, Eli, lama sabachthani?" This means, "My God, my God, why have you abandoned me?"

47Some of the people standing there who heard this said, "He is calling Elijah."

48Quickly one of them ran and got a sponge and filled it with vinegar and tied it to a stick and gave it to Jesus to drink. 49But the others said, "Don't bother him. We want to see if Elijah will come to save him."

50But Jesus cried out again in a loud voice and died.

51Then the curtain in the Temple[n] was torn into two pieces, from the top to the bottom. Also, the earth shook and rocks broke apart. 52The graves opened, and many of God's people who had died were raised from the dead. 53They came out of the graves after Jesus was raised from the dead and went into the holy city, where they appeared to many people.

54When the army officer and the soldiers guarding Jesus saw this earthquake and everything else that happened, they were very frightened and said, "He really was the Son of God!"

55Many women who had followed Jesus from Galilee to help him were standing at a distance from the cross, watching. 56Mary Magdalene, and Mary the mother of James and Joseph, and the mother of James and John were there.

JESUS IS BURIED

57That evening a rich man named Joseph, a follower of Jesus from the town of Arimathea, came to Jerusalem. 58Joseph went to Pilate and asked to have Jesus' body. So Pilate gave orders for the soldiers to give it to Joseph. 59Then Joseph took the body and wrapped it in a clean linen cloth. 60He put Jesus' body in a new tomb that he had cut out of a wall of rock, and he rolled a very large stone to block the entrance of the tomb. Then Joseph went away. 61Mary Magdalene and the other woman named Mary were sitting near the tomb.

THE TOMB OF JESUS IS GUARDED

62The next day, the day after Preparation Day, the leading priests and the Pharisees went to Pilate. 63They said, "Sir, we remember that while that liar was still alive he said, 'After three days I will rise from the dead.' 64So give the order for the tomb to be guarded closely till the third day. Otherwise, his followers might come and steal the body and tell people that he has risen from the dead. That lie would be even worse than the first one."

65Pilate said, "Take some soldiers and go guard the tomb the best way you know." 66So they all went to the tomb and made it safe from thieves by sealing the stone in the entrance and putting soldiers there to guard it.

27:24 washed his hands He did this as a sign to show that he wanted no part in what the people did. **27:34 gall** Probably a drink of wine mixed with drugs to help a person feel less pain. **27:35 clothes** Some Greek copies continue, "So what God said through the prophet came true, 'They divided my clothes among them, and they threw lots for my clothing.' " See Psalm 22:18. **27:51 curtain in the Temple** A curtain divided the Most Holy Place from the other part of the Temple. That was the special building in Jerusalem where God commanded the Jewish people to worship him.

JESUS RISES FROM THE DEAD

28

The day after the Sabbath day was the first day of the week. At dawn on the first day, Mary Magdalene and another woman named Mary went to look at the tomb.

²At that time there was a strong earthquake. An angel of the Lord came down from heaven, went to the tomb, and rolled the stone away from the entrance. Then he sat on the stone. ³He was shining as bright as lightning, and his clothes were white as snow. ⁴The soldiers guarding the tomb shook with fear because of the angel, and they became like dead men.

⁵The angel said to the women, "Don't be afraid. I know that you are looking for Jesus, who has been crucified. ⁶He is not here. He has risen from the dead as he said he would. Come and see the place where his body was. ⁷And go quickly and tell his followers, 'Jesus has risen from the dead. He is going into Galilee ahead of you, and you will see him there.' " Then the angel said, "Now I have told you."

⁸The women left the tomb quickly. They were afraid, but they were also very happy. They ran to tell Jesus' followers what had happened. ⁹Suddenly, Jesus met them and said, "Greetings." The women came up to him, took hold of his feet, and worshiped him. ¹⁰Then Jesus said to them, "Don't be afraid. Go and tell my followers to go on to Galilee, and they will see me there."

THE SOLDIERS REPORT TO THE LEADERS

¹¹While the women went to tell Jesus' followers, some of the soldiers who had been guarding the tomb went into the city to tell the leading priests everything that had happened. ¹²Then the priests met with the elders and made a plan. They paid the soldiers a large amount of money ¹³and said to them, "Tell the people that Jesus' followers came during the night and stole the body while you were asleep. ¹⁴If the governor hears about this, we will satisfy him and save you from trouble." ¹⁵So the soldiers kept the money and did as they were told. And that story is still spread among the people even today.

JESUS TALKS TO HIS FOLLOWERS

¹⁶The eleven followers went to Galilee to the mountain where Jesus had told them to go. ¹⁷On the mountain they saw Jesus and worshiped him, but some of them did not believe it was really Jesus. ¹⁸Then Jesus came to them and said, "All power in heaven and on earth is given to me. ¹⁹So go and make followers of all people in the world. Baptize them in the name of the Father and the Son and the Holy Spirit. ²⁰Teach them to obey everything that I have taught you, and I will be with you always, even until the end of this age."

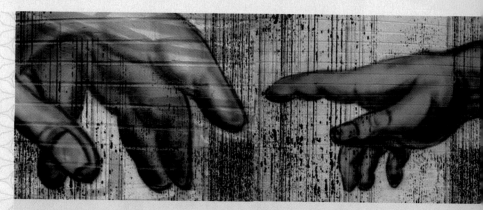

HeartCry

Identity Do you dislike yourself and sometimes wish you could be someone else? Do you wish you could be different or better? Be honest and let your heart cry . . .

Lord, I'm always struggling with my identity. I have such a poor view of myself. I don't think I'm smart enough, talented enough, or tight enough to do anything. I'm not the finest person in the world, and I'm always being hated on by people. They are always talking about me, and I just can't seem to get a break. I began to let people use me so that I would have some friends. I don't even want to tell you what all I've done to get attention, but you're God and you already know the low down. I'm so ashamed of who I am and how low I've stooped to gain the approval of the world. I know you are supposed to love me, but why did you make me the way I am? Thanks for listening again. Till next time.

I do love you, child. I formed all that you are with my own hands. I did not make a mistake, you are exactly the person I created you to be. I had a plan for your life before you were ever born and a future that is uniquely yours awaits. Trust in my love for you and I will make something beautiful of your life. **Ephesians 1:3–14**

MARK

JESUS WASN'T A SUPERSTAR LEADER

Most of us have experienced what Prejudice and Persecution feels like. Many of us have felt it because of the way we look. Some of us may have even felt it because we represented our faith. The Book of Mark was written during a time of some ill persecution. People left and right were being dissed because of their belief in Jesus. Not only were the average folks disrespecting Christians, but the Roman government and the police were putting some serious heat on believers. My man Mark knew the deal, so he quickly cut straight to the point. He pulled out his canvas and his spray can and painted an incredible picture of the life of Jesus. You'll quickly see that Jesus wasn't a superstar leader; he was a leader who served others. Jesus wasn't afraid to go to the local hood and get his hands dirty. As you read Mark's fast-paced chapters you'll see Jesus was constantly giving, teaching, healing, feeding, encouraging, and restoring people who were messed up. Jesus was a true role model. Mark wastes no time in displaying his mural, picturing a Jesus who kept it real and gave himself to others.

JOHN PREPARES FOR JESUS

1 This is the beginning of the Good News about Jesus Christ, the Son of God,[n] [2]as the prophet Isaiah wrote:

"I will send my messenger
ahead of you,
who will prepare your way."

Malachi 3:1

[3]"This is a voice of one
who calls out in the desert:
'Prepare the way for the Lord.
Make the road straight for him.' "

Isaiah 40:3

[4]John was baptizing people in the desert and preaching a baptism of changed hearts and lives for the forgiveness of sins. [5]All the people from Judea and Jerusalem were going out to him. They confessed their sins and were baptized by him in the Jordan River. [6]John wore clothes made from camel's hair, had a leather belt around his waist, and ate locusts and wild honey. [7]This is what John preached to the people: "There is one coming after me who is greater than I; I am not good enough even to kneel down and untie his sandals. [8]I baptize you with water, but he will baptize you with the Holy Spirit."

JESUS IS BAPTIZED

[9]At that time Jesus came from the town of Nazareth in Galilee and was baptized by John in the Jordan River. [10]Immediately, as Jesus was coming up out of the water, he saw heaven open. The Holy Spirit came down on him like a dove, [11]and a voice came from heaven: "You are my Son, whom I love, and I am very pleased with you."

[12]Then the Spirit sent Jesus into the desert. [13]He was in the desert forty days and was tempted by Satan. He was with the wild animals, and the angels came and took care of him.

JESUS CHOOSES SOME FOLLOWERS

[14]After John was put in prison, Jesus went into Galilee, preaching the Good News from God. [15]He said, "The right time has come. The kingdom of God is near. Change your hearts and lives and believe the Good News!"

[16]When Jesus was walking by Lake Galilee, he saw Simon[n] and his brother Andrew throwing a net into the lake because they were fishermen. [17]Jesus said to them, "Come follow me, and I will make you fish for people." [18]So Simon and Andrew immediately left their nets and followed him.

[19]Going a little farther, Jesus saw two more brothers, James and John, the sons of Zebedee. They were in a boat, mending their nets. [20]Jesus immediately called them, and they left their father in the boat with the hired workers and followed Jesus.

JESUS FORCES OUT AN EVIL SPIRIT

[21]Jesus and his followers went to Capernaum. On the Sabbath day He went to the synagogue and began to teach. [22]The people were amazed at his teaching, because he taught like a person who had authority, not like their teachers of the law. [23]Just then, a man was

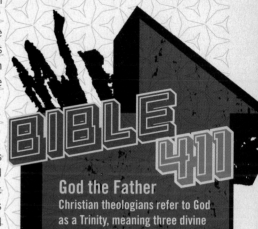

BIBLE 411

God the Father

Christian theologians refer to God as a Trinity, meaning three divine Persons making up one Godhead. God the Father, God the Son, and God the Holy Spirit are the names of those three Persons. God the Father is the ultimate source of all that is: the heavens, the earth, and everything in them. The unseen part of creation, such as the heavenly realms, angels, and cherubim, has its source in God the Father. God the Father is all-powerful, always present, and all-knowing. He has no beginning and no ending. He has always been and always will be; He is eternal. But there is one more very important fact about God the Father. According to 1 John 4:8, God is love. Not that God has love or gives love, but love is who and what God is. He showed his love by sending his Son into the world so we could have life through Him. Having life like this means we, too, become love, just like God. The culmination, then, of God's fatherhood is that we love each other. Now that will change the world!

JESUS KEPT it REAL AND GAVE HimSelf to OTHERS

  1:1 the Son of God Some Greek copies do not have this phrase.   **1:16 Simon** Simon's other name was Peter.

there in the synagogue who had an evil spirit in him. He shouted, [24]"Jesus of Nazareth! What do you want with us? Did you come to destroy us? I know who you are—God's Holy One!"

[25]Jesus commanded the evil spirit, "Be quiet! Come out of the man!" [26]The evil spirit shook the man violently, gave a loud cry, and then came out of him.

[27]The people were so amazed they asked each other, "What is happening here? This man is teaching something new, and with authority. He even gives commands to evil spirits, and they obey him." [28]And the news about Jesus spread quickly everywhere in the area of Galilee.

JESUS HEALS MANY PEOPLE

[29]As soon as Jesus and his followers left the synagogue, they went with James and John to the home of Simon[n] and Andrew. [30]Simon's mother-in-law was sick in bed with a fever, and the people told Jesus about her. [31]So Jesus went to her bed, took her hand, and helped her up. The fever left her, and she began serving them.

[32]That evening, after the sun went down, the people brought to Jesus all who were sick and had demons in them. [33]The whole town gathered at the door.

He's got answers

If I believe in Jesus, am I okay? Is that all there is to it?

At first glance, someone might answer, "Yes, believing in Jesus is enough." But, believing is head knowledge and that is not enough. The Bible says that demons believe in God and tremble with fear (James 2:19).

There are several more things you need:

- You have to realize that you have sinned and that your best falls short of God's glory.
- You have to realize that when people sin, they earn the payment of sin—eternal death, but that God has given us the free gift of eternal life through Jesus Christ.
- Realize that while we were sinners, Jesus died for us.
- Confess that Jesus is Lord and believe God raised him from the dead.

Once you confess and believe, you then build a relationship with Christ. As you get to know him, all the ill things you used to do and all the nasty desires begin to fade as your relationship with him grows. Believing in him becomes a lifestyle.

Read on: Romans 3:23, 5:8, 6:23, 10:9-10; James 2:19

PEEP THIS:

Seventy-eight percent of college students said they discuss religion or spirituality with friends; 73 percent stated religious and spiritual beliefs have helped develop their identity; 70 percent attended religious services in the past year.

[34]Jesus healed many who had different kinds of sicknesses, and he forced many demons to leave people. But he would not allow the demons to speak, because they knew who he was.

[35]Early the next morning, while it was still dark, Jesus woke and left the house. He went to a lonely place, where he prayed. [36]Simon and his friends went to look for Jesus. [37]When they found him, they said, "Everyone is looking for you!"

[38]Jesus answered, "We should go to other towns around here so I can preach there too. That is the reason I came." [39]So he went everywhere in Galilee, preaching in the synagogues and forcing out demons.

JESUS HEALS A SICK MAN

[40]A man with a skin disease came to Jesus. He fell to his knees and begged Jesus, "You can heal me if you will."

[41]Jesus felt sorry for the man, so he reached out his hand and touched him and said, "I will. Be healed!" [42]Immediately the disease left the man, and he was healed.

[43]Jesus told the man to go away

1:29 Simon Simon's other name was Peter.

at once, but he warned him strongly, [44]"Don't tell anyone about this. But go and show yourself to the priest. And offer the gift Moses commanded for people who are made well." This will show the people what I have done." [45]The man left there, but he began to tell everyone that Jesus had healed him, and so he spread the news about Jesus. As a result, Jesus could not enter a town if people saw him. He stayed in places where nobody lived, but people came to him from everywhere.

JESUS HEALS A PARALYZED MAN

2 A few days later, when Jesus came back to Capernaum, the news spread that he was at home. [2]Many people gathered together so that there was no room in the house, not even outside the door. And Jesus was teaching them God's message. [3]Four people came, carrying a paralyzed man. [4]Since they could not get to Jesus because of the crowd, they dug a hole in the roof right above where he was speaking. When they got through, they lowered the mat with the paralyzed man on it. [5]When Jesus saw the faith of these people, he said to the paralyzed man, "Young man, your sins are forgiven."

[6]Some of the teachers of the law were sitting there, thinking to themselves, [7]"Why does this man say things like that? He is speaking as if he were God. Only God can forgive sins."

[8]Jesus knew immediately what these teachers of the law were thinking. So he said to them, "Why are you thinking these things? [9]Which is easier: to tell this paralyzed man, 'Your sins are forgiven,' or to tell him, 'Stand up. Take your mat and walk'? [10]But I will prove to you that the Son of Man has authority on earth to forgive sins." So Jesus said to the paralyzed man, [11]"I tell you, stand up, take your mat, and go home." [12]Immediately the paralyzed man stood

up, took his mat, and walked out while everyone was watching him.

The people were amazed and praised God. They said, "We have never seen anything like this!"

[13]Jesus went to the lake again. The whole crowd followed him there, and he taught them. [14]While he was walking along, he saw a man named Levi son of Alphaeus, sitting in the tax collector's booth. Jesus said to him, "Follow me," and he stood up and followed Jesus.

[15]Later, as Jesus was having dinner at Levi's house, many tax collectors and "sinners" were eating there with Jesus and his followers. Many people like this followed Jesus. [16]When the teachers of the law who were Pharisees saw Jesus eating with the tax collectors and "sinners," they asked his followers, "Why does he eat with tax collectors and sinners?"

> I DID NOT COME TO INVITE GOOD PEOPLE BUT TO INVITE SINNERS.

[17]Jesus heard this and said to them, "It is not the healthy people who need a doctor, but the sick. I did not come to invite good people but to invite sinners."

JESUS' FOLLOWERS ARE CRITICIZED

[18]Now the followers of John[n] and the Pharisees often fasted[n] for a certain time. Some people came to Jesus and said, "Why do John's followers and the followers of the Pharisees often fast, but your followers don't?"

[19]Jesus answered, "The friends of the bridegroom do not fast while the bride-

groom is still with them. As long as the bridegroom is with them, they cannot fast. [20]But the time will come when the bridegroom will be taken from them, and then they will fast.

[21]"No one sews a patch of unshrunk cloth over a hole in an old coat. Otherwise, the patch will shrink and pull away—the new patch will pull away from the old coat. Then the hole will be worse. [22]Also, no one ever pours new wine into old leather bags. Otherwise, the new wine will break the bags, and the wine will be ruined along with the bags. But new wine should be put into new leather bags."

JESUS IS LORD OF THE SABBATH

[23]One Sabbath day, as Jesus was walking through some fields of grain, his followers began to pick some grain to eat. [24]The Pharisees said to Jesus, "Why are your followers doing what is not lawful on the Sabbath day?"

[25]Jesus answered, "Have you never read what David did when he and those with him were hungry and needed food? [26]During the time of Abiathar the high priest, David went into God's house and ate the holy bread, which is lawful only for priests to eat. And David also gave some of the bread to those who were with him."

[27]Then Jesus said to the Pharisees, "The Sabbath day was made to help people; they were not made to be ruled by the Sabbath day. [28]So then, the Son of Man is Lord even of the Sabbath day."

JESUS HEALS A MAN'S HAND

3 Another time when Jesus went into a synagogue, a man with a crippled hand was there. [2]Some people watched Jesus closely to see if he would heal the man on the Sabbath day so they could accuse him.

[3]Jesus said to the man with the crippled hand, "Stand up here in the middle of everyone."

1:44 Moses . . . well Read about this in Leviticus 14:1-32. **2:18 John** John the Baptist, who preached to the Jewish people about Christ's coming (Mark 1:4-8). **2:18 fasted** The people would give up eating for a special time of prayer and worship to God. It was also done to show sadness and disappointment.

VIEWPOINT

WHAT IS THE BIGGEST ISSUE PREVENTING WORLD PEACE?

Racism is the main problem in the world and is currently at the root of war. The division of races is a major issue. The wars occurring in the world today are based on territorial ownership, racial divisions, and the misconception of superiority of certain races.

⁴Then Jesus asked the people, "Which is lawful on the Sabbath day: to do good or to do evil, to save a life or to kill?" But they said nothing to answer him. ⁵Jesus was angry as he looked at the people, and he felt very sad because they were stubborn. Then he said to the man, "Hold out your hand." The man held out his hand and it was healed. ⁶Then the Pharisees left and began making plans with the Herodians[n] about a way to kill Jesus.

MANY PEOPLE FOLLOW JESUS

⁷Jesus left with his followers for the lake, and a large crowd from Galilee followed him. ⁸Also many people came from Judea, from Jerusalem, from Idumea, from the lands across the Jordan River, and from the area of Tyre and Sidon. When they heard what Jesus was doing, many people came to him. ⁹When Jesus saw the crowds, he told his followers to get a boat ready for him to keep people from crowding against him. ¹⁰He had healed many people, so all the sick were pushing toward him to touch him. ¹¹When evil spirits saw Jesus, they fell down before him and shouted, "You are the Son of God!" ¹²But Jesus strongly warned them not to tell who he was.

JESUS CHOOSES HIS TWELVE APOSTLES

¹³Then Jesus went up on a mountain and called to him those he wanted, and they came to him. ¹⁴Jesus chose twelve and called them apostles.[n] He wanted them to be with him, and he wanted to send them out to preach ¹⁵and to have the authority to force demons out of people. ¹⁶These are the twelve men he chose: Simon (Jesus named him Peter), ¹⁷James and John, the sons of Zebedee (Jesus named them Boanerges, which means "Sons of Thunder"), ¹⁸Andrew, Philip, Bartholomew, Matthew, Thomas, James the son of Alphaeus, Thaddaeus, Simon the Zealot, ¹⁹and Judas Iscariot, who later turned against Jesus.

SOME PEOPLE SAY JESUS HAS A DEVIL

²⁰Then Jesus went home, but again a crowd gathered. There were so many people that Jesus and his followers could not eat. ²¹When his family heard this, they went to get him because they thought he was out of his mind. ²²But the teachers of the law from Jerusalem were saying, "Beelzebul is living inside him! He uses power from the ruler of demons to force demons out of people."

²³So Jesus called the people together and taught them with stories. He said, "Satan will not force himself out of people. ²⁴A kingdom that is divided cannot continue, ²⁵and a family that is divided cannot continue. ²⁶And if Satan is against himself and fights against his own people, he cannot continue; that is the end of Satan. ²⁷No one can enter a strong person's house and steal his things unless he first ties up the strong person. Then he can steal things from the house. ²⁸I tell you the truth, all sins that people do and all the things people say against God can be forgiven. ²⁹But anyone who speaks against the Holy Spirit will never be forgiven; he is guilty of a sin that continues forever."

³⁰Jesus said this because the teachers of the law said that he had an evil spirit inside him.

JESUS' TRUE FAMILY

³¹Then Jesus' mother and brothers arrived. Standing outside, they sent someone in to tell him to come out. ³²Many people were sitting around Jesus, and they said to him, "Your mother and brothers[n] are waiting for you outside."

³³Jesus asked, "Who are my mother and my brothers?" ³⁴Then he looked at those sitting around him and said, "Here are my mother and my brothers! ³⁵My true brother and sister and mother are those who do what God wants."

A STORY ABOUT PLANTING SEED

4 Again Jesus began teaching by the lake. A great crowd gathered around him, so he sat down in a boat near the shore. All the people stayed on the shore close to the water. ²Jesus taught them many things, using stories. He said, ³"Listen! A farmer went out to plant his seed. ⁴While he was planting, some seed fell by the road, and the birds came and ate it up. ⁵Some seed fell on rocky ground where there wasn't much dirt. That seed grew very fast, because the ground was not deep. ⁶But when the sun rose, the plants dried up because they did not have deep roots. ⁷Some

---

3:6 Herodians A political group that followed Herod and his family.   **3:14 and called them apostles** Some Greek copies do not have this phrase.   **3:32 brothers** Some Greek copies continue, "and sisters."

WORLD SAYS, WORD SAYS

LOOKING FOR ANSWERS

If you have questions about love, life, or relationships, just look to the stars. There's nothing wrong with reading your horoscope. Go to a psychic and get your palm read. It's okay to believe in astrology; there are many answers you can find through the stars. Take a deep breath and just meditate in your best yoga position. The answer will come.

"As the Scripture says, 'Anyone who calls on the Lord will be saved'" (Romans 10:13).

"Idols tell lies; fortune-tellers see false visions and tell about false dreams. The comfort they give is worth nothing. So the people are like lost sheep. They are abused, because there is no shepherd" (Zechariah 10:2).

---

other seed fell among thorny weeds, which grew and choked the good plants. So those plants did not produce a crop. [8]Some other seed fell on good ground and began to grow. It got taller and produced a crop. Some plants made thirty times more, some made sixty times more, and some made a hundred times more."

[9]Then Jesus said, "Let those with ears use them and listen!"

JESUS TELLS WHY HE USED STORIES

[10]Later, when Jesus was alone, the twelve apostles and others around him asked him about the stories.

[11]Jesus said, "You can know the secret about the kingdom of God. But to other people I tell everything by using stories [12]so that:

'They will look and look, but they
    will not learn.
They will listen and listen, but
    they will not understand.
If they did learn and understand,
    they would come back to me and
    be forgiven.'"   *Isaiah 6:9-10*

JESUS EXPLAINS THE SEED STORY

[13]Then Jesus said to his followers, "Don't you understand this story? If you don't, how will you understand any story? [14]The farmer is like a person who plants God's message in people. [15]Sometimes the teaching falls on the road. This is like the people who hear the teaching of God, but Satan quickly comes and takes away the teaching that was planted in them. [16]Others are like the seed planted on rocky ground. They hear the teaching and quickly accept it with joy. [17]But since they don't allow the teaching to go deep into their lives, they keep it only a short time. When trouble or persecution comes because of the teaching they accepted, they quickly give up. [18]Others are like the seed planted among the thorny weeds. They hear the teaching, [19]but the worries of this life, the temptation of wealth, and many other evil desires keep the teaching from growing and producing fruit[n] in their lives. [20]Others are like the seed planted in the good ground. They hear the teaching and accept it. Then they grow and produce fruit—sometimes thirty times more, sometimes sixty times more, and sometimes a hundred times more."

USE WHAT YOU HAVE

[21]Then Jesus said to them, "Do you hide a lamp under a bowl or under a bed? No! You put the lamp on a lampstand. [22]Everything that is hidden will be made clear and every secret thing will be made known. [23]Let those with ears use them and listen!

[24]"Think carefully about what you hear. The way you give to others is the way God will give to you, but God will give you even more. [25]Those who have understanding will be given more. But those who do not have understanding, even what they have will be taken away from them."

JESUS USES A STORY ABOUT SEED

[26]Then Jesus said, "The kingdom of God is like someone who plants seed in the ground. [27]Night and day, whether the person is asleep or awake, the seed still grows, but the person does not know how it grows. [28]By itself the earth produces grain. First the plant grows, then the head, and then all the grain in the head. [29]When the grain is ready, the farmer cuts it, because this is the harvest time."

A STORY ABOUT MUSTARD SEED

[30]Then Jesus said, "How can I show you what the kingdom of God is like? What story can I use to explain it? [31]The kingdom of God is like a mustard seed, the smallest seed you plant in the ground. [32]But when planted, this seed grows and becomes the largest of all garden plants. It produces large branches, and the wild birds can make nests in its shade."

[33]Jesus used many stories like these to teach the crowd God's message—as much as they could understand. [34]He always used stories to teach them. But when he and his followers were alone, Jesus explained everything to them.

 4:19 producing fruit To produce fruit means to have in your life the good things God wants.

JESUS CALMS A STORM

[35] That evening, Jesus said to his followers, "Let's go across the lake." [36] Leaving the crowd behind, they took him in the boat just as he was. There were also other boats with them. [37] A very strong wind came up on the lake. The waves came over the sides and into the boat so that it was already full of water. [38] Jesus was at the back of the boat, sleeping with his head on a cushion. His followers woke him and said, "Teacher, don't you care that we are drowning!"

[39] Jesus stood up and commanded the wind and said to the waves, "Quiet! Be still!" Then the wind stopped, and it became completely calm.

[40] Jesus said to his followers, "Why are you afraid? Do you still have no faith?"

[41] The followers were very afraid and asked each other, "Who is this? Even the wind and the waves obey him!"

A MAN WITH DEMONS INSIDE HIM

5 Jesus and his followers went to the other side of the lake to the area of the Gerasene[n] people. [2] When Jesus got out of the boat, instantly a man with an evil spirit came to him from the burial caves. [3] This man lived in the caves, and no one could tie him up, not even with a chain. [4] Many times people had used chains to tie the man's hands and feet, but he always broke them off. No one was strong enough to control him. [5] Day and night he would wander around the burial caves and on the hills, screaming and cutting himself with stones. [6] While Jesus was still far away, the man saw him, ran to him, and fell down before him.

[7] The man shouted in a loud voice, "What do you want with me, Jesus, Son

5:1 Gerasene From Gerasa, an area southeast of Lake Galilee. The exact location is uncertain and some Greek copies read "Gergesene"; others read "Gadarene."

HOW YA TRAVELIN'?

FAITH

Faith is our active demonstration of belief. Three dimensions of faith are: faith is unseen, it is absolute, and it bears fruit. Unfortunately, faith has gotten a bad rep because it does rely on the unseen. Folks in the world say that intelligent people should rely on only what they can see and, therefore, know. People miss the fact that having faith is the essence of knowing . . . knowing that God is supremely trustworthy to do all that he has promised. "Faith means being sure of the things we hope for and knowing that something is real even if we do not see it" (Hebrews 11:1).

Faith is a powerful force. It takes very little to move the "mountains" in your life. The Bible says that if "your faith is as big as a mustard seed [a very tiny seed], you can say to this mountain, 'Move from here to there,' and it will move. All things will be possible for you" (Matthew 17:20). If you don't have faith, it will be impossible to please God (Hebrews 11:6).

Faith in Jesus Christ brings life-changing results. Faithless characteristics such as fear, anger, worry, and greed are replaced with fruit: attributes such as joy, patience, peace, hope, and understanding. Ultimately, faith is about God revealing more of himself to you when you place your trust in him (Romans 1:17).

WE LIVE BY WHAT WE BELIEVE – 2 CORINTHIANS 5:7

of the Most High God? I command you in God's name not to torture me!" [8]He said this because Jesus was saying to him, "You evil spirit, come out of the man."

[9]Then Jesus asked him, "What is your name?"

He answered, "My name is Legion,[n] because we are many spirits." [10]He begged Jesus again and again not to send them out of that area.

[11]A large herd of pigs was feeding on a hill near there. [12]The demons begged Jesus, "Send us into the pigs; let us go into them." [13]So Jesus allowed them to do this. The evil spirits left the man and went into the pigs. Then the herd of pigs—about two thousand of them—rushed down the hill into the lake and were drowned.

[14]The herdsmen ran away and went to the town and to the countryside, telling everyone about this. So people went out to see what had happened. [15]They came to Jesus and saw the man who used to have the many evil spirits, sitting, clothed, and in his right mind. And they were frightened. [16]The people who saw this told the others what had happened to the man who had the demons living in him, and they told about the pigs. [17]Then the people began to beg Jesus to leave their area.

[18]As Jesus was getting back into the boat, the man who was freed from the demons begged to go with him.

[19]But Jesus would not let him. He said, "Go home to your family and tell them how much the Lord has done for you and how he has had mercy on you." [20]So the man left and began to tell the people in the Ten Towns[n] about what Jesus had done for him. And everyone was amazed.

JESUS GIVES LIFE TO A DEAD GIRL AND HEALS A SICK WOMAN

[21]When Jesus went in the boat back to the other side of the lake, a large crowd gathered around him there. [22]A leader of the synagogue, named Jairus, came there, saw Jesus, and fell at his feet. [23]He begged Jesus, saying again and again,

hot 10

Biblical Attributes of a Good Man

10. Deals straight

9. Gives generously

8. Keeps his body pure

7. Forgives others

6. Is faithful

5. Stands with God

4. His word is his bond

3. Feels for others

2. Tries to do right

1. Walks with Jesus

"My daughter is dying. Please come and put your hands on her so she will be healed and will live." [24]So Jesus went with him.

A large crowd followed Jesus and pushed very close around him. [25]Among them was a woman who had been bleeding for twelve years. [26]She had suffered very much from many doctors and had spent all the money she had, but instead of improving, she was getting worse. [27]When the woman heard about Jesus, she came up behind him in the crowd and touched his coat. [28]She thought, "If I can just touch his clothes, I will be healed." [29]Instantly her bleeding stopped, and she felt in her body that she was healed from her disease.

[30]At once Jesus felt power go out from him. So he turned around in the crowd and asked, "Who touched my clothes?"

[31]His followers said, "Look at how many people are pushing against you! And you ask, 'Who touched me?'"

[32]But Jesus continued looking around to see who had touched him. [33]The woman, knowing that she was healed, came and fell at Jesus' feet. Shaking with fear, she told him the whole truth. [34]Jesus said to her, "Dear woman, you are made well because you believed. Go in peace; be healed of your disease."

[35]While Jesus was still speaking, some people came from the house of the synagogue leader. They said, "Your daughter is dead. There is no need to bother the teacher anymore."

[36]But Jesus paid no attention to what they said. He told the synagogue leader, "Don't be afraid; just believe."

[37]Jesus let only Peter, James, and John the brother of James go with him. [38]When they came to the house of the synagogue leader, Jesus found many people there making lots of noise and crying loudly. [39]Jesus entered the house and said to them, "Why are you crying and making so much noise? The child is not dead, only asleep." [40]But they laughed at him. So, after throwing them out of the house, Jesus took the child's father and mother and his three followers into the room where the child was. [41]Taking hold of the girl's hand, he said to her, "Talitha, koum!" (This means, "Young girl, I tell you to stand up!") [42]At once the girl stood right up and

5:9 Legion Means very many. A legion was about five thousand men in the Roman army. **5:20 Ten Towns** In Greek, called "Decapolis." It was an area east of Lake Galilee that once had ten main towns.

REAL RHYMES:

STRANGE WOMAN

BY JOHN MOORER AKA JOHN THE BAPTIST

WHAT IS IT, SON? LET ME SHED SOME WISDOM ON THIS ONE BEFORE YA DEAD OR IN PRISON.
DON'T BE FOOLED BY HER TRICK FLATTERY—THE EYES, THE THIGHS, THE HIPS, AND THICK ANATOMY.
SHE TRIED TO FLATTER ME LATE ON SATURDAY, DRESSED LIKE THE HARLOT, HOOO, WHATEVER YOU WANNA CALL IT.
BUT THE TRAP, I SAW IT COMIN'. ALL OF A SUDDEN, I'M BEING APPROACHED BY THIS STRANGE WOMAN.
TALKIN' ABOUT, "UHH YOU FLY TO ME. JOHN THE BAPTIST, WILL YOU COME LIE WITH ME?
PLEASE COME ON INSIDE WITH ME, HUSBAND'S OUTTA TOWN.
TOOK A LOT A DOUGH. HE WON'T BE AROUND FOR A WHILE."
I SMILED AND SAID, "YOU'VE SLAIN MANY MEN WITH YOUR LINEN OF CINNAMON.
THERE'S SINFUL VENOM IN YOUR ADRENALIN. I WON'T BE LED OFF LIKE COOKED VENISON.
YOU KILL THE INNOCENT.

GOTTA FEELIN' IF I GO, THAT A BROTHER WON'T BE BACK NO MORE.
TO ALL THE YOUNG ONES, STAY FROM HER DO. SHE'LL HEM YOU UP MAN AND THAT'S FO SHO.
AND UM, THAT PRETTY YOUNG THING WITH THE TONGUE RING, SHE AIN'T THE ONE KING.
MESS AROUND AND LOSE YOUR ANOINTING. YEP, YOU LOSE YOUR HOUSE, THEN YOUR LIFE.
WOULDN'T THAT BE DISAPPOINTING?
SNEAKING AND FREAKING WITH THIS ONE AND THAT ONE.
SOME STUFF YOU CATCH NOW, MAN, YOU DON'T COME BACK FROM.
FOR A FEW MOMENTS OF ACTION, THE COST TOO GREAT OF A LOSS.
IT WON'T BE WORTH THE SATISFACTION.
IT'S JUST FOOD FOR THOUGHT. IF YOU LIVE AS YOU OUGHT, THEN YOU WOULDN'T GET CAUGHT.
AND WHEN YOU GET OLDER AND GIVE LIFE SOME THOUGHT.
WHEN YOU LOOK BACK, IT WAS ALL FOR NAUGHT. MMMMPHH.

JOHN THE BAPTIST, "FELLAS HEY, I GOT TO WARN YA. FROM DELAWARE ON TO CALIFORNIA.
YEAH SHE LOOKS GOOD AND THE BODY'S BANGIN'. SHE'LL LEAVE YOU HANGIN'.
DON'T DO IT.

TO MY EAST COAST MAN, DON'T DO IT.
TO MY WEST COAST MAN DON'T DO IT.
TO MY MIDWEST MAN DON'T DO IT, DON'T DO IT, DON'T DO IT.
TO MY DIRTY SOUTH MAN DON'T DO IT.
ALL CARIBBEAN MON DON'T DO IT, DON'T DO IT, DON'T DO IT.
DON'T DO IT SON, NOPE.

TAKE IT FROM ME. THE LIPS DRIP WITH HONEY. THE THICK HIPS ARE MONEY.
THE TRICK TRICKS THE DUMMIES. THE PILLOW DRIPS WITH ALOE TO SLAY THE SHALLOW MINDED, OH NO!
FIRST YOU LOSE MONEY AND THEN YOUR HONOR, THEN ALL OF YOUR WEALTH GOES TO THE FOREIGNER.
THEN YOU GET TO RIDE IN THE BACK OF THE CORONER. ALL BECAUSE OF LACK OF SELF-CONTROL.

began walking. (She was twelve years old.) Everyone was completely amazed. [43]Jesus gave them strict orders not to tell people about this. Then he told them to give the girl something to eat.

JESUS GOES TO HIS HOMETOWN

6 Jesus left there and went to his hometown, and his followers went with him. [2]On the Sabbath day he taught in the synagogue. Many people heard him and were amazed, saying, "Where did this man get these teachings? What is this wisdom that has been given to him? And where did he get the power to do miracles? [3]He is just the carpenter, the son of Mary and the brother of James, Joseph, Judas, and Simon. And his sisters are here with us." So the people were upset with Jesus.

[4]Jesus said to them, "A prophet is honored everywhere except in his hometown and with his own people and in his own home." [5]So Jesus was not able to work any miracles there except to heal a few sick people by putting his hands on them. [6]He was amazed at how many people had no faith.

Then Jesus went to other villages in that area and taught. [7]He called his twelve followers together and got ready to send them out two by two and gave them authority over evil spirits. [8]This is what Jesus commanded them: "Take nothing for your trip except a walking stick. Take no bread, no bag, and no money in your pockets. [9]Wear sandals, but take only the clothes you are wearing. [10]When you enter a house, stay there until you leave that town. [11]If the people in a certain place refuse to welcome you or listen to you, leave that place. Shake its dust off your feet[n] as a warning to them."[n]

[12]So the followers went out and preached that people should change their hearts and lives. [13]They forced many demons out and put olive oil on many sick people and healed them.

HOW JOHN THE BAPTIST WAS KILLED

[14]King Herod heard about Jesus, because he was now well known. Some people said,[n] "He is John the Baptist, who has risen from the dead. That is why he can work these miracles."

[15]Others said, "He is Elijah."[n]

Other people said, "Jesus is a prophet, like the prophets who lived long ago."

[16]When Herod heard this, he said, "I killed John by cutting off his head. Now he has risen from the dead!"

[17]Herod himself had ordered his soldiers to arrest John and put him in prison in order to please his wife, Herodias. She had been the wife of Philip, Herod's brother, but then Herod had married her. [18]John had been telling Herod, "It is not lawful for you to be married to your brother's wife." [19]So Herodias hated John and wanted to kill him. But she couldn't, [20]because Herod was afraid of John and protected him. He knew John was a good and holy man. Also, though John's preaching always bothered him, he enjoyed listening to John.

[21]Then the perfect time came for Herodias to cause John's death. On Herod's birthday, he gave a dinner party for the most important government leaders, the commanders of his army, and the most important people in Galilee. [22]When the daughter of Herodias[n] came in and danced, she pleased Herod and the people eating with him.

So King Herod said to the girl, "Ask me for anything you want, and I will give it to you." [23]He promised her, "Anything you ask for I will give to you—up to half of my kingdom."

[24]The girl went to her mother and asked, "What should I ask for?"

Her mother answered, "Ask for the head of John the Baptist."

[25]At once the girl went back to the king and said to him, "I want the head of John the Baptist right now on a platter."

[26]Although the king was very sad, he had made a promise, and his dinner guests had heard it. So he did not want to refuse what she asked. [27]Immediately the king sent a soldier to bring John's head. The soldier went and cut off John's head in the prison [28]and brought it back on a platter. He gave it to the girl, and the girl gave it to her mother. [29]When John's followers heard this, they came and got John's body and put it in a tomb.

MORE THAN FIVE THOUSAND FED

[30]The apostles gathered around Jesus and told him about all the things they had done and taught. [31]Crowds of people were coming and going so that Jesus and his followers did not even have time to eat. He said to them, "Come away by yourselves, and we will go to a lonely place to get some rest."

[32]So they went in a boat by themselves to a lonely place. [33]But many people saw them leave and recognized them. So from all the towns they ran to the place where Jesus was going, and they got there before him. [34]When he arrived, he saw a great crowd waiting. He felt sorry for them, because they were like sheep without a shepherd. So he began to teach them many things.

[35]When it was late in the day, his followers came to him and said, "No one lives in this place, and it is already very late. [36]Send the people away so they can go to the countryside and towns around here to buy themselves something to eat."

[37]But Jesus answered, "You give them something to eat."

They said to him, "We would all have to work a month to earn enough money to buy that much bread!"

[38]Jesus asked them, "How many loaves of bread do you have? Go and see."

When they found out, they said, "Five loaves and two fish."

[39]Then Jesus told his followers to have the people sit in groups on the green grass. [40]So they sat in groups of fifty or a hundred. [41]Jesus took the five loaves and two fish and, looking up to heaven,

6:11 Shake . . . feet A warning. It showed that they were rejecting these people. **6:11 them** Some Greek copies continue, "I tell you the truth, on the Judgment Day it will be better for the towns of Sodom and Gomorrah than for the people of that town." See Matthew 10:15. **6:14 Some people said** Some Greek copies read "He said." **6:15 Elijah** A great prophet who spoke for God and who lived hundreds of years before Christ. See 1 Kings 17. **6:22 When . . . Herodias** Some Greek copies read "When his daughter Herodias."

he thanked God for the food. He divided the bread and gave it to his followers for them to give to the people. Then he divided the two fish among them all. [42]All the people ate and were satisfied. [43]The followers filled twelve baskets with the leftover pieces of bread and fish. [44]There were five thousand men who ate.

JESUS WALKS ON THE WATER

[45]Immediately Jesus told his followers to get into the boat and go ahead of him to Bethsaida across the lake. He stayed there to send the people home. [46]After sending them away, he went into the hills to pray.

> STEALING, MURDER, . . . GREED, . . . THESE EVIL THINGS COME FROM INSIDE AND MAKE PEOPLE UNCLEAN.

[47]That night, the boat was in the middle of the lake, and Jesus was alone on the land. [48]He saw his followers struggling hard to row the boat, because the wind was blowing against them. Between three and six o'clock in the morning, Jesus came to them, walking on the water, and he wanted to walk past the boat. [49]But when they saw him walking on the water, they thought he was a ghost and cried out. [50]They all saw him and were afraid. But quickly Jesus spoke to them and said, "Have courage! It is I. Do not be afraid." [51]Then he got into the boat with them, and the wind became calm. The followers were greatly amazed. [52]They did not understand about the miracle of the five loaves, because their minds were closed.

[53]When they had crossed the lake, they came to shore at Gennesaret and tied the boat there. [54]When they got out of the boat, people immediately recognized Jesus. [55]They ran everywhere in that area and began to bring sick people on mats wherever they heard he was. [56]And everywhere he went—into towns, cities, or countryside—the people brought the sick to the marketplaces. They begged him to let them touch just the edge of his coat, and all who touched it were healed.

OBEY GOD'S LAW

7When some Pharisees and some teachers of the law came from Jerusalem, they gathered around Jesus. [2]They saw that some of Jesus' followers ate food with hands that were not clean, that is, they hadn't washed them. [3](The Pharisees and all the Jews never eat before washing their hands in the way required by their unwritten laws. [4]And when they buy something in the market, they never eat it until they wash themselves in a special way. They also follow many other unwritten laws, such as the washing of cups, pitchers, and pots.[n])

[5]The Pharisees and the teachers of the law said to Jesus, "Why don't your followers obey the unwritten laws which have been handed down to us? Why do your followers eat their food with hands that are not clean?"

[6]Jesus answered, "Isaiah was right when he spoke about you hypocrites. He wrote,

'These people show honor to me
    with words,
    but their hearts are far from me.
[7]Their worship of me is worthless.
    The things they teach are nothing
        but human rules.'   *Isaiah 29:13*
[8]You have stopped following the commands of God, and you follow only human teachings."[n]

[9]Then Jesus said to them, "You clev-erly ignore the commands of God so you can follow your own teachings. [10]Moses said, 'Honor your father and your mother,'[n] and 'Anyone who says cruel things to his father or mother must be put to death.'[n] [11]But you say a person can tell his father or mother, 'I have something I could use to help you, but it is Corban—a gift to God.' [12]You no longer let that person use that money for his father or his mother. [13]By your own rules, which you teach people, you are rejecting what God said. And you do many things like that."

[14]After Jesus called the crowd to him again, he said, "Every person should listen to me and understand what I am saying. [15]There is nothing people put into their bodies that makes them unclean. People are made unclean by the things that come out of them. [[16]Let those with ears use them and listen.]"[n]

[17]When Jesus left the people and went into the house, his followers asked him about this story. [18]Jesus said, "Do you still not understand? Surely you know that nothing that enters someone from the outside can make that person unclean. [19]It does not go into the mind, but into the stomach. Then it goes out of the body." (When Jesus said this, he meant that no longer was any food unclean for people to eat.)

[20]And Jesus said, "The things that come out of people are the things that make them unclean. [21]All these evil things begin inside people, in the mind: evil thoughts, sexual sins, stealing, murder, adultery, [22]greed, evil actions, lying, doing sinful things, jealousy, speaking evil of others, pride, and foolish living. [23]All these evil things come from inside and make people unclean."

JESUS HELPS A NON-JEWISH WOMAN

[24]Jesus left that place and went to the area around Tyre.[n] When he went into a house, he did not want anyone to know he was there, but he could not stay hidden. [25]A woman whose daughter had an evil spirit in her heard that he was there.

7:4 pots Some Greek copies continue, "and dining couches." **7:8 teachings** Some Greek copies continue, "You wash pitchers and jugs and do many other such things." **7:10 'Honor . . . mother.'** Quotation from Exodus 20:12; Deuteronomy 5:16. **7:10 'Anyone . . . death.'** Quotation from Exodus 21:17. **7:16 Let . . . listen.** Some Greek copies do not contain the bracketed text. **7:24 Tyre** Some Greek copies continue, "and Sidon."

60

So she quickly came to Jesus and fell at his feet. [26]She was Greek, born in Phoenicia, in Syria. She begged Jesus to force the demon out of her daughter.

[27]Jesus told the woman, "It is not right to take the children's bread and give it to the dogs. First let the children eat all they want."

[28]But she answered, "Yes, Lord, but even the dogs under the table can eat the children's crumbs."

[29]Then Jesus said, "Because of your answer, you may go. The demon has left your daughter."

[30]The woman went home and found her daughter lying in bed; the demon was gone.

JESUS HEALS A DEAF MAN

[31]Then Jesus left the area around Tyre and went through Sidon to Lake Galilee, to the area of the Ten Towns.[n] [32]While he was there, some people brought a man to him who was deaf and could not talk plainly. The people begged Jesus to put his hand on the man to heal him.

[33]Jesus led the man away from the crowd, by himself. He put his fingers in the man's ears and then spit and touched the man's tongue. [34]Looking up to heaven, he sighed and said to the man, "Ephphatha!" (This means, "Be opened.") [35]Instantly the man was able to hear and to use his tongue so that he spoke clearly.

[36]Jesus commanded the people not to tell anyone about what happened. But the more he commanded them, the more they told about it. [37]They were completely amazed and said, "Jesus does everything well. He makes the deaf hear! And those who can't talk he makes able to speak."

 7:31 Ten Towns In Greek, called "Decapolis." It was an area east of Lake Galilee that once had ten main towns.

THE SCRIPT

Rise Up and Walk
Mark 2:1-12

When Jesus was healing folks of demons and diseases,
He told folks not to tell, but everyone did what they pleased.
So people found out and followed Jesus out to where he roamed desert places.
Whenever Jesus came back to his home,
It didn't take long for word to spread around Capernaum.
"He's at his house." So a large crowd gathered round for a look-see,
Packing Jesus' place up to maximum capacity,
To hear his teaching while he was preaching,
Four brought forth a paraplegic; they were strategic.
The sick man was carried on a mat by his friends.
The scene was dismal and grim 'cause there was no way for them to enter in,
To get their friend close to Jesus to experience healing. So . . .
They broke in by removing roof tiles and made a hole in the ceiling,
Rappelling the ill dude down through the hole, atop his mat.
But Jesus wasn't mad, in fact, he was feelin' that!
"Your faith is great my son, I forgive your sins."
But some of the religious teachers couldn't let it end. (They were whisperin' and hissin':
"Why, Jesus is misleading him, feeding this sick man fabrications.
Only God can take man's sins and give preferred adjudication.")
Right away, Jesus knew they was hatin' and said, "What's up? Oh, you think I'm mistaken. Humph.
Well, maybe you can make end of which is the easiest statement:

Should I choose to say to the man, 'Son, I forgive your sins'
Or should I flip the script and heal him by saying,
'Get up, grab your stuff, and walk again?' I can't call it.
But just so it's comprehended that the Son of Man's power extends to make sins amended . . ."
Jesus bent down, looked at the man's face and said, "Your paralysis is ended.
Get up. Grab your bed and go to your house fully independent!"
Everyone watched as the sick man got up, got his stuff, and got out.
And once again all the people had that look: the wide-open mouth,
And praised God saying, "This is something we can't figure out!"

Take this with you: Jesus grants us freedom from the root of our problems—sin. He came to overrule the law of sin and death, bring us hope and healing, and offer us a way out.

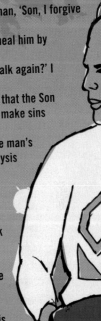

MORE THAN FOUR THOUSAND PEOPLE FED

8 Another time there was a great crowd with Jesus that had nothing to eat. So Jesus called his followers and said, [2]"I feel sorry for these people, because they have already been with me for three days, and they have nothing to eat. [3]If I send them home hungry, they will faint on the way. Some of them live a long way from here."

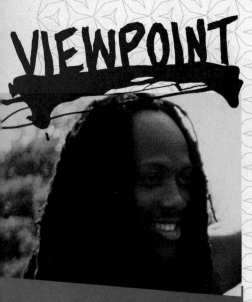

VIEWPOINT

WHAT IS THE NUMBER ONE QUESTION YOU WANT TO ASK GOD?

Why do we have people who are stupid rich and others who are stank poor? Everyday I see people begging on the street. I can't even go to the drive-thru at McDonald's without getting hit up for some ends.

[4]Jesus' followers answered, "How can we get enough bread to feed all these people? We are far away from any town."

[5]Jesus asked, "How many loaves of bread do you have?"

They answered, "Seven."

[6]Jesus told the people to sit on the ground. Then he took the seven loaves, gave thanks to God, and divided the bread. He gave the pieces to his followers to give to the people, and they did so. [7]The followers also had a few small fish. After Jesus gave thanks for the fish, he told his followers to give them to the people also. [8]All the people ate and were satisfied. Then his followers filled seven baskets with the leftover pieces of food. [9]There were about four thousand people who ate. After they had eaten, Jesus sent them home. [10]Then right away he got into a boat with his followers and went to the area of Dalmanutha.

THE LEADERS ASK FOR A MIRACLE

[11]The Pharisees came to Jesus and began to ask him questions. Hoping to trap him, they asked Jesus for a miracle from God. [12]Jesus sighed deeply and said, "Why do you people ask for a miracle as a sign? I tell you the truth, no sign will be given to you." [13]Then Jesus left the Pharisees and went in the boat to the other side of the lake.

GUARD AGAINST WRONG TEACHINGS

[14]His followers had only one loaf of bread with them in the boat; they had forgotten to bring more. [15]Jesus warned them, "Be careful! Beware of the yeast of the Pharisees and the yeast of Herod."

[16]His followers discussed the meaning of this, saying, "He said this because we have no bread."

[17]Knowing what they were talking about, Jesus asked them, "Why are you talking about not having bread? Do you still not see or understand? Are your minds closed? [18]You have eyes, but you don't really see. You have ears, but you don't really listen. Remember when [19]I divided five loaves of bread for the five thousand? How many baskets did you fill with leftover pieces of food?"

They answered, "Twelve."

[20]"And when I divided seven loaves of bread for the four thousand, how many baskets did you fill with leftover pieces of food?"

They answered, "Seven."

[21]Then Jesus said to them, "Don't you understand yet?"

JESUS HEALS A BLIND MAN

[22]Jesus and his followers came to Bethsaida. There some people brought a blind man to Jesus and begged him to touch the man. [23]So Jesus took the blind man's hand and led him out of the village. Then he spit on the man's eyes and put his hands on the man and asked, "Can you see now?"

[24]The man looked up and said, "Yes, I see people, but they look like trees walking around."

[25]Again Jesus put his hands on the man's eyes. Then the man opened his eyes wide and they were healed, and he was able to see everything clearly. [26]Jesus told him to go home, saying, "Don't go into the town."[n]

PETER SAYS JESUS IS THE CHRIST

[27]Jesus and his followers went to the towns around Caesarea Philippi. While they were traveling, Jesus asked them, "Who do people say I am?"

[28]They answered, "Some say you are John the Baptist. Others say you are Elijah,[n] and others say you are one of the prophets."

[29]Then Jesus asked, "But who do you say I am?"

Peter answered, "You are the Christ."

[30]Jesus warned his followers not to tell anyone who he was.

[31]Then Jesus began to teach them that the Son of Man must suffer many things and that he would be rejected by the Jewish elders, the leading priests, and the teachers of the law. He told them that the Son of Man must be killed and

---

 8:26 town Some Greek copies continue, "Don't even go and tell anyone in the town." **8:28 Elijah** A man who spoke for God and who lived hundreds of years before Christ. See 1 Kings 17.

CONNECTED

DISCONNECTING FROM A "SEXY" WORLD:

YOU CAN DO IT

We live in a time when it seems that everything is "sexed up." Movies, television programs, commercials, music lyrics, and videos— sex is everywhere you look and much of what you hear. Having sexual messages all around us makes us more vulnerable and, at the same time, numbs us to their impact. You can't get away from it. So, you are going to have to decide for yourself how you will live your life in this sexed-up world.

Jesus knows that those who have accepted him still remain in the world, so he prayed for those who "are still in the world" that his Father would "keep them safe" (John 17:11). He doesn't ask the Father to take his people out of the world, but asks that they be empowered to live their lives for him. Jesus wants you to be a demonstration of his power in you.

God didn't call Christians to disengage from the realities of the world. Instead, he calls Christians to live their lives for him in the nitty-gritty of a sometimes dark, dirty, and sexed-up world. He has not called you to be isolated; he has called you to be insulated. He desires to give you the power of his Spirit to live a holy and pure life—even in a world that *is* sexed-up. You cannot do this by yourself. There is too much pressure on you. You live in a world that is against you. But the good news is that God never intended for you to handle sexual temptation alone. He offers you his *own power* to resist all types of temptation and to live a life that pleases him.

Temptation is not a sin. You know that because Jesus Christ himself was tempted. The Bible says he was tempted just the way you are (Hebrews 4:15). Jesus was a man in the flesh, which means that he knows what it is like to be tempted. He can relate to what you go through when you struggle with sexual temptation.

then rise from the dead after three days. [32]Jesus told them plainly what would happen. Then Peter took Jesus aside and began to tell him not to talk like that. [33]But Jesus turned and looked at his followers. Then he told Peter not to talk that way. He said, "Go away from me, Satan!" You don't care about the things of God, but only about things people think are important."

[34]Then Jesus called the crowd to him, along with his followers. He said, "If people want to follow me, they must give up the things they want. They must be willing even to give up their lives to follow me. [35]Those who want to save their lives will give up true life. But those who give up their lives for me and for the Good News will have true life. [36]It is worthless to have the whole world if they lose their souls. [37]They could never pay enough to buy back their souls. [38]The people who live now are living in a sinful and evil time. If people are ashamed of me and my teaching, the Son of Man will be ashamed of them when he comes with his Father's glory and with the holy angels."

9 Then Jesus said to the people, "I tell you the truth, some people standing here will see the kingdom of God come with power before they die."

JESUS TALKS WITH MOSES AND ELIJAH

[2]Six days later, Jesus took Peter, James, and John up on a high mountain by themselves. While they watched, Jesus' appearance was changed. [3]His clothes became shining white, whiter than any person could make them. [4]Then Elijah and Moses[n] appeared to them, talking with Jesus.

[5]Peter said to Jesus, "Teacher, it is good that we are here. Let us make three tents—one for you, one for Moses, and one for Elijah." [6]Peter did not know what to say, because he and the others were so frightened.

 8:33 Satan Name for the devil meaning "the enemy." Jesus means that Peter was talking like Satan. **9:4 Elijah and Moses** Two of the most important Jewish leaders in the past. God had given Moses the Law, and Elijah was an important prophet.

OVERCOMING

▶ WORRYING

Many things in life don't go the way we would like. But worrying won't fix anything. Not only does it not help, but it will tie you up emotionally and hurt your relationship with God. When we worry about things, it's as if we are telling God that we are taking control of the situation and that we don't need him or trust him.

In Matthew 6:34 we read, "So don't worry about tomorrow, because tomorrow will have its own worries. Each day has enough trouble of its own." God knows what all our tomorrows hold, even though we cannot foresee the next minute. If we look to God, he will guide us and provide just what we need at just the right time. Doesn't it make sense to trust the One who knows the beginning from the end? He knows what's going on in your life and how to bring you through. Trust will cancel out worry. You can trust God. He's got your back!

⁷Then a cloud came and covered them, and a voice came from the cloud, saying, "This is my Son, whom I love. Listen to him!"

⁸Suddenly Peter, James, and John looked around, but they saw only Jesus there alone with them.

⁹As they were coming down the mountain, Jesus commanded them not to tell anyone about what they had seen until the Son of Man had risen from the dead.

¹⁰So the followers obeyed Jesus, but they discussed what he meant about rising from the dead.

¹¹Then they asked Jesus, "Why do the teachers of the law say that Elijah must come first?"

¹²Jesus answered, "They are right to say that Elijah must come first and make everything the way it should be. But why does the Scripture say that the Son of Man will suffer much and that people will treat him as if he were nothing? ¹³I tell you that Elijah has already come. And people did to him whatever they wanted to do, just as the Scriptures said it would happen."

JESUS HEALS A SICK BOY

¹⁴When Jesus, Peter, James, and John came back to the other followers, they saw a great crowd around them and the teachers of the law arguing with them. ¹⁵But as soon as the crowd saw Jesus, the people were surprised and ran to welcome him.

¹⁶Jesus asked, "What are you arguing about?"

¹⁷A man answered, "Teacher, I brought my son to you. He has an evil spirit in him that stops him from talking. ¹⁸When the spirit attacks him, it throws him on the ground. Then my son foams at the mouth, grinds his teeth, and becomes very stiff. I asked your followers to force the evil spirit out, but they couldn't."

¹⁹Jesus answered, "You people have no faith. How long must I stay with you? How long must I put up with you? Bring the boy to me."

²⁰So the followers brought him to Jesus. As soon as the evil spirit saw Jesus, it made the boy lose control of himself, and he fell down and rolled on the ground, foaming at the mouth.

²¹Jesus asked the boy's father, "How long has this been happening?"

The father answered, "Since he was very young. ²²The spirit often throws him into a fire or into water to kill him. If you can do anything for him, please have pity on us and help us."

²³Jesus said to the father, "You said, 'If you can!' All things are possible for the one who believes."

²⁴Immediately the father cried out, "I do believe! Help me to believe more!"

²⁵When Jesus saw that a crowd was quickly gathering, he ordered the evil spirit, saying, "You spirit that makes people unable to hear or speak, I command you to come out of this boy and never enter him again!"

²⁶The evil spirit screamed and caused the boy to fall on the ground again. Then the spirit came out. The boy looked as if he were dead, and many people said, "He is dead!" ²⁷But Jesus took hold of the boy's hand and helped him to stand up.

²⁸When Jesus went into the house, his followers began asking him privately, "Why couldn't we force that evil spirit out?"

²⁹Jesus answered, "That kind of spirit can only be forced out by prayer."[n]

JESUS TALKS ABOUT HIS DEATH

³⁰Then Jesus and his followers left that place and went through Galilee. He didn't want anyone to know where he was, ³¹because he was teaching his followers. He said to them, "The Son of Man will be handed over to people, and

---

 9:29 prayer Some Greek copies continue, "and fasting."

they will kill him. After three days, he will rise from the dead." ³²But the followers did not understand what Jesus meant, and they were afraid to ask him.

WHO IS THE GREATEST?

³³Jesus and his followers went to Capernaum. When they went into a house there, he asked them, "What were you arguing about on the road?" ³⁴But the followers did not answer, because their argument on the road was about which one of them was the greatest.

³⁵Jesus sat down and called the twelve apostles to him. He said, "Whoever wants to be the most important must be last of all and servant of all."

³⁶Then Jesus took a small child and had him stand among them. Taking the child in his arms, he said, ³⁷"Whoever accepts a child like this in my name accepts me. And whoever accepts me accepts the One who sent me."

ANYONE NOT AGAINST US IS FOR US

³⁸Then John said, "Teacher, we saw someone using your name to force demons out of a person. We told him to stop, because he does not belong to our group."

³⁹But Jesus said, "Don't stop him, because anyone who uses my name to do powerful things will not easily say evil things about me. ⁴⁰Whoever is not against us is with us. ⁴¹I tell you the truth, whoever gives you a drink of water because you belong to the Christ will truly get his reward.

⁴²"If one of these little children believes in me, and someone causes that child to sin, it would be better for that person to have a large stone tied around his neck and be drowned in the sea. ⁴³If your hand causes you to sin, cut it off. It is better for you to lose part of your body and live forever than to have two hands and go to hell, where the fire never goes out. [⁴⁴In hell the worm does not die; the fire is never put out.]ⁿ ⁴⁵If your foot causes you to sin, cut it off. It is better for you to lose part of your

body and to live forever than to have two feet and be thrown into hell. [⁴⁶In hell the worm does not die; the fire is never put out.]ⁿ ⁴⁷If your eye causes you to sin, take it out. It is better for you to enter the kingdom of God with only one eye than to have two eyes and be thrown into hell. ⁴⁸In hell the worm does not die; the fire is never put out. ⁴⁹Every person will be salted with fire.

⁵⁰"Salt is good, but if the salt loses its salty taste, you cannot make it salty again. So, be full of salt, and have peace with each other."

JESUS TEACHES ABOUT DIVORCE

10 Then Jesus left that place and went into the area of Judea and across the Jordan River. Again, crowds came to him, and he taught them as he usually did.

²Some Pharisees came to Jesus and tried to trick him. They asked, "Is it right for a man to divorce his wife?"

³Jesus answered, "What did Moses command you to do?"

⁴They said, "Moses allowed a man to write out divorce papers and send her away."ⁿ

⁵Jesus said, "Moses wrote that command for you because you were stubborn. ⁶But when God made the world, ʰe made them male and female.ⁿ ⁷So a man will leave his father and mother and be united with his wife,ⁿ ⁸and the two will become one body.ⁿ So there are not two, but one. ⁹God has joined the two together, so no one should separate them."

¹⁰Later, in the house, his followers asked Jesus again about the question of divorce. ¹¹He answered, "Anyone who divorces his wife and marries another woman is guilty of adultery against her. ¹²And the woman who divorces her husband and marries another man is also guilty of adultery."

JESUS ACCEPTS CHILDREN

¹³Some people brought their little children to Jesus so he could touch them, but his followers told them to stop. ¹⁴When Jesus saw this, he was upset and said to them, "Let the little children come to me. Don't stop them, because the kingdom of God belongs to people who are like these children. ¹⁵I tell you the truth, you must accept the kingdom of God as if you were a little child, or you will never enter it." ¹⁶Then Jesus took the children in his arms, put his hands on them, and blessed them.

A RICH YOUNG MAN'S QUESTION

¹⁷As Jesus started to leave, a man ran to him and fell on his knees before Jesus.

PEEP THIS:

Seventy-seven percent of Blacks over the age of 25 have a high school diploma. Fifteen percent have at least a bachelor's degree.

The man asked, "Good teacher, what must I do to have life forever?"

¹⁸Jesus answered, "Why do you call me good? Only God is good. ¹⁹You know the commands: 'You must not murder anyone. You must not be guilty of adultery. You must not steal. You must not tell lies about your neighbor. You must not cheat. Honor your father and mother.' "ⁿ

²⁰The man said, "Teacher, I have obeyed all these things since I was a boy."

²¹Jesus, looking at the man, loved him and said, "There is one more thing you

GOD UNIT

GETTING OVER AN ABORTION

I had turned away from God and become very promiscuous. Now I needed an easy solution to a nuisance problem. Little thought was necessary; abortion was the answer.

Though the room was cold and sterile, my mind was at ease. They would just suck out the growing "problem" inside of me. I refused to think of it as a baby. To me, it wasn't anything but a big blob. But if I didn't do something, it would be a baby and there was no way I was ready to be somebody's mamma. There were just too many things I wanted to do with my life and having a child would interfere with all my plans.

After the procedure was done, I had a few cramps. I was definitely relieved, but I did feel a little empty. I knew, however, that I'd get over the pain much more quickly than I would have gotten over having a baby I didn't want.

Slowly, over the years, the emptiness I felt turned into deep regret. Many questions often haunted me. I asked myself, *what could my child have been? What if my mom had killed me before I was born? What if I'm never able to get pregnant again? Would the father have helped if I had told him? What will the child say to me when I get to heaven? How could he ever forgive me? How could God ever forgive me?* The questions stung my soul.

I knew the way I had been living was sinful. After the abortion, I wanted to return to God, but I felt I couldn't. I was haunted by the life I had taken. I began to see clearly that I had murdered my own child. I desperately wanted God back in my life, but I could not see how God could ever accept me again.

I started going to church again and joined a Bible study class. My pastor's wife mentored me, and I began having daily devotional times with God. Yet still I wondered how God could forgive me. Then I came across this Scripture, Psalm 25:17–18 which says, "My troubles have grown larger; free me from my problems. Look at my suffering and troubles, and take away all my sins." I realized that if God could forgive David, who was also an adulterer and a murderer, then he could forgive me. I discovered that any time I felt despair, I could ask God for help. God loved me in spite of myself. I may have given up on my child, but God didn't give up on me. I was and am forgiven. With him helping me live on, I'm able to forgive myself and find joy in life again. I am able to move into a future with God in it.

1 John 1:9 — But if we confess our sins, he will forgive our sins, because we can trust God to do what is right.

---

need to do. Go and sell everything you have, and give the money to the poor, and you will have treasure in heaven. Then come and follow me."

[22] He was very sad to hear Jesus say this, and he left sorrowfully, because he was rich.

[23] Then Jesus looked at his followers and said, "How hard it will be for the rich to enter the kingdom of God!"

[24] The followers were amazed at what Jesus said. But he said again, "My children, it is very hard[n] to enter the kingdom of God! [25] It is easier for a camel to go through the eye of a needle than for a rich person to enter the kingdom of God."

[26] The followers were even more surprised and said to each other, "Then who can be saved?"

[27] Jesus looked at them and said, "For people this is impossible, but for God all things are possible."

[28] Peter said to Jesus, "Look, we have left everything and followed you."

[29] Jesus said, "I tell you the truth, all those who have left houses, brothers, sisters, mother, father, children, or farms for me and for the Good News [30] will get more than they left. Here in this world

 10:24 hard Some Greek copies continue, "for those who trust in riches."

they will have a hundred times more homes, brothers, sisters, mothers, children, and fields. And with those things, they will also suffer for their belief. But in this age they will have life forever. [31]Many who are first now will be last in the future. And many who are last now will be first in the future."

JESUS TALKS ABOUT HIS DEATH

[32]As Jesus and the people with him were on the road to Jerusalem, he was leading the way. His followers were amazed, but others in the crowd who followed were afraid. Again Jesus took the twelve apostles aside and began to tell them what was about to happen in Jerusalem. [33]He said, "Look, we are going to Jerusalem. The Son of Man will be turned over to the leading priests and the teachers of the law. They will say that he must die, and they will turn him over to the non-Jewish people, [34]who will laugh at him and spit on him. They will beat him with whips and crucify him. But on the third day, he will rise to life again."

TWO FOLLOWERS ASK JESUS A FAVOR

[35]Then James and John, sons of Zebedee, came to Jesus and said, "Teacher, we want to ask you to do something for us."

[36]Jesus asked, "What do you want me to do for you?"

[37]They answered, "Let one of us sit at your right side and one of us sit at your left side in your glory in your kingdom."

[38]Jesus said, "You don't understand what you are asking. Can you drink the cup that I must drink? And can you be baptized with the same kind of baptism that I must go through?"[n]

[39]They answered, "Yes, we can."

Jesus said to them, "You will drink the same cup that I will drink, and you will be baptized with the same baptism that I must go through. [40]But I cannot choose who will sit at my right or my left; those places belong to those for whom they have been prepared."

[41]When the other ten followers heard this, they began to be angry with James and John.

[42]Jesus called them together and said, "The other nations have rulers. You know that those rulers love to show their power over the people, and their important leaders love to use all their authority. [43]But it should not be that way among you. Whoever wants to become great among you must serve the rest of you like a servant. [44]Whoever wants to become the first among you must serve all of you like a slave. [45]In the same way, the Son of Man did not come to be served. He came to serve others and to give his life as a ransom for many people."

GOD BLESS THE ONE WHO COMES IN THE NAME OF THE LORD!

JESUS HEALS A BLIND MAN

[46]Then they came to the town of Jericho. As Jesus was leaving there with his followers and a great many people, a blind beggar named Bartimaeus son of Timaeus was sitting by the road. [47]When he heard that Jesus from Nazareth was walking by, he began to shout, "Jesus, Son of David, have mercy on me!"

[48]Many people warned the blind man to be quiet, but he shouted even more, "Son of David, have mercy on me!"

[49]Jesus stopped and said, "Tell the man to come here."

So they called the blind man, saying, "Cheer up! Get to your feet. Jesus is calling you." [50]The blind man jumped up, left his coat there, and went to Jesus.

[51]Jesus asked him, "What do you want me to do for you?"

The blind man answered, "Teacher, I want to see."

[52]Jesus said, "Go, you are healed because you believed." At once the man could see, and he followed Jesus on the road.

JESUS ENTERS JERUSALEM AS A KING

11 As Jesus and his followers were coming closer to Jerusalem, they came to the towns of Bethphage and Bethany near the Mount of Olives. From there Jesus sent two of his followers [2]and said to them, "Go to the town you can see there. When you enter it, you will quickly find a colt tied, which no one has ever ridden. Untie it and bring it here to me. [3]If anyone asks you why you are doing this, tell him its Master needs the colt, and he will send it at once."

[4]The followers went into the town, found a colt tied in the street near the door of a house, and untied it. [5]Some people were standing there and asked, "What are you doing? Why are you untying that colt?" [6]The followers answered the way Jesus told them to answer, and the people let them take the colt.

[7]They brought the colt to Jesus and put their coats on it, and Jesus sat on it. [8]Many people spread their coats on the road. Others cut branches in the fields and spread them on the road. [9]The people were walking ahead of Jesus and behind him, shouting,

"Praise God!
God bless the One who comes in the
    name of the Lord! *Psalm 118:26*
[10]God bless the kingdom of our father
    David!
That kingdom is coming!
Praise[n] to God in heaven!"

[11]Jesus entered Jerusalem and went into the Temple. After he had looked at everything, since it was already late, he went out to Bethany with the twelve apostles.

[12]The next day as Jesus was leaving

10:38 Can you . . . through? Jesus was asking if they could suffer the same terrible things that would happen to him. **11:10 Praise** Literally, "Hosanna," a Hebrew word used at first in praying to God for help, but at this time it was probably a shout of joy used in praising God or his Messiah.

▶ 67

365

MARCH

1
2 On This Day In History 1867—Howard University was chartered.
3
4 Encourage a **friend** who needs you.
5
6 It's your birthday, Shaquille O'Neil!
7
8 On This Day In History 1948—Supreme Court rules that religious education in public schools is unconstitutional.
9 Happy Birthday Lil Bow Wow!
10
11 Determine to spend
12 one entire day
13 thinking only
14 positive thoughts.
15
16
17 HOLIDAY—St. Patrick's Day
18 It's your birthday, Queen Latifah!
19
20 Happy Birthday Spike Lee!
21
22 Make a clothing donation to your local homeless shelter.
23
24 Think outside
25 the box:
26 What difference does the truth of
27 Christ's birth, death, and resurrection
28 make in your life?
29
30 On This Day in History 1867—Augusta Institute, later Morehouse College, opens in Atlanta, Georgia.
31

"You've really got to start hitting the books because it's no joke out here."
-Spike Lee

ARTIST: URBAN D.   ALBUM: THE IMMIGRANT

The argument as to whether or not rap is a true art form is heightened once again through the twenty-one tracks of *The Immigrant*. Urban D. creatively informs his audience about very real issues through his rap talents, appropriately announcing "hip-hop fresh off the boat."

Urban D. raps about the state of our society in a way that makes the listener want to back up the track and listen to his true statements again. His lyrics talk about everything from getting to know Jesus, to how we protect the environment but pollute our bodies and minds with the ways of the world.

There is no better example of a true art form or artist than one who can shed light on real issues, place them over a tight beat, and have it all come together to sound as good as this CD. I would suggest that anyone who is ready to listen to something with some "real" substance should pick up this CD.

"ACCEPTED"

Bethany, he became hungry. [13]Seeing a fig tree in leaf from far away, he went to see if it had any figs on it. But he found no figs, only leaves, because it was not the right season for figs. [14]So Jesus said to the tree, "May no one ever eat fruit from you again." And Jesus' followers heard him say this.

JESUS GOES TO THE TEMPLE

[15]When Jesus returned to Jerusalem, he went into the Temple and began to throw out those who were buying and selling there. He turned over the tables of those who were exchanging different kinds of money, and he upset the benches of those who were selling doves. [16]Jesus refused to allow anyone to carry goods through the Temple courts. [17]Then he taught the people, saying, "It is written in the Scriptures, 'My Temple will be called a house for prayer for people from all nations.'[n] But you are changing God's house into a 'hideout for robbers.'"[n]

[18]The leading priests and the teachers of the law heard all this and began trying to find a way to kill Jesus. They were afraid of him, because all the people were amazed at his teaching. [19]That evening, Jesus and his followers[n] left the city.

THE POWER OF FAITH

[20]The next morning as Jesus was passing by with his followers, they saw the fig tree dry and dead, even to the roots. [21]Peter remembered the tree and said to Jesus, "Teacher, look! The fig tree you cursed is dry and dead!"

[22]Jesus answered, "Have faith in God. [23]I tell you the truth, you can say to this mountain, 'Go, fall into the sea.' And if you have no doubts in your mind and believe that what you say will happen, God will do it for you. [24]So I tell you to believe that you have received the things you ask for in prayer, and God will give them to you. [25]When you are praying, if you are angry with someone, forgive him so that your Father in heaven will also forgive your sins. [[26]But if you don't forgive other people, then your Father in heaven will not forgive your sins.]"[n]

LEADERS DOUBT JESUS' AUTHORITY

[27]Jesus and his followers went again to Jerusalem. As Jesus was walking in the Temple, the leading priests, the teachers of the law, and the elders came to him. [28]They said to him, "What authority do you have to do these things? Who gave you this authority?"

[29]Jesus answered, "I will ask you one question. If you answer me, I will tell you what authority I have to do these things. [30]Tell me: When John baptized people, was that authority from God or just from other people?"

[31]They argued about Jesus' question, saying, "If we answer, 'John's baptism was from God,' Jesus will say, 'Then why didn't you believe him?' [32]But if we say, 'It was from other people,' the crowd will be against us." (These leaders were afraid of the people, because all the people believed that John was a prophet.)

[33]So they answered Jesus, "We don't know."[n]

Jesus said to them, "Then I won't tell you what authority I have to do these things."

 11:17 'My Temple . . . nations.' Quotation from Isaiah 56:7.   **11:17 'hideout for robbers'** Quotation from Jeremiah 7:11.   **11:19 his followers** Some Greek copies mention only Jesus here.   **11:26 But . . . sins.** Some Greek copies do not contain the bracketed text.

A STORY ABOUT GOD'S SON

12 Jesus began to use stories to teach the people. He said, "A man planted a vineyard. He put a wall around it and dug a hole for a winepress and built a tower. Then he leased the land to some farmers and left for a trip. [2]When it was time for the grapes to be picked, he sent a servant to the farmers to get his share of the grapes. [3]But the farmers grabbed the servant and beat him and sent him away empty-handed. [4]Then the man sent another servant. They hit him on the head and showed no respect for him. [5]So the man sent another servant, whom they killed. The man sent many other servants; the farmers beat some of them and killed others.

[6]"The man had one person left to send, his son whom he loved. He sent him last of all, saying, 'They will respect my son.'

[7]"But the farmers said to each other, 'This son will inherit the vineyard. If we kill him, it will be ours.' [8]So they took the son, killed him, and threw him out of the vineyard.

[9]"So what will the owner of the vineyard do? He will come and kill those farmers and will give the vineyard to other farmers. [10]Surely you have read this Scripture:

'The stone that the builders rejected
  became the cornerstone.
[11]The Lord did this,
  and it is wonderful to us.'"
Psalm 118:22-23

[12]The Jewish leaders knew that the story was about them. So they wanted to find a way to arrest Jesus, but they were afraid of the people. So the leaders left him and went away.

IS IT RIGHT TO PAY TAXES OR NOT?

[13]Later, the Jewish leaders sent some Pharisees and Herodians[n] to Jesus to trap him in saying something wrong.

[14]They came to him and said, "Teacher, we know that you are an honest man. You are not afraid of what other people think about you, because you pay no attention to who they are. And you teach the truth about God's way. Tell us: Is it right to pay taxes to Caesar or not? [15]Should we pay them, or not?"

But knowing what these men were really trying to do, Jesus said to them, "Why are you trying to trap me? Bring me a coin to look at." [16]They gave Jesus a coin, and he asked, "Whose image and name are on the coin?"

They answered, "Caesar's."

[17]Then Jesus said to them, "Give to Caesar the things that are Caesar's, and give to God the things that are God's." The men were amazed at what Jesus said.

SOME SADDUCEES TRY TO TRICK JESUS

[18]Then some Sadducees came to Jesus and asked him a question. (Sadducees believed that people would not rise from the dead.) [19]They said, "Teacher, Moses wrote that if a man's brother dies, leaving a wife but no children, then that man must marry the widow and have children for his brother. [20]Once there were seven brothers. The first brother married and died, leaving no children. [21]So the second brother married the widow, but he also died and had no children. The same thing happened with the third brother. [22]All seven brothers married her and died, and none of the brothers had any children. Finally the woman died too. [23]Since all seven brothers had married her, when people rise from the dead, whose wife will she be?"

[24]Jesus answered, "Why don't you understand? Don't you know what the Scriptures say, and don't you know about the power of God? [25]When people rise from the dead, they will not marry, nor will they be given to someone to marry. They will be like the angels in heaven. [26]Surely you have read what God said about people rising from the dead. In the book in which Moses wrote about the burning bush,[n] it says that God told Moses, 'I am the God of Abraham, the God of Isaac, and the God of Jacob.'[n] [27]God is the God of the living, not the dead. You Sadducees are wrong!"

THE MOST IMPORTANT COMMAND

[28]One of the teachers of the law came and heard Jesus arguing with the Sadducees. Seeing that Jesus gave good answers to their questions, he asked Jesus, "Which of the commands is most important?"

[29]Jesus answered, "The most important command is this: 'Listen, people of Israel! The Lord our God is the only Lord. [30]Love the Lord your God with all your heart, all your soul, all your mind, and all your strength.'[n] [31]The second command is this: 'Love your neighbor as you love yourself.'[n] There are no commands more important than these."

[32]The man answered, "That was a good answer, Teacher. You were right when you said God is the only Lord and there is no other God besides him. [33]One must love God with all his heart, all his mind, and all his strength. And one must love his neighbor as he loves himself. These commands are more important than all the animals and sacrifices we offer to God."

[34]When Jesus saw that the man answered him wisely, Jesus said to him, "You are close to the kingdom of God." And after that, no one was brave enough to ask Jesus any more questions.

[35]As Jesus was teaching in the Temple, he asked, "Why do the teachers of the law say that the Christ is the son of David? [36]David himself, speaking by the Holy Spirit, said:

'The Lord said to my Lord,
"Sit by me at my right side,
  until I put your enemies under
    your control."'   *Psalm 110:1*

[37]David himself calls the Christ 'Lord,' so how can the Christ be his son?" The large crowd listened to Jesus with pleasure.

[38]Jesus continued teaching and said, "Beware of the teachers of the

 12:13 Herodians A political group that followed Herod and his family.   **12:26 burning bush** Read Exodus 3:1-12 in the Old Testament.   **12:26 'I am . . . Jacob.'** Quotation from Exodus 3:6.   **12:30 'Listen . . . strength.'** Quotation from Deuteronomy 6:4-5.   **12:31 'Love . . . yourself.'** Quotation from Leviticus 19:18.

JAIL'S NO JOKE

Jail Makes You Crazy

Being on the inside sent me straight over the edge. I was certifiably crazy. I felt like a slave. Now believe me when I say that I am not condoning my ill behavior. I deserved everything I got after I robbed two convenience stores with my homeboy. We got away with the first one, so of course I was down when he came to me with a plan to get some loot from another one. But the second score wasn't an in and out job. There were some deep complications. The clerk pulled a gun out on us, so my buddy shot him dead. I was convicted and sent to prison. Don't believe it if anybody tells you that prison rehabilitates you. How could anybody be rehabilitated when they live like caged animals with about a hundred other angry men? I couldn't handle it. All the outward hostility finally sent me over the edge.

Picture long secured hallways with about 5-6 dormitories. Each dorm held enough beds for 24 inmates, but about 40 were crowded up in there. The overflow had to sleep on the floor in beds called "boats." I was on the floor when I first got to there, so sleep was out of the question. I only got to go outside for an hour each day, so I couldn't see whether it was night or day. I was told when to get up, when to go to sleep, and when to eat. My cell had a bathroom with no door, so I had to hope my celly (cellmate) understood when I really had to go. It was similar to a zoo. I could see out of the dormitory, but I could not leave. There was only this small area to sit, or maybe watch TV, I was constantly on guard, hoping nothing would go down that would force me to defend myself. C.O.'s (correctional officers) would constantly walk by and look at me like I was on display. Having no privacy was really hard to take. The inmates screaming, the foul odors, the stealing, the beat downs, the lack of fresh air and sunshine, the inmates constant clamoring on the bars, and no emotional or physical outlets definitely took its toll on me. But when I got thrown into solitary confinement for seven days I came out severely screwed up.

Now I admit there were times I felt I deserved to be treated like an animal because of what I did. But when I thought about it, (and I had plenty of time to think while doing time for three years) I was still God's creation. Though I made a bad choice, I didn't deserve cruelty. I had failed badly and needed a second chance, a fresh start. It was the prison chaplain who told me how to receive one. He didn't force religion on me, but he took time to listen. Then he told me he knew the one who could give me a fresh start and a chance to live a new life. He told me about Jesus Christ. Through many counseling sessions, I came to understand God's plan and, finally, I received God's Son into my heart. Now, I'm renewed. I know I am made in His image. I'm no longer crazy. Since I've met Jesus, I'm whole.

law. They like to walk around wearing fancy clothes, and they love for people to greet them with respect in the marketplaces. [39]They love to have the most important seats in the synagogues and at feasts. [40]But they cheat widows and steal their houses and then try to make themselves look good by saying long prayers. They will receive a greater punishment."

TRUE GIVING

[41]Jesus sat near the Temple money box and watched the people put in their money. Many rich people gave large sums of money. [42]Then a poor widow came and put in two small copper coins, which were only worth a few cents. [43]Calling his followers to him, Jesus said, "I tell you the truth, this poor widow gave more than all those rich people. [44]They gave only what they did not need. This woman is very poor, but she gave all she had; she gave all she had to live on."

THE TEMPLE WILL BE DESTROYED

13 As Jesus was leaving the Temple, one of his followers said to him, "Look, Teacher! How beautiful the buildings are! How big the stones are!"

[2]Jesus said, "Do you see all these great buildings? Not one stone will be left on another. Every stone will be thrown down to the ground."

[3]Later, as Jesus was sitting on the Mount of Olives, opposite the Temple, he was alone with Peter, James, John, and Andrew. They asked Jesus, [4]"Tell us, when will these things happen? And what will be the sign that they are going to happen?"

[5]Jesus began to answer them, "Be careful that no one fools you. [6]Many people will come in my name, saying, 'I am the One,' and they will fool many people. [7]When you hear about wars and stories of wars that are coming, don't be afraid. These things must happen before the end comes. [8]Nations will fight against other nations, and kingdoms against other kingdoms. There will be earthquakes in different places, and there will be times when there is no food for people to eat. These things are like

DEEP ISSUES

Parents

Sometimes our parents or our guardians are hard to get along with, even as adults. Many times we might feel they are out of touch or they just don't understand what we are going through. Believe it or not, our parents or guardians do have a lot of wisdom to share with us.

Things might have been different back in their day, but they faced a lot of the same decisions and temptations that we face. We need to learn to listen more to their advice and even learn from their mistakes. Every generation struggles with different issues in their relationships with their family. No relationship will be perfect because there are people involved, and people aren't perfect. Even parents can make mistakes, but God has put them in our lives to lead us and guide us. The Bible has several verses that tell us to honor and obey our father and mother. It even promises us that if we do this we will have a longer life.

Most people focus on the negative things about others. Sometimes we even do this with our parents or guardians. But we should take a minute and think about all the time, energy, effort, and money they've put into raising us. It's not easy raising kids in today's culture. Let's focus on ways we can be a blessing and an encouragement to our parents.

the first pains when something new is about to be born.

9"You must be careful. People will arrest you and take you to court and beat you in their synagogues. You will be forced to stand before kings and governors, to tell them about me. This will happen to you because you follow me. 10But before these things happen, the Good News must be told to all people. 11When you are arrested and judged, don't worry ahead of time about what you should say. Say whatever is given you to say at that time, because it will not really be you speaking; it will be the Holy Spirit.

> BE CAREFUL THAT NO ONE FOOLS YOU. MANY PEOPLE WILL COME IN MY NAME...

12"Brothers will give their own brothers to be killed, and fathers will give their own children to be killed. Children will fight against their own parents and cause them to be put to death. 13All people will hate you because you follow me, but those people who keep their faith until the end will be saved.

14"You will see 'a blasphemous object that brings destruction'[n] standing where it should not be." (You who read this should understand what it means.) "At that time, the people in Judea should run away to the mountains. 15If people are on the roofs[n] of their houses, they must not go down or go inside to get anything out of their houses. 16If people are in the fields, they must not go back to get their coats. 17At that time, how terrible it will be for women who are pregnant or have nursing babies! 18Pray that these things will not happen in winter, 19because those days will be full of trouble. There will be more trouble than there has ever been since the beginning, when God made the world, until now, and nothing as bad will

ever happen again. 20God has decided to make that terrible time short. Otherwise, no one would go on living. But God will make that time short to help the people he has chosen. 21At that time, someone might say to you, 'Look, there is the Christ!' Or another person might say, 'There he is!' But don't believe them. 22False Christs and false prophets will come and perform great wonders and miracles. They will try to fool even the people God has chosen, if that is possible. 23So be careful. I have warned you about all this before it happens.

24"During the days after this trouble comes,

'the sun will grow dark,
and the moon will not give its
light.
25The stars will fall from the sky.
And the powers of the heavens
will be shaken.' *Isaiah 13:10; 34:4*

26"Then people will see the Son of Man coming in clouds with great power and glory. 27Then he will send his angels all around the earth to gather his chosen people from every part of the earth and from every part of heaven.

28"Learn a lesson from the fig tree: When its branches become green and soft and new leaves appear, you know summer is near. 29In the same way, when you see these things happening, you will know that the time is near, ready to come. 30I tell you the truth, all these things will happen while the people of this time are still living. 31Earth and sky will be destroyed, but the words I have said will never be destroyed.

32"No one knows when that day or time will be, not the angels in heaven, not even the Son. Only the Father knows. 33Be careful! Always be ready,[n] because you don't know when that time will be. 34It is like a man who goes on a trip. He leaves his house and lets his servants take care of it, giving each one a special job to do. The man tells the servant guarding the door always to be watchful. 35So always be ready, because you don't know when the owner of the house will come back. It might be in the evening, or

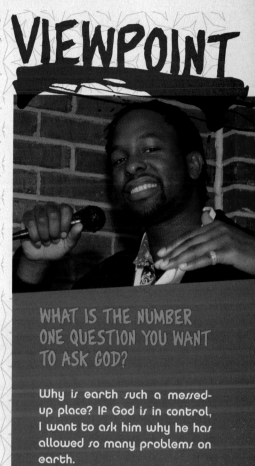

VIEWPOINT

WHAT IS THE NUMBER ONE QUESTION YOU WANT TO ASK GOD?

Why is earth such a messed-up place? If God is in control, I want to ask him why he has allowed so many problems on earth.

at midnight, or in the morning while it is still dark, or when the sun rises. 36Always be ready. Otherwise he might come back suddenly and find you sleeping. 37I tell you this, and I say this to everyone: 'Be ready!'"

THE PLAN TO KILL JESUS

14 It was now only two days before the Passover and the Feast of Unleavened Bread. The leading priests and teachers of the law were trying to find a trick to arrest Jesus and kill him. 2But they said, "We

---

13:14 'a blasphemous object that brings destruction' Mentioned in Daniel 9:27; 12:11 (cf. Daniel 11:31). **13:15 roofs** In Bible times houses were built with flat roofs. The roof was used for drying things such as flax and fruit. And it was used as an extra room, as a place for worship, and as a cool place to sleep in the summer. **13:33 ready** Some Greek copies continue, "and pray."

must not do it during the feast, because the people might cause a riot."

A WOMAN WITH PERFUME FOR JESUS

[3]Jesus was in Bethany at the house of Simon, who had a skin disease. While Jesus was eating there, a woman approached him with an alabaster jar filled with very expensive perfume, made of pure nard. She opened the jar and poured the perfume on Jesus' head.

[4]Some who were there became upset and said to each other, "Why waste that perfume? [5]It was worth a full year's work. It could have been sold and the money given to the poor." And they got very angry with the woman.

[6]Jesus said, "Leave her alone. Why are you troubling her? She did an excellent thing for me. [7]You will always have the poor with you, and you can help them anytime you want. But you will not always have me. [8]This woman did the only thing she could do for me; she poured perfume on my body to prepare me for burial. [9]I tell you the truth, wherever the Good News is preached in all the world, what this woman has done will be told, and people will remember her."

JUDAS BECOMES AN ENEMY OF JESUS

[10]One of the twelve apostles, Judas Iscariot, went to talk to the leading priests to offer to hand Jesus over to them. [11]These priests were pleased about this and promised to pay Judas money. So he watched for the best time to turn Jesus in.

JESUS EATS THE PASSOVER MEAL

[12]It was now the first day of the Feast of Unleavened Bread when the Passover lamb was sacrificed. Jesus' followers said to him, "Where do you want us to

THE SCRIPT

Touching the Hem of His Garment
Mark 5:21-42

And when they reached the ground on the other side of the shore,
Crowds came out the woodwork to the lake fendin' for more.
They wanted to hear and see him. One of the synagogue leaders named Jairus came to Jesus.
Soon as he seen him he dropped to his knees and pleaded out loud nearly screamin',
"My daughter's dying, right before my eyes her life is leavin'
So I'm beseechin', please come and lay your hands on her for healing."
Jesus conceded and followed Jairus who was leading Jesus to her house.
But they couldn't shake the crowd, the people were too rowdy, too loud.
In the midst of the pandemonium there was a certain woman
Who had suffered twelve years of hemorrhaging—
Abused by the highest M.D.'s and hustled out of her life savings battling her disease.
Instead of getting better, her health decreased by major degrees.
But she heard about this Jesus, so she saw a moment and seized it,
Came up from behind him, touched his robe, quietly sneaking, 'cause she was thinking,
"If I just touch the bottom of his robe with my finger,
I'd be healed of this disease and be at ease from this pain that lingers!"
So, taking a chance, she just reached out to touch Jesus.
The instant she did, her bleeding quit and remitted and she knew that she was whole.

That's when Jesus froze 'cause when she touched him felt energy flow . . .
He turned to the crowd asking his disciples, "Who touched my clothes?"
His disciples thought he was joking, so they mockingly prosed,
"Now who do you suppose?
With all these folks packed in like cattle and throwin' bows, who knows!"
But Jesus wasn't feeling all of their rigmarole.
He started scoping the souls to see who caused the virtue to go.
Timid and exposed, the woman knew that she was the reason that Jesus stopped his stroll
'Cause she had ceased from bleeding. So she came and bowed low
And told the full story from the opening to close.
Jesus told her, "Baby girl, your faith made you complete!
You're healed of that disease. Go on and live in peace!"
And Jesus still went on to check on Jairus' daughter, even though she was now dead.
He went into the house and told her to get up and she did just what Jesus said.

Take this with you: Our faith moves us. Faith allows us to move out of the prison of our present circumstance and into the land of God's infinite possibilities.

go and prepare for you to eat the Passover meal?"

[13]Jesus sent two of his followers and said to them, "Go into the city and a man carrying a jar of water will meet you. Follow him. [14]When he goes into a house, tell the owner of the house, 'The Teacher says: "Where is my guest room in which I can eat the Passover meal with my followers?" ' [15]The owner will show you a large room upstairs that is furnished and ready. Prepare the food for us there."

[16]So the followers left and went into the city. Everything happened as Jesus had said, so they prepared the Passover meal.

[17]In the evening, Jesus went to that house with the twelve. [18]While they were all eating, Jesus said, "I tell you the truth, one of you will turn against me—one of you eating with me now."

[19]The followers were very sad to hear this. Each one began to say to Jesus, "I am not the one, am I?"

[20]Jesus answered, "It is one of the twelve—the one who dips his bread into the bowl with me. [21]The Son of Man will die, just as the Scriptures say. But how terrible it will be for the person who hands the Son of Man over to be killed. It would be better for him if he had never been born."

THE LORD'S SUPPER

[22]While they were eating, Jesus took some bread and thanked God for it and broke it. Then he gave it to his followers and said, "Take it; this is my body."

[23]Then Jesus took a cup and thanked God for it and gave it to the followers, and they all drank from the cup.

[24]Then Jesus said, "This is my blood which is the new[n] agreement that God makes with his people. This blood is poured out for many. [25]I tell you the truth, I will not drink of this fruit of the vine[n] again until that day when I drink it new in the kingdom of God."

[26]After singing a hymn, they went out to the Mount of Olives.

JESUS' FOLLOWERS WILL LEAVE HIM

[27]Then Jesus told the followers, "You will all stumble in your faith, because it is written in the Scriptures:

'I will kill the shepherd,
    and the sheep will scatter.'
                          Zechariah 13:7

[28]But after I rise from the dead, I will go ahead of you into Galilee."

[29]Peter said, "Everyone else may stumble in their faith, but I will not."

[30]Jesus answered, "I tell you the truth, tonight before the rooster crows twice you will say three times you don't know me."

[31]But Peter insisted, "I will never say that I don't know you! I will even die with you!" And all the other followers said the same thing.

JESUS PRAYS ALONE

[32]Jesus and his followers went to a place called Gethsemane. He said to them, "Sit here while I pray." [33]Jesus took Peter, James, and John with him, and he began to be very sad and troubled. [34]He said to them, "My heart is full of sorrow, to the point of death. Stay here and watch."

[35]After walking a little farther away from them, Jesus fell to the ground and prayed that, if possible, he would not have this time of suffering. [36]He prayed, "Abba,[n] Father! You can do all things. Take away this cup[n] of suffering. But do what you want, not what I want."

[37]Then Jesus went back to his followers and found them asleep. He said to Peter, "Simon, are you sleeping? Couldn't you stay awake with me for one hour? [38]Stay awake and pray for strength against temptation. The spirit wants to do what is right, but the body is weak."

[39]Again Jesus went away and prayed the same thing. [40]Then he went back to his followers, and again he found them asleep, because their eyes were very heavy. And they did not know what to say to him.

[41]After Jesus prayed a third time, he went back to his followers and said to them, "Are you still sleeping and resting? That's enough. The time has come for the Son of Man to be handed over to sinful people. [42]Get up, we must go. Look, here comes the man who has turned against me."

JESUS IS ARRESTED

[43]At once, while Jesus was still speaking, Judas, one of the twelve apostles, came up. With him were many people carrying swords and clubs who had been sent from the leading priests, the teachers of the law, and the Jewish elders.

[44]Judas had planned a signal for them, saying, "The man I kiss is Jesus. Arrest him and guard him while you lead him away." [45]So Judas went straight to Jesus and said, "Teacher!" and kissed him. [46]Then the people grabbed Jesus and arrested him. [47]One of his followers standing nearby pulled out his sword and struck the servant of the high priest and cut off his ear.

[48]Then Jesus said, "You came to get me with swords and clubs as if I were a criminal. [49]Every day I was with you teaching in the Temple, and you did not arrest me there. But all these things have happened to make the Scriptures come true." [50]Then all of Jesus' followers left him and ran away.

[51]A young man, wearing only a linen cloth, was following Jesus, and the people also grabbed him. [52]But the cloth he was wearing came off, and he ran away naked.

JESUS BEFORE THE LEADERS

[53]The people who arrested Jesus led him to the house of the high priest, where all the leading priests, the elders, and the teachers of the law were gathered. [54]Peter followed far behind and entered the courtyard of the high priest's house. There he sat with the guards, warming himself by the fire.

[55]The leading priests and the whole Jewish council tried to find something that Jesus had done wrong so they could

---

14:24 new Some Greek copies do not have this word. Compare Luke 22:20.   **14:25 fruit of the vine** Product of the grapevine; this may also be translated "wine."   **14:36 Abba** Name that a Jewish child called his father.   **14:36 cup** Jesus is talking about the terrible things that will happen to him. Accepting these things will be very hard, like drinking a cup of something bitter.

kill him. But the council could find no proof of anything. ⁵⁶Many people came and told false things about him, but all said different things—none of them agreed.

⁵⁷Then some people stood up and lied about Jesus, saying, ⁵⁸"We heard this man say, 'I will destroy this Temple that people made. And three days later, I will build another Temple not made by people.' " ⁵⁹But even the things these people said did not agree.

⁶⁰Then the high priest stood before them and asked Jesus, "Aren't you going to answer? Don't you have something to say about their charges against you?" ⁶¹But Jesus said nothing; he did not answer.

The high priest asked Jesus another question: "Are you the Christ, the Son of the blessed God?"

⁶²Jesus answered, "I am. And in the future you will see the Son of Man sitting at the right hand of God, the Powerful One, and coming on clouds in the sky."

⁶³When the high priest heard this, he tore his clothes and said, "We don't need any more witnesses! ⁶⁴You all heard him say these things against God. What do you think?"

He's got answers

I've done so much wrong in my life. Can God forgive me?

One of the coolest things about God is that he loves to forgive. Just look at all the great heroes of the Bible. What a bunch of screw-ups! King David—the "man after God's own heart"—was a murderer and adulterer. The Apostle Paul spent the first part of his life persecuting the church. Rahab, a direct ancestor of Jesus, was a prostitute. God not only forgave their sins, but he changed their lives and gave them an incredible legacy.

God wants to forgive you too. All you have to do is admit that what you have been doing is wrong and trust God to help you do what is right. That is called repentance. And after he forgives your sins, God forgets them. The Bible says he throws them as far as the east is from the west.

But God doesn't stop there. He knows that unforgiveness is like shackles around your ankles; so while he forgives you, he also commands you to forgive those who have offended you. Jesus gave us the greatest example of this by asking God to forgive the people who put him to death. By forgiving others and receiving forgiveness from God, you can live a life of total freedom.

Read on: Matthew 6:12; Luke 17:4, 23:34; Acts 5:31; Ephesians 1:7; Hebrews 8:11-12; 1 John 1:9

PEEP THIS:

African-Americans total 35.1 million or 13 percent of the United States population. Most African-Americans live in the South (55 percent); 19 percent live in the Northeast; 18 percent live in the Midwest; 8 percent live in the West.

They all said that Jesus was guilty and should die. ⁶⁵Some of the people there began to spit at Jesus. They blindfolded him and beat him with their fists and said, "Prove you are a prophet!" Then the guards led Jesus away and beat him.

PETER SAYS HE DOESN'T KNOW JESUS

⁶⁶While Peter was in the courtyard, a servant girl of the high priest came there. ⁶⁷She saw Peter warming himself at the fire and looked closely at him.

Then she said, "You also were with Jesus, that man from Nazareth."

⁶⁸But Peter said that he was never with Jesus. He said, "I don't know or understand what you are talking about." Then Peter left and went toward the entrance of the courtyard. And the rooster crowed.ⁿ

⁶⁹The servant girl saw Peter there, and again she said to the people who were standing nearby, "This man is one of those who followed Jesus." ⁷⁰Again Peter said that it was not true.

A short time later, some people were standing near Peter saying, "Surely you are one of those who followed Jesus, because you are from Galilee, too."

⁷¹Then Peter began to place a curse on himself and swear, "I don't know this man you're talking about!"

⁷²At once, the rooster crowed the

 14:68 And the rooster crowed. Some Greek copies do not have this phrase.

second time. Then Peter remembered what Jesus had told him: "Before the rooster crows twice, you will say three times that you don't know me." Then Peter lost control of himself and began to cry.

PILATE QUESTIONS JESUS

15 Very early in the morning, the leading priests, the elders, the teachers of the law, and all the Jewish council decided what to do with Jesus. They tied him, led him away, and turned him over to Pilate, the governor.

[2]Pilate asked Jesus, "Are you the king of the Jews?"

Jesus answered, "Those are your words."

[3]The leading priests accused Jesus of many things. [4]So Pilate asked Jesus another question, "You can see that they are accusing you of many things. Aren't you going to answer?"

[5]But Jesus still said nothing, so Pilate was very surprised.

PILATE TRIES TO FREE JESUS

[6]Every year at the time of the Passover the governor would free one prisoner whom the people chose. [7]At that time, there was a man named Barabbas in prison who was a rebel and had committed murder during a riot. [8]The crowd came to Pilate and began to ask him to free a prisoner as he always did.

[9]So Pilate asked them, "Do you want me to free the king of the Jews?" [10]Pilate knew that the leading priests had turned Jesus in to him because they were jealous. [11]But the leading priests had persuaded the people to ask Pilate to free Barabbas, not Jesus.

[12]Then Pilate asked the crowd again, "So what should I do with this man you call the king of the Jews?"

[13]They shouted, "Crucify him!"

[14]Pilate asked, "Why? What wrong has he done?"

But they shouted even louder, "Crucify him!"

[15]Pilate wanted to please the crowd, so he freed Barabbas for them. After having Jesus beaten with whips, he handed Jesus over to the soldiers to be crucified.

[16]The soldiers took Jesus into the governor's palace (called the Praetorium) and called all the other soldiers together. [17]They put a purple robe on Jesus and used thorny branches to make a crown for his head. [18]They began to call out to him, "Hail, King of the Jews!" [19]The soldiers beat Jesus on the head many times with a stick. They spit on him and made fun of him by bowing on their knees and worshiping him. [20]After they finished, the soldiers took off the purple robe and put his own clothes on him again. Then they led him out of the palace to be crucified.

IN THE FUTURE YOU WILL SEE THE SON OF MAN SITTING AT THE RIGHT HAND OF GOD, THE POWERFUL ONE, AND COMING ON CLOUDS IN THE SKY.

JESUS IS CRUCIFIED

[21]A man named Simon from Cyrene, the father of Alexander and Rufus, was coming from the fields to the city. The soldiers forced Simon to carry the cross for Jesus. [22]They led Jesus to the place called Golgotha, which means the Place of the Skull. [23]The soldiers tried to give Jesus wine mixed with myrrh to drink, but he refused. [24]The soldiers crucified Jesus and divided his clothes among themselves, throwing lots to decide what each soldier would get.

[25]It was nine o'clock in the morning when they crucified Jesus. [26]There was a sign with this charge against Jesus written on it: THE KING OF THE JEWS. [27]They also put two robbers on crosses beside Jesus, one on the right, and the other on the left. [[28]And the Scripture came true that says, "They put him with criminals."] [29]People walked by and insulted Jesus and shook their heads, saying, "You said you could destroy the Temple and build it again in three days. [30]So save yourself! Come down from that cross!"

[31]The leading priests and the teachers of the law were also making fun of Jesus. They said to each other, "He saved other people, but he can't save himself. [32]If he is really the Christ, the king of Israel, let him come down now from the cross. When we see this, we will believe in him." The robbers who were being crucified beside Jesus also insulted him.

JESUS DIES

[33]At noon the whole country became dark, and the darkness lasted for three hours. [34]At three o'clock Jesus cried in a loud voice, "Eloi, Eloi, lama sabachthani." This means, "My God, my God, why have you abandoned me?"

[35]When some of the people standing there heard this, they said, "Listen! He is calling Elijah."

[36]Someone there ran and got a sponge, filled it with vinegar, tied it to a stick, and gave it to Jesus to drink. He said, "We want to see if Elijah will come to take him down from the cross."

[37]Then Jesus cried in a loud voice and died.

15:28 And . . . criminals." Some Greek copies do not contain the bracketed text, which quotes from Isaiah 53:12.

WORLD SAYS, WORD SAYS,

ABORTION

It's your body—do as you please. It's your choice. That thing inside of you is not a human being; it's just a fetus. Besides, you're not ready to have a baby or take care of one. You still have a life to live. And fellas, you're not ready to be fathers or pay anybody's child support. You're right in telling her not to have the baby. Go ahead, you're not hurting anybody.

"You must not murder anyone" (Exodus 20:13).

"Before I made you in your mother's womb, I chose you. Before you were born, I set you apart for a special work" (Jeremiah 1:5).

"Do not be fooled: You cannot cheat God. People harvest only what they plant" (Galatians 6:7).

"You should know that your body is a temple for the Holy Spirit who is in you. You have received the Holy Spirit from God. So you do not belong to yourselves, because you were bought by God for a price. So honor God with your bodies" (1 Corinthians 6:19-20).

---

[38]The curtain in the Temple[n] was torn into two pieces, from the top to the bottom. [39]When the army officer who was standing in front of the cross saw what happened when Jesus died,[n] he said, "This man really was the Son of God!"

[40]Some women were standing at a distance from the cross, watching; among them were Mary Magdalene, Salome, and Mary the mother of James and Joseph. (James was her youngest son.) [41]These women had followed Jesus in Galilee and helped him. Many other women were also there who had come with Jesus to Jerusalem.

JESUS IS BURIED

[42]This was Preparation Day. (That means the day before the Sabbath day.) That evening, [43]Joseph from Arimathea was brave enough to go to Pilate and ask for Jesus' body. Joseph, an important member of the Jewish council, was one of the people who was waiting for the kingdom of God to come. [44]Pilate was amazed that Jesus would have already died, so he called the army officer who had guarded Jesus and asked him if Jesus had already died. [45]The officer told Pilate that he was dead, so Pilate told Joseph he could have the body. [46]Jo-

seph bought some linen cloth, took the body down from the cross, and wrapped it in the linen. He put the body in a tomb that was cut out of a wall of rock. Then he rolled a very large stone to block the entrance of the tomb. [47]And Mary Magdalene and Mary the mother of Joseph saw the place where Jesus was laid.

JESUS RISES FROM THE DEAD

16 The day after the Sabbath day, Mary Magdalene, Mary the mother of James, and Salome bought some sweet-smelling spices to put on Jesus' body. [2]Very early on that day, the first day of the week, soon after sunrise, the women were on their way to the tomb. [3]They said to each other, "Who will roll away for us the stone that covers the entrance of the tomb?"

[4]Then the women looked and saw that the stone had already been rolled away, even though it was very large. [5]The women entered the tomb and saw a young man wearing a white robe and sitting on the right side, and they were afraid.

[6]But the man said, "Don't be afraid. You are looking for Jesus from Nazareth, who has been crucified. He has risen from the dead; he is not here. Look, here is the place they laid him. [7]Now go and tell his followers and Peter, 'Jesus is going into Galilee ahead of you, and you will see him there as he told you before.'"

[8]The women were confused and shaking with fear, so they left the tomb and ran away. They did not tell anyone about what happened, because they were afraid.

Verses 9-20 are not included in some of the earliest surviving Greek copies of Mark.

SOME FOLLOWERS SEE JESUS

[[9]After Jesus rose from the dead early on the first day of the week, he showed himself first to Mary Magdalene. One time in the past, he had forced seven demons out of her. [10]After Mary saw Jesus, she went and told his followers, who were very sad and were crying. [11]But Mary told them that Jesus was alive. She said that she had seen him, but the followers did not believe her.

[12]Later, Jesus showed himself to two of his followers while they were walking

---

 15:38 curtain in the Temple A curtain divided the Most Holy Place from the other part of the Temple. That was the special building in Jerusalem where God commanded the Jewish people to worship him.   **15:39 when Jesus died** Some Greek copies read "when Jesus cried out and died."

in the country, but he did not look the same as before. [13]These followers went back to the others and told them what had happened, but again, the followers did not believe them.

JESUS TALKS TO THE APOSTLES

[14]Later Jesus showed himself to the eleven apostles while they were eating, and he criticized them because they had no faith. They were stubborn and refused to believe those who had seen him after he had risen from the dead.

[15]Jesus said to his followers, "Go everywhere in the world, and tell the Good News to everyone. [16]Anyone who believes and is baptized will be saved, but anyone who does not believe will be punished. [17]And those who believe will be able to do these things as proof: They will use my name to force out demons. They will speak in new languages.[n] [18]They will pick up snakes and drink poison without being hurt. They will touch the sick, and the sick will be healed."

[19]After the Lord Jesus said these things to his followers, he was carried up into heaven, and he sat at the right side of God. [20]The followers went everywhere in the world and told the Good News to people, and the Lord helped them. The Lord proved that the Good News they told was true by giving them power to work miracles.]

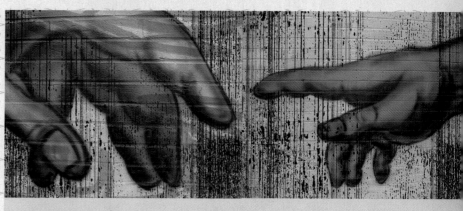

HeartCry

Regret Do you keep looking back at the past and wishing you had made different choices? Are there things you wish you could undo? Let your heart cry . . .

Lord, I need help with all this mess. There are so many things I would change if only I could. I don't like the way my life is turning out and I don't know how to change it. I've hurt my family and my friends and myself. I've just let everyone down. Please forgive me for all the wrong things I've done and help me make it right. Help me find a way to start over and make the right choices. I can't do this without you.

I forgive you, I love you and I will make all things new. I bring beautiful things out of burned out ashes and I will replace a broken spirit with a joyful heart. Isaiah 61:3; John 6:37; 2 Corinthians 5:17

16:17 languages This can also be translated "tongues."

LUKE

WHEN IT COMES TO JESUS, THERE ARE NO OUTSIDERS

We have all felt like outsiders before, at school, at work, in our neighborhoods, maybe even in our own home. Each one of us was made with a need to belong to something. Many people try to find this in sports teams, fraternities, community organizations, political groups, or even in street gangs. These groups can provide some form of belonging, but our Creator has something much more fulfilling for us. Unfortunately some of us have searched for God and even felt like outsiders at a local church. The atmosphere, the music, the dress code, or maybe even some of the members made us feel unwelcome. You may have wondered if you even fit in God's family. Luke has some dope news for all of us! When it comes to Jesus, there are no outsiders!

Luke can definitely relate to people who feel like outsiders. He was basically an outsider himself since he was the only Gentile in the whole crew of all Jewish New Testament writers. His angle on Jesus shows you a man who was quick to include people who were usually treated as outsiders: women, the poor and even racial minorities. Jesus showed these people love. Luke also did his homework on this piece! He didn't just rely on other writings or reports about Jesus. Luke did his own investigation and interviews. He was thorough! Many experts actually consider "Luke the outsider" to be one of the leading historical writers of his day.

LUKE WRITES ABOUT JESUS' LIFE

Many have tried to report on the things that happened among us. [2]They have written the same things that we learned from others—the people who saw those things from the beginning and served God by telling people his message. [3]Since I myself have studied everything carefully from the beginning, most excellent[n] Theophilus, it seemed good for me to write it out for you. I arranged it in order, [4]to help you know that what you have been taught is true.

ZECHARIAH AND ELIZABETH

[5]During the time Herod ruled Judea, there was a priest named Zechariah who belonged to Abijah's group.[n] Zechariah's wife, Elizabeth, came from the family of Aaron. [6]Zechariah and Elizabeth truly did what God said was good. They did everything the Lord commanded and were without fault in keeping his law. [7]But they had no children, because Elizabeth could not have a baby, and both of them were very old.

[8]One day Zechariah was serving as a priest before God, because his group was on duty. [9]According to the custom of the priests, he was chosen by lot to go into the Temple of the Lord and burn incense. [10]There were a great many people outside praying at the time the incense was offered. [11]Then an angel of the Lord appeared to Zechariah, standing on the right side of the incense table. [12]When he saw the angel, Zechariah was startled and frightened. [13]But the angel said to him, "Zechariah, don't be afraid. God has heard your prayer. Your wife, Elizabeth, will give birth to a son, and you will name him John. [14]He will bring you joy and gladness, and many people will be happy because of his birth. [15]John will be a great man for the Lord. He will never drink wine or beer, and even from birth, he will be filled with the Holy Spirit. [16]He will help many people of Israel return to the Lord their God. [17]He will go before the Lord in spirit and power like Elijah. He will make peace between parents and their children and will bring those who are not obeying God back to the right way of thinking, to make a people ready for the coming of the Lord."

[18]Zechariah said to the angel, "How can I know that what you say is true? I am an old man, and my wife is old, too."

[19]The angel answered him, "I am Gabriel. I stand before God, who sent me to talk to you and to tell you this good news. [20]Now, listen! You will not be able to speak until the day these things happen, because you did not believe what I told you. But they will really happen."

[21]Outside, the people were still waiting for Zechariah and were surprised that he was staying so long in the Temple. [22]When Zechariah came outside, he could not speak to them, and they knew he had seen a vision in the Temple. He could only make signs to them and remained unable to speak. [23]When his time of service at the Temple was finished, he went home.

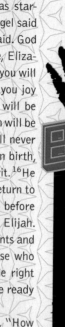

Holy Spirit

After Jesus' resurrection from the dead, just before He returned to heaven, He promised to send "a Helper," the Holy Spirit. The Holy Spirit is one of the three persons of the Trinity, the Godhead worshiped by Christians. The Holy Spirit resides within believers to:

- bring hope (Romans 5:5)
- help us to understand truth (1 Corinthians 2:6-16)
- help us to pray (Romans 8:26)
- enable us to operate in the spiritual gifts (1 Corinthians 12:4-11)
- convict us of sin (John 16:8)
- correct our attitudes and actions (Romans 14:17; 1 Corinthians 6:9-11)

The Holy Spirit gives the Christian real power.

WE WERE MADE WITH A NEED TO BELONG

1:3 excellent This word was used to show respect to an important person like a king or ruler. **1:5 Abijah's group** The Jewish priests were divided into twenty-four groups. See 1 Chronicles 24.

[24]Later, Zechariah's wife, Elizabeth, became pregnant and did not go out of her house for five months. Elizabeth said, [25]"Look what the Lord has done for me! My people were ashamed[n] of me, but now the Lord has taken away that shame."

AN ANGEL APPEARS TO MARY

[26]During Elizabeth's sixth month of pregnancy, God sent the angel Gabriel to Nazareth, a town in Galilee, [27]to a virgin. She was engaged to marry a man named Joseph from the family of David. Her name was Mary. [28]The angel came to her and said, "Greetings! The Lord has blessed you and is with you."

[29]But Mary was very startled by what the angel said and wondered what this greeting might mean.

[30]The angel said to her, "Don't be afraid, Mary; God has shown you his grace. [31]Listen! You will become pregnant and give birth to a son, and you will name him Jesus. [32]He will be great and will be called the Son of the Most High. The Lord God will give him the throne of King David, his ancestor. [33]He will rule over the people of Jacob forever, and his kingdom will never end."

Someone I loved just died. How do I cope? How do I keep going?

No matter what the circumstances, death is hard. The loss is so absolute, so shattering, and the heartache is so painful. But death is unavoidable; very few people will reach adulthood without experiencing the loss of someone they love.

How do you cope? First, you need to realize that there is no correct way to grieve. Some people will cry for hours on end; some won't shed a tear. Some people will sit and stare at the wall while others will release their pain through work, whether at home, at the office, or through volunteering. You might be fine for days, only to suddenly be overwhelmed with sadness. Talk to a friend or counselor or pastor—someone who can listen and help you sort through grief and any decisions you might have to face.

Above all, realize that death is not the end. Jesus came to give us life eternal. Those who belong to the Lord will be with their loved ones in heaven, and will never be separated from them again. We have Jesus' word on it.

Read on: Romans 8:35-39; 1 Corinthians 15; 1 Thessalonians 4:13-18

He's got answers

PEEP THIS:

African-Americans make up 13 percent of the total United States population, but make up 50 percent of the total U.S. prison population. This incarceration rate varies from state to state.

[34]Mary said to the angel, "How will this happen since I am a virgin?"

[35]The angel said to Mary, "The Holy Spirit will come upon you, and the power of the Most High will cover you. For this reason the baby will be holy and will be called the Son of God. [36]Now Elizabeth, your relative, is also pregnant with a son though she is very old. Everyone thought she could not have a baby, but she has been pregnant for six months. [37]God can do anything!"

[38]Mary said, "I am the servant of the Lord. Let this happen to me as you say!" Then the angel went away.

MARY VISITS ELIZABETH

[39]Mary got up and went quickly to a town in the hills of Judea. [40]She came to Zechariah's house and greeted Elizabeth. [41]When Elizabeth heard Mary's greeting, the unborn baby inside her jumped, and Elizabeth was filled with the Holy Spirit. [42]She cried out in a loud voice, "God has blessed you more than any other woman, and he has blessed the baby to which you will give birth. [43]Why has this good thing happened to me, that the mother of my Lord comes to me? [44]When I heard your voice, the baby inside me jumped with joy. [45]You are blessed because you believed that what the Lord said to you would really happen."

MARY PRAISES GOD

[46]Then Mary said,
"My soul praises the Lord;
[47] my heart rejoices in God my Savior,

1:25 ashamed The Jewish people thought it was a disgrace for women not to have children.

48because he has shown his concern
for his humble servant girl.
From now on, all people will say
that I am blessed,
49 because the Powerful One has done
great things for me.
His name is holy.
50God will show his mercy forever and
ever
to those who worship and serve
him.
51He has done mighty deeds by his
power.
He has scattered the people who
are proud
and think great things about
themselves.
52He has brought down rulers from
their thrones
and raised up the humble.
53He has filled the hungry with good
things
and sent the rich away with
nothing.
54He has helped his servant, the
people of Israel,
remembering to show them mercy
55as he promised to our ancestors,
to Abraham and to his children
forever."

56Mary stayed with Elizabeth for
about three months and then returned
home.

THE BIRTH OF JOHN

57When it was time for Elizabeth to
give birth, she had a boy. 58Her neighbors and relatives heard how good the
Lord was to her, and they rejoiced with
her.
59When the baby was eight days
old, they came to circumcise him. They
wanted to name him Zechariah because
this was his father's name, 60but his
mother said, "No! He will be named
John."
61The people said to Elizabeth, "But
no one in your family has this name."
62Then they made signs to his father
to find out what he would like to name
him.

63Zechariah asked for a writing tab-
let and wrote, "His name is John," and
everyone was surprised. 64Immediately
Zechariah could talk again, and he began praising God. 65All their neighbors
became alarmed, and in all the mountains of Judea people continued talking
about all these things. 66The people who
heard about them wondered, saying,
"What will this child be?" because the
Lord was with him.

ZECHARIAH PRAISES GOD

67Then Zechariah, John's father, was
filled with the Holy Spirit and prophesied:
68"Let us praise the Lord, the God of
Israel,
because he has come to help his
people and has given them
freedom.
69He has given us a powerful Savior
from the family of God's servant
David.
70He said that he would do this
through his holy prophets who
lived long ago:
71He promised he would save us from
our enemies
and from the power of all those
who hate us.
72He said he would give mercy to our
ancestors
and that he would remember his
holy promise.
73God promised Abraham, our father,
74 that he would save us from the
power of our enemies
so we could serve him without
fear,
75being holy and good before God as
long as we live.

76"Now you, child, will be called a
prophet of the Most High God.
You will go before the Lord to
prepare his way.
77You will make his people know that
they will be saved
by having their sins forgiven.
78With the loving mercy of our God,
a new day from heaven will dawn
upon us.

79It will shine on those who live in
darkness,
in the shadow of death.
It will guide us into the path of
peace."
80And so the child grew up and became strong in spirit. John lived in the
desert until the time when he came out
to preach to Israel.

THE BIRTH OF JESUS

2At that time, Augustus
Caesar sent an order that
all people in the countries
under Roman rule must
list their names in a reg-
ister. 2This was the first registration;[n]
it was taken while Quirinius was governor of Syria. 3And all went to their own
towns to be registered.
4So Joseph left Nazareth, a town in
Galilee, and went to the town of Bethlehem in Judea, known as the town of
David. Joseph went there because he
was from the family of David. 5Joseph
registered with Mary, to whom he was
engaged[n] and who was now pregnant.
6While they were in Bethlehem, the time
came for Mary to have the baby, 7and
she gave birth to her first son. Because
there were no rooms left in the inn, she
wrapped the baby with pieces of cloth
and laid him in a feeding trough.

SHEPHERDS HEAR ABOUT JESUS

8That night, some shepherds were in
the fields nearby watching their sheep.
9Then an angel of the Lord stood before
them. The glory of the Lord was shining around them, and they became very
frightened. 10The angel said to them, "Do
not be afraid. I am bringing you good
news that will be a great joy to all the
people. 11Today your Savior was born
in the town of David. He is Christ, the
Lord. 12This is how you will know him:
You will find a baby wrapped in pieces of
cloth and lying in a feeding box."
13Then a very large group of angels
from heaven joined the first angel, praising God and saying:

2:2 registration Census. A counting of all the people and the things they own.   **2:5 engaged** For the Jewish people, an engagement was a lasting agreement. It could only be broken by divorce.

[14]"Give glory to God in heaven,
    and on earth let there be peace
        among the people who please
        God.'"[n]

[15]When the angels left them and went back to heaven, the shepherds said to each other, "Let's go to Bethlehem. Let's see this thing that has happened which the Lord has told us about."

[16]So the shepherds went quickly and found Mary and Joseph and the baby, who was lying in a feeding trough. [17]When they had seen him, they told what the angels had said about this child. [18]Everyone was amazed at what the shepherds said to them. [19]But Mary treasured these things and continued to think about them. [20]Then the shepherds went back to their sheep, praising God and thanking him for everything they had seen and heard. It had been just as the angel had told them.

[21]When the baby was eight days old, he was circumcised and was named Jesus, the name given by the angel before the baby began to grow inside Mary.

JESUS IS PRESENTED IN THE TEMPLE

[22]When the time came for Mary and Joseph to do what the law of Moses taught about being made pure,[n] they took Jesus to Jerusalem to present him to the Lord. [23](It is written in the law of the Lord: "Every firstborn male shall be given to the Lord.")[n] [24]Mary and Joseph also went to offer a sacrifice, as the law of the Lord says: "You must sacrifice two doves or two young pigeons."[n]

SIMEON SEES JESUS

[25]In Jerusalem lived a man named Simeon who was a good man and godly. He was waiting for the time when God would take away Israel's sorrow, and the Holy Spirit was in him. [26]Simeon had been told by the Holy Spirit that he would not die before he saw the Christ promised by the Lord. [27]The Spirit led Simeon to the Temple. When Mary and Joseph brought the baby Jesus to the Temple to do what the law said they

hot|○

Biblical Attributes of a Good Woman

10. Doesn't gossip

9. Shows self-control

8. Takes care of her body and spirit

7. Protects her children

6. Uses time and energy efficiently

5. Has inner beauty

4. Is optimistic

3. Is faithful

2. Prays all the time

1. Walks with Jesus

must do, [28]Simeon took the baby in his arms and thanked God:
[29]"Now, Lord, you can let me, your servant,
    die in peace as you said.
[30]With my own eyes I have seen your salvation,
[31] which you prepared before all people.
[32]It is a light for the non-Jewish people to see
    and an honor for your people, the Israelites."

[33]Jesus' father and mother were amazed at what Simeon had said about him. [34]Then Simeon blessed them and said to Mary, "God has chosen this child to cause the fall and rise of many in Israel. He will be a sign from God that many people will not accept [35]so that the thoughts of many will be made known. And the things that will happen will make your heart sad, too."

ANNA SEES JESUS

[36]There was a prophetess, Anna, from the family of Phanuel in the tribe of Asher. Anna was very old. She had once been married for seven years. [37]Then her husband died, and she was a widow for eighty-four years. Anna never left the Temple but worshiped God, going without food and praying day and night. [38]Standing there at that time, she thanked God and spoke about Jesus to all who were waiting for God to free Jerusalem.

JOSEPH AND MARY RETURN HOME

[39]When Joseph and Mary had done everything the law of the Lord commanded, they went home to Nazareth, their own town in Galilee. [40]The little child grew and became strong. He was filled with wisdom, and God's goodness was upon him.

JESUS AS A BOY

[41]Every year Jesus' parents went to Jerusalem for the Passover Feast. [42]When he was twelve years old, they went to the feast as they always did. [43]After the feast

---

 2:14 and . . . God Some Greek copies read "and on earth let there be peace and goodwill among people." **2:22 pure** The Law of Moses said that forty days after a Jewish woman gave birth to a son, she must be cleansed by a ceremony at the Temple. Read Leviticus 12:2-8. **2:23 "Every . . . Lord."** Quotation from Exodus 13:2. **2:24 "You . . . pigeons."** Quotation from Leviticus 12:8.

days were over, they started home. The boy Jesus stayed behind in Jerusalem, but his parents did not know it. ⁴⁴Thinking that Jesus was with them in the group, they traveled for a whole day. Then they began to look for him among their family and friends. ⁴⁵When they did not find him, they went back to Jerusalem to look for him there. ⁴⁶After three days they found Jesus sitting in the Temple with the teachers, listening to them and asking them questions. ⁴⁷All who heard him were amazed at his understanding and answers. ⁴⁸When Jesus' parents saw him, they were astonished. His mother said to him, "Son, why did you do this to us? Your father and I were very worried about you and have been looking for you."

⁴⁹Jesus said to them, "Why were you looking for me? Didn't you know that I must be in my Father's house?" ⁵⁰But they did not understand the meaning of what he said.

⁵¹Jesus went with them to Nazareth and was obedient to them. But his mother kept in her mind all that had happened. ⁵²Jesus became wiser and grew physically. People liked him, and he pleased God.

THE PREACHING OF JOHN

3 It was the fifteenth year of the rule of Tiberius Caesar. These men were under Caesar: Pontius Pilate, the ruler of Judea; Herod, the ruler of Galilee; Philip, Herod's brother, the ruler of Iturea and Traconitis; and Lysanias, the ruler of Abilene. ²Annas and Caiaphas were the high priests. At this time, the word of God came to John son of Zechariah in the desert. ³He went all over the area around the Jordan River preaching a baptism of changed hearts and lives for the forgiveness of sins. ⁴As it is written in the book of Isaiah the prophet:

"This is a voice of one
    who calls out in the desert:
'Prepare the way for the Lord.
    Make the road straight for him.
⁵Every valley should be filled in,
    and every mountain and hill
        should be made flat.
Roads with turns should be made
        straight,
    and rough roads should be made
        smooth.
⁶And all people will know about the
        salvation of God!'" *Isaiah 40:3-5*

⁷To the crowds of people who came to be baptized by John, he said, "You are all snakes! Who warned you to run away from God's coming punishment? ⁸Do the things that show you really have changed your hearts and lives. Don't begin to say to yourselves, 'Abraham is our father.' I tell you that God could make children

IMPACT!

Concerned Black Men

Originally founded in Philadelphia to help find a way out for kids caught up in gang violence, Concerned Black Men is twenty-nine years strong and continues to provide enrichment and prevention programs for youth and their parents. Some of the programs they offer include teaching abstinence to teenage boys, HIV/AIDS prevention, help for low-income parents, substance abuse help, and educational initiatives. Concerned Black Men has several chapters in the United States and a chapter in South Africa. To get involved, call 1-888-395-7816 or visit their Web site at <u>www.cbmnational.org</u>.

GOD UNIT 0

GETTING OVER A PORN ADDICTION

I couldn't explain why, but something about watching folks get their groove on really turned me on. I was a newly married man. My wife was sexy to me, but the porn added a little somethin' to the mix. Porn was just easy. I didn't have to talk to it, take it out, make it feel good, or be sensitive to its needs. I never looked at porn as something that took my wife's place. It was something I did in addition to my wife. When she wouldn't join in, I did it in secret. She began to notice that I wasn't as sensitive to her needs as I used to be. She accused me of a "wham-bam, thank you ma'am" mentality. I just didn't see there was anything wrong with my enjoyment of pornography until my wife gave me an ultimatum. I had to choose—either her or my porn women. I told her she was crazy and that looking at a little porn sometimes wasn't hurting her or anyone else. I held onto that thought while my wife left me.

When she was gone, I went through a period when I thought, "Good, I didn't need her anyway." The women in the porn tapes didn't talk back. But those women also weren't real. Then one day, I figured out that I was all alone. I tried to date other women, but I just froze up. I still loved my wife, yet I had no idea how to relate to her any more.

I called up a dude who I used to roll with. We actually stopped hanging because he kept talking about Jesus. It took me three tries to finally get him, but once I did he came over and met with me. He shot straight, telling me that apart from God we were all sinners. I began to understand that only God could free me from my problems. I confessed my sins and became a believer. Now I'm learning to deny temptation. My wife hasn't come back, but I hope she will see that the love of God has changed me and believe when I say I still love her. For now, I'm cool with the fact that God's getting me straight so I'll be a better man when and if she returns.

2 Peter 2:9—The Lord knows how to save those who serve him when troubles [or temptations] come.

---

for Abraham from these rocks. [9]The ax is now ready to cut down the trees, and every tree that does not produce good fruit will be cut down and thrown into the fire."[n]

[10]The people asked John, "Then what should we do?"

[11]John answered, "If you have two shirts, share with the person who does not have one. If you have food, share that also."

[12]Even tax collectors came to John to be baptized. They said to him, "Teacher, what should we do?"

[13]John said to them, "Don't take more taxes from people than you have been ordered to take."

[14]The soldiers asked John, "What about us? What should we do?"

John said to them, "Don't force people to give you money, and don't lie about them. Be satisfied with the pay you get."

[15]Since the people were hoping for the Christ to come, they wondered if John might be the one.

[16]John answered everyone, "I baptize you with water, but there is one coming who is greater than I am. I am not good enough to untie his sandals. He will baptize you with the Holy Spirit and fire. [17]He will come ready to clean the grain, separating the good grain from the chaff. He will put the good part of the grain into his barn, but he will burn the chaff with a fire that cannot be put out."[n] [18]And John continued to preach the Good News, saying many other things to encourage the people.

[19]But John spoke against Herod, the governor, because of his sin with Herodias, the wife of Herod's brother, and because of the many other evil things Herod did. [20]So Herod did something even worse: He put John in prison.

 3:9 The ax . . . fire. This means that God is ready to punish his people who do not obey him.   **3:17 He will . . . out.** This means that Jesus will come to separate good people from bad people, saving the good and punishing the bad.

JESUS IS BAPTIZED BY JOHN

21When all the people were being baptized by John, Jesus also was baptized. While Jesus was praying, heaven opened 22and the Holy Spirit came down on him in the form of a dove. Then a voice came from heaven, saying, "You are my Son, whom I love, and I am very pleased with you."

THE FAMILY HISTORY OF JESUS

23When Jesus began his ministry, he was about thirty years old. People thought that Jesus was Joseph's son.

Joseph was the son[n] of Heli.
24Heli was the son of Matthat.
Matthat was the son of Levi.
Levi was the son of Melki.
Melki was the son of Jannai.
Jannai was the son of Joseph.
25Joseph was the son of Mattathias.
Mattathias was the son of Amos.
Amos was the son of Nahum.
Nahum was the son of Esli.
Esli was the son of Naggai.
26Naggai was the son of Maath.
Maath was the son of Mattathias.
Mattathias was the son of Semein.
Semein was the son of Josech.
Josech was the son of Joda.
27Joda was the son of Joanan.
Joanan was the son of Rhesa.
Rhesa was the son of Zerubbabel.
Zerubbabel was the grandson of Shealtiel.
Shealtiel was the son of Neri.
28Neri was the son of Melki.
Melki was the son of Addi.
Addi was the son of Cosam.
Cosam was the son of Elmadam.
Elmadam was the son of Er.
29Er was the son of Joshua.
Joshua was the son of Eliezer.
Eliezer was the son of Jorim.
Jorim was the son of Matthat.
Matthat was the son of Levi.
30Levi was the son of Simeon.
Simeon was the son of Judah.
Judah was the son of Joseph.
Joseph was the son of Jonam.
Jonam was the son of Eliakim.
31Eliakim was the son of Melea.
Melea was the son of Menna.
Menna was the son of Mattatha.
Mattatha was the son of Nathan.
Nathan was the son of David.
32David was the son of Jesse.
Jesse was the son of Obed.
Obed was the son of Boaz.
Boaz was the son of Salmon.[n]
Salmon was the son of Nahshon.
33Nahshon was the son of Amminadab.
Amminadab was the son of Admin.
Admin was the son of Arni.
Arni was the son of Hezron.
Hezron was the son of Perez.
Perez was the son of Judah.
34Judah was the son of Jacob.
Jacob was the son of Isaac.
Isaac was the son of Abraham.
Abraham was the son of Terah.
Terah was the son of Nahor.
35Nahor was the son of Serug.
Serug was the son of Reu.
Reu was the son of Peleg.
Peleg was the son of Eber.
Eber was the son of Shelah.
36Shelah was the son of Cainan.
Cainan was the son of Arphaxad.
Arphaxad was the son of Shem.
Shem was the son of Noah.
Noah was the son of Lamech.
37Lamech was the son of Methuselah.
Methuselah was the son of Enoch.
Enoch was the son of Jared.
Jared was the son of Mahalalel.
Mahalalel was the son of Kenan.
38Kenan was the son of Enosh.
Enosh was the son of Seth.
Seth was the son of Adam.
Adam was the son of God.

JESUS IS TEMPTED BY THE DEVIL

4Jesus, filled with the Holy Spirit, returned from the Jordan River. The Spirit led Jesus into the desert 2where the devil tempted Jesus for forty days. Jesus ate nothing during that time, and when those days were ended, he was very hungry.

3The devil said to Jesus, "If you are the Son of God, tell this rock to become bread."

4Jesus answered, "It is written in the Scriptures: 'A person does not live on bread alone.'"[n]

5Then the devil took Jesus and showed him all the kingdoms of the world in an instant. 6The devil said to Jesus, "I will give you all these kingdoms and all their power and glory. It has all been given to me, and I can give it to anyone I wish. 7If you worship me, then it will all be yours."

8Jesus answered, "It is written in the Scriptures: 'You must worship the Lord your God and serve only him.'"[n]

9Then the devil led Jesus to Jerusalem and put him on a high place of the Temple. He said to Jesus, "If you are the Son of God, jump down. 10It is written in the Scriptures:

'He has put his angels in charge of you
to watch over you.'   Psalm 91:11
11It is also written:
'They will catch you in their hands
so that you will not hit your foot
on a rock.'"   Psalm 91:12
12Jesus answered, "But it also says in the Scriptures: 'Do not test the Lord your God.'"[n]

13After the devil had tempted Jesus in every way, he left him to wait until a better time.

JESUS TEACHES THE PEOPLE

14Jesus returned to Galilee in the power of the Holy Spirit, and stories about him spread all through the area. 15He began to teach in their synagogues, and everyone praised him.

16Jesus traveled to Nazareth, where he had grown up. On the Sabbath day he went to the synagogue, as he always did, and stood up to read. 17The book of Isaiah the prophet was given to him. He opened the book and found the place where this is written:

18"The Lord has put his Spirit in me,
because he appointed me to tell the Good News to the poor.
He has sent me to tell the captives they are free

3:23 son "Son" in Jewish lists of ancestors can sometimes mean grandson or more distant relative. **3:32 Salmon** Some Greek copies read "Sala." **4:4 'A person . . . alone.'** Quotation from Deuteronomy 8:3. **4:8 'You . . . him.'** Quotation from Deuteronomy 6:13. **4:12 'Do . . . God.'** Quotation from Deuteronomy 6:16.

and to tell the blind that they can see again. *Isaiah 61:1*
God sent me to free those who have been treated unfairly *Isaiah 58:6*
¹⁹and to announce the time when the Lord will show his kindness." *Isaiah 61:2*

²⁰Jesus closed the book, gave it back to the assistant, and sat down. Everyone in the synagogue was watching Jesus closely. ²¹He began to say to them, "While you heard these words just now, they were coming true!"

²²All the people spoke well of Jesus and were amazed at the words of grace he spoke. They asked, "Isn't this Joseph's son?"

²³Jesus said to them, "I know that you will tell me the old saying: 'Doctor, heal yourself.' You want to say, 'We heard about the things you did in Capernaum. Do those things here in your own town!'" ²⁴Then Jesus said, "I tell you the truth, a prophet is not accepted in his hometown. ²⁵But I tell you the truth, there were many widows in Israel during the time of Elijah. It did not rain in Israel for three and one-half years, and there was no food anywhere in the whole country. ²⁶But Elijah was sent to none of those widows, only to a widow in Zarephath, a town in Sidon. ²⁷And there were many with skin diseases living in Israel during the time of the prophet Elisha. But none of them were healed, only Naaman, who was from the country of Syria."

²⁸When all the people in the synagogue heard these things, they became very angry. ²⁹They got up, forced Jesus out of town, and took him to the edge of the cliff on which the town was built. They planned to throw him off the edge, ³⁰but Jesus walked through the crowd and went on his way.

JESUS FORCES OUT AN EVIL SPIRIT

³¹Jesus went to Capernaum, a city in Galilee, and on the Sabbath day, he taught the people. ³²They were amazed at his teaching, because he spoke with authority. ³³In the synagogue a man who had within him an evil spirit shouted in a loud voice, ³⁴"Jesus of Nazareth! What do you want with us? Did you come to destroy us? I know who you are—God's Holy One!"

³⁵Jesus commanded the evil spirit, "Be quiet! Come out of the man!" The evil spirit threw the man down to the

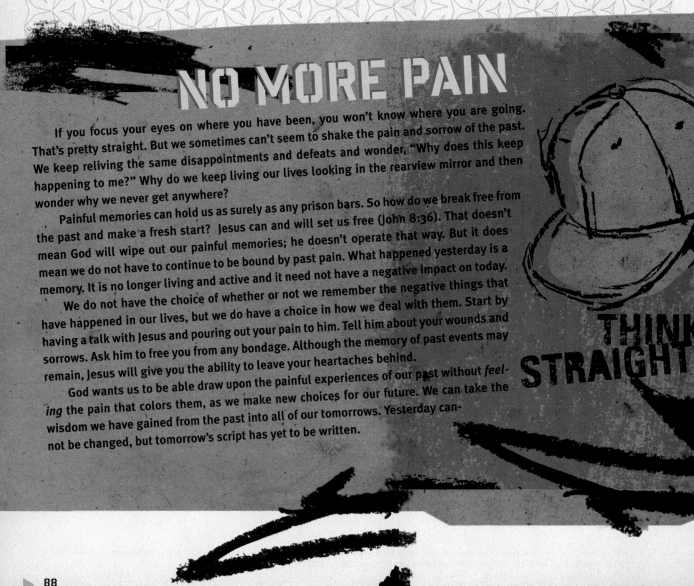

NO MORE PAIN

If you focus your eyes on where you have been, you won't know where you are going. That's pretty straight. But we sometimes can't seem to shake the pain and sorrow of the past. We keep reliving the same disappointments and defeats and wonder, "Why does this keep happening to me?" Why do we keep living our lives looking in the rearview mirror and then wonder why we never get anywhere?

Painful memories can hold us as surely as any prison bars. So how do we break free from the past and make a fresh start? Jesus can and will set us free (John 8:36). That doesn't mean God will wipe out our painful memories; he doesn't operate that way. But it does mean we do not have to continue to be bound by past pain. What happened yesterday is a memory. It is no longer living and active and it need not have a negative impact on today.

We do not have the choice of whether or not we remember the negative things that have happened in our lives, but we do have a choice in how we deal with them. Start by having a talk with Jesus and pouring out your pain to him. Tell him about your wounds and sorrows. Ask him to free you from any bondage. Although the memory of past events may remain, Jesus will give you the ability to leave your heartaches behind.

God wants us to be able draw upon the painful experiences of our past without *feel-ing* the pain that colors them, as we make new choices for our future. We can take the wisdom we have gained from the past into all of our tomorrows. Yesterday cannot be changed, but tomorrow's script has yet to be written.

THINK STRAIGHT

LONELINESS

No one loves you; you're better off being by yourself. Just go and have a couple of drinks because it will make you feel better. Drink, eat, and sleep your loneliness away. Stop trying to be right all the time; just flow with what everyone else is doing and maybe people will like you more. *Live* a little.

"Turn to me and have mercy on me, because I am lonely and hurting. . . . Protect me and save me. I trust you, so do not let me be disgraced. My hope is in you, so may goodness and honesty guard me" (Psalm 25:16, 20–21).

"People will hate you, shut you out, insult you, and say you are evil because you follow the Son of Man. But when they do, you will be happy" (Luke 6:22).

"I will never leave you; I will never forget you" (Hebrews 13:5b).

ground before all the people and then left the man without hurting him.

[36] The people were amazed and said to each other, "What does this mean? With authority and power he commands evil spirits, and they come out." [37] And so the news about Jesus spread to every place in the whole area.

JESUS HEALS MANY PEOPLE

[38] Jesus left the synagogue and went to the home of Simon.[n] Simon's mother-in-law was sick with a high fever, and they asked Jesus to help her. [39] He came to her side and commanded the fever to leave. It left her, and immediately she got up and began serving them.

[40] When the sun went down, the people brought those who were sick to Jesus. Putting his hands on each sick person, he healed every one of them. [41] Demons came out of many people, shouting, "You are the Son of God." But Jesus commanded the demons and would not allow them to speak, because they knew Jesus was the Christ.

[42] At daybreak, Jesus went to a lonely place, but the people looked for him. When they found him, they tried to keep him from leaving. [43] But Jesus said to them, "I must preach about God's kingdom to other towns, too. This is why I was sent."

[44] Then he kept on preaching in the synagogues of Judea.[n]

JESUS' FIRST FOLLOWERS

5 One day while Jesus was standing beside Lake Galilee, many people were pressing all around him to hear the word of God. [2] Jesus saw two boats at the shore of the lake. The fishermen had left them and were washing their nets. [3] Jesus got into one of the boats, the one that belonged to Simon,[n] and asked him to push off a little from the land. Then Jesus sat down and continued to teach the people from the boat.

[4] When Jesus had finished speaking, he said to Simon, "Take the boat into deep water, and put your nets in the water to catch some fish."

[5] Simon answered, "Master, we worked hard all night trying to catch fish, and we caught nothing. But you say to put the nets in the water, so I will." [6] When the fishermen did as Jesus told them, they caught so many fish that the nets began to break. [7] They called to their partners in the other boat to come and help them. They came and filled both boats so full that they were almost sinking.

[8] When Simon Peter saw what had happened, he bowed down before Jesus and said, "Go away from me, Lord. I am a sinful man!" [9] He and the other fishermen were amazed at the many fish they caught, as were [10] James and John, the sons of Zebedee, Simon's partners.

Jesus said to Simon, "Don't be afraid. From now on you will fish for people." [11] When the men brought their boats to the shore, they left everything and followed Jesus.

JESUS HEALS A SICK MAN

[12] When Jesus was in one of the towns, there was a man covered with a skin disease. When he saw Jesus, he bowed before him and begged him, "Lord, you can heal me if you will."

[13] Jesus reached out his hand and touched the man and said, "I will. Be healed!" Immediately the disease disappeared. [14] Then Jesus said, "Don't tell anyone about this, but go and show yourself to the priest[n] and offer a gift for your healing, as Moses commanded.[n] This will show the people what I have done."

[15] But the news about Jesus spread even more. Many people came to hear Jesus and to be healed of their sicknesses, [16] but Jesus often slipped away to be alone so he could pray.

 4:38; 5:3 Simon Simon's other name was Peter. **4:44 Judea** Some Greek copies read "Galilee." **5:14 show . . . priest** The Law of Moses said a priest must say when a Jewish person with a skin disease was well. **5:14 Moses commanded** Read about this in Leviticus 14:1-32.

JESUS HEALS A PARALYZED MAN

[17]One day as Jesus was teaching the people, the Pharisees and teachers of the law from every town in Galilee and Judea and from Jerusalem were there. The Lord was giving Jesus the power to heal people. [18]Just then, some men were carrying on a mat a man who was paralyzed. They tried to bring him in and put him down before Jesus. [19]But because there were so many people there, they could not find a way in. So they went up on the roof and lowered the man on his mat through the ceiling into the middle of the crowd right before Jesus. [20]Seeing their faith, Jesus said, "Friend, your sins are forgiven."

[21]The Jewish teachers of the law and the Pharisees thought to themselves, "Who is this man who is speaking as if he were God? Only God can forgive sins."

PEEP THIS:

In 2000, cardiovascular disease accounted for 33.5 percent of deaths among African-American men and 40.6 percent of African-American women.

[22]But Jesus knew what they were thinking and said, "Why are you thinking these things? [23]Which is easier: to say, 'Your sins are forgiven,' or to say, 'Stand up and walk'? [24]But I will prove to you that the Son of Man has authority on earth to forgive sins." So Jesus said to the paralyzed man, "I tell you, stand up, take your mat, and go home."

[25]At once the man stood up before them, picked up his mat, and went home, praising God. [26]All the people were fully amazed and began to praise God. They were filled with much respect and said, "Today we have seen amazing things!"

LEVI FOLLOWS JESUS

[27]After this, Jesus went out and saw a tax collector named Levi sitting in the tax collector's booth. Jesus said to him, "Follow me!" [28]So Levi got up, left everything, and followed him.

[29]Then Levi gave a big dinner for Jesus at his house. Many tax collectors and other people were eating there, too. [30]But the Pharisees and the men who taught the law for the Pharisees began to complain to Jesus' followers, "Why do you eat and drink with tax collectors and sinners?"

[31]Jesus answered them, "It is not the healthy people who need a doctor, but the sick. [32]I have not come to invite good people but sinners to change their hearts and lives."

JESUS ANSWERS A QUESTION

[33]They said to Jesus, "John's followers often fast[n] for a certain time and pray, just as the Pharisees do. But your followers eat and drink all the time."

[34]Jesus said to them, "You cannot make the friends of the bridegroom fast while he is still with them. [35]But the time will come when the bridegroom will be taken away from them, and then they will fast."

[36]Jesus told them this story: "No one takes cloth off a new coat to cover a hole in an old coat. Otherwise, he ruins the new coat, and the cloth from the new coat will not be the same as the old cloth. [37]Also, no one ever pours new wine into old leather bags. Otherwise, the new wine will break the bags, the wine will spill out, and the leather bags will be ruined. [38]New wine must be put into new leather bags. [39]No one after drinking old wine wants new wine, because he says, 'The old wine is better.' "

JESUS IS LORD OVER THE SABBATH

6One Sabbath day Jesus was walking through some fields of grain. His followers picked the heads of grain, rubbed them in their hands, and ate them. [2]Some Pharisees said, "Why do you do what is not lawful on the Sabbath day?"

[3]Jesus answered, "Have you not read what David did when he and those with him were hungry? [4]He went into God's house and took and ate the holy bread, which is lawful only for priests to eat. And he gave some to the people who were with him." [5]Then Jesus said to the Pharisees, "The Son of Man is Lord of the Sabbath day."

JESUS HEALS A MAN'S HAND

[6]On another Sabbath day Jesus went into the synagogue and was teaching, and a man with a crippled right hand was there. [7]The teachers of the law and the Pharisees were watching closely to see if Jesus would heal on the Sabbath day so they could accuse him. [8]But he knew what they were thinking, and he said to the man with the crippled hand, "Stand up here in the middle of everyone." The man got up and stood there. [9]Then Jesus said to them, "I ask you, which is lawful on the Sabbath day: to do good or to do evil, to save a life or to destroy it?" [10]Jesus looked around at all of them and said to the man, "Hold out your hand." The man held out his hand, and it was healed.

[11]But the Pharisees and the teachers of the law were very angry and discussed with each other what they could do to Jesus.

JESUS CHOOSES HIS APOSTLES

[12]At that time Jesus went off to a mountain to pray, and he spent the night praying to God. [13]The next morning, Jesus called his followers to him and chose twelve of them, whom he named apostles: [14]Simon (Jesus named him Peter),

---

5:33 fast The people would give up eating for a special time of prayer and worship to God. It was also done to show sadness and disappointment.

CONNECTED

CONNECTED TO FRIENDS:

FRIENDS DON'T PLAY

John 15:13 says, "The greatest love a person can show is to die for his friends." Jesus was criticized because he was a friend to sinners. He even called Judas, the man who betrayed him, "friend." And he called others, including everyday people like Lazarus, his friends.

What makes a good friend? Do you stand by your friend during both good and bad times, or do you bail out at the first sign of trouble? Do you talk about your friends behind their backs? Proverbs 16:28 says that "a gossip ruins friendships." Are you loyal? The fastest way to break up a friendship is by not knowing how to remain. Does your love for your friends change based on how you feel or what they might have done? Proverbs 17:17 says that "a friend loves you all the time"—unconditionally. Do you love your friend wholeheartedly? Do you have the strength to tell a friend the truth about himself, even though you know that sometimes the truth will hurt? Are you willing to listen when something is wrong and give sound, godly advice? These are the most vital components of a good friendship and the foundation for building a healthy relationship.

God loves you no matter what—simply because you are his child. You should love your friends in the same way. Love them for who they are, not because of what they do. Love them in spite of their flaws, remembering that you aren't perfect either. There are times when you will be required to give wise counsel. Listen first, and then speak truth out of love. Speaking the truth is sometimes the hardest part of a being a friend. But if you keep God first in your relationships, you will grow in the process and your friendships will grow stronger than you ever could have imagined.

his brother Andrew, James, John, Philip, Bartholomew, [15]Matthew, Thomas, James son of Alphaeus, Simon (called the Zealot), [16]Judas son of James, and Judas Iscariot, who later turned Jesus over to his enemies.

JESUS TEACHES AND HEALS

[17]Jesus and the apostles came down from the mountain, and he stood on level ground. A large group of his followers was there, as well as many people from all around Judea, Jerusalem, and the seacoast cities of Tyre and Sidon. [18]They all came to hear Jesus teach and to be healed of their sicknesses, and he healed those who were troubled by evil spirits. [19]All the people were trying to touch Jesus, because power was coming from him and healing them all.

[20]Jesus looked at his followers and said,

"You people who are poor are blessed,
   because the kingdom of God belongs to you.
[21]You people who are now hungry are blessed,
   because you will be satisfied.
You people who are now crying are blessed,
   because you will laugh with joy.
[22]"People will hate you, shut you out, insult you, and say you are evil because you follow the Son of Man. But when they do, you will be blessed. [23]Be full of joy at that time, because you have a great reward in heaven. Their ancestors did the same things to the prophets.
[24]"But how terrible it will be for you who are rich,
   because you have had your easy life.
[25]How terrible it will be for you who are full now,
   because you will be hungry.
How terrible it will be for you who are laughing now,
   because you will be sad and cry.
[26]"How terrible when everyone says only good things about you, because

their ancestors said the same things about the false prophets.

LOVE YOUR ENEMIES

27"But I say to you who are listening, love your enemies. Do good to those who hate you, 28bless those who curse you, pray for those who are cruel to you. 29If anyone slaps you on one cheek, offer him the other cheek, too. If someone takes your coat, do not stop him from taking your shirt. 30Give to everyone who asks you, and when someone takes something that is yours, don't ask for it back. 31Do to others what you would want them to do to you. 32If you love only the people who love you, what praise should you get? Even sinners love the people who love them. 33If you do good only to those who do good to you, what praise should you get? Even sinners do that! 34If you lend things to people, always hoping to get something back, what praise should you get? Even sinners lend to other sinners so that they can get back the same amount! 35But love your enemies, do good to them, and lend to them without hoping to get anything back. Then you will have a great reward, and you will be children of the Most High God, because he is kind even to people who are ungrateful and full of sin. 36Show mercy, just as your Father shows mercy.

LOOK AT YOURSELVES

37"Don't judge others, and you will not be judged. Don't accuse others of being guilty, and you will not be accused of being guilty. Forgive, and you will be forgiven. 38Give, and you will receive. You will be given much. Pressed down, shaken together, and running over, it will spill into your lap. The way you give to others is the way God will give to you."

39Jesus told them this story: "Can a blind person lead another blind person? No! Both of them will fall into a ditch. 40A student is not better than the teacher, but the student who has been fully trained will be like the teacher.

41"Why do you notice the little piece of dust in your friend's eye, but you don't notice the big piece of wood in your own eye? 42How can you say to your friend, 'Friend, let me take that little piece of dust out of your eye' when you cannot see that big piece of wood in your own eye! You hypocrite! First, take the wood out of your own eye. Then you will see clearly to take the dust out of your friend's eye.

TWO KINDS OF FRUIT

43"A good tree does not produce bad fruit, nor does a bad tree produce good fruit. 44Each tree is known by its own fruit. People don't gather figs from thornbushes, and they don't get grapes from bushes. 45Good people bring good things out of the good they stored in their hearts. But evil people bring evil things out of the evil they stored in their hearts. People speak the things that are in their hearts.

> WHY DO YOU CALL ME, 'LORD, LORD,' BUT DO NOT DO WHAT I SAY?

TWO KINDS OF PEOPLE

46"Why do you call me, 'Lord, Lord,' but do not do what I say? 47I will show you what everyone is like who comes to me and hears my words and obeys. 48That person is like a man building a house who dug deep and laid the foundation on rock. When the floods came, the water tried to wash the house away, but it could not shake it, because the house was built well. 49But the one who hears my words and does not obey is like a man who built his house on the ground without a foundation. When the floods came, the house quickly fell and was completely destroyed."

JESUS HEALS A SOLDIER'S SERVANT

7 When Jesus finished saying all these things to the people, he went to Capernaum. 2There was an army officer who had a servant who was very important to him. The servant was so sick he was nearly dead. 3When the officer heard about Jesus, he sent some Jewish elders to him to ask Jesus to come and heal his servant. 4The men went to Jesus and begged him, saying, "This officer is worthy of your help. 5He loves our people, and he built us a synagogue."

6So Jesus went with the men. He was getting near the officer's house when the officer sent friends to say, "Lord, don't trouble yourself, because I am not worthy to have you come into my house. 7That is why I did not come to you myself. But you only need to command it, and my servant will be healed. 8I, too, am a man under the authority of others, and I have soldiers under my command. I tell one soldier, 'Go,' and he goes. I tell another soldier, 'Come,' and he comes. I say to my servant, 'Do this,' and my servant does it."

9When Jesus heard this, he was amazed. Turning to the crowd that was following him, he said, "I tell you, this is the greatest faith I have found anywhere, even in Israel."

10Those who had been sent to Jesus went back to the house where they found the servant in good health.

JESUS BRINGS A MAN BACK TO LIFE

11Soon afterwards Jesus went to a town called Nain, and his followers and a large crowd traveled with him. 12When he came near the town gate, he saw a funeral. A mother, who was a widow, had lost her only son. A large crowd from the town was with the mother while her son was being carried out. 13When the Lord saw her, he felt very sorry for her and said, "Don't cry." 14He went up and touched the coffin, and the people who were carrying it stopped. Jesus said, "Young man, I tell you, get up!" [15]And the son sat up and began to talk. Then Jesus gave him back to his mother.

[16]All the people were amazed and began praising God, saying, "A great prophet has come to us! God has come to help his people."

[17]This news about Jesus spread through all Judea and into all the places around there.

JOHN ASKS A QUESTION

[18]John's followers told him about all these things. He called for two of his followers [19]and sent them to the Lord to ask, "Are you the One who is to come, or should we wait for someone else?"

[20]When the men came to Jesus, they said, "John the Baptist sent us to you with this question: 'Are you the One who is to come, or should we wait for someone else?'"

[21]At that time, Jesus healed many people of their sicknesses, diseases, and evil spirits, and he gave sight to many blind people. [22]Then Jesus answered John's followers, "Go tell John what you saw and heard here. The blind can see, the crippled can walk, and people with skin diseases are healed. The deaf can hear, the dead are raised to life, and the Good News is preached to the poor. [23]Those who do not stumble in their faith because of me are blessed!"

[24]When John's followers left, Jesus began talking to the people about John: "What did you go out into the desert to see? A reed[n] blown by the wind? [25]What did you go out to see? A man dressed in fine clothes? No, people who have fine clothes and much wealth live in kings' palaces. [26]But what did you go out to

7:24 reed It means that John was not ordinary or weak like grass blown by the wind.

THE SCRIPT

The Three Wise Men
Luke 2:1-20

Back in the day around Jesus' birth, right before he appeared on earth-
Caesar Augustus was the big-time sire; ruling the entire Roman
    Empire—
He inquired to check the stretch of his rule from city to shire.
So he issued a census covering all his areas; it was mad hysteria.
Everyone had to travel back to their original habitat just to pay a
    senseless tax.
So Joseph trekked all the way from Galilee out of Nazareth;
Making it down to Bethlehem, David's town, to represent his tribe.
He traveled with his brand new bride, Mary,
Who was already pregnant in full, approaching delivery time.
And . . . you know the way things go when it's raining;
Contractions started hitting Mary—pouring down on her without
    restraining—
Minute-by-minute, fighting the pain, and feeling the hurt.
Mary brought forth her first—a son . . .
And they wrapped him up in worn out rags to keep him warm.
See that's all they had—no loot for fancy blankets—just 'the clothes
    off their backs' ripped and torn. A little baby thrown to vagrancy
    cause the Inn had no vacancy.
Homeless but not hopeless Joseph and Mary waited it out patiently,
And finally made do 'cause they refused to lose,
And laid the baby in a drinking trench that cattle used to use.
Now there just happened to be in that same country
Some shepherds who had their sheep with them on the same premises.
Watching their flocks by the night that evening,
They got caught up in epiphany, seeing angelic images.
Amazed and terrified at the very same time,

The angel eased their troubled minds,
Saying, "Don't be afraid, be filled with joy, today in
    Bethlehem
Is born the Savior who is Christ—Lord and Master
    over all men.
And this is the sign so you're gonna know him for
    yourselves:
Look for the baby ragged-out, lying in the trench,
    that's Emanuel.
And quicker than their eyes could tell,
All blinders fell from the shepherds'
    view, revealing the spirit-u-el:
Angels by the zillions, filling the
    skies with God's praises,
"Glory to God in the most high
    places!
May the earth know peace and
    all men share his graces."
When those shepherds went to
    find Mary and Joseph right
    at the spoken destination
They celebrated, too, and began
    their declaration.
They just shouted it out; giving God
    the glory with no doubt!

Take this with you: God's love is real and
    strategic. The next time you think that
    he's not real, just remember that he has
    surrounded you with a plan for your life,
    just like he had a plan for Mary's. The only
    thing left for you to do is surrender. So...get
    your hands up!

see? A prophet? Yes, and I tell you, John is more than a prophet. [27]This was written about him:

'I will send my messenger ahead of you,
who will prepare the way for you.'

Malachi 3:1

[28]I tell you, John is greater than any other person ever born, but even the least important person in the kingdom of God is greater than John."

[29](When the people, including the tax collectors, heard this, they all agreed that God's teaching was good, because they had been baptized by John. [30]But the Pharisees and experts on the law refused to accept God's plan for themselves; they did not let John baptize them.)

[31]Then Jesus said, "What shall I say about the people of this time? What are they like? [32]They are like children sitting in the marketplace, calling to one another and saying,

'We played music for you, but you did not dance;
we sang a sad song, but you did not cry.'

He's got answers

Do people of all religions go to heaven?

Heaven, as defined by the Bible, is the place created by God for those who have accepted Jesus as their Savior. You can be a religious-acting person and not go to heaven. You can belong to a Christian church and not go to heaven. You can live a good life and not go to heaven. Religions, churches, and good lives do not determine who goes to heaven and who doesn't. God decides and, according to the Bible, he has set only one way into heaven . . . through his son, Jesus Christ.

Jesus died a horrible death on the cross to pay for the sins of the world, so that anyone who accepts him as their savior can be with him in heaven. Christianity is the only religion where the one worshiped died for his believers and then rose from the dead so they could spend eternity with him in heaven. Think about this: If there were any other way to get into heaven, there would have been no reason for Jesus to die.

Read on: John 14:1-3; Acts 4:10; 1 Corinthians 15:35-57

PEEP THIS:

One in 3 (33 percent) African-American males will be incarcerated or under the supervision of the criminal justice system at some point between the ages of 15 and 25.

[33]John the Baptist came and did not eat bread or drink wine, and you say, 'He has a demon in him.' [34]The Son of Man came eating and drinking, and you say, 'Look at him! He eats too much and drinks too much wine, and he is a friend of tax collectors and sinners!' [35]But wisdom is proved to be right by what it does."

A WOMAN WASHES JESUS' FEET

[36]One of the Pharisees asked Jesus to eat with him, so Jesus went into the Pharisee's house and sat at the table. [37]A sinful woman in the town learned that Jesus was eating at the Pharisee's house. So she brought an alabaster jar of perfume [38]and stood behind Jesus at his feet, crying. She began to wash his feet with her tears, and she dried them with her hair, kissing them many times and rubbing them with the perfume. [39]When the Pharisee who asked Jesus to come to his house saw this, he thought to himself, "If Jesus were a prophet, he would know that the woman touching him is a sinner!"

[40]Jesus said to the Pharisee, "Simon, I have something to say to you."

Simon said, "Teacher, tell me."

[41]Jesus said, "Two people owed money to the same banker. One owed five hundred coins[n] and the other owed fifty. [42]They had no money to pay what they owed, but the banker told both of them they did not have to pay him. Which person will love the banker more?"

[43]Simon, the Pharisee, answered, "I think it would be the one who owed him the most money."

Jesus said to Simon, "You are right." [44]Then Jesus turned toward the woman and said to Simon, "Do you see this woman? When I came into your house, you gave me no water for my feet, but she washed my feet with her tears and dried them with her hair. [45]You gave

---

7:41 coins Roman denarii. One coin was the average pay for one day's work.

me no kiss of greeting, but she has been kissing my feet since I came in. ⁴⁶You did not put oil on my head, but she poured perfume on my feet. ⁴⁷I tell you that her many sins are forgiven, so she showed great love. But the person who is forgiven only a little will love only a little."

⁴⁸Then Jesus said to her, "Your sins are forgiven."

⁴⁹The people sitting at the table began to say among themselves, "Who is this who even forgives sins?"

⁵⁰Jesus said to the woman, "Because you believed, you are saved from your sins. Go in peace."

THE GROUP WITH JESUS

8 After this, while Jesus was traveling through some cities and small towns, he preached and told the Good News about God's kingdom. The twelve apostles were with him, ²and also some women who had been healed of sicknesses and evil spirits: Mary, called Magdalene, from whom seven demons had gone out; ³Joanna, the wife of Cuza (the manager of Herod's house); Susanna; and many others. These women used their own money to help Jesus and his apostles.

A STORY ABOUT PLANTING SEED

⁴When a great crowd was gathered, and people were coming to Jesus from every town, he told them this story:

⁵"A farmer went out to plant his seed. While he was planting, some seed fell by the road. People walked on the seed, and the birds ate it up. ⁶Some seed fell on rock, and when it began to grow, it died because it had no water. ⁷Some seed fell among thorny weeds, but the weeds grew up with it and choked the good plants. ⁸And some seed fell on good ground and grew and made a hundred times more."

As Jesus finished the story, he called out, "Let those with ears use them and listen!"

⁹Jesus' followers asked him what this story meant.

¹⁰Jesus said, "You have been chosen to know the secrets about the kingdom of God. But I use stories to speak to other people so that:

'They will look, but they may not see.

They will listen, but they may not understand.'   *Isaiah 6:9*

¹¹"This is what the story means: The seed is God's message. ¹²The seed that fell beside the road is like the people who hear God's teaching, but the devil comes and takes it away from them so they cannot believe it and be saved. ¹³The seed that fell on rock is like those who hear God's teaching and accept it gladly, but they don't allow the teaching to go deep into their lives. They believe for a while, but when trouble comes, they give up. ¹⁴The seed that fell among the thorny weeds is like those who hear God's teaching, but they let the worries, riches, and pleasures of this life keep them from growing and producing good fruit. ¹⁵And the seed that fell on the good ground is like those who hear God's teaching with good, honest hearts and obey it and patiently produce good fruit.

USE WHAT YOU HAVE

¹⁶"No one after lighting a lamp covers it with a bowl or hides it under a bed. Instead, the person puts it on a lampstand so those who come in will see the light. ¹⁷Everything that is hidden will become clear, and every secret thing will be made known. ¹⁸So be careful how you listen. Those who have understanding will be given more. But those who do not have understanding, even what they think they have will be taken away from them."

JESUS' TRUE FAMILY

¹⁹Jesus' mother and brothers came to see him, but there was such a crowd they could not get to him. ²⁰Someone said to Jesus, "Your mother and your brothers are standing outside, wanting to see you."

VIEWPOINT

WHAT HAS BEEN THE GREATEST SOURCE OF PAIN IN YOUR LIFE AND HOW HAS IT HELPED YOU TO GROW?

Seeing my homeboy get shot. His girl was pregnant, too. He didn't get to see his little girl. That made me change. I'm not all the way there, but I'm getting there.

²¹Jesus answered them, "My mother and my brothers are those who listen to God's teaching and obey it!"

JESUS CALMS A STORM

²²One day Jesus and his followers got into a boat, and he said to them, "Let's go across the lake." And so they started across. ²³While they were sailing, Jesus fell asleep. A very strong wind blew up on the lake, causing the boat to fill with water, and they were in danger.

²⁴The followers went to Jesus and

woke him, saying, "Master! Master! We will drown!"

Jesus got up and gave a command to the wind and the waves. They stopped, and it became calm. [25]Jesus said to his followers, "Where is your faith?"

The followers were afraid and amazed and said to each other, "Who is this that commands even the wind and the water, and they obey him?"

A MAN WITH DEMONS INSIDE HIM

[26]Jesus and his followers sailed across the lake from Galilee to the area of the Gerasene[n] people. [27]When Jesus got out on the land, a man from the town who had demons inside him came to Jesus. For a long time he had worn no clothes and had lived in the burial caves, not in a house. [28]When he saw Jesus, he cried out and fell down before him. He said with a loud voice, "What do you want with me, Jesus, Son of the Most High God? I beg you, don't torture me!" [29]He said this because Jesus was commanding the evil spirit to come out of the man. Many times it had taken hold of him. Though he had been kept under guard and chained hand and foot, he had broken his chains and had been forced by the demon out into a lonely place.

[30]Jesus asked him, "What is your name?"

He answered, "Legion,"[n] because many demons were in him. [31]The demons begged Jesus not to send them into eternal darkness.[n] [32]A large herd of pigs was feeding on a hill, and the demons begged Jesus to allow them to go into the pigs. So Jesus allowed them to do this. [33]When the demons came out of the man, they went into the pigs, and the herd ran down the hill into the lake and was drowned.

[34]When the herdsmen saw what had happened, they ran away and told about this in the town and the countryside. [35]And people went to see what had happened. When they came to Jesus, they found the man sitting at Jesus' feet, clothed and in his right mind, because

the demons were gone. But the people were frightened. [36]The people who saw this happen told the others how Jesus had made the man well. [37]All the people of the Gerasene country asked Jesus to leave, because they were all very afraid. So Jesus got into the boat and went back to Galilee.

[38]The man whom Jesus had healed begged to go with him, but Jesus sent him away, saying, [39]"Go back home and tell people how much God has done for you." So the man went all over town telling how much Jesus had done for him.

GO BACK HOME AND TELL PEOPLE HOW MUCH GOD HAS DONE FOR YOU.

JESUS GIVES LIFE TO A DEAD GIRL AND HEALS A SICK WOMAN

[40]When Jesus got back to Galilee, a crowd welcomed him, because everyone was waiting for him. [41]A man named Jairus, a leader of the synagogue, came to Jesus and fell at his feet, begging him to come to his house. [42]Jairus' only daughter, about twelve years old, was dying.

While Jesus was on his way to Jairus' house, the people were crowding all around him. [43]A woman was in the crowd who had been bleeding for twelve years,[n] but no one was able to heal her. [44]She came up behind Jesus and touched the edge of his coat, and instantly her bleeding stopped. [45]Then Jesus said, "Who touched me?"

When all the people said they had not touched him, Peter said, "Master, the people are all around you and are pushing against you."

[46]But Jesus said, "Someone did touch

me, because I felt power go out from me." [47]When the woman saw she could not hide, she came forward, shaking, and fell down before Jesus. While all the people listened, she told why she had touched him and how she had been instantly healed. [48]Jesus said to her, "Dear woman, you are made well because you believed. Go in peace."

[49]While Jesus was still speaking, someone came from the house of the synagogue leader and said to him, "Your daughter is dead. Don't bother the teacher anymore."

[50]When Jesus heard this, he said to Jairus, "Don't be afraid. Just believe, and your daughter will be well."

[51]When Jesus went to the house, he let only Peter, John, James, and the girl's father and mother go inside with him. [52]All the people were crying and feeling sad because the girl was dead, but Jesus said, "Stop crying. She is not dead, only asleep."

[53]The people laughed at Jesus because they knew the girl was dead. [54]But Jesus took hold of her hand and called to her, "My child, stand up!" [55]Her spirit came back into her, and she stood up at once. Then Jesus ordered that she be given something to eat. [56]The girl's parents were amazed, but Jesus told them not to tell anyone what had happened.

JESUS SENDS OUT THE APOSTLES

9 Jesus called the twelve apostles together and gave them power and authority over all demons and the ability to heal sicknesses. [2]He sent the apostles out to tell about God's kingdom and to heal the sick. [3]He said to them, "Take nothing for your trip, neither a walking stick, bag, bread, money, or extra clothes. [4]When you enter a house, stay there until it is time to leave. [5]If people do not welcome you, shake the dust off of your feet[n] as you leave the town, as a warning to them." [6]So the apostles went out and

---

8:26 Gerasene From Gerasa, an area southeast of Lake Galilee. The exact location is uncertain and some Greek copies read "Gadarene"; others read "Gergesene." **8:30 "Legion"** Means very many. A legion was about five thousand men in the Roman army. **8:31 eternal darkness** Literally, "the abyss," something like a pit or a hole that has no end. **8:43 years** Some Greek copies continue, "and she had spent all the money she had on doctors." **9:5 shake . . . feet** A warning. It showed that they had rejected these people.

REAL RHYMES:

JESUS

BY PLATINUM SOULS

HE OFFERED LIGHT IN MY WORLD OF DARKNESS. ACCEPTED ME WHEN I WAS CRUEL—EVEN HEARTLESS.
KNEW I WASN'T FLAWLESS, YET NEVER THOUGHT LESS OF ME.
SHOWED NOTHING BUT LOVE, AND PROTECTED ME FROM MY ENEMY.
HE WAS THE REMEDY FOR ALL OF MY PAIN. HIS BLOOD WASHED AWAY ALL OF MY SHAME.
GAVE ME A NEW NAME. NOW HE'S THE ONE I CLAIM.

I DROP—JESUS—ON MY FOES, JESUS—IN MY FLOWS, JESUS—ON MY CLOTHES, JESUS—ONLY HE KNOWS.
JESUS—THE WAY TO GO, JESUS—GIMME SOME MORE, JESUS—IS LIKE WHOA, JESUS—STAYS IN CONTROL. JESUS—IS IN MY SOUL, JESUS—IS WHAT I SOW, I
    REAP JESUS—YALL AIN'T KNOW. AWIGHT YO.
JESUS—THE MAGNIFICENT. THE SIGNIFICANT OTHER.
JESUS IS WHO I DISCOVERED WHEN I WAS SEARCHIN' FOR A LOVER.
JESUS—PLEASES US, RELIEVES US, BELIEVES IN US, RECEIVES US.
NEVER GRIEVES US, LEAVES US—NEVER.
CLEVER OPPOSITION TRIES TO STOP THE PROVISION, BUT WE'RE FOREVER ON A MISSION FOR JESUS: THE WAY, THE TRUTH, THE LIFE, THE LIGHT, THE PROOF.
ABSOLUTELY, JESUS—SEES US AT ALL TIMES.
SEASONING, SEIZING, THROUGH THE SEASONS WE REIGN.
EVEN WHEN THE RAIN FALLS THE SUN SHINES AND JESUS IS HIS NAME YALL.

AT 33 HE DIED. ALLOWED HIMSELF TO BE CRUCIFIED.
LAID ASIDE ALL PRIDE SO THAT HIS FAITH COULD BE TRIED.
FOR US HE CRIED—AND NEVER RAN.
INSTEAD HE CARRIED HIS CROSS LIKE A MAN—WITH PURPOSE.
FOR HE KNEW THAT HIS LIFE WAS NOT WORTHLESS.
HE PAID NO ATTENTION WHEN SOME WOULD MOCK.
THE LIES OF THE PHARISEES NEVER CAME AS A SHOCK.
NOT EVEN THE BETRAYAL OF A FRIEND COULD CAUSE HIS COMPASSION TO STOP.
HE IS THE ORIGINAL ROCK.
UNSHAKABLE, UNBREAKABLE, UNMISTAKABLE SAVIOR.
SO SAVE YOUR CONTRADICTIONS, PREDICTIONS, AND THEORIES BECAUSE IF THEY SAY THAT: "JESUS IS NOT THE CHRIST," THEN THEY'RE UNFOUNDATIONAL
    FALLACIES.
AT 33, WHEN TRIED, HE ALLOWED HIMSELF TO BE CRUCIFIED.
WE ARE THE REASON HE DIED.

JESUS—THE NOCTURNAL, INFERNAL IN MY HEART. TURNIN' THIS, BURNIN' THIS, ETERNAL, ETERNALIST.
I'M LEARNIN' THIS 'CAUSE IT'S P—P—PERMANENT, LIKE THE FIRMAMENT. FIRM—NESS.
GOT THAT JESUS GERM AND IT'S CONTAGIOUS. OUTRAGEOUS, THE STAGES OF LIFE, THE PAGES OF CHRIST.
AMAZIN' IT'S SAVIN' BLACKS, CAUCASIANS, ASIANS, KOREANS, CHINESE, LOS, PUERTO RICANS, SOMALIANS, THE WHOLE BODY—AND JESUS THE GUARDIAN.
PARDON, MAKE WAY WHILE I MOVE SOMETHIN'.
ALL YALL KNOW JESUS—STOP FRONTIN'.
SO TAKE YOUR BIG BODY AND BIG STAKES OF DOUGH AND HOPE THAT WHEN JESUS COMES BACK THAT YOU CAN GO.
THE J TO THE C, THE BIG MAC ON THE THRONE.
JESUS—THE NAME ITSELF, ENOUGH SAID WHEN IT'S SOWN.
JESUS—HE'S NOT A BULLY AND HIS LOVE IS FULLY BLOWN.
IF YOU'RE OUT THERE AND YOU'RE LOST—HE'S THE PATHWAY HOME.
    JESUS.

THE WAY, THE TRUTH, THE LIFE. ALWAYS BY MY SIDE.
KEEPS ME SATISFIED. HE IS MY GOD.
ALWAYS PROVIDES FOR ME IT'S JESUS, JESUS.

OVERCOMING

▶ MAKING TIME FOR GOD

In this day and time, life seems to be moving so fast. From the moment you wake up in the morning until the time you go to sleep at night, it's as if you're fighting for more time to get things done. So how could you possibly have time for God?

It is so important to spend a part of your day in fellowship with God. Take Jesus as an example. He was always busy; he could hardly get a moment's rest. So what did he do? He withdrew. We are told in Matthew 14:23, "After he had sent them away, he went by himself up into the hills to pray. It was late, and Jesus was there alone" (See also Luke 5:16.) Jesus took control by finding a time to get away from the things that demanded his time and energy.

You must put everything to the side and make your time with God a priority. When you do, you'll find that throughout every crazy day, you'll feel God with you.

---

traveled through all the towns, preaching the Good News and healing people everywhere.

HEROD IS CONFUSED ABOUT JESUS

[7] Herod, the governor, heard about all the things that were happening and was confused, because some people said, "John the Baptist has risen from the dead." [8] Others said, "Elijah has come to us." And still others said, "One of the prophets who lived long ago has risen from the dead." [9] Herod said, "I cut off John's head, so who is this man I hear such things about?" And Herod kept trying to see Jesus.

MORE THAN FIVE THOUSAND FED

[10] When the apostles returned, they told Jesus everything they had done. Then Jesus took them with him to a town called Bethsaida where they could be alone together. [11] But the people learned where Jesus went and followed him. He welcomed them and talked with them about God's kingdom and healed those who needed to be healed.

[12] Late in the afternoon, the twelve apostles came to Jesus and said, "Send the people away. They need to go to the towns and countryside around here and find places to sleep and something to eat, because no one lives in this place."

[13] But Jesus said to them, "You give them something to eat."

They said, "We have only five loaves of bread and two fish, unless we go buy food for all these people." [14] (There were about five thousand men there.)

Jesus said to his followers, "Tell the people to sit in groups of about fifty people."

[15] So the followers did this, and all the people sat down. [16] Then Jesus took the five loaves of bread and two fish, and looking up to heaven, he thanked God for the food. Then he divided the food and gave it to the followers to give to the people. [17] They all ate and were satisfied, and what was left over was gathered up, filling twelve baskets.

JESUS IS THE CHRIST

[18] One time when Jesus was praying alone, his followers were with him, and he asked them, "Who do the people say I am?"

[19] They answered, "Some say you are John the Baptist. Others say you are Elijah." And others say you are one of the prophets from long ago who has come back to life."

[20] Then Jesus asked, "But who do you say I am?"

Peter answered, "You are the Christ from God."

[21] Jesus warned them not to tell anyone, saying, [22] "The Son of Man must suffer many things. He will be rejected by the Jewish elders, the leading priests, and the teachers of the law. He will be killed and after three days will be raised from the dead."

[23] Jesus said to all of them, "If people want to follow me, they must give up the things they want. They must be willing to give up their lives daily to follow me. [24] Those who want to save their lives will give up true life. But those who give up their lives for me will have true life. [25] It is worthless to have the whole world if they themselves are destroyed or lost. [26] If people are ashamed of me and my teaching, then the Son of Man will be ashamed of them when he comes in his glory and with the glory of the Father and the holy angels. [27] I tell you the truth, some people standing here will see the kingdom of God before they die."

JESUS TALKS WITH MOSES AND ELIJAH

[28] About eight days after Jesus said these things, he took Peter, John, and James and went up on a mountain to pray. [29] While Jesus was praying, the ap-

---

 9:19 Elijah A man who spoke for God and who lived hundreds of years before Christ. See 1 Kings 17.

pearance of his face changed, and his clothes became shining white. [30]Then two men, Moses and Elijah,[n] were talking with Jesus. [31]They appeared in heavenly glory, talking about his departure which he would soon bring about in Jerusalem. [32]Peter and the others were very sleepy, but when they awoke fully, they saw the glory of Jesus and the two men standing with him. [33]When Moses and Elijah were about to leave, Peter said to Jesus, "Master, it is good that we are here. Let us make three tents—one for you, one for Moses, and one for Elijah." (Peter did not know what he was talking about.)

[34]While he was saying these things, a cloud came and covered them, and they became afraid as the cloud covered them. [35]A voice came from the cloud, saying, "This is my Son, whom I have chosen. Listen to him!"

[36]When the voice finished speaking, only Jesus was there. Peter, John, and James said nothing and told no one at that time what they had seen.

JESUS HEALS A SICK BOY

[37]The next day, when they came down from the mountain, a large crowd met Jesus. [38]A man in the crowd shouted to him, "Teacher, please come and look at my son, because he is my only child. [39]An evil spirit seizes my son, and suddenly he screams. It causes him to lose control of himself and foam at the mouth. The evil spirit keeps on hurting him and almost never leaves him. [40]I begged your followers to force the evil spirit out, but they could not do it."

[41]Jesus answered, "You people have no faith, and your lives are all wrong. How long must I stay with you and put up with you? Bring your son here."

[42]While the boy was coming, the demon threw him on the ground and made him lose control of himself. But Jesus gave a strong command to the evil spirit and healed the boy and gave him back to his father. [43]All the people were amazed at the great power of God.

JESUS TALKS ABOUT HIS DEATH

While everyone was wondering about all that Jesus did, he said to his followers, [44]"Don't forget what I tell you now: The Son of Man will be handed over to people." [45]But the followers did not understand what this meant; the meaning was hidden from them so they could not understand. But they were afraid to ask Jesus about it.

WHO IS THE GREATEST?

[46]Jesus' followers began to have an argument about which one of them was the greatest. [47]Jesus knew what they were thinking, so he took a little child and stood the child beside him. [48]Then Jesus said, "Whoever accepts this little

IMPACT!

Holy Hip Hop

Taking gospel to the streets, Holy Hip Hop is a ministry that showcases artists who use their skills in music and entertainment to glorify God. You can view the latest music videos, buy CDs, download ring tones, and buy Holy Hip Hop gear right from their Web site, www.holyhiphop.com. There you can also share your testimony in the free-style chat room with other brothers and sisters, or book an artist for an upcoming event. While surfing the site, you can get information about their annual Hip Hop Artist Showcase and Music Awards and Holy Hip Hop Week activities.

9:30 Moses and Elijah Two of the most important Jewish leaders in the past. God had given Moses the Law, and Elijah was an important prophet.

HEARING GOD'S VOICE

I'll never forget it. It was the first time I'd ever heard God speak to me. Let me start at the beginning. I was in college and I had been approached by one of the fraternities on campus. This fraternity was full of good brothers who were involved in campus activities. I liked their involvement in the community and I was eager to join their "family". I had a friend or two already in the frat and another couple of friends who were going to join with me. It was a great opportunity, or so I thought.

For some reason, I never did feel comfortable joining the group. I wrestled with the idea for days, even weeks. I liked what the group had to offer, and it was just a college organization, right? But I never felt settled about being a part of the frat. I figured that if I felt so much uneasiness about this decision, I should talk to God about it. It seemed silly really, but I bothered God about joining this fraternity for days. Finally, one evening as I was about to go to an interest meeting for

the group, I heard a voice. It was so loud that I jumped and looked to see if someone else was in the room with me. The only thing I heard was, "First Corinthians 2:9!" It was a booming voice, and that's all it said. I immediately found a Bible and looked up the Scripture. It was my answer: "But as it is written in the Scriptures: 'No one has ever seen this, and no one has ever heard about it. No one has ever imagined what God has prepared for those who love him.'"

I know it sounds strange, but that's how it happened. Somehow I knew I was not to join the fraternity. It was much later that I found out why. A few years after I graduated, members of that same fraternity at my college were arrested for hazing. A young man almost died during a fraternity ritual. I watched the news in awe as I saw people I went to school with—people who joined before and after I would have—escorted to police vehicles in handcuffs. God had protected me years earlier from ruining my life and career. Had I joined, I could have been in handcuffs with all the others. I'm not knocking fraternities; my father was in one, and I'm friends with several of the older guys from the fraternity I considered joining. But because I listened to God's voice one evening, I avoided a huge pitfall and found out that God's plans for me are always best.

child in my name accepts me. And whoever accepts me accepts the One who sent me, because whoever is least among you all is really the greatest."

ANYONE NOT AGAINST US IS FOR US

[49]John answered, "Master, we saw someone using your name to force demons out of people. We told him to stop, because he does not belong to our group."

[50]But Jesus said to him, "Don't stop him, because whoever is not against you is for you."

A TOWN REJECTS JESUS

[51]When the time was coming near for Jesus to depart, he was determined to go to Jerusalem. [52]He sent some messengers ahead of him, who went into a town in Samaria to make everything ready for him. [53]But the people there would not welcome him, because he was set on going to Jerusalem. [54]When James and John, followers of Jesus, saw this, they said, "Lord, do you want us to call fire down from heaven and destroy those people?"[n]

[55]But Jesus turned and scolded them. [And Jesus said, "You don't know what kind of spirit you belong to. [56]The Son of Man did not come to destroy the souls of people but to save them."][n] Then they went to another town.

FOLLOWING JESUS

[57]As they were going along the road, someone said to Jesus, "I will follow you any place you go."

[58]Jesus said to them, "The foxes have holes to live in, and the birds have nests, but the Son of Man has no place to rest his head."

[59]Jesus said to another man, "Follow me!"

But he said, "Lord, first let me go and bury my father."

[60]But Jesus said to him, "Let the people who are dead bury their own dead. You must go and tell about the kingdom of God."

[61]Another man said, "I will follow you, Lord, but first let me go and say good-bye to my family."

[62]Jesus said, "Anyone who begins to plow a field but keeps looking back is of no use in the kingdom of God."

 9:54 people Some Greek copies continue "as Elijah did." **9:55-56 And . . . them.** Some Greek copies do not contain the bracketed text.

JESUS SENDS OUT THE SEVENTY-TWO

10 After this, the Lord chose seventy-two[n] others and sent them out in pairs ahead of him into every town and place where he planned to go. [2]He said to them, "There are a great many people to harvest, but there are only a few workers. So pray to God, who owns the harvest, that he will send more workers to help gather his harvest. [3]Go now, but listen! I am sending you out like sheep among wolves. [4]Don't carry a purse, a bag, or sandals, and don't waste time talking with people on the road. [5]Before you go into a house, say, 'Peace be with this house.' [6]If peace-loving people live there, your blessing of peace will stay with them, but if not, then your blessing will come back to you. [7]Stay in the same house, eating and drinking what the people there give you. A worker should be given his pay. Don't move from house to house. [8]If you go into a town and the people welcome you, eat what they give you. [9]Heal the sick who live there, and tell them, 'The kingdom of God is near you.' [10]But if you go into a town, and the people don't welcome you, then go into the streets and say, [11]'Even the dirt from your town that sticks to our feet we wipe off against you.[n] But remember that the kingdom of God is near.' [12]I tell you, on the Judgment Day it will be better for the people of Sodom[n] than for the people of that town.

JESUS WARNS UNBELIEVERS

[13]"How terrible for you, Korazin! How terrible for you, Bethsaida! If the miracles I did in you had happened in Tyre and Sidon,[n] those people would have changed their lives long ago. They would have worn rough cloth and put ashes on themselves to show they had changed. [14]But on the Judgment Day it will be better for Tyre and Sidon than for you. [15]And you, Capernaum,[n] will you be lifted up to heaven? No! You will be thrown down to the depths!

[16]"Whoever listens to you listens to me, and whoever refuses to accept you refuses to accept me. And whoever refuses to accept me refuses to accept the One who sent me."

SATAN FALLS

[17]When the seventy-two[n] came back, they were very happy and said, "Lord, even the demons obeyed us when we used your name!"

[18]Jesus said, "I saw Satan fall like lightning from heaven. [19]Listen, I have given you power to walk on snakes and scorpions, power that is greater than the enemy has. So nothing will hurt you. [20]But you should not be happy because the spirits obey you but because your names are written in heaven."

JESUS PRAYS TO THE FATHER

[21]Then Jesus rejoiced in the Holy Spirit and said, "I praise you, Father, Lord of heaven and earth, because you have hidden these things from the people who are wise and smart. But you have shown them to those who are like little children. Yes, Father, this is what you really wanted.

[22]"My Father has given me all things. No one knows who the Son is, except the Father. And no one knows who the Father is, except the Son and those whom the Son chooses to tell."

[23]Then Jesus turned to his followers and said privately, "You are blessed to see what you now see. [24]I tell you, many prophets and kings wanted to see what you now see, but they did not, and they wanted to hear what you now hear, but they did not."

THE GOOD SAMARITAN

[25]Then an expert on the law stood up to test Jesus, saying, "Teacher, what must I do to get life forever?"

[26]Jesus said, "What is written in the law? What do you read there?"

[27]The man answered, "Love the Lord your God with all your heart, all your soul, all your strength, and all your mind."[n] Also, "Love your neighbor as you love yourself."[n]

[28]Jesus said to him, "Your answer is right. Do this and you will live."

[29]But the man, wanting to show the importance of his question, said to Jesus, "And who is my neighbor?"

PEEP THIS:

African-Americans have the highest rate of infection with sexually transmitted diseases in the nation. Compared to Whites, African-Americans are 24 times more likely to have gonorrhea and 8 times more likely to have syphilis.

[30]Jesus answered, "As a man was going down from Jerusalem to Jericho, some robbers attacked him. They tore off his clothes, beat him, and left him lying there, almost dead. [31]It happened that a priest was going down that road. When he saw the man, he walked by on the other side. [32]Next, a Levite[n] came there, and after he went over and looked at the man, he walked by on the other side of the road. [33]Then a Samaritan[n] traveling down the road came to where the hurt man was. When he saw the man, he felt very sorry for him. [34]The Samaritan went to him, poured olive oil and wine[n] on his wounds, and bandaged them. Then he put the hurt man on his own donkey and took him to an inn where he cared

10:1, 17 seventy-two Some Greek copies read "seventy." **10:11 dirt . . . you** A warning. It showed that they had rejected these people. **10:12 Sodom** City that God destroyed because the people were so evil. **10:13 Tyre and Sidon** Towns where wicked people lived. **10:13, 15 Korazin, Bethsaida, Capernaum** Towns by Lake Galilee where Jesus preached to the people. **10:27 "Love . . . mind."** Quotation from Deuteronomy 6:5. **10:27 "Love . . . yourself."** Quotation from Leviticus 19:18. **10:32 Levite** Levites were members of the tribe of Levi who helped the Jewish priests with their work in the Temple. Read 1 Chronicles 23:24-32. **10:33 Samaritan** Samaritans were people from Samaria. These people were part Jewish, but the Jews did not accept them as true Jews. Samaritans and Jews disliked each other. **10:34 olive oil and wine** Oil and wine were used like medicine to soften and clean wounds.

for him. [35]The next day, the Samaritan brought out two coins,[n] gave them to the innkeeper, and said, 'Take care of this man. If you spend more money on him, I will pay it back to you when I come again.' "

[36]Then Jesus said, "Which one of these three men do you think was a neighbor to the man who was attacked by the robbers?"

[37]The expert on the law answered, "The one who showed him mercy."

Jesus said to him, "Then go and do what he did."

MARY AND MARTHA

[38]While Jesus and his followers were traveling, Jesus went into a town. A woman named Martha let Jesus stay at her house. [39]Martha had a sister named Mary, who was sitting at Jesus' feet and listening to him teach. [40]But Martha was busy with all the work to be done. She went in and said, "Lord, don't you care that my sister has left me alone to do all the work? Tell her to help me."

[41]But the Lord answered her, "Martha, Martha, you are worried and upset about many things. [42]Only one thing is important. Mary has chosen the better thing, and it will never be taken away from her."

JESUS TEACHES ABOUT PRAYER

11 One time Jesus was praying in a certain place. When he finished, one of his followers said to him, "Lord, teach us to pray as John taught his followers."

[2]Jesus said to them, "When you pray, say:

'Father, may your name always be kept holy.
May your kingdom come.
[3]Give us the food we need for each day.
[4]Forgive us for our sins,
because we forgive everyone who has done wrong to us.

And do not cause us to be tempted.' "[n]

CONTINUE TO ASK

[5]Then Jesus said to them, "Suppose one of you went to your friend's house at midnight and said to him, 'Friend, loan me three loaves of bread. [6]A friend of mine has come into town to visit me, but I have nothing for him to eat.' [7]Your friend inside the house answers, 'Don't bother me! The door is already locked, and my children and I are in bed. I cannot get up and give you anything.' [8]I tell you, if friendship is not enough to make him get up to give you the bread, your boldness will make him get up and give you whatever you need. [9]So I tell you, ask, and God will give to you. Search, and you will find. Knock, and the door will open for you. [10]Yes, everyone who asks will receive. The one who searches will find. And everyone who knocks will have the door opened. [11]If your children ask for[n] a fish, which of you would give them a snake instead? [12]Or, if your children ask for an egg, would you give them a scorpion? [13]Even though you are bad, you know how to give good things to your children. How much more your heavenly Father will give the Holy Spirit to those who ask him!"

JESUS' POWER IS FROM GOD

[14]One time Jesus was sending out a demon who could not talk. When the demon came out, the man who had been unable to speak, then spoke. The people were amazed. [15]But some of them said, "Jesus uses the power of Beelzebul, the ruler of demons, to force demons out of people."

[16]Other people, wanting to test Jesus, asked him to give them a sign from heaven. [17]But knowing their thoughts, he said to them, "Every kingdom that is divided against itself will be destroyed. And a family that is divided against itself will not continue. [18]So if Satan is divided against himself, his kingdom will not continue. You say that I use the power of Beelzebul to force out demons.

[19]But if I use the power of Beelzebul to force out demons, what power do your people use to force demons out? So they will be your judges. [20]But if I use the power of God to force out demons, then the kingdom of God has come to you.

[21]"When a strong person with many weapons guards his own house, his possessions are safe. [22]But when someone stronger comes and defeats him, the stronger one will take away the weapons the first man trusted and will give away the possessions.

[23]"Anyone who is not with me is against me, and anyone who does not work with me is working against me.

THE EMPTY PERSON

[24]"When an evil spirit comes out of a person, it travels through dry places, looking for a place to rest. But when it finds no place, it says, 'I will go back to the house I left.' [25]And when it comes back, it finds that house swept clean and made neat. [26]Then the evil spirit goes out and brings seven other spirits more evil than it is, and they go in and live there. So the person has even more trouble than before."

PEOPLE WHO ARE TRULY BLESSED

[27]As Jesus was saying these things, a woman in the crowd called out to Jesus, "Blessed is the mother who gave birth to you and nursed you."

[28]But Jesus said, "No, blessed are those who hear the teaching of God and obey it."

THE PEOPLE WANT A MIRACLE

[29]As the crowd grew larger, Jesus said, "The people who live today are evil. They want to see a miracle for a sign, but no sign will be given them, except the sign of Jonah.[n] [30]As Jonah was a sign for those people who lived in Nineveh, the Son of Man will be a sign for the people of this time. [31]On the Judgment Day the Queen of the South[n] will stand up with the people who live now. She will show they are guilty, because she came from far away to listen to Solomon's wise

10:35 coins Roman denarii. One coin was the average pay for one day's work.   **11:2–4 'Father . . . tempted.'** Some Greek copies include phrases from Matthew's version of this prayer (Matthew 6:9–13).   **11:11 for** Some Greek copies include the phrase "for bread, which of you would give them a stone, or if they ask for . . ."   **11:29 sign of Jonah** Jonah's three days in the fish are like Jesus' three days in the tomb. See Matthew 12:40.   **11:31 Queen of the South** The Queen of Sheba. She traveled a thousand miles to learn God's wisdom from Solomon. Read 1 Kings 10:1–3.

▶ **102**

CONNECTED

THE RIGHT CONNECTION TO MONEY:
ROOT OF ALL EVIL.

We tend to put a high value on money and not much else. People pull scams and rob stores for "quick cash" or get into marriages because they want to gain more of their most prized possession: money. Ask yourself, "How shallow am I if the only thing I want in life is money?" It's okay to enjoy money and the many wonderful things it can provide, but do you tend to take it a bit too far? Do you actually love money? Loving money can leave you open and vulnerable for the many attacks of the enemy. You begin to separate yourself from your family, your friends, and most importantly, from God. You hold yourself in higher esteem than the rest of the world. You begin to forget who you are, where you have come from, and who helped get you where you are.

Many people think that money equals success, but the definition of success really varies from person to person. For some people, success is graduating from college and getting a good job. For others it may be having a great marriage or an effective ministry. Even then, the point is to never get too dependent on any of these *things* in your life.

In Luke 18, there was a rich man who told Jesus that he wanted eternal life. Jesus told the man to sell everything, distribute the proceeds to the poor, and then follow Jesus. The man just couldn't part with his stuff.

Is there something that you think you just can't live without—something that you'd give up God for? There is really nothing you need in your life but Christ. He'll provide everything else (Matthew 6:33-34). Don't let anything else go to your head. Stay grounded through God. Material things only last for a season, but God is forever. Everything you have belongs to him anyway, and he can take it away if it's not used wisely. Be successful, enjoy money, but always keep God first, and don't take your success for granted or abuse your privileges. Remember greediness is at the root of evil. Why add on extra drama?

teaching. And I tell you that someone greater than Solomon is here. [32]On the Judgment Day the people of Nineveh will stand up with the people who live now, and they will show that you are guilty. When Jonah preached to them, they were sorry and changed their lives. And I tell you that someone greater than Jonah is here.

BE A LIGHT FOR THE WORLD

[33]"No one lights a lamp and puts it in a secret place or under a bowl, but on a lampstand so the people who come in can see. [34]Your eye is a light for the body. When your eyes are good, your whole body will be full of light. But when your eyes are evil, your whole body will be full of darkness. [35]So be careful not to let the light in you become darkness. [36]If your whole body is full of light, and none of it is dark, then you will shine bright, as when a lamp shines on you."

JESUS ACCUSES THE PHARISEES

[37]After Jesus had finished speaking, a Pharisee asked Jesus to eat with him. So Jesus went in and sat at the table. [38]But the Pharisee was surprised when he saw that Jesus did not wash his hands[n] before the meal. [39]The Lord said to him, "You Pharisees clean the outside of the cup and the dish, but inside you are full of greed and evil. [40]You foolish people! The same one who made what is outside also made what is inside. [41]So give what is in your dishes to the poor, and then you will be fully clean. [42]How terrible for you Pharisees! You give God one-tenth of even your mint, your rue, and every other plant in your garden. But you fail to be fair to others and to love God. These are the things you should do while continuing to do those other things. [43]How terrible for you Pharisees, because you love to have the most important seats in the synagogues, and you love to be greeted with respect in the marketplaces. [44]How terrible for you, because you are like hidden graves, which people walk on without knowing."

11:38 wash his hands This was a Jewish religious custom that the Pharisees thought was very important.

JESUS TALKS TO EXPERTS ON THE LAW

[45]One of the experts on the law said to Jesus, "Teacher, when you say these things, you are insulting us, too."

[46]Jesus answered, "How terrible for you, you experts on the law! You make strict rules that are very hard for people to obey, but you yourselves don't even try to follow those rules. [47]How terrible for you, because you build tombs for the prophets whom your ancestors killed! [48]And now you show that you approve of what your ancestors did. They killed the prophets, and you build tombs for them! [49]This is why in his wisdom God said, 'I will send prophets and apostles to them. They will kill some, and they will treat others cruelly.' [50]So you who live now will be punished for the deaths of all the prophets who were killed since the beginning of the world— [51]from the killing of Abel to the killing of Zechariah,[n] who died between the altar and the Temple. Yes, I tell you that you who are alive now will be punished for them all.

[52]"How terrible for you, you experts on the law. You have taken away the key to learning about God. You yourselves would not learn, and you stopped others from learning, too."

[53]When Jesus left, the teachers of the law and the Pharisees began to give him trouble, asking him questions about many things, [54]trying to catch him saying something wrong.

11:51 Abel . . . Zechariah In the Hebrew Old Testament, the first and last men to be murdered.

DON'T BE LIKE THE PHARISEES

12 So many thousands of people had gathered that they were stepping on each other. Jesus spoke

THE SCRIPT

The Parable of the Lost Son
Luke 15:11-32

A story Jesus told, about two brothers and their dad, who loved their souls.
"Now the younger one had a hunger for wealth and wanted his props.
So he said to Pops, 'I know I got a lot of money coming to me later; but I want mine now.'
So his daddy reluctantly took his inheritance and cashed the young brother out.
With plenty yens, he moved from home to far away. Livin' loud, eatin' and carousin' everyday;
Burning grain cause money just wasn't a thang.
Til them ends started to drain and then thangs started to change!
Hard times came right to his town, and all his money ran out! Oww!
So he found a gig feeding some pigs.
Once, when he was hungry, he tried to steal pig slop.
Nobody cared about him. Then he came to himself. He woke up!
He stopped and began to compare, 'My daddy's slaves got food to spare
And I'm on welfare. Man, yo, I'm outta here!'
Now headed on the right road, still a good ways off,
His father saw him. His heart had remained soft.
Pops got up, ran out to greet his son with much love, big kisses, and bear hugs.
Son said, 'Daddy, I've missed you, dissed you, and dissed God.'
But his father wasn't listenin',
Instead called his staff members to quickly make provisions!
Let's get the fattest calf we got and kill him!
This is a new holiday that I've just written in.
'Cause my son's back! He was dead and now he lives again.'
Now, when the day was ended, the older son finally came home through the kitchen;
Tired from all day long tending to the family business.
Hearing all the ruckus, he was like, 'Wait a minute . . .'

Music blasting, people dancing, so he asked one of the valets, 'What is this?'
Little man said, 'Your brother just made it back home uninjured and safe,
And your daddy's so happy that he's celebrating with a fat, juicy steak.'
The news hit the older brother hard 'tween the shoulders!
He said, 'Hold-up, this is how you gone' play me?
All these years I served you, no complaining, nearly slavery!
Then this thang you call a son, who wasted all your chips
On partying, clothes, and wild women comes back and you ready to turn flips?'
His father said, 'Son, you don't think I see that you're the faithful one?
And everything I got belongs to you 'cause you're the stable one?
But a good fate has come and we have to celebrate the blessing.
Your brother wrestled death and came out alive possessing
The best thing he could ever own. See, he lost his way but he finally found home.'"

Take this with you: No matter how badly you mess things up, no matter how dirty and lost you become, God will always be waiting to welcome you back. His love doesn't end even when you turn away from him and destroy the good things he has given you. He will always be there to welcome you back home.

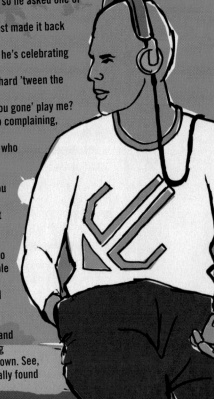

first to his followers, saying, "Beware of the yeast of the Pharisees, because they are hypocrites. [2]Everything that is hidden will be shown, and everything that is secret will be made known. [3]What you have said in the dark will be heard in the light, and what you have whispered in an inner room will be shouted from the housetops.

[4]"I tell you, my friends, don't be afraid of people who can kill the body but after that can do nothing more to hurt you. [5]I will show you the one to fear. Fear the one who has the power to kill you and also to throw you into hell. Yes, this is the one you should fear.

[6]"Five sparrows are sold for only two pennies, and God does not forget any of them. [7]But God even knows how many hairs you have on your head. Don't be afraid. You are worth much more than many sparrows.

DON'T BE ASHAMED OF JESUS

[8]"I tell you, all those who stand before others and say they believe in me, I, the Son of Man, will say before the angels of God that they belong to me. [9]But all who stand before others and say they do not believe in me, I will say before the angels of God that they do not belong to me.

[10]"Anyone who speaks against the Son of Man can be forgiven, but anyone who speaks against the Holy Spirit will not be forgiven.

[11]"When you are brought into the synagogues before the leaders and other powerful people, don't worry about how to defend yourself or what to say. [12]At that time the Holy Spirit will teach you what you must say."

JESUS WARNS AGAINST SELFISHNESS

[13]Someone in the crowd said to Jesus, "Teacher, tell my brother to divide with me the property our father left us."

[14]But Jesus said to him, "Who said I should judge or decide between you?" [15]Then Jesus said to them, "Be careful and guard against all kinds of greed.

Life is not measured by how much one owns."

[16]Then Jesus told this story: "There was a rich man who had some land, which grew a good crop. [17]He thought to himself, 'What will I do? I have no place to keep all my crops.' [18]Then he said, 'This is what I will do: I will tear down my barns and build bigger ones, and there I will store all my grain and other goods. [19]Then I can say to myself, "I have enough good things stored to last for many years. Rest, eat, drink, and enjoy life!" '

[20]"But God said to him, 'Foolish man! Tonight your life will be taken from you. So who will get those things you have prepared for yourself?'

[21]"This is how it will be for those who store up things for themselves and are not rich toward God."

> LIFE IS NOT MEASURED BY HOW MUCH ONE OWNS.

DON'T WORRY

[22]Jesus said to his followers, "So I tell you, don't worry about the food you need to live, or about the clothes you need for your body. [23]Life is more than food, and the body is more than clothes. [24]Look at the birds. They don't plant or harvest, they don't have storerooms or barns, but God feeds them. And you are worth much more than birds. [25]You cannot add any time to your life by worrying about it. [26]If you cannot do even the little things, then why worry about the big things? [27]Consider how the lilies grow; they don't work or make clothes for themselves. But I tell you that even Solomon with his riches was not dressed as beautifully as one of these flowers. [28]God clothes the grass in the field,

which is alive today but tomorrow is thrown into the fire. So how much more will God clothe you? Don't have so little faith! [29]Don't always think about what you will eat or what you will drink, and don't keep worrying. [30]All the people in the world are trying to get these things, and your Father knows you need them. [31]But seek God's kingdom, and all your other needs will be met as well.

DON'T TRUST IN MONEY

[32]"Don't fear, little flock, because your Father wants to give you the kingdom. [33]Sell your possessions and give to the poor. Get for yourselves purses that will not wear out, the treasure in heaven that never runs out, where thieves can't steal and moths can't destroy. [34]Your heart will be where your treasure is.

ALWAYS BE READY

[35]"Be dressed, ready for service, and have your lamps shining. [36]Be like servants who are waiting for their master to come home from a wedding party. When he comes and knocks, the servants immediately open the door for him. [37]They will be blessed when their master comes home, because he sees that they were watching for him. I tell you the truth, the master will dress himself to serve and tell the servants to sit at the table, and he will serve them. [38]Those servants will be blessed when he comes in and finds them still waiting, even if it is midnight or later.

[39]"Remember this: If the owner of the house knew what time a thief was coming, he would not allow the thief to enter his house. [40]So you also must be ready, because the Son of Man will come at a time when you don't expect him!"

WHO IS THE TRUSTED SERVANT?

[41]Peter said, "Lord, did you tell this story to us or to all people?"

[42]The Lord said, "Who is the wise and trusted servant that the master trusts to give the other servants their food at the right time? [43]When the master comes and finds the servant doing his work, the

servant will be blessed. [44]I tell you the truth, the master will choose that servant to take care of everything he owns. [45]But suppose the servant thinks to himself, 'My master will not come back soon,' and he begins to beat the other servants, men and women, and to eat and drink and get drunk. [46]The master will come when that servant is not ready and is not expecting him. Then the master will cut him in pieces and send him away to be with the others who don't obey.

[47]"The servant who knows what his master wants but is not ready, or who does not do what the master wants, will be beaten with many blows! [48]But the servant who does not know what his master wants and does things that should be punished will be beaten with few blows. From everyone who has been given much, much will be demanded. And from the one trusted with much, much more will be expected.

JESUS CAUSES DIVISION

[49]"I came to set fire to the world, and I wish it were already burning! [50]I have a baptism[n] to suffer through, and I feel

He's got answers

Can Christians be involved in politics? Is there a right and wrong way to vote?

There is nothing in the Bible to indicate that Christians shouldn't be involved in politics. According to the scriptures, all authority comes from God and Christians are commanded to be good citizens.

What should Christians do politically? Pray for your country and your leaders, whether you agree with them or not. Respect the positions they hold even if you can't respect the persons or their views. Christians should exercise all of the rights granted them under the law.

Is there a right and wrong way to vote? Of course there is. Does it reside with one political party over another? No, it doesn't. There are godly people and issues on both sides of the political fence, and many of them are quite loud in expressing their views. So, what is the right way to vote? According to what the Bible teaches, even if this is unpopular. How do you figure out what that is? Read God's Word regarding the issues.

Read on: Matthew 22:17-21; Romans 13:1-6; Titus 3:1; 1 Peter 2:13-17

PEEP THIS:

In 2000, HIV/AIDS was among the top three causes of death for African-American men aged 25 to 54 and African-American women aged 35 to 44. African-Americans have accounted for 39 percent of the AIDS cases diagnosed since the beginning of the epidemic.

very troubled until it is over. [51]Do you think I came to give peace to the earth? No, I tell you, I came to divide it. [52]From now on, a family with five people will be divided, three against two, and two against three. [53]They will be divided: father against son and son against father, mother against daughter and daughter against mother, mother-in-law against daughter-in-law and daughter-in-law against mother-in-law."

UNDERSTANDING THE TIMES

[54]Then Jesus said to the people, "When you see clouds coming up in the west, you say, 'It's going to rain,' and it happens. [55]When you feel the wind begin to blow from the south, you say, 'It will be a hot day,' and it happens. [56]Hypocrites! You know how to understand the appearance of the earth and sky. Why don't you understand what is happening now?

SETTLE YOUR PROBLEMS

[57]"Why can't you decide for yourselves what is right? [58]If your enemy is taking you to court, try hard to settle it on the way. If you don't, your enemy might take you to the judge, and the judge might turn you over to the officer, and the officer might throw you into jail. [59]I tell you, you will not get out of there until you have paid everything you owe."

12:50 I . . . baptism Jesus was talking about the suffering he would soon go through.

CHANGE YOUR HEARTS

13 At that time some people were there who told Jesus that Pilate[n] had killed some people from Galilee while they were worshiping. He mixed their blood with the blood of the animals they were sacrificing to God. [2]Jesus answered, "Do you think this happened to them because they were more sinful than all others from Galilee? [3]No, I tell you. But unless you change your hearts and lives, you will be destroyed as they were! [4]What about those eighteen people who died when the tower of Siloam fell on them? Do you think they were more sinful than all the others who live in Jerusalem? [5]No, I tell you. But unless you change your hearts and lives, you will all be destroyed too!"

THE USELESS TREE

[6]Jesus told this story: "A man had a fig tree planted in his vineyard. He came looking for some fruit on the tree, but he found none. [7]So the man said to his gardener, 'I have been looking for fruit on this tree for three years, but I never find any. Cut it down. Why should it waste the ground?' [8]But the servant answered, 'Master, let the tree have one more year to produce fruit. Let me dig up the dirt around it and put on some fertilizer. [9]If the tree produces fruit next year, good. But if not, you can cut it down.'"

JESUS HEALS ON THE SABBATH

[10]Jesus was teaching in one of the synagogues on the Sabbath day. [11]A woman was there who, for eighteen years, had an evil spirit in her that made her crippled. Her back was always bent; she could not stand up straight. [12]When Jesus saw her, he called her over and

13:1 **Pilate** Pontius Pilate was the Roman governor of Judea from A.D. 26 to A.D. 36.

HOW YA TRAVELIN'?

HANDLING CONFLICT

"You will know the truth, and the truth will make you free" (John 8:32).

Why do people lie? Chances are that every fictional account you ever came up with was designed to help you avoid some conflict. You felt that if you told the truth, somebody was going to start trippin'. You couldn't handle that kind of reaction, so you lied. Half-truth, outright denial, cover-up—whatever—you compromised the truth in order to avoid conflict. Why? Most likely because the ugliest, deepest, and most painful wounds that Satan has ever inflicted in your life came through conflicts with other human beings.

God has a better way. Don't be afraid of conflict, and don't lie to avoid it. When someone is sweatin' you, ask them this question: "Do I understand you to say . . . ?" (The reason playas hate these words is because they don't want to understand anybody else's point of view. They don't care. They just want to win the argument.) If you want to resolve your arguments quickly, try presenting your opponent's case. That's right. Try to state the other person's argument in your own words. Start with his or her strongest point. And don't be half-hearted about doing so. When you feed back his precise argument, he will know that you have heard him. Then, he may be more willing and able to hear what you have to say, even if you disagree with him. Tell him the truth, whether he agrees with you or not. God wants you to live in freedom.

A GENTLE ANSWER WILL CALM ANGER – PROVERBS 15:1

365

1 HOLIDAY—April Fools Day

2

3

4 On This Day In History 1968—Martin Luther King, Jr. assassinated in
   Memphis, Tennessee.

5 It's your birthday, Colin Powell!

6

7

8 On This Day In History 1974—Henry "Hank"
   Aaron set new homerun record.

9

"No one is immune
to the trials and
tribulations of life."
- Martin Lawrence

10 Think outside
11 the box:
12 How can I best use
13 the talents God has
14 given me?
15

16 Happy Birthday Martin Lawrence!

17

18

19 Visit a local nursing home
20 and bring cheer.

21

22 HOLIDAY—Earth Day

23

24 Participate in an Earth Day activity

25

26 It's your birthday, Tionne Watkins (aka T-Boz)!

27

28

29 Daylight Savings Time begins—spring foward (move your clock up 1 hour).

30

31

MUSIC REVIEWS

ARTIST: BONE THUGS N HARMONY   **ALBUM:** EAST 1999
CUT: "HELL SENT"

Here are some lyrics from Bone Thugs N Harmony that live up to their name: "Hell sent, they call me rip for a reason. I'm on a road to see bloody bodies, just call me a demon."

Bone Thugs N Harmony are some of the most influential rappers of our era. Their hip-hop style is very unique and captivating, but their lyrics are hellish. They mix claims of alliance to the devil with mesmerizing vocals and chants. They also perform "witchcraft"-type practices in their video and photos—such as levitation, crystal ball readings, Ouija board séances, and plenty of weed smokin', murda, and dope selling. In one of their videos, they even mock the cloven tongues of fire that appeared upon the disciples' heads in the New Testament, while gathered around a crystal ball. They are way out there.

"REJECTED"

---

said, "Woman, you are free from your sickness." [13]Jesus put his hands on her, and immediately she was able to stand up straight and began praising God.

[14]The synagogue leader was angry because Jesus healed on the Sabbath day. He said to the people, "There are six days when one has to work. So come to be healed on one of those days, and not on the Sabbath day."

[15]The Lord answered, "You hypocrites! Doesn't each of you untie your work animals and lead them to drink water every day—even on the Sabbath day? [16]This woman that I healed, a daughter of Abraham, has been held by Satan for eighteen years. Surely it is not wrong for her to be freed from her sickness on a Sabbath day!" [17]When Jesus said this, all of those who were criticizing him were ashamed, but the entire crowd rejoiced at all the wonderful things Jesus was doing.

STORIES OF MUSTARD SEED AND YEAST

[18]Then Jesus said, "What is God's kingdom like? What can I compare it with? [19]It is like a mustard seed that a man plants in his garden. The seed grows and becomes a tree, and the wild birds build nests in its branches."

[20]Jesus said again, "What can I compare God's kingdom with? [21]It is like yeast that a woman took and hid in a large tub of flour until it made all the dough rise."

THE NARROW DOOR

[22]Jesus was teaching in every town and village as he traveled toward Jerusalem. [23]Someone said to Jesus, "Lord, will only a few people be saved?"

Jesus said, [24]"Try hard to enter through the narrow door, because many people will try to enter there, but they will not be able. [25]When the owner of the house gets up and closes the door, you can stand outside and knock on the door and say, 'Sir, open the door for us.' But he will answer, 'I don't know you or where you come from.' [26]Then you will say, 'We ate and drank with you, and you taught in the streets of our town.' [27]But he will say to you, 'I don't know you or where you come from. Go away

from me, all you who do evil!' [28]You will cry and grind your teeth with pain when you see Abraham, Isaac, Jacob, and all the prophets in God's kingdom, but you yourselves thrown outside. [29]People will come from the east, west, north, and south and will sit down at the table in the kingdom of God. [30]There are those who are last now who will be first in the future. And there are those who are first now who will be last in the future."

JESUS WILL DIE IN JERUSALEM

[31]At that time some Pharisees came to Jesus and said, "Go away from here! Herod wants to kill you!"

[32]Jesus said to them, "Go tell that fox Herod, 'Today and tomorrow I am forcing demons out and healing people. Then, on the third day, I will reach my goal.' [33]Yet I must be on my way today and tomorrow and the next day. Surely it cannot be right for a prophet to be killed anywhere except in Jerusalem.

[34]"Jerusalem, Jerusalem! You kill the prophets and stone to death those who are sent to you. Many times I wanted to gather your people as a hen gath-

ers her chicks under her wings, but you would not let me. [35] Now your house is left completely empty. I tell you, you will not see me until that time when you will say, 'God bless the One who comes in the name of the Lord.' "[n]

HEALING ON THE SABBATH

 On a Sabbath day, when Jesus went to eat at the home of a leading Pharisee, the people were watching Jesus very closely. [2] And in front of him was a man with dropsy.[n] [3] Jesus said to the Pharisees and experts on the law, "Is it right or wrong to heal on the Sabbath day?" [4] But they would not answer his question. So Jesus took the man, healed him, and sent him away. [5] Jesus said to the Pharisees and teachers of the law, "If your child[n] or ox falls into a well on the Sabbath day, will you not pull him out quickly?" [6] And they could not answer him.

DON'T MAKE YOURSELF IMPORTANT

[7] When Jesus noticed that some of the guests were choosing the best places to sit, he told this story: [8] "When someone invites you to a wedding feast, don't take the most important seat, because someone more important than you may have been invited. [9] The host, who invited both of you, will come to you and say, 'Give this person your seat.' Then you will be embarrassed and will have to move to the last place. [10] So when you are invited, go sit in a seat that is not important. When the host comes to you, he may say, 'Friend, move up here to a more important place.' Then all the other guests

13:35 'God . . . Lord.' Quotation from Psalm 118:26. **14:2 dropsy** A sickness that causes the body to swell larger and larger. **14:5 child** Some Greek copies read "donkey."

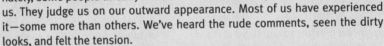

DEEP ISSUES

Racism

We are defined in various ways—by our skin color, our background, our nationality, our neighborhood, our clothes, our music, and our faith. At first glance, people can pick out some things that describe us. They can look at us and know our skin color and maybe guess our nationality. But they can never truly know the real us by just a casual look. Unfortunately, some people already have their minds made up about us. They judge us on our outward appearance. Most of us have experienced it—some more than others. We've heard the rude comments, seen the dirty looks, and felt the tension.

No, it's not fair. How do we usually respond? Let's be real! We feel angry and discriminated against, and many times we feed others' stereotypes. It feels good to lash back with words like, "What you looking at?" Or to respond with an ice grill or some hand motions. But think about it for a minute. Does that change anything? That person just walked away thinking we are exactly what they had imagined, and so is everybody *else* who looks similar to us. So did we solve anything? Nope! And, instead of feeling better about the situation and ourselves, we probably walked away feeling even more frustrated.

So, what's the answer to racism and discrimination? There isn't an overnight solution. We have to realize that most people were raised and influenced by their families to think certain things about people who are different from them. We have to show them different! Let's be real again. At some point in our lives, we all have judged people by the way they look. If somebody doesn't look hip-hop, then we may not even talk to them. Think about it. We just did the same thing that people do to us. We say we want things to change, but many times we aren't any part of that change. We just help the problems continue.

Check out what Christ says in Luke 6:27-36. He talks about loving our enemies, doing good to them, and even praying for them. It's not always easy, but try it! Many times, when we respond in love, it totally changes the atmosphere. They're shocked! It's funny to watch the confused expressions on their faces. Next time someone gives you a look or makes an unfriendly comment, smile! Go up and start a positive conversation. We might be surprised at how God can use us to change their view of who we really are!

will respect you. [11]All who make themselves great will be made humble, but those who make themselves humble will be made great."

YOU WILL BE REWARDED

[12]Then Jesus said to the man who had invited him, "When you give a lunch or a dinner, don't invite only your friends, your family, your other relatives, and your rich neighbors. At another time they will invite you to eat with them, and you will be repaid. [13]Instead, when you give a feast, invite the poor, the crippled, the lame, and the blind. [14]Then you will be blessed, because they have nothing and cannot pay you back. But you will be repaid when the good people rise from the dead."

A STORY ABOUT A BIG BANQUET

[15]One of those at the table with Jesus heard these things and said to him, "Blessed are the people who will share in the meal in God's kingdom."

[16]Jesus said to him, "A man gave a big banquet and invited many people. [17]When it was time to eat, the man sent his servant to tell the guests, 'Come. Everything is ready.'

[18]"But all the guests made excuses. The first one said, 'I have just bought a field, and I must go look at it. Please excuse me.' [19]Another said, 'I have just bought five pairs of oxen; I must go and try them. Please excuse me.' [20]A third person said, 'I just got married; I can't come.' [21]So the servant returned and told his master what had happened. Then the master became angry and said, 'Go at once into the streets and alleys of the town, and bring in the poor, the crippled, the blind, and the lame.' [22]Later the servant said to him, 'Master, I did what you commanded, but we still have room.' [23]The master said to the servant, 'Go out to the roads and country lanes, and urge the people there to come so my house will be full. [24]I tell you, none of those whom I invited first will eat with me.' "

THE COST OF BEING JESUS' FOLLOWER

[25]Large crowds were traveling with Jesus, and he turned and said to them, [26]"If anyone comes to me but loves his father, mother, wife, children, brothers, or sisters—or even life—more than me, he cannot be my follower. [27]Whoever is not willing to carry his cross and follow me cannot be my follower. [28]If you want to build a tower, you first sit down and decide how much it will cost, to see if you have enough money to finish the job. [29]If you don't, you might lay the foundation, but you would not be able to finish. Then all who would see it would make fun of you, [30]saying, 'This person began to build but was not able to finish.'

[31]"If a king is going to fight another king, first he will sit down and plan. He will decide if he and his ten thousand soldiers can defeat the other king who has twenty thousand soldiers. [32]If he can't, then while the other king is still far away, he will send some people to speak to him and ask for peace. [33]In the same way, you must give up everything you have to be my follower.

DON'T LOSE YOUR INFLUENCE

[34]"Salt is good, but if it loses its salty taste, you cannot make it salty again. [35]It is no good for the soil or for manure; it is thrown away.

"Let those with ears use them and listen."

A LOST SHEEP, A LOST COIN

15 The tax collectors and sinners all came to listen to Jesus. [2]But the Pharisees and the teachers of the law began to complain: "Look, this man welcomes sinners and even eats with them."

[3]Then Jesus told them this story: [4]"Suppose one of you has a hundred sheep but loses one of them. Then he will leave the other ninety-nine sheep in the open field and go out and look for the lost sheep until he finds it. [5]And when he finds it, he happily puts it on his shoulders [6]and goes home. He calls to his friends and neighbors and says, 'Be happy with me because I found my lost sheep.' [7]In the same way, I tell you there is more joy in heaven over one sinner who changes his heart and life, than over ninety-nine good people who don't need to change.

[8]"Suppose a woman has ten silver coins,[n] but loses one. She will light a lamp, sweep the house, and look carefully for the coin until she finds it. [9]And when she finds it, she will call her friends and neighbors and say, 'Be happy with me because I have found the coin that I lost.' [10]In the same way, there is joy in the presence of the angels of God when one sinner changes his heart and life."

THE SON WHO LEFT HOME

[11]Then Jesus said, "A man had two sons. [12]The younger son said to his father, 'Give me my share of the property.' So the father divided the property between his two sons. [13]Then the younger son gathered up all that was his and traveled far away to another country. There he wasted his money in foolish living. [14]After he had spent everything, a time came when there was no food anywhere in the country, and the son was poor and hungry. [15]So he got a job with one of the citizens there who sent the son into the fields to feed pigs. [16]The son was so hungry that he wanted to eat the pods the pigs were eating, but no one gave him anything. [17]When he realized what he was doing, he thought, 'All of my father's servants have plenty of food. But I am here, almost dying with hunger. [18]I will leave and return to my father and say to him, "Father, I have sinned against God and against you. [19]I am no longer worthy to be called your son, but let me be like one of your servants." ' [20]So the son left and went to his father.

"While the son was still a long way off, his father saw him and felt sorry for his son. So the father ran to him and hugged and kissed him. [21]The son said,

---

 15:8 silver coins Roman denarii. One coin was the average pay for one day's work.

'Father, I have sinned against God and against you. I am no longer worthy to be called your son.'[n] ²²But the father said to his servants, 'Hurry! Bring the best clothes and put them on him. Also, put a ring on his finger and sandals on his feet. ²³And get our fat calf and kill it so we can have a feast and celebrate. ²⁴My son was dead, but now he is alive again! He was lost, but now he is found!' So they began to celebrate.

²⁵"The older son was in the field, and as he came closer to the house, he heard the sound of music and dancing. ²⁶So he called to one of the servants and asked what all this meant. ²⁷The servant said, 'Your brother has come back, and your father killed the fat calf, because your brother came home safely.' ²⁸The older son was angry and would not go in to the feast. So his father went out and begged him to come in. ²⁹But the older son said to his father, 'I have served you like a slave for many years and have always obeyed your commands. But you never gave me even a young goat to have at a feast with my friends. ³⁰But your other son, who wasted all your money on prostitutes, comes home, and you kill the fat calf for him!' ³¹The father said to him, 'Son, you are always with me, and all that I have is yours. ³²We had to celebrate and be happy because your brother was dead, but now he is alive. He was lost, but now he is found.'"

PEEP THIS:

In 2003, the music industry shipped 745,900,000 units, representing $11,232,900,000 in sales for the year.

He's got answers

It seems as if even preachers don't agree with each other. How can I know what's true?

You're right; many preachers—and other Christians—don't agree with each other. God created each person to be unique, with different life experiences and tastes. When you become a Christian, God doesn't change that. One Christian might like rock and roll while another likes classical. One might like a set pattern for their church services and another may want to go with the flow. One might like several different translations of the Bible, while another may want only one. Although there are fundamental truths within Christianity, God may reveal himself differently to different people. Also, remember that we are fallible people who can make mistakes in our interpretations and applications.

Don't let somebody else's mistakes become your excuse for not getting to know your creator. Everyone makes mistakes and someday God will separate the fake from the real! You must always read the Bible for yourself and ask God to show you what is true. The scriptures promise that those who seek truth will find it.

Read on: Matthew 7:1-7; 1 Corinthians 1:10-13, 14

TRUE WEALTH

'16 Jesus also said to his followers, "Once there was a rich man who had a manager to take care of his business. This manager was accused of cheating him. ²So he called the manager in and said to him, 'What is this I hear about you? Give me a report of what you have done with my money, because you can't be my manager any longer.' ³The manager thought to himself, 'What will I do since my master is taking my job away from me? I am not strong enough to dig ditches, and I am ashamed to beg. ⁴I know what I'll do so that when I lose my job people will welcome me into their homes.'

⁵"So the manager called in everyone who owed the master any money. He asked the first one, 'How much do you owe?' ⁶He answered, 'Eight hundred gallons of olive oil.' The manager said to him, 'Take your bill, sit down quickly,

15:21 son Some Greek copies continue, "but let me be like one of your servants" (see verse 19).

and write four hundred gallons.' [7]Then the manager asked another one, 'How much do you owe?' He answered, 'One thousand bushels of wheat.' Then the manager said to him, 'Take your bill and write eight hundred bushels.' [8]So, the master praised the dishonest manager for being clever. Yes, worldly people are more clever with their own kind than spiritual people are.

[9]"I tell you, make friends for yourselves using worldly riches so that when those riches are gone, you will be welcomed in those homes that continue forever. [10]Whoever can be trusted with a little can also be trusted with a lot, and whoever is dishonest with a little is dishonest with a lot. [11]If you cannot be trusted with worldly riches, then who will trust you with true riches? [12]And if you cannot be trusted with things that belong to someone else, who will give you things of your own?

[13]"No servant can serve two masters. The servant will hate one master and love the other, or will follow one master and refuse to follow the other. You cannot serve both God and worldly riches."

GOD'S LAW CANNOT BE CHANGED

[14]The Pharisees, who loved money, were listening to all these things and made fun of Jesus. [15]He said to them, "You make yourselves look good in front of people, but God knows what is really in your hearts. What is important to people is hateful in God's sight.

[16]"The law of Moses and the writings of the prophets were preached until John[n] came. Since then the Good News about the kingdom of God is being told, and everyone tries to enter it by force. [17]It would be easier for heaven and earth to pass away than for the smallest part of a letter in the law to be changed.

DIVORCE AND REMARRIAGE

[18]"If a man divorces his wife and marries another woman, he is guilty of adultery, and the man who marries a divorced woman is also guilty of adultery."

THE RICH MAN AND LAZARUS

[19]Jesus said, "There was a rich man who always dressed in the finest clothes and lived in luxury every day. [20]And a very poor man named Lazarus, whose body was covered with sores, was laid at the rich man's gate. [21]He wanted to eat only the small pieces of food that fell from the rich man's table. And the dogs would come and lick his sores. [22]Later, Lazarus died, and the angels carried him to the arms of Abraham. The rich man died, too, and was buried. [23]In the place of the dead, he was in much pain. The rich man saw Abraham far away with Lazarus at his side. [24]He called, 'Father Abraham, have mercy on me! Send Lazarus to dip his finger in water and cool my tongue, because I am suffering in this fire!' [25]But Abraham said, 'Child, remember when you were alive you had the good things in life, but bad things happened to Lazarus. Now he is comforted here, and you are suffering. [26]Besides, there is a big pit between you and us, so no one can cross over to you, and no one can leave there and come here.' [27]The rich man said, 'Father, then please send Lazarus to my father's house. [28]I have five brothers, and Lazarus could warn them so that they will not come to this place of pain.' [29]But Abraham said, 'They have the law of Moses and the writings of the prophets; let them learn from them.' [30]The rich man said, 'No, father Abraham! If someone goes to them from the dead, they would believe and change their hearts and lives.' [31]But Abraham said to him, 'If they will not listen to Moses and the prophets, they will not listen to someone who comes back from the dead.'"

SIN AND FORGIVENESS

17 Jesus said to his followers, "Things that cause people to sin will happen, but how terrible for the person who causes them to happen! [2]It would be better for you to be thrown

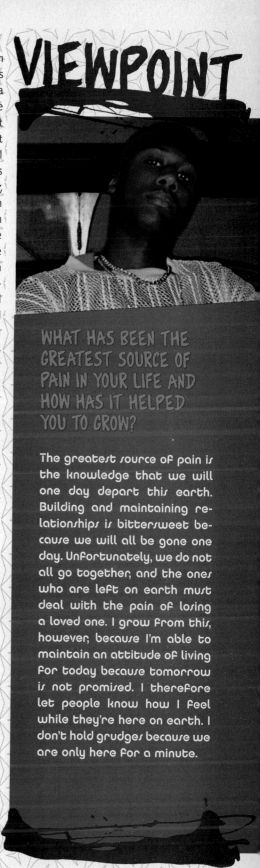

VIEWPOINT

WHAT HAS BEEN THE GREATEST SOURCE OF PAIN IN YOUR LIFE AND HOW HAS IT HELPED YOU TO GROW?

The greatest source of pain is the knowledge that we will one day depart this earth. Building and maintaining relationships is bittersweet because we will all be gone one day. Unfortunately, we do not all go together, and the ones who are left on earth must deal with the pain of losing a loved one. I grow from this, however, because I'm able to maintain an attitude of living for today because tomorrow is not promised. I therefore let people know how I feel while they're here on earth. I don't hold grudges because we are only here for a minute.

 16:16 John John the Baptist, who preached to people about Christ's coming (Matthew 3, Luke 3).

into the sea with a large stone around your neck than to cause one of these little ones to sin. ³So be careful!

"If another follower sins, warn him, and if he is sorry and stops sinning, forgive him. ⁴If he sins against you seven times in one day and says that he is sorry each time, forgive him."

HOW BIG IS YOUR FAITH?

⁵The apostles said to the Lord, "Give us more faith!"

⁶The Lord said, "If your faith were the size of a mustard seed, you could say to this mulberry tree, 'Dig yourself up and plant yourself in the sea,' and it would obey you.

BE GOOD SERVANTS

⁷"Suppose one of you has a servant who has been plowing the ground or caring for the sheep. When the servant comes in from working in the field, would you say, 'Come in and sit down to eat'? ⁸No, you would say to him, 'Prepare something for me to eat. Then get yourself ready and serve me. After I finish eating and drinking, you can eat.' ⁹The servant does not get any special thanks for doing what his master commanded. ¹⁰It is the same with you. When you have done everything you are told to do, you should say, 'We are unworthy servants; we have only done the work we should do.' "

BE THANKFUL

¹¹While Jesus was on his way to Jerusalem, he was going through the area between Samaria and Galilee. ¹²As he came into a small town, ten men who had a skin disease met him there. They did not come close to Jesus ¹³but called to him, "Jesus! Master! Have mercy on us!"

¹⁴When Jesus saw the men, he said, "Go and show yourselves to the priests."ⁿ

As the ten men were going, they were healed. ¹⁵When one of them saw that he was healed, he went back to Jesus, praising God in a loud voice. ¹⁶Then he

bowed down at Jesus' feet and thanked him. (And this man was a Samaritan.) ¹⁷Jesus said, "Weren't ten men healed? Where are the other nine? ¹⁸Is this Samaritan the only one who came back to thank God?" ¹⁹Then Jesus said to him, "Stand up and go on your way. You were healed because you believed."

GOD'S KINGDOM IS WITHIN YOU

²⁰Some of the Pharisees asked Jesus, "When will the kingdom of God come?"

Jesus answered, "God's kingdom is coming, but not in a way that you will be able to see with your eyes. ²¹People will not say, 'Look, here it is!' or, 'There it is!' because God's kingdom is withinⁿ you."

²²Then Jesus said to his followers, "The time will come when you will want very much to see one of the days of the Son of Man. But you will not see it. ²³People will say to you, 'Look, there he is!' or, 'Look, here he is!' Stay where you are; don't go away and search.

WHEN JESUS COMES AGAIN

²⁴"When the Son of Man comes again, he will shine like lightning, which flashes across the sky and lights it up from one side to the other. ²⁵But first he must suffer many things and be rejected by the people of this time. ²⁶When the Son of Man comes again, it will be as it was when Noah lived. ²⁷People were eating, drinking, marrying, and giving their children to be married until the day Noah entered the boat. Then the flood came and killed them all. ²⁸It will be the same as during the time of Lot. People were eating, drinking, buying, selling, planting, and building. ²⁹But the day Lot left Sodom,ⁿ fire and sulfur rained down from the sky and killed them all. ³⁰This is how it will be when the Son of Man comes again.

³¹"On that day, a person who is on the roof and whose belongings are in the house should not go inside to get them. A person who is in the field should not go back home. ³²Remember Lot's wife.ⁿ ³³Those who try to keep their lives will

lose them. But those who give up their lives will save them. ³⁴I tell you, on that night two people will be sleeping in one bed; one will be taken and the other will be left. ³⁵There will be two women grinding grain together; one will be taken, and the other will be left. [³⁶Two people will be in the field. One will be taken, and the other will be left.]ⁿ

³⁷The followers asked Jesus, "Where will this be, Lord?"

Jesus answered, "Where there is a dead body, there the vultures will gather."

GOD WILL ANSWER HIS PEOPLE

18 Then Jesus used this story to teach his followers that they should always pray and never lose hope. ²"In a certain town there was a judge who did not respect God or care about people. ³In that same town there was a widow who kept coming to this judge, saying, 'Give me my rights against my enemy.' ⁴For a while the judge refused to help her. But afterwards, he thought to himself, 'Even though I don't respect God or care about people, ⁵I will see that she gets her rights. Otherwise she will continue to bother me until I am worn out.' "

⁶The Lord said, "Listen to what the unfair judge said. ⁷God will always give what is right to his people who cry to him night and day, and he will not be slow to answer them. ⁸I tell you, God will help his people quickly. But when the Son of Man comes again, will he find those on earth who believe in him?"

BEING RIGHT WITH GOD

⁹Jesus told this story to some people who thought they were very good and looked down on everyone else: ¹⁰"A Pharisee and a tax collector both went to the Temple to pray. ¹¹The Pharisee stood alone and prayed, 'God, I thank you that I am not like other people who steal, cheat, or take part in adultery,

---

17:14 show . . . priests The Law of Moses said a priest must say when a person with a skin disease became well.   **17:21 within** Or "among."   **17:29 Sodom** City that God destroyed because the people were so evil.   **17:32 Lot's wife** A story about what happened to Lot's wife is found in Genesis 19:15-17, 26.   **17:36 Two . . . left.** Some Greek copies do not contain the bracketed text.

WORLD SAYS, WORD SAYS

BEAUTY

You are considered beautiful if you look like the girl in the magazine, or the guy on the b-ball courts, or people in the music video. Buy the latest gear, make sure your face is just right, and get your weight down to model perfect, because then and only then are you beautiful.

"I praise you because you made me in an amazing and wonderful way. What you have done is wonderful. I know this very well" (Psalm 139:14).

"But the LORD said to Samuel, 'Don't look at how handsome Eliab is or how tall he is, because I have not chosen him. God does not see the same way people see. People look at the outside of a person, but the LORD looks at the heart'" (1 Samuel 16:7).

"Charm can fool you, and beauty can trick you, but a woman who respects the LORD should be praised" (Proverbs 31:30).

---

or even like this tax collector. [12] I fast[n] twice a week, and I give one-tenth of everything I get!'

[13] "The tax collector, standing at a distance, would not even look up to heaven. But he beat on his chest because he was so sad. He said, 'God, have mercy on me, a sinner.' [14] I tell you, when this man went home, he was right with God, but the Pharisee was not. All who make themselves great will be made humble, but all who make themselves humble will be made great."

WHO WILL ENTER GOD'S KINGDOM?

[15] Some people brought even their babies to Jesus so he could touch them. When the followers saw this, they told them to stop. [16] But Jesus called for the children, saying, "Let the little children come to me. Don't stop them, because the kingdom of God belongs to people who are like these children. [17] I tell you the truth, you must accept the kingdom of God as if you were a child, or you will never enter it."

A RICH MAN'S QUESTION

[18] A certain leader asked Jesus, "Good Teacher, what must I do to have life forever?"

[19] Jesus said to him, "Why do you call me good? Only God is good. [20] You know the commands: 'You must not be guilty of adultery. You must not murder anyone. You must not steal. You must not tell lies about your neighbor. Honor your father and mother.'"[n]

[21] But the leader said, "I have obeyed all these commands since I was a boy."

[22] When Jesus heard this, he said to him, "There is still one more thing you need to do. Sell everything you have and give it to the poor, and you will have treasure in heaven. Then come and follow me." [23] But when the man heard this, he became very sad, because he was very rich.

[24] Jesus looked at him and said, "It is very hard for rich people to enter the kingdom of God. [25] It is easier for a camel to go through the eye of a needle than for a rich person to enter the kingdom of God."

WHO CAN BE SAVED?

[26] When the people heard this, they asked, "Then who can be saved?"

[27] Jesus answered, "The things impossible for people are possible for God."

[28] Peter said, "Look, we have left everything and followed you."

[29] Jesus said, "I tell you the truth, all those who have left houses, wives, brothers, parents, or children for the kingdom of God [30] will get much more in this life. And in the age that is coming, they will have life forever."

JESUS WILL RISE FROM THE DEAD

[31] Then Jesus took the twelve apostles aside and said to them, "We are going to Jerusalem. Everything the prophets wrote about the Son of Man will happen. [32] He will be turned over to those who are evil. They will laugh at him, insult him, spit on him, [33] beat him with whips, and kill him. But on the third day, he will rise to life again." [34] The apostles did not understand this; the meaning was hidden from them, and they did not realize what was said.

JESUS HEALS A BLIND MAN

[35] As Jesus came near the city of Jericho, a blind man was sitting beside the road, begging. [36] When he heard the people coming down the road, he asked, "What is happening?"

[37] They told him, "Jesus, from Nazareth, is going by."

[38] The blind man cried out, "Jesus, Son of David, have mercy on me!"

[39] The people leading the group warned the blind man to be quiet. But the blind man shouted even more, "Son of David, have mercy on me!"

 18:12 fast The people would give up eating for a special time of prayer and worship to God. It was also done to show sadness and disappointment. **18:20 'You . . . mother.'** Quotation from Exodus 20:12-16; Deuteronomy 5:16-20.

⁴⁰Jesus stopped and ordered the blind man to be brought to him. When he came near, Jesus asked him, ⁴¹"What do you want me to do for you?"

He said, "Lord, I want to see."

⁴²Jesus said to him, "Then see. You are healed because you believed."

⁴³At once the man was able to see, and he followed Jesus, thanking God. All the people who saw this praised God.

ZACCHAEUS MEETS JESUS

19 Jesus was going through the city of Jericho. ²A man was there named Zacchaeus, who was a very important tax collector, and he was wealthy. ³He wanted to see who Jesus was, but he was not able because he was too short to see above the crowd. ⁴He ran ahead to a place where Jesus would come, and he climbed a sycamore tree so he could see him. ⁵When Jesus came to that place, he looked up and said to him, "Zacchaeus, hurry and come down! I must stay at your house today."

⁶Zacchaeus came down quickly and welcomed him gladly. ⁷All the people saw this and began to complain, "Jesus is staying with a sinner!"

⁸But Zacchaeus stood and said to the Lord, "I will give half of my possessions to the poor. And if I have cheated anyone, I will pay back four times more."

⁹Jesus said to him, "Salvation has come to this house today, because this man also belongs to the family of Abraham. ¹⁰The Son of Man came to find lost people and save them."

A STORY ABOUT THREE SERVANTS

¹¹As the people were listening to this, Jesus told them a story because he was near Jerusalem and they thought God's kingdom would appear immediately. ¹²He said: "A very important man went to a country far away to be made a king and then to return home. ¹³So he called ten of his servants and gave a coin[n] to each

servant. He said, 'Do business with this money until I get back.' ¹⁴But the people in the kingdom hated the man. So they sent a group to follow him and say, 'We don't want this man to be our king.'

¹⁵"But the man became king. When he returned home, he said, 'Call those servants who have my money so I can know how much they earned with it.'

¹⁶"The first servant came and said, 'Sir, I earned ten coins with the one you gave me.' ¹⁷The king said to the servant, 'Excellent! You are a good servant. Since I can trust you with small things, I will let you rule over ten of my cities.'

¹⁸"The second servant said, 'Sir, I earned five coins with your one.' ¹⁹The king said to this servant, 'You can rule over five cities.'

²⁰"Then another servant came in and said to the king, 'Sir, here is your coin which I wrapped in a piece of cloth and hid. ²¹I was afraid of you, because you are a hard man. You even take money that you didn't earn and gather food that you didn't plant.' ²²Then the king said to the servant, 'I will condemn you by your own words, you evil servant. You knew that I am a hard man, taking money that I didn't earn and gathering food that I didn't plant. ²³Why then didn't you put my money in the bank? Then when I came back, my money would have earned some interest.'

²⁴"The king said to the men who were standing by, 'Take the coin away from this servant and give it to the servant who earned ten coins.' ²⁵They said, 'But sir, that servant already has ten coins.' ²⁶The king said, 'Those who have will be given more, but those who do not have anything will have everything taken away from them. ²⁷Now where are my enemies who didn't want me to be king? Bring them here and kill them before me.' "

JESUS ENTERS JERUSALEM AS A KING

²⁸After Jesus said this, he went on toward Jerusalem. ²⁹As Jesus came near Bethphage and Bethany, towns near the hill called the Mount of Olives, he sent out two of his followers. ³⁰He said, "Go

to the town you can see there. When you enter it, you will find a colt tied there, which no one has ever ridden. Untie it and bring it here to me. ³¹If anyone asks you why you are untying it, say that the Master needs it."

³²The two followers went into town and found the colt just as Jesus had told them. ³³As they were untying it, its owners came out and asked the followers, "Why are you untying our colt?"

³⁴The followers answered, "The Master needs it." ³⁵So they brought it to Jesus, threw their coats on the colt's back, and put Jesus on it. ³⁶As Jesus rode toward Jerusalem, others spread their coats on the road before him.

³⁷As he was coming close to Jerusalem, on the way down the Mount of Olives, the whole crowd of followers began joyfully shouting praise to God for all the miracles they had seen. ³⁸They said,

"God bless the king who comes in the name of the Lord!

Psalm 118:26

There is peace in heaven and glory to God!"

³⁹Some of the Pharisees in the crowd said to Jesus, "Teacher, tell your followers not to say these things."

⁴⁰But Jesus answered, "I tell you, if my followers didn't say these things, then the stones would cry out."

JESUS CRIES FOR JERUSALEM

⁴¹As Jesus came near Jerusalem, he saw the city and cried for it, ⁴²saying, "I wish you knew today what would bring you peace. But now it is hidden from you. ⁴³The time is coming when your enemies will build a wall around you and will hold you in on all sides. ⁴⁴They will destroy you and all your people, and not one stone will be left on another. All this will happen because you did not recognize the time when God came to save you."

JESUS GOES TO THE TEMPLE

⁴⁵Jesus went into the Temple and began to throw out the people who were selling things there. ⁴⁶He said, "It is written in the Scriptures, 'My Temple

---

 19:13 coin A Greek "mina." One mina was enough money to pay a person for working three months.

will be a house for prayer.'" But you have changed it into a 'hideout for robbers'!'"

⁴⁷Jesus taught in the Temple every day. The leading priests, the experts on the law, and some of the leaders of the people wanted to kill Jesus. ⁴⁸But they did not know how they could do it, because all the people were listening closely to him.

JEWISH LEADERS QUESTION JESUS

20 One day Jesus was in the Temple, teaching the people and telling them the Good News. The leading priests, teachers of the law, and elders came up to talk with him, ²saying, "Tell us what authority you have to do these things? Who gave you this authority?"

³Jesus answered, "I will also ask you a question. Tell me: ⁴When John baptized people, was that authority from God or just from other people?"

⁵They argued about this, saying, "If we answer, 'John's baptism was from God,' Jesus will say, 'Then why did you not believe him?' ⁶But if we say, 'It was from other people,' all the people will stone us to death, because they believe John was a prophet." ⁷So they answered that they didn't know where it came from.

⁸Jesus said to them, "Then I won't tell you what authority I have to do these things."

A STORY ABOUT GOD'S SON

⁹Then Jesus told the people this story: "A man planted a vineyard and leased it to some farmers. Then he went away for a long time. ¹⁰When it was time for the grapes to be picked, he sent a servant to the farmers to get some of the grapes. But they beat the servant and sent him away empty-handed. ¹¹Then he sent another servant. They beat this servant also, and showed no respect for him, and sent him away empty-handed. ¹²So the man sent a third servant. The farmers wounded him and threw him out. ¹³The

19:46 'My Temple . . . prayer.' Quotation from Isaiah 56:7.   **19:46 'hideout for robbers'** Quotation from Jeremiah 7:11.

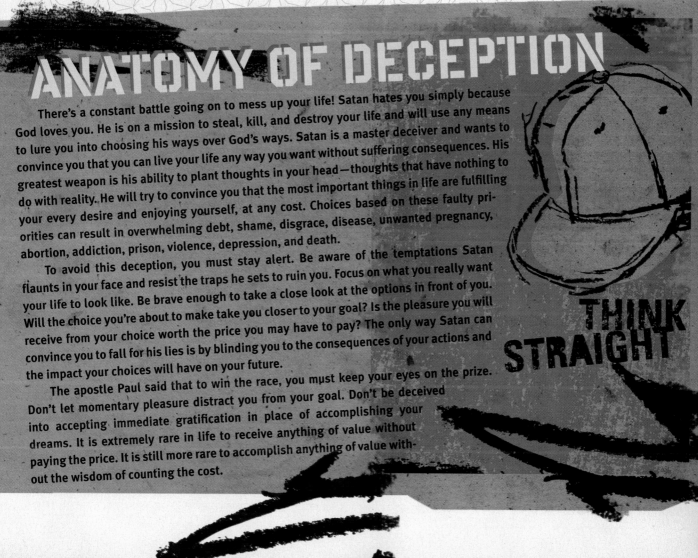

ANATOMY OF DECEPTION

There's a constant battle going on to mess up your life! Satan hates you simply because God loves you. He is on a mission to steal, kill, and destroy your life and will use any means to lure you into choosing his ways over God's ways. Satan is a master deceiver and wants to convince you that you can live your life any way you want without suffering consequences. His greatest weapon is his ability to plant thoughts in your head—thoughts that have nothing to do with reality. He will try to convince you that the most important things in life are fulfilling your every desire and enjoying yourself, at any cost. Choices based on these faulty priorities can result in overwhelming debt, shame, disgrace, disease, unwanted pregnancy, abortion, addiction, prison, violence, depression, and death.

To avoid this deception, you must stay alert. Be aware of the temptations Satan flaunts in your face and resist the traps he sets to ruin you. Focus on what you really want your life to look like. Be brave enough to take a close look at the options in front of you. Will the choice you're about to make take you closer to your goal? Is the pleasure you will receive from your choice worth the price you may have to pay? The only way Satan can convince you to fall for his lies is by blinding you to the consequences of your actions and the impact your choices will have on your future.

The apostle Paul said that to win the race, you must keep your eyes on the prize. Don't let momentary pleasure distract you from your goal. Don't be deceived into accepting immediate gratification in place of accomplishing your dreams. It is extremely rare in life to receive anything of value without paying the price. It is still more rare to accomplish anything of value without the wisdom of counting the cost.

THINK STRAIGHT

owner of the vineyard said, 'What will I do now? I will send my son whom I love. Maybe they will respect him.' [14]But when the farmers saw the son, they said to each other, 'This son will inherit the vineyard. If we kill him, it will be ours.' [15]So the farmers threw the son out of the vineyard and killed him.

"What will the owner of this vineyard do to them? [16]He will come and kill those farmers and will give the vineyard to other farmers."

When the people heard this story, they said, "Let this never happen!"

[17]But Jesus looked at them and said, "Then what does this verse mean:

'The stone that the builders rejected became the cornerstone'?

Psalm 118:22

[18]Everyone who falls on that stone will be broken, and the person on whom it falls, that person will be crushed!"

[19]The teachers of the law and the leading priests wanted to arrest Jesus at once, because they knew the story was about them. But they were afraid of what the people would do.

IS IT RIGHT TO PAY TAXES OR NOT?

[20]So they watched Jesus and sent some spies who acted as if they were sin-

He's got answers

Are heaven and hell real places?

Most religions believe in some place where the spirit goes to dwell after death, and many have a place of punishment for those who have gone against their teachings. However, we will answer this question based on what the Bible says about heaven and hell.

Heaven is mentioned more than 200 times in the New Testament. It is the place God created for those who have accepted Jesus as their Savior. Whenever Jesus spoke of it, he described it as real. There are many beautiful descriptions of heaven, but where it is or what it is exactly, no one knows for sure. We only know that this is the place where we will live forever with God, if we know him.

Jesus also spoke many times of hell—or hades or gehenna—as a real place. He described it as a place made for Satan and Satan's followers. The descriptions of hell are numerous, and all of them describe a place of darkness and torment. All that is good and holy is absent in hell. It is a place where God is not.

Read on: Matthew 3:12; Mark 9:48; Luke 23:42-43; Revelation 21

PEEP THIS:

Music listening is extremely or very important to half of Hispanic consumers. Another 41 percent consider music listening fairly important, with only 9 percent reporting music to be not very or not at all important to them.

cere. They wanted to trap Jesus in saying something wrong so they could hand him over to the authority and power of the governor. [21]So the spies asked Jesus, "Teacher, we know that what you say and teach is true. You pay no attention to who people are, and you always teach the truth about God's way. [22]Tell us, is it right for us to pay taxes to Caesar or not?"

[23]But Jesus, knowing they were trying to trick him, said, [24]"Show me a coin. Whose image and name are on it?"

They said, "Caesar's."

[25]Jesus said to them, "Then give to Caesar the things that are Caesar's, and give to God the things that are God's."

[26]So they were not able to trap Jesus in anything he said in the presence of the people. And being amazed at his answer, they became silent.

SOME SADDUCEES TRY TO TRICK JESUS

[27]Some Sadducees, who believed people would not rise from the dead, came to Jesus. [28]They asked, "Teacher, Moses wrote that if a man's brother dies and leaves a wife but no children, then that man must marry the widow and have

children for his brother. [29]Once there were seven brothers. The first brother married and died, but had no children. [30]Then the second brother married the widow, and he died. [31]And the third brother married the widow, and he died. The same thing happened with all seven brothers; they died and had no children. [32]Finally, the woman died also. [33]Since all seven brothers had married her, whose wife will she be when people rise from the dead?"

[34]Jesus said to them, "On earth, people marry and are given to someone to marry. [35]But those who will be worthy to be raised from the dead and live again will not marry, nor will they be given to someone to marry. [36]In that life they are like angels and cannot die. They are children of God, because they have been raised from the dead. [37]Even Moses clearly showed that the dead are raised to life. When he wrote about the burning bush,[n] he said that the Lord is 'the God of Abraham, the God of Isaac, and the God of Jacob.'[n] [38]God is the God of the living, not the dead, because all people are alive to him."

[39]Some of the teachers of the law said, "Teacher, your answer was good." [40]No one was brave enough to ask him another question.

IS THE CHRIST THE SON OF DAVID?

[41]Then Jesus said, "Why do people say that the Christ is the Son of David? [42]In the book of Psalms, David himself says:

'The Lord said to my Lord,
  "Sit by me at my right side,
[43] until I put your enemies under your
      control."'[n]   *Psalm 110:1*

[44]David calls the Christ 'Lord,' so how can the Christ be his son?"

JESUS ACCUSES SOME LEADERS

[45]While all the people were listening, Jesus said to his followers, [46]"Beware of the teachers of the law. They like to walk around wearing fancy clothes, and they love for people to greet them with respect in the marketplaces. They love to have the most important seats in the synagogues and at feasts. [47]But they cheat widows and steal their houses and then try to make themselves look good by saying long prayers. They will receive a greater punishment."

TRUE GIVING

21 As Jesus looked up, he saw some rich people putting their gifts into the Temple money box.[n] [2]Then he saw a poor widow putting two small copper coins into the box. [3]He said, "I tell you the truth, this poor widow gave more than all those rich people. [4]They gave only what they

IMPACT!

Holy Rollerz Christian Car Club

Are you a car enthusiast but you can't get down with the promiscuity and profanity sometimes associated with car clubs? You need to check out Holy Rollerz Christian Car Club. The Holy Rollerz are about fellowship with God and one another. They feature both project vehicles and show-quality vehicles. Even if you don't have a tight ride, you can join Holy Rollerz as an honorary member and participate in the ministry. Shine up your chrome and contact a Holy Rollerz chapter near you. Information is available on their Web site www.holyrollerz.org.

 20:37 burning bush Read Exodus 3:1-12 in the Old Testament.   **20:37 'the God of . . . Jacob'** These words are taken from Exodus 3:6.   **20:43 until . . . control** Literally, "until I make your enemies a footstool for your feet."   **21:1 money box** A special box in the Jewish place of worship where people put their gifts to God.

did not need. This woman is very poor, but she gave all she had to live on."

THE TEMPLE WILL BE DESTROYED

[5]Some people were talking about the Temple and how it was decorated with beautiful stones and gifts offered to God.

But Jesus said, [6]"As for these things you are looking at, the time will come when not one stone will be left on another. Every stone will be thrown down."

[7]They asked Jesus, "Teacher, when will these things happen? What will be the sign that they are about to take place?"

[8]Jesus said, "Be careful so you are not fooled. Many people will come in my name, saying, 'I am the One' and, 'The time has come!' But don't follow them. [9]When you hear about wars and riots, don't be afraid, because these things must happen first, but the end will come later."

[10]Then he said to them, "Nations will fight against other nations, and kingdoms against other kingdoms. [11]In various places there will be great earthquakes, sicknesses, and a lack of food. Fearful events and great signs will come from heaven.

[12]"But before all these things happen, people will arrest you and treat you cruelly. They will judge you in their synagogues and put you in jail and force you to stand before kings and governors, because you follow me. [13]But this will give you an opportunity to tell about me. [14]Make up your minds not to worry ahead of time about what you will say. [15]I will give you the wisdom to say things that none of your enemies will be able to stand against or prove wrong. [16]Even your parents, brothers, relatives, and friends will turn against you, and they will kill some of you. [17]All people will hate you because you follow me. [18]But none of these things can really harm you. [19]By continuing to have faith you will save your lives.

JERUSALEM WILL BE DESTROYED

[20]"When you see armies all around Jerusalem, you will know it will soon be

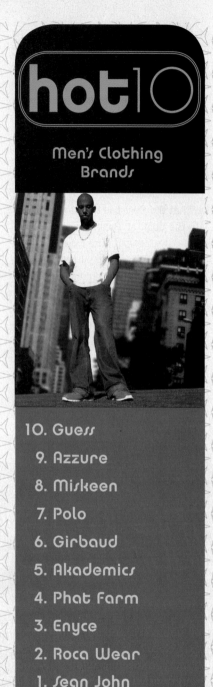

hot 10

Men's Clothing Brands

10. Guess

9. Azzure

8. Miskeen

7. Polo

6. Girbaud

5. Akademics

4. Phat Farm

3. Enyce

2. Roca Wear

1. Sean John

destroyed. [21]At that time, the people in Judea should run away to the mountains. The people in Jerusalem must get out, and those who are near the city should not go in. [22]These are the days of punishment to bring about all that is written in the Scriptures. [23]How terrible it will be for women who are pregnant or have nursing babies! Great trouble will come

upon this land, and God will be angry with these people. [24]They will be killed by the sword and taken as prisoners to all nations. Jerusalem will be crushed by non-Jewish people until their time is over.

DON'T FEAR

[25]"There will be signs in the sun, moon, and stars. On earth, nations will be afraid and confused because of the roar and fury of the sea. [26]People will be so afraid they will faint, wondering what is happening to the world, because the powers of the heavens will be shaken. [27]Then people will see the Son of Man coming in a cloud with power and great glory. [28]When these things begin to happen, look up and hold your heads high, because the time when God will free you is near!"

JESUS' WORDS WILL LIVE FOREVER

[29]Then Jesus told this story: "Look at the fig tree and all the other trees. [30]When their leaves appear, you know that summer is near. [31]In the same way, when you see these things happening, you will know that God's kingdom is near. [32]"I tell you the truth, all these things will happen while the people of this time are still living. [33]Earth and sky will be destroyed, but the words I have spoken will never be destroyed.

BE READY ALL THE TIME

[34]"Be careful not to spend your time feasting, drinking, or worrying about worldly things. If you do, that day might come on you suddenly, [35]like a trap on all people on earth. [36]So be ready all the time. Pray that you will be strong enough to escape all these things that will happen and that you will be able to stand before the Son of Man."

[37]During the day, Jesus taught the people in the Temple, and at night he went out of the city and stayed on the Mount of Olives. [38]Every morning all the people got up early to go to the Temple to listen to him.

JUDAS BECOMES AN ENEMY OF JESUS

22 It was almost time for the Feast of Unleavened Bread, called the Passover Feast. [2]The leading priests and teachers of the law were trying to find a way to kill Jesus, because they were afraid of the people.

[3]Satan entered Judas Iscariot, one of Jesus' twelve apostles. [4]Judas went to the leading priests and some of the soldiers who guarded the Temple and talked to them about a way to hand Jesus over to them. [5]They were pleased and agreed to give Judas money. [6]He agreed and watched for the best time to hand Jesus over to them when he was away from the crowd.

JESUS EATS THE PASSOVER MEAL

[7]The Day of Unleavened Bread came when the Passover lambs had to be sacrificed. [8]Jesus said to Peter and John, "Go and prepare the Passover meal for us to eat."

[9]They asked, "Where do you want us to prepare it?" [10]Jesus said to them, "After you go into the city, a man carrying a jar of water will meet you. Follow him into the house that he enters, [11]and tell the owner of the house, 'The Teacher says: "Where is the guest room in which I may eat the Passover meal with my followers?"' [12]Then he will show you a large, furnished room upstairs. Prepare the Passover meal there."

[13]So Peter and John left and found everything as Jesus had said. And they prepared the Passover meal.

THE LORD'S SUPPER

[14]When the time came, Jesus and the apostles were sitting at the table. [15]He said to them, "I wanted very much to eat this Passover meal with you before I suffer. [16]I will not eat another Passover meal until it is given its true meaning in the kingdom of God."

[17]Then Jesus took a cup, gave thanks, and said, "Take this cup and share it among yourselves. [18]I will not drink again from the fruit of the vine[n] until God's kingdom comes."

[19]Then Jesus took some bread, gave thanks, broke it, and gave it to the apostles, saying, "This is my body,[n] which I am giving for you. Do this to remember me." [20]In the same way, after supper, Jesus took the cup and said, "This cup is the new agreement that God makes with his people. This new agreement begins with my blood which is poured out for you.

WHO WILL TURN AGAINST JESUS?

[21]"But one of you will turn against me, and his hand is with mine on the table. [22]What God has planned for the Son of Man will happen, but how terrible it will be for that one who turns against the Son of Man."

[23]Then the apostles asked each other which one of them would do that.

BE LIKE A SERVANT

[24]The apostles also began to argue about which one of them was the most important. [25]But Jesus said to them, "The kings of the non-Jewish people rule over them, and those who have authority over others like to be called 'friends of the people.' [26]But you must not be like that. Instead, the greatest among you should be like the youngest, and the leader should be like the servant. [27]Who is more important: the one sitting at the table or the one serving? You think the one at the table is more important, but I am like a servant among you.

[28]"You have stayed with me through my struggles. [29]Just as my Father has given me a kingdom, I also give you a kingdom [30]so you may eat and drink at my table in my kingdom. And you will sit on thrones, judging the twelve tribes of Israel.

DON'T LOSE YOUR FAITH!

[31]"Simon, Simon, Satan has asked to test all of you as a farmer sifts his wheat. [32]I have prayed that you will not lose your faith! Help your brothers be stronger when you come back to me."

[33]But Peter said to Jesus, "Lord, I am ready to go with you to prison and even to die with you!"

[34]But Jesus said, "Peter, before the rooster crows this day, you will say three times that you don't know me."

BE READY FOR TROUBLE

[35]Then Jesus said to the apostles, "When I sent you out without a purse, a bag, or sandals, did you need anything?"

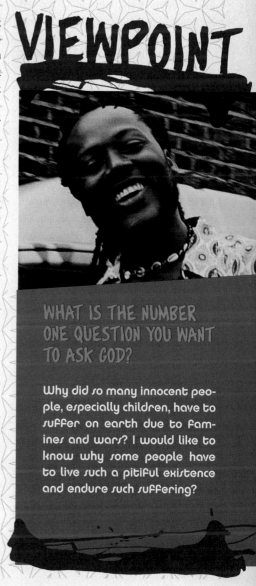

VIEWPOINT

WHAT IS THE NUMBER ONE QUESTION YOU WANT TO ASK GOD?

Why did so many innocent people, especially children, have to suffer on earth due to famines and wars? I would like to know why some people have to live such a pitiful existence and endure such suffering?

 22:18 fruit of the vine Product of the grapevine; this may also be translated "wine." **22:19b-20 body** Some Greek copies do not have the rest of verse 19 or verse 20.

They said, "No."

[36]He said to them, "But now if you have a purse or a bag, carry that with you. If you don't have a sword, sell your coat and buy one. [37]The Scripture says, 'He was treated like a criminal,'[n] and I tell you this scripture must have its full meaning. It was written about me, and it is happening now."

[38]His followers said, "Look, Lord, here are two swords."

He said to them, "That is enough."

JESUS PRAYS ALONE

[39]Jesus left the city and went to the Mount of Olives, as he often did, and his followers went with him. [40]When he reached the place, he said to them, "Pray for strength against temptation."

[41]Then Jesus went about a stone's throw away from them. He kneeled down and prayed, [42]"Father, if you are willing, take away this cup[n] of suffering. But do what you want, not what I want." [43]Then an angel from heaven appeared to him to strengthen him. [44]Being full of pain, Jesus prayed even harder. His sweat was like drops of blood falling to the ground. [45]When he finished praying, he went to his followers and found them asleep because of their sadness. [46]Jesus said to them, "Why are you sleeping? Get up and pray for strength against temptation."

JESUS IS ARRESTED

[47]While Jesus was speaking, a crowd came up, and Judas, one of the twelve apostles, was leading them. He came close to Jesus so he could kiss him.

[48]But Jesus said to him, "Judas, are you using the kiss to give the Son of Man to his enemies?"

[49]When those who were standing around him saw what was happening, they said, "Lord, should we strike them with our swords?" [50]And one of them struck the servant of the high priest and cut off his right ear.

[51]Jesus said, "Stop! No more of this." Then he touched the servant's ear and healed him.

[52]Those who came to arrest Jesus were the leading priests, the soldiers who guarded the Temple, and the elders. Jesus said to them, "You came out here with swords and clubs as though I were a criminal. [53]I was with you every day in the Temple, and you didn't arrest me there. But this is your time—the time when darkness rules."

PETER SAYS HE DOESN'T KNOW JESUS

[54]They arrested Jesus, and led him away, and brought him into the house of the high priest. Peter followed far behind them. [55]After the soldiers started a fire in the middle of the courtyard and sat together, Peter sat with them. [56]A servant girl saw Peter sitting there in the firelight, and looking closely at him, she said, "This man was also with him."

> FATHER, IF YOU ARE WILLING, TAKE AWAY THIS CUP OF SUFFERING. BUT DO WHAT YOU WANT, NOT WHAT I WANT.

[57]But Peter said this was not true; he said, "Woman, I don't know him."

[58]A short time later, another person saw Peter and said, "You are also one of them."

But Peter said, "Man, I am not!"

[59]About an hour later, another man insisted, "Certainly this man was with him, because he is from Galilee, too."

[60]But Peter said, "Man, I don't know what you are talking about!"

At once, while Peter was still speaking, a rooster crowed. [61]Then the Lord turned and looked straight at Peter. And Peter remembered what the Lord had said: "Before the rooster crows this day, you will say three times that you don't know me." [62]Then Peter went outside and cried painfully.

THE PEOPLE MAKE FUN OF JESUS

[63]The men who were guarding Jesus began making fun of him and beating him.

[64]They blindfolded him and said, "Prove that you are a prophet, and tell us who hit you." [65]They said many cruel things to Jesus.

JESUS BEFORE THE LEADERS

[66]When day came, the council of the elders of the people, both the leading priests and the teachers of the law, came together and led Jesus to their highest court. [67]They said, "If you are the Christ, tell us."

Jesus said to them, "If I tell you, you will not believe me. [68]And if I ask you, you will not answer. [69]But from now on, the Son of Man will sit at the right hand of the powerful God."

[70]They all said, "Then are you the Son of God?"

Jesus said to them, "You say that I am."

[71]They said, "Why do we need witnesses now? We ourselves heard him say this."

PILATE QUESTIONS JESUS

23 Then the whole group stood up and led Jesus to Pilate.[n] [2]They began to accuse Jesus, saying, "We caught this man telling things that mislead our people. He says that we should not pay taxes to Caesar, and he calls himself the Christ, a king."

[3]Pilate asked Jesus, "Are you the king of the Jews?"

22:37 'He . . . criminal.' Quotation from Isaiah 53:12. **22:42 cup** Jesus is talking about the painful things that will happen to him. Accepting these things will be hard, like drinking a cup of something bitter. **23:1 Pilate** Pontius Pilate was the Roman governor of Judea from A.D. 26 to A.D. 36.

Jesus answered, "Those are your words."

[4]Pilate said to the leading priests and the people, "I find nothing against this man."

[5]They were insisting, saying, "But Jesus makes trouble with the people, teaching all around Judea. He began in Galilee, and now he is here."

PILATE SENDS JESUS TO HEROD

[6]Pilate heard this and asked if Jesus was from Galilee. [7]Since Jesus was under Herod's authority, Pilate sent Jesus to Herod, who was in Jerusalem at that time. [8]When Herod saw Jesus, he was very glad, because he had heard about Jesus and had wanted to meet him for a long time. He was hoping to see Jesus work a miracle. [9]Herod asked Jesus many questions, but Jesus said nothing. [10]The leading priests and teachers of the law were standing there, strongly accusing Jesus. [11]After Herod and his soldiers had made fun of Jesus, they dressed him in a kingly robe and sent him back to Pilate. [12]In the past, Pilate and Herod had always been enemies, but on that day they became friends.

JESUS MUST DIE

[13]Pilate called the people together with the leading priests and the rulers. [14]He said to them, "You brought this man to me, saying he makes trouble among the people. But I have questioned him before you all, and I have not found him guilty of what you say. [15]Also, Herod found nothing wrong with him; he sent him back to us. Look, he has done nothing for which he should die. [16]So, after I punish him, I will let him go free." [[17]Every year at the Passover Feast, Pilate had to release one prisoner to the people.][n]

[18]But the people shouted together, "Take this man away! Let Barabbas go free!" [19](Barabbas was a man who was in prison for his part in a riot in the city and for murder.)

[20]Pilate wanted to let Jesus go free and told this to the crowd. [21]But they shouted again, "Crucify him! Crucify him!"

[22]A third time Pilate said to them, "Why? What wrong has he done? I can find no reason to kill him. So I will have him punished and set him free."

[23]But they continued to shout, demanding that Jesus be crucified. Their yelling became so loud that [24]Pilate decided to give them what they wanted. [25]He set free the man who was in jail for rioting and murder, and he handed Jesus over to them to do with him as they wished.

JESUS IS CRUCIFIED

[26]As they led Jesus away, Simon, a man from Cyrene, was coming in from the fields. They forced him to carry Jesus' cross and to walk behind him.

[27]A large crowd of people was following Jesus, including some women who were sad and crying for him. [28]But Jesus turned and said to them, "Women of Jerusalem, don't cry for me. Cry for yourselves and for your children. [29]The time is coming when people will say, 'Blessed are the women who cannot have children and who have no babies to nurse.' [30]Then people will say to the mountains, 'Fall on us!' And they will say to the hills, 'Cover us!' [31]If they act like this now when life is good, what will happen when bad times come?"[n]

[32]There were also two criminals led out with Jesus to be put to death. [33]When they came to a place called the Skull, the soldiers crucified Jesus and the criminals—one on his right and the other on his left. [34]Jesus said, "Father, forgive them, because they don't know what they are doing."[n]

The soldiers threw lots to decide who would get his clothes. [35]The people stood there watching. And the leaders made fun of Jesus, saying, "He saved others. Let him save himself if he is God's Chosen One, the Christ."

[36]The soldiers also made fun of him, coming to Jesus and offering him some vinegar. [37]They said, "If you are the king of the Jews, save yourself!" [38]At the top of the cross these words were written: THIS IS THE KING OF THE JEWS.

[39]One of the criminals on a cross began to shout insults at Jesus: "Aren't you the Christ? Then save yourself and us."

[40]But the other criminal stopped him and said, "You should fear God! You are getting the same punishment he is. [41]We are punished justly, getting what we deserve for what we did. But this man has done nothing wrong." [42]Then he said, "Jesus, remember me when you come into your kingdom."

[43]Jesus said to him, "I tell you the truth, today you will be with me in paradise."[n]

JESUS DIES

[44]It was about noon, and the whole land became dark until three o'clock in the afternoon, [45]because the sun did not shine. The curtain in the Temple[n] was torn in two. [46]Jesus cried out in a loud voice, "Father, I give you my life." After Jesus said this, he died.

[47]When the army officer there saw what happened, he praised God, saying, "Surely this was a good man!"

[48]When all the people who had gathered there to watch saw what happened, they returned home, beating their chests because they were so sad. [49]But those who were close friends of Jesus, including the women who had followed him from Galilee, stood at a distance and watched.

JOSEPH TAKES JESUS' BODY

[50]There was a good and religious man named Joseph who was a member of the council. [51]But he had not agreed to the other leaders' plans and actions against Jesus. He was from the town of Arimathea and was waiting for the kingdom of God to come. [52]Joseph went to Pilate to ask for the body of Jesus. [53]He took the body down from the cross, wrapped it in cloth, and put it in a tomb that was cut out of a wall of rock. This tomb had never been used before. [54]This was late on Preparation Day, and when the sun went down, the Sabbath day would begin.

[55]The women who had come from

23:17 Every . . . people. Some Greek copies do not contain the bracketed text. **23:31 If . . . come?** Literally, "If they do these things in the green tree, what will happen in the dry?" **23:34 Jesus . . . doing.** Some Greek copies do not have this first part of verse 34. **23:43 paradise** Another word for heaven. **23:45 curtain in the Temple** A curtain divided the Most Holy Place from the other part of the Temple, the special building in Jerusalem where God commanded the Jewish people to worship him.

Galilee with Jesus followed Joseph and saw the tomb and how Jesus' body was laid. [56]Then the women left to prepare spices and perfumes.

On the Sabbath day they rested, as the law of Moses commanded.

JESUS RISES FROM THE DEAD

24 Very early on the first day of the week, at dawn, the women came to the tomb, bringing the spices they had prepared. [2]They found the stone rolled away from the entrance of the tomb, [3]but when they went in, they did not find the body of the Lord Jesus. [4]While they were wondering about this, two men in shining clothes suddenly stood beside them. [5]The women were very afraid and bowed their heads to the ground. The men said to them, "Why are you looking for a living person in this place for the dead? [6]He is not here; he has risen from the dead. Do you remember what he told you in Galilee? [7]He said the Son of Man must be handed over to sinful people, be crucified, and rise from the dead on the third day." [8]Then the women remembered what Jesus had said.

[9]The women left the tomb and told all these things to the eleven apostles and the other followers. [10]It was Mary Magdalene, Joanna, Mary the mother of James, and some other women who told the apostles everything that had happened at the tomb. [11]But they did not believe the women, because it sounded like nonsense. [12]But Peter got up and ran to the tomb. Bending down and looking in, he saw only the cloth that Jesus' body had been wrapped in. Peter went away to his home, wondering about what had happened.

JESUS ON THE ROAD TO EMMAUS

[13]That same day two of Jesus' followers were going to a town named Emmaus, about seven miles from Jerusalem. [14]They were talking about everything that had happened. [15]While they were talking and discussing, Jesus himself came near and began walking with them, [16]but they were kept from recognizing him. [17]Then he said, "What are these things you are talking about while you walk?"

The two followers stopped, looking very sad. [18]The one named Cleopas answered, "Are you the only visitor in Jerusalem who does not know what just happened there?"

[19]Jesus said to them, "What are you talking about?"

> **IT IS WRITTEN THAT THE CHRIST WOULD SUFFER AND RISE FROM THE DEAD ON THE THIRD DAY.**

They said, "About Jesus of Nazareth. He was a prophet who said and did many powerful things before God and all the people. [20]Our leaders and the leading priests handed him over to be sentenced to death, and they crucified him. [21]But we were hoping that he would free Israel. Besides this, it is now the third day since this happened. [22]And today some women among us amazed us. Early this morning they went to the tomb, [23]but they did not find his body there. They came and told us that they had seen a vision of angels who said that Jesus was alive! [24]So some of our group went to the tomb, too. They found it just as the women said, but they did not see Jesus."

[25]Then Jesus said to them, "You are foolish and slow to believe everything the prophets said. [26]They said that the Christ must suffer these things before he enters his glory." [27]Then starting with what Moses and all the prophets had said about him, Jesus began to explain everything that had been written about himself in the Scriptures.

[28]They came near the town of Emmaus, and Jesus acted as if he were going farther. [29]But they begged him, "Stay with us, because it is late; it is almost night." So he went in to stay with them.

[30]When Jesus was at the table with them, he took some bread, gave thanks, divided it, and gave it to them. [31]And then, they were allowed to recognize Jesus. But when they saw who he was, he disappeared. [32]They said to each other, "It felt like a fire burning in us when Jesus talked to us on the road and explained the Scriptures to us."

[33]So the two followers got up at once and went back to Jerusalem. There they found the eleven apostles and others gathered. [34]They were saying, "The Lord really has risen from the dead! He showed himself to Simon."

[35]Then the two followers told what had happened on the road and how they recognized Jesus when he divided the bread.

JESUS APPEARS TO HIS FOLLOWERS

[36]While the two followers were telling this, Jesus himself stood right in the middle of them and said, "Peace be with you."

[37]They were fearful and terrified and thought they were seeing a ghost. [38]But Jesus said, "Why are you troubled? Why do you doubt what you see? [39]Look at my hands and my feet. It is I myself! Touch me and see, because a ghost does not have a living body as you see I have."

[40]After Jesus said this, he showed them his hands and feet. [41]While they

still could not believe it because they were amazed and happy, Jesus said to them, "Do you have any food here?" [42]They gave him a piece of broiled fish. [43]While the followers watched, Jesus took the fish and ate it.

[44]He said to them, "Remember when I was with you before? I said that everything written about me must happen—everything in the law of Moses, the books of the prophets, and the Psalms."

[45]Then Jesus opened their minds so they could understand the Scriptures. [46]He said to them, "It is written that the Christ would suffer and rise from the dead on the third day [47]and that a change of hearts and lives and forgiveness of sins would be preached in his name to all nations, starting at Jerusalem. [48]You are witnesses of these things. [49]I will send you what my Father has promised, but you must stay in Jerusalem until you have received that power from heaven."

JESUS GOES BACK TO HEAVEN

[50]Jesus led his followers as far as Bethany, and he raised his hands and blessed them. [51]While he was blessing them, he was separated from them and carried into heaven. [52]They worshiped him and returned to Jerusalem very happy. [53]They stayed in the Temple all the time, praising God.

HeartCry

Time with God   Would you really like to get to know God? Would you really like to have him speak to you? All it takes is spending time with him. Tell him your thoughts and feelings and then listen. He wants to talk with you. Let your heart cry . . .

What's up Lord? Sorry that we haven't talked in a while. I've been on the go all the time. I know that I've been saying that I'm going to holla at you a lot lately. There has been so much stuff going on in my life and I have to get to it. I always make time for my homies, my family, and especially my boo, but I never seem to make time for you. Deepen my desire to hook up with you. I know that we need to rap constantly because when we ain't talking, Satan starts doing his thing with me. Protect me and help me to make you a priority. Hit me back.

I'm always here. Closer than your next breath.   Acts 17:28; Hebrews 13:5

WHO DO YOU LOOK LIKE?

Breaking the Chains of the Past
By Bishop Kenneth Ulmer

In our church, there is a family that is four generations deep and they all look alike. The baby girl is a spitting image of her great granny. Their eyes, their lips, their cheeks, noses, smile – identical. This is because the traits of the parents are the tendencies of the children. What you do see in the parents you may see in the children.

We know this is true on the medical tip. When you go to a doctor for the first time, the first thing you must do is fill out a medical history. The doctor wants to know the low down on all the family. For example, children of parents who have heart problems or high blood pressure are more likely to develop similar challenges. Women with certain kinds of cancers in their family tree should be on a regular with their doctor. That is because, medically, the traits of the parents are the tendencies of the children.

Check it! An A-1 lesson in Sociology 101. A few years ago one of the television networks did a study on the welfare system and found an interesting family in the eastern United States. They told the story of four generations of women on welfare. They traced the family history through the high-rise projects, where all four generations had lived. They told the sad stories of faded dreams and lifeless hopes as each successive generation had plans to get out and break the cycle of poverty. However, the closing shot of the family was of a teen-age girl holding a newborn baby girl. The teenage mother was standing next to a mother who looked to be in her early 30's. All were standing around the furrow-filled, frozen face of the eldest female who was the first of the four to live with the aid of public assistance. It is painfully true that, in many cases, the traits of the parents become the tendencies of the children.

However, it is interesting that this same principle is true in the spirit realm. When Jesus gets accused of being a devil, he launches into an explanation of how demonic forces come to lock down the crib and the devil takes charge of the house. Here, the word "house" has at least two meanings. On the one hand it means a literal, physical house; a place of dwelling. However, the same word also means a family or even an individual. In either case, Jesus says that in order to gain freedom, the strong man (the devil) who locks down the crib must first be bound.

Exodus 20 in the Old Testament puts it this way: God declares that he is a jealous God and that he wants all of our worship. He says, if you bow down and worship other gods, the results will continue to the next three or four generations. The results and residue of sin are passed down to your children, your grandchildren and your great grandchildren. When applied to the unrighteous act or activity by a person, it has this meaning: When a parent habitually and continually commits a sin it puts his or her children in spiritual danger. The danger is that what the parent did do, the child may do. It means that what you do see in the life of the parent, you may see in the life of the child. The tendency toward the same characteristics will exist in the next generation.

In the Bible, Abraham came to be known as the father of the faithful. But Abraham had a tendency to lie. He told a lie about his wife (Gen 20:2). Abraham had a son named Isaac who also had a tendency to lie. In fact, he also lied about his wife (Gen 26:7). Then Isaac had a son whose name was Jacob. Jacob turned out to be both a liar and a cheat. He lied to his father Isaac and gaffled his brother out of his inheritance (Genesis 25, 27). Abraham was a liar, his son Isaac was a liar, his grandson Jacob was a liar. The traits of the parent became the tendencies of the children.

In another example, when Jesus was born there was foul leader named Herod the Great. He fought against God and his kingdom. He heard that Jesus had been born and that Jesus was prophesied to be the King of the Jews. Herod was so threatened and jealous that he had all the first born, baby boys in Jerusalem killed (Matt 2). He was trying to kill Jesus because he was hatin' on the Kingdom of God.

Herod the Great had a son named Herod Antipas (Luke 9:7, 9) who had an affair with his brother's wife. John the Baptist, the cousin of Jesus, was a prophet who called Herod Antipas out about his sin (Luke 3:19-20). Herod Antipas threw John into jail, eventually, ordering his murder. He was so committed to living his life against the will, word and Kingdom of God that he killed a man.

Herod Antipas had a son named Herod Agrippa. By the time Herod Agrippa came to power, both Jesus and John the Baptist had long been dead. The church of

What habits or actions in your life did you pick up from your father or mother?
Have people ever said to you, "You're just like your daddy?"

Jesus Christ had been born on the day of Pentecost and the church was beginning to grow under the powerful preaching of Peter and the leadership of James. Herod Antipas, like his father and grandfather, hated the Kingdom of God and was an enemy of the church. Not only did he lead the persecution of Christians in Jerusalem, but he had James killed (Acts 12:1-2). He would have killed Peter too, but an angel released Peter from jail in response to the prayers of the saints. Again we see the traits of the parents become the tendencies of the children.

Who do you act like? Why do you get down like that? What habits or actions in your life did you pick up from you father or mother? Have people ever said to you, "You're just like your daddy?" The bad news about what Jesus said is that a house, a family, or a life can be entered by and influenced by ungodly, unrighteous, demonic spirits. However, Jesus also says that demons can be cast out of the house and the spot can be cleaned up! The Lord is solid. Maybe you stuggle with something in your life. Maybe, if you think about it, you see that same thing in your father's life, or your mother's life.

Jesus says the strong man, who has taken charge of the house, can be bound, tied up, and cast out. He goes on to say that the spot must be kept clean or the

demon spirit will return with some of his imps and the crib will be in worse shape than it was in the first place.

There may be things in your life that do not honor the Lord. Most of all, there may be things in your life that you noticed were present in one or more of your parents. It may be a particular sin tendency that makes you just like your mama or your daddy. Maybe you have a tendency to put a lot on it – just like your pops. Maybe you abuse women and disrespect them – just like your father. Maybe you allow men to disrespect you and abuse you because that is the way you saw your mother deal with men in her life. Maybe you are a brotha who always chases skirts and yet never makes a commitment to any significant relationship; just like your pops. Maybe you have low goals, or no goals at all for your life because living an average life, just trying to get by, is all you know and all you have been exposed to. If so, you are an example of the truth that the traits of the parents become the tendencies of the children.

Don't sleep, Jesus has a word for you. The ungodly influences in your life that have been passed down from generation to generation can be broken off your life. You have the authority to bind the spirits that would make you a slave. You have been given authority by God to release hope, success, achievement, prosperity, and freedom from guilt and sin into your life (Luke 9:1; Matt. 16:19; 18:18). You can stop the cycle of ungodliness and sin that has been passed down to you. It can stop with you. You can break the chain. You can have a clean house. By the power of Christ in you, you can overcome the tendencies you feel to do dirt and have the kind of negative attitudes that your parents had. By the power of the resurrected Christ who dwells in you, your life can be a testimony. You can declare, by faith, the power and word of God:

Heavenly Father, I thank you that you have the power to break the pattern of sin and ungodliness that has been passed down to me from previous generations. Dear Lord, by faith I declare: It ends here! By your power, I break the generational curses of sin and ungodliness over my life. By your power, I bind the influence of parental sins and any involvement in the occult and demonic activity that my fore parents may have been involved in. I declare that my life and my generation will be clean. I trust you, my God, to cleanse my thoughts and my life of those things that were bad in the lives of those before me. I will live my life day by day trusting you to keep my life clean. I thank you, Father, for the power to cleanse me and forgive me. Amen ★

JOHN

WE CAN EXPERIENCE FORGIVENESS

Stress, Pressure, Drama... these are all things we would like to avoid. When we go through this type of stuff sometimes an uglier side of us will suddenly appear. Well, if we are all honest, we'll admit that it almost always appears. John's scripts highlight the final week of Jesus' life. Almost half of the book focuses on the Stress, Pressure, and Drama that Jesus had to roll with the last couple days of his life. Most people can represent and make the right choices when things are going well, but when it gets crazy, many times we can't think straight. Not Jesus. John shows us what a true leader looks like when the heat is turned up. As we read these pages we'll catch a glimpse of a man who stayed real and displayed peace even through the most stressful situations you could imagine. But while John shows us a real man, a role model, and someone who welcomes everyone, he especially talks about Jesus as the Son of God. He stresses that Jesus suffered through all this so that we can experience forgiveness and a new life with our creator that will last forever. It all starts with being real with Jesus and being real with ourselves as we say, "I believe."

CHRIST COMES TO THE WORLD

1 In the beginning there was the Word.[n] The Word was with God, and the Word was God. [2]He was with God in the beginning. [3]All things were made by him, and nothing was made without him. [4]In him there was life, and that life was the light of all people. [5]The Light shines in the darkness, and the darkness has not overpowered[n] it.

[6]There was a man named John[n] who was sent by God. [7]He came to tell people the truth about the Light so that through him all people could hear about the Light and believe. [8]John was not the Light, but he came to tell people the truth about the Light. [9]The true Light that gives light to all was coming into the world!

[10]The Word was in the world, and the world was made by him, but the world did not know him. [11]He came to the world that was his own, but his own people did not accept him. [12]But to all who did accept him and believe in him he gave the right to become children of God. [13]They did not become his children in any human way—by any human parents or human desire. They were born of God.

[16]Because he was full of grace and truth, from him we all received one gift after another. [17]The law was given through Moses, but grace and truth came through Jesus Christ. [18]No one has ever seen God. But God the only Son is very close to the Father,[n] and he has shown us what God is like.

JOHN TELLS PEOPLE ABOUT JESUS

[19]Here is the truth John[n] told when the leaders in Jerusalem sent priests and Levites to ask him, "Who are you?"

[20]John spoke freely and did not refuse to answer. He said, "I am not the Christ."

[21]So they asked him, "Then who are you? Are you Elijah?"[n]

He answered, "No, I am not."

"Are you the Prophet?"[n] they asked.

He answered, "No."

[22]Then they said, "Who are you? Give us an answer to tell those who sent us. What do you say about yourself?"

[23]John told them in the words of the prophet Isaiah:

"I am the voice of one
    calling out in the desert:
'Make the road straight for the
    Lord.'" *Isaiah 40:3*

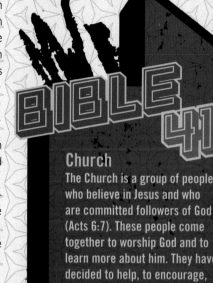

Church

The Church is a group of people who believe in Jesus and who are committed followers of God (Acts 6:7). These people come together to worship God and to learn more about him. They have decided to help, to encourage, and to love each other unconditionally—truly they can call each other "brother" and "sister." God's love is among them. They have a message for a world that needs truth, they give hope to the hopeless, and they comfort those who are in despair.

Church is not a building; it is wherever God's people gather together to share in his love and to live out his truth.

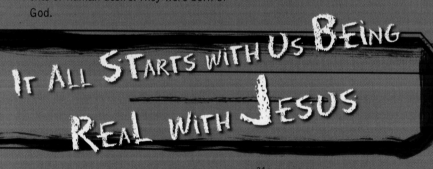
IT ALL STARTS WITH US BEING REAL WITH JESUS

[14]The Word became a human and lived among us. We saw his glory—the glory that belongs to the only Son of the Father—and he was full of grace and truth. [15]John tells the truth about him and cries out, saying, "This is the One I told you about: 'The One who comes after me is greater than I am, because he was living before me.'"

[24]Some Pharisees who had been sent asked John: [25]"If you are not the Christ or Elijah or the Prophet, why do you baptize people?"

[26]John answered, "I baptize with water, but there is one here with you that you don't know about. [27]He is the One who comes after me. I am not good enough to untie the strings of his sandals."

1:1 Word The Greek word is "logos," meaning any kind of communication; it could be translated "message." Here, it means Christ, because Christ was the way God told people about himself. **1:5 overpowered** This can also be translated, "understood." **1:6, 19 John** John the Baptist, who preached to people about Christ's coming (Matthew 3, Luke 3). **1:18 But . . . Father** This could be translated, "But the only God is very close to the Father." Also, some Greek copies read "But the only Son is very close to the Father." **1:21 Elijah** A prophet who spoke for God. He lived hundreds of years before Christ and was expected to return before Christ (Malachi 4:5-6). **1:21 Prophet** They probably meant the prophet that God told Moses he would send (Deuteronomy 18:15-19).

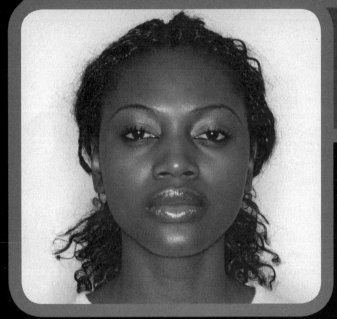

GOD UNIT 0

STRONGER FROM RAPE

Uncles are supposed to be good people, right? Not always. When I was nine years old, my mother left her younger brother to baby-sit for me one night while she went clubbing. Actually, I was really excited because I was tired of all the girls my mom used to leave me with. I looked forward to my unc and me having some male bonding time. Things were cool at first. We played video games. We played with my race cars. Then we wrestled. He let me win the first couple of times. Then he pinned me down and wouldn't let me up. Before I knew it, he'd snatched down my pants and violated me.

Afterward he socked me in the ribs, telling me that he would beat me far worse if I ever told what he had done. I would have killed him if I had known how. My momma was on my hit list as well. She had left me with her nasty-tail brother to go and get her groove on. And I was very angry that I didn't have a dad. I believed a father would have protected me from my uncle. But of course I didn't know who my dad was. And God—I knew then that he didn't exist or he would not have let that happen to me. Thankfully, threatening my uncle with telling the world he was a fag if he touched me again, made him back up off me, like the punk he really was.

For years I was bitter, keeping it all inside. I was full of anger, and I took it out on everyone around me. It wasn't until I bumped into a cat that I used to roll with that I was able to release some of my hurt. He had given his life to the Lord. He told me to cast my mess on Jesus. Just having someone talk to me in-depth about God was what I needed in order to understand how deep God's love was for me. I wept letting go of all that old pain. After growing closer to God, I now know that though something bad happened to me in my childhood, God was there all along. He helped me grow stronger through the ordeal. My love for God has helped me to forgive where I once hated and allowed me to be happy instead of angry 24/7. Now whatever I go through, I don't handle it alone. I call on him, and I he carries it with me.

Matthew 6:14—If you forgive others for their sins, your Father in heaven will also forgive you for your sins.

[28]This all happened at Bethany on the other side of the Jordan River, where John was baptizing people.

[29]The next day John saw Jesus coming toward him. John said, "Look, the Lamb of God,[n] who takes away the sin of the world! [30]This is the One I was talking about when I said, 'A man will come after me, but he is greater than I am, because he was living before me.' [31]Even I did not know who he was, although I came baptizing with water so that the people of Israel would know who he is."

[32-33]Then John said, "I saw the Spirit come down from heaven in the form of a dove and rest on him. Until then I did not know who the Christ was. But the God who sent me to baptize with water told me, 'You will see the Spirit come down and rest on a man; he is the One who will baptize with the Holy Spirit.' [34]I have seen this happen, and I tell you the truth: This man is the Son of God.'"[n]

THE FIRST FOLLOWERS OF JESUS

[35]The next day John[n] was there again with two of his followers. [36]When he saw Jesus walking by, he said, "Look, the Lamb of God!"[n]

[37]The two followers heard John say this, so they followed Jesus. [38]When Jesus turned and saw them following him, he asked, "What are you looking for?"

They said, "Rabbi, where are you staying?" ("Rabbi" means "Teacher.")

[39]He answered, "Come and see." So the two men went with Jesus and saw where he was staying and stayed there with him that day. It was about four o'clock in the afternoon.

[40]One of the two men who followed Jesus after they heard John speak about him was Andrew, Simon Peter's brother.

 1:29, 36 Lamb of God Name for Jesus. Jesus is like the lambs that were offered for a sacrifice to God. **1:34 the Son of God** Some Greek copies read "God's Chosen One." **1:35 John** John the Baptist, who preached to people about Christ's coming (Matthew 3, Luke 3).

⁴¹The first thing Andrew did was to find his brother Simon and say to him, "We have found the Messiah." ("Messiah" means "Christ.")

⁴²Then Andrew took Simon to Jesus. Jesus looked at him and said, "You are Simon son of John. You will be called Cephas." ("Cephas" means "Peter."ⁿ)

⁴³The next day Jesus decided to go to Galilee. He found Philip and said to him, "Follow me."

⁴⁴Philip was from the town of Bethsaida, where Andrew and Peter lived. ⁴⁵Philip found Nathanael and told him, "We have found the man that Moses wrote about in the law, and the prophets also wrote about him. He is Jesus, the son of Joseph, from Nazareth."

⁴⁶But Nathanael said to Philip, "Can anything good come from Nazareth?"

Philip answered, "Come and see."

⁴⁷As Jesus saw Nathanael coming toward him, he said, "Here is truly an Israelite. There is nothing false in him."

⁴⁸Nathanael asked, "How do you know me?"

Jesus answered, "I saw you when you were under the fig tree, before Philip told you about me."

⁴⁹Then Nathanael said to Jesus, "Teacher, you are the Son of God; you are the King of Israel."

⁵⁰Jesus said to Nathanael, "Do you believe simply because I told you I saw you under the fig tree? You will see greater things than that." ⁵¹And Jesus said to them, "I tell you the truth, you will all see heaven open and 'angels of God going up and coming down'ⁿ on the Son of Man."

THE WEDDING AT CANA

2 Two days later there was a wedding in the town of Cana in Galilee. Jesus' mother was there, ²and Jesus and his followers were also invited to the wedding. ³When all the wine was gone, Jesus' mother said to him, "They have no more wine."

⁴Jesus answered, "Dear woman, why come to me? My time has not yet come."

⁵His mother said to the servants, "Do whatever he tells you to do."

⁶In that place there were six stone water jars that the Jews used in their washing ceremony.ⁿ Each jar held about twenty or thirty gallons.

⁷Jesus said to the servants, "Fill the jars with water." So they filled the jars to the top.

⁸Then he said to them, "Now take some out and give it to the master of the feast."

So they took the water to the master. ⁹When he tasted it, the water had become wine. He did not know where the wine came from, but the servants who had brought the water knew. The master of the wedding called the bridegroom ¹⁰and said to him, "People always serve the best wine first. Later, after the guests have been drinking awhile, they serve the cheaper wine. But you have saved the best wine till now."

¹¹So in Cana of Galilee Jesus did his first miracle. There he showed his glory, and his followers believed in him.

JESUS IN THE TEMPLE

¹²After this, Jesus went to the town of Capernaum with his mother, brothers, and followers. They stayed there for just a few days. ¹³When it was almost time for the Jewish Passover Feast, Jesus went to Jerusalem. ¹⁴In the Temple he found people selling cattle, sheep, and doves. He saw others sitting at tables, exchanging different kinds of money. ¹⁵Jesus made a whip out of cords and forced all of them, both the sheep and cattle, to leave the Temple. He turned over the tables and scattered the money of those who were exchanging it. ¹⁶Then he said to those who were selling pigeons, "Take these things out of here! Don't make my Father's house a place for buying and selling!"

¹⁷When this happened, the followers remembered what was written in the Scriptures: "My strong love for your Temple completely controls me."ⁿ

¹⁸Some of his people said to Jesus, "Show us a miracle to prove you have the right to do these things."

¹⁹Jesus answered them, "Destroy this temple, and I will build it again in three days."

²⁰They answered, "It took forty-six years to build this Temple! Do you really believe you can build it again in three days?"

²¹(But the temple Jesus meant was his own body. ²²After Jesus was raised from the dead, his followers remembered that Jesus had said this. Then they believed the Scripture and the words Jesus had said.)

²³When Jesus was in Jerusalem for the Passover Feast, many people believed in him because they saw the miracles he did. ²⁴But Jesus did not believe in them because he knew them all. ²⁵He did not need anyone to tell him about people, because he knew what was in people's minds.

NICODEMUS COMES TO JESUS

3 There was a man named Nicodemus who was one of the Pharisees and an important Jewish leader. ²One night Nicodemus came to Jesus and said, "Teacher, we know you are a teacher sent from God, because no one can do the miracles you do unless God is with him."

³Jesus answered, "I tell you the truth, unless you are born again, you cannot be in God's kingdom."

⁴Nicodemus said, "But if a person is already old, how can he be born again? He cannot enter his mother's womb again. So how can a person be born a second time?"

⁵But Jesus answered, "I tell you the truth, unless you are born from water and the Spirit, you cannot enter God's kingdom. ⁶Human life comes from human parents, but spiritual life comes

 1:42 Peter The Greek name "Peter," like the Aramaic name "Cephas," means "rock." **1:51 'angels . . . down'** These words are from Genesis 28:12. **2:6 washing ceremony** The Jewish people washed themselves in special ways before eating, before worshiping in the Temple, and at other special times. **2:17 "My . . . me."** Quotation from Psalm 69:9.

from the Spirit. [7]Don't be surprised when I tell you, 'You must all be born again.' [8]The wind blows where it wants to and you hear the sound of it, but you don't know where the wind comes from or where it is going. It is the same with every person who is born from the Spirit."

[9]Nicodemus asked, "How can this happen?"

[10]Jesus said, "You are an important teacher in Israel, and you don't understand these things? [11]I tell you the truth, we talk about what we know, and we tell about what we have seen, but you don't accept what we tell you. [12]I have told you about things here on earth, and you do not believe me. So you will not believe me if I tell you about things of heaven. [13]The only one who has ever gone up to heaven is the One who came down from heaven—the Son of Man.[n]

[14]"Just as Moses lifted up the snake in the desert,[n] the Son of Man must also be lifted up. [15]So that everyone who believes can have eternal life in him.

[16]"God loved the world so much that he gave his one and only Son so that whoever believes in him may not be lost, but have eternal life. [17]God did not send his Son into the world to judge the world guilty, but to save the world through him. [18]People who believe in God's Son are not judged guilty. Those who do not believe have already been judged guilty, because they have not believed in God's

He's got answers

I heard someone say that Christians shouldn't have credit cards. What's up with that?

When used correctly, credit can be a good thing. Without a mortgage, only a few people would be able to buy a home. For those who pay their balances at the end of the month, credit cards are not a problem.

But it doesn't take a financial expert to see that debt is a big problem for many people. For some, it becomes an addiction. One of the problems with credit is that it can feed into a need for instant gratification. Instead of using it only for their needs, many people whip out a credit card to buy wants. They don't have money to see the latest movie, so they charge the tickets. They don't want to wait and save up the money for a new computer; so they charge it. They don't have extra money in their budget to eat out, so they charge burgers. There are few places where credit cards are not accepted.

Few people pay the balance of their bills at the end of the month. Those who can't end up having huge interest rates tacked onto a bill for things they didn't need and didn't have the money to buy in the first place. It's not uncommon for many people to end up borrowing from one card to pay the bill on another. What started as a snowball becomes an avalanche of debt. Bankruptcy courts are full of people who have monstrous credit-card debt.

The Bible doesn't say a lot about debt, but what it does say is deep. It says that the person who borrows is a slave to the lender. It also says that the only thing you should owe anyone is love.

Read on: Romans 13:7-8; Hebrews 13:5

PEEP THIS:

Forty-three percent of consumers entering a music store or music section of a store bought music; 57 percent left empty-handed.

one and only Son. [19]They are judged by this fact: The Light has come into the world, but they did not want light. They wanted darkness, because they were doing evil things. [20]All who do evil hate the light and will not come to the light, be-cause it will show all the evil things they do. [21]But those who follow the true way come to the light, and it shows that the things they do were done through God."

JESUS AND JOHN THE BAPTIST

[22]After this, Jesus and his followers went into the area of Judea, where he stayed with his followers and baptized people. [23]John was also baptizing in Aenon, near Salim, because there was plenty of water there. People were going there to be baptized. [24](This was before John was put into prison.)

[25]Some of John's followers had an argument with a Jew about religious wash-

---

3:13 the Son of Man Some Greek copies continue, "who is in heaven." **3:14 Moses . . . desert** When the Israelites were dying from snakebites, God told Moses to put a bronze snake on a pole. The people who looked at the snake were healed (Numbers 21:4-9).

ing." ²⁶So they came to John and said, "Teacher, remember the man who was with you on the other side of the Jordan River, the one you spoke about so much? He is baptizing, and everyone is going to him."

²⁷John answered, "A man can get only what God gives him. ²⁸You yourselves heard me say, 'I am not the Christ, but I am the one sent to prepare the way for him.' ²⁹The bride belongs only to the bridegroom. But the friend who helps the bridegroom stands by and listens to him. He is thrilled that he gets to hear the bridegroom's voice. In the same way, I am really happy. ³⁰He must become greater, and I must become less important.

THE ONE WHO COMES FROM HEAVEN

³¹"The One who comes from above is greater than all. The one who is from the earth belongs to the earth and talks about things on the earth. But the One who comes from heaven is greater than all. ³²He tells what he has seen and heard, but no one accepts what he says. ³³Whoever accepts what he says has proven that God is true. ³⁴The One whom God sent speaks the words of God, because God gives him the Spirit fully. ³⁵The Father loves the Son and has given him power over everything. ³⁶Those who believe in the Son have eternal life, but those who do not obey the Son will never have life. God's anger stays on them."

3:25 religious washing The Jewish people washed themselves in special ways before eating, before worshiping in the Temple, and at other special times.

THE SCRIPT

Water to Wine
John 1:29-33; 2:1-13

Down in Cana of Galilee; A wedding took place on day three
After Jesus was baptized by his cousin John,
In the Jordan when the Holy Spirit on Jesus came down,
Jesus and his disciples got called to a ceremony.
It was a festive matrimony, a time to drink some wine
But there was only one catch-22, and that became a sign,
'Cause they ran out of wine early so . . . what cha gone' do?
Mary pulled Jesus to the side and told him the news:
"Jesus, they're out of wine" but Jesus said in her view,
"Ma, you're pursuing me like this is my issue; it's not time for my debut!"
Mary was like, "Cool." But she told the serving crew,
"Whatever Jesus says, make sure that it's what cha gone' do!"
Now check the plot: standing in the room were six big stone water pots
Jews used them to wash their face, feet, and hands—to purify
Jesus had the servants fill them with water to the top, and they didn't ask, "Why?"
Jesus told them to pour out some liquid for the bridegroom's homies.

The servants served water turned to wine to the master of the ceremony.
Not knowing what really had taken place,
The ruler sipped the wine and had a look on his face like:
"Man, wait! This was the best wine in the place!
I'm captured by the taste! Why did we wait to break this case?"
(He just didn't know it was once water that Jesus miraculously replaced),
But the staff knew the case because they saw it all take place,
And they all testified to Jesus' amazing grace!
It was the first of many miracles revealing a glimpse of God's face.
This was just the beginning of Jesus showing God's glory
And his disciples started to believe on Jesus and his story.
Then Jesus' mother, brothers, and followers headed down to Capernaum
It was Jewish Passover and Jesus headed straight for Jerusalem.

Take this with you: Don't worry about what other people think when God speaks to you and gives you direction. Following his instructions will set the stage for God to perform great transforming miracles in your life.

OVERCOMING

▶ SEXUAL ABUSE

One of every five girls and one of every eight boys is sexually abused by age 12. In the US alone, it's estimated that from 200,000 to 500,000 children are sexually abused each year and only 100,000 of these cases are reported (Lueders, Beth J. "The Painful Truth: Statistics About Abuse." Christianity Today International/ Leadership Journal. Summer, 1997). Survivors of sexual abuse carry the resulting pain, sorrow and false sense of shame with them into their adult lives. These wounded ones find it very difficult to form relationships. They have built walls of self-protection that are nearly invincible.

If I am talking about you, please believe me, you do not have to continue living with this hidden pain. There is a life available to you that offers the security and peace you so desire. You can overcome the overwhelming effects of abuse. It is important that you find a counselor or pastor to help you on your journey out of pain. Talk to him or her; be honest and open. But even more importantly, pour your heart out to God. He's listening. He cares. And he will lead you to a place where your bruised heart can find healing.

JESUS AND A SAMARITAN WOMAN

4 The Pharisees heard that Jesus was making and baptizing more followers than John, [2]although Jesus himself did not baptize people, but his followers did. [3]Jesus knew that the Pharisees had heard about him, so he left Judea and went back to Galilee. [4]But on the way he had to go through the country of Samaria.

[5]In Samaria Jesus came to the town called Sychar, which is near the field Jacob gave to his son Joseph. [6]Jacob's well was there. Jesus was tired from his long trip, so he sat down beside the well. It was about twelve o'clock noon. [7]When a Samaritan woman came to the well to get some water, Jesus said to her, "Please give me a drink." [8](This happened while Jesus' followers were in town buying some food.)

[9]The woman said, "I am surprised that you ask me for a drink, since you are a Jewish man and I am a Samaritan woman." (Jewish people are not friends with Samaritans.")

[10]Jesus said, "If you only knew the free gift of God and who it is that is asking you for water, you would have asked him, and he would have given you living water."

[11]The woman said, "Sir, where will you get this living water? The well is very deep, and you have nothing to get water with. [12]Are you greater than Jacob, our father, who gave us this well and drank from it himself along with his sons and flocks?"

[13]Jesus answered, "Everyone who drinks this water will be thirsty again, [14]but whoever drinks the water I give will never be thirsty. The water I give will become a spring of water gushing up inside that person, giving eternal life."

[15]The woman said to him, "Sir, give me this water so I will never be thirsty again and will not have to come back here to get more water."

[16]Jesus told her, "Go get your husband and come back here."

[17]The woman answered, "I have no husband."

Jesus said to her, "You are right to say you have no husband. [18]Really you have

had five husbands, and the man you live with now is not your husband. You told the truth."

[19]The woman said, "Sir, I can see that you are a prophet. [20]Our ancestors worshiped on this mountain, but you say that Jerusalem is the place where people must worship."

[21]Jesus said, "Believe me, woman. The time is coming when neither in Jerusalem nor on this mountain will you actually worship the Father. [22]You Samaritans worship something you don't understand. We understand what we worship, because salvation comes from the Jews. [23]The time is coming when the true worshipers will worship the Father in spirit and truth, and that time is here already. You see, the Father too is actively seeking such people to worship him. [24]God is spirit, and those who worship him must worship in spirit and truth."

[25]The woman said, "I know that the Messiah is coming." (Messiah is the One called Christ.) "When the Messiah comes, he will explain everything to us."

[26]Then Jesus said, "I am he—I, the one talking to you."

4:9 Jewish people . . . Samaritans. This can also be translated "Jewish people don't use things that Samaritans have used."

²⁷Just then his followers came back from town and were surprised to see him talking with a woman. But none of them asked, "What do you want?" or "Why are you talking with her?"

²⁸Then the woman left her water jar and went back to town. She said to the people, ²⁹"Come and see a man who told me everything I ever did. Do you think he might be the Christ?" ³⁰So the people left the town and went to see Jesus.

³¹Meanwhile, his followers were begging him, "Teacher, eat something."

³²But Jesus answered, "I have food to eat that you know nothing about."

³³So the followers asked themselves, "Did somebody already bring him food?"

³⁴Jesus said, "My food is to do what the One who sent me wants me to do and to finish his work. ³⁵You have a saying, 'Four more months till harvest.' But I tell you, open your eyes and look at the fields ready for harvest now. ³⁶Already, the one who harvests is being paid and is gathering crops for eternal life. So the one who plants and the one who harvests celebrate at the same time. ³⁷Here the saying is true, 'One person plants, and another harvests.' ³⁸I sent you to harvest a crop that you did not work on. Others did the work, and you get to finish up their work."ⁿ

³⁹Many of the Samaritans in that town believed in Jesus because of what the woman said: "He told me everything I ever did." ⁴⁰When the Samaritans came to Jesus, they begged him to stay with them, so he stayed there two more days. ⁴¹And many more believed because of the things he said.

⁴²They said to the woman, "First we believed in Jesus because of what you said, but now we believe because we heard him ourselves. We know that this man really is the Savior of the world."

JESUS HEALS AN OFFICER'S SON

⁴³Two days later, Jesus left and went to Galilee. ⁴⁴(Jesus had said before that a prophet is not respected in his own country.) ⁴⁵When Jesus arrived in Galilee, the people there welcomed him. They had seen all the things he did at the Passover Feast in Jerusalem, because they had been there, too.

⁴⁶Jesus went again to visit Cana in Galilee where he had changed the water into wine. One of the king's important officers lived in the city of Capernaum, and his son was sick. ⁴⁷When he heard that Jesus had come from Judea to Galilee, he went to Jesus and begged him to come to Capernaum and heal his son, because his son was almost dead. ⁴⁸Jesus said to him, "You people must see signs and miracles before you will believe in me."

> ## WHOEVER DRINKS THE WATER I GIVE WILL NEVER BE THIRSTY.

⁴⁹The officer said, "Sir, come before my child dies."

⁵⁰Jesus answered, "Go. Your son will live."

The man believed what Jesus told him and went home. ⁵¹On the way the man's servants came and met him and told him, "Your son is alive."

⁵²The man asked, "What time did my son begin to get well?"

They answered, "Yesterday at one o'clock the fever left him."

⁵³The father knew that one o'clock was the exact time that Jesus had said, "Your son will live." So the man and all the people who lived in his house believed in Jesus.

⁵⁴That was the second miracle Jesus did after coming from Judea to Galilee.

JESUS HEALS A MAN AT A POOL

5 Later Jesus went to Jerusalem for a special feast. ²In Jerusalem there is a pool with five covered porches, which is called Bethesdaⁿ in the Hebrew language.ⁿ This pool is near the Sheep Gate. ³Many sick people were lying on the porches beside the pool. Some were blind, some were crippled, and some were paralyzed [, and they waited for the water to move. ⁴Sometimes an angel of the Lord came down to the pool and stirred up the water. After the angel did this, the first person to go into the pool was healed from any sickness he had].ⁿ ⁵A man was lying there who had been sick for thirty-eight years. ⁶When Jesus saw the man and knew that he had been sick for such a long time, Jesus asked him, "Do you want to be well?"

⁷The sick man answered, "Sir, there is no one to help me get into the pool when the water starts moving. While I am coming to the water, someone else always gets in before me."

⁸Then Jesus said, "Stand up. Pick up your mat and walk." ⁹And immediately the man was well; he picked up his mat and began to walk.

The day this happened was a Sabbath day. ¹⁰So the Jews said to the man who had been healed, "Today is the Sabbath. It is against our law for you to carry your mat on the Sabbath day."

¹¹But he answered, "The man who made me well told me, 'Pick up your mat and walk.'"

¹²Then they asked him, "Who is the man who told you to pick up your mat and walk?"

¹³But the man who had been healed did not know who it was, because there were many people in that place, and Jesus had left.

¹⁴Later, Jesus found the man at the Temple and said to him, "See, you are well now. Stop sinning so that something worse does not happen to you."

4:38 I . . . their work. As a farmer sends workers to harvest grain, Jesus sends his followers out to bring people to God. **5:2 Bethesda** Some Greek copies read "Bethzatha" or "Bethsaida," different names for the pool of Bethesda. **5:2 Hebrew language** Or Aramaic, the languages of many people in this region in the first century. **5:3-4 and . . . had** Some Greek copies do not contain all or most of the bracketed text.

▶ 135

¹⁵Then the man left and told his people that Jesus was the one who had made him well.

¹⁶Because Jesus was doing this on the Sabbath day, some evil people began to persecute him. ¹⁷But Jesus said to them, "My Father never stops working, and so I keep working, too."

¹⁸This made them try still harder to kill him. They said, "First Jesus was breaking the law about the Sabbath day. Now he says that God is his own Father, making himself equal with God!"

JESUS HAS GOD'S AUTHORITY

¹⁹But Jesus said, "I tell you the truth, the Son can do nothing alone. The Son does only what he sees the Father doing, because the Son does whatever the Father does. ²⁰The Father loves the Son and shows the Son all the things he himself does. But the Father will show the Son even greater things than this so that you can all be amazed. ²¹Just as the Father raises the dead and gives them life, so also the Son gives life to those he wants to. ²²In fact, the Father judges no one, but he has given the Son power to do all the judging ²³so that all people will honor the Son as much as they honor the Father. Anyone who does not honor the Son does not honor the Father who sent him.

²⁴"I tell you the truth, whoever hears what I say and believes in the One who sent me has eternal life. That person will not be judged guilty but has already left death and entered life. ²⁵I tell you the truth, the time is coming and is already here when the dead will hear the voice of the Son of God, and those who hear will have life. ²⁶Life comes from the Father himself, and he has allowed the Son to have life in himself as well. ²⁷And the Father has given the Son the approval to judge, because he is the Son of Man. ²⁸Don't be surprised at this: A time is coming when all who are dead and in their graves will hear his voice. ²⁹Then they will come out of their graves. Those who did good will rise and have life for-

hot 10

Movies You Should Have in Your Collection

10. Dogma

9. It's a Wonderful Life

8. The Ten Commandments

7. Chariots of Fire

6. The Apostle

5. The Green Mile

4. Soul Food

3. Lord of the Rings (Trilogy)

2. Remember the Titans

1. The Passion of the Christ

ever, but those who did evil will rise to be judged guilty.

JESUS IS GOD'S SON

³⁰"I can do nothing alone. I judge only the way I am told, so my judgment is fair. I don't try to please myself, but I try to please the One who sent me.

³¹"If only I tell people about myself, what I say is not true. ³²But there is another who tells about me, and I know that the things he says about me are true.

³³"You have sent people to John, and he has told you the truth. ³⁴It is not that I need what humans say; I tell you this so you can be saved. ³⁵John was like a burning and shining lamp, and you were happy to enjoy his light for a while.

³⁶"But I have a proof about myself that is greater than that of John. The things I do, which are the things my Father gave me to do, prove that the Father sent me. ³⁷And the Father himself who sent me has given proof about me. You have never heard his voice or seen what he looks like. ³⁸His teaching does not live in you, because you don't believe in the One the Father sent. ³⁹You carefully study the Scriptures because you think they give you eternal life. They do in fact tell about me, ⁴⁰but you refuse to come to me to have that life.

⁴¹"I don't need praise from people. ⁴²But I know you—I know that you don't have God's love in you. ⁴³I have come from my Father and speak for him, but you don't accept me. But when another person comes, speaking only for himself, you will accept him. ⁴⁴You try to get praise from each other, but you do not try to get the praise that comes from the only God. So how can you believe? ⁴⁵Don't think that I will stand before the Father and say you are wrong. The one who says you are wrong is Moses, the one you hoped would save you. ⁴⁶If you really believed Moses, you would believe me, because Moses wrote about me. ⁴⁷But if you don't believe what Moses wrote, how can you believe what I say?"

MORE THAN FIVE THOUSAND FED

6 After this, Jesus went across Lake Galilee (or, Lake Tiberias). [2]Many people followed him because they saw the miracles he did to heal the sick. [3]Jesus went up on a hill and sat down there with his followers. [4]It was almost the time for the Jewish Passover Feast.

[5]When Jesus looked up and saw a large crowd coming toward him, he said to Philip, "Where can we buy enough bread for all these people to eat?" [6](Jesus asked Philip this question to test him, because Jesus already knew what he planned to do.)

[7]Philip answered, "Someone would have to work almost a year to buy enough bread for each person to have only a little piece."

[8]Another one of his followers, Andrew, Simon Peter's brother, said, [9]"Here is a boy with five loaves of barley bread and two little fish, but that is not enough for so many people."

[10]Jesus said, "Tell the people to sit down." There was plenty of grass there, and about five thousand men sat down there. [11]Then Jesus took the loaves of bread, thanked God for them, and gave them to the people who were sitting there. He did the same with the fish, giving as much as the people wanted.

[12]When they had all had enough to eat, Jesus said to his followers, "Gather the leftover pieces of fish and bread so that nothing is wasted." [13]So they gathered up the pieces and filled twelve baskets with the pieces left from the five barley loaves.

[14]When the people saw this miracle that Jesus did, they said, "He must truly be the Prophet[n] who is coming into the world."

[15]Jesus knew that the people planned to come and take him by force and make him their king, so he left and went into the hills alone.

JESUS WALKS ON THE WATER

[16]That evening Jesus' followers went down to Lake Galilee. [17]It was dark now, and Jesus had not yet come to them. The followers got into a boat and started across the lake to Capernaum. [18]By now a strong wind was blowing, and the waves on the lake were getting bigger. [19]When they had rowed the boat about three or four miles, they saw Jesus walking on the water, coming toward the boat. The followers were afraid, [20]but Jesus said to them, "It is I. Do not be afraid." [21]Then they were glad to take him into the boat. At once the boat came to land at the place where they wanted to go.

THE PEOPLE SEEK JESUS

[22]The next day the people who had stayed on the other side of the lake knew that Jesus had not gone in the boat with his followers but that they had left without him. And they knew that only one boat had been there. [23]But then some boats came from Tiberias and landed near the place where the people had eaten the bread after the Lord had given thanks. [24]When the people saw that Jesus and his followers were not there now, they got into boats and went to Capernaum to find Jesus.

JESUS, THE BREAD OF LIFE

[25]When the people found Jesus on the other side of the lake, they asked him, "Teacher, when did you come here?"

[26]Jesus answered, "I tell you the truth, you aren't looking for me because you saw me do miracles. You are looking for me because you ate the bread and were satisfied. [27]Don't work for the food that spoils. Work for the food that stays good always and gives eternal life. The Son of Man will give you this food, because on him God the Father has put his power."

[28]The people asked Jesus, "What are the things God wants us to do?"

[29]Jesus answered, "The work God wants you to do is this: Believe the One he sent."

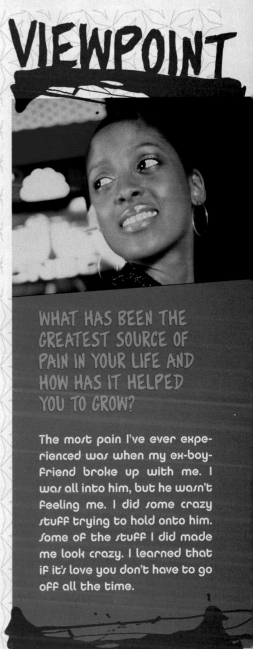

VIEWPOINT

WHAT HAS BEEN THE GREATEST SOURCE OF PAIN IN YOUR LIFE AND HOW HAS IT HELPED YOU TO GROW?

The most pain I've ever experienced was when my ex-boyfriend broke up with me. I was all into him, but he wasn't feeling me. I did some crazy stuff trying to hold onto him. Some of the stuff I did made me look crazy. I learned that if it's love you don't have to go off all the time.

[30]So the people asked, "What miracle will you do? If we see a miracle, we will believe you. What will you do? [31]Our ancestors ate the manna in the desert. This is written in the Scriptures: 'He gave them bread from heaven to eat.'"

[32]Jesus said, "I tell you the truth, it was not Moses who gave you bread from heaven; it is my Father who is giving you the true bread from heaven. [33]God's

---

 6:14 Prophet They probably meant the prophet that God told Moses he would send (Deuteronomy 18:15-19).   **6:31 'He gave . . . eat.'** Quotation from Psalm 78:24.

365

1 On This Day In History 1961—Fidel Castro announces that elections in Cuba will cease.

2

3 It's your birthday, James Brown and Damon Dash!

4

5 HOLIDAY—Cinco de Mayo   Lil Romeo's Birthday

6 HOLIDAY—Mother's Day

7 HOLIDAY—Memorial Day

8

9 Think outside the box:
What can I do to make my mother proud?

10

11

12

13

14

15

"It is my belief that we all have the need to feel special. It is this need that can bring out the best in us, yet the worst in us."
—Janet Jackson

16 It's your birthday, Janet Jackson!

17 Take your mother or a special lady in your life out to lunch.

18

19

20

21

22 Who has had the greatest positive impact in your life and how?

23

24

25

26 On This Day In History 1965—Voting Rights Bill passed.

27

28 Celebrate Cinco de Mayo—
appreciate the culture by preparing a dish

29

30

31

ARTIST: JT   ALBUM: BUMP THIS

Bump This is an encouraging rap and R&B album by JT. The vocals are amazing, and JT has a righteous voice that is smooth and easy to listen to. This is a CD that's best listened to with a group ready to act up. Each song is carefully formulated for a perfect sound. I know I couldn't help but put my hands together in time to the rhythms when I listened to this CD. Each cut has a great message about praise and worship. There were so many tracks that I liked, it is hard to pinpoint a favorite. But, "Do You Wanna Know" has to win out. If you're looking for an album that you can get your praise on with, this is the CD for you. Be sure to pick up a copy of this album to share with others.

"ACCEPTED"

bread is the One who comes down from heaven and gives life to the world."

[34] The people said, "Sir, give us this bread always."

[35] Then Jesus said, "I am the bread that gives life. Whoever comes to me will never be hungry, and whoever believes in me will never be thirsty. [36] But as I told you before, you have seen me and still don't believe. [37] The Father gives me the people who are mine. Every one of them will come to me, and I will always accept them. [38] I came down from heaven to do what God wants me to do, not what I want to do. [39] Here is what the One who sent me wants me to do: I must not lose even one whom God gave me, but I must raise them all on the last day. [40] Those who see the Son and believe in him have eternal life, and I will raise them on the last day. This is what my Father wants."

[41] Some people began to complain about Jesus because he said, "I am the bread that comes down from heaven." [42] They said, "This is Jesus, the son of Joseph. We know his father and mother. How can he say, 'I came down from heaven'?"

[43] But Jesus answered, "Stop complaining to each other. [44] The Father is the One who sent me. No one can come to me unless the Father draws him to me, and I will raise that person up on the last day. [45] It is written in the prophets, 'They will all be taught by God.'[n] Everyone who listens to the Father and learns from him comes to me. [46] No one has seen the Father except the One who is from God; only he has seen the Father. [47] I tell you the truth, whoever believes has eternal life. [48] I am the bread that gives life. [49] Your ancestors ate the manna in the desert, but still they died. [50] Here is the bread that comes down from heaven. Anyone who eats this bread will never die. [51] I am the living bread that came down from heaven. Anyone who eats this bread will live forever. This bread is my flesh, which I will give up so that the world may have life."

[52] Then the evil people began to argue among themselves, saying, "How can this man give us his flesh to eat?"

[53] Jesus said, "I tell you the truth, you must eat the flesh of the Son of Man and drink his blood. Otherwise, you won't have real life in you. [54] Those who eat my flesh and drink my blood have eternal life, and I will raise them up on the last day. [55] My flesh is true food, and my blood is true drink. [56] Those who eat my flesh and drink my blood live in me, and I live in them. [57] The living Father sent me, and I live because of the Father. So whoever eats me will live because of me. [58] I am not like the bread your ancestors ate. They ate that bread and still died. I am the bread that came down from heaven, and whoever eats this bread will live forever." [59] Jesus said all these things while he was teaching in the synagogue in Capernaum.

THE WORDS OF ETERNAL LIFE

[60] When the followers of Jesus heard this, many of them said, "This teaching is hard. Who can accept it?"

[61] Knowing that his followers were complaining about this, Jesus said, "Does this teaching bother you? [62] Then will it also bother you to see the Son of Man going back to the place where he came from? [63] It is the Spirit that gives life. The flesh doesn't give life. The words

6:45 'They . . . God.' Quotation from Isaiah 54:13.

I told you are spirit, and they give life. [64]But some of you don't believe." (Jesus knew from the beginning who did not believe and who would turn against him.) [65]Jesus said, "That is the reason I said, 'If the Father does not bring a person to me, that one cannot come.'"

[66]After Jesus said this, many of his followers left him and stopped following him.

[67]Jesus asked the twelve followers, "Do you want to leave, too?"

[68]Simon Peter answered him, "Lord, who would we go to? You have the words that give eternal life. [69]We believe and know that you are the Holy One from God."

[70]Then Jesus answered, "I chose all twelve of you, but one of you is a devil." [71]Jesus was talking about Judas, the son of Simon Iscariot. Judas was one of the twelve, but later he was going to turn against Jesus.

JESUS' BROTHERS DON'T BELIEVE

7 After this, Jesus traveled around Galilee. He did not want to travel in Judea, because some evil people there wanted to kill him. [2]It was time for the Feast of Shelters. [3]So Jesus' brothers said to him, "You should leave here and go to Judea so your followers there can see the miracles you do. [4]Anyone who wants to be well known does not hide what he does. If you are doing these things, show yourself to the world." [5](Even Jesus' brothers did not believe in him.)

[6]Jesus said to his brothers, "The right time for me has not yet come, but any time is right for you. [7]The world cannot hate you, but it hates me, because I tell it the evil things it does. [8]So you go to the feast. I will not go yet[n] to this feast, because the right time for me has not yet come." [9]After saying this, Jesus stayed in Galilee.

[10]But after Jesus' brothers had gone to the feast, Jesus went also. But he did not let people see him. [11]At the feast some people were looking for him and saying, "Where is that man?"

[12]Within the large crowd there, many people were whispering to each other about Jesus. Some said, "He is a good man."

Others said, "No, he fools the people." [13]But no one was brave enough to talk about Jesus openly, because they were afraid of the elders.

JESUS TEACHES AT THE FEAST

[14]When the feast was about half over, Jesus went to the Temple and began to teach. [15]The people were amazed and said, "This man has never studied in school. How did he learn so much?"

STOP JUDGING BY THE WAY THINGS LOOK, BUT JUDGE BY WHAT IS REALLY RIGHT.

[16]Jesus answered, "The things I teach are not my own, but they come from him who sent me. [17]If people choose to do what God wants, they will know that my teaching comes from God and not from me. [18]Those who teach their own ideas are trying to get honor for themselves. But those who try to bring honor to the one who sent them speak the truth, and there is nothing false in them. [19]Moses gave you the law,[n] but none of you obeys that law. Why are you trying to kill me?"

[20]The people answered, "A demon has come into you. We are not trying to kill you."

[21]Jesus said to them, "I did one miracle, and you are all amazed. [22]Moses gave you the law about circumcision. (But really Moses did not give you circumcision; it came from our ancestors.) And yet you circumcise a baby boy on a Sabbath day. [23]If a baby boy can be circumcised on a Sabbath day to obey the law of Moses, why are you angry at me for healing a person's whole body on the Sabbath day? [24]Stop judging by the way things look, but judge by what is really right."

IS JESUS THE CHRIST?

[25]Then some of the people who lived in Jerusalem said, "This is the man they are trying to kill. [26]But he is teaching where everyone can see and hear him, and no one is trying to stop him. Maybe the leaders have decided he really is the Christ. [27]But we know where this man is from. Yet when the real Christ comes, no one will know where he comes from."

[28]Jesus, teaching in the Temple, cried out, "Yes, you know me, and you know where I am from. But I have not come by my own authority. I was sent by the One who is true, whom you don't know. [29]But I know him, because I am from him, and he sent me."

[30]When Jesus said this, they tried to seize him. But no one was able to touch him, because it was not yet the right time. [31]But many of the people believed in Jesus. They said, "When the Christ comes, will he do more miracles than this man has done?"

THE LEADERS TRY TO ARREST JESUS

[32]The Pharisees heard the crowd whispering these things about Jesus. So the leading priests and the Pharisees sent some Temple guards to arrest him. [33]Jesus said, "I will be with you a little while longer. Then I will go back to the One who sent me. [34]You will look for me, but you will not find me. And you cannot come where I am."

[35]Some people said to each other, "Where will this man go so we cannot find him? Will he go to the Greek cities where our people live and teach the Greek people there? [36]What did he

7:8 yet Some Greek copies do not have this word. **7:19 law** Moses gave God's people the Law that God gave him on Mount Sinai (Exodus 34:29–32).

WORLD SAYS, WORD SAYS,

RELIGION

There are many pathways to God. You must search within yourself and find the god within you. Who can really say that there is only one true god? Believe in what makes you feel good and what brings you peace. There's nothing wrong with Buddha or Allah. Find what works for *you*.

"Jesus answered, 'I am the way, and the truth, and the life. The only way to the Father is through me' " (John 14:6).

"You must not have any other gods except me" (Exodus 20:3).

mean when he said, 'You will look for me, but you will not find me,' and 'You cannot come where I am'?"

JESUS TALKS ABOUT THE SPIRIT

[37]On the last and most important day of the feast Jesus stood up and said in a loud voice, "Let anyone who is thirsty come to me and drink. [38]If anyone believes in me, rivers of living water will flow out from that person's heart, as the Scripture says." [39]Jesus was talking about the Holy Spirit. The Spirit had not yet been given, because Jesus had not yet been raised to glory. But later, those who believed in Jesus would receive the Spirit.

THE PEOPLE ARGUE ABOUT JESUS

[40]When the people heard Jesus' words, some of them said, "This man really is the Prophet."[n]

[41]Others said, "He is the Christ."

Still others said, "The Christ will not come from Galilee. [42]The Scripture says that the Christ will come from David's family and from Bethlehem, the town where David lived." [43]So the people did not agree with each other about Jesus. [44]Some of them wanted to arrest him, but no one was able to touch him.

SOME LEADERS WON'T BELIEVE

[45]The Temple guards went back to the leading priests and the Pharisees, who asked, "Why didn't you bring Jesus?"

[46]The guards answered, "The words he says are greater than the words of any other person who has ever spoken!"

[47]The Pharisees answered, "So Jesus has fooled you also! [48]Have any of the leaders or the Pharisees believed in him? No! [49]But these people, who know nothing about the law, are under God's curse."

[50]Nicodemus, who had gone to see Jesus before, was in that group.[n] He said, [51]"Our law does not judge a person without hearing him and knowing what he has done."

[52]They answered, "Are you from Galilee, too? Study the Scriptures, and you will learn that no prophet comes from Galilee."

Some of the earliest surviving Greek copies do not contain 7:53—8:11.

[[53]And everyone left and went home.

THE WOMAN CAUGHT IN ADULTERY

8 Jesus went to the Mount of Olives. [2]But early in the morning he went back to the Temple, and all the people came to him, and he sat and taught them. [3]The teachers of the law and the Pharisees brought a woman who had been caught in adultery. They forced her to stand before the peo-

ple. [4]They said to Jesus, "Teacher, this woman was caught having sexual relations with a man who is not her husband. [5]The law of Moses commands that we stone to death every woman who does this. What do you say we should do?" [6]They were asking this to trick Jesus so that they could have some charge against him.

But Jesus bent over and started writing on the ground with his finger. [7]When they continued to ask Jesus their question, he raised up and said, "Anyone here who has never sinned can throw the first stone at her." [8]Then Jesus bent over again and wrote on the ground.

[9]Those who heard Jesus began to leave one by one, first the older men and then the others. Jesus was left there alone with the woman standing before him. [10]Jesus raised up again and asked her, "Woman, where are they? Has no one judged you guilty?"

[11]She answered, "No one, sir."

Then Jesus said, "I also don't judge you guilty. You may go now, but don't sin anymore."]

JESUS IS THE LIGHT OF THE WORLD

[12]Later, Jesus talked to the people again, saying, "I am the light of the world. The person who follows me will never live in darkness but will have the light that gives life."

 7:40 Prophet They probably meant the prophet God told Moses he would send (Deuteronomy 18:15-19). **7:50 Nicodemus . . . group.** The story about Nicodemus going and talking to Jesus is in John 3:1-21.

VIEWPOINT

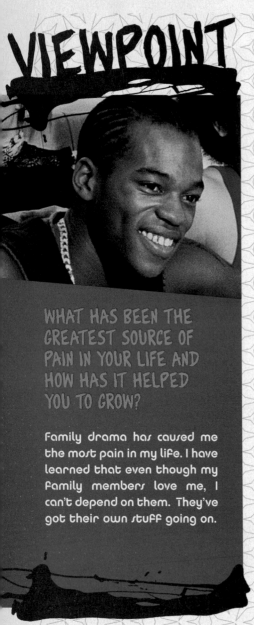

WHAT HAS BEEN THE GREATEST SOURCE OF PAIN IN YOUR LIFE AND HOW HAS IT HELPED YOU TO GROW?

Family drama has caused me the most pain in my life. I have learned that even though my family members love me, I can't depend on them. They've got their own stuff going on.

[13]The Pharisees said to Jesus, "When you talk about yourself, you are the only one to say these things are true. We cannot accept what you say."

[14]Jesus answered, "Yes, I am saying these things about myself, but they are true. I know where I came from and where I am going. But you don't know where I came from or where I am going. [15]You judge by human standards. I am not judging anyone. [16]But when I do judge, I judge truthfully, because I am not alone. The Father who sent me is with me. [17]Your own law says that when two witnesses say the same thing, you must accept what they say. [18]I am one of the witnesses who speaks about myself, and the Father who sent me is the other witness."

[19]They asked, "Where is your father?"

Jesus answered, "You don't know me or my Father. If you knew me, you would know my Father, too." [20]Jesus said these things while he was teaching in the Temple, near where the money is kept. But no one arrested him, because the right time for him had not yet come.

THE PEOPLE MISUNDERSTAND JESUS

[21]Again, Jesus said to the people, "I will leave you, and you will look for me, but you will die in your sins. You cannot come where I am going."

[22]So the Jews asked, "Will he kill himself? Is that why he said, 'You cannot come where I am going'?"

[23]Jesus said, "You people are from here below, but I am from above. You belong to this world, but I don't belong to this world. [24]So I told you that you would die in your sins. Yes, you will die in your sins if you don't believe that I am he."

[25]They asked, "Then who are you?"

Jesus answered, "I am what I have told you from the beginning. [26]I have many things to say and decide about you. But I tell people only the things I have heard from the One who sent me, and he speaks the truth."

[27]The people did not understand that he was talking to them about the Father. [28]So Jesus said to them, "When you lift up the Son of Man, you will know that I am he. You will know that these things I do are not by my own authority but that I say only what the Father has taught me. [29]The One who sent me is with me. I always do what is pleasing to him, so he has not left me alone." [30]While Jesus was saying these things, many people believed in him.

FREEDOM FROM SIN

[31]So Jesus said to the Jews who believed in him, "If you continue to obey my teaching, you are truly my followers. [32]Then you will know the truth, and the truth will make you free."

[33]They answered, "We are Abraham's children, and we have never been anyone's slaves. So why do you say we will be free?"

[34]Jesus answered, "I tell you the truth, everyone who lives in sin is a slave to sin. [35]A slave does not stay with a family forever, but a son belongs to the family forever. [36]So if the Son makes you free, you will be truly free. [37]I know you are Abraham's children, but you want to kill me because you don't accept my teaching. [38]I am telling you what my Father has shown me, but you do what your father has told you."

[39]They answered, "Our father is Abraham."

Jesus said, "If you were really Abraham's children, you would do[n] the things Abraham did. [40]I am a man who has told you the truth which I heard from God, but you are trying to kill me. Abraham did nothing like that. [41]So you are doing the things your own father did."

But they said, "We are not like children who never knew who their father was. God is our Father; he is the only Father we have."

[42]Jesus said to them, "If God were really your Father, you would love me, because I came from God and now I am here. I did not come by my own authority; God sent me. [43]You don't understand what I say, because you cannot accept my teaching. [44]You belong to your father the devil, and you want to do what he wants. He was a murderer from the beginning and was against the truth, because there is no truth in him. When he tells a lie, he shows what he is really like, because he is a liar and the father of lies. [45]But because I speak the truth, you don't believe me. [46]Can any of you prove that I am guilty of sin? If I am telling the truth, why don't you believe

---

8:39 If . . . do Some Greek copies read "If you are really Abraham's children, you will do."

me? [47]The person who belongs to God accepts what God says. But you don't accept what God says, because you don't belong to God."

JESUS IS GREATER THAN ABRAHAM

[48]They answered, "We say you are a Samaritan and have a demon in you. Are we not right?"

[49]Jesus answered, "I have no demon in me. I give honor to my Father, but you dishonor me. [50]I am not trying to get honor for myself. There is One who wants this honor for me, and he is the judge. [51]I tell you the truth, whoever obeys my teaching will never die."

[52]They said to Jesus, "Now we know that you have a demon in you! Even Abraham and the prophets died. But you say, 'Whoever obeys my teaching will never die.' [53]Do you think you are greater than our father Abraham, who died? And the prophets died, too. Who do you think you are?"

[54]Jesus answered, "If I give honor to myself, that honor is worth nothing. The One who gives me honor is my Father, and you say he is your God. [55]You don't really know him, but I know him. If I said I did not know him, I would be a liar like you. But I do know him, and I obey what he says. [56]Your father Abraham was very happy that he would see my day. He saw that day and was glad."

[57]They said to him, "You have never seen Abraham! You are not even fifty years old."

[58]Jesus answered, "I tell you the truth, before Abraham was even born, I am!" [59]When Jesus said this, the people picked up stones to throw at him. But Jesus hid himself, and then he left the Temple.

JESUS HEALS A MAN BORN BLIND

9 As Jesus was walking along, he saw a man who had been born blind. [2]His followers asked him, "Teacher, whose sin caused this man to be born blind—his own sin or his parents' sin?"

[3]Jesus answered, "It is not this man's sin or his parents' sin that made him blind. This man was born blind so that God's power could be shown in him.

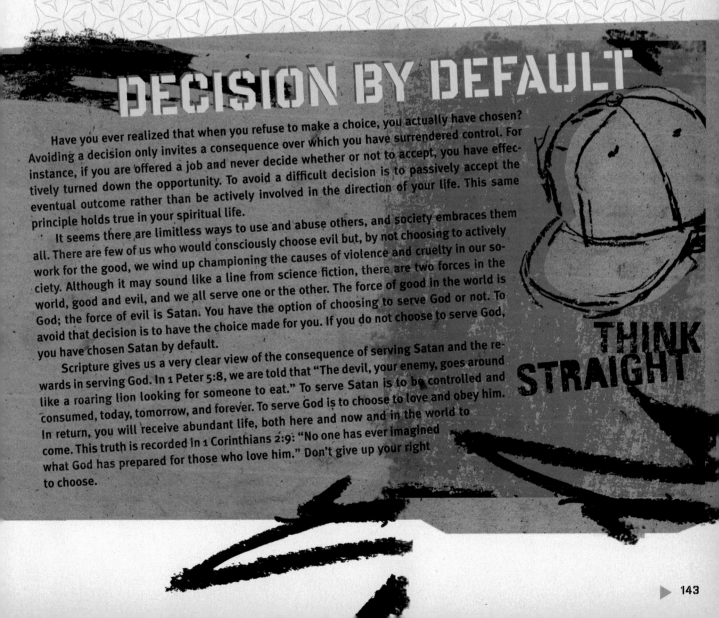

DECISION BY DEFAULT

Have you ever realized that when you refuse to make a choice, you actually have chosen? Avoiding a decision only invites a consequence over which you have surrendered control. For instance, if you are offered a job and never decide whether or not to accept, you have effectively turned down the opportunity. To avoid a difficult decision is to passively accept the eventual outcome rather than be actively involved in the direction of your life. This same principle holds true in your spiritual life.

It seems there are limitless ways to use and abuse others, and society embraces them all. There are few of us who would consciously choose evil but, by not choosing to actively work for the good, we wind up championing the causes of violence and cruelty in our society. Although it may sound like a line from science fiction, there are two forces in the world, good and evil, and we all serve one or the other. The force of good in the world is God; the force of evil is Satan. You have the option of choosing to serve God or not. To avoid that decision is to have the choice made for you. If you do not choose to serve God, you have chosen Satan by default.

Scripture gives us a very clear view of the consequence of serving Satan and the rewards in serving God. In 1 Peter 5:8, we are told that "The devil, your enemy, goes around like a roaring lion looking for someone to eat." To serve Satan is to be controlled and consumed, today, tomorrow, and forever. To serve God is to choose to love and obey him. In return, you will receive abundant life, both here and now and in the world to come. This truth is recorded in 1 Corinthians 2:9: "No one has ever imagined what God has prepared for those who love him." Don't give up your right to choose.

THINK STRAIGHT

[4]While it is daytime, we must continue doing the work of the One who sent me. Night is coming, when no one can work. [5]While I am in the world, I am the light of the world."

[6]After Jesus said this, he spit on the ground and made some mud with it and put the mud on the man's eyes. [7]Then he told the man, "Go and wash in the Pool of Siloam." (Siloam means Sent.) So the man went, washed, and came back seeing.

[8]The neighbors and some people who had earlier seen this man begging said, "Isn't this the same man who used to sit and beg?"

[9]Some said, "He is the one," but others said, "No, he only looks like him."

The man himself said, "I am the man."

[10]They asked, "How did you get your sight?"

[11]He answered, "The man named Jesus made some mud and put it on my eyes. Then he told me to go to Siloam and wash. So I went and washed, and then I could see."

[12]They asked him, "Where is this man?"

"I don't know," he answered.

Is there really a devil?

The devil has been a character in books, stories, legends, and movies, and is portrayed as everything from a handsome man or woman to a red cartoon figure with horns and a tail, poking people with a pitchfork. He has many names: Satan, Beelzebul, Abaddon, the devil, the enemy, the accuser of the brothers and sisters are just a few of them. He is mentioned in the New Testament nearly a hundred times and is always spoken of in Scripture as a real being. According to the Bible, the devil is a fallen angel who tried to overthrow God. When he lost, he set out to hurt God through the people God loves.

Jesus speaks of Satan as a tempter; in fact, the first time Satan appears in the New Testament is when he tried to tempt Jesus. Anytime Satan is mentioned, it is always as an evil creature and the Bible warns us to be on guard against him.

But the devil is not all-knowing or all-powerful like God. He manipulates lives through lies and deception. The Bible says that "The devil, your enemy, goes around like a roaring lion looking for someone to eat. Refuse to give in to him, by standing strong in your faith" (1 Peter 5:8-9).

Read on: Matthew 4:1-11, 12:22-28; John 12:31; 1 Peter 5:8-9; Revelation 12:10

He's got answers

PEEP THIS:

Thirty-one percent of all records are sold to 20 to 34 year olds.

PHARISEES QUESTION THE HEALING

[13]Then the people took to the Pharisees the man who had been blind. [14]The day Jesus had made mud and healed his eyes was a Sabbath day. [15]So now the Pharisees asked the man, "How did you get your sight?"

He answered, "He put mud on my eyes, I washed, and now I see."

[16]So some of the Pharisees were saying, "This man does not keep the Sabbath day, so he is not from God."

But others said, "A man who is a sinner can't do miracles like these." So they could not agree with each other.

[17]They asked the man again, "What do you say about him since it was your eyes he opened?"

The man answered, "He is a prophet."

[18]These leaders did not believe that he had been blind and could now see again. So they sent for the man's parents [19]and asked them, "Is this your son who you say was born blind? Then how does he now see?"

[20]His parents answered, "We know that this is our son and that he was born blind. [21]But we don't know how he can now see. We don't know who opened his eyes. Ask him. He is old enough to speak for himself." [22]His parents said this because they were afraid of the elders, who had already decided that anyone who said Jesus was the Christ would be avoided. [23]That is why his parents said, "He is old enough. Ask him."

[24]So for the second time, they called the man who had been blind. They said, "You should give God the glory by tell-

ing the truth. We know that this man is a sinner."

²⁵He answered, "I don't know if he is a sinner. One thing I do know: I was blind, and now I see."

²⁶They asked, "What did he do to you? How did he make you see again?"

²⁷He answered, "I already told you, and you didn't listen. Why do you want to hear it again? Do you want to become his followers, too?"

²⁸Then they insulted him and said, "You are his follower, but we are followers of Moses. ²⁹We know that God spoke to Moses, but we don't even know where this man comes from."

³⁰The man answered, "This is a very strange thing. You don't know where he comes from, and yet he opened my eyes. ³¹We all know that God does not listen to sinners, but he listens to anyone who worships and obeys him. ³²Nobody has ever heard of anyone giving sight to a man born blind. ³³If this man were not from God, he could do nothing."

³⁴They answered, "You were born full of sin! Are you trying to teach us?" And they threw him out.

SPIRITUAL BLINDNESS

³⁵When Jesus heard that they had thrown him out, Jesus found him and said, "Do you believe in the Son of Man?"

³⁶He asked, "Who is the Son of Man, sir, so that I can believe in him?"

³⁷Jesus said to him, "You have seen him. The Son of Man is the one talking with you."

³⁸He said, "Lord, I believe!" Then the man worshiped Jesus.

³⁹Jesus said, "I came into this world so that the world could be judged. I came so that the blind[n] would see and so that those who see will become blind."

⁴⁰Some of the Pharisees who were nearby heard Jesus say this and asked, "Are you saying we are blind, too?"

⁴¹Jesus said, "If you were blind, you would not be guilty of sin. But since you keep saying you see, your guilt remains."

THE SHEPHERD AND HIS SHEEP

10 Jesus said, "I tell you the truth, the person who does not enter the sheepfold by the door, but climbs in some other way, is a thief and a robber. ²The one who enters by the door is the shepherd of the sheep. ³The one who guards the door opens it for him. And the sheep listen to the voice of the shepherd. He calls his own sheep by name and leads them out. ⁴When he brings all his sheep out, he goes ahead of them, and they follow him

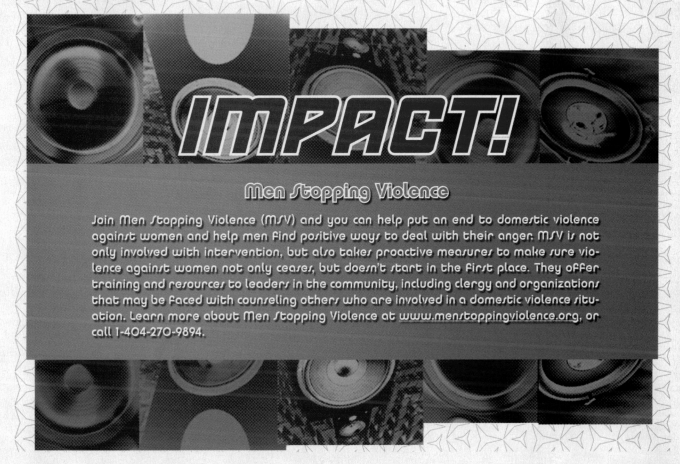

IMPACT!

Men Stopping Violence

Join Men Stopping Violence (MSV) and you can help put an end to domestic violence against women and help men find positive ways to deal with their anger. MSV is not only involved with intervention, but also takes proactive measures to make sure violence against women not only ceases, but doesn't start in the first place. They offer training and resources to leaders in the community, including clergy and organizations that may be faced with counseling others who are involved in a domestic violence situation. Learn more about Men Stopping Violence at www.menstoppingviolence.org, or call 1-404-270-9894.

9:39 blind Jesus is talking about people who are spiritually blind, not physically blind.

REAL RHYMES:

AMERICAN DREAM

BY C. SULLIVAN, T. KYLLONEN, R. YOUNG

WHERE I'M FROM IF YOU POOR AND YOU BLACK,
YOU GET TWO GATS AND PULL YOURSELF UP BY YOUR BOOT
  STRAPS.
FOR THE LOVE OF MONEY, CAP EM' AND KILL EM'.
IF YOU BLACK YOU A VILLAIN, BUT, IF YOU A BANKER, IT'S
  CAPITALISM.
IN THE STREETS, THEY FIGURE CRIME PAYS.
THEY MILITANT 'CUZ WE WAS X-SLAVES. TREATED WORSE
  THAN THE IMMIGRANTS.
BUT WE KNOW HOW THIS STORY ENDS. WITHOUT CHRIST
  THEY DIE AND GO TO HELL.
SO ON THIS RHYME I'M A PUT A SPIN.
NOW LET'S SAY YOU A GREAT GUY. NEVER DRANK. NEVER
  CURSED.
SON IS LAWYER, DAUGHTER A NURSE.
A BIG WIG EXEC, FOR CHRISTMAS YOUR WIFE GET A LEX.
YOU TOO BUSY MAKING MONEY TO GIVE HER SEX.
NO PEACE IN THE MIDDLE EAST. THE RISE OF THE BEAST.
IT'S HORRIFYING WATCHING CNN LIVE IN YOUR STREET.
POLICE RUSH YOUR HOUSE. BUST YOUR MOUTH.
AS BURGUNDY BLOOD STREAMS, YOU WAKE UP FROM YOUR
  AMERICAN DREAM.

THE FIRST IMMIGRANTS CAME IN SEARCH OF RELIGIOUS
  FREEDOM.
THEY FOUND WEALTH AND SAID, "FORGET GOD. WE DON'T
  NEED HIM.
WE CAN BEAT HIM. NEVER LET THEY LITTLE KIDS MEET HIM.
SEND EM' TO COLLEGE. IT'S ALL ABOUT SUCCEEDING.
GET RICH OR DIE TRYING AS THE GREED KEEPS FEEDING.
BUT, THEY CAN TAKE THEY WORDS AND EAT EM'.
WHEN THIS WORLD LEAVES EM' BLEEDING. I'LL PULL THEY CARD
  MEANING.
THIS AIN'T HALLMARK OR AMERICAN GREETING. JAMES
  5—YA'LL BETTER DO SOME READING.
AND TURN YOUR LIGHTS ON. YOUR FINANCES WILL BE GONE
  LIKE WORLDCOM AND ENRON.
HEADS GOT CONNED, LIKE SELLING DRUGS ON THE CORNER
  TILL DAWN.
NOW THEY BOTH WRITING LETTERS TO MOM FROM AN 8X10.

TURNING SELFISH LITTLE BOYS TO MEN. NOW SUDDENLY
  GOD'S THEY FRIEND.
IT'S HUMBLING, LIKE THE PRODIGAL SON IN THE PIG PEN.
YOU CAN'T TRUST BIG BEN, CUZ GREEN PAPER WILL BURN.
WAKE UP AND SEE THAT ELOHIM MAKE THE WORLD TURN.

SHE WAS A PRETTY GIRL, YOUNG THING, HOUR GLASS SHAPED
  UP.
FACE ALL CAKED WITH MARY KAY MAKE-UP. TEEN, AMERICAN
  DREAM.
TRAVELED THE GLOBE. WALKED THE CATWALK. COVER SHOTS
  POSE AND VOGUE.
YOUNG GIRL, AND COUNTRY GIRL, HIT THE BIG APPLE.
BEDAZZLED BY BROADWAY'S LIGHTS AND HELLS' CASTLE.
MET A FAST TALKER, PLAYER, RIGHT CONNECTS. PARTIED
  WITH HER—LATE NIGHT DRUGS AND SEX.
NOW SHE FIENDED OUT. POCKETS ARE BROKE.
NEED A HIT, TURNED OUT FREEZING COLD WORKING THE
  STRIP.
THAT BODY USED TO JIGGLE LIKE GELATIN, NOW LOOK LIKE
  A SKELETON.
MAKING PEANUTS LIKE A ELEPHANT.
AMERICAN DREAM, NOW A NIGHTMARE THAT SHE CAN'T
  AWAKE FROM.
AND SHE GOT SHACKLES SHE CAN'T BREAK FROM.
I WISH SHE KNEW JESUS. HOLY GHOST FREES US AND PUTS
  BACK TOGETHER THE BROKE PIECES.

THE AMERICAN DREAM. IT'S NOT ALL THAT IT SEEMS.
FROM THE GHETTO TO WALL STREET IT'S MONEY MAKING
  SCHEMES.
WHETHER THEY SELL TO FIENDS OR WORK ON CORPORATE
  TEAMS.
MOST JUST NEED TO BE REDEEMED.
THE AMERICAN DREAM. IT'S NOT ALL THAT IT SEEMS.
FROM THE GHETTO TO WALL STREET ITS MONEY MAKING
  SCHEMES.
FROM SUITS AND TIES TO TIMBS AND JEANS, MOST JUST
  NEED TO BE REDEEMED.

because they know his voice. ⁵But they will never follow a stranger. They will run away from him because they don't know his voice." ⁶Jesus told the people this story, but they did not understand what it meant.

JESUS IS THE GOOD SHEPHERD

⁷So Jesus said again, "I tell you the truth, I am the door for the sheep. ⁸All the people who came before me were thieves and robbers. The sheep did not listen to them. ⁹I am the door, and the person who enters through me will be saved and will be able to come in and go out and find pasture. ¹⁰A thief comes to steal and kill and destroy, but I came to give life—life in all its fullness.

¹¹"I am the good shepherd. The good shepherd gives his life for the sheep. ¹²The worker who is paid to keep the sheep is different from the shepherd who owns them. When the worker sees a wolf coming, he runs away and leaves the sheep alone. Then the wolf attacks the sheep and scatters them. ¹³The man runs away because he is only a paid worker and does not really care about the sheep.

¹⁴"I am the good shepherd. I know my sheep, and my sheep know me, ¹⁵just as the Father knows me, and I know the Father. I give my life for the sheep. ¹⁶I have other sheep that are not in this flock, and I must bring them also. They will listen to my voice, and there will be one flock and one shepherd. ¹⁷The Father loves me because I give my life so that I can take it back again. ¹⁸No one takes it away from me; I give my own life freely. I have the right to give my life, and I have the right to take it back. This is what my Father commanded me to do."

¹⁹Again the leaders did not agree with each other because of these words of Jesus. ²⁰Many of them said, "A demon has come into him and made him crazy. Why listen to him?"

²¹But others said, "A man who is crazy with a demon does not say things like this. Can a demon open the eyes of the blind?"

JESUS IS REJECTED

²²The time came for the Feast of Dedication at Jerusalem. It was winter, ²³and Jesus was walking in the Temple in Solomon's Porch. ²⁴Some people gathered around him and said, "How long will you make us wonder about you? If you are the Christ, tell us plainly."

²⁵Jesus answered, "I told you already, but you did not believe. The miracles I do in my Father's name show who I am. ²⁶But you don't believe, because you are not my sheep. ²⁷My sheep listen to my voice; I know them, and they follow me. ²⁸I give them eternal life, and they will never die, and no one can steal them out of my hand. ²⁹My Father gave my sheep to me. He is greater than all, and no person can steal my sheep out of my Father's hand. ³⁰The Father and I are one."

³¹Again some of the people picked up stones to kill Jesus. ³²But he said to them, "I have done many good works from the Father. Which of these good works are you killing me for?"

³³They answered, "We are not killing you because of any good work you did, but because you speak against God. You are only a human, but you say you are the same as God!"

³⁴Jesus answered, "It is written in your law that God said, 'I said, you are gods.'* ³⁵This Scripture called those people gods who received God's message, and Scripture is always true. ³⁶So why do you say that I speak against God because I said, 'I am God's Son'? I am the one God chose and sent into the world. ³⁷If I don't do what my Father does, then don't believe me. ³⁸But if I do what my Father does, even though you don't believe in me, believe what I do. Then you will know and understand that the Father is in me and I am in the Father."

³⁹They tried to take Jesus again, but he escaped from them.

⁴⁰Then he went back across the Jordan River to the place where John had first baptized. Jesus stayed there, ⁴¹and many people came to him and said, "John never did a miracle, but everything John said about this man is true." ⁴²And in that place many believed in Jesus.

THE DEATH OF LAZARUS

11 A man named Lazarus was sick. He lived in the town of Bethany, where Mary and her sister Martha lived. ²Mary was the woman who later put perfume on the Lord and wiped his feet with her hair. Mary's brother was Lazarus, the man who was now sick. ³So Mary and Martha sent someone to tell Jesus, "Lord, the one you love is sick."

⁴When Jesus heard this, he said, "This sickness will not end in death. It is for the glory of God, to bring glory to the Son of God." ⁵Jesus loved Martha and her sister and Lazarus. ⁶But when he heard that Lazarus was sick, he stayed where he was for two more days. ⁷Then Jesus said to his followers, "Let's go back to Judea."

⁸The followers said, "But Teacher, some people there tried to stone you to death only a short time ago. Now you want to go back there?"

⁹Jesus answered, "Are there not twelve hours in the day? If anyone walks in the daylight, he will not stumble, because he can see by this world's light. ¹⁰But if anyone walks at night, he stumbles because there is no light to help him see."

¹¹After Jesus said this, he added, "Our friend Lazarus has fallen asleep, but I am going there to wake him."

¹²The followers said, "But Lord, if he is only asleep, he will be all right."

¹³Jesus meant that Lazarus was dead, but his followers thought he meant Lazarus was really sleeping. ¹⁴So then Jesus said plainly, "Lazarus is dead. ¹⁵And I am glad for your sakes I was not there

10:34 'I . . . gods.' Quotation from Psalm 82:6.

GOD

HEALING FROM REJECTION

ship is not necessarily a beneficial one. I soon found that chasing after people, whether I caught them or not, did not work. It caused inner turmoil. I just spent the entire relationship, whether a friendship or a romance, working as hard to keep the person as I had to get the person.

When I met God, I came to a conclusion: God had a purpose in the rejection I had faced. God wouldn't allow me to get tangled up with everyone, because he had his own plans for me. God gave me a childhood spent with those older than me so that I could learn wisdom. And the time I spent with young, broken kids gave me a passion to defend and encourage those who were rejected by others. I also found the personal relationship that I'd always longed for. God knew me inside and out and accepted me no matter what. I'd been picked last for most teams in life, except one: God's team. He chose me then kept me from the distractions that would deter me from my life's mission. I'm on his team. And it's a team that always wins.

Ephesians 1:11—In Christ we were chosen to be God's people, because from the very beginning God had decided this in keeping with his plan. . . . We were chosen so that we would bring praise to God's glory.

Take the youngest of three boys, mix in a quirky personality, and toss in a desire to please people, and you'll have me. I have two older brothers, both of whom were athletic, charismatic, and good looking. Then there was me—kinda chubby, musically inclined, and definitely not normal. I tried to do everything that the older boys did, but somehow my chubby legs wouldn't quite let me. I was always picked last for teams, and just assumed I would always be picked last in life as well. I was accepted in the oddest circles, like adults over age 55 and kids half my age.

As a result, I spent my childhood and early young adult years wandering after the people I thought would give me the attention I needed. I desperately wanted the approval of the guys, and the attraction of the girls. As an adult, I began to befriend anyone who paid any sort of attention to me, and I found out that every warm relation-

---

so that you may believe. But let's go to him now."

[16]Then Thomas (the one called Didymus) said to the other followers, "Let us also go so that we can die with him."

JESUS IN BETHANY

[17]When Jesus arrived, he learned that Lazarus had already been dead and in the tomb for four days. [18]Bethany was about two miles from Jerusalem. [19]Many of the Jews had come there to comfort Martha and Mary about their brother. [20]When Martha heard that Jesus was coming, she went out to meet him, but

Mary stayed home. [21]Martha said to Jesus, "Lord, if you had been here, my brother would not have died. [22]But I know that even now God will give you anything you ask."

[23]Jesus said, "Your brother will rise and live again."

[24]Martha answered, "I know that he will rise and live again in the resurrection on the last day."

[25]Jesus said to her, "I am the resurrection and the life. Those who believe in me will have life even if they die. [26]And everyone who lives and believes in me

will never die. Martha, do you believe this?"

[27]Martha answered, "Yes, Lord. I believe that you are the Christ, the Son of God, the One coming to the world."

JESUS CRIES

[28]After Martha said this, she went back and talked to her sister Mary alone. Martha said, "The Teacher is here and he is asking for you." [29]When Mary heard this, she got up quickly and went to Jesus. [30]Jesus had not yet come into the town but was still at the place where Martha had met him. [31]The Jews

---

 11:24 resurrection Being raised from the dead to live again.

were with Mary in the house, comforting her. When they saw her stand and leave quickly, they followed her, thinking she was going to the tomb to cry there.

³²But Mary went to the place where Jesus was. When she saw him, she fell at his feet and said, "Lord, if you had been here, my brother would not have died."

³³When Jesus saw Mary crying and the Jews who came with her also crying, he was upset and was deeply troubled. ³⁴He asked, "Where did you bury him?"

"Come and see, Lord," they said.

³⁵Jesus cried.

³⁶So the Jews said, "See how much he loved him."

³⁷But some of them said, "If Jesus opened the eyes of the blind man, why couldn't he keep Lazarus from dying?"

JESUS RAISES LAZARUS

³⁸Again feeling very upset, Jesus came to the tomb. It was a cave with a large stone covering the entrance. ³⁹Jesus said, "Move the stone away."

Martha, the sister of the dead man, said, "But, Lord, it has been four days since he died. There will be a bad smell."

⁴⁰Then Jesus said to her, "Didn't I tell you that if you believed you would see the glory of God?"

⁴¹So they moved the stone away from the entrance. Then Jesus looked up and said, "Father, I thank you that you heard me. ⁴²I know that you always hear me, but I said these things because of the people here around me. I want them to believe that you sent me." ⁴³After Jesus said this, he cried out in a loud voice, "Lazarus, come out!" ⁴⁴The dead man came out, his hands and feet wrapped with pieces of cloth, and a cloth around his face.

Jesus said to them, "Take the cloth off of him and let him go."

THE PLAN TO KILL JESUS

⁴⁵Many of the people, who had come to visit Mary and saw what Jesus did, believed in him. ⁴⁶But some of them went to the Pharisees and told them what Jesus had done. ⁴⁷Then the leading priests and Pharisees called a meeting of the council. They asked, "What should we do? This man is doing many miracles. ⁴⁸If we let him continue doing these things, everyone will believe in him. Then the Romans will come and take away our Temple and our nation."

⁴⁹One of the men there was Caiaphas, the high priest that year. He said, "You people know nothing! ⁵⁰You don't realize that it is better for one man to die for the people than for the whole nation to be destroyed."

⁵¹Caiaphas did not think of this himself. As high priest that year, he was really prophesying that Jesus would die for their nation ⁵²and for God's scattered children to bring them all together and make them one.

PEEP THIS:

Stores other than music stores account for 52.8 percent of all records sold. Five percent of all records sold are purchased over the Internet (not including club purchases).

⁵³That day they started planning to kill Jesus. ⁵⁴So Jesus no longer traveled openly among the people. He left there and went to a place near the desert, to a town called Ephraim and stayed there with his followers.

⁵⁵It was almost time for the Passover Feast. Many from the country went up to Jerusalem before the Passover to do the special things to make themselves pure. ⁵⁶The people looked for Jesus and stood in the Temple asking each other, "Is he coming to the Feast? What do you think?" ⁵⁷But the leading priests and the Pharisees had given orders that if anyone knew where Jesus was, he must tell them. Then they could arrest him.

JESUS WITH FRIENDS IN BETHANY

12 Six days before the Passover Feast, Jesus went to Bethany, where Lazarus lived. (Lazarus is the man Jesus raised from the dead.) ²There they had a dinner for Jesus. Martha served the food, and Lazarus was one of the people eating with Jesus. ³Mary brought in a pint of very expensive perfume made from pure nard. She poured the perfume on Jesus' feet, and then she wiped his feet with her hair. And the sweet smell from the perfume filled the whole house.

⁴Judas Iscariot, one of Jesus' followers who would later turn against him, was there. Judas said, ⁵"This perfume was worth an entire year's wages. Why wasn't it sold and the money given to the poor?" ⁶But Judas did not really care about the poor; he said this because he was a thief. He was the one who kept the money box, and he often stole from it.

⁷Jesus answered, "Leave her alone. It was right for her to save this perfume for today, the day for me to be prepared for burial. ⁸You will always have the poor with you, but you will not always have me."

THE PLOT AGAINST LAZARUS

⁹A large crowd of people heard that Jesus was in Bethany. So they went there to see not only Jesus but Lazarus, whom Jesus raised from the dead. ¹⁰So the leading priests made plans to kill Lazarus, too. ¹¹Because of Lazarus

many of the Jews were leaving them and believing in Jesus.

JESUS ENTERS JERUSALEM

[12]The next day a great crowd who had come to Jerusalem for the Passover Feast heard that Jesus was coming there. [13]So they took branches of palm trees and went out to meet Jesus, shouting,

"Praise[n] God!
God bless the One who comes in the name of the Lord!
God bless the King of Israel!"

Psalm 118:25-26

[14]Jesus found a colt and sat on it. This was as the Scripture says,

[15]"Don't be afraid, people of Jerusalem!

Your king is coming, sitting on the colt of a donkey."

Zechariah 9:9

[16]The followers of Jesus did not understand this at first. But after Jesus was raised to glory, they remembered that this had been written about him and that they had done these things to him.

PEOPLE TELL ABOUT JESUS

[17]There had been many people with Jesus when he raised Lazarus from the dead and told him to come out of the tomb. Now they were telling others about what Jesus did. [18]Many people went out to meet Jesus, because they had heard about this miracle. [19]So the Pharisees said to each other, "You can see that

nothing is going right for us. Look! The whole world is following him."

JESUS TALKS ABOUT HIS DEATH

[20]There were some Greek people, too, who came to Jerusalem to worship at the Passover Feast. [21]They went to Philip, who was from Bethsaida in Galilee, and said, "Sir, we would like to see Jesus." [22]Philip told Andrew, and then Andrew and Philip told Jesus.

[23]Jesus said to them, "The time has come for the Son of Man to receive his glory. [24]I tell you the truth, a grain of wheat must fall to the ground and die to make many seeds. But if it never dies, it remains only a single seed. [25]Those who love their lives will lose them, but those

12:13 Praise Literally, "Hosanna," a Hebrew word used at first in praying to God for help, but at this time it was probably a shout of joy used in praising God or his Messiah.

DEEP ISSUES

Abortion

Everybody's got a different opinion about abortion. In the political world, it's been known to make or break a candidate's successful bid for office. Biological science only defines development phases and viability. Legal cases turn on whether the woman is carrying a mass of tissue or nurturing a baby. The business community concerns itself with providing services to meet the demand for abortions. Medical research wants to experiment with fetal tissue with the hope of finding cures for diseases.

Science supports the view that the beginning of life is at conception. When the sperm meets the egg, the resulting cell immediately begins to multiply. At the very moment of conception, there is a transfer of DNA from both the mother and the father, determining from the first spark of life the physical attributes of this tiny new person. The amount of genetic information transferred in the first moment of life boggles the mind! The baby quickly grows and, within weeks, has its own heartbeat and even its own facial features.

What does God say about life? Genesis 2:7 says God is the author of human life. In Jeremiah 1:5 God says, "Before I made you in your mother's womb, I chose you. Before you were born, I set you apart." God recognizes the existence of a personal life before birth. No one questions the justice of the Commandment that tells us not to murder (Exodus 20:13), yet the burden of an unwanted pregnancy seems to blur the clear message of the Bible that abortion is murder. Abortion takes the life of another.

God loves and honors every single life—the tiny, helpless life inside a mother's womb and the man and woman with the responsibility of father and mother. Abortion only appears to be a quick fix, but doesn't take into account the long-term effects of a life lost and the simmering guilt of all parties involved. God is in the business of creating and blessing life, even life in difficult circumstances. Who knows what good things can come from the life of an unplanned child? Never sell God short. He can turn a desperate situation into a most hopeful circumstance. Read Romans 8:28-39.

who hate their lives in this world will keep true life forever. ²⁶Whoever serves me must follow me. Then my servant will be with me everywhere I am. My Father will honor anyone who serves me.

²⁷"Now I am very troubled. Should I say, 'Father, save me from this time'? No, I came to this time so I could suffer. ²⁸Father, bring glory to your name!"

Then a voice came from heaven, "I have brought glory to it, and I will do it again."

²⁹The crowd standing there, who heard the voice, said it was thunder.

But others said, "An angel has spoken to him."

³⁰Jesus said, "That voice was for your sake, not mine. ³¹Now is the time for the world to be judged; now the ruler of this world will be thrown down. ³²If I am lifted up from the earth, I will draw all people toward me." ³³Jesus said this to show how he would die.

³⁴The crowd said, "We have heard from the law that the Christ will live forever. So why do you say, 'The Son of Man must be lifted up'? Who is this 'Son of Man'?"

³⁵Then Jesus said, "The light will be with you for a little longer, so walk while you have the light. Then the darkness will not catch you. If you walk in the darkness, you will not know where you are going. ³⁶Believe in the light while you still have it so that you will become children of light." When Jesus had said this, he left and hid himself from them.

SOME PEOPLE WON'T BELIEVE IN JESUS

³⁷Though Jesus had done many miracles in front of the people, they still did not believe in him. ³⁸This was to bring about what Isaiah the prophet had said:

"Lord, who believed what we told them?
Who saw the Lord's power in this?"   *Isaiah 53:1*

³⁹This is why the people could not believe: Isaiah also had said,

⁴⁰"He has blinded their eyes,

and he has closed their minds.
Otherwise they would see with their eyes
and understand in their minds
and come back to me and be healed."   *Isaiah 6:10*

⁴¹Isaiah said this because he saw Jesus' glory and spoke about him.

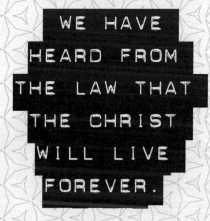

WE HAVE HEARD FROM THE LAW THAT THE CHRIST WILL LIVE FOREVER.

⁴²But many believed in Jesus, even many of the leaders. But because of the Pharisees, they did not say they believed in him for fear they would be put out of the synagogue. ⁴³They loved praise from people more than praise from God.

⁴⁴Then Jesus cried out, "Whoever believes in me is really believing in the One who sent me. ⁴⁵Whoever sees me sees the One who sent me. ⁴⁶I have come as light into the world so that whoever believes in me would not stay in darkness.

⁴⁷"Anyone who hears my words and does not obey them, I do not judge, because I did not come to judge the world, but to save the world. ⁴⁸There is a judge for those who refuse to believe in me and do not accept my words. The word I have taught will be their judge on the last day. ⁴⁹The things I taught were not from myself. The Father who sent me told me what to say and what to teach. ⁵⁰And I know that eternal life comes from what the Father commands. So whatever I say is what the Father told me to say."

JESUS WASHES HIS FOLLOWERS' FEET

13 It was almost time for the Passover Feast. Jesus knew that it was time for him to leave this world and go back to the Father. He had always loved those who were his own in the world, and he loved them all the way to the end.

²Jesus and his followers were at the evening meal. The devil had already persuaded Judas Iscariot, the son of Simon, to turn against Jesus. ³Jesus knew that the Father had given him power over everything and that he had come from God and was going back to God. ⁴So during the meal Jesus stood up and took off his outer clothing. Taking a towel, he wrapped it around his waist. ⁵Then he poured water into a bowl and began to wash the followers' feet, drying them with the towel that was wrapped around him.

⁶Jesus came to Simon Peter, who said to him, "Lord, are you going to wash my feet?"

⁷Jesus answered, "You don't understand now what I am doing, but you will understand later."

⁸Peter said, "No, you will never wash my feet."

Jesus answered, "If I don't wash your feet, you are not one of my people."

⁹Simon Peter answered, "Lord, then wash not only my feet, but wash my hands and my head, too!"

¹⁰Jesus said, "After a person has had a bath, his whole body is clean. He needs only to wash his feet. And you men are clean, but not all of you." ¹¹Jesus knew who would turn against him, and that is why he said, "Not all of you are clean."

¹²When he had finished washing their feet, he put on his clothes and sat down again. He asked, "Do you understand what I have just done for you? ¹³You call me 'Teacher' and 'Lord,' and you are right, because that is what I am. ¹⁴If I,

your Lord and Teacher, have washed your feet, you also should wash each other's feet. [15] I did this as an example so that you should do as I have done for you. [16] I tell you the truth, a servant is not greater than his master. A messenger is not greater than the one who sent him. [17] If you know these things, you will be blessed if you do them.

[18] "I am not talking about all of you. I know those I have chosen. But this is to bring about what the Scripture said: 'The man who ate at my table has turned against me.'[n] [19] I am telling you this now before it happens so that when it happens, you will believe that I am he. [20] I tell you the truth, whoever accepts anyone I send also accepts me. And whoever accepts me also accepts the One who sent me."

JESUS TALKS ABOUT HIS DEATH

[21] After Jesus said this, he was very troubled. He said openly, "I tell you the truth, one of you will turn against me."

[22] The followers all looked at each other, because they did not know whom Jesus was talking about. [23] One of the followers sitting[n] next to Jesus was the follower Jesus loved. [24] Simon Peter motioned to him to ask Jesus whom he was talking about.

[25] That follower leaned closer to Jesus and asked, "Lord, who is it?"

[26] Jesus answered, "I will dip this bread into the dish. The man I give it to is the man who will turn against me." So Jesus took a piece of bread, dipped it, and gave it to Judas Iscariot, the son of Simon. [27] As soon as Judas took the bread, Satan entered him. Jesus said to him, "The thing that you will do—do it quickly."

13:18 'The man . . . me.' Quotation from Psalm 41:9. **13:23 sitting** Literally, "lying." The people of that time ate lying down and leaning on one arm.

THE SCRIPT

Jesus Heals the Blind Man
John Chapter 9:1-12

As the master walked the dusty streets of Jerusalem,
He saw a man who was in the grossest of states.
Groping in the full light of day; Blind since birth, he'd always been that way.
The disciples asked their Rabbi, "Does this man have to be that way and why?
Did he or his folks sin so bad that this is how he must pay?"
Jesus said, "Hold up. Wait a minute! No one's paying penance!
Since you're paying close attention, watch till God is finished with him!
That's why I'm on a mission to finish the job I was given.
The night is still coming when all assignments diminish.
And in this world, I'm the brightest Light as long as I'm in it.
        And when Jesus was finished, he bent over and in the ground did spit,
            Reached down and made some clay, and that was it.
            Rubbing the clay into the man's eyes he said,
                "Now I want you to get.

Go wash this off in the pool of Siloam." (The name of the place means 'sent.')
The blind man did just as Jesus said and he came back seeing!
His sight was two-O, two-O! The whole town flipped like Judo!
People both near and far came and was like,
"Ain't this the blind beggar that our whole crew knew?"
Some of them 'fessed up, "True that."
But others was like, "Naw, wait a minute. Who that?
We know it can't be that blind kid. He's got to be a new cat!"
But he said, "Nah, it's me, for real!" So they asked him, "What the deal?
If you were born without sight, then how'd you get this miracle?"
He said, "Scope this. A man named Jesus healed me, straight up no joking.
He spit and made clay, rubbed it in my eyes, and he told me,
'I want you to get going. Wash this off in the pool of Siloam.'
I did so and now my sight is two-O, two-O, man!"
They was like, "Whoa, man! Where is he then?"
He said, "I don't know man.
All I know is that I was blind but now I see, and life is golden."

Take this with you: Sometimes the biggest problem in our lives is in the way we look at the problem. Jesus can touch your eyes and help you to see what's really important.

²⁸No one at the table understood why Jesus said this to Judas. ²⁹Since he was the one who kept the money box, some of the followers thought Jesus was telling him to buy what was needed for the feast or to give something to the poor.

³⁰Judas took the bread Jesus gave him and immediately went out. It was night.

³¹When Judas was gone, Jesus said, "Now the Son of Man receives his glory, and God receives glory through him. ³²If God receives glory through him,ⁿ then God will give glory to the Son through himself. And God will give him glory quickly."

³³Jesus said, "My children, I will be with you only a little longer. You will look for me, and what I told the Jews, I tell you now: Where I am going you cannot come.

³⁴"I give you a new command: Love each other. You must love each other as I have loved you. ³⁵All people will know that you are my followers if you love each other."

PETER WILL SAY HE DOESN'T KNOW JESUS

³⁶Simon Peter asked Jesus, "Lord, where are you going?"

Jesus answered, "Where I am going you cannot follow now, but you will follow later."

³⁷Peter asked, "Lord, why can't I follow you now? I am ready to die for you!"

³⁸Jesus answered, "Are you ready to die for me? I tell you the truth, before the rooster crows, you will say three times that you don't know me."

JESUS COMFORTS HIS FOLLOWERS

'14 Jesus said, "Don't let your hearts be troubled. Trust in God, and trust in me. ²There are many rooms in my Father's house; I would not tell you this if it were not true. I am going there to prepare a place for you. ³After I go and prepare a place for you, I will come back and take you to be with me so that you may be where I am. ⁴You know the way to the place where I am going."ⁿ

⁵Thomas said to Jesus, "Lord, we don't know where you are going. So how can we know the way?"

⁶Jesus answered, "I am the way, and the truth, and the life. The only way to the Father is through me. ⁷If you really knew me, you would know my Father, too. But now you do know him, and you have seen him."

⁸Philip said to him, "Lord, show us the Father. That is all we need."

⁹Jesus answered, "I have been with you a long time now. Do you still not know me, Philip? Whoever has seen me has seen the Father. So why do you say, 'Show us the Father'? ¹⁰Don't you believe that I am in the Father and the Father is in me? The words I say to you don't come from me, but the Father lives in me and does his own work. ¹¹Believe me when I say that I am in the Father and the Father is in me. Or believe because of the miracles I have done. ¹²I tell you the truth, whoever believes in me will do the same things that I do. Those who believe will do even greater things than these, because I am going to the Father. ¹³And if you ask for anything in my name, I will do it for you so that the Father's glory will be shown through the Son. ¹⁴If you ask me for anything in my name, I will do it.

THE PROMISE OF THE HOLY SPIRIT

¹⁵"If you love me, you will obey my commands. ¹⁶I will ask the Father, and he will give you another Helperⁿ to be with you forever— ¹⁷the Spirit of truth. The world cannot accept him, because it does not see him or know him. But you know him, because he lives with you and he will be in you.

¹⁸"I will not leave you all alone like orphans; I will come back to you. ¹⁹In a little while the world will not see me anymore, but you will see me. Because I live, you will live, too. ²⁰On that day you will know that I am in my Father, and that you are in me and I am in you. ²¹Those who know my commands and obey them are the ones who love me, and my Father will love those who love me. I will love them and will show myself to them."

²²Then Judas (not Judas Iscariot) said, "But, Lord, why do you plan to show yourself to us and not to the rest of the world?"

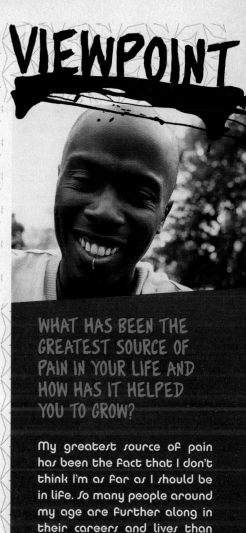

VIEWPOINT

WHAT HAS BEEN THE GREATEST SOURCE OF PAIN IN YOUR LIFE AND HOW HAS IT HELPED YOU TO GROW?

My greatest source of pain has been the fact that I don't think I'm as far as I should be in life. So many people around my age are further along in their careers and lives than I am. I often wonder what I could have done differently to have been more successful by now.

 13:32 If . . . him Some Greek copies do not have this phrase. **14:4 You . . . going.** Some Greek copies read "You know where I am going and the way to the place I am going." **14:16 Helper** "Counselor" or "Comforter." Jesus is talking about the Holy Spirit.

²³Jesus answered, "If people love me, they will obey my teaching. My Father will love them, and we will come to them and make our home with them. ²⁴Those who do not love me do not obey my teaching. This teaching that you hear is not really mine; it is from my Father, who sent me.

²⁵"I have told you all these things while I am with you. ²⁶But the Helper will teach you everything and will cause you to remember all that I told you. This Helper is the Holy Spirit whom the Father will send in my name.

²⁷"I leave you peace; my peace I give you. I do not give it to you as the world does. So don't let your hearts be troubled or afraid. ²⁸You heard me say to you, 'I am going, but I am coming back to you.' If you loved me, you should be happy that I am going back to the Father, because he is greater than I am. ²⁹I have told you this now, before it happens, so that when it happens, you will believe. ³⁰I will

not talk with you much longer, because the ruler of this world is coming. He has no power over me, ³¹but the world must know that I love the Father, so I do exactly what the Father told me to do.

"Come now, let us go.

JESUS IS LIKE A VINE

15 "I am the true vine; my Father is the gardener. ²He cuts off every branch of mine that does not produce fruit. And he trims and cleans every branch that produces fruit so that it will produce even more fruit. ³You are already clean because of the words I have spoken to you. ⁴Remain in me, and I will remain in you. A branch cannot produce fruit alone but must remain in the vine. In the same way, you cannot produce fruit alone but must remain in me.

⁵"I am the vine, and you are the branches. If any remain in me and I remain in them, they produce much fruit. But without me they can do nothing. ⁶If any do not remain in me, they are like a branch that is thrown away and then dies. People pick up dead branches, throw them into the fire, and burn them. ⁷If you remain in me and follow my teachings, you can ask anything you want, and it will be given to you. ⁸You should produce much fruit and show that you are my followers, which brings glory to my Father. ⁹I loved you as the Father loved me. Now remain in my love. ¹⁰I have obeyed my Father's commands, and I remain in his love. In the same way, if you obey my commands, you will remain in my love. ¹¹I have told you these things so that you can have the same joy I have and so that your joy will be the fullest possible joy.

¹²"This is my command: Love each other as I have loved you. ¹³The greatest love a person can show is to die for

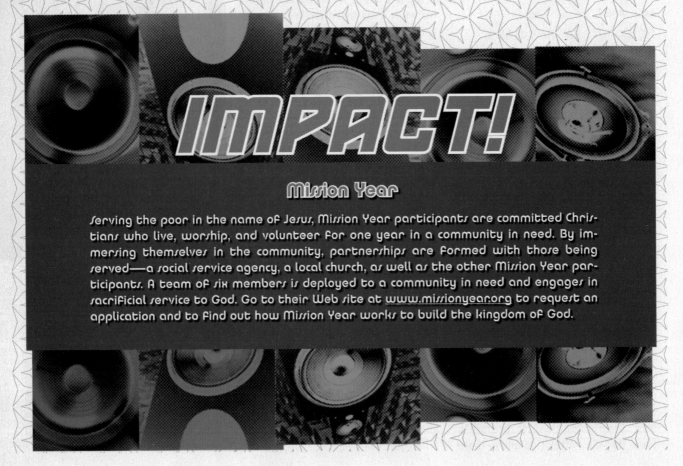

IMPACT!

Mission Year

Serving the poor in the name of Jesus, Mission Year participants are committed Christians who live, worship, and volunteer for one year in a community in need. By immersing themselves in the community, partnerships are formed with those being served—a social service agency, a local church, as well as the other Mission Year participants. A team of six members is deployed to a community in need and engages in sacrificial service to God. Go to their Web site at www.missionyear.org to request an application and to find out how Mission Year works to build the kingdom of God.

his friends. ¹⁴You are my friends if you do what I command you. ¹⁵I no longer call you servants, because a servant does not know what his master is doing. But I call you friends, because I have made known to you everything I heard from my Father. ¹⁶You did not choose me; I chose you. And I gave you this work: to go and produce fruit, fruit that will last. Then the Father will give you anything you ask for in my name. ¹⁷This is my command: Love each other.

JESUS WARNS HIS FOLLOWERS

¹⁸"If the world hates you, remember that it hated me first. ¹⁹If you belonged to the world, it would love you as it loves its own. But I have chosen you out of the world, so you don't belong to it. That is why the world hates you. ²⁰Remember what I told you: A servant is not greater than his master. If people did wrong to me, they will do wrong to you, too. And if they obeyed my teaching, they will obey yours, too. ²¹They will do all this to you on account of me, because they do not know the One who sent me. ²²If I had not come and spoken to them, they would not be guilty of sin, but now they have no excuse for their sin. ²³Whoever hates me also hates my Father. ²⁴I did works among them that no one else has ever done. If I had not done these works, they would not be guilty of sin. But now they have seen what I have done, and yet they have hated both me and my Father. ²⁵But this happened so that what is written in their law would be true: 'They hated me for no reason.'ⁿ

²⁶"I will send you the Helperⁿ from the Father; he is the Spirit of truth who comes from the Father. When he comes, he will tell about me, ²⁷and you also must tell people about me, because you have been with me from the beginning.

'16 "I have told you these things to keep you from giving up. ²People will put you out of their syna-gogues. Yes, the time is coming when those who kill you will think they are offering service to God. ³They will do this because they have not known the Father and they have not known me. ⁴I have told you these things now so that when the time comes you will remember that I warned you.

THE WORK OF THE HOLY SPIRIT

"I did not tell you these things at the beginning, because I was with you then. ⁵Now I am going back to the One who sent me. But none of you asks me, 'Where are you going?' ⁶Your hearts are filled with sadness because I have told you these things. ⁷But I tell you the truth, it is better for you that I go away. When I go away, I will send the Helperⁿ to you. If I do not go away, the Helper will not come. ⁸When the Helper comes, he will prove to the people of the world the truth about sin, about being right with God, and about judgment. ⁹He will prove to them that sin is not believing in me. ¹⁰He will prove to them that being right with God comes from my going to the Father and not being seen anymore. ¹¹And the Helper will prove to them that judgment happened when the ruler of this world was judged.

¹²"I have many more things to say to you, but they are too much for you now. ¹³But when the Spirit of truth comes, he will lead you into all truth. He will not speak his own words, but he will speak only what he hears, and he will tell you what is to come. ¹⁴The Spirit of truth will bring glory to me, because he will take what I have to say and tell it to you. ¹⁵All that the Father has is mine. That is why I said that the Spirit will take what I have to say and tell it to you.

SADNESS WILL BECOME HAPPINESS

¹⁶"After a little while you will not see me, and then after a little while you will see me again."

¹⁷Some of the followers said to each other, "What does Jesus mean when he says, 'After a little while you will not see

hot 10

Things to Do on a Saturday Night

10. Go to a house jam
9. Host a dinner party
8. Go bowling
7. Go to the movies
6. Watch boxing on "Pay-Per-View"
5. Hang out with friends
4. Play video games
3. Workout/play basketball
2. Watch "Sports Center"
1. Go out with your date

15:25 'They . . . reason.' These words could be from Psalm 35:19 or Psalm 69:4. **15:26; 16:7 Helper** "Counselor" or "Comforter." Jesus is talking about the Holy Spirit.

me, and then after a little while you will see me again'? And what does he mean when he says, 'Because I am going to the Father'?" [18]They also asked, "What does he mean by 'a little while'? We don't understand what he is saying."

[19]Jesus saw that the followers wanted to ask him about this, so he said to them, "Are you asking each other what I meant when I said, 'After a little while you will not see me, and then after a little while you will see me again'? [20]I tell you the truth, you will cry and be sad, but the world will be happy. You will be sad, but your sadness will become joy. [21]When a woman gives birth to a baby, she has pain, because her time has come. But when her baby is born, she forgets the pain, because she is so happy that a child has been born into the world. [22]It is the same with you. Now you are sad, but I will see you again and you will be happy, and no one will take away your joy. [23]In that day you will not ask me for anything. I tell you the truth, my Father will give you anything you ask for in my name. [24]Until now you have not asked for anything in my name. Ask and you will receive, so that your joy will be the fullest possible joy.

VICTORY OVER THE WORLD

[25]"I have told you these things indirectly in stories. But the time will come when I will not use stories like that to

tell you things; I will speak to you in plain words about the Father. [26]In that day you will ask the Father for things in my name. I mean, I will not need to ask the Father for you. [27]The Father himself loves you. He loves you because you loved me and believed that I came from God. [28]I came from the Father into the world. Now I am leaving the world and going back to the Father."

[29]Then the followers of Jesus said, "You are speaking clearly to us now and are not using stories that are hard to understand. [30]We can see now that you know all things. You can answer a person's question even before it is asked. This makes us believe you came from God."

[31]Jesus answered, "So now you believe? [32]Listen to me; a time is coming when you will be scattered, each to your own home. That time is now here. You will leave me alone, but I am never really alone, because the Father is with me.

[33]"I told you these things so that you can have peace in me. In this world you

PEEP THIS:

In 1982, the word "Internet" was used for the first time.

will have trouble, but be brave! I have defeated the world."

JESUS PRAYS FOR HIS FOLLOWERS

17 After Jesus said these things, he looked toward heaven and prayed, "Father, the time has come. Give glory to your Son so that the Son can give glory to you. ²You gave the Son power over all people so that the Son could give eternal life to all those you gave him. ³And this is eternal life: that people know you, the only true God, and that they know Jesus Christ, the One you sent. ⁴Having finished the work you gave me to do, I brought you glory on earth. ⁵And now, Father, give me glory with you; give me the glory I had with you before the world was made.

⁶"I showed what you are like to those you gave me from the world. They belonged to you, and you gave them to me, and they have obeyed your teaching. ⁷Now they know that everything you gave me comes from you. ⁸I gave them the teachings you gave me, and they accepted them. They knew that I truly came from you, and they believed that you sent me. ⁹I am praying for them. I am not praying for people in the world but for those you gave me, because they are yours. ¹⁰All I have is yours, and all you have is mine. And my glory is shown through them. ¹¹I am coming to you; I will not stay in the world any longer. But they are still in the world. Holy Father, keep them safe by the power of your name, the name you gave me, so that they will be one, just as you and I are one. ¹²While I was with them, I kept them safe by the power of your name, the name you gave me. I protected them, and only one of them, the one worthy of destruction, was lost so that the Scripture would come true.

¹³"I am coming to you now. But I pray these things while I am still in the world so that these followers can have all of my joy in them. ¹⁴I have given them your teaching. And the world has hated them, because they don't belong to the world, just as I don't belong to the world. ¹⁵I am not asking you to take them out of the world but to keep them safe from the Evil One. ¹⁶They don't belong to the world, just as I don't belong to the world. ¹⁷Make them ready for your service through your truth; your teaching is truth. ¹⁸I have sent them into the world, just as you sent me into the world. ¹⁹For their sake, I am making myself ready to serve so that they can be ready for their service of the truth.

> JESUS SAID TO PETER, "PUT YOUR SWORD BACK. SHOULDN'T I DRINK THE CUP THE FATHER GAVE ME?"

²⁰"I pray for these followers, but I am also praying for all those who will believe in me because of their teaching. ²¹Father, I pray that they can be one. As you are in me and I am in you, I pray that they can also be one in us. Then the world will believe that you sent me. ²²I have given these people the glory that you gave me so that they can be one, just as you and I are one. ²³I will be in them and you will be in me so that they will be completely one. Then the world will know that you sent me and that you loved them just as much as you loved me.

²⁴"Father, I want these people that you gave me to be with me where I am. I want them to see my glory, which you gave me because you loved me before the world was made. ²⁵Father, you are the One who is good. The world does not know you, but I know you, and these people know you sent me. ²⁶I showed them what you are like, and I will show them again. Then they will have the same love that you have for me, and I will live in them."

JESUS IS ARRESTED

18 When Jesus finished praying, he went with his followers across the Kidron Valley. On the other side there was a garden, and Jesus and his followers went into it.

²Judas knew where this place was, because Jesus met there often with his followers. Judas was the one who turned against Jesus. ³So Judas came there with a group of soldiers and some guards from the leading priests and the Pharisees. They were carrying torches, lanterns, and weapons.

⁴Knowing everything that would happen to him, Jesus went out and asked, "Who is it you are looking for?"

⁵They answered, "Jesus from Nazareth."

"I am he," Jesus said. (Judas, the one who turned against Jesus, was standing there with them.) ⁶When Jesus said, "I am he," they moved back and fell to the ground.

⁷Jesus asked them again, "Who is it you are looking for?"

They said, "Jesus of Nazareth."

⁸"I told you that I am he," Jesus said. "So if you are looking for me, let the others go." ⁹This happened so that the words Jesus said before would come true: "I have not lost any of the ones you gave me."

¹⁰Simon Peter, who had a sword, pulled it out and struck the servant of the high priest, cutting off his right ear. (The servant's name was Malchus.) ¹¹Jesus said to Peter, "Put your sword back. Shouldn't I drink the cupⁿ the Father gave me?"

 18:11 cup Jesus is talking about the painful things that will happen to him. Accepting these things will be very hard, like drinking a cup of something bitter.

365

JUNE

1
2 **Think** outside
3 **the box:**
4 Service is the rent we pay to
5 live on earth. What
6 can I do to give back?

7 It's your birthday, Allen Iverson!

8
9

10 Happy Birthday Faith Evans!

11 On This Day In History 1911—Marcus Garvey
    founded U.N.I.A. (Universal Negro
12   Improvement Association).

13
14

15 Take your **dad** or a special man in your
16 life to dinner

17 It's your birthday, Venus Williams!

18

19 On This Day In History 1865—"Juneteenth" celebration commemorates
                           Emancipation in Texas.

20 Summer begins today!

21 On This Day In History 1948—The "long playing" record is first introduced
                           by Dr. Peter Goldmark.

22 HOLIDAY—Father's Day

23

24

25 On This Day In History 1962—U.S. Supreme Court bans prayer in public schools.

26 Happy Birthday Derek Jeter!

27

28 Summer begins June 20th. How can you
29 make this season **special?**

"In my mind, I'm
always the best. If I
walk out on the court
(and) I think the next
person is better,
I've already lost."
- *Venus Williams*

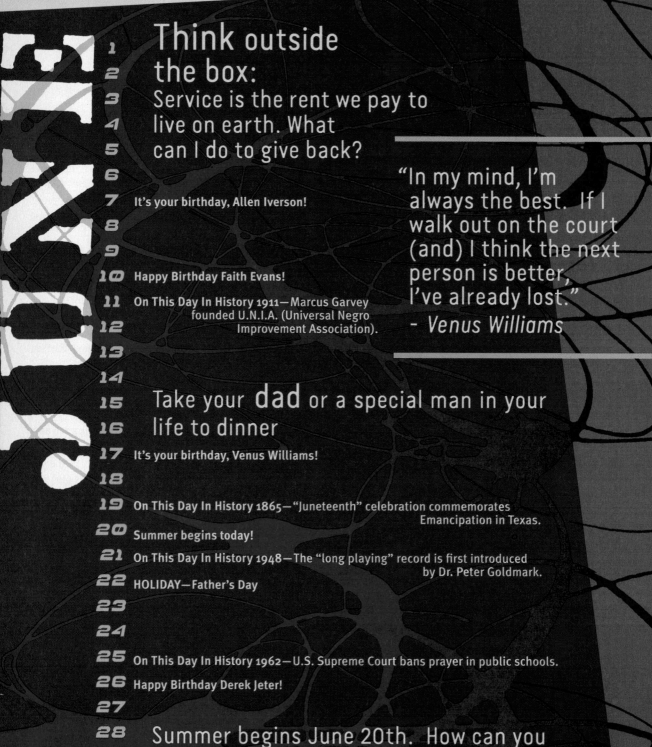

MUSIC REVIEWS

ARTIST: BUSTA RHYMES **ALBUM:** ANARCHY
CUT: "SALUTE DA GODS"

Busta Rhymes is just plain profane! Cussin' up a storm in all his lyrics. It stops meaning something after awhile and just starts to hurt your ears. So, it shouldn't surprise you that what few lyrics I can quote here say, "My niggaz tell me (why) tell me (we die) because we gods nigga (and) we go the yard nigga because I walk the ground under my feet and keep it live and stay in tune with the street now let me ask my niggaz (why?)"

Busta's rhyme let out a false word that we are gods. So what does that say about the real God?

"REJECTED"

JESUS IS BROUGHT BEFORE ANNAS

[12]Then the soldiers with their commander and the guards arrested Jesus. They tied him [13]and led him first to Annas, the father-in-law of Caiaphas, the high priest that year. [14]Caiaphas was the one who told the Jews that it would be better if one man died for all the people.

PETER SAYS HE DOESN'T KNOW JESUS

[15]Simon Peter and another one of Jesus' followers went along after Jesus. This follower knew the high priest, so he went with Jesus into the high priest's courtyard. [16]But Peter waited outside near the door. The follower who knew the high priest came back outside, spoke to the girl at the door, and brought Peter inside. [17]The girl at the door said to Peter, "Aren't you also one of that man's followers?"

Peter answered, "No, I am not!"

[18]It was cold, so the servants and guards had built a fire and were standing around it, warming themselves. Peter also was standing with them, warming himself.

THE HIGH PRIEST QUESTIONS JESUS

[19]The high priest asked Jesus questions about his followers and his teaching. [20]Jesus answered, "I have spoken openly to everyone. I have always taught in synagogues and in the Temple, where all the Jews come together. I never said anything in secret. [21]So why do you question me? Ask the people who heard my teaching. They know what I said."

[22]When Jesus said this, one of the guards standing there hit him. The guard said, "Is that the way you answer the high priest?"

[23]Jesus answered him, "If I said something wrong, then show what it was. But if what I said is true, why do you hit me?"

[24]Then Annas sent Jesus, who was still tied, to Caiaphas the high priest.

PETER SAYS AGAIN HE DOESN'T KNOW JESUS

[25]As Simon Peter was standing and warming himself, they said to him, "Aren't you one of that man's followers?"

Peter said it was not true; he said, "No, I am not."

[26]One of the servants of the high priest was there. This servant was a relative of the man whose ear Peter had cut off. The servant said, "Didn't I see you with him in the garden?"

[27]Again Peter said it wasn't true. At once a rooster crowed.

JESUS IS BROUGHT BEFORE PILATE

[28]Early in the morning they led Jesus from Caiaphas's house to the Roman governor's palace. They would not go inside the palace, because they did not want to make themselves unclean;[n] they wanted to eat the Passover meal. [29]So Pilate went outside to them and asked, "What charges do you bring against this man?"

[30]They answered, "If he were not a criminal, we wouldn't have brought him to you."

[31]Pilate said to them, "Take him yourselves and judge him by your own law."

 18:28 unclean Going into the Roman palace would make them unfit to eat the Passover Feast, according to their Law.

WORLD SAYS, WORD SAYS

AUTHORITY

You are your own boss. You're in charge. Don't let *nobody* tell you what to do! Forget what your boss said; you'll get to work when you get there. Take control of your own life. Don't listen to your parents, either. After all, what do they know? You are grown. You make your *own* rules. And if some people don't like it, tough.

"All of you must yield to the government rulers. No one rules unless God has given him the power to rule, and no one rules now without that power from God. So those who are against the government are really against what God has commanded. And they will bring punishment on themselves" (Romans 13:1-2).

"But we are not allowed to put anyone to death," the Jews answered. [32](This happened so that what Jesus said about how he would die would come true.)

[33]Then Pilate went back inside the palace and called Jesus to him and asked, "Are you the king of the Jews?"

[34]Jesus said, "Is that your own question, or did others tell you about me?"

[35]Pilate answered, "I am not one of you. It was your own people and their leading priests who handed you over to me. What have you done wrong?"

[36]Jesus answered, "My kingdom does not belong to this world. If it belonged to this world, my servants would have fought to keep me from being given over to the Jewish leaders. But my kingdom is from another place."

[37]Pilate said, "So you are a king!"

Jesus answered, "You are the one saying I am a king. This is why I was born and came into the world: to tell people the truth. And everyone who belongs to the truth listens to me."

[38]Pilate said, "What is truth?" After he said this, he went out to the crowd again and said to them, "I find nothing against this man. [39]But it is your custom that I free one prisoner to you at Passover time. Do you want me to free the 'king of the Jews'?"

[40]They shouted back, "No, not him! Let Barabbas go free!" (Barabbas was a robber.)

'19 Then Pilate ordered that Jesus be taken away and whipped. [2]The soldiers made a crown from some thorny branches and put it on Jesus' head and put a purple robe around him. [3]Then they came to him many times and said, "Hail, King of the Jews!" and hit him in the face.

[4]Again Pilate came out and said to them, "Look, I am bringing Jesus out to you. I want you to know that I find nothing against him." [5]So Jesus came out, wearing the crown of thorns and the purple robe. Pilate said to them, "Here is the man!"

[6]When the leading priests and the guards saw Jesus, they shouted, "Crucify him! Crucify him!"

But Pilate answered, "Crucify him yourselves, because I find nothing against him."

[7]The leaders answered, "We have a law that says he should die, because he said he is the Son of God."

[8]When Pilate heard this, he was even more afraid. [9]He went back inside the palace and asked Jesus, "Where do you come from?" But Jesus did not answer him. [10]Pilate said, "You refuse to speak to me? Don't you know I have power to set you free and power to have you crucified?"

[11]Jesus answered, "The only power you have over me is the power given to you by God. The man who turned me in to you is guilty of a greater sin."

[12]After this, Pilate tried to let Jesus go. But some in the crowd cried out, "Anyone who makes himself king is against Caesar. If you let this man go, you are no friend of Caesar."

[13]When Pilate heard what they were saying, he brought Jesus out and sat down on the judge's seat at the place called The Stone Pavement. (In the Hebrew language[n] the name is Gabbatha.) [14]It was about noon on Preparation Day of Passover week. Pilate said to the crowd, "Here is your king!"

[15]They shouted, "Take him away! Take him away! Crucify him!"

Pilate asked them, "Do you want me to crucify your king?"

The leading priests answered, "The only king we have is Caesar."

[16]So Pilate handed Jesus over to them to be crucified.

JESUS IS CRUCIFIED

The soldiers took charge of Jesus. [17]Carrying his own cross, Jesus went out to a place called The Place of the Skull, which in the Hebrew language[n] is called Golgotha. [18]There they crucified Jesus. They also crucified two other men, one on each side, with Jesus in the middle. [19]Pilate wrote a sign and put it on the cross. It read: JESUS OF NAZARETH, THE

 19:13, 17 Hebrew language Or Aramaic, the languages of many people in this region in the first century.

CONNECTED

DISCONNECTING FROM PEER PRESSURE:

NO MATTER WHAT THEY SAY

I had a hidden desire to become a writer, but that just wasn't the way my life was moving. Mostly, I was worried about what people would say if I changed up on them to follow some fantasy. I was on the same roll as most of my friends and it would totally throw them for a loop if I were to make a change now. Deep down, it kept gnawing at me to write, until I finally made the switch. It was amazing to see how much peace I had with that decision.

Likewise, Mary of Bethany actually got some heat from her peeps for doing what she knew she should be doing. Mary knew her place was at the feet of Jesus, but her sister, Martha, jumped all over her for not helping in the kitchen when Jesus came to visit (Luke 10:39-40). At another time, the disciples really thought she was crazy when Mary lavished Jesus with some top-of-the-line fragrant oil (John 12:1-3). But Jesus made all of them back way up off of her because he understood that Mary was using her unique gift to honor him before he went to the cross (Matthew 26:10-13).

You've got a unique fragrance, too. Have you ever been surprised to find out that when other people wear your favorite perfume or cologne, it smells so different on them? Don't be intimidated by other people's fragrances, or by the gifts that God has placed in them. Just focus on your own gift. Are you using it? You have something inside of you that God wants to share with the world, but only through you.

Trust that you will be criticized when you give your best to the Lord. Someone will pop lip, but don't let that stop you. People will not always understand what God is doing through you and in you. Don't let friends or foes, peers or haters keep you from walking in the fullness of what God has for you. He has prepared a place just for you. Sit at his feet and pour out your fragrant oil. That negative stuff? Don't even sweat it.

KING OF THE JEWS. [20]The sign was written in Hebrew, in Latin, and in Greek. Many of the people read the sign, because the place where Jesus was crucified was near the city. [21]The leading priests said to Pilate, "Don't write, 'The King of the Jews.' But write, 'This man said, "I am the King of the Jews." ' "

[22]Pilate answered, "What I have written, I have written."

[23]After the soldiers crucified Jesus, they took his clothes and divided them into four parts, with each soldier getting one part. They also took his long shirt, which was all one piece of cloth, woven from top to bottom. [24]So the soldiers said to each other, "We should not tear this into parts. Let's throw lots to see who will get it." This happened so that this Scripture would come true:

"They divided my clothes among
     them,
   and they threw lots for my
     clothing."   *Psalm 22:18*

So the soldiers did this.

[25]Standing near his cross were Jesus' mother, his mother's sister, Mary the wife of Clopas, and Mary Magdalene. [26]When Jesus saw his mother and the follower he loved standing nearby, he said to his mother, "Dear woman, here is your son." [27]Then he said to the follower, "Here is your mother." From that time on, the follower took her to live in his home.

JESUS DIES

[28]After this, Jesus knew that everything had been done. So that the Scripture would come true, he said, "I am thirsty."[n] [29]There was a jar full of vinegar there, so the soldiers soaked a sponge in it, put the sponge on a branch of a hyssop plant, and lifted it to Jesus' mouth. [30]When Jesus tasted the vinegar, he said, "It is finished." Then he bowed his head and died.

[31]This day was Preparation Day, and the next day was a special Sabbath day. Since the religious leaders did not want the bodies to stay on the cross on the

 19:28 "I am thirsty." Read Psalms 22:15; 69:21.

Sabbath day, they asked Pilate to order that the legs of the men be broken[n] and the bodies be taken away. [32]So the soldiers came and broke the legs of the first man on the cross beside Jesus. Then they broke the legs of the man on the other cross beside Jesus. [33]But when the soldiers came to Jesus and saw that he was already dead, they did not break his legs. [34]But one of the soldiers stuck his spear into Jesus' side, and at once blood and water came out. [35](The one who saw this happen is the one who told us this, and whatever he says is true. And he knows that he tells the truth, and he tells it so that you might believe.) [36]These things happened to make the Scripture come true: "Not one of his bones will be broken."[n] [37]And another Scripture says, "They will look at the one they stabbed."[n]

JESUS IS BURIED

[38]Later, Joseph from Arimathea asked Pilate if he could take the body of Jesus. (Joseph was a secret follower of Jesus, because he was afraid of some of the leaders.) Pilate gave his permission, so Joseph came and took Jesus' body away. [39]Nicodemus, who earlier had come to Jesus at night, went with Joseph. He brought about seventy-five pounds of myrrh and aloes. [40]These two men took Jesus' body and wrapped it with the spices in pieces of linen cloth, which is how they bury the dead. [41]In the place where Jesus was crucified, there was a garden. In the garden was a new tomb that had never been used before. [42]The men laid Jesus in that tomb because it was nearby, and they were preparing to start their Sabbath day.

19:31 broken The breaking of their bones would make them die sooner. **19:36 "Not one . . . broken."** Quotation from Psalm 34:20. The idea is from Exodus 12:46; Numbers 9:12. **19:37 "They . . . stabbed."** Quotation from Zechariah 12:10.

HOW YA TRAVELIN'?

REAL POWER

Do you want power? The greatest power doesn't come from one person standing alone. Instead, it comes from joining forces with God's people to form a powerful gang. In this gang, you have weapons: prayer and accountability to God and to the other gang members. Joy, love, and unity of spirit, is where the power comes from. But, like any gang, you have to commit and sign a blood oath. The blood of Jesus Christ enables you to overcome.

The Word of God says, "If two or three people come together in my name, I am there with them" (Matthew 18:20). It doesn't matter whether you call them a gang, a church, or prayer partners. They are others who have accepted Jesus Christ as their Lord you stand strong to reach the spiritual goals you set for yourself. Of course, your prayer partner needs to be someone you want to hang with, but who isn't trying to overdub you or put you down. A prayer partner is not somebody who is trying to get you straight; instead, he's got your back unconditionally. Most important, a prayer partner is somebody who won't put your business out in the street. But you've got to be real with your partner because, remember, God's up in this, too. You've got to be willing to be exposed.

Being a part of God's gang helps you focus on your life goal of staying tight with Jesus Christ. Having Christ as your number one is the only way to tap into

JESUS' TOMB IS EMPTY

20 Early on the first day of the week, Mary Magdalene went to the tomb while it was still dark. When she saw that the large stone had been moved away from the tomb, ²she ran to Simon Peter and the follower whom Jesus loved. Mary said, "They have taken the Lord out of the tomb, and we don't know where they have put him."

³So Peter and the other follower started for the tomb. ⁴They were both running, but the other follower ran faster than Peter and reached the tomb first. ⁵He bent down and looked in and saw the strips of linen cloth lying there, but he did not go in. ⁶Then following him, Simon Peter arrived and went into the tomb and saw the strips of linen lying there. ⁷He also saw the cloth that had been around Jesus' head, which was folded up and laid in a different place from the strips of linen. ⁸Then the other follower, who had reached the tomb first, also went in. He saw and believed. ⁹(They did not yet understand from the Scriptures that Jesus must rise from the dead.)

JESUS APPEARS TO MARY MAGDALENE

¹⁰Then the followers went back home. ¹¹But Mary stood outside the tomb, crying. As she was crying, she bent down and looked inside the tomb. ¹²She saw two angels dressed in white, sitting where Jesus' body had been, one at the head and one at the feet.

¹³They asked her, "Woman, why are you crying?"

She answered, "They have taken away my Lord, and I don't know where they have put him." ¹⁴When Mary said this, she turned around and saw Jesus standing there, but she did not know it was Jesus.

¹⁵Jesus asked her, "Woman, why are you crying? Whom are you looking for?"

Thinking he was the gardener, she said to him, "Did you take him away, sir? Tell me where you put him, and I will get him."

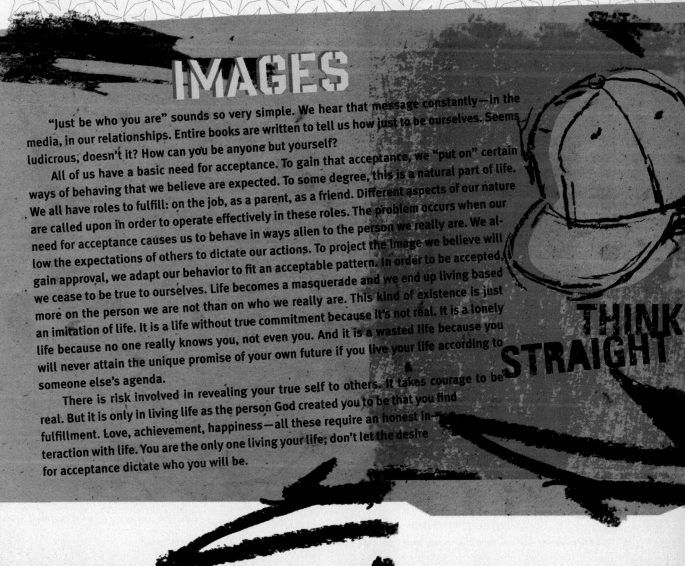

IMAGES

"Just be who you are" sounds so very simple. We hear that message constantly—in the media, in our relationships. Entire books are written to tell us how just to be ourselves. Seems ludicrous, doesn't it? How can you be anyone but yourself?

All of us have a basic need for acceptance. To gain that acceptance, we "put on" certain ways of behaving that we believe are expected. To some degree, this is a natural part of life. We all have roles to fulfill: on the job, as a parent, as a friend. Different aspects of our nature are called upon in order to operate effectively in these roles. The problem occurs when our need for acceptance causes us to behave in ways alien to the person we really are. We allow the expectations of others to dictate our actions. To project the image we believe will gain approval, we adapt our behavior to fit an acceptable pattern. In order to be accepted, we cease to be true to ourselves. Life becomes a masquerade and we end up living based more on the person we are not than on who we really are. This kind of existence is just an imitation of life. It is a life without true commitment because it's not real. It is a lonely life because no one really knows you, not even you. And it is a wasted life because you will never attain the unique promise of your own future if you live your life according to someone else's agenda.

There is risk involved in revealing your true self to others. It takes courage to be real. But it is only in living life as the person God created you to be that you find fulfillment. Love, achievement, happiness—all these require an honest interaction with life. You are the only one living your life; don't let the desire for acceptance dictate who you will be.

THINK STRAIGHT

OVERCOMING

▶ NEVER SATISFIED

Holding us hostage within ourselves is a yearning, a whispering voice. It speaks regardless of who we are, chasing us like a mad dog that needs to be put to sleep. It is the struggle to obtain and acquire because we are never satisfied. Fame and fortune are never enough. The love you choose is never enough. Jobs that give you opportunities to excel are never enough. We will lie to have more, cheat to get more, and steal to accumulate more. We struggle to get ahead only to discover it's never

enough. Consider God's servant Job (Job 1:20-22). He was satisfied with what he had. His soul was right with his creator because he understood a principle summed up in three little words: Hold everything loosely!

Circumstances may change tomorrow. We will gain and lose; we will know times of plenty and times of need. But the love of God is changeless and constant. Only God himself is enough to satisfy—to fill up that place within us that ceaselessly searches for more.

---

[16] Jesus said to her, "Mary."

Mary turned toward Jesus and said in the Hebrew language,[n] "Rabboni." (This means "Teacher.")

[17] Jesus said to her, "Don't hold on to me, because I have not yet gone up to the Father. But go to my brothers and tell them, 'I am going back to my Father and your Father, to my God and your God.'"

[18] Mary Magdalene went and said to the followers, "I saw the Lord!" And she told them what Jesus had said to her.

JESUS APPEARS TO HIS FOLLOWERS

[19] When it was evening on the first day of the week, Jesus' followers were together. The doors were locked, because they were afraid of the elders. Then Jesus came and stood right in the middle of them and said, "Peace be with you." [20] After he said this, he showed them his hands and his side. His followers were thrilled when they saw the Lord.

[21] Then Jesus said again, "Peace be with you. As the Father sent me, I now send you." [22] After he said this, he breathed on them and said, "Receive the Holy Spirit. [23] If you forgive anyone his sins, they are forgiven. If you don't forgive them, they are not forgiven."

JESUS APPEARS TO THOMAS

[24] Thomas (called Didymus), who was one of the twelve, was not with them when Jesus came. [25] The other followers kept telling Thomas, "We saw the Lord."

But Thomas said, "I will not believe it until I see the nail marks in his hands and put my finger where the nails were and put my hand into his side."

[26] A week later the followers were in the house again, and Thomas was with them. The doors were locked, but Jesus came in and stood right in the middle of them. He said, "Peace be with you." [27] Then he said to Thomas, "Put your finger here, and look at my hands. Put your hand here in my side. Stop being an unbeliever and believe."

[28] Thomas said to him, "My Lord and my God!"

[29] Then Jesus told him, "You believe because you see me. Those who believe without seeing me will be truly blessed."

WHY JOHN WROTE THIS BOOK

[30] Jesus did many other miracles in the presence of his followers that are not written in this book. [31] But these are written so that you may believe that Je-

sus is the Christ, the Son of God. Then, by believing, you may have life through his name.

JESUS APPEARS TO SEVEN FOLLOWERS

21 Later, Jesus showed himself to his followers again—this time at Lake Galilee.[n] This is how he showed himself: [2] Some of the followers were together: Simon Peter, Thomas (called Didymus), Nathanael from Cana in Galilee, the two sons of Zebedee, and two other followers. [3] Simon Peter said, "I am going out to fish."

The others said, "We will go with you." So they went out and got into the boat. They fished that night but caught nothing.

[4] Early the next morning Jesus stood on the shore, but the followers did not know it was Jesus. [5] Then he said to them, "Friends, did you catch any fish?"

They answered, "No."

[6] He said, "Throw your net on the right side of the boat, and you will find some."

  20:16 Hebrew language Or Aramaic, the languages of many people in this region in the first century.   **21:1 Lake Galilee** Literally, "Sea of Tiberias."

JAIL'S NO JOKE

Jail Separates Mothers and Babies

As soon as I gave birth to my baby, the system took him away. I don't know what I was thinking selling my body for money. Well, actually that was how I got pregnant in the first place, prostituting for cash and drugs. Guess I wasn't thinking. I was only four months pregnant when I got busted for the third time in one year. I was still hustling on the streets cause I didn't even know I was carrying a child. After I got arrested, I got real sick, so they did a physical and that's when I first found out.

Guess I thought I'd get off like all the other times, especially because I was pregnant. I thought that they wouldn't and couldn't lock up a pregnant woman. Man, was I wrong. My court-appointed lawyer didn't even try to argue my case. When my name got called, he rambled off some stuff to the judge and the clerk and they rambled some stuff back. I don't even remember having a chance to say whether I was guilty or not. (I was guilty, but that was beside the point.) Next thing I know, I had received a mandatory sentence because of how many times I'd been brought in. Five years! I couldn't believe it. I was sentenced to five years in prison, and I'd be eligible for parole in 18 months. But what about my baby? When I was sentenced, I dropped to the floor and cried so hard that the judge had to order someone to remove me. I knew my baby would become a ward of the state, because I had no family that the DFCS would approve to care for the child. Nothing had prepared me for that dreaded moment. I hadn't talked to Jesus since I was twelve and got saved in the church, but now I was pleading with him to help me.

Jesus didn't keep me from going to jail or having the state take away my son, so I got hard and defiant in prison. No one could mess with me. I was so bitter and hateful. I don't believe I said a hundred words to anyone for six months. One day I was out in the courtyard at a church service and the minister preached about releasing pent up anger. All of a sudden, rain started pouring down and everyone else ran inside. I stood to my feet, stretched out my arms and wailed. It felt like Jesus was crying with me. I knew then that he was sad, too, that I didn't have my baby. I had caused this situation and I couldn't blame him. The minister started working with me and I began to understand more about Jesus and his love for me.

I'm now able to trust God with my life and the life of my son. I got out of jail about two years ago and now I'm licensed to do hair. My DFCS caseworker is working with me to try to get my son back. Living a reckless, sinful life cost me my son. But now, living my life for God, I have hope that I may get him back. Whatever happens, I know that God's got my back.

GOD UNIT ✚

THE CYCLE OF VIEOLENCE

he first time I hit my girl it felt natural. What did I expect? My pops was in jail for killing my mother. My maternal grandma raised me, and every time I acted out of hand, she told me I had a temper just like my dad. Really, I didn't intend to hit my lady that day, but she had such a mouth! It seemed she was always nagging about nothing. She knew which buttons to push, and I had to show her who was boss. Didn't I?

Then my eyes were opened. Seeing the bruises I left on my girl's body from the beat down I gave her, I was torn up in a way I didn't expect. She curled up in a ball and bawled. When I reached down to help, she yelled for me to leave her be. "I'm not going to take this," I remember her screaming. "You're crazy!"

Her words hit me in the face. Since my mom's death, I had vowed that I'd break the cycle of domestic violence that plagued my family. I wasn't gonna be like the man who'd taken all my mom's hugs and kisses away. But what could I do to change? Violence was in my blood. I was doomed to repeat the sins of my father.

In my sadness, with my girl weeping behind me, I fell to my knees and asked God for help. I don't remember what I said; I just remember knowing God was by me, hearing my pleas. I accepted Jesus into my heart, and I admitted that I needed help to control my negative ways. Immediately I felt a calming peace that zapped my anger away. I hadn't realized that my girl heard me give my life to Christ, but then she helped me from the floor and told me she'd been praying that I'd find the Lord. I apologized to her with a sincere heart. She forgave me, and I started going to church with her. I got into counseling with the pastor. God brought him into my life to teach me how to handle my rage and need to control others. After a year of counseling with my pastor, my girl and I got married. It's now been four years since I hit her, and by God's grace, it only happened that one time. Thanks to the Holy Spirit living inside me, the cycle is broken!

James 5:16 — Confess your sins to each other and pray for each other so God can heal you. When a believing person prays, great things happen.

So they did, and they caught so many fish they could not pull the net back into the boat.

[7]The follower whom Jesus loved said to Peter, "It is the Lord!" When Peter heard him say this, he wrapped his coat around himself. (Peter had taken his clothes off.) Then he jumped into the water. [8]The other followers went to shore in the boat, dragging the net full of fish. They were not very far from shore, only about a hundred yards. [9]When the followers stepped out of the boat and onto the shore, they saw a fire of hot coals. There were fish on the fire, and there was bread.

[10]Then Jesus said, "Bring some of the fish you just caught."

[11]Simon Peter went into the boat and pulled the net to the shore. It was full of big fish, one hundred fifty-three in all, but even though there were so many, the net did not tear. [12]Jesus said to them, "Come and eat." None of the followers dared ask him, "Who are you?" because they knew it was the Lord. [13]Jesus came and took the bread and gave it to them, along with the fish.

[14]This was now the third time Jesus showed himself to his followers after he was raised from the dead.

JESUS TALKS TO PETER

[15]When they finished eating, Jesus said to Simon Peter, "Simon son of John, do you love me more than these?"

He answered, "Yes, Lord, you know that I love you."

Jesus said, "Feed my lambs."

[16]Again Jesus said, "Simon son of John, do you love me?"

He answered, "Yes, Lord, you know that I love you."

Jesus said, "Take care of my sheep."

¹⁷A third time he said, "Simon son of John, do you love me?"

Peter was hurt because Jesus asked him the third time, "Do you love me?" Peter said, "Lord, you know everything; you know that I love you!"

He said to him, "Feed my sheep. ¹⁸I tell you the truth, when you were younger, you tied your own belt and went where you wanted. But when you are old, you will put out your hands and someone else will tie you and take you where you don't want to go." ¹⁹(Jesus said this to show how Peter would die to give glory to God.) Then Jesus said to Peter, "Follow me!"

²⁰Peter turned and saw that the follower Jesus loved was walking behind them. (This was the follower who had leaned against Jesus at the supper and had said, "Lord, who will turn against you?") ²¹When Peter saw him behind them, he asked Jesus, "Lord, what about him?"

²²Jesus answered, "If I want him to live until I come back, that is not your business. You follow me."

²³So a story spread among the followers that this one would not die. But Jesus did not say he would not die. He only said, "If I want him to live until I come back, that is not your business."

²⁴That follower is the one who is telling these things and who has now written them down. We know that what he says is true.

²⁵There are many other things Jesus did. If every one of them were written down, I suppose the whole world would not be big enough for all the books that would be written.

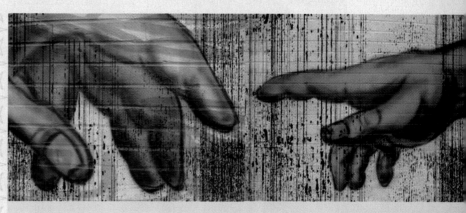

HeartCry

Bondage **Do memories of the past haunt you? Does all the pain from yesterday keep you from really living today? Let your heart cry . . .**

Jesus, please make this go away! I keep hearing all the voices and feeling all the pain from before. I get so angry about the things that happened to me. How can I leave all that garbage behind me? It's like it follows me wherever I go. The Bible says you carried all my sorrows —PLEASE—carry these because I can't. I need you. I need to be free from all this.

I did carry all your sorrows, my child. But you must choose to let go of your pain and give it to me. I will not force it from your hand. If you will believe in my love for you, the freedom you seek will be yours. John 8:36; 1 Peter 5:6, 7

ACTS

Actions Speak Louder Than Words

Actions speak louder than words. We all know people who just like to talk a good game but then they never actually do anything. That's not what these upcoming pages are about. The book of Acts is all about Action! The writer, Luke, lets us know that the early disciples pulled together and rocked entire cities and even countries with the message of Christ. They were like one big street team getting the word out to the masses. The story of Jesus didn't end after he resurrected and went up to heaven. It continued through all the people who believed in him. The book of Acts records the beginning of a community of believers, drawn together for fellowship, worship, teaching, serving, and spreading the message. This was the birth of the Church in its purest form. The really dope thing to notice is that all of the people involved in the action are just average folks like you and me. Jesus was all about using every day people from around the way. Many of the young leaders of the early Church started out scared, unsure, and even ignorant. But, after God sent his Spirit they were given power to accomplish incredible things. Check out the action in Acts . . . it gets no more real!

LUKE WRITES ANOTHER BOOK

1 To Theophilus.

The first book I wrote was about everything Jesus began to do and teach [2]until the day he was taken up into heaven. Before this, with the help of the Holy Spirit, Jesus told the apostles he had chosen what they should do. [3]After his death, he showed himself to them and proved in many ways that he was alive. The apostles saw Jesus during the forty days after he was raised from the dead, and he spoke to them about the kingdom of God. [4]Once when he was eating with them, he told them not to leave Jerusalem. He said, "Wait here to receive the promise from the Father which I told you about. [5]John baptized people with water, but in a few days you will be baptized with the Holy Spirit."

JESUS IS TAKEN UP INTO HEAVEN

[6]When the apostles were all together, they asked Jesus, "Lord, are you now going to give the kingdom back to Israel?"

[7]Jesus said to them, "The Father is the only One who has the authority to decide dates and times. These things are not for you to know. [8]But when the Holy Spirit comes to you, you will receive power. You will be my witnesses—in Jerusalem, in all of Judea, in Samaria, and in every part of the world."

[9]After he said this, as they were watching, he was lifted up, and a cloud hid him from their sight. [10]As he was going, they were looking into the sky. Suddenly, two men wearing white clothes stood beside them. [11]They said, "Men of Galilee, why are you standing here looking into the sky? Jesus, whom you saw taken up from you into heaven, will come back in the same way you saw him go."

A NEW APOSTLE IS CHOSEN

[12]Then they went back to Jerusalem from the Mount of Olives. (This mountain is about half a mile from Jerusalem.) [13]When they entered the city, they went to the upstairs room where they were staying. Peter, John, James, Andrew, Philip, Thomas, Bartholomew, Matthew, James son of Alphaeus, Simon (known as the Zealot), and Judas son of James were there. [14]They all continued praying together with some women, including Mary the mother of Jesus, and Jesus' brothers.

[15]During this time there was a meeting of the believers (about one hundred twenty of them). Peter stood up and said, [16-17]"Brothers and sisters, in the Scriptures the Holy Spirit said through David something that must happen involving Judas. He was one of our own group and served together with us. He led those who arrested Jesus." [18](Judas bought a field with the money he got for his evil act. But he fell to his death, his body burst open, and all his intestines poured out. [19]Everyone in Jerusalem learned about this so they named this place Akeldama. In their language Akeldama means "Field of Blood.") [20]"In the Book of Psalms," Peter said, "this is written:

JESUS WAS ALL ABOUT USING EVERYDAY PEOPLE

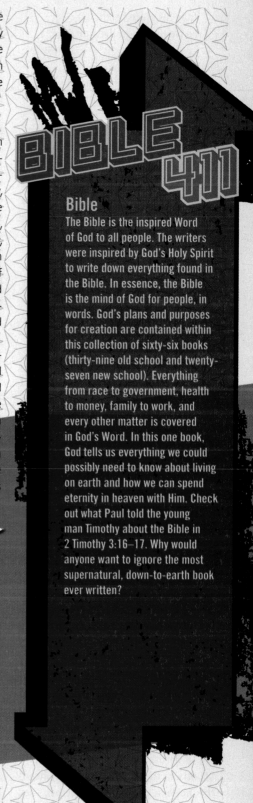

Bible

The Bible is the inspired Word of God to all people. The writers were inspired by God's Holy Spirit to write down everything found in the Bible. In essence, the Bible is the mind of God for people, in words. God's plans and purposes for creation are contained within this collection of sixty-six books (thirty-nine old school and twenty-seven new school). Everything from race to government, health to money, family to work, and every other matter is covered in God's Word. In this one book, God tells us everything we could possibly need to know about living on earth and how we can spend eternity in heaven with Him. Check out what Paul told the young man Timothy about the Bible in 2 Timothy 3:16–17. Why would anyone want to ignore the most supernatural, down-to-earth book ever written?

'May his place be empty;
leave no one to live in it.'

Psalm 69:25

And it is also written:

'Let another man replace him as
leader.'

Psalm 109:8

21-22"So now a man must become a witness with us of Jesus' being raised from the dead. He must be one of the men who were part of our group during all the time the Lord Jesus was among us—from the time John was baptizing people until the day Jesus was taken up from us to heaven."

23They put the names of two men before the group. One was Joseph Barsabbas, who was also called Justus. The other was Matthias. 24-25The apostles prayed, "Lord, you know the thoughts of everyone. Show us which one of these two you have chosen to do this work. Show us who should be an apostle in place of Judas, who turned away and went where he belongs." 26Then they used lots to choose between them, and the lots showed that Matthias was the one. So he became an apostle with the other eleven.

THE COMING OF THE HOLY SPIRIT

2 When the day of Pentecost came, they were all together in one place. 2Suddenly a noise like a strong, blowing wind came from heaven and filled the whole house where they were sitting. 3They saw something like flames of fire that were separated and stood over each person there. 4They were all filled with the Holy Spirit, and they began to speak different languages[n] by the power the Holy Spirit was giving them.

5There were some religious Jews staying in Jerusalem who were from every country in the world. 6When they heard this noise, a crowd came together. They were all surprised, because each one heard them speaking in his own language. 7They were completely amazed at this. They said, "Look! Aren't all these people that we hear speaking from Galilee? 8Then how is it possible that we each hear them in our own languages? We are from different places: 9Parthia, Media, Elam, Mesopotamia, Judea, Cappadocia, Pontus, Asia, 10Phrygia, Pamphylia, Egypt, the areas of Libya near Cyrene, Rome 11(both Jews and those who had become Jews), Crete, and Arabia. But we hear them telling in our own languages about the great things God has done!" 12They were all amazed and confused, asking each other, "What does this mean?"

13But others were making fun of them, saying, "They have had too much wine."

PETER SPEAKS TO THE PEOPLE

14But Peter stood up with the eleven apostles, and in a loud voice he spoke to the crowd: "My fellow Jews, and all of you who are in Jerusalem, listen to me. Pay attention to what I have to say. 15These people are not drunk, as you think; it is only nine o'clock in the morning! 16But Joel the prophet wrote about what is happening here today:

17'God says: In the last days
I will pour out my Spirit on all
kinds of people.
Your sons and daughters will
prophesy.
Your young men will see visions,
and your old men will dream
dreams.
18At that time I will pour out my
Spirit
also on my male slaves and female
slaves,
and they will prophesy.
19I will show miracles
in the sky and on the earth:
blood, fire, and thick smoke.
20The sun will become dark,
the moon red as blood,
before the overwhelming and
glorious day of the Lord will
come.
21Then anyone who calls on the Lord
will be saved.'

Joel 2:28-32

22"People of Israel, listen to these words: Jesus from Nazareth was a very special man. God clearly showed this to you by the miracles, wonders, and signs he did through Jesus. You all know this, because it happened right here among you. 23Jesus was given to you, and with the help of those who don't know the law, you put him to death by nailing him to a cross. But this was God's plan which he had made long ago; he knew all this would happen. 24God raised Jesus from the dead and set him free from the pain of death, because death could not hold him. 25For David said this about him:

'I keep the Lord before me always.
Because he is close by my side,
I will not be hurt.
26So I am glad, and I rejoice.
Even my body has hope,
27because you will not leave me in the
grave.
You will not let your Holy One rot.
28You will teach me how to live a holy
life.
Being with you will fill me with
joy.'

Psalm 16:8-11

29"Brothers and sisters, I can tell you truly that David, our ancestor, died and was buried. His grave is still here with us today. 30He was a prophet and knew God had promised him that he would make a person from David's family a king just as he was.[n] 31Knowing this before it happened, David talked about the Christ rising from the dead. He said:

'He was not left in the grave.
His body did not rot.'

32So Jesus is the One whom God raised from the dead. And we are all witnesses to this. 33Jesus was lifted up to heaven and is now at God's right side. The Father has given the Holy Spirit to Jesus as he promised. So Jesus has poured out that Spirit, and this is what you now see and hear. 34David was not the one who was lifted up to heaven, but he said:

'The Lord said to my Lord,
"Sit by me at my right side,
35until I put your enemies under your
control." '[n]

Psalm 110:1

2:4 languages This can also be translated "tongues." **2:30 God . . . was** See 2 Samuel 7:13; Psalm 132:11. **2:35 until . . . control** Literally, "until I make your enemies a footstool for your feet."

[36]"So, all the people of Israel should know this truly: God has made Jesus— the man you nailed to the cross—both Lord and Christ."

[37]When the people heard this, they felt guilty and asked Peter and the other apostles, "What shall we do?"

[38]Peter said to them, "Change your hearts and lives and be baptized, each one of you, in the name of Jesus Christ for the forgiveness of your sins. And you will receive the gift of the Holy Spirit. [39]This promise is for you, for your children, and for all who are far away. It is for everyone the Lord our God calls to himself."

[40]Peter warned them with many other words. He begged them, "Save yourselves from the evil of today's people!" [41]Then those people who accepted what Peter said were baptized. About three thousand people were added to the number of believers that day. [42]They spent their time learning the apostles' teaching, sharing, breaking bread,[n] and praying together.

THE BELIEVERS SHARE

[43]The apostles were doing many miracles and signs, and everyone felt great respect for God. [44]All the believers were together and shared everything. [45]They would sell their land and the things they owned and then divide the money and give it to anyone who needed it. [46]The believers met together in the Temple every day. They ate together in their homes, happy to share their food with joyful hearts. [47]They praised God and were liked by all the people. Every day the Lord added those who were being saved to the group of believers.

PETER HEALS A CRIPPLED MAN

3 One day Peter and John went to the Temple at three o'clock, the time set each day for the afternoon prayer service. [2]There, at the Temple gate called Beautiful Gate, was a man who had been crippled all his life. Every day he was carried to this gate to beg for money from the people going into the Temple. [3]The man saw Peter and John going into the Temple and asked them for money. [4]Peter and John looked straight at him and said, "Look at us!" [5]The man looked at them, thinking they were going to give him some money. [6]But Peter said, "I don't have any silver or gold, but I do have something else I can give you. By the power of Jesus Christ from Nazareth, stand up and walk!" [7]Then Peter took the man's right hand and lifted him up. Immediately the man's feet and ankles became strong. [8]He jumped up, stood on his feet, and began to walk. He went into the Temple with them, walking and jumping and praising God. [9-10]All the people recognized him as the crippled man who always sat by the Beautiful Gate begging for money. Now they saw this same man walking and praising God, and they were amazed. They wondered how this could happen.

PETER SPEAKS TO THE PEOPLE

[11]While the man was holding on to Peter and John, all the people were amazed and ran to them at Solomon's Porch. [12]When Peter saw this, he said to them, "People of Israel, why are you surprised? You are looking at us as if it were our own power or goodness that made this man walk. [13]The God of Abraham, Isaac, and Jacob, the God of our ancestors, gave glory to Jesus, his servant. But you handed him over to be killed. Pilate decided to let him go free, but you told Pilate you did not want Jesus. [14]You did not want the One who is holy and good but asked Pilate to give you a murderer[n] instead. [15]And so you killed the One who gives life, but God raised him from the dead. We are witnesses to this. [16]It was faith in Jesus that made this crippled man well. You can see this man, and you know him. He was made completely well because of trust in Jesus, and you all saw it happen!

[17]"Brothers and sisters, I know you did those things to Jesus because neither you nor your leaders understood what you were doing. [18]God said through the prophets that his Christ would suffer and die. And now God has made these things come true in this way. [19]So you must change your hearts and lives! Come back to God, and he will forgive your sins. Then the Lord will send the time of rest. [20]And he will send Jesus, the One he chose to be the Christ. [21]But Jesus must stay in heaven until the time comes when all things will be made right again. God told about this time long ago when he spoke through his holy prophets. [22]Moses said, 'The Lord your God will give you a prophet like me, who is one of your own people. You must listen to everything he tells you. [23]Anyone who does not listen to that prophet will die, cut off from God's people.'[n] [24]Samuel, and all the other prophets who spoke for God after Samuel, told about this time now. [25]You are descendants of the prophets. You have received the agreement God made with your ancestors. He said to your father Abraham, 'Through your descendants all the nations on the earth will be blessed.'[n] [26]God has raised up his servant Jesus and sent him to you first to bless you by turning each of you away from doing evil."

> # PEEP THIS:
>
> As of January, 2002, 58.5 percent of the U.S. population (164.14 million people) was using the Internet. Worldwide there are 544.2 million users.

2:42 breaking bread This may mean a meal as in verse 46, or the Lord's Supper, the special meal Jesus told his followers to eat to remember him (Luke 22:14-20). **3:14 murderer** Barabbas, the man the crowd asked Pilate to set free instead of Jesus (Luke 23:18). **3:22-23 'The Lord . . . people.'** Quotation from Deuteronomy 18:15, 19. **3:25 'Through . . . blessed.'** Quotation from Genesis 22:18; 26:4.

PETER AND JOHN AT THE COUNCIL

While Peter and John were speaking to the people, priests, the captain of the soldiers that guarded the Temple, and Sadducees came up to them. [2]They were upset because the two apostles were teaching the people and were preaching that people will rise from the dead through the power of Jesus. [3]The older leaders grabbed Peter and John and put them in jail. Since it was already night, they kept them in jail until the next day. [4]But many of those who had heard Peter and John preach believed the things they said. There were now about five thousand in the group of believers.

[5]The next day the rulers, the elders, and the teachers of the law met in Jerusalem. [6]Annas the high priest, Caiaphas, John, and Alexander were there, as well as everyone from the high priest's family. [7]They made Peter and John stand before them and then asked them, "By what power or authority did you do this?"

[8]Then Peter, filled with the Holy Spirit, said to them, "Rulers of the people and you elders, [9]are you questioning us about a good thing that was done to a crippled man? Are you asking us who made him well? [10]We want all of you and all the people to know that this man was made well by the power of Jesus Christ from Nazareth. You crucified him, but God raised him from the dead. This man was crippled, but he is now well and able to stand here before you because of the power of Jesus. [11]Jesus is

'the stone[n] that you builders
  rejected,
which has become the
  cornerstone.'   *Psalm 118:22*

[12]Jesus is the only One who can save people. No one else in the world is able to save us."

[13]The leaders saw that Peter and John were not afraid to speak, and they understood that these men had no special training or education. So they were

4:11 stone A symbol meaning Jesus.

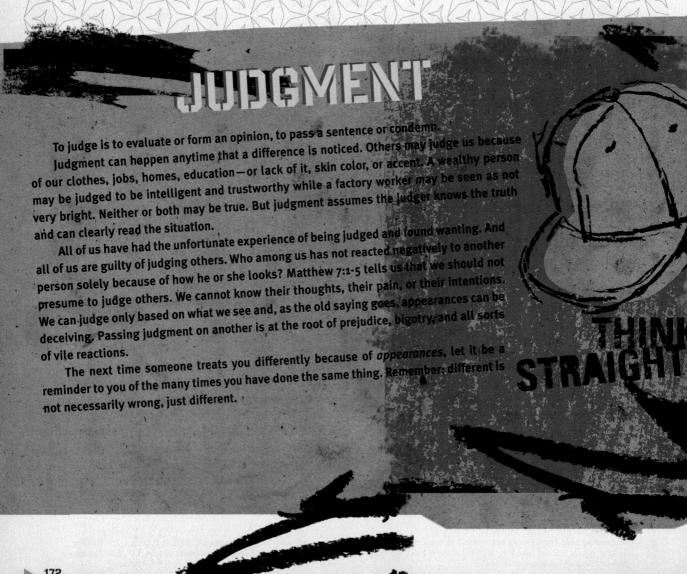

JUDGMENT

To judge is to evaluate or form an opinion, to pass a sentence or condemn. Judgment can happen anytime that a difference is noticed. Others may judge us because of our clothes, jobs, homes, education—or lack of it, skin color, or accent. A wealthy person may be judged to be intelligent and trustworthy while a factory worker may be seen as not very bright. Neither or both may be true. But judgment assumes the judger knows the truth and can clearly read the situation.

All of us have had the unfortunate experience of being judged and found wanting. And all of us are guilty of judging others. Who among us has not reacted negatively to another person solely because of how he or she looks? Matthew 7:1-5 tells us that we should not presume to judge others. We cannot know their thoughts, their pain, or their intentions. We can judge only based on what we see and, as the old saying goes, appearances can be deceiving. Passing judgment on another is at the root of prejudice, bigotry, and all sorts of vile reactions.

The next time someone treats you differently because of *appearances*, let it be a reminder to you of the many times you have done the same thing. Remember: different is not necessarily wrong, just different.

THINK STRAIGHT

REAL RHYMES:

ALWAYS BESIDE YOU

BY JOANNA ROBINSON

SHOULD I BE EXACTLY WHAT THEY EXPECT ME TO BE?
IS IT WORTH THE HASSLE OF AVOIDING UGLY CIRCUMSTANCES?
OF BEING MISUNDERSTOOD BY EVERYBODY?
OR SHOULD I KEEP THE FAITH AND BE WHO YOU HAVE CALLED ME TO BE?

WHY DOES MY HEART NOT KNOW WHICH WAY TO CHOOSE AND WHY,
WHY IS THERE SUCH A HUGE BATTLE OVER MY MIND?
TELL ME LORD, DO YOU SEE AND HEAR MY TROUBLED CRIES?
IF YOU DO, THEN WOULD YOU WALK ME THROUGH THIS TRIAL?

BUT YOU SAY: "DON'T WASTE YOUR WORRIES ON TOMORROW.
TAKE IT STEP BY STEP. IN TIME I'LL BE COMFORT FOR YOUR SORROWS.
JUST RELAX. I'LL EASE YOUR MIND.
WHEN YOUR JOURNEY GETS HARDER, I'LL REMIND YOU THAT I'M NEAR.
IT DOESN'T MATTER WHAT YOU CHOOSE NOW, 'CAUSE I'M ALWAYS BESIDE YOU."

SO MANY QUESTIONS GO UNANSWERED IN MY MIND.
AND LORD CAN YOU SEE THE DOUBT THAT'S GROWING UP DEEP INSIDE?
MY HEART'S BEEN ACHING FOR YOU A LONG TIME. BUT THROUGH MY PAIN I STILL HEAR YOU SAY:
"DON'T WASTE YOUR WORRIES ON TOMORROW. TAKE IT STEP BY STEP IN TIME.
I'LL BE COMFORT FOR YOUR SORROWS. JUST RELAX, I'LL EASE YOUR MIND.
WHEN YOUR JOURNEY GETS HARDER, I'LL REMIND YOU THAT I'M NEAR.
IT DOESN'T MATTER WHAT YOU CHOOSE NOW, 'CAUSE I'M ALWAYS BESIDE YOU."

amazed. Then they realized that Peter and John had been with Jesus. [14]Because they saw the healed man standing there beside the two apostles, they could say nothing against them. [15]After the leaders ordered them to leave the meeting, they began to talk to each other. [16]They said, "What shall we do with these men? Everyone in Jerusalem knows they have done a great miracle, and we cannot say it is not true. [17]But to keep it from spreading among the people, we must warn them not to talk to people anymore using that name."

[18]So they called Peter and John in again and told them not to speak or to teach at all in the name of Jesus. [19]But Peter and John answered them, "You decide what God would want. Should we obey you or God? [20]We cannot keep quiet. We must speak about what we have seen and heard." [21]The leaders warned the apostles again and let them go free. They could not find a way to punish them, because all the people were praising God for what had been done. [22]The man who received the miracle of healing was more than forty years old.

THE BELIEVERS PRAY

[23]After Peter and John left the meeting of leaders, they went to their own group and told them everything the leading priests and the elders had said to

He's got answers

I keep hearing that trials make us better. How can anything good come out of horrible experiences?

A young wife learns her husband has been killed in an accident, leaving her alone to raise two little boys. A doctor tells parents their newborn daughter has spina bifida. Tragedies hit like a ton of bricks.

Trials don't make you better; it's how you react to them that can make you better. Many times you do what you do just because it has to be done. As much as she would like to shut herself away from life, the young mother doesn't have many choices. She must feed her sons, get them to school, and learn to make hundreds of decisions alone. The new parents don't have the time to just sit and wonder why their daughter will never be able to walk. They need to quickly educate themselves and their family to be prepared to take care of their little girl's special needs.

In each of these situations—which happen every day—these people faced each moment, each decision, as it came. One thing they didn't do was try to make it on their own. They learned to lean on family and friends for help, advice, and a shoulder to cry on. They also learned the real power of prayer: not only that God would change their situation, but also that God would change them to be able to cope.

Read on: John 16:33; Hebrews 2:18; James 1:2-5; 1 Peter 1:6-9

PEEP THIS:

It is estimated that Internet users illegally download about 2.6 billion music files each month.

them. [24]When the believers heard this, they prayed to God together, "Lord, you are the One who made the sky, the earth, the sea, and everything in them. [25]By the Holy Spirit, through our father David your servant, you said:

'Why are the nations so angry?
    Why are the people making
        useless plans?
[26]The kings of the earth prepare to
        fight,
    and their leaders make plans
        together
    against the Lord
        and his Christ.'   *Psalm 2:1-2*
[27]These things really happened when Herod, Pontius Pilate, and some Jews and non-Jews all came together against

Jesus here in Jerusalem. Jesus is your holy servant, the One you made to be the Christ. [28]These people made your plan happen because of your power and your will. [29]And now, Lord, listen to their threats. Lord, help us, your servants, to speak your word without fear. [30]Show us your power to heal. Give proofs and make miracles happen by the power of Jesus, your holy servant."

[31]After they had prayed, the place

where they were meeting was shaken. They were all filled with the Holy Spirit, and they spoke God's word without fear.

THE BELIEVERS SHARE

[32]The group of believers were united in their hearts and spirit. All those in the group acted as though their private property belonged to everyone in the group. In fact, they shared everything. [33]With great power the apostles were telling people that the Lord Jesus was truly raised from the dead. And God blessed all the believers very much. [34]There were no needy people among them. From time to time those who owned fields or houses sold them, brought the money, [35]and gave it to the apostles. Then the money was given to anyone who needed it.

[36]One of the believers was named Joseph, a Levite born in Cyprus. The apostles called him Barnabas (which means "one who encourages"). [37]Joseph owned a field, sold it, brought the money, and gave it to the apostles.

ANANIAS AND SAPPHIRA DIE

5 But a man named Ananias and his wife Sapphira sold some land. [2]He kept back part of the money for himself; his wife knew about this and agreed to it. But he brought the rest of the money and gave it to the apostles. [3]Peter said, "Ananias, why did you let Satan rule your thoughts to lie to the Holy Spirit and to keep for yourself part of the money you received for the land? [4]Before you sold the land, it belonged to you. And even after you sold it, you could have used the money any way you wanted. Why did you think of doing this? You lied to God, not to us!" [5-6]When Ananias heard this, he fell down and died. Some young men came in, wrapped up his body, carried it out, and buried it. And everyone who heard about this was filled with fear.

[7]About three hours later his wife came in, but she did not know what had happened. [8]Peter said to her, "Tell me, was the money you got for your field this much?"

Sapphira answered, "Yes, that was the price."

[9]Peter said to her, "Why did you and your husband agree to test the Spirit of the Lord? Look! The men who buried your husband are at the door, and they will carry you out." [10]At that moment Sapphira fell down by his feet and died. When the young men came in and saw that she was dead, they carried her out and buried her beside her husband. [11]The whole church and all the others who heard about these things were filled with fear.

THE APOSTLES HEAL MANY

[12]The apostles did many signs and miracles among the people. And they would all meet together on Solomon's Porch. [13]None of the others dared to join them, but all the people respected them. [14]More and more men and women believed in the Lord and were added to the group of believers. [15]The people placed their sick on beds and mats in the streets, hoping that when Peter passed by at least his shadow might fall on them. [16]Crowds came from all the towns around Jerusalem, bringing their sick and those who were bothered by evil spirits, and all of them were healed.

LEADERS TRY TO STOP THE APOSTLES

[17]The high priest and all his friends (a group called the Sadducees) became very jealous. [18]They took the apostles and put them in jail. [19]But during the night, an angel of the Lord opened the doors of the jail and led the apostles outside. The angel said, [20]"Go stand in the Temple and tell the people everything about this new life." [21]When the apostles heard this, they obeyed and went into the Temple early in the morning and continued teaching.

When the high priest and his friends arrived, they called a meeting of the leaders and all the important elders. They sent some men to the jail to bring the apostles to them. [22]But, upon arriving, the officers could not find the apostles. So they went back and reported to the leaders. [23]They said, "The jail was closed and locked, and the guards were standing at the doors. But when we opened the doors, the jail was empty!" [24]Hearing this, the captain of the Temple guards and the leading priests were confused and wondered what was happening.

[25]Then someone came and told them, "Listen! The men you put in jail are standing in the Temple teaching the people." [26]Then the captain and his men went out and brought the apostles back. But the soldiers did not use force, because they were afraid the people would stone them to death.

[27]The soldiers brought the apostles to the meeting and made them stand before the leaders. The high priest questioned them, [28]saying, "We gave you strict orders not to continue teaching in that name. But look, you have filled Jerusalem with your teaching and are trying to make us responsible for this man's death."

[29]Peter and the other apostles answered, "We must obey God, not human authority! [30]You killed Jesus by hanging him on a cross. But God, the God of our ancestors, raised Jesus up from the dead! [31]Jesus is the One whom God raised to be on his right side, as Leader and Savior. Through him, all people could change their hearts and lives and have their sins forgiven. [32]We saw all these things happen. The Holy Spirit, whom God has given to all who obey him, also proves these things are true."

[33]When the leaders heard this, they became angry and wanted to kill them. [34]But a Pharisee named Gamaliel stood up in the meeting. He was a teacher of the law, and all the people respected him. He ordered the apostles to leave the meeting for a little while. [35]Then he said, "People of Israel, be careful what you are planning to do to these men. [36]Remember when Theudas appeared?

WORLD SAYS, WORD SAYS,

He said he was a great man, and about four hundred men joined him. But he was killed, and all his followers were scattered; they were able to do nothing. [37]Later, a man named Judas came from Galilee at the time of the registration.[n] He also led a group of followers and was killed, and all his followers were scattered. [38]And so now I tell you: Stay away from these men, and leave them alone. If their plan comes from human authority, it will fail. [39]But if it is from God, you will not be able to stop them. You might even be fighting against God himself!"

The leaders agreed with what Gamaliel said. [40]They called the apostles in, beat them, and told them not to speak in the name of Jesus again. Then they let them go free. [41]The apostles left the meeting full of joy because they were given the honor of suffering disgrace for Jesus. [42]Every day in the Temple and in people's homes they continued teaching the people and telling the Good News—that Jesus is the Christ.

SEVEN LEADERS ARE CHOSEN

6 The number of followers was growing. But during this same time, the Greek-speaking followers had an argument with the other followers. The Greek-speaking widows were not getting their share of the food that was given out every day. [2]The twelve apostles called the whole group of followers together and said, "It is not right for us to stop our work of teaching God's word in order to serve tables. [3]So, brothers and sisters, choose seven of your own men who are good, full of the Spirit and full of wisdom. We will put them in charge of this work. [4]Then we can continue to pray and to teach the word of God."

[5]The whole group liked the idea, so they chose these seven men: Stephen (a man with great faith and full of the Holy Spirit), Philip,[n] Procorus, Nicanor, Timon, Parmenas, and Nicolas (a man from Antioch who had become a follower of the Jewish religion). [6]Then they put these men before the apostles, who prayed and laid their hands[n] on them.

[7]The word of God was continuing to spread. The group of followers in Jerusalem increased, and a great number of the Jewish priests believed and obeyed.

STEPHEN IS ACCUSED

[8]Stephen was richly blessed by God who gave him the power to do great miracles and signs among the people. [9]But some people were against him. They belonged to the synagogue of Free Men[n] (as it was called), which included people from Cyrene, Alexandria, Cilicia, and Asia. They all came and argued with Stephen.

[10]But the Spirit was helping him to speak with wisdom, and his words were so strong that they could not argue with him. [11]So they secretly urged some men to say, "We heard Stephen speak against Moses and against God."

[12]This upset the people, the elders, and the teachers of the law. They came and grabbed Stephen and brought him to a meeting of the leaders. [13]They brought in some people to tell lies about Stephen, saying, "This man is always speaking against this holy place and the law of Moses. [14]We heard him say that Jesus from Nazareth will destroy this place and that Jesus will change the customs Moses gave us." [15]All the people in the meeting were watching Stephen closely and saw that his face looked like the face of an angel.

STEPHEN'S SPEECH

7 The high priest said to Stephen, "Are these things true?"

[2]Stephen answered, "Brothers and fathers, listen to me. Our glorious God appeared to Abraham, our ancestor, in Mesopotamia before he lived in Haran. [3]God said to Abraham, 'Leave your country and your relatives, and go to the land I will show you.'[n] [4]So Abraham left the country of Chaldea and went to live in Haran. After

---

5:37 registration Census. A counting of all the people and the things they own.   **6:5 Philip** Not the apostle named Philip.   **6:6 laid their hands** The laying on of hands had many purposes, including the giving of a blessing, power, or authority.   **6:9 Free Men** Jewish people who had been slaves or whose fathers had been slaves, but were now free.   **7:3 'Leave . . . you.'** Quotation from Genesis 12:1.

Abraham's father died, God sent him to this place where you now live. [5]God did not give Abraham any of this land, not even a foot of it. But God promised that he would give this land to him and his descendants, even before Abraham had a child. [6]This is what God said to him: 'Your descendants will be strangers in a land they don't own. The people there will make them slaves and will mistreat them for four hundred years. [7]But I will punish the nation where they are slaves. Then your descendants will leave that land and will worship me in this place.'[n] [8]God made an agreement with Abraham, the sign of which was circumcision. And so when Abraham had his son Isaac, Abraham circumcised him when he was eight days old. Isaac also circumcised his son Jacob, and Jacob did the same for his sons, the twelve ancestors[n] of our people.

[9]"Jacob's sons became jealous of Joseph and sold him to be a slave in Egypt. But God was with him [10]and saved him from all his troubles. The king of Egypt liked Joseph and respected him because of the wisdom God gave him. The king made him governor of Egypt and put him in charge of all the people in his palace.

[11]"Then all the land of Egypt and Canaan became so dry that nothing would grow, and the people suffered very much. Jacob's sons, our ancestors, could not find anything to eat. [12]But when Jacob heard there was grain in Egypt, he sent his sons there. This was their first trip to Egypt. [13]When they went there a second time, Joseph told his brothers who he was, and the king learned about Joseph's family. [14]Then Joseph sent messengers to invite Jacob, his father, to come to Egypt along with all his relatives (seventy-five persons altogether). [15]So Jacob went down to Egypt, where he and his sons died. [16]Later their bodies were moved to Shechem and put in a grave

7:6-7 'Your descendants . . . place.' Quotation from Genesis 15:13-14 and Exodus 3:12.   7:8 twelve ancestors Important ancestors of the people of Israel; the leaders of the twelve tribes of Israel.

HOW YA TRAVELIN'?

CARING AIN'T A PUNK

The word *caring* seems like such a punk word, very "sweet." But it's really a strong word that produces change. It is a powerful word; it means that you have caused somebody else's life to be profitable or useful. Don't make the mistake of thinking that caring is simply giving; it must be giving in the greatest area of need in someone's life.

Here are four great acts of caring that one person can give to another:

Provide safety. The need for safety is one of the greatest needs in anyone's life. To make someone feel safe means living by a creed that says, "I will *never* attack, criticize, or sweat anyone." Additionally, we should do all we can to protect those around us from the attacks of others, giving them the assurance that we will stand up for them.

Pour out praise. Pour into people; encourage them. Go out of your way to say good things about others. "So encourage each other and give each other strength" (1 Thessalonians 5:11).

Offer help. Help comes from a servant's heart. The goal is to give your heart to do something to benefit someone else and to let the love of God flow through you while giving him the glory.

Give an honest response. Go beyond being nice or telling people what they want to hear. Be bold enough to speak the truth in love, and stand firmly on the principles in which you believe.

BE WISE IN THE WAY YOU ACT – COLOSSIANS 4:5, 6

VIEWPOINT

WHAT HAS BEEN THE GREATEST SOURCE OF PAIN IN YOUR LIFE AND HOW HAS IT HELPED YOU TO GROW?

Unforgiveness is the greatest source of pain in my life. I have been hurt numerous times by people and sometimes it is not easy to forgive them. Consequently, I hold on to the pain. However, I have learned that I must forgive others in order to receive forgiveness from God and to release myself from the pain of unforgiveness. Holding on to hurt prolongs the pain while a simple act of forgiveness can ease the hurt and release peace into my heart.

there. (It was the same grave Abraham had bought for a sum of money from the sons of Hamor in Shechem.) ¹⁷"The promise God made to Abraham

was soon to come true, and the number of people in Egypt grew large. ¹⁸Then a new king, who did not know who Joseph was, began to rule Egypt. ¹⁹This king tricked our people and was cruel to our ancestors, forcing them to leave their babies outside to die. ²⁰At this time Moses was born, and he was very beautiful. For three months Moses was cared for in his father's house. ²¹When they put Moses outside, the king's daughter adopted him and raised him as if he were her own son. ²²The Egyptians taught Moses everything they knew, and he was a powerful man in what he said and did.

²³"When Moses was about forty years old, he thought it would be good to visit his own people, the people of Israel. ²⁴Moses saw an Egyptian mistreating one of his people, so he defended the Israelite and punished the Egyptian by killing him. ²⁵Moses thought his own people would understand that God was using him to save them, but they did not. ²⁶The next day when Moses saw two men of Israel fighting, he tried to make peace between them. He said, 'Men, you are brothers. Why are you hurting each other?' ²⁷The man who was hurting the other pushed Moses away and said, 'Who made you our ruler and judge? ²⁸Are you going to kill me as you killed the Egyptian yesterday?'ⁿ ²⁹When Moses heard him say this, he left Egypt and went to live in the land of Midian where he was a stranger. While Moses lived in Midian, he had two sons.

³⁰"Forty years later an angel appeared to Moses in the flames of a burning bush as he was in the desert near Mount Sinai. ³¹When Moses saw this, he was amazed and went near to look closer. Moses heard the Lord's voice say, ³²'I am the God of your ancestors, the God of Abraham, Isaac, and Jacob.'ⁿ Moses began to shake with fear and was afraid to look. ³³The Lord said to him, 'Take off your sandals, because you are standing on holy ground. ³⁴I have seen the troubles my people have suffered in Egypt. I have heard their cries and have

come down to save them. And now, Moses, I am sending you back to Egypt.'ⁿ

³⁵"This Moses was the same man the two men of Israel rejected, saying, 'Who made you a ruler and judge?'ⁿ Moses is the same man God sent to be a ruler and savior, with the help of the angel that Moses saw in the burning bush. ³⁶So Moses led the people out of Egypt. He worked miracles and signs in Egypt, at the Red Sea, and then in the desert for forty years. ³⁷This is the same Moses that said to the people of Israel, 'God will give you a prophet like me, who is one of your own people.'ⁿ ³⁸This is the Moses who was with the gathering of the Israelites in the desert. He was with the angel that spoke to him at Mount Sinai, and he was with our ancestors. He received commands from God that give life, and he gave those commands to us.

³⁹"But our ancestors did not want to obey Moses. They rejected him and wanted to go back to Egypt. ⁴⁰They said to Aaron, 'Make us gods who will lead us. Moses led us out of Egypt, but we don't know what has happened to him.'ⁿ ⁴¹So the people made an idol that looked like a calf. Then they brought sacrifices to it and were proud of what they had made with their own hands. ⁴²But God turned against them and did not try to stop them from worshiping the sun, moon, and stars. This is what is written in the book of the prophets: God says,

'People of Israel, you did not bring
    me sacrifices and offerings
    while you traveled in the desert
    for forty years.
⁴³You have carried with you
    the tent to worship Molech
    and the idols of the star god
    Rephan that you made to
    worship.
So I will send you away beyond
    Babylon.'   *Amos 5:25-27*

⁴⁴"The Holy Tent where God spoke to our ancestors was with them in the desert. God told Moses how to make this Tent, and he made it like the plan God showed him. ⁴⁵Later, Joshua led our ancestors to

7:27-28 'Who . . . yesterday?' Quotation from Exodus 2:14. **7:32** 'I am . . . Jacob.' Quotation from Exodus 3:6. **7:33-34** 'Take . . . Egypt.' Quotation from Exodus 3:5-10. **7:35** 'Who . . . judge?' Quotation from Exodus 2:14. **7:37** 'God . . . people.' Quotation from Deuteronomy 18:15. **7:40** 'Make . . . him.' Quotation from Exodus 32:1.

CONNECTED

DISCONNECTING FROM SEXUAL IMMORALITY:

HOW FAR IS TOO FAR?

"It's not penetration." "I'm still a virgin." "Everybody's doing it." "If oral sex were a sin then wouldn't God have listed it with all the other sins in the Bible?" Spoken with great conviction, statements like these are frequently made by unmarried people struggling with the tension of living a life of sexual purity.

Oral sex can be hurtful to your reputation and your witness. Whether or not there is penetration, you have still *used* your body and that of another person purely for physical pleasure without the benefit of marriage. You have not valued, loved, or committed to that other person. You have used that person and that body for the moment. Sexual immorality makes the Lord very sad. He says that your body is a temple for the Holy Spirit (1 Corinthians 6:19). God's plan for sex is within the context of marriage. When you start trying to get the benefits without the commitment and then play word games in the gray area, you run the risk of taking the Lord and his grace for granted. If you are not looking for ways to please God, then you are looking for ways to see what you can get away with.

Are you doing something that you'd be embarrassed to have the Lord witness? If you don't have a line, you have a price. Is a moment of pleasure worth the price of sin? Ask yourself, "How far will I go? How far is too far?" It all comes down to who is in control of your flesh. If you are too weak to be in control of it, stay away from situations where you may be tempted. Don't give away something precious because of some raging hormones. The Lord is well able to keep you sexually pure if you just ask him and trust him to help you do so. How far is too far? Well if you think it's wrong, disconnect from it.

capture the lands of the other nations. Our people went in, and God forced the other people out. When our people went into this new land, they took with them this same Tent they had received from their ancestors. They kept it until the time of David, [46]who pleased God and asked God to let him build a house for him, the God of Jacob.[n] [47]But Solomon was the one who built the Temple.

[48]"But the Most High does not live in houses that people build with their hands. As the prophet says:

[49]'Heaven is my throne,
    and the earth is my footstool.
So do you think you can build a
    house for me? says the Lord.
Do I need a place to rest?
[50]Remember, my hand made all these
    things!'"   *Isaiah 66:1-2*

[51]Stephen continued speaking: "You stubborn people! You have not given your hearts to God, nor will you listen to him! You are always against what the Holy Spirit is trying to tell you, just as your ancestors were. [52]Your ancestors tried to hurt every prophet who ever lived. Those prophets said long ago that the One who is good would come, but your ancestors killed them. And now you have turned against and killed the One who is good. [53]You received the law of Moses, which God gave you through his angels, but you haven't obeyed it."

STEPHEN IS KILLED

[54]When the leaders heard this, they became furious. They were so mad they were grinding their teeth at Stephen. [55]But Stephen was full of the Holy Spirit. He looked up to heaven and saw the glory of God and Jesus standing at God's right side. [56]He said, "Look! I see heaven open and the Son of Man standing at God's right side."

[57]Then they shouted loudly and covered their ears and all ran at Stephen. [58]They took him out of the city and began to throw stones at him to kill him. And those who told lies against Stephen left their coats with a young man named

7:46 Jacob Some Greek copies read "the house of Jacob." This means the people of Israel.

Saul. [59]While they were throwing stones, Stephen prayed, "Lord Jesus, receive my spirit." [60]He fell on his knees and cried in a loud voice, "Lord, do not hold this sin against them." After Stephen said this, he died.

8

Saul agreed that the killing of Stephen was good.

TROUBLES FOR THE BELIEVERS

On that day the church of Jerusalem began to be persecuted, and all the believers, except the apostles, were scattered throughout Judea and Samaria.

[2]And some religious people buried Stephen and cried loudly for him. [3]Saul was also trying to destroy the church, going from house to house, dragging out men and women and putting them in jail. [4]And wherever they were scattered, they told people the Good News.

PHILIP PREACHES IN SAMARIA

[5]Philip went to the city of Samaria and preached about the Christ. [6]When the people there heard Philip and saw the miracles he was doing, they all listened carefully to what he said. [7]Many of these people had evil spirits in them, but Philip made the evil spirits leave. The spirits made a loud noise when they came out. Philip also healed many weak and crippled people there. [8]So the people in that city were very happy.

[9]But there was a man named Simon in that city. Before Philip came there, Simon had practiced magic and amazed all the people of Samaria. He bragged and called himself a great man. [10]All the people—the least important and the most important—paid attention to Simon, saying, "This man has the power of God, called 'the Great Power'!" [11]Simon had amazed them with his magic so long that the people became his followers. [12]But when Philip told them the Good News about the kingdom of God and the power of Jesus Christ, men and women believed Philip and were baptized. [13]Simon him-self believed, and after he was baptized, he stayed very close to Philip. When he saw the miracles and the powerful things Philip did, Simon was amazed.

[14]When the apostles who were still in Jerusalem heard that the people of Samaria had accepted the word of God, they sent Peter and John to them. [15]When Peter and John arrived, they prayed that the Samaritan believers might receive the Holy Spirit. [16]These people had been baptized in the name of the Lord Jesus, but the Holy Spirit had not yet come upon any of them. [17]Then, when the two apostles began laying their hands on the people, they received the Holy Spirit.

[18]Simon saw that the Spirit was given to people when the apostles laid their hands on them. So he offered the apostles money, [19]saying, "Give me also this power so that anyone on whom I lay my hands will receive the Holy Spirit."

[20]Peter said to him, "You and your money should both be destroyed, because you thought you could buy God's gift with money. [21]You cannot share with us in this work since your heart is not right before God. [22]Change your heart! Turn away from this evil thing you have done, and pray to the Lord. Maybe he will forgive you for thinking this. [23]I see that you are full of bitter jealousy and ruled by sin."

[24]Simon answered, "Both of you pray for me to the Lord so the things you have said will not happen to me."

[25]After Peter and John told the people what they had seen Jesus do and after they had spoken the message of the Lord, they went back to Jerusalem. On the way, they went through many Samaritan towns and preached the Good News to the people.

PHILIP TEACHES AN ETHIOPIAN

[26]An angel of the Lord said to Philip, "Get ready and go south to the road that leads down to Gaza from Jerusalem—the desert road." [27]So Philip got ready and went. On the road he saw a man from Ethiopia, a eunuch. He was an important officer in the service of Candace, the queen of the Ethiopians; he was responsible for taking care of all her money. He had gone to Jerusalem to worship. [28]Now, as he was on his way home, he was sitting in his chariot reading from the Book of Isaiah, the prophet. [29]The Spirit said to Philip, "Go to that chariot and stay near it."

[30]So when Philip ran toward the chariot, he heard the man reading from Isaiah the prophet. Philip asked, "Do you understand what you are reading?"

[31]He answered, "How can I understand unless someone explains it to me?" Then he invited Philip to climb in and sit with him. [32]The portion of Scripture he was reading was this:

"He was like a sheep being led to be killed.
He was quiet, as a lamb is quiet while its wool is being cut;
he never opened his mouth.
[33] He was shamed and was treated unfairly.
He died without children to continue his family.
His life on earth has ended."

Isaiah 53:7-8

[34]The officer said to Philip, "Please tell me, who is the prophet talking about—himself or someone else?" [35]Philip began to speak, and starting with this same Scripture, he told the man the Good News about Jesus.

[36]While they were traveling down the road, they came to some water. The officer said, "Look, here is water. What is stopping me from being baptized?" [[37]Philip answered, "If you believe with all your heart, you can." The officer said, "I believe that Jesus Christ is the Son of God."][n] [38]Then the officer commanded the chariot to stop. Both Philip and the officer went down into the water, and Philip baptized him. [39]When they came up out of the water, the Spirit of the Lord took Philip away; the officer never saw him again. And the officer continued on his way home, full of joy. [40]But Philip

---

8:37 **Philip . . . God."** Some Greek copies do not contain the bracketed text.

appeared in a city called Azotus and preached the Good News in all the towns on the way from Azotus to Caesarea.

SAUL IS CONVERTED

9

In Jerusalem Saul was still threatening the followers of the Lord by saying he would kill them. So he went to the high priest [2]and asked him to write letters to the synagogues in the city of Damascus. Then if Saul found any followers of Christ's Way, men or women, he would arrest them and bring them back to Jerusalem.

[3]So Saul headed toward Damascus. As he came near the city, a bright light from heaven suddenly flashed around him. [4]Saul fell to the ground and heard a voice saying to him, "Saul, Saul! Why are you persecuting me?"

[5]Saul said, "Who are you, Lord?"

The voice answered, "I am Jesus, whom you are persecuting. [6]Get up now and go into the city. Someone there will tell you what you must do."

[7]The people traveling with Saul stood there but said nothing. They heard the voice, but they saw no one. [8]Saul got up from the ground and opened his eyes, but he could not see. So those with Saul took his hand and led him into Damascus. [9]For three days Saul could not see and did not eat or drink.

[10]There was a follower of Jesus in Damascus named Ananias. The Lord spoke to Ananias in a vision, "Ananias!"

Ananias answered, "Here I am, Lord."

[11]The Lord said to him, "Get up and go to Straight Street. Find the house of Judas,[n] and ask for a man named Saul from the city of Tarsus. He is there now,

9:11 Judas This is not either of the apostles named Judas.

THE SCRIPT

The Parable of the Mustard Seed
Matthew 13:31-32

Jesus dropped another parable 'bout the heavenly kingdom—
How it spreads through hearts and heads; he had them all clinging
   to his scenario.
He said, "How can I describe the heavenly realm of God's rule,
   what is comparable?
I got something here that comes near to the sum."
He reached down on the ground and picked up a little seed.
"It's like this mustard seed. In its infancy, it's just tiny,
Hardly seen, small as it can be, an oddity among trees. But here's
   the farmer's story:
He pairs the seed with some dirty earth. In time, this herb gives
   birth,
'Cause time brings growth as it feeds below the surface where
   nobody sees.
All the other trees never would've thought
   they'd get caught.
The growth process takes too long and they
   all got head starts.
But here's the cool part! Remember that little seed that was
   planted,
That insignificant, disenfranchised, and taken for granted?
Now the other trees are taking heed. 'Cause what was once a seed

Is now a twig and gaining speed! 'No need to
   panic,' the other trees scanted,
'We rule these botanics.'
But before they knew it, they looked up and lil'
   mustard was like gigantic!
It's just ill-matic! The way the story happens
   is romantic!
From seed, to twig, to tree, to the titanic
   of the forest!
Birds from all around hear about it
   and come to make their nest.
And once again, if you're
   feeling Me, you know what
   this means."
Picture this seed as the
   beginning of the kingdom
   Jesus brings.

Take this with you: Take time to slow down and pay attention to the small seeds of change that God has planted in your life. Stay with God and watch the invisible and remote possibilities grow into observable fact of God's presence in your life.

praying. [12]Saul has seen a vision in which a man named Ananias comes to him and lays his hands on him. Then he is able to see again."

[13]But Ananias answered, "Lord, many people have told me about this man and the terrible things he did to your holy people in Jerusalem. [14]Now he has come here to Damascus, and the leading priests have given him the power to arrest everyone who worships you."

[15]But the Lord said to Ananias, "Go! I have chosen Saul for an important work. He must tell about me to those who are not Jews, to kings, and to the people of Israel. [16]I will show him how much he must suffer for my name."

[17]So Ananias went to the house of Judas. He laid his hands on Saul and said, "Brother Saul, the Lord Jesus sent me. He is the one you saw on the road on your way here. He sent me so that you can see again and be filled with the Holy Spirit." [18]Immediately, something that looked like fish scales fell from Saul's eyes, and he was able to see again! Then Saul got up and was baptized. [19]After he ate some food, his strength returned.

SAUL PREACHES IN DAMASCUS

Saul stayed with the followers of Jesus in Damascus for a few days. [20]Soon he began to preach about Jesus in the synagogues, saying, "Jesus is the Son of God."

[21]All the people who heard him were amazed. They said, "This is the man who was in Jerusalem trying to destroy those who trust in this name! He came here to arrest the followers of Jesus and take them back to the leading priests."

[22]But Saul grew more powerful. His proofs that Jesus is the Christ were so strong that his own people in Damascus could not argue with him.

[23]After many days, they made plans to kill Saul. [24]They were watching the city gates day and night, but Saul learned about their plan. [25]One night some followers of Saul helped him leave the city by lowering him in a basket through an opening in the city wall.

SAUL PREACHES IN JERUSALEM

[26]When Saul went to Jerusalem, he tried to join the group of followers, but they were all afraid of him. They did not believe he was really a follower. [27]But Barnabas accepted Saul and took him to the apostles. Barnabas explained to them that Saul had seen the Lord on the road and the Lord had spoken to Saul. Then he told them how boldly Saul had preached in the name of Jesus in Damascus.

[28]And so Saul stayed with the followers, going everywhere in Jerusalem, preaching boldly in the name of the Lord. [29]He would often talk and argue with the Jewish people who spoke Greek, but they were trying to kill him. [30]When the followers learned about this,

IMPACT!

National Urban League

Founded in 1910, the National Urban League seeks to educate children, help adults attain self-sufficiency, and eradicate barriers that infringe on equal rights. The organization is devoted to many causes, including closing the homeownership gap, developing leadership skills in youth, and increasing computer access in the community. The National Urban League serves more than 2 million African-Americans and others in need. To find out how to be a volunteer, make a donation, or benefit from one of their many services, find a branch near you on their Web site, www.nul.org, or call 1-212-558-5300.

they took Saul to Caesarea and from there sent him to Tarsus.

³¹The church everywhere in Judea, Galilee, and Samaria had a time of peace and became stronger. Respecting the Lord by the way they lived, and being encouraged by the Holy Spirit, the group of believers continued to grow.

PETER HEALS AENEAS

³²As Peter was traveling through all the area, he visited God's people who lived in Lydda. ³³There he met a man named Aeneas, who was paralyzed and had not been able to leave his bed for the past eight years. ³⁴Peter said to him, "Aeneas, Jesus Christ heals you. Stand up and make your bed." Aeneas stood up immediately. ³⁵All the people living in Lydda and on the Plain of Sharon saw him and turned to the Lord.

PETER HEALS TABITHA

³⁶In the city of Joppa there was a follower named Tabitha (whose Greek name was Dorcas). She was always doing good deeds and kind acts. ³⁷While Peter was in Lydda, Tabitha became sick and died. Her body was washed and put in a room upstairs. ³⁸Since Lydda is near Joppa and the followers in Joppa heard that Peter was in Lydda, they sent two messengers to Peter. They begged him, "Hurry, please come to us!" ³⁹So Peter got ready and went with them. When he arrived, they took him to the upstairs room where all the widows stood around Peter, crying. They showed him the shirts and coats Tabitha had made when she was still alive. ⁴⁰Peter sent everyone out of the room and kneeled and prayed. Then he turned to the body and said, "Tabitha, stand up." She opened her eyes, and when she saw Peter, she sat up. ⁴¹He gave her his hand and helped her up. Then he called the saints and the widows into the room and showed them that Tabitha was alive. ⁴²People everywhere in Joppa learned about this, and many believed in the Lord. ⁴³Peter stayed in Joppa for many days with a man named Simon who was a tanner.

PETER TEACHES CORNELIUS

10 At Caesarea there was a man named Cornelius, an officer in the Italian group of the Roman army. ²Cornelius was a religious man. He and all the other people who lived in his house worshiped the true God. He gave much of his money to the poor and prayed to God often. ³One afternoon about three o'clock, Cornelius clearly saw a vision. An angel of God came to him and said, "Cornelius!"

⁴Cornelius stared at the angel. He became afraid and said, "What do you want, Lord?"

The angel said, "God has heard your prayers. He has seen that you give to the poor, and he remembers you. ⁵Send some men now to Joppa to bring back a man named Simon who is also called Peter. ⁶He is staying with a man, also named Simon, who is a tanner and has a house beside the sea." ⁷When the angel who spoke to Cornelius left, Cornelius called two of his servants and a soldier, a religious man who worked for him. ⁸Cornelius explained everything to them and sent them to Joppa.

⁹About noon the next day as they came near Joppa, Peter was going up to the roofⁿ to pray. ¹⁰He was hungry and wanted to eat, but while the food was being prepared, he had a vision. ¹¹He saw heaven opened and something coming down that looked like a big sheet being lowered to earth by its four corners. ¹²In it were all kinds of animals, reptiles, and birds. ¹³Then a voice said to Peter, "Get up, Peter; kill and eat."

¹⁴But Peter said, "No, Lord! I have never eaten food that is unholy or unclean."

¹⁵But the voice said to him again, "God has made these things clean, so don't call them unholy!" ¹⁶This happened three times, and at once the sheet was taken back to heaven.

¹⁷While Peter was wondering what this vision meant, the men Cornelius sent had found Simon's house and were standing at the gate. ¹⁸They asked, "Is Simon Peter staying here?"

¹⁹While Peter was still thinking about the vision, the Spirit said to him, "Listen, three men are looking for you. ²⁰Get up and go downstairs. Go with them without doubting, because I have sent them to you."

²¹So Peter went down to the men and said, "I am the one you are looking for. Why did you come here?"

²²They said, "A holy angel spoke to Cornelius, an army officer and a good man; he worships God. All the people respect him. The angel told Cornelius to ask you to come to his house so that he can hear what you have to say." ²³So Peter asked the men to come in and spend the night.

The next day Peter got ready and went with them, and some of the followers from Joppa joined him. ²⁴On the following day they came to Caesarea. Cornelius was waiting for them and had called together his relatives and close friends. ²⁵When Peter entered, Cornelius met him, fell at his feet, and worshiped him. ²⁶But Peter helped him up, saying, "Stand up. I too am only a human." ²⁷As he talked with Cornelius, Peter went inside where he saw many people gathered. ²⁸He said, "You people understand that it is against our law for Jewish people to associate with or visit anyone who is not Jewish. But God has shown me that I should not call any person 'unholy' or 'unclean.' ²⁹That is why I did not argue when I was asked to come here. Now, please tell me why you sent for me."

³⁰Cornelius said, "Four days ago, I was praying in my house at this same time—three o'clock in the afternoon. Suddenly, there was a man standing before me wearing shining clothes. ³¹He said, 'Cornelius, God has heard your prayer and has seen that you give to the poor and remembers you. ³²So send some men to Joppa and ask Simon Peter to come.

10:9 roof In Bible times houses were built with flat roofs. The roof was used for drying things such as flax and fruit. And it was used as an extra room, as a place for worship, and as a cool place to sleep in the summer.

GOD UNIT

LOSS OF A DREAM

I was finally starting in the NFL and was just plays away from a 1000-yard season. I was "the man" for the team. With five more games to go, my dream of signing a bigger contract was right around the corner. While traveling to an away game, the general manager of the team said he wanted to sit down with my agent and me to ink a big deal before the off-season hit. During the game, I was on a roll, but in the fourth quarter, I got seriously hurt. Suddenly, all my hopes and dreams for a fat contract and NFL security were gone.

I was angry at the world. I'd worked for years to get to where I was. God had been with me from the projects to the NFL, and now suddenly it seemed I was alone. Though my knee healed, the team had doubts that I could still run north and south like a Mack truck, so they didn't sign me at all. After all the touchdowns and one-yarders I'd made to keep drives going, I wasn't picked up by a team until well into the next season. With my peace gone, I knew I needed to get closer to the One who'd always been there for me.

In my darkest hour, I called on God and he showed me that he'd already given me the desire of my heart. My dream wasn't lost. I'd achieved it. As a poor high-school kid, I had walked to the gym everyday just hoping to be drafted one day by a pro team. The Lord had allowed me to achieve that goal. I decided to focus on his promises and see what God would do.

It's been a few years since my NFL days. I used to want millions so I'd never have to worry about being poor again. I never got that kind of money, but I got something greater. Through my pro playing days, I learned how to take Philippians 4:6-7 and apply it to my daily living. It was sometimes a struggle, but I learned that all I had to do was pray, be thankful, and trust in God to supply my needs. That was—and is—true peace. I'm signed on to the Lord's team. I've got the best deal possible.

Philippians 4:6-7—Do not worry about anything, but pray and ask God for everything you need, always giving thanks. And God's peace, which is so great we cannot understand it, will keep your hearts and minds in Christ Jesus.

Peter is staying in the house of a man, also named Simon, who is a tanner and has a house beside the sea.' [33] So I sent for you immediately, and it was very good of you to come. Now we are all here before God to hear everything the Lord has commanded you to tell us."

[34] Peter began to speak: "I really understand now that to God every person is the same. [35] In every country God accepts anyone who worships him and does what is right. [36] You know the message that God has sent to the people of Israel is the Good News that peace has come through Jesus Christ. Jesus is the Lord of all people! [37] You know what has happened all over Judea, beginning in Galilee after John[n] preached to the people about baptism. [38] You know about Jesus from Nazareth, that God gave him the Holy Spirit and power. You know how Jesus went everywhere doing good and healing those who were ruled by the devil, because God was with him. [39] We saw what Jesus did in Judea and in Jerusalem, but the Jews in Jerusalem killed him by hanging him on a cross. [40] Yet, on the third day, God raised Jesus to life and caused him to be seen, [41] not by all the people, but only by the witnesses God had already chosen. And we are those witnesses who ate and drank with him after he was raised from the dead. [42] He told us to preach to the people and to tell them that he is the one whom God chose to be the judge of the living and the dead. [43] All the prophets say it is true that all who believe in Jesus will be forgiven of their sins through Jesus' name."

[44] While Peter was still saying this, the Holy Spirit came down on all those who were listening. [45] The Jewish believers who came with Peter were amazed that the gift of the Holy Spirit had been

  10:37 John John the Baptist, who preached to people about Christ's coming (Luke 3).

given even to the nations. [46]These believers heard them speaking in different languages[n] and praising God. Then Peter said, [47]"Can anyone keep these people from being baptized with water? They have received the Holy Spirit just as we did!" [48]So Peter ordered that they be baptized in the name of Jesus Christ. Then they asked Peter to stay with them for a few days.

PETER RETURNS TO JERUSALEM

11 The apostles and the believers in Judea heard that some who were not Jewish had accepted God's teaching too. [2]But when Peter came to Jerusalem, some people argued with him. [3]They said, "You went into the homes of people who are not circumcised and ate with them!"

[4]So Peter explained the whole story to them. [5]He said, "I was in the city of Joppa, and while I was praying, I had a vision. I saw something that looked like a big sheet being lowered from heaven by its four corners. It came very close to me. [6]I looked inside it and saw animals, wild beasts, reptiles, and birds. [7]I heard a voice say to me, 'Get up, Peter. Kill and eat.' [8]But I said, 'No, Lord! I have never eaten anything that is unholy or unclean.' [9]But the voice from heaven spoke again, 'God has made these things clean, so don't call them unholy.' [10]This happened three times. Then the whole thing was taken back to heaven. [11]Right then three men who were sent to me from Caesarea came to the house where I was staying. [12]The Spirit told me to go with them without doubting. These six believers here also went with me, and we entered the house of Cornelius. [13]He told us about the angel he saw standing in his house. The angel said to him, 'Send some men to Joppa and invite Simon Peter to come. [14]By the words he will say to you, you and all your family will be saved.' [15]When I began my

speech, the Holy Spirit came on them just as he came on us at the beginning. [16]Then I remembered the words of the Lord. He said, 'John baptized with water, but you will be baptized with the Holy Spirit.' [17]Since God gave them the same gift he gave us who believed in the Lord Jesus Christ, how could I stop the work of God?"

[18]When the believers heard this, they stopped arguing. They praised God and said, "So God is allowing even other nations to turn to him and live."

THE GOOD NEWS COMES TO ANTIOCH

[19]Many of the believers were scattered when they were persecuted after Stephen was killed. Some of them went as far as Phoenicia, Cyprus, and Antioch telling the message to others, but only to Jews. [20]Some of these believers were people from Cyprus and Cyrene. When they came to Antioch, they spoke also to Greeks,[n] telling them the Good News about the Lord Jesus. [21]The Lord was helping the believers, and a large group of people believed and turned to the Lord.

[22]The church in Jerusalem heard about all of this, so they sent Barnabas to Antioch. [23-24]Barnabas was a good man, full of the Holy Spirit and full of faith. When he reached Antioch and saw how God had blessed the people, he was glad. He encouraged all the believers in Antioch always to obey the Lord with all their hearts, and many people became followers of the Lord.

[25]Then Barnabas went to the city of Tarsus to look for Saul, [26]and when he found Saul, he brought him to Antioch.

For a whole year Saul and Barnabas met with the church and taught many people there. In Antioch the followers were called Christians for the first time.

[27]About that time some prophets came from Jerusalem to Antioch. [28]One of them, named Agabus, stood up and spoke with the help of the Holy Spirit. He said, "A very hard time is coming to the whole world. There will be no food to eat." (This happened when Claudius ruled.) [29]The followers all decided to help the believers who lived in Judea, as much as each one could. [30]They gathered the money and gave it to Barnabas and Saul, who brought it to the elders in Judea.

HEROD AGRIPPA HURTS THE CHURCH

12 During that same time King Herod began to mistreat some who belonged to the church. [2]He ordered James, the brother of John, to be killed by the sword. [3]Herod saw that some of the people liked this, so he decided to arrest Peter, too. (This happened during the time of the Feast of Unleavened Bread.) [4]After Herod arrested Peter, he put him in jail and handed him over to be guarded by sixteen soldiers. Herod planned to bring Peter before the people for trial after the Passover Feast. [5]So Peter was kept in jail, but the church prayed earnestly to God for him.

PEEP THIS:

The first national rap hit was "Rapper's Delight" by the Sugar Hill Gang in 1979. The Association of Record Retailers named it single of the year.

PETER LEAVES THE JAIL

[6]The night before Herod was to bring him to trial, Peter was sleeping between two soldiers, bound with two chains.

 10:46 languages This can also be translated "tongues." **11:20 Greeks** Some Greek copies read "Hellenists," non-Greeks who spoke Greek.

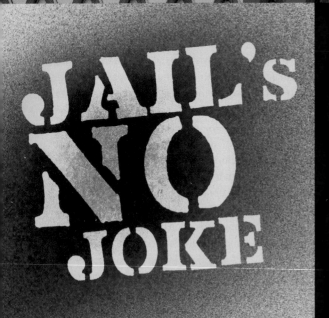

JAIL'S NO JOKE

How can a young person live a pure life? By obeying your word. With all my heart I try to obey you. Don't let me break your commands. Psalm 119:9-10

But the Spirit produces the fruit of love, joy, peace, patience, kindness, goodness, faithfulness, gentleness, self-control. There is no law that says these things are wrong. Galatians 5:22-23

Jail Makes You a Target

I got turned out in jail. I was a loner at first, staying away from all the chaos. Then one guy befriended me and we became boys. I had no idea that he wanted us to be an item. He was a regular cool cat, and we would just hang. Some guys tried to get at me when I was in the shower one day, and this dude fought them off. He asked me about being my cellmate. He said he had pull and that he could protect me. I was down with that. He was my only friend and I didn't know moving in together meant I owed him. One night when I was asleep, he forced himself on me. At first I fought him with everything I had, but it was no use. I'm ashamed now to say that even while my mind was resisting, my body was responding.

After he had me, our relationship became abusive. I was known as his wife. I knew it was wrong and I watched while my life spun even further out of control. The sorriest part was that I was a Christian. An imprisoned man having sex with other men, but on some level, still a Christian. Only six months before I had been a straight, God-fearing man. At first, I couldn't even pray. I was too low down for God to help. But finally, I hurt so bad that God was my only chance. It was weird, but as I prayed, it felt like

poison was coming out of me and I prayed for hours. Afterward, I got the courage to ask to be moved. But when my cellmate heard that I was trying to leave him, I got another beat down. This time, through the terror, I just kept praying. Eventually, the warden got wind of my situation. Thankfully, he got me moved to another wing with more security and I haven't seen my cellmate since. I began working for the warden, schooling new inmates on what to look out for inside. I teach them that even friendship behind bars comes with a price here.

God took my sin and is helping me help others. Every now and then, I battle with my flesh. In those tough times, I pray even harder, confessing to God that I can't do this without him. Amazingly, he leads me to an out every time. Sometimes, I am helped by remembering a scripture that settles my flesh. Sometimes, I sing a spiritual song that moves my mind into thinking about the Lord. Often, I read a letter from my girl and I write to her. I don't know if she'll be waiting when I get out in three years, but I now know I don't ever plan to have sex with any man again. In the book of Galatians, I read that one of the fruits of the Spirit is self-control. You really need it in here.

Other soldiers were guarding the door of the jail. [7]Suddenly, an angel of the Lord stood there, and a light shined in the cell. The angel struck Peter on the side and woke him up. "Hurry! Get up!" the angel said. And the chains fell off Peter's hands. [8]Then the angel told him, "Get dressed and put on your sandals." And Peter did. Then the angel said, "Put on your coat and follow me." [9]So Peter followed him out, but he did not know if what the angel was doing was real; he thought he might be seeing a vision. [10]They went past the first and second guards and came to the iron gate that separated them from the city. The gate opened by itself for them, and they went through it. When they had walked down one street, the angel suddenly left him.

[11]Then Peter realized what had happened. He thought, "Now I know that the Lord really sent his angel to me. He rescued me from Herod and from all the things the people thought would happen."

[12]When he considered this, he went to the home of Mary, the mother of John Mark. Many people were gathered there, praying. [13]Peter knocked on the outside door, and a servant girl named Rhoda came to answer it. [14]When she recognized Peter's voice, she was so happy she forgot to open the door. Instead, she ran inside and told the group, "Peter is at the door!"

[15]They said to her, "You are crazy!" But she kept on saying it was true, so they said, "It must be Peter's angel."

[16]Peter continued to knock, and when they opened the door, they saw him and were amazed. [17]Peter made a sign with his hand to tell them to be quiet. He explained how the Lord led him out of the jail, and he said, "Tell James and the other believers what happened." Then he left to go to another place.

[18]The next day the soldiers were very upset and wondered what had happened to Peter. [19]Herod looked everywhere for him but could not find him. So he questioned the guards and ordered that they be killed.

THE DEATH OF HEROD AGRIPPA

Later Herod moved from Judea and went to the city of Caesarea, where he stayed. [20]Herod was very angry with the people of Tyre and Sidon, but the people of those cities all came in a group to him. After convincing Blastus, the king's

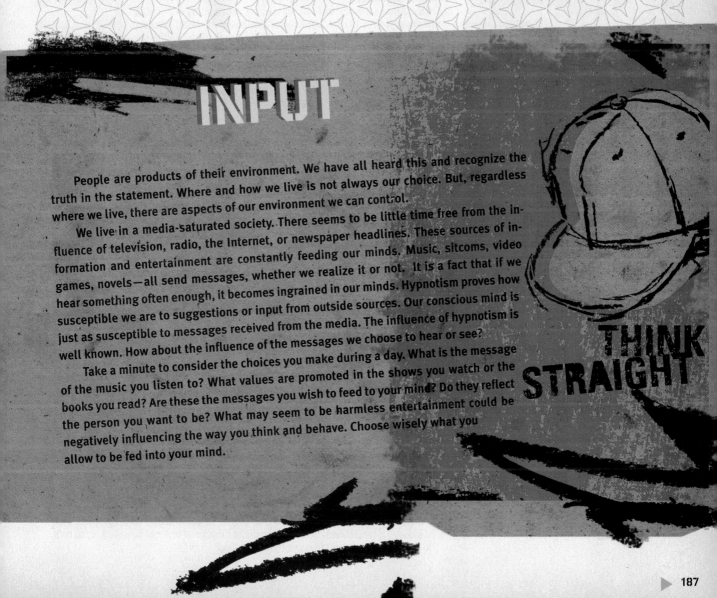

INPUT

People are products of their environment. We have all heard this and recognize the truth in the statement. Where and how we live is not always our choice. But, regardless where we live, there are aspects of our environment we can control.

We live in a media-saturated society. There seems to be little time free from the influence of television, radio, the Internet, or newspaper headlines. These sources of information and entertainment are constantly feeding our minds. Music, sitcoms, video games, novels—all send messages, whether we realize it or not. It is a fact that if we hear something often enough, it becomes ingrained in our minds. Hypnotism proves how susceptible we are to suggestions or input from outside sources. Our conscious mind is just as susceptible to messages received from the media. The influence of hypnotism is well known. How about the influence of the messages we choose to hear or see?

Take a minute to consider the choices you make during a day. What is the message of the music you listen to? What values are promoted in the shows you watch or the books you read? Are these the messages you wish to feed to your mind? Do they reflect the person you want to be? What may seem to be harmless entertainment could be negatively influencing the way you think and behave. Choose wisely what you allow to be fed into your mind.

THINK STRAIGHT

personal servant, to be on their side, they asked Herod for peace, because their country got its food from his country.

[21] On a chosen day Herod put on his royal robes, sat on his throne, and made a speech to the people. [22] They shouted, "This is the voice of a god, not a human!" [23] Because Herod did not give the glory to God, an angel of the Lord immediately caused him to become sick, and he was eaten by worms and died.

[24] God's message continued to spread and reach people.

[25] After Barnabas and Saul finished their task in Jerusalem, they returned to Antioch, taking John Mark with them.

BARNABAS AND SAUL ARE CHOSEN

13 In the church at Antioch there were these prophets and teachers: Barnabas, Simeon (also called Niger), Lucius (from the city of Cyrene), Manaen (who had grown up with Herod, the ruler), and Saul. [2] They were all worshiping the Lord and fasting[n] for a certain time. During this time the Holy Spirit said to them, "Set apart for me Barnabas and Saul to do a special work for which I have chosen them."

[3] So after they fasted and prayed, they laid their hands on[n] Barnabas and Saul and sent them out.

13:2 fasting The people would give up eating for a special time of prayer and worship to God. It was also done sometimes to show sadness and disappointment. **13:3 laid their hands on** The laying on of hands had many purposes, including the giving of a blessing, power, or authority.

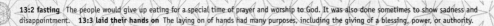

DEEP ISSUES

Homosexuality

"These times are pivotal/ The masses are captured by the digital/ The message is usually subliminal/ But never minimal/ The way they pimp the propaganda's criminal/ Push their views on the culture/ As they loungin' on the sofa/ The Sitcoms, The Music Channels, The News, got you thinkin' that you supposed to/ Just accept this as normal/ A few years back we would have never thought same sex marriage would be official and formal/ Well I'm not here to be cordial. . . ." (*"The Big Screen"—Urban D. Fla.vor Alliance Album.*).

Check out Romans 1:18-32. It's a tough message when it says homosexual acts are evidence of the rebellious state of humanity against God. So are acts of murder, jealousy, fighting, and lying. Before that the Old Testament spoke at Leviticus 18:22. But while nobody is saying murder and lying are OK, we have folks saying homosexual behavior is OK. It's debated in state legislatures in the form of same-sex marriages. It's the subject of constitutional discussions about defining marriage. Work place laws may see homosexuals become a legally protected group, confusing the line between civil rights and moral choices. "Coming out of the closet" is painted as a courageous act.

Two of the most profound statements on sexuality are Genesis 1:27-28 and Genesis 2:18-25. "So God created human beings in his image. . . . He created them male and female." "It is not good for the man to be alone. . . . So a man will leave his father and mother and be united with his wife, and the two will become one body." The face of male and female most perfectly reflects the character of God and the sexual union of a man and a woman in marriage is the ultimate form of companionship and mutual help.

If heterosexuality is the plan of God, then what to make of homosexuality? Let's be clear. Homosexuality as a condition is one thing; homosexual acts are something else. A person may have a sexual desire for and sexual responsiveness to persons of the same sex in the same way a person may have an inordinate desire for power or possessions. In either case, it's a matter of the inherent state of rebellion in all of us. Be it murder, lying, jealousy, fighting, homosexuality or disobedience, we each have our individual struggles with sin. We can follow the pull or urge of sin or we can fight against the urges which disrupt and destroy the original plan of God for the world. It is possible to live without acting on the sinful urges within us.

Do you know someone engaged in a homosexual lifestyle? Keep praying for them. And remember that none of is without some sin. You can treat someone with respect without having to agree with their life choices.

Is there hope for the person who struggles to overcome homosexual urges? Without doubt! Just as the one who struggles with anger or lust or resentment can find help in God to overcome powerful urges, so can the one who struggles with homosexual tendencies. God wants to restore the good order of his creation, so he'll do his part. It's our part to come to him for help.

BARNABAS AND SAUL IN CYPRUS

[4] Barnabas and Saul, sent out by the Holy Spirit, went to the city of Seleucia. From there they sailed to the island of Cyprus. [5] When they came to Salamis, they preached the Good News of God in the synagogues. John Mark was with them to help.

[6] They went across the whole island to Paphos where they met a magician named Bar-Jesus. He was a false prophet [7] who always stayed close to Sergius Paulus, the governor and a smart man. He asked Barnabas and Saul to come to him, because he wanted to hear the message of God. [8] But Elymas, the magician, was against them. (Elymas is the name for Bar-Jesus in the Greek language.) He tried to stop the governor from believing in Jesus. [9] But Saul, who was also called Paul, was filled with the Holy Spirit. He looked straight at Elymas [10] and said, "You son of the devil! You are an enemy of everything that is right! You are full of evil tricks and lies, always trying to change the Lord's truths into lies. [11] Now the Lord will touch you, and you will be blind. For a time you will not be able to see anything—not even the light from the sun."

Then everything became dark for Elymas, and he walked around, trying to find someone to lead him by the hand. [12] When the governor saw this, he believed because he was amazed at the teaching about the Lord.

PAUL AND BARNABAS LEAVE CYPRUS

[13] Paul and those with him sailed from Paphos and came to Perga, in Pamphylia. There John Mark left them to return to Jerusalem. [14] They continued their trip from Perga and went to Antioch, a city in Pisidia. On the Sabbath day they went into the synagogue and sat down. [15] After the law of Moses and the writings of the prophets were read, the leaders of the synagogue sent a message to Paul and Barnabas: "Brothers, if you have any message that will encourage the people, please speak."

[16] Paul stood up, raised his hand, and said, "You Israelites and you who worship God, please listen! [17] The God of the Israelites chose our ancestors. He made the people great during the time they lived in Egypt, and he brought them out of that country with great power. [18] And he was patient with them[n] for forty years in the desert. [19] God destroyed seven nations in the land of Canaan and gave the land to his people. [20] All this happened in about four hundred fifty years.

"After this, God gave them judges until the time of Samuel the prophet. [21] Then the people asked for a king, so God gave them Saul son of Kish. Saul was from the tribe of Benjamin and was king for forty years. [22] After God took him away, God made David their king. God said about him: 'I have found in David son of Jesse the kind of man I want. He will do all I want him to do.' [23] So God has brought Jesus, one of David's descendants, to Israel to be its Savior, as he promised. [24] Before Jesus came, John[n] preached to all the people of Israel about a baptism of changed hearts and lives. [25] When he was finishing his work, he said, 'Who do you think I am? I am not the Christ. He is coming later, and I am not worthy to untie his sandals.'

[26] "Brothers, sons of the family of Abraham, and others who worship God, listen! The news about this salvation has been sent to us. [27] Those who live in Jerusalem and their leaders did not realize that Jesus was the Savior. They did not understand the words that the prophets wrote, which are read every Sabbath day. But they made them come true when they said Jesus was guilty. [28] They could not find any real reason for Jesus to be put to death, but they asked Pilate to have him killed. [29] When they had done to him all that the Scriptures had said, they took him down from the cross and laid him in a tomb. [30] But God raised him up from the dead! [31] After this, for many days, those who had gone with Jesus from Galilee to Jerusalem saw him. They are now his witnesses to

the people. [32] We tell you the Good News about the promise God made to our ancestors. [33] God has made this promise come true for us, his children, by raising Jesus from the dead. We read about this also in Psalm 2:

'You are my Son.
Today I have become your
Father.'   Psalm 2:7

[34] God raised Jesus from the dead, and he will never go back to the grave and become dust. So God said:

'I will give you the holy and sure
blessings
that I promised to David.'
Isaiah 55:3

[35] But in another place God says:

'You will not let your Holy One
rot.'
Psalm 16:10

[36] David did God's will during his lifetime. Then he died and was buried beside his ancestors, and his body did rot in the grave. [37] But the One God raised from the dead did not rot in the grave. [38-39] Brothers, understand what we are telling you: You can have forgiveness of your sins through Jesus. The law of Moses could not free you from your sins. But through Jesus everyone who believes is free from all sins. [40] Be careful! Don't let what the prophets said happen to you:

[41] 'Listen, you people who doubt!
You can wonder, and then die.
I will do something in your lifetime
that you won't believe even when
you are told about it!' "
Habakkuk 1:5

[42] While Paul and Barnabas were leaving the synagogue, the people asked them to tell them more about these things on the next Sabbath. [43] When the meeting was over, many people with those who had changed to worship God followed Paul and Barnabas from that place. Paul and Barnabas were persuading them to continue trusting in God's grace.

[44] On the next Sabbath day, almost everyone in the city came to hear the

---

13:18 And . . . them Some Greek copies read "And he cared for them."   **13:24 John** John the Baptist, who preached to people about Christ's coming (Luke 3).

WANTING MORE

There's *gotta* be more to life than this. You can never be satisfied where you're at; you must have more. You must never stop until you've reached the top, and then you must climb higher. It's not enough to just have a roof over your head and food to eat. You must continue to move from job to job, place to place, or person to person.

"I have learned to be satisfied with the things I have and with everything that happens" (Philippians 4:11).

"Serving God does make us very rich, if we are satisfied with what we have. . . . If we have food and clothes, we will be satisfied with that" (1 Timothy 6:6, 8).

---

word of the Lord. [45]Seeing the crowd, the Jewish people became very jealous and said insulting things and argued against what Paul said. [46]But Paul and Barnabas spoke very boldly, saying, "We must speak the message of God to you first. But you refuse to listen. You are judging yourselves not worthy of having eternal life! So we will now go to the people of other nations. [47]This is what the Lord told us to do, saying:

'I have made you a light for the
        nations;
you will show people all over the
        world the way to be saved.' "

Isaiah 49:6

[48]When those who were not Jewish heard Paul say this, they were happy and gave honor to the message of the Lord. And the people who were chosen to have life forever believed the message.

[49]So the message of the Lord was spreading through the whole country. [50]But the Jewish people stirred up some of the important religious women and the leaders of the city. They started trouble against Paul and Barnabas and forced them out of their area. [51]So Paul and Barnabas shook the dust off their feet[n] and went to Iconium. [52]But the followers were filled with joy and the Holy Spirit.

PAUL AND BARNABAS IN ICONIUM

14 In Iconium, Paul and Barnabas went as usual to the synagogue. They spoke so well that a great many Jews and Greeks believed. [2]But some people who did not believe excited the others and turned them against the believers. [3]Paul and Barnabas stayed in Iconium a long time and spoke bravely for the Lord. He showed that their message about his grace was true by giving them the power to work miracles and signs. [4]But the city was divided. Some of the people agreed with the Jews, and others believed the apostles.

[5]Some who were not Jews, some Jews, and some of their rulers wanted to mistreat Paul and Barnabas and to stone them to death. [6]When Paul and Barnabas learned about this, they ran away to Lystra and Derbe, cities in Lycaonia, and to the areas around those cities. [7]They announced the Good News there, too.

PAUL IN LYSTRA AND DERBE

[8]In Lystra there sat a man who had been born crippled; he had never walked. [9]As this man was listening to Paul speak, Paul looked straight at him and saw that he believed God could heal him. [10]So he cried out, "Stand up on your feet!" The man jumped up and began walking around. [11]When the crowds saw what Paul did, they shouted in the Lycaonian language, "The gods have become like humans and have come down to us!" [12]Then the people began to call Barnabas "Zeus"[n] and Paul "Hermes,"[n] because he was the main speaker. [13]The priest in the temple of Zeus, which was near the city, brought some bulls and flowers to the city gates. He and the people wanted to offer a sacrifice to Paul and Barnabas. [14]But when the apostles, Barnabas and Paul, heard about it, they tore their clothes. They ran in among the people, shouting, [15]"Friends, why are you doing these things? We are only human beings like you. We are bringing you the Good News and are telling you to turn away from these worthless things and turn to the living God. He is the One who made the sky, the earth, the sea, and everything in them. [16]In the past, God let all the nations do what they wanted. [17]Yet he proved he is real by showing kindness, by giving you rain from heaven and crops at the right times, by giving you food and filling your hearts with joy." [18]Even with these words, they were barely able to keep the crowd from offering sacrifices to them.

13:51 shook . . . feet A warning. It showed that they had rejected these people.   **14:12 "Zeus"** The Greeks believed in many false gods, of whom Zeus was most important.   **14:12 "Hermes"** The Greeks believed he was a messenger for the other gods.

[19] Then some evil people came from Antioch and Iconium and persuaded the people to turn against Paul. So they threw stones at him and dragged him out of town, thinking they had killed him. [20] But the followers gathered around him, and he got up and went back into the town. The next day he and Barnabas left and went to the city of Derbe.

THE RETURN TO ANTIOCH IN SYRIA

[21] Paul and Barnabas told the Good News in Derbe, and many became followers. Paul and Barnabas returned to Lystra, Iconium, and Antioch, [22] making the followers of Jesus stronger and helping them stay in the faith. They said, "We must suffer many things to enter God's kingdom." [23] They chose elders for each church, by praying and fasting[n] for a certain time. These elders had trusted the Lord, so Paul and Barnabas put them in the Lord's care.

[24] Then they went through Pisidia and came to Pamphylia. [25] When they had preached the message in Perga, they went down to Attalia. [26] And from there they sailed away to Antioch where the believers had put them into God's care and had sent them out to do this work. Now they had finished.

[27] When they arrived in Antioch, Paul and Barnabas gathered the church together. They told the church all about what God had done with them and how God had made it possible for those who were not Jewish to believe. [28] And they stayed there a long time with the followers.

THE MEETING AT JERUSALEM

'15 Then some people came to Antioch from Judea and began teaching the non-Jewish believers: "You cannot be saved if you are not circumcised as Moses taught us." [2] Paul and Barnabas were against this teaching and argued with them about

it. So the church decided to send Paul, Barnabas, and some others to Jerusalem where they could talk more about this with the apostles and elders.

[3] The church helped them leave on the trip, and they went through the countries of Phoenicia and Samaria, telling all about how the other nations had turned to God. This made all the believers very happy. [4] When they arrived in Jerusalem, they were welcomed by the apostles, the elders, and the church. Paul, Barnabas, and the others told about everything God had done with them. [5] But some of the believers who belonged to the Pharisee group came forward and said, "The non-Jewish believers must be circumcised. They must be told to obey the law of Moses."

[6] The apostles and the elders gathered to consider this problem. [7] After a long debate, Peter stood up and said to them, "Brothers, you know that in the early days God chose me from among you to preach the Good News to the nations. They heard the Good News from me, and they believed. [8] God, who knows the thoughts of everyone, accepted them. He showed this to us by giving them the Holy Spirit, just as he did to us. [9] To God, those people are not different from us. When they believed, he made their hearts pure. [10] So now why are you testing God by putting a heavy load around the necks of the non-Jewish believers? It is a load that neither we nor our ancestors were able to carry. [11] But we believe that we and they too will be saved by the grace of the Lord Jesus."

[12] Then the whole group became quiet. They listened to Paul and Barnabas tell about all the miracles and signs that God did through them among the people. [13] After they finished speaking, James said, "Brothers, listen to me. [14] Simon has told us how God showed his love for those people. For the first time he is accepting from among them a people to be his own. [15] The words of the prophets agree with this too:

[16] 'After these things I will return.

The kingdom of David is like a fallen tent.
But I will rebuild its ruins,
and I will set it up.
[17] Then those people who are left alive
may ask the Lord for help,
and the other nations that belong to me,
says the Lord,
who will make it happen.
[18] And these things have been known for a long time.' *Amos 9:11-12*

[19] "So I think we should not bother the other people who are turning to God. [20] Instead, we should write a letter to them telling them these things: Stay away from food that has been offered to idols (which makes it unclean), any kind of sexual sin, eating animals that have been strangled, and blood. [21] They should do these things, because for a long time in every city the law of Moses has been taught. And it is still read in the synagogue every Sabbath day."

LETTER TO NON-JEWISH BELIEVERS

[22] The apostles, the elders, and the whole church decided to send some of their men with Paul and Barnabas to Antioch. They chose Judas Barsabbas and Silas, who were respected by the believers. [23] They sent the following letter with them:

From the apostles and elders, your brothers.
To all the non-Jewish believers in Antioch, Syria, and Cilicia:
Greetings!
[24] We have heard that some of our group have come to you and said things that trouble and upset you. But we did not tell them to do this. [25] We have all agreed to choose some messengers and send them to you with our dear friends Barnabas and Paul— [26] people who have given their lives to serve our Lord Jesus Christ. [27] So we are sending Judas and Silas, who will tell you the same things. [28] It has pleased the Holy Spirit that you should not have a heavy load to carry,

---

14:23 fasting The people would give up eating for a special time of prayer and worship to God. It was also done sometimes to show sadness and disappointment.

and we agree. You need to do only these things: [29]Stay away from any food that has been offered to idols, eating any animals that have been strangled, and blood, and any kind of sexual sin. If you stay away from these things, you will do well.

Good-bye.

[30]So they left Jerusalem and went to Antioch where they gathered the church and gave them the letter. [31]When they read it, they were very happy because of the encouraging message. [32]Judas and Silas, who were also prophets, said many things to encourage the believers and make them stronger. [33]After some time Judas and Silas were sent off in peace by the believers, and they went back to those who had sent them [, [34]but Silas decided to remain there].[n]

[35]But Paul and Barnabas stayed in Antioch and, along with many others, preached the Good News and taught the people the message of the Lord.

PAUL AND BARNABAS SEPARATE

[36]After some time, Paul said to Barnabas, "We should go back to all those towns where we preached the message of the Lord. Let's visit the believers and see how they are doing."

[37]Barnabas wanted to take John Mark with them, [38]but he had left them at Pamphylia; he did not continue with them in the work. So Paul did not think it was a good idea to take him. [39]Paul and

He's got answers

I am a pretty good person. Why do I need God?

What do you mean by pretty good? Do you mean that you don't steal or kill? That's pretty good. Do you mean that you don't cheat on your spouse or sell drugs? That's pretty good, too, at least by the world's standards.

There are many people in the Bible that lived good lives and were even praised by God for it. However, these people were not interested in just living a good life on this earth. They were determined to spend eternity with God, and, according to the Bible, being pretty good isn't enough in order to be with God forever.

Have you ever told a half-truth—a lie? Have you ever done something you regretted? Have you ever had to say, "I'm sorry . . . I just lost my temper." Have you ever been so mad at someone that you enjoyed the thought of beating them to a pulp? Those things—mild according to most people—keep you from being good enough in the eyes of God.

The Bible says that there is no one who is righteous. It says that everyone has committed a sin. It says that our sin—even a little one—is enough to condemn us to spend eternity away from God. Only spotless, sinless perfection can live in the presence of God. And only one person has ever lived that way: Jesus.

Think of it this way . . . if God's righteousness is one hundred percent and a mass murderer's is two percent, then where does your life fit in? Eighty percent? Jesus came to make up that difference.

Read on: John 3:16; Romans 3:10, 23; 6:23

PEEP THIS:

In England, East Indian youth blend Indian melodies and Hindi with English rap as a street form of protest.

TIMOTHY GOES WITH PAUL

Barnabas had such a serious argument about this that they separated and went different ways. Barnabas took Mark and sailed to Cyprus, [40]but Paul chose Silas and left. The believers in Antioch put Paul into the Lord's care, [41]and he went through Syria and Cilicia, giving strength to the churches.

16 Paul came to Derbe and Lystra, where a follower named Timothy lived. Timothy's mother was Jewish and a believer, but his father was a Greek.

[2]The believers in Lystra and Iconium respected Timothy and said good things about him. [3]Paul wanted Timothy to travel with him, but all the people living in that area knew that Timothy's father was Greek. So Paul circumcised Timothy to please his mother's people. [4]Paul and those with him traveled from town to town and gave the decisions made by the apostles and elders in Jerusalem

15:34 but . . . there Some Greek copies do not contain the bracketed text.

for the people to obey. ⁵So the churches became stronger in the faith and grew larger every day.

PAUL IS CALLED OUT OF ASIA

⁶Paul and those with him went through the areas of Phrygia and Galatia since the Holy Spirit did not let them preach the Good News in Asia. ⁷When they came near the country of Mysia, they tried to go into Bithynia, but the Spirit of Jesus did not let them. ⁸So they passed by Mysia and went to Troas. ⁹That night Paul saw in a vision a man from Macedonia. The man stood and begged, "Come over to Macedonia and help us." ¹⁰After Paul had seen the vision, we immediately prepared to leave for Macedonia, understanding that God had called us to tell the Good News to those people.

LYDIA BECOMES A CHRISTIAN

¹¹We left Troas and sailed straight to the island of Samothrace. The next day we sailed to Neapolis.ⁿ ¹²Then we went by land to Philippi, a Roman colonyⁿ and the leading city in that part of Macedonia. We stayed there for several days.

¹³On the Sabbath day we went outside the city gate to the river where we thought we would find a special place for prayer. Some women had gathered there, so we sat down and talked with them. ¹⁴One of the listeners was a woman named Lydia from the city of Thyatira whose job was selling purple cloth. She worshiped God, and he opened her mind to pay attention to what Paul was saying. ¹⁵She and all the people in her house were baptized. Then she invited us to her home, saying, "If you think I am truly a believer in the Lord, then come stay in my house." And she persuaded us to stay with her.

PAUL AND SILAS IN JAIL

¹⁶Once, while we were going to the place for prayer, a servant girl met us.

16:11 Neapolis City in Macedonia. It was the first city Paul visited on the continent of Europe. **16:12 Roman colony** A town begun by Romans with Roman laws, customs, and privileges.

HOW YA TRAVELIN'?

MENTORS

We are created for community, fashioned for fellowship, and formed for a family. None of us can fulfill God's purposes by ourselves. Isolation breeds deceitfulness because it's easy to fool ourselves into thinking we are wonderful if there is no one to challenge us. We get a real gauge on where we are when we are in relationships.

God uses his Word, people, and circumstances to mold you. Think about it: You can't practice being like Jesus without being in relationship with other people. The book of Proverbs has much to say about this: "If you have lots of good advice, you will win" (Proverbs 24:6). "Without leadership a nation falls, but lots of good advice will save it" (Proverbs 11:14). "Plans fail without good advice, but they succeed with the advice of many others" (Proverbs 15:22). You will grow faster and stronger by learning from and being accountable to others.

Finding God's will involves seeking advice. If you're wise, you will find advice that comes from those with experience. Seek mentors who have already traveled some of the roads you're traveling and who can help you navigate around the "potholes." Mentors can help you during times of decision and when you're facing life's problems. Mentors can help fortify your faith, help you find and refine your talents, and assist you as you begin fulfilling your mission on this earth. All of us are more consistent in our faith when others walk with us and encourage us. The Bible commands mutual accountability, mutual encouragement, mutual serving, and mutual honoring. God's Word tells us to love, serve, and help one another—to carry each other's burdens (Galatians 6:2). Seek out relationships with people who can offer you godly wisdom and advice. When you do this, you'll gain life-long relationships that can grow deeper in the Lord.

BE VERY HUMBLE WITH EACH OTHER – I PETER 5:5

VIEWPOINT

WHAT HAS BEEN THE GREATEST SOURCE OF PAIN IN YOUR LIFE AND HOW HAS IT HELPED YOU TO GROW?

I lost my brother. Losing him has been very painful for my family and me. But his memory and suffering his loss has inspired my future.

She had a special spirit" in her, and she earned a lot of money for her owners by telling fortunes. 17This girl followed Paul and us, shouting, "These men are servants of the Most High God. They are telling you how you can be saved."

18She kept this up for many days. This bothered Paul, so he turned and said to the spirit, "By the power of Jesus Christ, I command you to come out of her!" Immediately, the spirit came out.

19When the owners of the servant girl saw this, they knew that now they could not use her to make money. So they grabbed Paul and Silas and dragged them before the city rulers in the marketplace. 20They brought Paul and Silas to the Roman rulers and said, "These men are Jews and are making trouble in our city. 21They are teaching things that are not right for us as Romans to do."

22The crowd joined the attack against them. The Roman officers tore the clothes of Paul and Silas and had them beaten with rods. 23Then Paul and Silas were thrown into jail, and the jailer was ordered to guard them carefully. 24When he heard this order, he put them far inside the jail and pinned their feet down between large blocks of wood.

25About midnight Paul and Silas were praying and singing songs to God as the other prisoners listened. 26Suddenly, there was a strong earthquake that shook the foundation of the jail. Then all the doors of the jail broke open, and all the prisoners were freed from their chains. 27The jailer woke up and saw that the jail doors were open. Thinking that the prisoners had already escaped, he got his sword and was about to kill himself." 28But Paul shouted, "Don't hurt yourself! We are all here."

29The jailer told someone to bring a light. Then he ran inside and, shaking with fear, fell down before Paul and Silas. 30He brought them outside and said, "Men, what must I do to be saved?"

31They said to him, "Believe in the Lord Jesus and you will be saved—you and all the people in your house." 32So Paul and Silas told the message of the Lord to the jailer and all the people in his house. 33At that hour of the night the jailer took Paul and Silas and washed their wounds. Then he and all his people were baptized immediately. 34After this the jailer took Paul and Silas home and gave them food. He and his family were very happy because they now believed in God.

35The next morning, the Roman officers sent the police to tell the jailer, "Let these men go free."

36The jailer said to Paul, "The officers have sent an order to let you go free. You can leave now. Go in peace."

37But Paul said to the police, "They beat us in public without a trial, even though we are Roman citizens." And they threw us in jail. Now they want to make us go away quietly. No! Let them come themselves and bring us out."

38The police told the Roman officers what Paul said. When the officers heard that Paul and Silas were Roman citizens, they were afraid. 39So they came and told Paul and Silas they were sorry and took them out of jail and asked them to leave the city. 40So when they came out of the jail, they went to Lydia's house where they saw some of the believers and encouraged them. Then they left.

PAUL AND SILAS IN THESSALONICA

17 Paul and Silas traveled through Amphipolis and Apollonia and came to Thessalonica where there was a synagogue. 2Paul went into the synagogue as he always did, and on each Sabbath day for three weeks, he talked with his fellow Jews about the Scriptures. 3He explained and proved that the Christ must die and then rise from the dead. He said, "This Jesus I am telling you about is the Christ." 4Some of them were convinced and joined Paul and Silas, along with many of the Greeks who worshiped God and many of the important women.

5But some others became jealous. So they got some evil men from the marketplace, formed a mob, and started a riot. They ran to Jason's house, looking for Paul and Silas, wanting to bring them out to the people. 6But when they did not find them, they dragged Jason and some other believers to the leaders of the city. The people were yelling, "These people have made trouble everywhere in the world, and now they have come here too! 7Jason is keeping them in his house. All of them do things against the laws

---

 16:16 spirit This was a spirit from the devil, which caused her to say she had special knowledge.   **16:27 kill himself** He thought the leaders would kill him for letting the prisoners escape.   **16:37 Roman citizens** Roman law said that Roman citizens must not be beaten before they had a trial.

of Caesar, saying there is another king, called Jesus."

[8] When the people and the leaders of the city heard these things, they became very upset. [9] They made Jason and the others put up a sum of money. Then they let the believers go free.

PAUL AND SILAS GO TO BEREA

[10] That same night the believers sent Paul and Silas to Berea where they went to the synagogue. [11] These people were more willing to listen than the people in Thessalonica. The Bereans were eager to hear what Paul and Silas said and studied the Scriptures every day to find out if these things were true. [12] So, many of them believed, as well as many important Greek women and men. [13] But the people in Thessalonica learned that Paul was preaching the word of God in Berea, too. So they came there, upsetting the people and making trouble. [14] The believ-

ers quickly sent Paul away to the coast, but Silas and Timothy stayed in Berea. [15] The people leading Paul went with him to Athens. Then they carried a message from Paul back to Silas and Timothy for them to come to him as soon as they could.

PAUL PREACHES IN ATHENS

[16] While Paul was waiting for Silas and Timothy in Athens, he was troubled because he saw that the city was full of idols. [17] In the synagogue, he talked with the Jews and the Greeks who worshiped God. He also talked every day with people in the marketplace. [18] Some of the Epicurean and Stoic philosophers[n] argued with him, saying, "This man doesn't know what he is talking about. What is he trying to say?" Others said, "He seems to be telling us about some other gods," because Paul was telling them about Jesus and his ris-

ing from the dead. [19] They got Paul and took him to a meeting of the Areopagus,[n] where they said, "Please explain to us this new idea you have been teaching. [20] The things you are saying are new to us, and we want to know what this teaching means." [21] (All the people of Athens and those from other countries who lived there always used their time to talk about the newest ideas.)

[22] Then Paul stood before the meeting of the Areopagus and said, "People of Athens, I can see you are very religious in all things. [23] As I was going through your city, I saw the objects you worship. I found an altar that had these words written on it: TO A GOD WHO IS NOT KNOWN. You worship a god that you don't know, and this is the God I am telling you about! [24] The God who made the whole world and everything in it is the Lord of the land and the sky. He does not live in temples built by human hands. [25] This

IMPACT!

Urban Gospel Alliance

The Urban Gospel Alliance (UGA) unites urban gospel artists and provides them with the exposure they wouldn't get on a major record label or in mainstream music. Not just for musicians, UGA also supports the ministries of Christian spoken word artists and comedians. It doesn't matter whether you are an artist, manager, publicist, or label owner trying to find your niche in urban gospel, you have to hook up with the UGA. For membership information, check out their Web site at www.urbangospelal-liance.com.

 17:18 Epicurean and Stoic philosophers Philosophers were those who searched for truth. Epicureans believed that pleasure, especially pleasures of the mind, were the goal of life. Stoics believed that life should be without feelings of joy or grief.   **17:19 Areopagus** A council or group of important leaders in Athens. They were like judges.

God is the One who gives life, breath, and everything else to people. He does not need any help from them; he has everything he needs. [26]God began by making one person, and from him came all the different people who live everywhere in the world. God decided exactly when and where they must live. [27]God wanted them to look for him and perhaps search all around for him and find him, though he is not far from any of us: [28]'By his power we live and move and exist.' Some of your own poets have said: 'For we are his children.' [29]Since we are God's children, you must not think that God is like something that people imagine or make from gold, silver, or rock. [30]In the past, people did not understand God, and he ignored this. But now, God tells all people in the world to change their hearts and lives. [31]God has set a day that he will judge all the world with fairness, by the man he chose long ago. And God has proved this to everyone by raising that man from the dead!"

[32]When the people heard about Jesus being raised from the dead, some of them laughed. But others said, "We will hear more about this from you later." [33]So Paul went away from them. [34]But some of the people believed Paul and joined him. Among those who believed was Dionysius, a member of the Areopagus, a woman named Damaris, and some others.

PAUL IN CORINTH

18 Later Paul left Athens and went to Corinth. [2]Here he met a Jew named Aquila who had been born in the country of Pontus. But Aquila and his wife, Priscilla, had

THE SCRIPT

The Parable of the Treasure
Matthew 13:44-46

Jesus asked, "Can I explain heaven's domain?
It's like a treasure hidden in a field that's never been claimed.
One day a man was crossing terrain and felt kinda strange;
Optimistic like the vibe you get when things 'bout to change.
He thought he saw a gleam in his eye.
And, instead of passing by, kid decided to turn back and, "Oh my!"
On the double-take, that's when he saw this large crate full of stacked cake.
Son didn't wait! You know how we operate!
He hid the freight from others' eyes so nobody passing by would see it and confiscate.

Then he skated to the crib, tickled to the ribs,
Gathered all his chips, went and bought that field!
Oh, I got another ideal to spill.
You want to know what the kingdom is like? Well, let me reveal!
It's like a jeweler digging for the right find;
Looking for the perfect pearl, a one-of-a-kind.
Then he finds the baddest pearl, shining eloquently.
So he took all he owned and pawned it immediately.
Just enough to pay for that pearl and so he bought it!
Anybody caught it? See I'm talking 'bout selling out yo' heart, kid!
If you can't give it all, then you've already forfeit.

Take this with you: God's kingdom is here. Don't miss it because you don't take time to seek it. Only he has the treasure that's true.

recently moved to Corinth from Italy, because Claudius[n] commanded that all Jews must leave Rome. Paul went to visit Aquila and Priscilla. [3]Because they were tentmakers, just as he was, he stayed with them and worked with them. [4]Every Sabbath day he talked with the Jews and Greeks in the synagogue, trying to persuade them to believe in Jesus.

[5]Silas and Timothy came from Macedonia and joined Paul in Corinth. After this, Paul spent all his time telling people the Good News, showing them that Jesus is the Christ. [6]But they would not accept Paul's teaching and said some evil things. So he shook off the dust from his clothes[n] and said to them, "If you are not saved, it will be your own fault! I have done all I can do! After this, I will go to other nations." [7]Paul left the synagogue and moved into the home of Titius Justus, next to the synagogue. This man worshiped God. [8]Crispus was the leader of that synagogue, and he and all the people living in his house believed in the Lord. Many others in Corinth also listened to Paul and believed and were baptized.

[9]During the night, the Lord told Paul in a vision: "Don't be afraid. Continue talking to people and don't be quiet. [10]I am with you, and no one will hurt you because many of my people are in this city." [11]Paul stayed there for a year and a half, teaching God's word to the people.

PAUL IS BROUGHT BEFORE GALLIO

[12]When Gallio was the governor of the country of Southern Greece, some people came together against Paul and took him to the court. [13]They said, "This man is teaching people to worship God in a way that is against our law."

[14]Paul was about to say something, but Gallio spoke, saying, "I would listen to you if you were complaining about a crime or some wrong. [15]But the things you are saying are only questions about words and names—arguments about

hot10

Ways to Know If a Man Is into You

10. Takes care of you when you're sick

9. Listens to you

8. Washes your car

7. Surprises you with gifts

6. Brings you around his boys

5. Cooks for you

4. Remembers significant dates

3. Takes you out more than twice

2. Calls all the time

1. Introduces you to his mother

your own law. So you must solve this problem yourselves. I don't want to be a judge of these things." [16]And Gallio made them leave the court.

[17]Then they all grabbed Sosthenes, the leader of the synagogue, and beat him there before the court. But this did not bother Gallio.

PAUL RETURNS TO ANTIOCH

[18]Paul stayed with the believers for many more days. Then he left and sailed for Syria, with Priscilla and Aquila. At Cenchrea Paul cut off his hair,[n] because he had made a promise to God. [19]Then they went to Ephesus, where Paul left Priscilla and Aquila. While Paul was there, he went into the synagogue and talked with the people. [20]When they asked him to stay with them longer, he refused. [21]But as he left, he said, "I will come back to you again if God wants me to." And so he sailed away from Ephesus.

[22]When Paul landed at Caesarea, he went and gave greetings to the church in Jerusalem. After that, Paul went to Antioch. [23]He stayed there for a while and then left and went through the regions of Galatia and Phrygia. He traveled from town to town in these regions, giving strength to all the followers.

APOLLOS IN EPHESUS AND CORINTH

[24]A Jew named Apollos came to Ephesus. He was born in the city of Alexandria and was a good speaker who knew the Scriptures well. [25]He had been taught about the way of the Lord and was always very excited when he spoke and taught the truth about Jesus. But the only baptism Apollos knew about was the baptism that John[n] taught. [26]Apollos began to speak very boldly in the synagogue, and when Priscilla and Aquila heard him, they took him to their home and helped him better understand the way of God. [27]Now Apollos wanted to go to the country of Southern Greece. So the believers helped him and wrote a letter to the followers there, asking them

---

 18:2 Claudius The emperor (ruler) of Rome, A.D. 41-54.   **18:6 shook . . . clothes** This was a warning to show that Paul was finished talking to the people in that city.   **18:18 cut . . . hair** Jews did this to show that the time of a special promise to God was finished.   **18:25 John** John the Baptist, who preached to people about Christ's coming (Luke 3).

365

1   Try to reach out in friendship to at least two new people this month.

2

3

4   HOLIDAY—Independence Day

5

6

7

8   Attend your family reunion or a family reunion of a friend.

9

10

11

12   It's your birthday, Bill Cosby!

13   Create a family tree and share it with your family.

14

15

16

17

18

19

20   Happy Birthday Omar Epps!

21

22   On This Day In History 1814—Five Native American tribes make peace with the United States and declare war on Britain.

23   On This Day In History 1968—Fourteenth Amendment is ratified, making African-Americans citizens of the United States. **Marlon Wayans' birthday.**

24   Happy Birthday Jennifer Lopez!

25

26   On This Day In History 1847—Liberia becomes the first African colony to become an independent state.

27

28   Use creative thoughts wisely (start a journal, write some lyrics, etc.)

29

30   It's your birthday, Vivica Fox!

31

"I talked to Jesus the other day, and he said he's tired of you. There is a book out there called the Bible. It's got lessons in there on how to live. Ten Commandments. They make a lot of sense, but you've thrown all of it out."
—Bill Cosby

Think outside the box: "...I know what I am planning for you," says the Lord. I have good plans for you, not plans to hurt you. I will give you hope and a good future." (Jeremiah 29:11)

Head to the beach

MUSIC REVIEWS

ARTIST: GRITS   ALBUM: DICHOTOMY A

Laced with upbeat sounds, *Dichotomy A* is a groundbreaking album by the rap duo, GRITS. In my opinion, this CD is better than most secular rap albums. The vocals over top of the instrumentals evoke emotion based on the sound alone, and then the lyrics speak to your soul. The lyrics are tight and witty, not just a bunch of words that rhyme.

I have to say this is my favorite album by a Christian rap artist. This is a perfect album for the car. It is definitely one of those CDs that you can leave in your player and let it play through each track. My favorite track is "Shawty" featuring Lisa Kimmey of Out of Eden, a popular Christian R&B female group. GRITS goes on tour often, so don't miss them when they show up in your neighborhood.

"ACCEPTED"

---

to accept him. These followers had believed in Jesus because of God's grace, and when Apollos arrived, he helped them very much. [28]He argued very strongly with the Jews before all the people, clearly proving with the Scriptures that Jesus is the Christ.

PAUL IN EPHESUS

19 While Apollos was in Corinth, Paul was visiting some places on the way to Ephesus. There he found some followers [2]and asked them, "Did you receive the Holy Spirit when you believed?"

They said, "We have never even heard of a Holy Spirit."

[3]So he asked, "What kind of baptism did you have?"

They said, "It was the baptism that John taught."

[4]Paul said, "John's baptism was a baptism of changed hearts and lives. He told people to believe in the one who

would come after him, and that one is Jesus."

[5]When they heard this, they were baptized in the name of the Lord Jesus. [6]Then Paul laid his hands on them,[n] and the Holy Spirit came upon them. They began speaking different languages[n] and prophesying. [7]There were about twelve people in this group.

[8]Paul went into the synagogue and spoke out boldly for three months. He talked with the people and persuaded them to accept the things he said about the kingdom of God. [9]But some of them became stubborn. They refused to believe and said evil things about the Way of Jesus before all the people. So Paul left them, and taking the followers with him, he went to the school of a man named Tyrannus. There Paul talked with people every day [10]for two years. Because of his work, every Jew and Greek in Asia heard the word of the Lord.

THE SONS OF SCEVA

[11]God used Paul to do some very special miracles. [12]Some people took hand-

kerchiefs and clothes that Paul had used and put them on the sick. When they did this, the sick were healed and evil spirits left them.

[13]But some people also were traveling around and making evil spirits go out of people. They tried to use the name of the Lord Jesus to force the evil spirits out. They would say, "By the same Jesus that Paul talks about, I order you to come out!" [14]Seven sons of Sceva, a leading priest, were doing this.

[15]But one time an evil spirit said to them, "I know Jesus, and I know about Paul, but who are you?"

[16]Then the man who had the evil spirit jumped on them. Because he was so much stronger than all of them, they ran away from the house naked and hurt. [17]All the people in Ephesus—Jews and Greeks—learned about this and were filled with fear and gave great honor to the Lord Jesus. [18]Many of the believers began to confess openly and tell all the evil things they had done. [19]Some of them who had used magic brought their magic books and burned them before

---

19:6 laid his hands on them The laying on of hands had many purposes, including the giving of a blessing, power, or authority.   **19:6 languages** This can also be translated "tongues."

everyone. Those books were worth about fifty thousand silver coins.[n]

[20]So in a powerful way the word of the Lord kept spreading and growing.

[21]After these things, Paul decided to go to Jerusalem, planning to go through the countries of Macedonia and Southern Greece and then on to Jerusalem. He said, "After I have been to Jerusalem, I must also visit Rome." [22]Paul sent Timothy and Erastus, two of his helpers, ahead to Macedonia, but he himself stayed in Asia for a while.

TROUBLE IN EPHESUS

[23]And during that time, there was some serious trouble in Ephesus about the Way of Jesus. [24]A man named Demetrius, who worked with silver, made little silver models that looked like the temple of the goddess Artemis.[n] Those who did this work made much money. [25]Demetrius had a meeting with them and some others who did the same kind of work. He told them, "Men, you know that we make a lot of money from our business. [26]But look at what this man Paul is doing. He has convinced and turned away many people in Ephesus and in almost all of Asia! He says the gods made by human hands are not real. [27]There is a danger that our business will lose its good name, but there is also another danger: People will begin to think that the temple of the great goddess Artemis is not important. Her greatness will be destroyed, and Artemis is the goddess that everyone in Asia and the whole world worships."

[28]When the others heard this, they became very angry and shouted, "Artemis, the goddess of Ephesus, is great!" [29]The whole city became confused. The people grabbed Gaius and Aristarchus, who were from Macedonia and were traveling with Paul, and ran to the theater. [30]Paul wanted to go in and talk to the crowd, but the followers did not let him. [31]Also, some leaders of Asia who were friends of Paul sent him a message, begging him not to go into the theater. [32]Some peo-

ple were shouting one thing, and some were shouting another. The meeting was completely confused; most of them did not know why they had come together. [33]They put a man named Alexander in front of the people, and some of them told him what to do. Alexander waved his hand so he could explain things to the people. [34]But when they saw that Alexander was a Jew, they all shouted the same thing for two hours: "Great is Artemis of Ephesus!"

[35]Then the city clerk made the crowd be quiet. He said, "People of Ephesus, everyone knows that Ephesus is the city that keeps the temple of the great goddess Artemis and her holy stone[n] that fell from heaven. [36]Since no one can say this is not true, you should be quiet. Stop and think before you do anything. [37]You brought these men here, but they have not said anything evil against our goddess or stolen anything from her temple. [38]If Demetrius and those who work with him have a charge against anyone they should go to the courts and judges where they can argue with each other. [39]If there is something else you want to talk about, it can be decided at the regular town meeting of the people. [40]I say this because some people might see this trouble today and say that we are rioting. We could not explain this, because there is no real reason for this meeting." [41]After the city clerk said these things, he told the people to go home.

PAUL IN MACEDONIA AND GREECE

20 When the trouble stopped, Paul sent for the followers to come to him. After he encouraged them and then told them good-bye, he left and went to the country of Macedonia. [2]He said many things to strengthen the followers in the different places on his way through Macedonia. Then he went to Greece, [3]where he stayed for three months. He

was ready to sail for Syria, but some evil people were planning something against him. So Paul decided to go back through Macedonia to Syria. [4]The men who went with him were Sopater son of Pyrrhus, from the city of Berea; Aristarchus and Secundus, from the city of Thessalonica; Gaius, from Derbe; Timothy; and Tychicus and Trophimus, two men from Asia. [5]These men went on ahead and waited for us at Troas. [6]We sailed from Philippi after the Feast of Unleavened Bread. Five days later we met them in Troas, where we stayed for seven days.

PAUL'S LAST VISIT TO TROAS

[7]On the first day of the week,[n] we all met together to break bread,[n] and Paul spoke to the group. Because he was planning to leave the next day, he kept on talking until midnight. [8]We were all together in a room upstairs, and there were many lamps in the room. [9]A young man named Eutychus was sitting in the window. As Paul continued talking, Eutychus was falling into a deep sleep. Finally, he went sound asleep and fell to the ground from the third floor. When they picked him up, he was dead. [10]Paul went down to Eutychus, knelt down, and put his arms around him. He said, "Don't worry. He is alive now." [11]Then Paul went upstairs again, broke bread, and ate. He spoke to them a long time, until it was early morning, and then he left. [12]They took the young man home alive and were greatly comforted.

THE TRIP FROM TROAS TO MILETUS

[13]We went on ahead of Paul and sailed for the city of Assos, where he wanted to join us on the ship. Paul planned it this way because he wanted to go to Assos by land. [14]When he met us there, we took him aboard and went to Mitylene. [15]We sailed from Mitylene and the next day came to a place near Kios. The following day we sailed to Samos, and the next day we reached Miletus. [16]Paul had already decided not to stop at Ephesus, because he did not want to stay too long

 19:19 fifty thousand silver coins Probably drachmas. One coin was enough to pay a worker for one day's labor. **19:24 Artemis** A Greek goddess that the people of Asia Minor worshiped. **19:35 holy stone** Probably a meteorite or stone that the people thought looked like Artemis. **20:7 first day of the week** Sunday, which for Jews began at sunset on our Saturday. But if in this part of Asia a different system of time was used, then the meeting was on our Sunday night. **20:7 break bread** Probably the Lord's Supper, the special meal that Jesus told his followers to eat to remember him (Luke 22:14-20).

GOD UNIT

OVERCOMING PRIDE

I've learned a lot since my snot-nosed teen years. As I entered into adulthood, I really began to smell myself, ya know? Couldn't nobody tell me nothing, man! So as a result, I bumped my big head several times too many. When you're twenty, you really think you know something. But as time rolls on, you find out you don't know nearly as much as you thought. Find yourself faced with losing a job, your reputation, or your health—all from bad decisions—and you'll be willing to take some advice!

I almost screwed up my life. An affair with a married woman, unprotected sex, and downright stupidity could have cost me everything. No one wants to admit it, but I will. I thought I was invincible! Even after I had quit using drugs and stopped drinking alcohol, I couldn't (actually a better word would be *wouldn't*) curb my own physical desires. My problem wasn't really lust; it was pride. In my book, I had subconsciously placed myself right up there with God. I knew what was right and wrong, but I just chose to do what I wanted. I could control everything in my world, and no one would get hurt. Well, sad to say, that's not true. A family was torn apart because of the affair and other issues, and everyone involved hit rock bottom in some way. I didn't want to go to work, church, or anywhere else and risk facing anyone who had heard about the incident. That's when I ran headlong into God.

I was isolated, by choice and by circumstance, and I just wanted the chance to start all over. I had no one to turn to except God. He allowed my situation to get so bad that there was nowhere to look but up—to him. In God I found more comfort than I'd known in all the years of playing dangerous games. I asked God to forgive me, and he did! But he also allowed me to go through my period of suffering. Friends stopped talking to me, and I was ashamed of myself. During that time, he taught me to forgive myself and respect others more. Now, I actually feel forgiven, and I'm even about to get married. God has the controls in my life. I learned that I'm not God, I just know him. As the Bible says, "If someone wants to brag, he should brag only about the Lord." Pride often precipitates a fall but God will pick us up. We only have to ask.

1 Corinthians 1:31—If someone wants to brag, he should brag only about the Lord.

---

in Asia. He was hurrying to be in Jerusalem on the day of Pentecost, if that were possible.

THE ELDERS FROM EPHESUS

[17]Now from Miletus Paul sent to Ephesus and called for the elders of the church. [18]When they came to him, he said, "You know about my life from the first day I came to Asia. You know the way I lived all the time I was with you. [19]The evil people made plans against me, which troubled me very much. But you know I always served the Lord unselfishly, and I often cried. [20]You know I preached to you and did not hold back anything that would help you. You know that I taught you in public and in your homes. [21]I warned both Jews and Greeks to change their lives and turn to God and believe in our Lord Jesus. [22]But now I must obey the Holy Spirit and go to Jerusalem. I don't know what will happen to me there. [23]I know only that in every city the Holy Spirit tells me that troubles and even jail wait for me. [24]I don't care about my own life. The most important thing is that I complete my mission, the work that the Lord Jesus gave me—to tell people the Good News about God's grace.

[25]"And now, I know that none of you among whom I was preaching the kingdom of God will ever see me again. [26]So today I tell you that if any of you should be lost, I am not responsible, [27]because I have told you everything God wants you to know. [28]Be careful for yourselves and for all the people the Holy Spirit has given to you to oversee. You must be like shepherds to the church of God,[n] which he bought with the death of his own son.

 20:28 of God Some Greek copies read "of the Lord."

[29]I know that after I leave, some people will come like wild wolves and try to destroy the flock. [30]Also, some from your own group will rise up and twist the truth and will lead away followers after them. [31]So be careful! Always remember that for three years, day and night, I never stopped warning each of you, and I often cried over you.

[32]"Now I am putting you in the care of God and the message about his grace. It is able to give you strength, and it will give you the blessings God has for all his holy people. [33]When I was with you, I never wanted anyone's money or fine clothes. [34]You know I always worked to take care of my own needs and the needs of those who were with me. [35]I showed you in all things that you should work as I did and help the weak. I taught you to remember the words Jesus said: 'It is more blessed to give than to receive.' "

[36]When Paul had said this, he knelt down with all of them and prayed. [37-38]And they all cried because Paul had said they would never see him again. They put their arms around him and kissed him. Then they went with him to the ship.

PAUL GOES TO JERUSALEM

21

After we all said good-bye to them, we sailed straight to the island of Cos. The next day we reached Rhodes, and from there we went to Patara. [2]There we found a ship going to Phoenicia, so we went aboard and sailed away. [3]We sailed near the island of Cyprus, seeing it to the north, but we sailed on to Syria. We stopped at Tyre because the ship needed to unload its cargo there. [4]We found some followers in Tyre and stayed with them for seven days. Through the Holy Spirit they warned Paul not to go to Jerusalem. [5]When we finished our visit, we left and continued our trip. All the followers, even the women and children,

came outside the city with us. After we all knelt on the beach and prayed, [6]we said good-bye and got on the ship, and the followers went back home.

[7]We continued our trip from Tyre and arrived at Ptolemais, where we greeted the believers and stayed with them for a day. [8]The next day we left Ptolemais

and went to the city of Caesarea. There we went into the home of Philip the preacher, one of the seven helpers,[n] and stayed with him. [9]He had four unmarried daughters who had the gift of prophesying. [10]After we had been there for some time, a prophet named Agabus arrived from Judea. [11]He came to us and borrowed Paul's belt and used it to tie his own hands and feet. He said, "The Holy Spirit says, 'This is how evil people in Jerusalem will tie up the man who wears this belt. Then they will give him to the older leaders.' "

[12]When we all heard this, we and the people there begged Paul not to go to Jerusalem. [13]But he said, "Why are you crying and making me so sad? I am not only ready to be tied up in Jerusalem, I am ready to die for the Lord Jesus!"

[14]We could not persuade him to stay away from Jerusalem. So we stopped begging him and said, "We pray that what the Lord wants will be done."

[15]After this, we got ready and started on our way to Jerusalem. [16]Some of the followers from Caesarea went with us and took us to the home of Mnason, where we would stay. He was from Cyprus and was one of the first followers.

PAUL VISITS JAMES

[17]In Jerusalem the believers were glad to see us. [18]The next day Paul went with us to visit James, and all the elders were there. [19]Paul greeted them and told them everything God had done among the other nations through him. [20]When they heard this, they praised God. Then they said to Paul, "Brother, you can see that many thousands of our people have become believers. And they think it is very important to obey the law of Moses. [21]They have heard about your teaching, that you tell our people who live among the nations to leave the law of Moses. They have heard that you tell them not to circumcise their children and not to obey customs. [22]What should we do? They will learn that you have come. [23]So we will tell you what to do:

hot 10

Best Cars

10. Rolls Royce Phantom

9. Escalade

8. Lexus

7. Jag

6. BMW

5. Benz

4. Lamborghini

3. Ferrari

2. Bentley

1. Maybach

21:8 helpers The seven men chosen for a special work described in Acts 6:1-6. Sometimes they are called "deacons."

Four of our men have made a promise to God. [24]Take these men with you and share in their cleansing ceremony.[n] Pay their expenses so they can shave their heads.[n] Then it will prove to everyone that what they have heard about you is not true and that you follow the law of Moses in your own life. [25]We have already sent a letter to the non-Jewish believers. The letter said: 'Do not eat food that has been offered to idols, or blood, or animals that have been strangled. Do not take part in sexual sin.' "

[26]The next day Paul took the four men and shared in the cleansing ceremony with them. Then he went to the Temple and announced the time when the days of the cleansing ceremony would be finished. On the last day an offering would be given for each of the men.

[27]When the seven days were almost over, some of his people from Asia saw Paul at the Temple. They caused all the people to be upset and grabbed Paul. [28]They shouted, "People of Israel, help us! This is the man who goes everywhere teaching against the law of Moses, against our people, and against this Temple. Now he has brought some Greeks into the Temple and has made this holy place unclean!" [29](They said this because they had seen Trophimus, a man from Ephesus, with Paul in Jerusalem. They thought that Paul had brought him into the Temple.)

[30]All the people in Jerusalem became upset. Together they ran, took Paul, and dragged him out of the Temple. The Temple doors were closed immediately. [31]While they were trying to kill Paul, the commander of the Roman army in Jerusalem learned that there was trouble in the whole city. [32]Immediately he took some officers and soldiers and ran to the place where the crowd was gathered. When the people saw them, they stopped beating Paul. [33]The commander went to Paul and arrested him. He told his soldiers to tie Paul with two chains. Then he asked who he was and what he had done wrong. [34]Some in the crowd were yelling one thing, and some were yelling another. Because of all this confusion and shouting, the commander could not learn what had happened. So he ordered the soldiers to take Paul to the army building. [35]When Paul came to the steps, the soldiers had to carry him because the people were ready to hurt him. [36]The whole mob was following them, shouting, "Kill him!"

[37]As the soldiers were about to take Paul into the army building, he spoke to the commander, "May I say something to you?"

The commander said, "Do you speak Greek? [38]I thought you were the Egyptian who started some trouble against the government not long ago and led

IMPACT!

PEACE CORPS

The Peace Corps is an organization where volunteers serve in 71 countries in Africa, Asia, the Caribbean, Central and South America, Europe, and the Middle East. Collaborating with local community members, volunteers work in areas like education, youth outreach and community development, the environment, and information technology. You could be teaching English to elementary school children in Zambia or launching a computer learning center in Moldova, promoting HIV/AIDS awareness in South Africa or working on soil conservation in Panama. Volunteers bring their skills and life experiences where they are needed most. As a member of the Peace Corps, you could truly make a different in this world. For more information, call 1-800-424-8580 or go to www.peacecorps.gov where you can apply online.

 21:24 cleansing ceremony The special things Jews did to end the Nazirite promise.   **21:24 shave their heads** Jews did this to show that their promise was finished.

four thousand killers out to the desert."

[39]Paul said, "No, I am a Jew from Tarsus in the country of Cilicia. I am a citizen of that important city. Please, let me speak to the people."

[40]The commander gave permission, so Paul stood on the steps and waved his hand to quiet the people. When there was silence, he spoke to them in the Hebrew language.

PAUL SPEAKS TO THE PEOPLE

22 Paul said, "Brothers and fathers, listen to my defense to you." [2]When they heard him speaking the Hebrew language,[n] they became very quiet. Paul said, [3]"I am a Jew, born in Tarsus in the country of Cilicia, but I grew up in this city. I was a student of Gamaliel,[n] who carefully taught me everything about the law of our ancestors. I was very serious about serving God, just as are all of you here today. [4]I persecuted the people who followed the Way of Jesus, and some of them were even killed. I arrested men and women and put them in jail. [5]The high priest and the whole council of elders can tell you this is true. They gave me letters to the brothers in Damascus. So I was going there to arrest these people and bring them back to Jerusalem to be punished.

[6]"About noon when I came near Damascus, a bright light from heaven suddenly flashed all around me. [7]I fell to the ground and heard a voice saying, 'Saul, Saul, why are you persecuting me?' [8]I asked, 'Who are you, Lord?' The voice said, 'I am Jesus from Nazareth whom you are persecuting.' [9]Those who were with me did not understand the voice, but they saw the light. [10]I said, 'What shall I do, Lord?' The Lord answered, 'Get up and go to Damascus. There you will be told about all the things I have planned for you to do.' [11]I could not see, because the bright light had made me blind. So my companions led me into Damascus.

[12]"There a man named Ananias came to me. He was a religious man; he obeyed

He's got answers

It makes me angry when people get up in my business. What's wrong with making people back up off me?

The Bible says it's okay to get angry, as long as that anger doesn't lead to sin. The problem with anger is that, many times, it leads to a loss of self-control, which leads to rage, hatred, insults, filthy language, and violence. Violence can lead to more violence, and then you have a fight on your hands.

Jesus said there is a better way to live. You've heard the Golden Rule: "Do unto others as you would have them do unto you." Many times a quiet answer has a stronger effect than a shouted one. There is nothing wrong with making people back off if they are intruding into areas of your life that are not their concern. If your boss criticizes how you handle your personal money that is none of his business. But if you get mad at him because he tells you that you're slacking off at work, then you're wrong. If you get furious when someone who loves you expresses concern, then you're wrong. If you get angry because you get a speeding ticket, then you're wrong.

The next time someone gets up in your business, try listening to what they are saying. If you react in anger, you'll gain nothing from what they've said. Maybe they're wrong and they need to back off. But then again, maybe they're right and you need to listen.

Read on: Proverbs 15:1-2; Ephesians 4:26; Ephesians 4:31; Colossians 3:8; James 1:20

PEEP THIS:

Theodore Livingston (or Grand Wizard Theodore) of the South Bronx became the first scratcher when he just happened to stop a record with his hand.

22:2 Hebrew language Or Aramaic, the languages of many people in this region in the first century. **22:3 Gamaliel** A very important teacher of the Pharisees, a Jewish religious group (Acts 5:34).

the law of Moses, and all the Jews who lived there respected him. [13]He stood by me and said, 'Brother Saul, see again!' Immediately I was able to see him. [14]He said, 'The God of our ancestors chose you long ago to know his plan, to see the Righteous One, and to hear words from him. [15]You will be his witness to all people, telling them about what you have seen and heard. [16]Now, why wait any longer? Get up, be baptized, and wash your sins away, trusting in him to save you.'

[17]"Later, when I returned to Jerusalem, I was praying in the Temple, and I saw a vision. [18]I saw the Lord saying to me, 'Hurry! Leave Jerusalem now! The people here will not accept the truth about me.' [19]But I said, 'Lord, they know that in every synagogue I put the believers in jail and beat them. [20]They also know I was there when Stephen, your witness, was killed. I stood there agreeing and holding the coats of those who were killing him!' [21]But the Lord said to me, 'Leave now. I will send you far away to the other nations.'"

[22]The crowd listened to Paul until he said this. Then they began shouting, "Get rid of him! He doesn't deserve to live!" [23]They shouted, threw off their coats,[n] and threw dust into the air.[n]

[24]Then the commander ordered the soldiers to take Paul into the army building and beat him. He wanted to make Paul tell why the people were shouting against him like this. [25]But as the soldiers were tying him up, preparing to beat him, Paul said to an officer nearby, "Do you have the right to beat a Roman citizen[n] who has not been proven guilty?"

[26]When the officer heard this, he went to the commander and reported it. The officer said, "Do you know what you are doing? This man is a Roman citizen."

[27]The commander came to Paul and said, "Tell me, are you really a Roman citizen?"

He answered, "Yes."

[28]The commander said, "I paid a lot of money to become a Roman citizen."

But Paul said, "I was born a citizen." [29]The men who were preparing to question Paul moved away from him immediately. The commander was frightened because he had already tied Paul, and Paul was a Roman citizen.

PAUL SPEAKS TO LEADERS

[30]The next day the commander decided to learn why the Jews were accusing Paul. So he ordered the leading priests and the council to meet. The commander took Paul's chains off. Then he brought Paul out and stood him before their meeting.

23 Paul looked at the council and said, "Brothers, I have lived my life without guilt feelings before God up to this day." [2]Ananias,[n] the high priest, heard this and told the men who were standing near Paul to hit him on the mouth. [3]Paul said to Ananias, "God will hit you, too! You are like a wall that has been painted white. You sit there and judge me, using the law of Moses, but you are telling them to hit me, and that is against the law."

[4]The men standing near Paul said to him, "You cannot insult God's high priest like that!"

[5]Paul said, "Brothers, I did not know this man was the high priest. It is written in the Scriptures, 'You must not curse a leader of your people.'"[n]

[6]Some of the men in the meeting were Sadducees, and others were Pharisees. Knowing this, Paul shouted to them, "My brothers, I am a Pharisee, and my father was a Pharisee. I am on trial here because I believe that people will rise from the dead."

[7]When Paul said this, there was an argument between the Pharisees and the Sadducees, and the group was divided. [8](The Sadducees do not believe in angels or spirits or that people will rise from the dead. But the Pharisees believe in them all.) [9]So there was a great uproar.

Some of the teachers of the law, who were Pharisees, stood up and argued, "We find nothing wrong with this man. Maybe an angel or a spirit did speak to him."

[10]The argument was beginning to turn into such a fight that the commander was afraid some evil people would tear Paul to pieces. So he told the soldiers to go down and take Paul away and put him in the army building.

[11]The next night the Lord came and stood by Paul. He said, "Be brave! You have told people in Jerusalem about me. You must do the same in Rome."

[12]In the morning some evil people made a plan to kill Paul, and they took an oath not to eat or drink anything until they had killed him. [13]There were more than forty men who made this plan. [14]They went to the leading priests and the elders and said, "We have taken an oath not to eat or drink until we have killed Paul. [15]So this is what we want you to do: Send a message to the commander to bring Paul out to you as though you want to ask him more questions. We will be waiting to kill him while he is on the way here."

[16]But Paul's nephew heard about this plan and went to the army building and told Paul. [17]Then Paul called one of the officers and said, "Take this young man to the commander. He has a message for him."

[18]So the officer brought Paul's nephew to the commander and said, "The prisoner, Paul, asked me to bring this young man to you. He wants to tell you something."

[19]The commander took the young man's hand and led him to a place where they could be alone. He asked, "What do you want to tell me?"

[20]The young man said, "The Jews have decided to ask you to bring Paul down to their council meeting tomorrow. They want you to think they are going to ask him more questions. [21]But don't believe them! More than forty men are hiding and waiting to kill Paul. They have all

22:23 threw off their coats This showed that the people were very angry with Paul. **22:23 threw dust into the air** This showed even greater anger. **22:25 Roman citizen** Roman law said that Roman citizens must not be beaten before they had a trial. **23:2 Ananias** This is not the same man named Ananias in Acts 22:12. **23:5 'You . . . people.'** Quotation from Exodus 22:28.

taken an oath not to eat or drink until they have killed him. Now they are waiting for you to agree."

[22] The commander sent the young man away, ordering him, "Don't tell anyone that you have told me about their plan."

PAUL IS SENT TO CAESAREA

[23] Then the commander called two officers and said, "I need some men to go to Caesarea. Get two hundred soldiers, seventy horsemen, and two hundred men with spears ready to leave at nine o'clock tonight. [24] Get some horses for Paul to ride so he can be taken to Governor Felix safely." [25] And he wrote a letter that said:

[26] From Claudius Lysias.
To the Most Excellent Governor Felix:
Greetings.
[27] Some of the Jews had taken this man and planned to kill him. But I learned that he is a Roman citizen, so I went with my soldiers and saved him. [28] I wanted to know why they were accusing him, so I brought him before their council meeting. [29] I learned that these people said Paul did some things that were wrong by their own laws, but no charge was worthy of jail or death. [30] When I was told that some of them were planning to kill Paul, I sent him to you at once. I also told them to tell you what they have against him.

[31] So the soldiers did what they were told and took Paul and brought him to the city of Antipatris that night. [32] The next day the horsemen went with Paul to Caesarea, but the other soldiers went back to the army building in Jerusalem.

THE SCRIPT

The Parable of the Farmer's Seeds
Matthew 12:1–13:23

One day Jesus had been eatin' with his disciples
Pharisees had been troublin', and and spittin' mess about the trifles.
Later, Jesus stepped out the house and sat by the sea
And many people followed Jesus to see what they could see.
The crowds gathered 'bout, people came from 'round the entire settlement,
Pressing Jesus towards the beach so that he had to jettison
To a vessel in the lake, a boat.
And as the crowds did congregate, Jesus would narrate anecdotes.
Like, "Once upon a time, not long ago,
In the country on a farm where people lived life slow,
A farmer went out and planted some grain.
Reaching in his bag, he pulled out seeds and started to slang.
Some seeds hit the road where birds ate 'em up.
And some fell onto the gravel with little luck.
Yea, of course they quickly sprouted, no doubt,
But with a weak root system, when the sun rose, them sprouts died out!
And some of them seeds fell into the weeds; and when they tried to feed,
The weeds sucked up what the seeds needed to breed!
But some seed succeeded, indeed, they fell on good ground,
Producing crops far beyond the farmer's dreams.
Now, if you feeling me, you know what I mean.
So his disciples asked him, "What's up with these stories and themes?"
Jesus said, "This knowledge 'bout the "rule of the king" is a heavenly thing,
Not something everyone's seen.
I'm being honest, it's just God's economics. 'Cause if you get it, you've got it, but if you miss it, you've lost it;
It won't even come back through logic. That's the reason I drop it in code.
It's to get their hearts in the right mode; have them searching for the next episode.
You know their hearts are cold:
Like the deaf, dumb, and blind; Isaiah wasn't lying,

When that prophet described em' right down to the line:
He said there'd come a time when people's ears and eyes
Would be open but still stymied; disconnected from their minds.
These people are just that kind: hard-headed and hard hearted;
Or else they'd listen to me and let true healing get started.
But look at you: you've got it. God's blessed your ears and your optics.
A lot of people would hop at the chance to witness these topics you're observing.
But I'm gone' still break it down for those stuck on the curb.
Jesus cleared his throat, looked up and said, "The farmer is planting God's Word:
Anybody that hears my message but can't receive it
Is like a street immediately getting sweeping but didn't need it.
It was the evil one that swept up what they should have kept up in their soul.
And the seed thrown in the gravel is the kid that gets on the quick roll.
They're with me for a short stroll till the word they're holding takes its toll . . .
And before you known it, they've taken my words and thrown it—just tossed it.
Now bout' the seeds and weeds, let's get on it.
If the seed are my words that are heard and observed,
The weeds are the people that never put me first. No wonder they thirst.
They got the whole thing in reverse.
They wanna let go and let God, but letting go is too odd,
So they hold on to this world forever chasing facades.
But now the good sod is the one who has heard the good news,
Takes it in till it fuses in his heart and produces bumper crops of souls:
Yielding a hundred, sixty, or thirty times in others who are told.

Take this with you: It's not enough to hear truth. You must absorb it, keep it, and be true to live it. Don't be distracted from what's real. Dedicate prime real estate in your heart for the words of God.

[33]When the horsemen came to Caesarea and gave the letter to the governor, they turned Paul over to him. [34]The governor read the letter and asked Paul, "What area are you from?" When he learned that Paul was from Cilicia, [35]he said, "I will hear your case when those who are against you come here, too." Then the governor gave orders for Paul to be kept under guard in Herod's palace.

PAUL IS ACCUSED

24 Five days later Ananias, the high priest, went to the city of Caesarea with some of the elders and a lawyer named Tertullus. They had come to make charges against Paul before the governor. [2]Paul was called into the meeting, and Tertullus began to accuse him, saying, "Most Excellent Felix! Our people enjoy much peace because of you, and many wrong things in our country are being made right through your wise help. [3]We accept these things always and in every place, and we are thankful for them. [4]But not wanting to take any more of your time, I beg you to be kind and listen to our few words. [5]We have found this man to be a troublemaker, stirring up his people everywhere in the world. He is a leader of the Nazarene group. [6]Also, he was trying to make the Temple unclean, but we stopped him. [And we wanted to judge him by our own law. [7]But the officer Lysias came and used much force to take him from us. [8]And Lysias commanded those who wanted to accuse Paul to come to you.][n] By asking him questions yourself, you can decide if all these things are true." [9]The others agreed and said that all of this was true.

[10]When the governor made a sign for Paul to speak, Paul said, "Governor Felix, I know you have been a judge over this nation for a long time. So I am happy to defend myself before you.

[11]You can learn for yourself that I went to worship in Jerusalem only twelve days ago. [12]Those who are accusing me did not find me arguing with anyone in the Temple or stirring up the people in the synagogues or in the city. [13]They cannot prove the things they are saying against me now. [14]But I will tell you this: I worship the God of our ancestors as a follower of the Way of Jesus. The others say that the Way of Jesus is not the right way. But I believe everything that is taught in the law of Moses and that is written in the books of the Prophets. [15]I have the same hope in God that they have—the hope that all people, good and bad, will surely be raised from the dead. [16]This is why I always try to do what I believe is right before God and people.

[17]"After being away from Jerusalem for several years, I went back to bring money to my people and to offer sacrifices. [18]I was doing this when they found me in the Temple. I had finished the cleansing ceremony and had not made any trouble; no people were gathering around me. [19]But there were some people from Asia who should be here, standing before you. If I have really done anything wrong, they are the ones who should accuse me. [20]Or ask these people here if they found any wrong in me when I stood before the council in Jerusalem. [21]But I did shout one thing when I stood before them: 'You are judging me today because I believe that people will rise from the dead!'"

[22]Felix already understood much about the Way of Jesus. He stopped the trial and said, "When commander Lysias comes here, I will decide your case." [23]Felix told the officer to keep Paul guarded but to give him some freedom and to let his friends bring what he needed.

PAUL SPEAKS TO FELIX AND HIS WIFE

[24]After some days Felix came with his wife, Drusilla, who was Jewish, and asked for Paul to be brought to him. He listened to Paul talk about believing in Christ Jesus. [25]But Felix became afraid when Paul spoke about living right, self-control, and the time when God will judge the world. He said, "Go away now. When I have more time, I will call for you." [26]At the same time Felix hoped that Paul would give him some money, so he often sent for Paul and talked with him.

[27]But after two years, Felix was

VIEWPOINT

WHAT HAS BEEN THE GREATEST SOURCE OF JOY IN YOUR LIFE?

I'm glad I'm still living. As a brother living in this world, I'm glad I haven't been shot and killed. I know some of my boys who got killed at 17 and 18. Now that I'm a little older, I can see that hanging out on the street wasn't the life I thought it was. But, I'm a young cat, so I still have time to catch my dreams. Each day I try to be joyful about that.

 24:6-8 And . . . you. Some Greek copies do not contain the bracketed text.

replaced by Porcius Festus as governor. But Felix had left Paul in prison to please the Jews.

PAUL ASKS TO SEE CAESAR

25 Three days after Festus became governor, he went from Caesarea to Jerusalem. ²There the leading priests and the important leaders made charges against Paul before Festus. ³They asked Festus to do them a favor. They wanted him to send Paul back to Jerusalem, because they had a plan to kill him on the way. ⁴But Festus answered that Paul would be kept in Caesarea and that he himself was returning there soon. ⁵He said, "Some of your leaders should go with me. They can accuse the man there in Caesarea, if he has really done something wrong."

⁶Festus stayed in Jerusalem another eight or ten days and then went back to Caesarea. The next day he told the soldiers to bring Paul before him. Festus was seated on the judge's seat ⁷when Paul came into the room. The people who had come from Jerusalem stood around him, making serious charges against him, which they could not prove. ⁸This is what Paul said to defend himself: "I have done nothing wrong against the law, against the Temple, or against Caesar."

⁹But Festus wanted to please the people. So he asked Paul, "Do you want to go to Jerusalem for me to judge you there on these charges?"

¹⁰Paul said, "I am standing at Caesar's judgment seat now, where I should be judged. I have done nothing wrong to them; you know this is true. ¹¹If I have done something wrong and the law says I must die, I do not ask to be saved from death. But if these charges are not true, then no one can give me to them. I want Caesar to hear my case!"

¹²Festus talked about this with his ad-visers. Then he said, "You have asked to see Caesar, so you will go to Caesar!"

PAUL BEFORE KING AGRIPPA

¹³A few days later King Agrippa and Bernice came to Caesarea to visit Festus. ¹⁴They stayed there for some time, and Festus told the king about Paul's case. Festus said, "There is a man that Felix left in prison. ¹⁵When I went to Jerusalem, the leading priests and the elders there made charges against him, asking me to sentence him to death. ¹⁶But I answered, 'When a man is accused of a crime, Romans do not hand him over until he has been allowed to face his accusers and defend himself against their charges.' ¹⁷So when these people came here to Caesarea for the trial, I did not waste time. The next day I sat on the judge's seat and commanded that the man be brought in. ¹⁸They stood up and accused him, but not of any serious crime as I thought they would. ¹⁹The things they said were about their own religion and about a man named Jesus who died. But Paul said that he is still alive. ²⁰Not knowing how to find out about these questions, I asked Paul, 'Do you want to go to Jerusalem and be judged there?' ²¹But he asked to be kept in Caesarea. He wants a decision from the emperor." So I ordered that he be held until I could send him to Caesar."

²²Agrippa said to Festus, "I would also like to hear this man myself."

Festus said, "Tomorrow you will hear him."

²³The next day Agrippa and Bernice appeared with great show, acting like very important people. They went into the judgment room with the army leaders and the important men of Caesarea. Then Festus ordered the soldiers to bring Paul in. ²⁴Festus said, "King Agrippa and all who are gathered here with us, you see this man. All the people, here and in Jerusalem, have complained to me about him, shouting that he should not live any longer. ²⁵When I judged him, I found no reason to order his death. But

since he asked to be judged by Caesar, I decided to send him. ²⁶But I have nothing definite to write the emperor about him. So I have brought him before all of you—especially you, King Agrippa. I hope you can question him and give me something to write. ²⁷I think it is foolish to send a prisoner to Caesar without telling what charges are against him."

PAUL DEFENDS HIMSELF

26 Agrippa said to Paul, "You may now speak to defend yourself."

Then Paul raised his hand and began to speak. ²He said, "King Agrippa, I am very blessed to stand before you and will answer all the charges the evil people make against me. ³You know so much about all the customs and the things they argue about, so please listen to me patiently.

⁴"All my people know about my whole life, how I lived from the beginning in my own country and later in Jerusalem. ⁵They have known me for a long time. If they want to, they can tell you that I was a good Pharisee. And the Pharisees obey the laws of my tradition more carefully than any other group. ⁶Now I am on trial because I hope for the promise that God made to our ancestors. ⁷This is the promise that the twelve tribes of our people hope to receive as they serve God day and night. My king, they have accused me because I hope for this same promise! ⁸Why do any of you people think it is impossible for God to raise people from the dead?

⁹"I, too, thought I ought to do many things against Jesus from Nazareth. ¹⁰And that is what I did in Jerusalem. The leading priests gave me the power to put many of God's people in jail, and when they were being killed, I agreed it was a good thing. ¹¹In every synagogue, I often punished them and tried to make them speak against Jesus. I was so an-

25:21 emperor The ruler of the Roman Empire, which was almost all the known world.

gry against them I even went to other cities to find them and punish them.

[12]"One time the leading priests gave me permission and the power to go to Damascus. [13]On the way there, at noon, I saw a light from heaven. It was brighter than the sun and flashed all around me and those who were traveling with me. [14]We all fell to the ground. Then I heard a voice speaking to me in the Hebrew language,[n] saying, 'Saul, Saul, why are you persecuting me? You are only hurting yourself by fighting me.' [15]I said, 'Who are you, Lord?' The Lord said, 'I am Jesus, the one you are persecuting. [16]Stand up! I have chosen you to be my servant and my witness—you will tell people the things that you have seen and the things that I will show you. This is why I have come to you today. [17]I will keep you safe from your own people and also from the others. I am sending you to them [18]to open their eyes so that they may turn away from darkness to the light, away from the power of Satan and to God. Then their sins can be forgiven, and they can have a place with those people who have been made holy by believing in me.'

[19]"King Agrippa, after I had this vision from heaven, I obeyed it. [20]I began telling people that they should change their hearts and lives and turn to God and do things to show they really had changed. I told this first to those in Damascus, then in Jerusalem, and in every part of Judea, and also to the other people. [21]This is why the Jews took me and were trying to kill me in the Temple. [22]But God has helped me, and so I stand here today, telling all people, small and great, what I have seen. But I am saying only what Moses and the prophets said would happen— [23]that the Christ would die, and as the first to rise from the dead, he would bring light to all people."

PAUL TRIES TO PERSUADE AGRIPPA

[24]While Paul was saying these things to defend himself, Festus said loudly, "Paul, you are out of your mind! Too much study has driven you crazy!"

[25]Paul said, "Most excellent Festus, I am not crazy. My words are true and sensible. [26]King Agrippa knows about these things, and I can speak freely to him. I know he has heard about all of these things, because they did not happen off in a corner. [27]King Agrippa, do you believe what the prophets wrote? I know you believe."

[28]King Agrippa said to Paul, "Do you think you can persuade me to become a Christian in such a short time?"

> I PRAY TO GOD THAT NOT ONLY YOU BUT EVERY PERSON LISTENING TO ME TODAY WOULD BE SAVED.

[29]Paul said, "Whether it is a short or a long time, I pray to God that not only you but every person listening to me today would be saved and be like me—except for these chains I have."

[30]Then King Agrippa, Governor Festus, Bernice, and all the people sitting with them stood up [31]and left the room. Talking to each other, they said, "There is no reason why this man should die or be put in jail." [32]And Agrippa said to Festus, "We could let this man go free, but he has asked Caesar to hear his case."

PAUL SAILS FOR ROME

27 It was decided that we would sail for Italy. An officer named Julius, who served in the emperor's[n] army, guarded Paul and some other prisoners. [2]We got on a ship that was from the city of Adramyttium and was about to sail to different ports in Asia. Aristarchus, a man from the city of Thessalonica in Macedonia, went with us. [3]The next day we came to Sidon. Julius was very good to Paul and gave him freedom to go visit his friends, who took care of his needs. [4]We left Sidon and sailed close to the island of Cyprus, because the wind was blowing against us. [5]We went across the sea by Cilicia and Pamphylia and landed at the city of Myra, in Lycia. [6]There the officer found a ship from Alexandria that was going to Italy, so he put us on it.

[7]We sailed slowly for many days. We had a hard time reaching Cnidus because the wind was blowing against us, and we could not go any farther. So we sailed by the south side of the island of Crete near Salmone. [8]Sailing past it was hard. Then we came to a place called Fair Havens, near the city of Lasea.

[9]We had lost much time, and it was now dangerous to sail, because it was already after the Day of Cleansing.[n] So Paul warned them, [10]"Men, I can see there will be a lot of trouble on this trip. The ship, the cargo, and even our lives may be lost." [11]But the captain and the owner of the ship did not agree with Paul, and the officer believed what the captain and owner of the ship said. [12]Since that harbor was not a good place for the ship to stay for the winter, most of the men decided that the ship should leave. They hoped we could go to Phoenix and stay there for the winter. Phoenix, a city on the island of Crete, had a harbor which faced southwest and northwest.

THE STORM

[13]When a good wind began to blow from the south, the men on the ship thought, "This is the wind we wanted, and now we have it." So they pulled up the anchor, and we sailed very close to the island of Crete. [14]But then a very strong wind named the "northeaster"

 26:14 Hebrew language Or Aramaic, the languages of many people in this region in the first century. **27:1 emperor** The ruler of the Roman Empire, which was almost all the known world. **27:9 Day of Cleansing** An important Jewish holy day in the fall of the year. This was the time of year that bad storms arose on the sea.

came from the island. [15]The ship was caught in it and could not sail against it. So we stopped trying and let the wind carry us. [16]When we went below a small island named Cauda, we were barely able to bring in the lifeboat. [17]After the men took the lifeboat in, they tied ropes around the ship to hold it together. The men were afraid that the ship would hit the sandbanks of Syrtis,[n] so they lowered the sail and let the wind carry the ship. [18]The next day the storm was blowing us so hard that the men threw out some of the cargo. [19]A day later with their own hands they threw out the ship's equipment. [20]When we could not see the sun or the stars for many days, and the storm was very bad, we lost all hope of being saved.

[21]After the men had gone without food for a long time, Paul stood up before them and said, "Men, you should have listened to me. You should not have sailed from Crete. Then you would not have all this trouble and loss. [22]But now I tell you to cheer up because none of you will die. Only the ship will be lost. [23]Last night an angel came to me from the God I belong to and worship. [24]The angel said, 'Paul, do not be afraid. You must stand before Caesar. And God has promised you that he will save the lives of everyone sailing with you.' [25]So men, have courage. I trust in God that everything will happen as his angel told me. [26]But we will crash on an island."

[27]On the fourteenth night we were still being carried around in the Adriatic Sea.[n] About midnight the sailors thought we were close to land, [28]so they lowered a rope with a weight on the end of it into the water. They found that the water was one hundred twenty feet deep. They went a little farther and lowered the rope again. It was ninety feet deep. [29]The sailors were afraid that we would hit the rocks, so they threw four anchors into the water and prayed for daylight to come. [30]Some of the sailors wanted to leave the ship, and they lowered the lifeboat, pretending they were throwing more anchors from the front of the ship. [31]But Paul told the officer and the other soldiers, "If these men do not stay in the ship, your lives cannot be saved." [32]So the soldiers cut the ropes and let the lifeboat fall into the water.

[33]Just before dawn Paul began persuading all the people to eat something. He said, "For the past fourteen days you have been waiting and watching and not eating. [34]Now I beg you to eat something. You need it to stay alive. None of you will lose even one hair off your heads." [35]After he said this, Paul took some bread and thanked God for it before all of them. He broke off a piece and began eating. [36]They all felt better and started eating, too. [37]There were two hundred seventy-six people on the ship. [38]When they had eaten all they wanted, they began making the ship lighter by throwing the grain into the sea.

THE SHIP IS DESTROYED

[39]When daylight came, the sailors saw land. They did not know what land it was, but they saw a bay with a beach and wanted to sail the ship to the beach if they could. [40]So they cut the ropes to the anchors and left the anchors in the sea. At the same time, they untied the ropes that were holding the rudders. Then they raised the front sail into the wind and sailed toward the beach. [41]But the ship hit a sandbank. The front of the ship stuck there and could not move, but the back of the ship began to break up from the big waves.

[42]The soldiers decided to kill the prisoners so none of them could swim away and escape. [43]But Julius, the officer, wanted to let Paul live and did not allow the soldiers to kill the prisoners. Instead he ordered everyone who could swim to jump into the water first and swim to land. [44]The rest were to follow using wooden boards or pieces of the ship. And this is how all the people made it safely to land.

PAUL ON THE ISLAND OF MALTA

28 When we were safe on land, we learned that the island was called Malta. [2]The people who lived there were very good to us. Because it was raining and very cold, they made a fire and welcomed all of us. [3]Paul gathered a pile of sticks and was putting them on the fire when a poisonous snake came out because of the heat and bit him on the hand. [4]The people living on the island saw the snake hanging from Paul's hand and said to each other, "This man must be a murderer! He did not die in the sea, but Justice[n] does not want him to live." [5]But Paul shook the snake off into the fire and was not hurt. [6]The people thought that Paul would swell up or fall down dead. They waited and watched him for a long time, but nothing bad happened to him. So they changed their minds and said, "He is a god!"

[7]There were some fields around there owned by Publius, an important man on the island. He welcomed us into his home and was very good to us for three days. [8]Publius' father was sick with a fever and dysentery.[n] Paul went to him, prayed, and put his hands on the man and healed him. [9]After this, all the other sick people on the island came to Paul, and he healed them, too. [10-11]The people on the island gave us many honors. When we were ready to leave, three months later, they gave us the things we needed.

PAUL GOES TO ROME

We got on a ship from Alexandria that had stayed on the island during the winter. On the front of the ship was the sign of the twin gods.[n] [12]We stopped at Syracuse for three days. [13]From there we sailed to Rhegium. The next day a wind began to blow from the south, and a day later we came to Puteoli. [14]We found some believers there who asked us to stay with them for a week. Finally, we came

---

27:17 Syrtis Shallow area in the sea near the Libyan coast.   **27:27 Adriatic Sea** The sea between Greece and Italy, including the central Mediterranean.   **28:4 Justice** The people thought there was a god named Justice who would punish bad people.   **28:8 dysentery** A sickness like diarrhea.   **28:10-11 twin gods** Statues of Castor and Pollux, gods in old Greek tales.

to Rome. [15]The believers in Rome heard that we were there and came out as far as the Market of Appius[n] and the Three Inns[n] to meet us. When Paul saw them, he was encouraged and thanked God.

PAUL IN ROME

[16]When we arrived at Rome, Paul was allowed to live alone, with the soldier who guarded him.

[17]Three days later Paul sent for the leaders there. When they came together, he said, "Brothers, I have done nothing against our people or the customs of our ancestors. But I was arrested in Jerusalem and given to the Romans. [18]After they asked me many questions, they could find no reason why I should be killed. They wanted to let me go free, [19]but the evil people there argued against that. So I had to ask to come to Rome to have my trial before Caesar. But I have no charge to bring against my own people. [20]That is why I wanted to see you and talk with you. I am bound with this chain because I believe in the hope of Israel."

[21]They answered Paul, "We have received no letters from Judea about you. None of our Jewish brothers who have come from there brought news or told us anything bad about you. [22]But we want to hear your ideas, because we know that people everywhere are speaking against this religious group."

[23]Paul and the people chose a day for a meeting and on that day many more of the Jews met with Paul at the place he was staying. He spoke to them all day long. Using the law of Moses and the prophets' writings, he explained the kingdom of God, and he tried to persuade them to believe these things about Jesus. [24]Some believed what Paul said, but others did not. [25]So they argued and began leaving after Paul said one more thing to them: "The Holy Spirit spoke the truth to your ancestors through Isaiah the prophet, saying,
[26]'Go to this people and say:
You will listen and listen, but you will not understand.

HeartCry

More **Are you never satisfied with your life? Is what you have never enough? Let your heart cry . . .**

What's up, God? I need to talk to you about my life. I'm never satisfied. I always want more. More money, status, things, and power. I want to conquer everything and be the big dawg. But no matter how much I get, it's never enough. I still feel so empty. All my stuff is just tomorrow's junkyard trash and I can lose everything in a heartbeat. Then what? It seems I'm trading my life for things that just don't really matter, things that just won't last. Help me find a better reason to live.

Things that do not last can never fill the emptiness in your heart. The emptiness you feel is the desire in your heart for meaning and purpose. You will find contentment when you allow me to fill the void in your life. I am the author of your life and I alone can satisfy your soul. John 10:7-10

You will look and look, but you will not learn,
[27]because these people have become stubborn.
They don't hear with their ears, and they have closed their eyes.
Otherwise, they might really understand
what they see with their eyes and hear with their ears.
They might really understand in their minds
and come back to me and be healed.' *Isaiah 6:9–10*

[28]"I want you to know that God has also sent his salvation to all nations, and they will listen!" [[29]After Paul said this, the Jews left. They were arguing very much with each other.][n]

[30]Paul stayed two full years in his own rented house and welcomed all people who came to visit him. [31]He boldly preached about the kingdom of God and taught about the Lord Jesus Christ, and no one stopped him.

28:15 Market of Appius A town about twenty-seven miles from Rome. **28:15 Three Inns** A town about thirty miles from Rome. **28:29 After . . . other.** Some Greek copies do not contain the bracketed text.

HIP HOP AND CHRISTIAN?

Rap music as an art form has been around for 50 years or more. Some say it actually stands for Rhyme and Poetry. In the mid-1970s a new genre of rap music called "emceeing" (rhyming to the beat of a bass line) appeared on the scene. It is the authentic voice of a disenfranchised segment of society; a group whose pursuit of the "American dream" was denied.

Emceeing is one of the original elements of the hip-hop culture along with breakdancing, graffiti, and deejaying. Through these forms of expression, the disenfranchised, urban, young adult gained a powerful presence that is still here 25 years later despite the opposition of mainstream America. The irony is that the hip-hop culture has now been incorporated into the very fabric of American life and is now the "pop culture" of this generation. Boasting sales of more than four billion dollars per year, yesterday's "step-child" of the music industry has gained wide-ranging acceptance. The design and marketing of big-ticket consumer items, from jewelry to luxury automobiles, are influenced by the hip-hop culture. Major fashion designers have incorporated the hip-hop look into their clothing lines. It appears as if the underdog has triumphed on the world scene. The disenfranchised have risen to the top. The message of rap music is quickly becoming the worldview of an entire generation. But can you be into the hip-hop culture and be a follower of Jesus Christ at the same time? To discover the answer, we must

first define the hip-hop culture. In "The Power of Rap" (www.Daveyd.com), Dave "Davey D" Cook says this about emceeing (still the cornerstone of the hip-hop culture): "Ideally a rap is a group of rhymes that are thrown together so everything has meaning. Nothing said is frivolous. It reflects the here and now and ideally the lifestyle of the one rapping. Raps ideally projected the emotions and feelings experienced by the rapper. Ultimately and historically, an artist rapped for no one but himself. His rap was a call for attention to himself. He was ideally saying, 'Hey look, here I am world. Somebody hear my song!'" This means that the message of hip hop is supposed to be real—not fantasy, not made up, not glamorized, but representative of the real life experienced by its originator.

Some of the original emcees had agendas beyond the sheer expression of their own experience. Afrika Bambaataa, credited by most historians with founding hip-hop music (along with Kool Herc and Grandmaster Flash), saw hip-hop music as a vehicle to disseminate the views of a belief system or religion called the "Universal Zulu Nation" (UZN). UZN is based upon the principles of the ancient Zulu empire, led by its chieftain, Shaka Zulu. UZN believes in a god, known by many names: Allah, Jehovah, Yahweh, God, etc. It teaches that "your mind is as powerful as God Himself in Knowledge, Wisdom, and Understanding." According to Bambaataa's website, it was his "idea to use music to spread the message of the UZN. He knew that music is universal and crosses all barriers. So with the birth of hip hop, Bambaataa and members of the Zulu Nation started to travel throughout the world to spread hip-hop culture and uplift communities everywhere." While it is true that the spread of the hip-hop culture helped stem the tide of gang violence by channeling frusrations and discontentment into creative areas, the belief system spread by Bambaataa and the UZN exalts man to the level of God. The overriding message in the present hip-hop culture is still the supremacy of self.

Music is a powerful tool and a perfect vehicle to carry a message to the masses. Music is one of the few things that we just can't block out. We may try to block out lyrics, but we cannot stop them from being recorded in our minds. Messages repeatedly fed into our minds become ingrained in our subconscious. One proof of this is the lingering affect of television commercial jingles. How many of them do you know by heart and how many of those did you set out to memorize? The same is true with hip-hop music. When we listen to any music over and over again our minds and spirits are affected. How many of us run around singing songs while ignoring the fact that the lyrics make a definite spiritual statement? How much of what we have heard has influenced us? How many women started listening to hip-hop music believing that they were b's and ho's? How many now not only regularly listen to those words, but even sing along with them? How many little children run around the house singing sexually explicit phrases because there is no filter on what they listen to on the radio? We've got pastors in the pulpit quoting songs like "ya'll gon' make me lose my mind, up in here, up in here" when the rest of the lyrics to that song by DMX are the most vile words you could hear. Clearly, not everyone who listens to, performs or writes hip-hop music plans to participate in a religious activity, but every person who participates in any culture is influenced by it's message.

The worldview and value system of hip hop has far-reaching influence. Baggy pants with boxers showing has become one of the looks of hip hop. That fashion came from prison wear. Prisoners cannot wear belts, so their pants ride low. So many Black and Hispanic men are in prison or have been in prison that it has become a familiar lifestyle. To this culture that rejects traditional society, a prison term is seen as a badge of honor. The look is indicative of a mindset that says, "There are no rules for me. I am my own god. My mind is "as powerful as God Himself in Knowledge, Wisdom, and Understanding." Straight out of UZN's teachings. It is a mindset that denies the supremacy of the one true God.

Let's take a look at the legacy the themes from hip-hop have left on a generation.

- Prison is a good place.
- Teen pregnancy is acceptable.
- Free sex with multiple partners is okay.
- Homosexuality and bi-sexuality are no big deal.
- Being a Christian does not mean you have to change your lifestyle.
- Foul language is just a way of expressing yourself.
- Abusive behavior is normal.
- Drugs and alcohol are an expected part of life.
- Murder is an option, if deserved.
- Jesus Christ is just one of many gods.
- Love is just a word.
- The white man is not fair and holds the black man down.
- You find our own path to god and don't need the Church or the Bible.
- Anything goes as long as you are feeling it.
- No accountability.
- No sense of responsibility.

When we are self (or flesh) focused, we cannot be God (or spirit) focused. "If they plant to satisfy their sinful selves, their sinful selves will bring them ruin. But if they plant to please the Spirit, they will receive eternal life from the Spirit" (Galatians 6:8).

Want to know if the music you're listening to lines up with Christian principles? Take a close look at the artist and messages they bring. If they use profanity, sex, drugs, violence, or any other sinful things to sell records then they cannot be working for Christ. Count the number of songs that glorify sin on their albums. Do any glorify God? If so, how can you reconcile the two messages? In Luke 16:13, Jesus tells us we cannot serve two masters; we cannot serve God and sin. How many lives are in confusion and turmoil because they have embraced the themes contained in music written and performed by those who do not serve God? They are making music and the world is buying it.

Nothing that demands a compromise of the teachings of Christ is of God. Being a Christian means you love Christ, try to do things that will please him, and strive to be more like him. In return, he promises to replace the chaos and conflicts of this world with his peace, his joy, his wisdom, and his understanding. Only in him can we find salvation and discover eternal life. Listen, none of us are sinless. But the difference is in whether you embrace sin as a lifestyle or repent of it and strive to be more like Christ. We don't dis people who are into hip-hop music, but neither do we embrace a message that is bringing so many to spiritual ruin. Pay attention to the lyrics you listen to. Don't allow a message of sin and death to take root in your mind. There are some very godly people whose ministries go out in the form of Christian rap music. The beat is the same as secular hip-hop, but this message brings life. "You must choose for yourselves today whom you will serve" *(Joshua 24:15).* ★

ROMANS

The book of Romans is a letter written by Paul to all the Christians in the city of Rome, the capital of the Roman Empire. The Roman Empire was running things and Rome was the hot spot of culture on the planet. It was the place to be for poetry, art, philosophy, and literature. When Paul's letter arrived hardly anyone heard about it . . . at first. There were so many other things popping off around the city: concerts, parties, intellectual gatherings, and art shows. Nobody had heard of this guy named Paul, and not many had yet heard about Jesus. But, even with no promotion or marketing dollars, Paul's letter soon became bigger than anything Rome had ever seen.

The few Romans who had heard about Christianity thought it was just a Jewish thing. Paul shared that both Jews and Gentiles have made real mistakes and are in need of a real relationship with a real Christ. The book of Romans breaks it down and explains how we've all messed up and sinned and no matter how we try, we can't make things right on our own. Only belief in Christ can provide forgiveness and a reconnection with our creator. Paul lyrically takes the stage in this letter, bringing up potential objections and questions and spitting back the answers. Check out this underground writer who breaks into the mainstream and takes over with his message of hope.

WE CAN'T MAKE THINGS RIGHT ON OUR OWN

1 From Paul, a servant of Christ Jesus. God called me to be an apostle and chose me to tell the Good News.

[2]God promised this Good News long ago through his prophets, as it is written in the Holy Scriptures. [3-4]The Good News is about God's Son, Jesus Christ our Lord. As a man, he was born from the family of David. But through the Spirit of holiness he was declared to be God's Son with great power by rising from the dead. [5]Through Christ, God gave me the special work of an apostle, which was to lead people of all nations to believe and obey. I do this work for him. [6]And you who are in Rome are also called to belong to Jesus Christ.

[7]To all of you in Rome whom God loves and has called to be his holy people:

Grace and peace to you from God our Father and the Lord Jesus Christ.

A PRAYER OF THANKS

[8]First I want to say that I thank my God through Jesus Christ for all of you, because people everywhere in the world are talking about your faith. [9]God, whom I serve with my whole heart by telling the Good News about his Son, knows that I always mention you [10]every time I pray. I pray that I will be allowed to

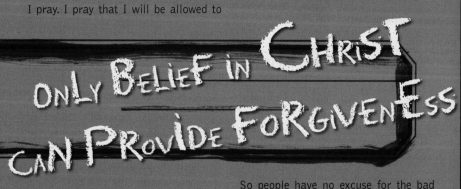

come to you, and this will happen if God wants it. [11]I want very much to see you, to give you some spiritual gift to make you strong. [12]I mean that I want us to help each other with the faith we have. Your faith will help me, and my faith will help you. [13]Brothers and sisters, I want you to know that I planned many times to come to you, but this has not

been possible. I wanted to come so that I could help you grow spiritually as I have helped the other non-Jewish people.

[14]I have a duty to all people—Greeks and those who are not Greeks, the wise and the foolish. [15]That is why I want so much to preach the Good News to you in Rome.

[16]I am not ashamed of the Good News, because it is the power God uses to save everyone who believes—to save the Jews first, and then to save non-Jews. [17]The Good News shows how God makes people right with himself—that it begins and ends with faith. As the Scripture says, "But those who are right with God will live by faith."[n]

ALL PEOPLE HAVE DONE WRONG

[18]God's anger is shown from heaven against all the evil and wrong things people do. By their own evil lives they hide the truth. [19]God shows his anger because some knowledge of him has been made clear to them. Yes, God has shown himself to them. [20]There are things about him that people cannot see—his eternal power and all the things that make him God. But since the beginning of the world those things have been easy to understand by what God has made.

So people have no excuse for the bad things they do. [21]They knew God, but they did not give glory to God or thank him. Their thinking became useless. Their foolish minds were filled with darkness. [22]They said they were wise, but they became fools. [23]They traded the glory of God who lives forever for the worship of idols made to look like earthly people, birds, animals, and snakes.

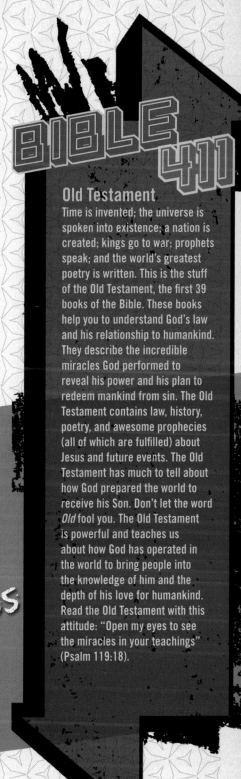

Old Testament

Time is invented; the universe is spoken into existence; a nation is created; kings go to war; prophets speak; and the world's greatest poetry is written. This is the stuff of the Old Testament, the first 39 books of the Bible. These books help you to understand God's law and his relationship to humankind. They describe the incredible miracles God performed to reveal his power and his plan to redeem mankind from sin. The Old Testament contains law, history, poetry, and awesome prophecies (all of which are fulfilled) about Jesus and future events. The Old Testament has much to tell about how God prepared the world to receive his Son. Don't let the word *Old* fool you. The Old Testament is powerful and teaches us about how God has operated in the world to bring people into the knowledge of him and the depth of his love for humankind. Read the Old Testament with this attitude: "Open my eyes to see the miracles in your teachings" (Psalm 119:18).

ONLY BELIEF IN CHRIST CAN PROVIDE FORGIVENESS

1:17 **"But those . . . faith."** Quotation from Habakkuk 2:4.

24Because they did these things, God left them and let them go their sinful way, wanting only to do evil. As a result, they became full of sexual sin, using their bodies wrongly with each other. 25They traded the truth of God for a lie. They worshiped and served what had been created instead of the God who created those things, who should be praised forever. Amen.

26Because people did those things, God left them and let them do the shameful things they wanted to do. Women stopped having natural sex and started having sex with other women. 27In the same way, men stopped having natural sex and began wanting each other. Men did shameful things with other men, and in their bodies they received the punishment for those wrongs.

28People did not think it was important to have a true knowledge of God. So God left them and allowed them to have their own worthless thinking and to do things they should not do. 29They are

He's got answers

What happens if you used to go to church, but now you don't live God's way?

That depends. Did you go to church because you thought you were supposed to? Or did you go to church because you love the Lord? It all boils down to the reason behind the action.

Simply going through religious steps has never pleased God. Jesus said the temple leaders' worship was worthless because they followed a bunch of rules for show only; their hearts were not in it.

However, if you love the Lord, but have allowed things to get between you and him, there is hope. The story of the prodigal son shows that God is always waiting for his children to return to him. Just take the first step and he'll welcome you with open arms.

Read on: Matthew 12:7, 23; Luke 15:4-6

PEEP THIS:

Hip-hop was founded by three Bronx DJ's: Cool Herk, Grandmaster Flash, and Africa Bambatta.

filled with every kind of sin, evil, selfishness, and hatred. They are full of jealousy, murder, fighting, lying, and thinking the worst about each other. They gossip 30and say evil things about each other. They hate God. They are rude and conceited and brag about themselves. They invent ways of doing evil. They do not obey their parents. 31They are foolish, they do not keep their promises, and they show no kindness or mercy to others. 32They know God's law says that those who live like this should die. But they themselves not only continue to do these evil things, they applaud others who do them.

YOU PEOPLE ALSO ARE SINFUL

2 If you think you can judge others, you are wrong. When you judge them, you are really judging yourself guilty, because you do the same things they do. 2God judges those who do wrong things, and we know that his judging is right. 3You judge those who do wrong, but you do wrong yourselves. Do you think you will be able to escape the judgment of God? 4He has been very kind and patient, waiting for you to change, but you think nothing of his kindness. Perhaps you do not understand that God is kind to you so you will

change your hearts and lives. 5But you are stubborn and refuse to change, so you are making your own punishment even greater on the day he shows his anger. On that day everyone will see God's right judgments. 6God will reward or punish every person for what that person has done. 7Some people, by always continuing to do good, live for God's glory, for honor, and for life that has no end. God will give them life forever. 8But other people are selfish. They refuse to follow truth and, instead, follow evil. God will give them his punishment and anger. 9He will give trouble and suffering to everyone who does evil—to the Jews first and also to those who are not Jews. 10But he will give glory, honor, and peace to everyone who does good—to the Jews first and also to those who are not Jews. ¹¹For God judges all people in the same way. ¹²People who do not have the law and who are sinners will be lost, although they do not have the law. And, in the same way, those who have the law and are sinners will be judged by the law. ¹³Hearing the law does not make people right with God. It is those who obey the law who will be right with him. ¹⁴(Those who are not Jews do not have the law, but when they freely do what the law commands, they are the law for themselves. This is true even though they do not have the law. ¹⁵They show that in their hearts they know what is right and wrong, just as the law commands. And they show this by their consciences. Sometimes their thoughts tell them they did wrong, and sometimes their thoughts tell them they did right.) ¹⁶All these things will happen on the day when God, through Christ Jesus, will judge people's secret thoughts. The Good News that I preach says this.

THE JEWS AND THE LAW

¹⁷What about you? You call yourself a Jew. You trust in the law of Moses and brag that you are close to God. ¹⁸You know what he wants you to do and what is important, because you have learned the law. ¹⁹You think you are a guide for the blind and a light for those who are in darkness. ²⁰You think you can show foolish people what is right and teach those who know nothing. You have the law; so you think you know everything and have all truth. ²¹You teach others, so why don't you teach yourself? You tell others not to steal, but you steal. ²²You say that others must not take part in adultery, but you are guilty of that sin. You hate idols, but you steal from temples. ²³You brag about having God's law, but you bring shame to God by breaking his law, ²⁴just as the Scriptures say: "Those who are not Jews speak against God's name because of you."

²⁵If you follow the law, your circumcision has meaning. But if you break the law, it is as if you were never circum-

cised. ²⁶People who are not Jews are not circumcised, but if they do what the law says, it is as if they were circumcised. ²⁷You Jews have the written law and circumcision, but you break the law. So those who are not circumcised in their bodies, but still obey the law, will show that you are guilty. ²⁸They can do this because a person is not a true Jew if he is only a Jew in his physical body; true circumcision is not only on the outside of the body. ²⁹A person is a Jew only if he is a Jew inside; true circumcision is done in the heart by the Spirit, not by the written law. Such a person gets praise from God rather than from people.

3 So, do Jews have anything that other people do not have? Is there anything special about being circumcised? ²Yes, of course, there is in every way. The most important thing is this: God trusted the Jews with his teachings. ³If some Jews were not faithful to him, will that stop God from doing what he promised? ⁴No! God will continue to be true even when every person is false. As the Scriptures say:

"So you will be shown to be right
      when you speak,
   and you will win your case."
                                    Psalm 51:4

⁵When we do wrong, that shows more clearly that God is right. So can we say that God is wrong to punish us? (I am talking as people might talk.) ⁶No! If God could not punish us, he could not judge the world.

⁷A person might say, "When I lie, it really gives him glory, because my lie shows God's truth. So why am I judged a sinner?" ⁸It would be the same to say, "We should do evil so that good will come." Some people find fault with us and say we teach this, but they are wrong and deserve the punishment they will receive.

ALL PEOPLE ARE GUILTY

⁹So are we Jews better than others? No! We have already said that Jews and

those who are not Jews are all guilty of sin. ¹⁰As the Scriptures say:

"There is no one who always does
      what is right,
   not even one.
¹¹There is no one who understands.
   There is no one who looks to God
      for help.
¹²All have turned away.
   Together, everyone has become
      useless.
   There is no one who does anything
      good;
   there is not even one."
                                    Psalm 14:1-3
¹³"Their throats are like open
      graves;
   they use their tongues for telling
      lies."   *Psalm 5:9*
"Their words are like snake
   poison."   *Psalm 140:3*
¹⁴ "Their mouths are full of cursing
   and hate."   *Psalm 10:7*
¹⁵"They are always ready to kill
   people.
¹⁶ Everywhere they go they cause
   ruin and misery.
¹⁷They don't know how to live in
   peace."   *Isaiah 59:7-8*
¹⁸ "They have no fear of God."
                                    Psalm 36:1

¹⁹We know that the law's commands are for those who have the law. This stops all excuses and brings the whole world under God's judgment, ²⁰because no one can be made right with God by following the law. The law only shows us our sin.

HOW GOD MAKES PEOPLE RIGHT

²¹But God has a way to make people right with him without the law, and he has now shown us that way which the law and the prophets told us about. ²²God makes people right with himself through their faith in Jesus Christ. This is true for all who believe in Christ, because all people are the same: ²³Everyone has sinned and fallen short of God's glorious standard, ²⁴and all need to be

---

 2:24 "Those . . . you." Quotation from Isaiah 52:5; Ezekiel 36:20.

made right with God by his grace, which is a free gift. They need to be made free from sin through Jesus Christ. [25]God sent him to die in our place to take away our sins. We receive forgiveness through faith in the blood of Jesus' death. This showed that God always does what is right and fair, as in the past when he was patient and did not punish people for their sins. [26]And God gave Jesus to show today that he does what is right. God did this so he could judge rightly and so he could make right any person who has faith in Jesus.

[27]So do we have a reason to brag about ourselves? No! And why not? It is the way of faith that stops all bragging, not the way of trying to obey the law. [28]A person is made right with God through faith, not through obeying the law. [29]Is God only the God of the Jews? Is he not also the God of those who are not Jews? [30]Of course he is, because there is only one God. He will make Jews right with him by their faith, and he will also make those who are not Jews right with him through their faith. [31]So do we destroy the law by following the way of faith? No! Faith causes us to be what the law truly wants.

THE EXAMPLE OF ABRAHAM

4 So what can we say that Abraham,[n] the father of our people, learned about faith? [2]If Abraham was made right by the things he did, he had a reason to brag. But this is not God's view, [3]because the Scripture says, "Abraham believed God, and God accepted Abraham's faith, and that faith made him right with God."[n]

[4]When people work, their pay is not given as a gift, but as something earned.

4:1 Abraham Most respected ancestor of the Jews. Every Jew hoped to see Abraham. **4:3 "Abraham . . . God."** Quotation from Genesis 15:6.

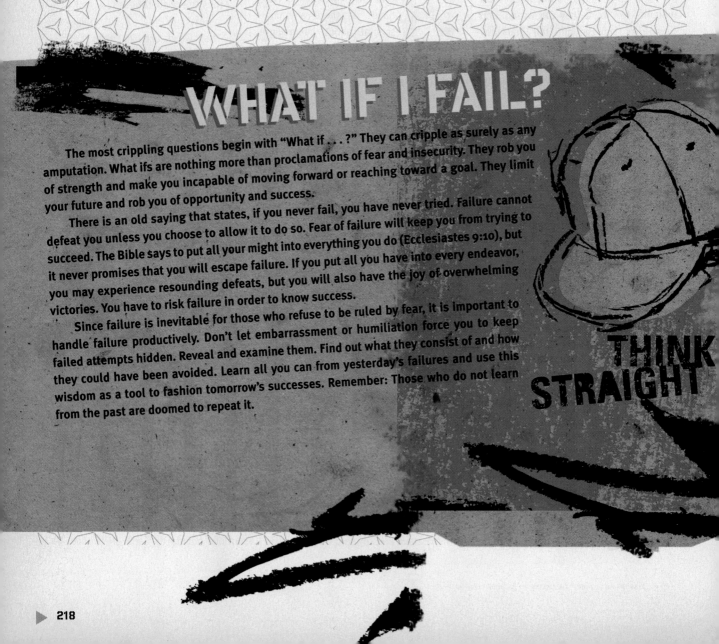

WHAT IF I FAIL?

The most crippling questions begin with "What if . . . ?" They can cripple as surely as any amputation. What ifs are nothing more than proclamations of fear and insecurity. They rob you of strength and make you incapable of moving forward or reaching toward a goal. They limit your future and rob you of opportunity and success.

There is an old saying that states, if you never fail, you have never tried. Failure cannot defeat you unless you choose to allow it to do so. Fear of failure will keep you from trying to succeed. The Bible says to put all your might into everything you do (Ecclesiastes 9:10), but it never promises that you will escape failure. If you put all you have into every endeavor, you may experience resounding defeats, but you will also have the joy of overwhelming victories. You have to risk failure in order to know success.

Since failure is inevitable for those who refuse to be ruled by fear, it is important to handle failure productively. Don't let embarrassment or humiliation force you to keep failed attempts hidden. Reveal and examine them. Find out what they consist of and how they could have been avoided. Learn all you can from yesterday's failures and use this wisdom as a tool to fashion tomorrow's successes. Remember: Those who do not learn from the past are doomed to repeat it.

THINK STRAIGHT

WORLD SAYS, WORD SAYS

WHAT TO WEAR

If it's short and tight, then it's got to be right. If it makes you look like the famous guy or girl on TV or in the music videos, then it must be the "in" thing to wear. Ladies, make sure that belly is showing and, no matter what size you are, wear that outfit so it fits—*really fits*. And fellas, you just got to have those pants hanging below the belt line. Forget that the history of sagging came from the jailhouse; "just do it" to look hip to the ladies, who will love you for it.

"Do not change yourselves to be like the people of this world, but be changed within by a new way of thinking. Then you will be able to decide what God wants for you; you will know what is good and pleasing to him and what is perfect" (Romans 12:2).

"A beautiful woman without good sense is like a gold ring in a pig's snout" (Proverbs 11:22).

---

[5]But people cannot do any work that will make them right with God. So they must trust in him, who makes even evil people right in his sight. Then God accepts their faith, and that makes them right with him. [6]David said the same thing. He said that people are truly blessed when God, without paying attention to their deeds, makes people right with himself.

[7]"Blessed are they
whose sins are forgiven,
whose wrongs are pardoned.
[8]Blessed is the person
whom the Lord does not consider
guilty." *Psalm 32:1-2*

[9]Is this blessing only for those who are circumcised or also for those who are not circumcised? We have already said that God accepted Abraham's faith and that faith made him right with God. [10]So how did this happen? Did God accept Abraham before or after he was circumcised? It was before his circumcision. [11]Abraham was circumcised to show that he was right with God through faith before he was circumcised. So Abraham is the father of all those who believe but are not circumcised; he is the father of all believers who are accepted as being right with God. [12]And Abraham is also the father of those who have been circumcised and who live following the faith that our father Abraham had before he was circumcised.

GOD KEEPS HIS PROMISE

[13]Abraham[n] and his descendants received the promise that they would get the whole world. He did not receive that promise through the law, but through being right with God by his faith. [14]If people could receive what God promised by following the law, then faith is worthless. And God's promise to Abraham is worthless, [15]because the law can only bring God's anger. But if there is no law, there is nothing to disobey.

[16]So people receive God's promise by having faith. This happens so the promise can be a free gift. Then all of Abraham's children can have that promise. It is not only for those who live under the law of Moses but for anyone who lives with faith like that of Abraham, who is the father of us all. [17]As it is written in the Scriptures: "I am making you a father of many nations."[n] This is true before God, the God Abraham believed, the God who gives life to the dead and who creates something out of nothing.

[18]There was no hope that Abraham would have children. But Abraham believed God and continued hoping, and so he became the father of many nations. As God told him, "Your descendants also will be too many to count."[n] [19]Abraham was almost a hundred years old, much past the age for having children, and Sarah could not have children. Abraham thought about all this, but his faith in God did not become weak. [20]He never doubted that God would keep his promise, and he never stopped believing. He grew stronger in his faith and gave praise to God. [21]Abraham felt sure that God was able to do what he had promised. [22]So, "God accepted Abraham's faith, and that faith made him right with God."[n] [23]Those words ("God accepted Abraham's faith") were written not only for Abraham [24]but also for us. God will accept us also because we believe in the One who raised Jesus our Lord from the dead. [25]Jesus was given to die for our sins, and he was raised from the dead to make us right with God.

RIGHT WITH GOD

5 Since we have been made right with God by our faith, we have[n] peace with God. This happened through our Lord Jesus Christ, [2]who through our faith[n] has brought us into

---

4:13 **Abraham** Most respected ancestor of the Jews. Every Jew hoped to see Abraham.   4:17 **"I . . . nations."** Quotation from Genesis 17:5.   4:18 **"Your . . . count."** Quotation from Genesis 15:5.   4:22 **"God . . . God."** Quotation from Genesis 15:6.   5:1 **we have** Some Greek copies read "let us have."   5:2 **through our faith** Some Greek copies do not have this phrase.

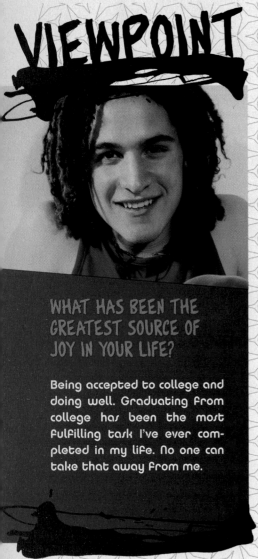

VIEWPOINT

WHAT HAS BEEN THE GREATEST SOURCE OF JOY IN YOUR LIFE?

Being accepted to college and doing well. Graduating from college has been the most fulfilling task I've ever completed in my life. No one can take that away from me.

that blessing of God's grace that we now enjoy. And we are happy because of the hope we have of sharing God's glory. [3]We also have joy with our troubles, because we know that these troubles produce patience. [4]And patience produces character, and character produces hope. [5]And this hope will never disappoint us, because God has poured out his love to fill our hearts. He gave us his love through the Holy Spirit, whom God has given to us.

[6]When we were unable to help ourselves, at the right time, Christ died for us, although we were living against God. [7]Very few people will die to save the life of someone else. Although perhaps for a good person someone might possibly die. [8]But God shows his great love for us in this way: Christ died for us while we were still sinners.

[9]So through Christ we will surely be saved from God's anger, because we have been made right with God by the blood of Christ's death. [10]While we were God's enemies, he made us his friends through the death of his Son. Surely, now that we are his friends, he will save us through his Son's life. [11]And not only that, but now we are also very happy in God through our Lord Jesus Christ. Through him we are now God's friends again.

ADAM AND CHRIST COMPARED

[12]Sin came into the world because of what one man did, and with sin came death. This is why everyone must die—because everyone sinned. [13]Sin was in the world before the law of Moses, but sin is not counted against us as breaking a command when there is no law. [14]But from the time of Adam to the time of Moses, everyone had to die, even those who had not sinned by breaking a command, as Adam had.

Adam was like the One who was coming in the future. [15]But God's free gift is not like Adam's sin. Many people died because of the sin of that one man. But the grace from God was much greater; many people received God's gift of life by the grace of the one man, Jesus Christ. [16]After Adam sinned once, he was judged guilty. But the gift of God is different. God's free gift came after many sins, and it makes people right with God. [17]One man sinned, and so death ruled all people because of that one man. But now those people who accept God's full grace and the great gift of being made right with him will surely have true life and rule through the one man, Jesus Christ.

[18]So as one sin of Adam brought the punishment of death to all people, one good act that Christ did makes all people right with God. And that brings true life for all. [19]One man disobeyed God, and many became sinners. In the same way, one man obeyed God, and many will be made right. [20]The law came to make sin worse. But when sin grew worse, God's grace increased. [21]Sin once used death to rule us, but God gave people more of his grace so that grace could rule by making people right with him. And this brings life forever through Jesus Christ our Lord.

DEAD TO SIN BUT ALIVE IN CHRIST

6 So do you think we should continue sinning so that God will give us even more grace? [2]No! We died to our old sinful lives, so how can we continue living with sin? [3]Did you forget that all of us became part of Christ when we were baptized? We shared his death in our baptism. [4]When we were baptized, we were buried with Christ and shared his death. So, just as Christ was raised from the dead by the wonderful power of the Father, we also can live a new life.

[5]Christ died, and we have been joined with him by dying too. So we will also be joined with him by rising from the dead as he did. [6]We know that our old life died with Christ on the cross so that our sinful selves would have no power over us and we would not be slaves to sin. [7]Anyone who has died is made free from sin's control.

[8]If we died with Christ, we know we will also live with him. [9]Christ was raised from the dead, and we know that he cannot die again. Death has no power over him now. [10]Yes, when Christ died, he died to defeat the power of sin one time—enough for all time. He now has a new life, and his new life is with God. [11]In the same way, you should see yourselves as being dead to the power of sin and alive with God through Christ Jesus.

[12]So, do not let sin control your life here on earth so that you do what your

REAL RHYMES:

ABOUT-FACE

BY JOSH ALSTON

IT'S MORE THAN MEETS THE EYE. I TRANSFORMED ON EVERY LEVEL.
SWITCHED MY STYLE, SWITCHED MY ATTITUDE, AND ALSO SWITCHED THE TREBLE.
MADE IT LOUDER THAN THE BASS TO HEAR JUST WHAT I'M SAYIN'.
HERE'S MY LIFE RIGHT IN YOUR FACE. SO ALLOW ME TO PORTRAY IT.
I JUST FADED WHILE JESUS CHRIST HAD TO BECOME MORE.
AND NOW I GET THE PLANET OPEN LIKE A NUCLEAR WAR.
I'M SO POOR TO THOSE OF YOU WHO LIVE IN THE WORLD AND JUDGE ACCORDING TO ITS STANDARDS.
WHILE IT SPINS AND IT TWIRLS, IT SENDS AND IT HURLS FIERY ARROWS.
WOMEN AND GIRLS, TWISTED AND CURLED BOYS TO MEN.
I'M SPITTIN' SOME PEARLS BECAUSE YOU LAUGHIN' AT GOD IN MY LIFE.
YOU HAD BIG MAC ATTACK AND BIT OFF MUCH MORE THAN YOU COULD CHEW.
I'M TAKIN' HALF OF THAT AND CASHIN' THAT IN RETURN FOR WISDOM FROM HEAVEN, BECAUSE TO ME IT'S MORE FILLING.
KINDA LIKE BREAD WHEN IT'S LEAVENED. HE CHANGED THE DIRECTION THAT MY LIFE WAS GOIN', 4REALZ.
HE GATHERED EVERYTHING I OWED HIM AND PAID ALL OF MY BILLS.
I'M DEBT-FREE AND I'VE ALSO BEEN SET FREE BY THE ONE WHO WALKED ON WATER WITHOUT USE OF A JET SKI.
AND NEXT HE SHOWED ME ALL THE LOVE THAT HE HAD AND THEN HE GAVE ME PEN AND PAPER AND STUCK ME IN THE LAB.
I'M SO GLAD THAT I HAD TO PUT INTO WRITING HOW HE RECONSTRUCTED ME LIKE VOLTRON WHEN HE'S FIGHTING.
'CUZ I'M WORSHIPIN' MY GOD NO MATTER WHO STANDS AGAINST ME AND TAKIN' UP MY SWORD WHEN THE ENEMY TEMPTS
    ME.
I'M MAKIN' MINCEMEAT OUTTA THE HORDES OF OPPOSITION AND PUSHIN' THE PAST ASIDE WITH THE THOUGHT OF MY
    MISSION 'CUZ I'M FORGIVEN.
24-7 NOTHIN' BUT LIVIN' AND I'M . . . THANKIN' THE LORD FOR THE CHANCE I WAS GIVEN.
A NEW BEGINNIN'. YO! CATS BARELY UNDERSTAND WHY.
BUT EVEN COMPARED TO CHEECH AND CHONG MY GOD'S THE MOST HIGH.
AND WHY HE CHOSE I IS STILL A MYSTERY TO MY BRAIN.
AND THOUGH I SIN FROM TIME TO TIME, HE LOVES ME THE SAME.
IT'S ALL IN HIS NAME. I SPREAD HIS GREAT GLORY AND FAME.
AND BEIN' A SERVANT OF GOD DOESN'T MEAN A BALL AND A CHAIN.
IT MEANS LIBERTY—FREEDOM FROM SIN. I MEAN IT LITERALLY.
THE HOLY SPIRIT ARRIVES INSIDE WITH ENERGY.
WHAT HE'S BEEN TO ME IS THE SOURCE OF PEACE IN THE NIGHT.
AND NOW MY HEART BELONGS TO HIM 'CUZ I GAVE HIM MY LIFE.
SO THANKFUL THAT CHRIST TONIGHT, CAME DOWN AS A BABE TO BEAR THE CURSE OF THE SINS OF THIS EARTH.
LET'S CELEBRATE. WE NEED TO ELEVATE.
PRAISE TO THE HEAVENS ABOVE AND SHOW HIM APPRECIATION FOR HIS EVIDENT LOVE.
IT'S NEVER ENOUGH TO RECOGNIZE GOD ONE DAY.
AND IT'S NEVER ENOUGH TO COME TO CHURCH EVERY SUNDAY BECAUSE THERE'S ONE WAY TO ETERNAL LIFE, AND THAT'S
    CHRIST.
AND I TRY TO EXPRESS THAT WHEN I'M CLUTCHIN' THE MIC.
AND THOUGH IT'S RIGHT, I STILL HAVE TO RUN IN THE RACE.
I DO IT WITH GOD'S HELP 'CUZ I'VE DONE AN ABOUT-FACE.

OVERCOMING

▶ OBESITY

The struggle to overcome obesity is all too common. Although there are many who suffer from physical disorders causing their obesity, most could banish it from their lives if they could retrain themselves. Today's society leads us to believe that we should always expect and achieve instant gratification. As a result, we have fast food, junk food, frozen dinners, and microwaves. Very little attention is given to the content of a meal, only to the time taken to prepare it. We have also become a society where exercise is an activity in and of itself. Gone are the days when your day's work provided more exercise than you could possibly want. We have become a sedentary society, and movement of any kind gets more unusual with every electronic advancement. We also tend to propagate the myth that food will make us feel better. We actually refer to them as comfort foods. It is no wonder that such a large percentage of Americans suffer with obesity.

The best plan for victory over obesity begins with a commitment to change. Consult your doctor to find a healthy new way of eating. Avoid dieting. Fad diets may not be good for you, and you will probably gain back all you lose as soon as the diet ends. Set small goals for yourself—goals you can achieve. Reaching attainable goals will give you incentive to continue. Probably the most life-altering plan for victory over obesity is the most simple. Whenever you find yourself wanting to reach for a comfort food, reach for the Bible instead. The Word of God will fill the emptiness within the way no other thing can.

sinful self wants to do. [13]Do not offer the parts of your body to serve sin, as things to be used in doing evil. Instead, offer yourselves to God as people who have died and now live. Offer the parts of your body to God to be used in doing good. [14]Sin will not be your master, because you are not under law but under God's grace.

BE SLAVES OF RIGHTEOUSNESS

[15]So what should we do? Should we sin because we are under grace and not under law? No! [16]Surely you know that when you give yourselves like slaves to obey someone, then you are really slaves of that person. The person you obey is your master. You can follow sin, which brings spiritual death, or you can obey God, which makes you right with him. [17]In the past you were slaves to sin—sin controlled you. But thank God, you fully obeyed the things that you were taught. [18]You were made free from sin, and now you are slaves to goodness. [19]I use this example because this is hard for you to understand. In the past you offered the parts of your body to be slaves to sin and evil; you lived only for evil. In the same way now you must give yourselves to be slaves of goodness. Then you will live only for God.

[20]In the past you were slaves to sin, and goodness did not control you. [21]You did evil things, and now you are ashamed of them. Those things only bring death. [22]But now you are free from sin and have become slaves of God. This brings you a life that is only for God, and this gives you life forever. [23]The payment for sin is death. But God gives us the free gift of life forever in Christ Jesus our Lord.

AN EXAMPLE FROM MARRIAGE

7 Brothers and sisters, all of you understand the law of Moses. So surely you know that the law rules over people only while they are alive. [2]For example, a woman must stay married to her husband as long as he is alive. But if her husband dies, she is free from the law of marriage. [3]But if she marries another man while her husband is still alive, the law says she is guilty of adultery. But if her husband dies, she is free from the law of marriage. Then if she marries another man, she is not guilty of adultery.

[4]In the same way, my brothers and sisters, your old selves died, and you became free from the law through the body of Christ. This happened so that you might belong to someone else—the One who was raised from the dead—and so that we might be used in service to God. [5]In the past, we were ruled by our sinful selves. The law made us want to do sinful things that controlled our bodies, so the things we did were bringing us death. [6]In the past, the law held us like prisoners, but our old selves died, and we were made free from the law. So now we serve God in a new way with the

Spirit, and not in the old way with written rules.

OUR FIGHT AGAINST SIN

[7]You might think I am saying that sin and the law are the same thing. That is not true. But the law was the only way I could learn what sin meant. I would never have known what it means to want to take something belonging to someone else if the law had not said, "You must not want to take your neighbor's things."[n] [8]And sin found a way to use that command and cause me to want all kinds of things I should not want. But without the law, sin has no power. [9]I was alive before I knew the law. But when the law's command came to me, then sin began to live, [10]and I died. The command was meant to bring life, but for me it brought death. [11]Sin found a way to fool me by using the command to make me die.

[12]So the law is holy, and the command is holy and right and good. [13]Does this mean that something that is good brought death to me? No! Sin used something that is good to bring death to me. This happened so that I could see what sin is really like; the command was used to show that sin is very evil.

THE WAR WITHIN US

[14]We know that the law is spiritual, but I am not spiritual since sin rules me as if I were its slave. [15]I do not understand the things I do. I do not do what I want to do, and I do the things I hate. [16]And if I do not want to do the hated things I do, that means I agree that the law is good. [17]But I am not really the one who is doing these hated things; it is sin living in me that does them. [18]Yes, I know that nothing good lives in me—I mean nothing good lives in the part of me that is earthly and sinful. I want to do the things that are good, but I do not do them. [19]I do not do the good things I want to do, but I do the bad things I do not want to do. [20]So if I do things I do not want to do, then I am not the one doing them. It is sin living in me that does those things.

[21]So I have learned this rule: When I want to do good, evil is there with me. [22]In my mind, I am happy with God's law. [23]But I see another law working in my body, which makes war against the law that my mind accepts. That other law working in my body is the law of sin, and it makes me its prisoner. [24]What a miserable man I am! Who will save me from this body that brings me death? [25]I thank God for saving me through Jesus Christ our Lord!

So in my mind I am a slave to God's law, but in my sinful self I am a slave to the law of sin.

> # I THANK GOD FOR SAVING ME THROUGH JESUS CHRIST OUR LORD!

BE RULED BY THE SPIRIT

8 So now, those who are in Christ Jesus are not judged guilty.[n] [2]Through Christ Jesus the law of the Spirit that brings life made you[n] free from the law that brings sin and death. [3]The law was without power, because the law was made weak by our sinful selves. But God did what the law could not do. He sent his own Son to earth with the same human life that others use for sin. By sending his Son to be an offering for sin, God used a human life to destroy sin. [4]He did this so that we could be the kind of people the law correctly wants us to be. Now we do not live following our sinful selves, but we live following the Spirit.

[5]Those who live following their sinful selves think only about things that their sinful selves want. But those who live following the Spirit are thinking about the things the Spirit wants them to do. [6]If people's thinking is controlled by the sinful self, there is death. But if their thinking is controlled by the Spirit, there is life and peace. [7]When people's thinking is controlled by the sinful self, they are against God, because they refuse to obey God's law and really are not even able to obey God's law. [8]Those people who are ruled by their sinful selves cannot please God.

[9]But you are not ruled by your sinful selves. You are ruled by the Spirit, if that Spirit of God really lives in you. But the person who does not have the Spirit of Christ does not belong to Christ. [10]Your body will always be dead because of sin. But if Christ is in you, then the Spirit gives you life, because Christ made you right with God. [11]God raised Jesus from the dead, and if God's Spirit is living in you, he will also give life to your bodies that die. God is the One who raised Christ from the dead, and he will give life through[n] his Spirit that lives in you.

[12]So, my brothers and sisters, we must not be ruled by our sinful selves or live the way our sinful selves want. [13]If you use your lives to do the wrong things your sinful selves want, you will die spiritually. But if you use the Spirit's help to stop doing the wrong things you do with your body, you will have true life.

[14]The true children of God are those who let God's Spirit lead them. [15]The Spirit we received does not make us slaves again to fear; it makes us children of God. With that Spirit we cry out, "Father."[n] [16]And the Spirit himself joins with our spirits to say we are God's children. [17]If we are God's children, we will receive blessings from God together with Christ. But we must suffer as Christ suffered so that we will have glory as Christ has glory.

OUR FUTURE GLORY

[18]The sufferings we have now are nothing compared to the great glory that will be shown to us. [19]Everything God

7:7 "You . . . things." Quotation from Exodus 20:17.   **8:1 guilty** Some Greek copies continue, "those who do not live in the power of their sinful selves, but in the power of the Spirit."
8:2 you Some Greek copies read "me."   **8:11 through** Some Greek copies read "because of."   **8:15 "Father"** Literally, "Abba, Father." Jewish children called their fathers "Abba."

made is waiting with excitement for God to show his children's glory completely. [20]Everything God made was changed to become useless, not by its own wish but because God wanted it and because all along there was this hope: [21]that everything God made would be set free from ruin to have the freedom and glory that belong to God's children.

[22]We know that everything God made has been waiting until now in pain, like a woman ready to give birth. [23]Not only the world, but we also have been waiting with pain inside us. We have the Spirit as the first part of God's promise. So we are waiting for God to finish making us his own children, which means our bodies will be made free. [24]We were saved, and we have this hope. If we see what we are waiting for, that is not really hope. People do not hope for something they already have. [25]But we are hoping for something we do not have yet, and we are waiting for it patiently.

[26]Also, the Spirit helps us with our weakness. We do not know how to pray as we should. But the Spirit himself speaks to God for us, even begs God for us with deep feelings that words cannot explain. [27]God can see what is in people's hearts. And he knows what is in the mind of the Spirit, because the Spirit speaks to God for his people in the way God wants.

[28]We know that in everything God works for the good of those who love him.[n] They are the people he called, because that was his plan. [29]God knew them before he made the world, and he chose them to be like his Son so that Jesus would be the firstborn[n] of many brothers and sisters. [30]God planned

8:28 We . . . him. Some Greek copies read "We know that everything works together for good for those who love God."
8:29 firstborn Here this probably means that Christ was the first in God's family to share God's glory.

THE SCRIPT

The Widow's Coins
Mark 12:41-44

In the synagogue, Jesus chose to sit in the spot right across from the offering box,
To cool out and watch how these people dropped their offerings:
Tossing them in the treasure with the pleasure of being seen and their money heard.
The rich in large measures, plush in their thick robes and leather,
Looking all together like proud cocks without the feathers.
But then there was a certain little widow who was so poor
She had no more than two skimpy coins to rub together.
She walked down the corridor all alone. Probably borrowed the coins;
'Cause widows never have plenty of anythang but pain and memories of the dead.
But no, she was there to have church instead and shook those thoughts out her head,
And headed for the offering plate. Moving slow, she was passionate,

There to celebrate with an attitude like, "I can't wait!"
Though she couldn't change the past,
She came once again. At last, she had a chance to pay God back for the good times.
I know it don't make sense to attempt to recompense God, but at least she was trying.
There was no denying this sacrifice right from a heart that was pure.
Jesus called his disciples to the floor and said, "I'm a tell ya the truth for sure:
This poor widow gave more with her pennies than all of these jokers with their
Good and their plenty! See, so many just gave a pinch of their abundance,
But this woman, still hungry and wanting, gave all her substance . . . and I love it."

Take this with you: God is not impressed with anything that we have. He is impressed with every motive with which we give.

for them to be like his Son; and those he planned to be like his Son, he also called; and those he called, he also made right with him; and those he made right, he also glorified.

GOD'S LOVE IN CHRIST JESUS

[31] So what should we say about this? If God is for us, no one can defeat us. [32] He did not spare his own Son but gave him for us all. So with Jesus, God will surely give us all things. [33] Who can accuse the people God has chosen? No one, because God is the One who makes them right. [34] Who can say God's people are guilty? No one, because Christ Jesus died, but he was also raised from the dead, and now he is on God's right side, appealing to God for us. [35] Can anything separate us from the love Christ has for us? Can troubles or problems or sufferings or hunger or nakedness or danger or violent death? [36] As it is written in the Scriptures:

"For you we are in danger of death
      all the time.
People think we are worth no
      more than sheep to be killed."

Psalm 44:22

[37] But in all these things we are completely victorious through God who showed his love for us. [38] Yes, I am sure that neither death, nor life, nor angels, nor ruling spirits, nothing now, nothing in the future, no powers, [39] nothing above us, nothing below us, nor anything else in the whole world will ever be able to separate us from the love of God that is in Christ Jesus our Lord.

GOD AND THE JEWISH PEOPLE

9 I am in Christ, and I am telling you the truth; I do not lie. My conscience is ruled by the Holy Spirit, and it tells me I am not lying. [2] I have great sorrow and always feel much sadness. [3] I wish I could help my Jewish brothers and sisters, my people. I would even wish that I were cursed and cut off from Christ if that would

help them. [4] They are the people of Israel, God's chosen children. They have seen the glory of God, and they have the agreements that God made between himself and his people. God gave them the law of Moses and the right way of worship and his promises. [5] They are the descendants of our great ancestors, and they are the earthly family into which Christ was born, who is God over all. Praise him forever![n] Amen.

[6] It is not that God failed to keep his promise to them. But only some of the people of Israel are truly God's people,[n] [7] and only some of Abraham's[n] descendants are true children of Abraham. But God said to Abraham: "The descendants I promised you will be from Isaac."[n] [8] This means that not all of Abraham's descendants are God's true children. Abraham's true children are those who become God's children because of the promise God made to Abraham. [9] God's promise to Abraham was this: "At the right time I will return, and Sarah will have a son."[n] [10] And that is not all. Rebekah's sons had the same father, our father Isaac. [11-12] But before the two boys were born, God told Rebekah, "The older will serve the younger."[n] This was before the boys had done anything good or bad. God said this so that the one chosen would be chosen because of God's own plan. He was chosen because he was the one God wanted to call, not because of anything he did. [13] As the Scripture says, "I loved Jacob, but I hated Esau."[n]

[14] So what should we say about this? Is God unfair? In no way. [15] God said to Moses, "I will show kindness to anyone to whom I want to show kindness, and I will show mercy to anyone to whom I want to show mercy."[n] [16] So God will choose the one to whom he decides to show mercy; his choice does not depend on what people want or try to do. [17] The Scripture says to the king of Egypt: "I made you king for this reason: to show my power in you so that my name will be talked about in all the earth."[n] [18] So God shows mercy where he wants to

show mercy, and he makes stubborn the people he wants to make stubborn.

[19] So one of you will ask me: "Then why does God blame us for our sins? Who can fight his will?" [20] You are only human, and human beings have no right to question God. An object should not ask the person who made it, "Why did you make me like this?" [21] The potter can make anything he wants to make. He can use the same clay to make one

VIEWPOINT

WHAT HAS BEEN THE GREATEST SOURCE OF JOY IN YOUR LIFE?

Up to this point, I believe my greatest source of joy would be the fact that I have family and friends who believe in me and support me in everything that I do. I can count on them to bring me joy when the cares of life try to bring me down. I, in turn, give support to my family and friends.

9:5 born . . . forever! This can also mean "born. May God, who rules over all things, be praised forever!" **9:6 God's people** Literally, "Israel," the people God chose to bring his blessings to the world. **9:7 Abraham** Most respected ancestor of the Jews. Every Jew hoped to see Abraham. **9:7 "The descendants . . . Isaac."** Quotation from Genesis 21:12. **9:9 "At . . . son."** Quotation from Genesis 18:10, 14. **9:11-12 "The older . . . younger."** Quotation from Genesis 25:23. **9:13 "I . . . Esau."** Quotation from Malachi 1:2-3. **9:15 "I . . . mercy."** Quotation from Exodus 33:19. **9:17 "I . . . earth."** Quotation from Exodus 9:16.

thing for special use and another thing for daily use.

²²It is the same way with God. He wanted to show his anger and to let people see his power. But he patiently stayed with those people he was angry with—people who were made ready to be destroyed. ²³He waited with patience so that he could make known his rich glory to the people who receive his mercy. He has prepared these people to have his glory, ²⁴and we are those people whom God called. He called us not from the Jews only but also from those who are not Jews. ²⁵As the Scripture says in Hosea:

"I will say, 'You are my people'
   to those I had called 'not my
   people.'
And I will show my love
   to those people I did not love."
                                    Hosea 2:1, 23

²⁶"They were called,
   'You are not my people,'
but later they will be called
   'children of the living God.'"
                                    Hosea 1:10

²⁷And Isaiah cries out about Israel:
"The people of Israel are many,
   like the grains of sand by the sea.
But only a few of them will be
   saved,
²⁸because the Lord will quickly and
   completely punish the
   people on the earth."
                                    Isaiah 10:22-23

²⁹It is as Isaiah said:
"The Lord All-Powerful
   allowed a few of our descendants
   to live.
Otherwise we would have been
   completely destroyed
like the cities of Sodom and
   Gomorrah."ⁿ   *Isaiah 1:9*

³⁰So what does all this mean? Those who are not Jews were not trying to make themselves right with God, but they were made right with God because of their faith. ³¹The people of Israel tried to follow a law to make themselves right with God. But they did not succeed,

³²because they tried to make themselves right by the things they did instead of trusting in God to make them right. They stumbled over the stone that causes people to stumble. ³³As it is written in the Scripture:

"I will put in Jerusalem a stone
   that causes people to stumble,
a rock that makes them fall.
Anyone who trusts in him will never
   be disappointed."
                                    Isaiah 8:14; 28:16

10 Brothers and sisters, the thing I want most is for all the Jews to be saved. That is my prayer to God. ²I can say this about them: They really try to follow God, but they do not know the right way. ³Because they did not know the way that God makes people right with him, they tried to make themselves right in their own way. So they did not accept God's way of making people right. ⁴Christ ended the law so that everyone who believes in him may be right with God.

⁵Moses writes about being made right by following the law. He says, "A person who obeys these things will live because of them."ⁿ ⁶But this is what the Scripture says about being made right through faith: "Don't say to yourself, 'Who will go up into heaven?'" (That means, "Who will go up to heaven and bring Christ down to earth?") ⁷"And do not say, 'Who will go down into the world below?'" (That means, "Who will go down and bring Christ up from the dead?") ⁸This is what the Scripture says: "The word is near you; it is in your mouth and in your heart."ⁿ That is the teaching of faith that we are telling. ⁹If you declare with your mouth, "Jesus is Lord," and if you believe in your heart that God raised Jesus from the dead, you will be saved. ¹⁰We believe with our hearts, and so we are made right with God. And we declare with our mouths that we believe, and so we are saved. ¹¹As the Scripture says, "Anyone who trusts in him will never be

disappointed."ⁿ ¹²That Scripture says "anyone" because there is no difference between those who are Jews and those who are not. The same Lord is the Lord of all and gives many blessings to all who trust in him, ¹³as the Scripture says, "Anyone who calls on the Lord will be saved."ⁿ

¹⁴But before people can ask the Lord for help, they must believe in him; and before they can believe in him, they must hear about him; and for them to hear about the Lord, someone must tell them; ¹⁵and before someone can go and tell them, that person must be sent. It is written, "How beautiful is the person who comes to bring good news."ⁿ ¹⁶But not all the Jews accepted the good news. Isaiah said, "Lord, who believed what we told them?"ⁿ ¹⁷So faith comes from hearing the Good News, and people hear the Good News when someone tells them about Christ.

¹⁸But I ask: Didn't people hear the Good News? Yes, they heard—as the Scripture says:

"Their message went out through
   all the world;
their words go everywhere on
   earth."   *Psalm 19:4*

¹⁹Again I ask: Didn't the people of Israel understand? Yes, they did understand. First, Moses says:

"I will use those who are not a
   nation to make you jealous.
I will use a nation that does
   not understand to make you
   angry."   *Deuteronomy 32:21*

²⁰Then Isaiah is bold enough to say:

"I was found by those who were not
   asking me for help.
I made myself known to people
   who were not looking for me."
                                    Isaiah 65:1

²¹But about Israel God says,

"All day long I stood ready to
   accept
people who disobey and are
   stubborn."   *Isaiah 65:2*

9:29 Sodom and Gomorrah Two cities that God destroyed because the people were so evil. **10:5 "A person . . . them."** Quotation from Leviticus 18:5. **10:6-8 But . . . heart."** Quotations from Deuteronomy 9:4; 30:12-14; Psalm 107:26. **10:11 "Anyone . . . disappointed."** Quotation from Isaiah 28:16. **10:13 "Anyone . . . saved."** Quotation from Joel 2:32. **10:15 "How . . . news."** Quotation from Isaiah 52:7. **10:16 "Lord, . . . them?"** Quotation from Isaiah 53:1.

GOD UNIT

GETTING OVER MYSELF

$\mathcal{W}$hen I was 14 years old, I professed faith in the Lord. *I'm saved*, I thought. *I'm going to church every week with my parents, aren't I? I'm doin' my best to do what the preacher says, so I must be okay.* But I wasn't. My faith—I didn't own it. It was just two years after I had "come to Christ" that I fell into doing what I wanted. If it felt good, I did it. I didn't deny myself anything that I wanted to do, 'cause that's what I saw so many of the other brothers around me doin'. In fact, my "relationship" with God was just a front for my parents and their friends at church.

It got bad. By age eighteen I had saved up a little money. I moved out of my parents' house, leaving behind my church family and everything Christian that I knew. I went from living under the influence of my parents and the church to living with some other dudes in the city. My Christian values (my parents' values) went out the window. There were no rules. I thought to myself, *this is all good*! I could stay out all night. I could say what I wanted to say. I chose who to hang with and did whatever dirt I felt like doing. As far as I was concerned, it was all about me. My

parents' lives were consumed with loving God and loving others for Christ's sake and I was havin' none of that. I was livin' large. I was getting drunk three times a week, hitting up every club on the weekend and sleeping around.

Then the strangest thing happened. I was out one Saturday night, kickin' it with some friends, and woke up the next morning at a stranger's house. It was the usual scene. We'd been smokin' dope, drinkin', and layin' around. I surveyed the scene. Suddenly, I had a flashback of my parents' house! I saw us at church together on Sunday morning, and I recalled the preacher's sermons and going forward to receive Christ. I remembered how the people at church treated each other and struggled to help each other. It was then that it struck me that I really didn't want this life. My friendships were not friendships at all. As quickly as folks came into my life they were gone, usually leaving some mess behind. I hadn't been raised to live like this and I didn't enjoy being buck wild.

I decided that I really wanted what my parents had. I asked them to allow me to come back home, and they did. The following Sunday, we went to church together. Everyone was glad to see me. It was obvious they really cared. Then and there I decided not to live half a life for Christ. I wanted to give him my whole life. And I did. For real.

Luke 9:23—Jesus said to all of them, "If people want to follow me, they must give up the things they want. They must be willing to give up their lives daily to follow me."

GOD SHOWS MERCY TO ALL PEOPLE

11 So I ask: Did God throw out his people? No! I myself am an Israelite from the family of Abraham, from the tribe of Benjamin. [2]God chose the Israelites to be his people before they were born, and he has not thrown his people out. Surely you know what the Scripture says about Elijah, how he prayed to God against the people of Israel. [3]"Lord," he said, "they have killed your prophets, and they have destroyed your altars. I am the only prophet left, and now they are trying to kill me, too."[n] [4]But what answer did God give Elijah? He said, "But I have left seven thousand people in Israel who have never bowed down before Baal."[n] [5]It is the same now. There are a few people that God has chosen by his grace. [6]And if he chose them by grace, it is not for the things they have done. If they could be made God's people by what they did, God's gift of grace would not really be a gift.

[7]So this is what has happened: Although the Israelites tried to be right

---

11:3 "they . . . too" Quotation from 1 Kings 19:10, 14.   **11:4 "But . . . Baal."** Quotation from 1 Kings 19:18.

365

AUGUST

1   Pray for world peace.

2   On This Day In History 1924—Track star Jess Owens wins four
Olympic gold medals at the Berlin Games.

3

4   It's your birthday, Marques Houston!

5

6

7   Think outside
the box:
What can you do
to improve your
community?

8

9

10

11

12

13

14   Happy Birthday Magic Johnson and Halle Berry!

15

16   Start a journal that
17   includes your 5-year goals.

18

19

20

21   Stay informed.
22   Subscribe to a favorite
23   magazine or the
24   local newspaper.

25

26   Share a favorite poem with a friend.

27   It's your birthday, Yolanda Adams!

28   On This Day In History 1963—Anniversary of historic March on Washington.

29

30

31   Happy Birthday Chris Tucker!

> "I think it's always
> best to be who
> you are."
> –Halle Berry

MUSIC REVIEWS

ARTIST: D'ANGELO   ALBUM: VOODOO   CUT: "DEVIL'S PIE"

D'Angelo is very sexual and explicit. He has a very X-rated video where he is naked during his sexual serenade. His album is ironically titled *Voodoo*, and his album cover has a picture of him in Haiti performing a voodoo ceremony with natives. He is playing the conga drum while a woman, possessed by a demon, is mangling a chicken. Don't believe the hype and don't make excuses for the voodoo. Here's what he wrote on his *Voodoo* album cover: "I personally believe in art as it exists in the context of the phrase 'thou art god.' In this phrase, art is the word that connects the individual (thou) to their higher self (god) or to that which is universal." His lyrics say, "Who am I to justify all the evil in our eye when I myself feel the high from all that I despise." D'Angelo is down with something, but I don't think it's God.

"REJECTED"

with God, they did not succeed, but the ones God chose did become right with him. The others were made stubborn and refused to listen to God. [8] As it is written in the Scriptures:

"God gave the people a dull mind so
   they could not understand."
                              Isaiah 29:10

"He closed their eyes so they could
   not see
and their ears so they could not
   hear.
This continues until today."
                           Deuteronomy 29:4

[9] And David says:

"Let their own feasts trap them and
   cause their ruin;
let their feasts cause them to
   stumble and be paid back.
[10] Let their eyes be closed so they
   cannot see
and their backs be forever weak
   from troubles."   *Psalm 69:22-23*

[11] So I ask: When the Jews fell, did that fall destroy them? No! But their failure brought salvation to those who are not Jews, in order to make the Jews jealous. [12] The Jews' failure brought rich blessings for the world, and the Jews' loss brought rich blessings for the non-Jewish people. So surely the world will receive much richer blessings when enough Jews become the kind of people God wants.

[13] Now I am speaking to you who are not Jews. I am an apostle to those who are not Jews, and since I have that work, I will make the most of it. [14] I hope I can make my own people jealous and, in that way, help some of them to be saved. [15] When God turned away from the Jews, he became friends with other people in the world. So when God accepts the Jews, surely that will bring them life after death.

[16] If the first piece of bread is offered to God, then the whole loaf is made holy. If the roots of a tree are holy, then the tree's branches are holy too.

[17] It is as if some of the branches from an olive tree have been broken off. You non-Jewish people are like the branch of a wild olive tree that has been joined to that first tree. You now share the strength and life of the first tree, the Jews. [18] So do not brag about those branches that were broken off. If you brag, remember that you do not support the root, but the root supports you. [19] You will say, "Branches were broken off so that I could be joined to their tree." [20] That is true. But those branches were broken off because they did not believe, and you continue to be part of the tree only because you believe. Do not be proud, but be afraid. [21] If God did not let the natural branches of that tree stay, then he will not let you stay if you don't believe.

[22] So you see that God is kind and also very strict. He punishes those who stop following him. But God is kind to you, if you continue following in his kindness. If you do not, you will be cut off from the tree. [23] And if the Jews will believe in God again, he will accept them back. God is able to put them back where they were. [24] It is not natural for a wild branch to be part of a good tree. And you who are not Jews are like a branch cut from a wild olive tree and joined to a

good olive tree. But since those Jews are like a branch that grew from the good tree, surely they can be joined to their own tree again.

²⁵I want you to understand this secret, brothers and sisters, so you will understand that you do not know everything: Part of Israel has been made stubborn, but that will change when many who are not Jews have come to God. ²⁶And that is how all Israel will be saved. It is written in the Scriptures:

"The Savior will come from
    Jerusalem;
    he will take away all evil from the
        family of Jacob.[n]
²⁷And I will make this agreement with
    those people
    when I take away their sins."
                        Isaiah 59:20–21; 27:9

²⁸The Jews refuse to accept the Good News, so they are God's enemies. This has happened to help you who are not Jews. But the Jews are still God's chosen people, and he loves them very much because of the promises he made to their ancestors. ²⁹God never changes his mind about the people he calls and the things he gives them. ³⁰At one time you refused to obey God. But now you have received mercy, because those people refused to obey. ³¹And now the Jews refuse to obey, because God showed mercy to you. But this happened so that they also can[n] receive mercy from him. ³²God has given all people over to their stubborn ways so that he can show mercy to all.

PRAISE TO GOD

³³Yes, God's riches are very great, and his wisdom and knowledge have no end! No one can explain the things God decides or understand his ways. ³⁴As the Scripture says,

"Who has known the mind of the
    Lord,
    or who has been able to give him
        advice?"   *Isaiah 40:13*
³⁵"No one has ever given God
    anything
    that he must pay back."
                        Job 41:11

hot10

Recommended
Reading List

10. Return to Glory: The Powerful Stirrings of the Black Race (Joel Freeman and Don Griffin)

9. Church Boy (Kirk Franklin)

8. The Left Behind Series (Tim LaHaye and Jerry B. Jenkins)

7. This Present Darkness (Frank Peretti)

6. The Screwtape Letters, Mere Christianity and anything else by C. S. Lewis

5. More Than a Carpenter (Josh McDowell)

4. The Measure of a Man (Martin Luther King, Jr.)

3. The Final Quest (Rick Joyner)

2. The Purpose Driven Life (Rick Warren)

1. The Bible

³⁶Yes, God made all things, and everything continues through him and for him. To him be the glory forever! Amen.

GIVE YOUR LIVES TO GOD

12 So brothers and sisters, since God has shown us great mercy, I beg you to offer your lives as a living sacrifice to him. Your offering must be only for God and pleasing to him, which is the spiritual way for you to worship. ²Do not be shaped by this world; instead be changed within by a new way of thinking. Then you will be able to decide what God wants for you; you will know what is good and pleasing to him and what is perfect. ³Because God has given me a special gift, I have something to say to everyone among you. Do not think you are better than you are. You must decide what you really are by the amount of faith God has given you. ⁴Each one of us has a body with many parts, and these parts all have different uses. ⁵In the same way, we are many, but in Christ we are all one body. Each one is a part of that body, and each part belongs to all the other parts. ⁶We all have different gifts, each of which came because of the grace God gave us. The person who has the gift of prophecy should use that gift in agreement with the faith. ⁷Anyone who has the gift of serving should serve. Anyone who has the gift of teaching should teach. ⁸Whoever has the gift of encouraging others should encourage. Whoever has the gift of giving to others should give freely. Anyone who has the gift of being a leader should try hard when he leads. Whoever has the gift of showing mercy to others should do so with joy.

⁹Your love must be real. Hate what is evil, and hold on to what is good. ¹⁰Love each other like brothers and sisters. Give each other more honor than you want for yourselves. ¹¹Do not be lazy

---

11:26 Jacob Father of the twelve family groups of Israel, the people God chose to be his people.   **11:31 can** Some Greek copies read "can now."

but work hard, serving the Lord with all your heart. [12]Be joyful because you have hope. Be patient when trouble comes, and pray at all times. [13]Share with God's people who need help. Bring strangers in need into your homes.

[14]Wish good for those who harm you; wish them well and do not curse them. [15]Be happy with those who are happy, and be sad with those who are sad. [16]Live in peace with each other. Do not be proud, but make friends with those who seem unimportant. Do not think how smart you are.

[17]If someone does wrong to you, do not pay him back by doing wrong to him. Try to do what everyone thinks is right. [18]Do your best to live in peace with everyone. [19]My friends, do not try to punish others when they wrong you, but wait for God to punish them with his anger. It is written: "I will punish those who do wrong; I will repay them,"[n] says the Lord. [20]But you should do this:

"If your enemy is hungry, feed him;
   if he is thirsty, give him a drink.
   Doing this will be like pouring
   burning coals on his head."
                    Proverbs 25:21-22

[21]Do not let evil defeat you, but defeat evil by doing good.

CHRISTIANS SHOULD OBEY THE LAW

13 All of you must yield to the government rulers. No one rules unless God has given him the power to rule, and no one rules now without that power from God. [2]So those who are against the government are really against what God has commanded. And they will bring punishment on themselves. [3]Those who do right do not have to fear the rulers; only those who do wrong fear them. Do you want to be unafraid of the rulers? Then do what is right, and they will praise you. [4]The ruler is God's servant to help you. But if you do wrong, then be afraid. He has the power to punish; he is God's servant to punish those who do wrong. [5]So you must yield to the government, not only because you might be punished, but because you know it is right.

[6]This is also why you pay taxes. Rulers are working for God and give their time to their work. [7]Pay everyone, then, what you owe. If you owe any kind of tax, pay it. Show respect and honor to them all.

LOVING OTHERS

[8]Do not owe people anything, except always owe love to each other, because the person who loves others has obeyed all the law. [9]The law says, "You must not be guilty of adultery. You must not murder anyone. You must not steal. You must not want to take your neighbor's things."[n] All these commands and all others are really only one rule: "Love your neighbor as you love yourself."[n] [10]Love never hurts a neighbor, so loving is obeying all the law.

[11]Do this because we live in an important time. It is now time for you to wake up from your sleep, because our salvation is nearer now than when we first believed. [12]The "night"[n] is almost finished, and the "day"[n] is almost here. So we should stop doing things that belong to darkness and take up the weapons used for fighting in the light. [13]Let us live in a right way, like people who belong to the day. We should not have wild parties or get drunk. There should be no sexual sins of any kind, no fighting or jealousy. [14]But clothe yourselves with the Lord Jesus Christ and forget about satisfying your sinful self.

DO NOT CRITICIZE OTHER PEOPLE

14 Accept into your group someone who is weak in faith, and do not argue about opinions. [2]One person believes it is right to eat all kinds of food.[n] But another, who is weak, believes it is right to eat only vegetables. [3]The one who knows that it is right to eat any kind of food must not reject the one who eats only vegetables. And the person who eats only vegetables must not think that the one who eats all foods is wrong, because God has accepted that person. [4]You cannot judge another person's servant. The master decides if the servant is doing well or not. And the

VIEWPOINT

WHAT HAS BEEN THE GREATEST SOURCE OF JOY IN YOUR LIFE?

My greatest source of joy would have to be my family—my wife of ten years, my daughter, and my son. We have lots of fun together. Even when things get a little tight, we are always there for each other. I believe a strong family is the foundation for a strong church.

12:19 "I . . . them." Quotation from Deuteronomy 32:35. **13:9 "You . . . things."** Quotation from Exodus 20:13-15, 17. **13:9 "Love . . . yourself."** Quotation from Leviticus 19:18. **13:12 "night"** This is used as a symbol of the sinful world we live in. This world will soon end. **13:12 "day"** This is used as a symbol of the good time that is coming, when we will be with God. **14:2 all . . . food** The Jewish law said there were some foods Jews should not eat. When Jews became Christians, some of them did not understand they could now eat all foods.

Lord's servant will do well because the Lord helps him do well.

[5]Some think that one day is more important than another, and others think that every day is the same. Let all be sure in their own mind. [6]Those who think one day is more important than other days are doing that for the Lord. And those who eat all kinds of food are doing that for the Lord, and they give thanks to God. Others who refuse to eat some foods do that for the Lord, and they give thanks to God. [7]We do not live or die for ourselves. [8]If we live, we are living for the Lord, and if we die, we are dying for the Lord. So living or dying, we belong to the Lord. [9]The reason Christ died and rose from the dead to live again was so he would be Lord over both the dead and the living. [10]So why do you judge your brothers or sisters in Christ? And why do you think you are better than they are? We will all stand before God to be judged, [11]because it is written in the Scriptures:

"'As surely as I live,' says the Lord,
'Everyone will bow before me;
everyone will say that I am God.'"

Isaiah 45:23

[12]So each of us will have to answer to God.

DO NOT CAUSE OTHERS TO SIN

[13]For that reason we should stop judging each other. We must make up our minds not to do anything that will make another Christian sin. [14]I am in the Lord Jesus, and I know that there is no food that is wrong to eat. But if a person believes something is wrong, that thing is wrong for him. [15]If you hurt your brother's or sister's faith because of something you eat, you are not really following the way of love. Do not destroy someone's faith by eating food he thinks is wrong, because Christ died for him. [16]Do not allow what you think is good to become what others say is evil. [17]In the kingdom of God, eating and drinking are not important. The important things

are living right with God, peace, and joy in the Holy Spirit. [18]Anyone who serves Christ by living this way is pleasing God and will be accepted by other people.

[19]So let us try to do what makes peace and helps one another. [20]Do not let the eating of food destroy the work of God. All foods are all right to eat, but it is wrong to eat food that causes someone else to sin. [21]It is better not to eat meat or drink wine or do anything that will cause your brother or sister to sin. [22]Your beliefs about these things should be kept secret between you and God. People are happy if they can do what they think is right without feeling guilty. [23]But those who eat something without being sure it is right are wrong because they did not believe it was right. Anything that is done without believing it is right is a sin.

15 We who are strong in faith should help the weak with their weaknesses, and not please only ourselves. [2]Let each of us please our neighbors for their good, to help them be stronger in faith. [3]Even Christ did not live to please himself. It was as the Scriptures said: "When people insult you, it hurts me."[n] [4]Everything that was written in the past was written to teach us. The Scriptures give us patience and encouragement so that we can have hope. [5]May the patience and encouragement that come from God allow you to live in harmony with each other the way Christ Jesus wants. [6]Then you will all be joined together, and you will give glory to God the Father of our Lord Jesus Christ. [7]Christ accepted you, so you should accept each other, which will bring glory to God. [8]I tell you that Christ became a servant of the Jews to show that God's promises to the Jewish ancestors are true. [9]And he also did this so that those who are not Jews could give glory to God for the mercy he gives to them. It is written in the Scriptures:

"So I will praise you among the
non-Jewish people.
I will sing praises to your name."

Psalm 18:49

[10]The Scripture also says,

"Be happy, you who are not Jews,
together with his people."

Deuteronomy 32:43

[11]Again the Scripture says,

"All you who are not Jews, praise
the Lord.
All you people, sing praises to
him."

Psalm 117:1

[12]And Isaiah says,

"A new king will come from the
family of Jesse.[n]
He will come to rule over the
non-Jewish people,
and they will have hope because of
him."

Isaiah 11:10

[13]I pray that the God who gives hope will fill you with much joy and peace while you trust in him. Then your hope will overflow by the power of the Holy Spirit.

PAUL TALKS ABOUT HIS WORK

[14]My brothers and sisters, I am sure that you are full of goodness. I know that you have all the knowledge you need and that you are able to teach each other. [15]But I have written to you very openly about some things I wanted you to remember. I did this because God gave me this special gift: [16]to be a minister of Christ Jesus to those who are not Jews. I served God by teaching his Good News, so that the non-Jewish people could be an offering that God would accept—an offering made holy by the Holy Spirit.

[17]So I am proud of what I have done for God in Christ Jesus. [18]I will not talk about anything except what Christ has done through me in leading those who are not Jews to obey God. They have obeyed God because of what I have said and done, [19]because of the power of miracles and the great things they saw, and because of the power of the Holy Spirit. I preached the Good News from

---

15:3 "When . . . me." Quotation from Psalm 69:9.   **15:12 Jesse** Jesse was the father of David, king of Israel. Jesus was from their family.

Jerusalem all the way around to Illyricum, and so I have finished that part of my work. [20]I always want to preach the Good News in places where people have never heard of Christ, because I do not want to build on the work someone else has already started. [21]But it is written in the Scriptures:

"Those who were not told about
     him will see,
  and those who have not heard
     about him will understand."

                              Isaiah 52:15

PAUL'S PLAN TO VISIT ROME

[22]This is the reason I was stopped many times from coming to you. [23]Now I have finished my work here. Since for many years I have wanted to come to you, [24]I hope to visit you on my way to Spain. After I enjoy being with you for a while, I hope you can help me on my trip. [25]Now I am going to Jerusalem to help God's people. [26]The believers in Macedonia and Southern Greece were happy to give their money to help the poor among God's people at Jerusalem. [27]They were happy to do this, and really they owe it to them. These who are not Jews have shared in the Jews' spiritual blessings, so they should use their material possessions to help the Jews. [28]After I am sure the poor in Jerusalem get the money that has been given for them, I will leave for Spain and stop and visit you. [29]I know that when I come to you I will bring Christ's full blessing.

[30]Brothers and sisters, I beg you to help me in my work by praying to God for me. Do this because of our Lord Jesus and the love that the Holy Spirit gives us. [31]Pray that I will be saved from the nonbelievers in Judea and that this help I bring to Jerusalem will please God's people there. [32]Then, if God wants me to, I will come to you with joy, and together you and I will have a time of rest. [33]The God who gives peace be with you all. Amen.

HOW YA TRAVELIN'?

LOVE AND CONQUERING

The plot or storyline of many of today's popular poems, plays, books, and movies revolves around two basic human drives: 1) love—in the form of friendship, romance, safety, warmth, tenderness, or affirmation, and 2) conquering—through productivity, aggressiveness, confidence, discipline, unity, or challenge.

Most of what you see in the media today has perverted love into lust and conquering into anger. As a result, this generation, which has made itself a slave to the media, also has adopted its viewpoints.

Christ meant for love to equal giving, and for conquering to equal confidence. With that equation, we can conquer through love. The whole book of Joshua is about conquering. Joshua is the Old Testament name that corresponds to the name of Jesus in the New Testament (Jesus saves). Jesus is the greatest conqueror of all time, because he conquered death and hell for us, and he did it out of love. With Jesus as our example, "we have full victory through God who showed his love for us" (Romans 8:37).

In this generation, we've confused love as a sign of weakness and conquering as a sign of violence. When we stop making the media our ultimate authority and instead allow Jesus to be our example, we'll understand that both words represent positive characteristics.

GREETINGS TO THE CHRISTIANS

16 I recommend to you our sister Phoebe, who is a helper[n] in the church in Cenchrea. [2]I ask you to accept her in the Lord in the way God's people should. Help her with anything she needs, because she has helped me and many other people also.

[3]Give my greetings to Priscilla and Aquila, who work together with me in Christ Jesus, [4]and who risked their own lives to save my life. I am thankful to them, and all the non-Jewish churches are thankful as well. [5]Also, greet for me the church that meets at their house.

Greetings to my dear friend Epenetus, who was the first person in Asia to follow Christ. [6]Greetings to Mary, who worked very hard for you. [7]Greetings to Andronicus and Junia, my relatives, who were in prison with me. They are very important apostles. They were believers in Christ before I was. [8]Greetings to Ampliatus, my dear friend in the Lord. [9]Greetings to Urbanus, a worker together with me for Christ. And greetings to my dear friend Stachys. [10]Greetings to Apelles, who was tested and proved that he truly loves Christ. Greetings to all those who are in the family of Aristobulus. [11]Greetings to Herodion, my fellow citizen. Greetings to all those in the family of Narcissus who belong to the Lord. [12]Greetings to Tryphena and Tryphosa, women who work very hard for the Lord. Greetings to my dear friend Persis, who also has worked very hard for the Lord. [13]Greetings to

16:1 helper Literally, "deaconess." This might mean the same as one of the special women helpers in 1 Timothy 3:11.

DEEP ISSUES

Peer Pressure

"What are you scared of?" "Stop being so soft!" "Don't sweat it, it's all good!" We've all heard comments like this when people are trying to get us to do something we are unsure that we should do. Maybe we *are* sure—sure that it is wrong. Yet we still want to do it because it seems like everyone is doing it and we just want to be down. We live in a culture where what is wrong is considered right and what is right is considered wrong. It's similar to Romans 1:25 where it says that evil people have "traded the truth of God for a lie." If we don't do what everyone else is doing we might be considered weak or corny. In reality, if we choose what is truly right and stand up for what we believe, we are the ones who are strong.

Everybody is always saying, "I'm original, I don't try to be like anyone else." But look around. Everyone is copying what they see on TV, in movies, and in the street. Look at the results of what "everyone" is doing! People sleeping around are getting pregnant, catching diseases, and catching mad drama. People smoking weed are burning up brain cells, getting addicted, and breaking the law. Girls dressing with less clothes are getting less respected and being called stuff way out of their names. People selling drugs or doing illegal things always have to watch their backs, and many get locked up every day and ruin their future.

Are those really the results we want? Do we really think that those people are happy in life? Are they really having a good time? That crowd is constantly searching and trying to find themselves. They are trying to find satisfaction and peace in all the wrong things. They all end up miserable. The book you hold in your hands is our instruction manual. This book has all the real answers on how to find real peace and real satisfaction as we build a real relationship with our Creator. Don't trade the truth for a lie. We can be what God wants us to be. If we are original, the pressure will be on our friends to follow us from the positive tip. So lead on, my brotha.

Rufus, who is a special person in the Lord, and to his mother, who has been like a mother to me also. [14]Greetings to Asyncritus, Phlegon, Hermes, Patrobas, Hermas, and all the brothers and sisters who are with them. [15]Greetings to Philologus and Julia, Nereus and his sister, and Olympas, and to all God's people with them. [16]Greet each other with a holy kiss. All of Christ's churches send greetings to you.

[17]Brothers and sisters, I ask you to look out for those who cause people to be against each other and who upset other people's faith. They are against the true teaching you learned, so stay away from them. [18]Such people are not serving our Lord Christ but are only doing what pleases themselves. They use fancy talk and fine words to fool the minds of those who do not know about evil. [19]All the believers have heard that you obey, so I am very happy because of you. But I want you to be wise in what is good and innocent in what is evil.

[20]The God who brings peace will soon defeat Satan and give you power over him.

The grace of our Lord Jesus be with you.

[21]Timothy, a worker together with me, sends greetings, as well as Lucius, Jason, and Sosipater, my relatives.

[22]I am Tertius, and I am writing this letter from Paul. I send greetings to you in the Lord.

[23]Gaius is letting me and the whole church here use his home. He also sends greetings to you, as do Erastus, the city treasurer, and our brother Quartus. [[24]The grace of our Lord Jesus Christ be with all of you. Amen.][n]

HeartCry

Loneliness **Are you feeling isolated? Do you feel like no one in the world understands or cares? Let your heart cry . . .**

What's up, Lord? I'm feeling pretty down. I'm so lonely I think it will kill me. I wish I had someone to really be down for me. I need to have some folks who've got my back. I can't seem to just relax and be real. It's like no one gets me. I feel like I'm alone even when I'm with people. I don't get it. Is something wrong with me? Why do I feel so rejected? I need help. I need you.

I've got your back, child. You are never alone; I am always with you. People will fail you, but I never will. **Psalm 68:6; John 8:29**

[25]Glory to God who can make you strong in faith by the Good News that I tell people and by the message about Jesus Christ. The message about Christ is the secret that was hidden for long ages past but is now made known. [26]It has been made clear through the writings of the prophets. And by the command of the eternal God it is made known to all nations that they might believe and obey.

[27]To the only wise God be glory forever through Jesus Christ! Amen.

16:24 The . . . Amen. Some Greek copies do not contain the bracketed text.

PAUL SPIT REAL TRUTH ABOUT REAL SIN

This book is a letter written by Paul to the church at Corinth. It is raw because it deals with *real* problems of *real* people. The church at Corinth was a new group of Christians. They were street and had every kind of sin issue you could think of. They were sleeping around (straight and gay), worshiping idols, having orgies, drinking and stealing right in the church! They needed to be taught how to live in the Kingdom of God. So, Paul dealt openly with their dirty laundry. Paul spit real truth about real sin: if you buy into certain lifestyles and practices you are "unrighteous" and "deceived." God straight up won't bless your mess!

Paul's letter makes it plain that the love of Jesus will outdo any sin you can imagine. It is a love that doesn't turn a blind eye but neither does it keep a laundry list of your sins. Jesus' real love doesn't bash you over the head when you are sincerely trying to kick a sin habit. Instead, it patiently speaks to the root cause to bring healing. The main reason Paul wrote this letter to the church at Corinth was to make it plain that folks in the church should live their lives based on the true Word of God; loving and honoring God and loving and respecting each other.

1 From Paul. God called me to be an apostle of Christ Jesus because that is what God wanted. Also from Sosthenes, our brother in Christ.

²To the church of God in Corinth, to you who have been made holy in Christ Jesus. You were called to be God's holy people with all people everywhere who pray in the name of the Lord Jesus Christ—their Lord and ours:

³Grace and peace to you from God our Father and the Lord Jesus Christ.

PAUL GIVES THANKS TO GOD

⁴I always thank my God for you because of the grace God has given you in Christ Jesus. ⁵I thank God because in Christ you have been made rich in every way, in all your speaking and in all your knowledge. ⁶Just as our witness about Christ has been guaranteed to you, ⁷so you have every gift from God while you wait for our Lord Jesus Christ to come again. ⁸Jesus will keep you strong until the end so that there will be no wrong in you on the day our Lord Jesus Christ comes again. ⁹God, who has called you into fellowship with his Son, Jesus Christ our Lord, is faithful.

of you says, "I follow Paul"; another says, "I follow Apollos"; another says, "I follow Peter"; and another says, "I follow Christ." ¹³Christ has been divided up into different groups! Did Paul die on the cross for you? No! Were you baptized in the name of Paul? No! ¹⁴I thank God I did not baptize any of you except Crispus and Gaius ¹⁵so that now no one can say you were baptized in my name. ¹⁶(I also baptized the family of Stephanas, but I do not remember that I baptized anyone else.) ¹⁷Christ did not send me to baptize people but to preach the Good News. And he sent me to preach the Good News without using words of human wisdom so that the cross[n] of Christ would not lose its power.

CHRIST IS GOD'S POWER AND WISDOM

¹⁸The teaching about the cross is foolishness to those who are being lost, but to us who are being saved it is the power of God. ¹⁹It is written in the Scriptures:

"I will cause the wise to lose their
    wisdom;
I will make the wise unable to
    understand."   *Isaiah 29:14*

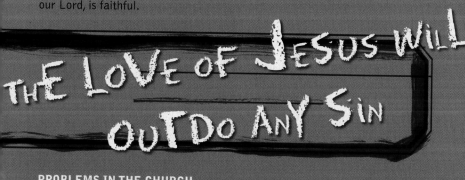

THE LOVE OF JESUS WILL OUTDO ANY SIN

PROBLEMS IN THE CHURCH

¹⁰I beg you, brothers and sisters, by the name of our Lord Jesus Christ that all of you agree with each other and not be split into groups. I beg that you be completely joined together by having the same kind of thinking and the same purpose. ¹¹My brothers and sisters, some people from Chloe's family have told me quite plainly that there are quarrels among you. ¹²This is what I mean: One

²⁰Where is the wise person? Where is the educated person? Where is the skilled talker of this world? God has made the wisdom of the world foolish. ²¹In the wisdom of God the world did not know God through its own wisdom. So God chose to use the message that sounds foolish to save those who believe. ²²The Jews ask for miracles, and the Greeks want wisdom. ²³But we preach a

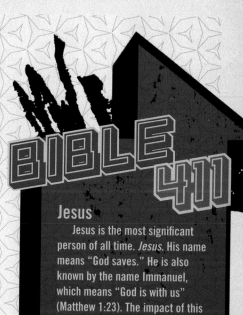

BIBLE 411

Jesus

Jesus is the most significant person of all time. *Jesus*. His name means "God saves." He is also known by the name Immanuel, which means "God is with us" (Matthew 1:23). The impact of this one life on our world is undeniable. He was at the same time truly God and truly a man, fully divine and fully human. He showed that all people are created equal and are important in God's sight. As a young adult, Jesus mixed with the poor, the oppressed, and sinners. He challenged the evils of the religious system of the day, taught the truth about God, and proved he was God's Son by his miracles of healing and even raising the dead. He did all that he did in order for people to know that there is forgiveness of sins through Jesus Christ alone. In fact, Jesus is also called "the second Adam." Just as sin came into the world by the first Adam, people are made right with God and have true life through relationship with this second Adam (Romans 5:12-19). Faith in Jesus produces a life infused with the character of God. By his life, death, and resurrection from the dead, Jesus truly lives up to his name— God is with us!

 1:17 cross Paul uses the cross as a picture of the Good News, the story of Christ's death and rising from the dead for people's sins. The cross, or Christ's death, was God's way to save people.

OVERCOMING

▶ JEALOUSY

Jealousy is a tricky sin. It doesn't seem like a sin at all, but the root of it and the affects of it go deep into your heart. Jealousy will cause you to envy those who may be more popular, better looking or richer than you. Jealousy can destroy your relationships, with God and others.

The Bible tells us in James 3:16, "Where jealousy and selfishness are, there will be confusion and every kind of evil." Envying others will cause you to be discontent with your own life. It can make you resentful and bitter. There will always be someone better off than you. Instead of bemoaning the things you don't have, try being thankful for what you have been given. A jealous spirit is greedy and demanding. It will alienate you from your world. A thankful heart brings joy and hope and will enable you to live life to the fullest and be at peace with those around you.

---

crucified Christ. This causes the Jews to stumble and is foolishness to non-Jews. [24] But Christ is the power of God and the wisdom of God to those people God has called—Jews and Greeks. [25] Even the foolishness of God is wiser than human wisdom, and the weakness of God is stronger than human strength.

[26] Brothers and sisters, look at what you were when God called you. Not many of you were wise in the way the world judges wisdom. Not many of you had great influence. Not many of you came from important families. [27] But God chose the foolish things of the world to shame the wise, and he chose the weak things of the world to shame the strong. [28] He chose what the world thinks is unimportant and what the world looks down on and thinks is nothing in order to destroy what the world thinks is important. [29] God did this so that no one can brag in his presence. [30] Because of God you are in Christ Jesus, who has become for us wisdom from God. In Christ we are put right with God, and have been made holy, and have been set free from sin. [31] So, as the Scripture says, "If people want to brag, they should brag only about the Lord."[n]

THE MESSAGE OF CHRIST'S DEATH

2 Dear brothers and sisters, when I came to you, I did not come preaching God's secret[n] with fancy words or a show of human wisdom. [2] I decided that while I was with you I would forget about everything except Jesus Christ and his death on the cross. [3] So when I came to you, I was weak and fearful and trembling. [4] My teaching and preaching were not with words of human wisdom that persuade people but with proof of the power that the Spirit gives. [5] This was so that your faith would be in God's power and not in human wisdom.

GOD'S WISDOM

[6] However, I speak a wisdom to those who are mature. But this wisdom is not from this world or from the rulers of this world, who are losing their power. [7] I speak God's secret wisdom, which he has kept hidden. Before the world began, God planned this wisdom for our glory. [8] None of the rulers of this world understood it. If they had, they would not have crucified the Lord of glory. [9] But as it is written in the Scriptures:

"No one has ever seen this,
   and no one has ever heard about it.
No one has ever imagined
   what God has prepared for those
   who love him."   *Isaiah 64:4*

[10] But God has shown us these things through the Spirit.

The Spirit searches out all things, even the deep secrets of God. [11] Who knows the thoughts that another person has? Only a person's spirit that lives within him knows his thoughts. It is the same with God. No one knows the thoughts of God except the Spirit of God. [12] Now we did not receive the spirit of the world, but we received the Spirit that is from God so that we can know all that God has given us. [13] And we speak about these things, not with words taught us by human wisdom but with words taught us by the Spirit. And so we explain spiritual truths to spiritual people. [14] A person who does not have the Spirit does not accept the truths that come from the Spirit of God. That person thinks they are foolish and cannot understand them, because they can only be judged to be true by the Spirit. [15] The spiritual person is able to judge all things, but no one can judge him. The Scripture says:

1:31 "If . . . Lord." Quotation from Jeremiah 9:24.   **2:1 God's secret** Some Greek copies read "God's message."

[16]"Who has known the mind of the Lord?
Who has been able to teach him?"   *Isaiah 40:13*
But we have the mind of Christ.

FOLLOWING PEOPLE IS WRONG

3 Brothers and sisters, in the past I could not talk to you as I talk to spiritual people. I had to talk to you as I would to people without the Spirit—babies in Christ. [2]The teaching I gave you was like milk, not solid food, because you were not able to take solid food. And even now you are not ready. [3]You are still not spiritual, because there is jealousy and quarreling among you, and this shows that you are not spiritual. You are acting like people of the world. [4]One of you says, "I belong to Paul," and another says, "I belong to Apollos." When you say things like this, you are acting like people of the world.

[5]Is Apollos important? No! Is Paul important? No! We are only servants of God who helped you believe. Each one of us did the work God gave us to do. [6]I planted the seed, and Apollos watered it. But God is the One who made it grow. [7]So the one who plants is not important, and the one who waters is not important. Only God, who makes things grow, is important. [8]The one who plants and the one who waters have the same purpose, and each will be rewarded for his own work. [9]We are God's workers, working together; you are like God's farm, God's house.

[10]Using the gift God gave me, I laid the foundation of that house like an expert builder. Others are building on that foundation, but all people should be careful how they build on it. [11]The foundation that has already been laid is Jesus Christ, and no one can lay down any other foundation. [12]But if people build on that foundation, using gold, silver, jewels, wood, grass, or straw, [13]their work will be clearly seen, because the Day of Judgment[n] will make it visible. That Day will appear with fire, and the fire will test everyone's work to show what sort of work it was. [14]If the building that has been put on the foundation still stands, the builder will get a reward. [15]But if the building is burned up, the builder will suffer loss. The builder will be saved, but it will be as one who escaped from a fire.

[16]Don't you know that you are God's temple and that God's Spirit lives in you? [17]If anyone destroys God's temple, God will destroy that person, because God's temple is holy and you are that temple.

[18]Do not fool yourselves. If you think you are wise in this world, you should become a fool so that you can become truly wise, [19]because the wisdom of this world is foolishness with God. It is written in the Scriptures, "He catches those who are wise in their own clever traps."[n] [20]It is also written in the Scriptures, "The Lord knows what wise people think. He knows their thoughts are just a puff of wind."[n] [21]So you should not brag about human leaders. All things belong to you: [22]Paul, Apollos, and Peter; the world, life, death, the present, and the future—all these belong to you. [23]And you belong to Christ, and Christ belongs to God.

APOSTLES ARE SERVANTS OF CHRIST

4 People should think of us as servants of Christ, the ones God has trusted with his secrets. [2]Now in this way those who are trusted with something valuable must show they are worthy of that trust. [3]As for myself, I do not care if I am judged by you or by any human court. I do not even judge myself. [4]I know of no wrong I have done, but this does not make me right before the Lord. The Lord is the One who judges me. [5]So do not judge before the right time; wait until the Lord comes. He will bring to light things that are now hidden in darkness, and will make known the secret purposes of people's hearts. Then God will praise each one of them.

[6]Brothers and sisters, I have used Apollos and myself as examples so you could learn through us the meaning of the saying, "Follow only what is written in the Scriptures." Then you will not be more proud of one person than another. [7]Who says you are better than others? What do you have that was not given to you? And if it was given to you, why do you brag as if you did not receive it as a gift?

[8]You think you already have everything you need. You think you are rich. You think you have become kings without us. I wish you really were kings so we could be kings together with you. [9]But it seems to me that God has put us apostles in last place, like those sentenced to die. We are like a show for the whole world to see—angels and people. [10]We are fools for Christ's sake, but you are very wise in Christ. We are weak, but you are strong. You receive honor, but we are shamed. [11]Even to this very hour we do not have enough to eat or drink or to wear. We are often beaten, and we have no homes in which to live. [12]We work hard with our own hands for our food. When people curse us, we bless them. When they hurt us, we put up with it. [13]When they tell evil lies about us, we speak nice words about them. Even today, we are treated as though we were the garbage of the world—the filth of the earth.

[14]I am not trying to make you feel ashamed. I am writing this to give you a warning as my own dear children. [15]For though you may have ten thousand teachers in Christ, you do not have many fathers. Through the Good News I became your father in Christ Jesus, [16]so I beg you, please follow my example. [17]That is why I am sending to you Timothy, my son in the Lord. I love Timothy, and he is faithful. He will help you remember my way of life in Christ Jesus, just as I teach it in all the churches everywhere.

[18]Some of you have become proud, thinking that I will not come to you again. [19]But I will come to you very soon

---

3:13 Day of Judgment The day Christ will come to judge all people and take his people home to live with him.   **3:19 "He . . . traps."** Quotation from Job 5:13.   **3:20 "The Lord . . . wind."** Quotation from Psalm 94:11.

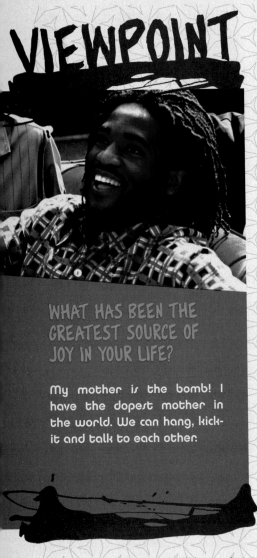

VIEWPOINT

WHAT HAS BEEN THE GREATEST SOURCE OF JOY IN YOUR LIFE?

My mother is the bomb! I have the dopest mother in the world. We can hang, kick-it and talk to each other.

if the Lord wishes. Then I will know what the proud ones do, not what they say, [20]because the kingdom of God is present not in talk but in power. [21]Which do you want: that I come to you with punishment or with love and gentleness?

WICKEDNESS IN THE CHURCH

5 It is actually being said that there is sexual sin among you. And it is a kind that does not happen even among people who do not know God. A man there has his father's wife. [2]And you are proud! You should have been filled with sadness so that the man who did this should be put out of your group. [3]I am not there with you in person, but I am with you in spirit. And I have already judged the man who did that sin as if I were really there. [4]When you meet together in the name of our Lord Jesus, and I meet with you in spirit with the power of our Lord Jesus, [5]then hand this man over to Satan. So his sinful self[n] will be destroyed, and his spirit will be saved on the day of the Lord.

[6]Your bragging is not good. You know the saying, "Just a little yeast makes the whole batch of dough rise." [7]Take out all the old yeast so that you will be a new batch of dough without yeast, which you really are. For Christ, our Passover lamb, has been sacrificed. [8]So let us celebrate this feast, but not with the bread that has the old yeast—the yeast of sin and wickedness. Let us celebrate this feast with the bread that has no yeast—the bread of goodness and truth.

[9]I wrote you in my earlier letter not to associate with those who sin sexually. [10]But I did not mean you should not associate with those of this world who sin sexually, or with the greedy, or robbers, or those who worship idols. To get away from them you would have to leave this world. [11]I am writing to tell you that you must not associate with those who call themselves believers in Christ but who sin sexually, or are greedy, or worship idols, or abuse others with words, or get drunk, or cheat people. Do not even eat with people like that.

[12-13]It is not my business to judge those who are not part of the church. God will judge them. But you must judge the people who are part of the church. The Scripture says, "You must get rid of the evil person among you."[n]

JUDGING PROBLEMS AMONG CHRISTIANS

6 When you have something against another Christian, how can you bring yourself to go before judges who are not right with God? Why do you not let God's people decide who is right? [2]Surely you know that God's people will judge the world. So if you are to judge the world, are you not able to judge small cases as well? [3]You know that in the future we will judge angels, so surely we can judge the ordinary things of this life. [4]If you have ordinary cases that must be judged, are you going to appoint people as judges who mean nothing to the church? [5]I say this to shame you. Surely there is someone among you wise enough to judge a complaint between believers. [6]But now one believer goes to court against another believer—and you do this in front of unbelievers!

[7]The fact that you have lawsuits against each other shows that you are already defeated. Why not let yourselves be wronged? Why not let yourselves be cheated? [8]But you yourselves do wrong and cheat, and you do this to other believers!

[9-10]Surely you know that the people who do wrong will not inherit God's kingdom. Do not be fooled. Those who sin sexually, worship idols, take part in adultery, those who are male prostitutes, or men who have sexual relations with other men, those who steal, are greedy, get drunk, lie about others, or rob—these people will not inherit God's kingdom. [11]In the past, some of you were like that, but you were washed clean. You were made holy, and you were made right with God in the name of the Lord Jesus Christ and in the Spirit of our God.

USE YOUR BODIES FOR GOD'S GLORY

[12]"I am allowed to do all things," but not all things are good for me to do. "I am allowed to do all things," but I will not let anything make me its slave. [13]"Food is for the stomach, and the stomach for food," but God will destroy them both. The body is not for sexual sin but for the Lord, and the Lord is for the body. [14]By his power God has raised the Lord from the dead and will also raise

5:5 sinful self Literally, "flesh." This could also mean his body.   **5:12-13 "You . . . you."** Quotation from Deuteronomy 17:7; 19:19; 22:21, 24; 24:7.

us from the dead. [15]Surely you know that your bodies are parts of Christ himself. So I must never take the parts of Christ and join them to a prostitute! [16]It is written in the Scriptures, "The two will become one body."[n] So you should know that anyone who joins with a prostitute becomes one body with the prostitute. [17]But the one who joins with the Lord is one spirit with the Lord.

[18]So run away from sexual sin. Every other sin people do is outside their bodies, but those who sin sexually sin against their own bodies. [19]You should know that your body is a temple for the Holy Spirit who is in you. You have received the Holy Spirit from God. So you do not belong to yourselves, [20]because you were bought by God for a price. So honor God with your bodies.

6:16 "The two . . . body." Quotation from Genesis 2:24.

ABOUT MARRIAGE

7 Now I will discuss the things you wrote me about. It is good for a man not to have sexual relations with a woman. [2]But because sexual sin is a danger, each man should have his own wife, and each woman should have her own husband. [3]The husband should give his wife all that he owes her as his wife. And the wife should give her husband all that she owes him as her husband. [4]The wife does not have full rights over her own body; her husband shares them. And the husband does not have full rights over his own body; his wife shares them. [5]Do not refuse to give your bodies to each other, unless you both agree to stay away from sexual relations for a time so you can give your time to prayer. Then come

THE SCRIPT

Jesus Heals the Lepers
Luke 17:11-19

Once again, Jesus headed toward Jerusalem,
Crossing the border between Galilee and the Samaritans.
This was a perilous piece of land full of prejudice and hate.
Incredulous were the Jews and the Samaritans were just as irate.
Never coming together to make their fate better,
They just lived in a mental ghetto; shackled by racism's fetters.
Jesus entered one town where he was run down by ten men
Accursed with leprosy-diseased skin.
They kept their distance 'cause they weren't supposed to get near men.
But they insisted that Jesus was gonna be hearing them.
So they screamed and shouted aloud, "Lord, have mercy!"
   Jesus heard it and he saw them and said,
      "First be obedient to the law: go and show
         yourselves to the priest!"

They all accepted what he told them and stepped out from first to least,
And while they were leaving him, they all became clean.
But one of the men, while it was happening, came back and fell at Jesus' feet!
"I praise ya, Masta. Thank ya, Jesus!" he repeated and repeated!
This man was Samaritan, so his accent was deep.
Jesus, clearly intrigued, said, "Hold up, wait a minute.
I healed ten men, where are the other nine so-called Israeli citizens?
Is this the new Jewish trend;
To be hateful and ungrateful to God; leaving true praise up to Samaritans?"
So then Jesus said to him, "Get on up and go my friend.
You're healed; your faith caused you to transcend.
No need to depend on racial files to get you in.
From now on I extend my favor to all men.

Take this with you: Be grateful to God for all he has done in your life. But more importantly, be grateful to God for who he is.

together again so Satan cannot tempt you because of a lack of self-control. [6]I say this to give you permission to stay away from sexual relations for a time. It is not a command to do so. [7]I wish that everyone were like me, but each person has his own gift from God. One has one gift, another has another gift.

[8]Now for those who are not married and for the widows I say this: It is good for them to stay unmarried as I am. [9]But if they cannot control themselves, they should marry. It is better to marry than to burn with sexual desire.

[10]Now I give this command for the married people. (The command is not from me; it is from the Lord.) A wife should not leave her husband. [11]But if she does leave, she must not marry again, or she should make up with her husband. Also the husband should not divorce his wife.

[12]For all the others I say this (I am saying this, not the Lord): If a Christian man has a wife who is not a believer, and she is happy to live with him, he must not divorce her. [13]And if a Christian woman has a husband who is not a believer, and he is happy to live with her, she must not divorce him. [14]The husband who is not a believer is made holy through his believing wife. And the wife who is not a be-

He's got answers

It seems as if a lot of people who call themselves Christian don't behave any better than anyone else. So what's the difference?

You go into a burger joint and there are two teenage guys standing side-by-side. They are dressed in the same uniform. Both do the same work. Both behave the same. You can't tell much difference between them. But one is a hired hand, working for minimum wage. The other is the owner's son. One day he will own the place.

One big difference is that Christians are called the children of God and are joint heirs with Christ. That means that, one day, regardless of what they look like on the outside, they will share in the unlimited wealth, power, and glory of God. When God saves a person, he changes him. He becomes a whole new creature. It doesn't mean he becomes better than the next guy. It means he becomes better than he used to be. What you are seeing is a work in progress. Everyone who says that he has an individual relationship with Jesus Christ may not; you can't really know the real believers from the pretenders until heaven. You can't look at what is happening in someone else's life and try to predict what God will do in yours.

Read on: Romans 7, 8:14-19; 2 Corinthians 5:17

PEEP THIS:

The 1993 debut of "Kirk Franklin & the Family," became the first gospel album to go platinum—1 million units sold.

liever is made holy through her believing husband. If this were not true, your children would not be clean, but now your children are holy.

[15]But if those who are not believers decide to leave, let them leave. When this happens, the Christian man or woman is free. But God called us[n] to live in peace. [16]Wife, you don't know; maybe you will save your husband. And husband, you don't know; maybe you will save your wife.

LIVE AS GOD CALLED YOU

[17]But in any case each one of you should continue to live the way God has given you to live—the way you were when God called you. This is a rule I make in all the churches. [18]If a man was already circumcised when he was called, he should not undo his circumcision. If a man was without circumcision when he was called, he should not be circumcised. [19]It is not important if a man is circumcised or not. The important thing is obeying God's commands. [20]Each one of you should stay the way you were when God called you. [21]If you were a slave when God called you, do not let that bother you. But if you can be free,

7:15 us Some Greek copies read "you."

then make good use of your freedom. [22]Those who were slaves when the Lord called them are free persons who belong to the Lord. In the same way, those who were free when they were called are now Christ's slaves. [23]You all were bought at a great price, so do not become slaves of people. [24]Brothers and sisters, each of you should stay as you were when you were called, and stay there with God.

QUESTIONS ABOUT GETTING MARRIED

[25]Now I write about people who are not married. I have no command from the Lord about this; I give my opinion. But I can be trusted, because the Lord has shown me mercy. [26]The present time is a time of trouble, so I think it is good for you to stay the way you are. [27]If you have a wife, do not try to become free from her. If you are not married, do not try to find a wife. [28]But if you decide to marry, you have not sinned. And if a girl who has never married decides to marry, she has not sinned. But those who marry will have trouble in this life, and I want you to be free from trouble.

[29]Brothers and sisters, this is what I mean: We do not have much time left. So starting now, those who have wives should live as if they had no wives. [30]Those who are crying should live as if they were not crying. Those who are happy should live as if they were not happy. Those who buy things should live as if they own nothing. [31]Those who use the things of the world should live as if they were not using them, because this world in its present form will soon be gone.

[32]I want you to be free from worry. A man who is not married is busy with the Lord's work, trying to please the Lord. [33]But a man who is married is busy with things of the world, trying to please his wife. [34]He must think about two things—pleasing his wife and pleasing the Lord. A woman who is not married or a girl who has never married is busy with the Lord's work. She wants to be holy in body and spirit. But a married woman is busy with things of the world,

as to how she can please her husband. [35]I am saying this to help you, not to limit you. But I want you to live in the right way, to give yourselves fully to the Lord without concern for other things.

[36]If a man thinks he is not doing the right thing with the girl he is engaged to, if she is almost past the best age to marry and he feels he should marry her, he should do what he wants. They should get married. It is no sin. [37]But if a man is sure in his mind that there is no need for marriage, and has his own desires under control, and has decided not to marry the one to whom he is engaged, he is doing the right thing. [38]So the man who marries his girl does right, but the man who does not marry will do better.

> # THERE IS ONLY ONE LORD— JESUS CHRIST. ALL THINGS WERE MADE THROUGH HIM.

[39]A woman must stay with her husband as long as he lives. But if her husband dies, she is free to marry any man she wants, but she must marry another believer. [40]The woman is happier if she does not marry again. This is my opinion, but I believe I also have God's Spirit.

ABOUT FOOD OFFERED TO IDOLS

8 Now I will write about meat that is sacrificed to idols. We know that "we all have knowledge." Knowledge puffs you up with pride, but love builds up. [2]If you think you know something, you do not yet know anything as you should. [3]But if any person loves God, that person is known by God.

[4]So this is what I say about eating meat sacrificed to idols: We know that an idol is really nothing in the world, and we know there is only one God. [5]Even though there are things called gods, in heaven or on earth (and there are many "gods" and "lords"), [6]for us there is only one God—our Father. All things came from him, and we live for him. And there is only one Lord—Jesus Christ. All things were made through him, and we also were made through him.

[7]But not all people know this. Some people are still so used to idols that when they eat meat, they still think of it as being sacrificed to an idol. Because their conscience is weak, when they eat it, they feel guilty. [8]But food will not bring us closer to God. Refusing to eat does not make us less pleasing to God, and eating does not make us better in God's sight.

[9]But be careful that your freedom does not cause those who are weak in faith to fall into sin. [10]Suppose one of you who has knowledge eats in an idol's temple.[n] Someone who is weak in faith might see you eating there and be encouraged to eat meat sacrificed to idols while thinking it is wrong to do so. [11]This weak believer for whom Christ died is ruined because of your "knowledge." [12]When you sin against your brothers and sisters in Christ like this and cause them to do what they feel is wrong, you are also sinning against Christ. [13]So if the food I eat causes them to fall into sin, I will never eat meat again so that I will not cause any of them to sin.

PAUL IS LIKE THE OTHER APOSTLES

9 I am a free man. I am an apostle. I have seen Jesus our Lord. You people are all an example of my work in the Lord. [2]If others do not accept me as an apostle, surely you do, because you are proof that I am an apostle in the Lord.

 8:10 idol's temple Building where a god is worshiped.

³This is the answer I give people who want to judge me: ⁴Do we not have the right to eat and drink? ⁵Do we not have the right to bring a believing wife with us when we travel as do the other apostles and the Lord's brothers and Peter? ⁶Are Barnabas and I the only ones who must work to earn our living? ⁷No soldier ever serves in the army and pays his own salary. No one ever plants a vineyard without eating some of the grapes. No person takes care of a flock without drinking some of the milk.

⁸I do not say this by human authority; God's law also says the same thing. ⁹It is written in the law of Moses: "When an ox is working in the grain, do not cover its mouth to keep it from eating."ⁿ When God said this, was he thinking only about oxen? No. ¹⁰He was really talking about us. Yes, that Scripture was written for us, because it goes on to say: "The one who plows and the one who works in the grain should hope to get some of the grain for their work." ¹¹Since we planted spiritual seed among you, is it too much if we should harvest material things? ¹²If others have the right to get something from you, surely we have this right, too. But we do not use it. No, we put up with everything ourselves so that we will not keep anyone from believing the Good News of Christ. ¹³Surely you know that those who work at the Temple get their food from the Temple, and those who serve at the altar get part of what is offered at the altar. ¹⁴In the same way, the Lord has commanded that those who tell the Good News should get their living from this work.

¹⁵But I have not used any of these rights. And I am not writing this now to get anything from you. I would rather die than to have my reason for bragging taken away. ¹⁶Telling the Good News does not give me any reason for bragging. Telling the Good News is my duty—something I must do. And how terrible it will be for me if I do not tell the Good News. ¹⁷If I preach because it is my own choice, I have a reward. But if I preach and it is not my choice to do so, I am only doing the duty that was given to me. ¹⁸So what reward do I get? This is my reward: that when I tell the Good News I can offer it freely. I do not use my full rights in my work of preaching the Good News.

> THE LORD HAS COMMANDED THAT THOSE WHO TELL THE GOOD NEWS SHOULD GET THEIR LIVING FROM THIS WORK.

¹⁹I am free and belong to no one. But I make myself a slave to all people to win as many as I can. ²⁰To the Jews I became like a Jew to win the Jews. I myself am not ruled by the law. But to those who are ruled by the law I became like a person who is ruled by the law. I did this to win those who are ruled by the law. ²¹To those who are without the law I became like a person who is without the law. I did this to win those people who are without the law. (But really, I am not without God's law—I am ruled by Christ's law.) ²²To those who are weak, I became weak so I could win the weak. I have become all things to all people so I could save some of them in any way possible. ²³I do all this because of the Good News and so I can share in its blessings.

²⁴You know that in a race all the runners run, but only one gets the prize. So run to win! ²⁵All those who compete in the games use self-control so they can win a crown. That crown is an earthly thing that lasts only a short time, but our crown will never be destroyed. ²⁶So I do not run without a goal. I fight like a boxer who is hitting something—not just the air. ²⁷I treat my body hard and make it my slave so that I myself will not be disqualified after I have preached to others.

WARNINGS FROM ISRAEL'S PAST

10 Brothers and sisters, I want you to know what happened to our ancestors who followed Moses. They were all under the cloud and all went through the sea. ²They were all baptized as followers of Moses in the cloud and in the sea. ³They all ate the same spiritual food, ⁴and all drank the same spiritual drink. They drank from that spiritual rock that followed them, and that rock was Christ. ⁵But God was not pleased with most of them, so they died in the desert.

⁶And these things happened as examples for us, to stop us from wanting evil things as those people did. ⁷Do not worship idols, as some of them did. Just as it is written in the Scriptures: "They sat down to eat and drink, and then they got up and sinned sexually."ⁿ ⁸We must not take part in sexual sins, as some of them did. In one day twenty-three thousand of them died because of their sins. ⁹We must not test Christ as some of them did; they were killed by snakes. ¹⁰Do not complain as some of them did; they were killed by the angel that destroys.

¹¹The things that happened to those people are examples. They were written down to teach us, because we live in a time when all these things of the past have reached their goal. ¹²If you think you are strong, you should be careful not to fall. ¹³The only temptation that has come to you is that which everyone has. But you can trust God, who will not permit you to be tempted more than you

---

9:9 "When an ox . . . eating." Quotation from Deuteronomy 25:4. 10:7 "They . . . sexually." Quotation from Exodus 32:6.

REAL RHYMES:

7 X 70

BY PLATINUM SOULS

THE PLACES I'VE BEEN IN THE MIDST OF SIN COULD HAVE SEPARATED ME FROM HIM.
BUT HIS CONSTANT ASSURANCE THAT HIS BLOOD WAS STILL THE CURE AND FOR SURE THE BALM FOR MY PAIN KEPT
  ME SANE.
FOR MANY WOULD HAVE LED ME TO BELIEVE THAT MY FALLS WERE UNFORGIVABLE—THAT I WAS UNDELIVERABLE.
BUT I CHOSE TO SEARCH THE WORD RATHER THAN TO BELIEVE EVERY PROPHETIC UTTERANCE I HEARD.
THEN, THROUGH MY TEARS, I FOUND PEACE FOR MY FEARS.
AND THE MORE I SOUGHT HIS WISDOM THE MORE HE DREW ME NEAR.
NOW, I SEE CLEAR. NO MORE DESPAIR.
SO I WANT ALL WHO CHOOSE TO LISTEN, TO DIGEST THIS LESSON HERE OF HOW ONE WITH TRANSGRESSIONS—
  LIKE ME—CAN BE FREE.
'CAUSE WHAT I SEE IS MANY PREACHING FALSE TEACHINGS THAT GOD IS VENGEFUL OR FULL OF SPITE.
BUT, HAVE COME TO DECLARE THAT HE STILL LOVE US WRONG OR RIGHT.
HE STILL SEES US AS PURE, IN SPITE OF WHAT WE DID THAT NIGHT.
FOR HE IS A GRACIOUS GOD AND HIS MERCY IS INFINITE.
CAN YOU FEEL IT? FORGIVENESS 7 X 70.
SEE, ONLY A HEAVENLY FATHER COULD UNFAILING BELIEVE THAT WHEN WE LEAVE HIM TO GO OUR OWN WAY, WE WILL
  COME BACK SOME DAY.
AND WHEN WE CRY OUT TO HIM, HE DOES NOT DELAY. NO ARGUMENT OR FUSS, HE JUST COMES AND RESCUES US.
HE IS WHAT SUPERMAN WISHES HE WAS OR COULD BE. EVERYDAY FOREVER GOOD TO ME.
SO IF WHAT I SPEAK GOES AGAINST YOUR RELIGIOSITY, HE WILL SILENCE YOUR TONGUE FROM RISING UP AGAINST THIS
  TREE.
FOR I HAVE GROWN IN THE GARDEN OF HE WHO CREATED MY SOUL.
AND ONLY HE KNOWS THAT, DESPITE MY FAULTS, HE HAS RESCUED ME FROM MY FOES.
GIVEN ME POETIC LICENSE TO TONGUE—LASH THOSE WHO VERBALLY BASH FALLEN SOLDIERS INSTEAD OF PRAYING
  FOR THEM.
WHEN WILL THE BACKBITING COME TO AN END?
BECAUSE IN THE END, THOSE WHO SPEAK ILL ARE EQUAL TO THE ONE WHO COMMITTED MURDER, ADULTERY, OR THE
  ONE WHO FORSOOK THE ASSEMBLY OF THE SAINTS.
IT'S IN EVERY BIBLE. DON'T TELL ME THAT IT AIN'T.
SO FOR THOSE WHO ARE TAINTED, LET ME SHOW YOU WHAT GOD'S WORD SAID HE DID:
"HE WAS WOUNDED FOR OUR TRANSGRESSIONS, BRUISED FOR OUR INIQUITIES, THE CHASTISEMENT FOR OUR PEACE
  WAS UPON HIM AND BY HIS STRIPES WE ARE ALL HEALED."
THUS IS WRITTEN IN THE FIFTH VERSE OF ISAIAH 53.
I DON'T WANT YOU TO BELIEVE ME. TAKE A LOOK FOR YOURSELF AND SEE.
BUT KNOW THAT HIS GRACE IS NOT A THING TO BE TAKEN LIGHTLY.
SO, IF YOU'RE GOING WHERE I'VE BEEN, JUST KNOW THAT I PRAY FOR YOU NIGHTLY,
THAT YOU WILL RIGHTLY DIVIDE THE WORD OF TRUTH
AND SURVIVE EVERY TEST AND TRIAL TO PRODUCE GOOD FRUIT.

can stand. But when you are tempted, he will also give you a way to escape so that you will be able to stand it.

[14]So, my dear friends, run away from the worship of idols. [15]I am speaking to you as to reasonable people; judge for yourselves what I say. [16]We give thanks for the cup of blessing,[n] which is a sharing in the blood of Christ. And the bread that we break is a sharing in the body of Christ. [17]Because there is one loaf of bread, we who are many are one body, because we all share that one loaf.

[18]Think about the Israelites: Do not those who eat the sacrifices share in the altar? [19]I do not mean that the food sacrificed to an idol is important. I do not mean that an idol is anything at all. [20]But I say that what is sacrificed to idols is offered to demons, not to God. And I do not want you to share anything with demons. [21]You cannot drink the cup of the Lord and the cup of demons also. You cannot share in the Lord's table and the table of demons. [22]Are we trying to make the Lord jealous? We are not stronger than he is, are we?

HOW TO USE CHRISTIAN FREEDOM

[23]"We are allowed to do all things," but not all things are good for us to do. "We are allowed to do all things," but not all things help others grow stronger. [24]Do not look out only for yourselves. Look out for the good of others also.

[25]Eat any meat that is sold in the meat market. Do not ask questions about it. [26]You may eat it, "because the earth belongs to the Lord, and everything in it."[n]

[27]Those who are not believers may invite you to eat with them. If you want to go, eat anything that is put before you. Do not ask questions about it. [28]But if anyone says to you, "That food was offered to idols," do not eat it. Do not eat it because of that person who told you and because eating it might be thought to be wrong. [29]I don't mean you think it is wrong, but the other person might. But why, you ask, should my freedom be judged by someone else's conscience? [30]If I eat the meal with thankfulness, why am I criticized because of something for which I thank God?

[31]The answer is, if you eat or drink, or if you do anything, do it all for the glory of God. [32]Never do anything that might hurt others—Jews, Greeks, or God's church—[33]just as I, also, try to please everybody in every way. I am not trying to do what is good for me but what is good for most people so they can be saved.

>
>
> "WE ARE ALLOWED TO DO ALL THINGS," BUT NOT ALL THINGS ARE GOOD FOR US TO DO.

11 Follow my example, as I follow the example of Christ.

BEING UNDER AUTHORITY

[2]I praise you because you remember me in everything, and you follow closely the teachings just as I gave them to you. [3]But I want you to understand this: The head of every man is Christ, the head of a woman is the man,[n] and the head of Christ is God. [4]Every man who prays or prophesies with his head covered brings shame to his head. [5]But every woman who prays or prophesies with her head uncovered brings shame to her head. She is the same as a woman who has her head shaved. [6]If a woman does not cover her head, she should have her hair cut off. But since it is shameful for a woman to cut off her hair or to shave her head, she should cover her head. [7]But a man should not cover his head, because he is the likeness and glory of God. But woman is man's glory. [8]Man did not come from woman, but woman came from man. [9]And man was not made for woman, but woman was made for man. [10]So that is why a woman should have a symbol of authority on her head, because of the angels.

[11]But in the Lord women are not independent of men, and men are not independent of women. [12]This is true because woman came from man, but also man is born from woman. But everything comes from God. [13]Decide this for yourselves: Is it right for a woman to pray to God with her head uncovered? [14]Even nature itself teaches you that wearing long hair is shameful for a man. [15]But long hair is a woman's glory. Long hair is given to her as a covering. [16]Some people may still want to argue about this, but I would add that neither we nor the churches of God have any other practice.

THE LORD'S SUPPER

[17]In the things I tell you now I do not praise you, because when you come together you do more harm than good. [18]First, I hear that when you meet together as a church you are divided, and I believe some of this. [19](It is necessary to have differences among you so that it may be clear which of you really have God's approval.) [20]When you come together, you are not really eating the Lord's Supper.[n] [21]This is because when you eat, each person eats without waiting for the others. Some people do not get enough to eat, while others have too much to drink. [22]You can eat and drink in your own homes! You seem to think God's church is not important, and you embarrass those who are poor. What should I tell you? Should I praise you? I do not praise you for doing this.

[23]The teaching I gave you is the same teaching I received from the Lord: On the night when the Lord Jesus was

---

 10:16 cup of blessing The cup of the fruit of the vine that Christians thank God for and drink at the Lord's Supper. **10:26 "because . . . it"** Quotation from Psalms 24:1; 50:12; 89:11. **11:3 the man** This could also mean "her husband." **11:20 Lord's Supper** The meal Jesus told his followers to eat to remember him (Luke 22:14-20).

handed over to be killed, he took bread [24]and gave thanks for it. Then he broke the bread and said, "This is my body; it is[n] for you. Do this to remember me." [25]In the same way, after they ate, Jesus took the cup. He said, "This cup is the new agreement that is sealed with the blood of my death. When you drink this, do it to remember me." [26]Every time you eat this bread and drink this cup you are telling others about the Lord's death until he comes.

[27]So a person who eats the bread or drinks the cup of the Lord in a way that is not worthy of it will be guilty of sinning against the body and the blood of the Lord. [28]Look into your own hearts before you eat the bread and drink the cup, [29]because all who eat the bread and drink the cup without recognizing the body eat and drink judgment against themselves. [30]That is why many in your group are sick and weak, and some of you have died. [31]But if we judged ourselves in the right way, God would not judge us. [32]But when the Lord judges us, he disciplines us so that we will not be destroyed along with the world.

[33]So my brothers and sisters, when you come together to eat, wait for each other. [34]Anyone who is too hungry should eat at home so that in meeting together you will not bring God's judgment on yourselves. I will tell you what to do about the other things when I come.

GIFTS FROM THE HOLY SPIRIT

'12 Now, brothers and sisters, I want you to understand about spiritual gifts. [2]You know the way you lived before you were believers. You let yourselves be influenced and led away to worship idols—things that could not speak. [3]So I want you to understand that no one who is speaking with the help of God's Spirit says, "Jesus be cursed." And no one can say, "Jesus is Lord," without the help of the Holy Spirit.

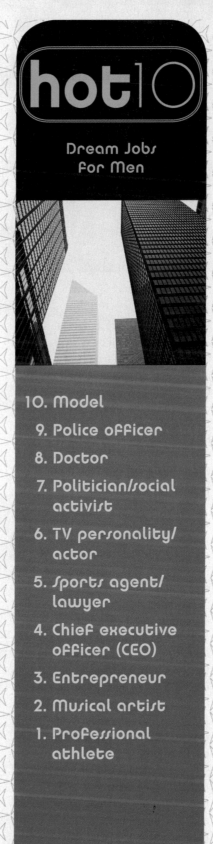

hot10

Dream Jobs for Men

10. Model

9. Police officer

8. Doctor

7. Politician/social activist

6. TV personality/actor

5. Sports agent/lawyer

4. Chief executive officer (CEO)

3. Entrepreneur

2. Musical artist

1. Professional athlete

[4]There are different kinds of gifts, but they are all from the same Spirit. [5]There are different ways to serve but the same Lord to serve. [6]And there are different ways that God works through people but the same God. God works in all of us in everything we do. [7]Something from the Spirit can be seen in each person, for the common good. [8]The Spirit gives one person the ability to speak with wisdom, and the same Spirit gives another the ability to speak with knowledge. [9]The same Spirit gives faith to one person. And, to another, that one Spirit gives gifts of healing. [10]The Spirit gives to another person the power to do miracles, to another the ability to prophesy. And he gives to another the ability to know the difference between good and evil spirits. The Spirit gives one person the ability to speak in different kinds of languages[n] and to another the ability to interpret those languages. [11]One Spirit, the same Spirit, does all these things, and the Spirit decides what to give each person.

THE BODY OF CHRIST WORKS TOGETHER

[12]A person's body is one thing, but it has many parts. Though there are many parts to a body, all those parts make only one body. Christ is like that also. [13]Some of us are Jews, and some are Greeks. Some of us are slaves, and some are free. But we were all baptized into one body through one Spirit. And we were all made to share in the one Spirit.

[14]The human body has many parts. [15]The foot might say, "Because I am not a hand, I am not part of the body." But saying this would not stop the foot from being a part of the body. [16]The ear might say, "Because I am not an eye, I am not part of the body." But saying this would not stop the ear from being a part of the body. [17]If the whole body were an eye, it would not be able to hear. If the whole body were an ear, it would not be able to smell. [18-19]If each part of the body were the same part, there would be no body.

11:24 it is Some Greek copies read "it is broken." **12:10 languages** This can also be translated "tongues."

WORLD SAYS, WORD SAYS,

FRIENDS ARE FRIENDS

It's important for you to be accepted by others, to be part of the crew. No one understands you like they do. Hang with those who look like they have it all together. So what if they have run-ins with the cops and get into trouble all the time? Who cares that they are messing around, having sex with every person they meet? They're your friends. Besides, you're not the one actually doing it.

"Whoever does not use good sense will end up among the dead" (Proverbs 21:16).

"Don't envy evil people or try to be friends with them" (Proverbs 24:1).

"I wrote you in my earlier letter not to associate with those who sin sexually" (1 Corinthians 5:9).

"Do not be fooled: 'Bad friends will ruin good habits'" (1 Corinthians 15:33).

But truly God put all the parts, each one of them, in the body as he wanted them. [20]So then there are many parts, but only one body.

[21]The eye cannot say to the hand, "I don't need you!" And the head cannot say to the foot, "I don't need you!" [22]No! Those parts of the body that seem to be the weaker are really necessary. [23]And the parts of the body we think are less deserving are the parts to which we give the most honor. We give special respect to the parts we want to hide. [24]The more respectable parts of our body need no special care. But God put the body together and gave more honor to the parts that need it [25]so our body would not be divided. God wanted the different parts to care the same for each other. [26]If one part of the body suffers, all the other parts suffer with it. Or if one part of our body is honored, all the other parts share its honor.

[27]Together you are the body of Christ, and each one of you is a part of that body. [28]In the church God has given a place first to apostles, second to prophets, and third to teachers. Then God has given a place to those who do miracles, those who have gifts of healing, those who can help others, those who are able to govern, and those who can speak in different languages.[n] [29]Not all are apostles. Not all are prophets. Not all are teachers. Not all do miracles. [30]Not all have gifts of healing. Not all speak in different languages. Not all interpret those languages. [31]But you should truly want to have the greater gifts.

LOVE IS THE GREATEST GIFT

And now I will show you the best way of all.

13 I may speak in different languages[n] of people or even angels. But if I do not have love, I am only a noisy bell or a crashing cymbal. [2]I may have the gift of prophecy. I may understand all the secret things of God and have all knowledge, and I may have faith so great I can move mountains. But even with all these things, if I do not have love, then I am nothing. [3]I may give away everything I have, and I may even give my body as an offering to be burned.[n] But I gain nothing if I do not have love.

[4]Love is patient and kind. Love is not jealous, it does not brag, and it is not proud. [5]Love is not rude, is not selfish, and does not get upset with others. Love does not count up wrongs that have been done. [6]Love takes no pleasure in evil but rejoices over the truth. [7]Love patiently accepts all things. It always trusts, always hopes, and always endures.

[8]Love never ends. There are gifts of prophecy, but they will be ended. There are gifts of speaking in different languages, but those gifts will stop. There is the gift of knowledge, but it will come to an end. [9]The reason is that our knowledge and our ability to prophesy are not perfect. [10]But when perfection comes, the things that are not perfect will end. [11]When I was a child, I talked like a child, I thought like a child, I reasoned like a child. When I became a man, I stopped those childish ways. [12]It is the same with us. Now we see a dim reflection, as if we were looking into a mirror, but then we shall see clearly. Now I know only a part, but then I will know fully, as God has known me. [13]So these three things continue forever: faith, hope, and love. And the greatest of these is love.

DESIRE SPIRITUAL GIFTS

14 You should seek after love, and you should truly want to have the spiritual gifts, especially the gift of prophecy. [2]I will explain why. Those who have the gift of speaking in

---

different languages[n] are not speaking to people; they are speaking to God. No one understands them; they are speaking secret things through the Spirit. [3]But those who prophesy are speaking to people to give them strength, encouragement, and comfort. [4]The ones who speak in different languages are helping only themselves, but those who prophesy are helping the whole church. [5]I wish all of you had the gift of speaking in different kinds of languages, but more, I wish you would prophesy. Those who prophesy are greater than those who can only speak in different languages—unless someone is there who can explain what is said so that the whole church can be helped.

[6]Brothers and sisters, will it help you if I come to you speaking in different languages? No! It will help you only if I bring you a new truth or some new knowledge, or prophecy, or teaching. [7]It is the same as with lifeless things that make sounds—like a flute or a harp. If they do not make clear musical notes, you will not know what is being played. [8]And in a war, if the trumpet does not give a clear sound, who will prepare for battle? [9]It is the same with you. Unless you speak clearly with your tongue, no one can understand what you are saying. You will be talking into the air! [10]It may be true that there are all kinds of sounds in the world, and none is without meaning. [11]But unless I understand the meaning of what someone says to me, we will be like foreigners to each other. [12]It is the same with you. Since you want spiritual gifts very much, seek most of all to have the gifts that help the church grow stronger.

[13]The one who has the gift of speaking in a different language should pray for the gift to interpret what is spoken. [14]If I pray in a different language, my spirit is praying, but my mind does nothing. [15]So what should I do? I will pray with my spirit, but I will also pray with my mind. I will sing with my spirit, but I will also sing with my mind. [16]If you praise God with your spirit, those persons there without understanding cannot say amen[n] to your prayer of thanks, because they do not know what you are saying. [17]You may be thanking God in a good way, but the other person is not helped.

> LOVE IS NOT RUDE, IS NOT SELFISH, AND DOES NOT GET UPSET WITH OTHERS. LOVE DOES NOT COUNT UP WRONGS THAT HAVE BEEN DONE.

[18]I thank God that I speak in different kinds of languages more than all of you. [19]But in the church meetings I would rather speak five words I understand in order to teach others than thousands of words in a different language.

[20]Brothers and sisters, do not think like children. In evil things be like babies, but in your thinking you should be like adults. [21]It is written in the Scriptures:

> "With people who use strange
> words and foreign languages
> I will speak to these people.
> But even then they will not listen to
> me," *Isaiah 28:11-12*
> says the Lord.

[22]So the gift of speaking in different kinds of languages is a sign for those who do not believe, not for those who do believe. And prophecy is for people who believe, not for those who do not believe. [23]Suppose the whole church meets together and everyone speaks in different languages. If some people come in who do not understand or do not believe, they will say you are crazy. [24]But suppose everyone is prophesying and some people come in who do not believe or do not understand. If everyone is prophesying, their sin will be shown to them, and they will be judged by all that they hear. [25]The secret things in their hearts will be made known. So they will bow down and worship God saying, "Truly, God is with you."

MEETINGS SHOULD HELP THE CHURCH

[26]So, brothers and sisters, what should you do? When you meet together, one person has a song, and another has a teaching. Another has a new truth from God. Another speaks in a different language,[n] and another person interprets that language. The purpose of all these things should be to help the church grow strong. [27]When you meet together, if anyone speaks in a different language, it should be only two, or not more than three, who speak. They should speak one after the other, and someone should interpret. [28]But if there is no interpreter, then those who speak in a different language should be quiet in the church meeting. They should speak only to themselves and to God.

[29]Only two or three prophets should speak, and the others should judge what they say. [30]If a message from God comes to another person who is sitting, the first speaker should stop. [31]You can all prophesy one after the other. In this way all the people can be taught and encouraged. [32]The spirits of prophets are under the control of the prophets themselves. [33]God is not a God of confusion but a God of peace.

As is true in all the churches of God's people, [34]women should keep quiet in the church meetings. They are not allowed to speak, but they must yield to this rule as the law says. [35]If they want to learn something, they should ask their own

---

 14:2, 26 languages This can also be translated "tongues." **14:16 amen** To say amen means to agree with the things that were said.

GOD UNIT ✝

BEING "THE MAN"

no peace. There were warning flags all along, but even an arrest, an "I may be pregnant," and an "I'd probably have an abortion if I am" episode didn't stop me. Though many of my childhood friends had been incarcerated or were running from the law, I wasn't really affected.

I'm a strong Christian man today, but it's only because God did something great for me. When I accepted God into my life, I put all of the crazy activities of the past behind and asked him to give me an example of a real man that I could follow. He did just that and more. He put several godly men—real men—in my life. They were fathers and brothers to me, a grown man, and they all helped me to find healing in different areas. Even more important, they let me know that I didn't have a thing to prove to them. They showed me how to be "The Man" God made me to be. I still needed a fresh start and God sent me other men to show me the way. As a new Christian, God and these men taught me to change how I viewed life, and they taught me that a real man doesn't take advantage of others or play dangerous games. Now I feel like a new person, and can truly say that I am "The Man."

Okay, okay. Let's admit it. We all want to be "The Man." Since we were little tykes, we were trained to seek handshakes and pats on the back. But we were getting our *props* the wrong way! I was told that being "The Man" was all about how much money I made, how many women I'd had, and what kind of car I drove. I didn't quite look like the infamous, spellbinding movie detective Shaft, but I still spent a lot of time trying to find ways to be like him. In my teens, I jumped in bed with the first girl who would join me. I drank alcohol and abused drugs because they were the things to do. I had a lot to prove and showing scrapes, cuts, and battle scars equaled successful manhood, right?

Add to the normal pressure to be a macho man the fact that I, like many guys my age, had childhood sexual experiences with both genders, and you'll understand why I was in a rush to be rich, well thought of, and "The Man." The road to disaster doesn't always look that bad on the outside. I was having tons of fun, but inside I had

2 Corinthians 5:17—If anyone belongs to Christ, there is a new creation. The old things have gone; everything is made new!

---

husbands at home. It is shameful for a woman to speak in the church meeting. [36]Did God's teaching come from you? Or are you the only ones to whom it has come?

[37]Those who think they are prophets or spiritual persons should understand that what I am writing to you is the Lord's command. [38]Those who ignore this will be ignored by God.[n]

[39]So my brothers and sisters, you should truly want to prophesy. But do not stop people from using the gift of speaking in different kinds of languages. [40]But let everything be done in a right and orderly way.

THE GOOD NEWS ABOUT CHRIST

15 Now, brothers and sisters, I want you to remember the Good News I brought to you. You received this Good News and continue strong in it. [2]And you are being saved by it if you continue believing what I told you. If you do not, then you believed for nothing.

[3]I passed on to you what I received, of which this was most important: that Christ died for our sins, as the Scriptures say; [4]that he was buried and was raised to life on the third day as the Scriptures say; [5]and that he was seen by Peter and then by the twelve apostles. [6]After that, Jesus was seen by more than five hundred of the believers at the same time. Most of them are still living today,

---

 14:38 Those . . . God. Some Greek copies read "Those who are ignorant of this will stay ignorant."

but some have died. [7]Then he was seen by James and later by all the apostles. [8]Last of all he was seen by me—as by a person not born at the normal time. [9]All the other apostles are greater than I am. I am not even good enough to be called an apostle, because I persecuted the church of God. [10]But God's grace has made me what I am, and his grace to me was not wasted. I worked harder than all the other apostles. (But it was not I really; it was God's grace that was with me.) [11]So if I preached to you or the other apostles preached to you, we all preach the same thing, and this is what you believed.

WE WILL BE RAISED FROM THE DEAD

[12]Now since we preached that Christ was raised from the dead, why do some of you say that people will not be raised from the dead? [13]If no one is ever raised from the dead, then Christ has not been raised. [14]And if Christ has not been raised, then our preaching is worth nothing, and your faith is worth nothing. [15]And also, we are guilty of lying about God, because we testified of him that he raised Christ from the dead. But if people are not raised from the dead, then God never raised Christ. [16]If the dead are not raised, Christ has not been raised either. [17]And if Christ has not been raised, then your faith has nothing to it; you are still guilty of your sins. [18]And those in Christ who have already died are lost. [19]If our hope in Christ is for this life only, we should be pitied more than anyone else in the world.

[20]But Christ has truly been raised from the dead—the first one and proof that those who sleep in death will also be raised. [21]Death has come because of what one man did, but the rising from death also comes because of one man. [22]In Adam all of us die. In the same way, in Christ all of us will be made alive again. [23]But everyone will be raised to life in the right order. Christ was first to be raised. When Christ comes again, those who belong to him will be raised to life, [24]and then the end will come. At that time Christ will destroy all rulers, authorities, and powers, and he will hand over the kingdom to God the Father. [25]Christ must rule until he puts all enemies under his control. [26]The last enemy to be destroyed will be death. [27]The Scripture says that God put all things under his control.[n] When it says "all things" are under him, it is clear this does not include God himself. God is the One who put everything under his control. [28]After everything has been put under the Son, then he will put himself under God, who had put all things under him. Then God will be the complete ruler over everything.

[29]If the dead are never raised, what will people do who are being baptized for the dead? If the dead are not raised at all, why are people being baptized for them?

[30]And what about us? Why do we put ourselves in danger every hour? [31]I die every day. That is true, brothers and sisters, just as it is true that I brag about you in Christ Jesus our Lord. [32]If I fought wild animals in Ephesus only with human hopes, I have gained nothing. If the dead are not raised, "Let us eat and drink, because tomorrow we will die."[n]

[33]Do not be fooled: "Bad friends will ruin good habits." [34]Come back to your right way of thinking and stop sinning. Some of you do not know God—I say this to shame you.

WHAT KIND OF BODY WILL WE HAVE?

[35]But someone may ask, "How are the dead raised? What kind of body will they have?" [36]Foolish person! When you sow a seed, it must die in the ground before it can live and grow. [37]And when you sow it, it does not have the same "body" it will have later. What you sow is only a bare seed, maybe wheat or something else. [38]But God gives it a body that he has planned for it, and God gives each kind of seed its own body. [39]All things made of flesh are not the same: People have one kind of flesh, animals have another, birds have another, and fish have another. [40]Also there are heavenly bodies and earthly bodies. But the beauty of the heavenly bodies is one kind, and the beauty of the earthly bodies is another. [41]The sun has one kind of beauty, the moon has another beauty, and the stars have another. And each star is different in its beauty.

[42]It is the same with the dead who are

15:27 God put . . . control. From Psalm 8:6. **15:32 "Let us . . . die."** Quotation from Isaiah 22:13; 56:12.

raised to life. The body that is "planted" will ruin and decay, but it is raised to a life that cannot be destroyed. [43]When the body is "planted," it is without honor, but it is raised in glory. When the body is "planted," it is weak, but when it is raised, it is powerful. [44]The body that is "planted" is a physical body. When it is raised, it is a spiritual body.

There is a physical body, and there is also a spiritual body. [45]It is written in the Scriptures: "The first man, Adam, became a living person."[n] But the last Adam became a spirit that gives life. [46]The spiritual did not come first, but the physical and then the spiritual. [47]The first man came from the dust of the earth. The second man came from heaven. [48]People who belong to the earth are like the first man of earth. But those people who belong to heaven are like the man of heaven. [49]Just as we were made like the man of earth, so we will[n] also be made like the man of heaven.

[50]I tell you this, brothers and sisters: Flesh and blood cannot have a part in the kingdom of God. Something that will ruin cannot have a part in something that never ruins. [51]But look! I tell you this secret: We will not all sleep in death, but we will all be changed. [52]It will take only a second—as quickly as an eye blinks—when the last trumpet sounds. The trumpet will sound, and those who have died will be raised to live forever, and we will all be changed. [53]This body that can be destroyed must clothe itself with something that can never be destroyed. And this body that dies must clothe itself with something that can never die. [54]So this body that can be destroyed will clothe itself with that which can never be destroyed, and this body that dies will clothe itself with that which can never die. When this happens, this Scripture will be made true:

"Death is destroyed forever in
    victory."   *Isaiah 25:8*
[55]"Death, where is your victory?
    Death, where is your pain?"
                               Hosea 13:14

[56]Death's power to hurt is sin, and the power of sin is the law. [57]But we thank God! He gives us the victory through our Lord Jesus Christ.

[58]So my dear brothers and sisters, stand strong. Do not let anything move you. Always give yourselves fully to the work of the Lord, because you know that your work in the Lord is never wasted.

THE GIFT FOR OTHER BELIEVERS

16 Now I will write about the collection of money for God's people. Do the same thing I told the Galatian churches to do: [2]On the first day of every week, each one of you should put aside money as you have been blessed. Save it up so you will not have to collect money after I come. [3]When I arrive, I will send whomever you approve to take your gift to Jerusalem. I will send them with letters of introduction, [4]and if it seems good for me to go also, they will go along with me.

PAUL'S PLANS

[5]I plan to go through Macedonia, so I will come to you after I go through there. [6]Perhaps I will stay with you for a time or even all winter. Then you can help me on my trip, wherever I go. [7]I do not want to see you now just in passing. I hope to stay a longer time with you if the

---

He's got answers

Life stinks. Just one letdown after another. How do I deal with that?

"Life is pain, and anyone who says different is selling something," says the hero in a popular movie. He's not far wrong. The brown-noser in the cubicle next to you gets that promotion that you really deserved. The bonus you got this month gets eaten up in car repairs. The dog bit the mailman, the kids have the flu, the washing machine is on the fritz, and it seems everybody is looking for a handout. The rich get richer, the poor get poorer, and only the good die young.

It doesn't seem fair, but then, nobody said life is fair. The bad news is that we live in a world where bad things happen to good people. The good news is that this is not all there is. This is not the end of the story. Life doesn't end with physical death and the Bible says we can't even imagine how cool heaven will be. As bad as things can get—and they can get pretty bad—trouble cannot overcome you unless you allow it to do so. Jesus came to give you full life, even in the middle of the bad times.

Read on: John 16:33; Romans 8:18, 31-39; 2 Corinthians 4:8-10; 2 Peter 2:20; 1 John 4:4

15:45 "The first . . . person." Quotation from Genesis 2:7.   15:49 so we will Some Greek copies read "so let us."

Lord allows it. [8]But I will stay at Ephesus until Pentecost, [9]because a good opportunity for a great and growing work has been given to me now. And there are many people working against me.

[10]If Timothy comes to you, see to it that he has nothing to fear with you, because he is working for the Lord just as I am. [11]So none of you should treat Timothy as unimportant, but help him on his trip in peace so that he can come back to me. I am expecting him to come with the brothers.

[12]Now about our brother Apollos: I strongly encouraged him to visit you with the other brothers. He did not at all want to come now; he will come when he has the opportunity.

PAUL ENDS HIS LETTER

[13]Be alert. Continue strong in the faith. Have courage, and be strong. [14]Do everything in love.

[15]You know that the family of Stephanas were the first believers in Southern Greece and that they have given themselves to the service of God's people. I ask you, brothers and sisters, [16]to follow the leading of people like these and anyone else who works and serves with them.

[17]I am happy that Stephanas, Fortunatus, and Achaicus have come. You are not here, but they have filled your place. [18]They have refreshed my spirit and yours. You should recognize the value of people like these.

[19]The churches in Asia send greetings to you. Aquila and Priscilla greet you in the Lord, as does the church that meets in their house. [20]All the brothers and sisters here send greetings. Give each other a holy kiss when you meet.

[21]I, Paul, am writing this greeting with my own hand.

HeartCry

Where's Mine? **Is the desire for money and things too important to you? Are you jealous when others get the things you want? Let your heart cry . . .**

God, I just wanted to come clean on a problem that I have. I resent that people around me have things I don't have. I sound like I'm hating, but it's how I feel. I see people with houses, cars, clothes, money—all the things I want—and it seems unfair. I want to be the number one stunner on the block. It seems that cash rules everything around me. I know it should be that Christ rules everything around me, but sometimes it's hard not to want what everybody else has. Lord, help me get it straight 'cause I want to represent for you. Holla.

The question is which is the ruler of your own heart? Seek my kingdom first and then all that you need will be given to you by my hand. Matthew 6:19-34

[22]If anyone does not love the Lord, let him be separated from God—lost forever!

Come, O Lord!

[23]The grace of the Lord Jesus be with you.

[24]My love be with all of you in Christ Jesus.[n]

 16:24 My . . . Jesus. Some Greek copies add "Amen."

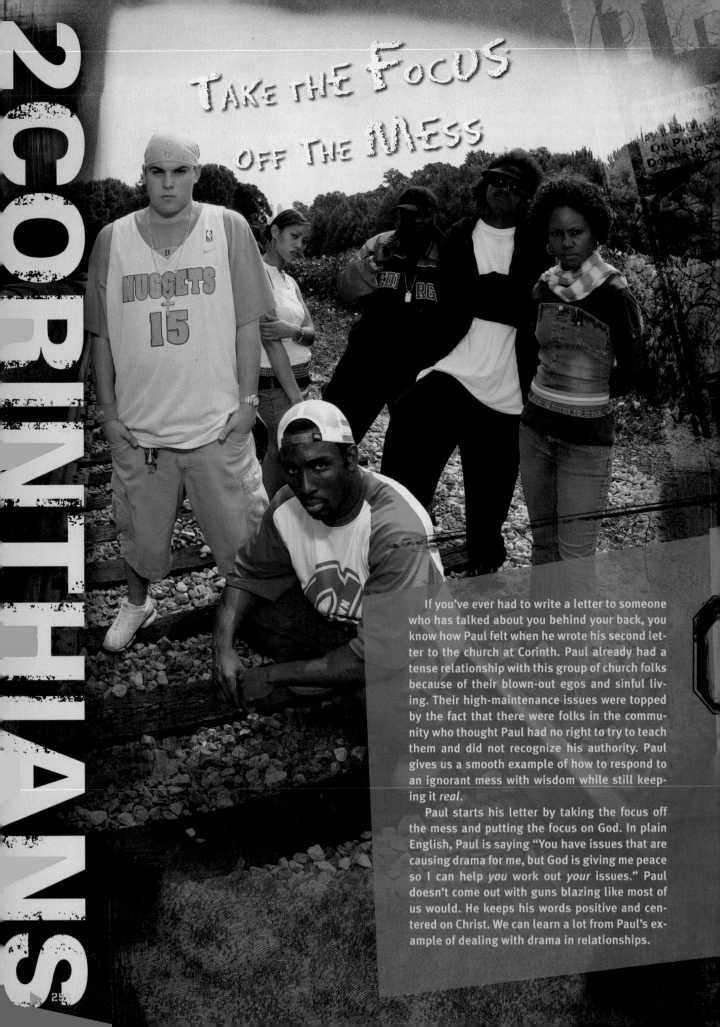

2CORINTHIANS

TAKE THE FOCUS OFF THE MESS

If you've ever had to write a letter to someone who has talked about you behind your back, you know how Paul felt when he wrote his second letter to the church at Corinth. Paul already had a tense relationship with this group of church folks because of their blown-out egos and sinful living. Their high-maintenance issues were topped by the fact that there were folks in the community who thought Paul had no right to try to teach them and did not recognize his authority. Paul gives us a smooth example of how to respond to an ignorant mess with wisdom while still keeping it *real*.

Paul starts his letter by taking the focus off the mess and putting the focus on God. In plain English, Paul is saying "You have issues that are causing drama for me, but God is giving me peace so I can help *you* work out *your* issues." Paul doesn't come out with guns blazing like most of us would. He keeps his words positive and centered on Christ. We can learn a lot from Paul's example of dealing with drama in relationships.

1

From Paul, an apostle of Christ Jesus. I am an apostle because that is what God wanted. Also from Timothy our brother in Christ.

To the church of God in Corinth, and to all of God's people everywhere in Southern Greece:

[2] Grace and peace to you from God our Father and the Lord Jesus Christ.

PAUL GIVES THANKS TO GOD

[3] Praise be to the God and Father of our Lord Jesus Christ. God is the Father who is full of mercy and all comfort. [4] He comforts us every time we have trouble, so when others have trouble, we can comfort them with the same comfort God gives us. [5] We share in the many sufferings of Christ. In the same way, much comfort comes to us through Christ. [6] If we have troubles, it is for your comfort and salvation, and if we have comfort, you also have comfort. This helps you to accept patiently the same sufferings we have. [7] Our hope for you is strong, knowing that you share in our sufferings and also in the comfort we receive.

[8] Brothers and sisters, we want you to know about the trouble we suffered in Asia. We had great burdens there that were beyond our own strength. We even gave up hope of living. [9] Truly, in our own hearts we believed we would die. But this happened so we would not trust in ourselves but in God, who raises people from the dead. [10] God saved us from these great dangers of death, and he will continue to save us. We have put our hope in him, and he will save us again. [11] And you can help us with your prayers.

Then many people will give thanks for us—that God blessed us because of their many prayers.

THE CHANGE IN PAUL'S PLANS

[12] This is what we are proud of, and I can say it with a clear conscience: In everything we have done in the world, and especially with you, we have had an honest[n] and sincere heart from God. We did this by God's grace, not by the kind of wisdom the world has. [13-14] We write to you only what you can read and understand. And I hope that as you have understood some things about us, you may come to know everything about us. Then you can be proud of us, as we will be proud of you on the day our Lord Jesus Christ comes again.

[15] I was so sure of all this that I made plans to visit you first so you could be blessed twice. [16] I planned to visit you on my way to Macedonia and again on my way back. I wanted to get help from you for my trip to Judea. [17] Do you think that I made these plans without really meaning it? Or maybe you think I make plans as the world does, so that I say yes, yes and at the same time no, no.

[18] But since you can believe God, you can believe that what we tell you is never both yes and no. [19] The Son of God, Jesus Christ, that Silas and Timothy and I preached to you, was not yes and no. In Christ it has always been yes. [20] The yes to all of God's promises is in Christ, and through Christ we say yes to the glory of God. [21] Remember, God is the One who makes you and us strong in Christ. God made us his chosen people. [22] He put his

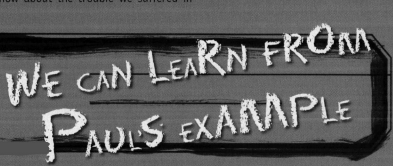

WE CAN LEARN FROM PAUL'S EXAMPLE

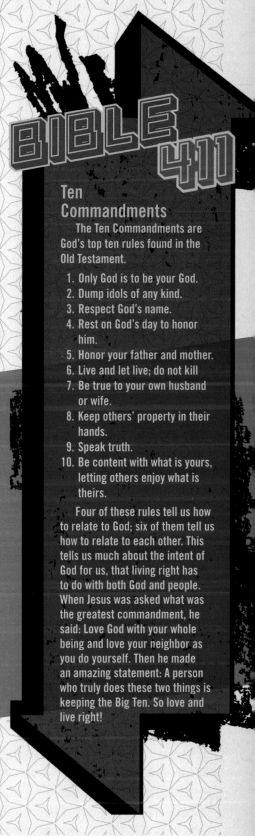

BIBLE 411

Ten Commandments

The Ten Commandments are God's top ten rules found in the Old Testament.

1. Only God is to be your God.
2. Dump idols of any kind.
3. Respect God's name.
4. Rest on God's day to honor him.
5. Honor your father and mother.
6. Live and let live; do not kill
7. Be true to your own husband or wife.
8. Keep others' property in their hands.
9. Speak truth.
10. Be content with what is yours, letting others enjoy what is theirs.

Four of these rules tell us how to relate to God; six of them tell us how to relate to each other. This tells us much about the intent of God for us, that living right has to do with both God and people. When Jesus was asked what was the greatest commandment, he said: Love God with your whole being and love your neighbor as you do yourself. Then he made an amazing statement: A person who truly does these two things is keeping the Big Ten. So love and live right!

1:12 honest Some Greek copies read "holy."

mark on us to show that we are his, and he put his Spirit in our hearts to be a guarantee for all he has promised.

²³I tell you this, and I ask God to be my witness that this is true: The reason I did not come back to Corinth was to keep you from being punished or hurt. ²⁴We are not trying to control your faith. You are strong in faith. But we are workers with you for your own joy.

2 So I decided that my next visit to you would not be another one to make you sad. ²If I make you sad, who will make me glad? Only you can make me glad—particularly the person whom I made sad. ³I wrote you a letter for this reason: that when I came to you I would not be made sad by the people who should make me happy. I felt sure of all of you, that you would share my joy. ⁴When I wrote to you before, I was very troubled and unhappy in my heart, and I wrote with many tears. I did not write to make you sad, but to let you know how much I love you.

FORGIVE THE SINNER

⁵Someone there among you has caused sadness, not to me, but to all of you. I mean he caused sadness to all in some way. (I do not want to make it sound worse than it really is.) ⁶The punishment that most of you gave him is enough for him. ⁷But now you should forgive him and comfort him to keep him from having too much sadness and giving up completely. ⁸So I beg you to show that you love him. ⁹I wrote you to test you and to see if you obey in everything. ¹⁰If you forgive someone, I also forgive him. And what I have forgiven—if I had anything to forgive—I forgave it for you, as if Christ were with me. ¹¹I did this so that Satan would not win anything from us, because we know very well what Satan's plans are.

PAUL'S CONCERN IN TROAS

¹²When I came to Troas to preach the Good News of Christ, the Lord gave me a good opportunity there. ¹³But I had no peace, because I did not find my brother Titus. So I said good-bye to them at Troas and went to Macedonia.

VICTORY THROUGH CHRIST

¹⁴But thanks be to God, who always leads us as captives in Christ's victory parade. God uses us to spread his knowledge everywhere like a sweet-smelling perfume. ¹⁵Our offering to God is this: We are the sweet smell of Christ among those who are being saved and among those who are being lost. ¹⁶To those who are lost, we are the smell of death that brings death, but to those who are being saved, we are the smell of life that brings life. So who is able to do this work? ¹⁷We do not sell the word of God for a profit as many other people do. But in Christ we speak the truth before God, as messengers of God.

SERVANTS OF THE NEW AGREEMENT

3 Are we starting to brag about ourselves again? Do we need letters of introduction to you or from you, like some other people? ²You yourselves are our letter, written on our hearts, known and read by everyone. ³You show that you are a letter from Christ sent through us. This letter is not written with ink but with the Spirit of the living God. It is not written on stone tablets[n] but on human hearts.

⁴We can say this, because through Christ we feel certain before God. ⁵We are not saying that we can do this work ourselves. It is God who makes us able to do all that we do. ⁶He made us able to be servants of a new agreement from himself to his people. This new agreement is not a written law, but it is of the Spirit. The written law brings death, but the Spirit gives life.

⁷The law that brought death was written in words on stone. It came with God's glory, which made Moses' face so bright that the Israelites could not continue to look at it. But that glory later disappeared. ⁸So surely the new way that brings the Spirit has even more glory. ⁹If the law that judged people guilty of sin had glory, surely the new way that makes people right with God has much greater glory. ¹⁰That old law had glory, but it really loses its glory when it is compared to the much greater glory of this new way. ¹¹If that law which disappeared came with glory, then this new way which continues forever has much greater glory.

¹²We have this hope, so we are very bold. ¹³We are not like Moses, who put a covering over his face so the Israelites would not see it. The glory was disappearing, and Moses did not want them to see it end. ¹⁴But their minds were closed, and even today that same covering hides the meaning when they read the old agreement. That covering is taken away only through Christ. ¹⁵Even today, when they read the law of Moses, there is a covering over their minds. ¹⁶But when a person changes and follows the Lord, that covering is taken away. ¹⁷The Lord is the Spirit, and where the Spirit of the Lord is, there is freedom. ¹⁸Our faces, then, are not covered. We all show the Lord's glory, and we are being changed to be like him. This change in us brings ever greater glory, which comes from the Lord, who is the Spirit.

PREACHING THE GOOD NEWS

4 God, with his mercy, gave us this work to do, so we don't give up. ²But we have turned away from secret and shameful ways. We use no trickery, and we do not change the teaching of God. We teach the truth plainly, showing everyone who we are. Then they can know in their hearts what kind of people we are in God's sight. ³If the Good News that we preach is hidden, it is hidden only to those who are lost. ⁴The devil who rules this world has blinded the minds of those who do not

---

 3:3 stone tablets Meaning the Law of Moses that was written on stone tablets (Exodus 24:12; 25:16).

JAIL'S NO JOKE

So what should we say about this? If God is with us, no one can defeat us. Romans 8:31

But in all these things we have full victory through God who showed his love for us. Romans 8:37

Loving God means obeying his commands. And God's commands are not too hard for us, because everyone who is a child of God conquers the world. 1 John 5:3,4

Jail Is Humiliating

When I got locked up I was humiliated. I had a serious problem with alcohol. It was my drug of choice. Often, I would get drunk and then drive myself home. I believed that I could manage it. After all, I may have been drinking, but I could still pull it all together when I got behind the wheel. One such night, it finally caught up with me and I was charged with a DUI. I didn't learn my lesson right away because I got another DUI about 6 months later. This time my license was taken away. I had given my life to the Lord, but I avoided talking to him about my drinking. I may have accepted him, but I wasn't ready to give up drinking. What would I do without it? All my friends drank and life would be really boring out at the club if I didn't have at least a little buzz. One night while reading the Bible, it dawned on me that I was acting like I loved alcohol more than God. No! That was all wrong. I gave it up on the spot and asked God to forgive me. But, I still wasn't out of the woods. I was caught driving on a suspended license and went straight to jail.

I had a decent job, a good family, I was a deacon in the church, and found myself behind bars because of stupidity. Well, my church family got the word that I was locked up and they couldn't understand it. I was a child of God but locked up for not paying all of my fines and not re-instating my license. I had to go through a program for alcohol abusers while serving one week in jail. Everyone else in the program was still battling alcohol, but I was clean. No one could believe that I was in jail because of a DUI that had happened years before. I was humiliated. When I had to speak to my wife through a plastic window, my heart was broken. I asked God to make me a better man.

I went through all of that embarrassment because of my laziness. It was so shameful, but I learned my lesson. As soon as I got out, I spent time with my pastor. I told him I was ashamed that folks knew. He admitted folks in our church were disappointed in me, but he said no one could cast the first stone. He said everyone in our congregation, including him, had issues the Lord had to help us overcome. He didn't let me off easy though. He got on me hard about my ways. I confessed that I wanted to have a stronger relationship with Christ. He then told me to spend time in the Word, come to church more regularly, tithe consistently, get a person to keep me accountable, fast more often, and stay in prayer. I've been following his advice and I am a better man. I am a better husband, father, businessman and deacon.

believe. They cannot see the light of the Good News—the Good News about the glory of Christ, who is exactly like God. [5]We do not preach about ourselves, but we preach that Jesus Christ is Lord and that we are your servants for Jesus. [6]God once said, "Let the light shine out of the darkness!" This is the same God who made his light shine in our hearts by letting us know the glory of God that is in the face of Christ.

SPIRITUAL TREASURE IN CLAY JARS

[7]We have this treasure from God, but we are like clay jars that hold the treasure. This shows that the great power is from God, not from us. [8]We have troubles all around us, but we are not defeated. We do not know what to do, but we do not give up the hope of living. [9]We are persecuted, but God does not leave us. We are hurt sometimes, but we are not destroyed. [10]We carry the death of Jesus in our own bodies so that the life of Jesus can also be seen in our bodies. [11]We are alive, but for Jesus we are always in danger of death so that the life of Jesus can be seen in our bodies that die. [12]So death is working in us, but life is working in you.

[13]It is written in the Scriptures, "I believed, so I spoke."[n] Our faith is like this, too. We believe, and so we speak. [14]God raised the Lord Jesus from the dead, and we know that God will also raise us with Jesus. God will bring us together with you, and we will stand before him. [15]All these things are for you. And so the grace of God that is being given to more and more people will bring increasing thanks to God for his glory.

LIVING BY FAITH

[16]So we do not give up. Our physical body is becoming older and weaker, but our spirit inside us is made new every day. [17]We have small troubles for a while now, but they are helping us gain an eternal glory that is much greater than the troubles. [18]We set our eyes not on what we see but on what we cannot

see. What we see will last only a short time, but what we cannot see will last forever.

5 We know that our body—the tent we live in here on earth—will be destroyed. But when that happens, God will have a house for us. It will not be a house made by human hands; instead, it will be a home in heaven that will last forever. [2]But now we groan in this tent. We want God to give us our heavenly home, [3]because it will clothe us so we will not be naked. [4]While we live in this body, we have burdens, and we groan. We do not want to be naked, but we want to be clothed with our heavenly home. Then this body that dies will be fully covered with life. [5]This

is what God made us for, and he has given us the Spirit to be a guarantee for this new life.

[6]So we always have courage. We know that while we live in this body, we are away from the Lord. [7]We live by what we believe, not by what we can see. [8]So I say that we have courage. We really want to be away from this body and be at home with the Lord. [9]Our only goal is to please God whether we live here or there, [10]because we must all stand before Christ to be judged. Each of us will receive what we should get—good or bad—for the things we did in the earthly body.

BECOMING FRIENDS WITH GOD

[11]Since we know what it means to fear the Lord, we try to help people ac-

He's got answers

Everybody around me is drinking, taking drugs, and having sex. How can I keep from being an outcast if I don't join in?

It sounds too easy, but just because other people are doing it, doesn't mean that you have to join in. It's important to be an independent thinker. Don't just follow the crowd. If you don't want to go where the crowd is going, then say no. The first time will be the hardest, but the more you say it, the less often you will have to. If the people headed in the wrong direction see you as an outcast, that's a good thing. Find different friends. There are more people out there than you think who don't pick their friends because they drink, do drugs, or have sex. However, if the problem is that you want to participate in these activities, then as the old saying goes, "Either you will change people or people will change you." Find a good counselor or a pastor to talk to. They can help you figure out why you've made destructive choices and how to change that pattern.

Read on: Matthew 28:20; 1 Corinthians 10:13; Hebrews 4:15; 13:5

4:13 "I . . . spoke." Quotation from Psalm 116:10.

cept the truth about us. God knows what we really are, and I hope that in your hearts you know, too. [12]We are not trying to prove ourselves to you again, but we are telling you about ourselves so you will be proud of us. Then you will have an answer for those who are proud about things that can be seen rather than what is in the heart. [13]If we are out of our minds, it is for God. If we have our right minds, it is for you. [14]The love of Christ controls us, because we know that One died for all, so all have died. [15]Christ died for all so that those who live would not continue to live for themselves. He died for them and was raised from the dead so that they would live for him.

[16]From this time on we do not think of anyone as the world does. In the past we thought of Christ as the world thinks, but we no longer think of him in that way. [17]If anyone belongs to Christ, there is a new creation. The old things have gone; everything is made new! [18]All this is from God. Through Christ, God made peace between us and himself, and God gave us the work of telling everyone about the peace we can have with him. [19]God was in Christ, making peace between the world and himself. In Christ, God did not hold the world guilty of its sins. And he gave us this message of peace. [20]So we have been sent to speak for Christ. It is as if God is calling to you through us. We speak for Christ when we beg you to be at peace with God. [21]Christ had no sin, but God made him become sin so that in Christ we could become right with God.

6 We are workers together with God, so we beg you: Do not let the grace that you received from God be for nothing. [2]God says,

"At the right time I heard your prayers.
On the day of salvation I helped you."
Isaiah 49:8

I tell you that the "right time" is now, and the "day of salvation" is now.

[3]We do not want anyone to find fault with our work, so nothing we do will be a problem for anyone. [4]But in every way we show we are servants of God: in accepting many hard things, in troubles, in difficulties, and in great problems. [5]We are beaten and thrown into prison. We meet those who become upset with us and start riots. We work hard, and sometimes we get no sleep or food. [6]We show we are servants of God by our pure lives, our understanding, patience, and kindness, by the Holy Spirit, by true love, [7]by speaking the truth, and by God's power. We use our right living to defend ourselves against everything. [8]Some people honor us, but others blame us. Some people say evil things about us, but others say good things. Some people say we are liars, but we speak the truth. [9]We are not known, but we are well known. We seem to be dying, but we continue to live. We are punished, but we are not killed. [10]We have much sadness, but we are always rejoicing. We are poor, but we are making many people rich in faith. We have nothing, but really we have everything.

[11]We have spoken freely to you in Corinth and have opened our hearts to you. [12]Our feelings of love for you have not stopped, but you have stopped your feelings of love for us. [13]I speak to you as if you were my children. Do to us as we have done—open your hearts to us.

WARNING ABOUT NON-CHRISTIANS

[14]You are not the same as those who do not believe. So do not join yourselves to them. Good and bad do not belong together. Light and darkness cannot share together. [15]How can Christ and Belial, the devil, have any agreement? What can a believer have together with a nonbeliever? [16]The temple of God cannot have any agreement with idols, and we are the temple of the living God. As God said: "I will live with them and walk with them. And I will be their God, and they will be my people."[n]

[17]"Leave those people,
and be separate, says the Lord.
Touch nothing that is unclean,
and I will accept you."
Isaiah 52:11; Ezekiel 20:34, 41

[18]"I will be your father,
and you will be my sons and daughters,
says the Lord Almighty."
2 Samuel 7:14

7 Dear friends, we have these promises from God, so we should make ourselves pure—free from anything that makes body or soul unclean.

We should try to become holy in the way we live, because we respect God.

PAUL'S JOY

[2]Open your hearts to us. We have not done wrong to anyone, we have not ruined the faith of anyone, and we have not cheated anyone. [3]I do not say this to blame you. I told you before that we love you so much we would live or die with you. [4]I feel very sure of you and am very proud of you. You give me much comfort,

---

6:16 "I . . . people." Quotation from Leviticus 26:11-12; Jeremiah 32:38; Ezekiel 37:27.

365

1 HOLIDAY—Labor Day

2 Visit a nursing home and adopt a grandparent.

3

4 ## Think outside the box:
   What difference has

5

6 9-11 made in

7 your life?

8

9

10

> "What is a soul? It's electricity—we don't really know what it is, but it's a force that can light a room."
> –Ray Charles

11 On This Day In History 2001—World Trade Center in New York City was bombed by terrorists.

12

13 Pray for those serving in the armed forces.

14

15 HOLIDAY—Hispanic Heritage Month begins

16 It's your birthday, Marc Anthony!

17

18 ## Pray for the victims of terrorism

19

20 On This Day In History 1979—Rapper's Delight was released and became the first rap song to ever hit the top 40

21

22 Autumn begins today

23 Happy Birthday Ray Charles!

24

25 ## Mentor a child

26 It's your birthday, Serena Williams!

27 On This Day In History 1950—Dr. Ralph Bunche receives Nobel Peace Prize.

28

29 Donate your old books to a local school.

30 Happy Birthday Jamal Anderson!

MUSIC REVIEWS

ARTIST: SPEC   ALBUM: IN YA EYE

In Ya Eye, the latest CD from Spec, is a wonderful compilation of creative rap lyrics and funky beats. The music on this album has a very Latin hip-hop sound which is popular among many rap listeners. The beats are original, yet have a familiar sound. The songs are very catchy and can get anyone rapping about the uplifting topics of Spec's music. Spec's lyrics speak powerfully about waging spiritual warfare in the name of the Lord. Every track is fun and comes off as light-hearted, but all have truly deep lyrics.

Christian or non-Christian, this is a great rap album. Anyone who thinks that Christian music or even Christian rap is boring will be proved wrong after listening to this great CD.

"ACCEPTED"

and in all of our troubles I have great joy.

[5]When we came into Macedonia, we had no rest. We found trouble all around us. We had fighting on the outside and fear on the inside. [6]But God, who comforts those who are troubled, comforted us when Titus came. [7]We were comforted, not only by his coming but also by the comfort you gave him. Titus told us about your wish to see me and that you are very sorry for what you did. He also told me about your great care for me, and when I heard this, I was much happier.

[8]Even if my letter made you sad, I am not sorry I wrote it. At first I was sorry, because it made you sad, but you were sad only for a short time. [9]Now I am happy, not because you were made sad, but because your sorrow made you change your lives. You became sad in the way God wanted you to, so you were not hurt by us in any way. [10]The kind of sorrow God wants makes people change their hearts and lives. This leads to salvation, and you cannot be sorry for

that. But the kind of sorrow the world has brings death. [11]See what this sorrow—the sorrow God wanted you to have—has done to you: It has made you very serious. It made you want to restore yourselves. It made you angry and afraid. It made you want to see me. It made you care. It made you want to do the right thing. In every way you have regained your innocence. [12]I wrote that letter, not because of the one who did the wrong or because of the person who was hurt. I wrote the letter so you could see, before God, the great care you have for us. [13]That is why we were comforted.

Not only were we very comforted, we were even happier to see that Titus was so happy. All of you made him feel much better. [14]I bragged to Titus about you, and you showed that I was right. Everything we said to you was true, and you have proved that what we bragged about to Titus is true. [15]And his love for you is stronger when he remembers that you were all ready to obey. You welcomed him with respect and fear. [16]I am very happy that I can trust you fully.

CHRISTIAN GIVING

8 And now, brothers and sisters, we want you to know about the grace God gave the churches in Macedonia. [2]They have been tested by great troubles, and they are very poor. But they gave much because of their great joy. [3]I can tell you that they gave as much as they were able and even more than they could afford. No one told them to do it. [4]But they begged and pleaded with us to let them share in this service for God's people. [5]And they gave in a way we did not expect: They first gave themselves to the Lord and to us. This is what God wants. [6]So we asked Titus to help you finish this special work of grace since he is the one who started it. [7]You are rich in everything—in faith, in speaking, in knowledge, in truly wanting to help, and in the love you learned from us.[n] In the same way, be strong also in the grace of giving.

[8]I am not commanding you to give.

8:7 in . . . us Some Greek copies read "in your love for us."

▶ **261**

But I want to see if your love is true by comparing you with others that really want to help. [9]You know the grace of our Lord Jesus Christ. You know that Christ was rich, but for you he became poor so that by his becoming poor you might become rich.

[10]This is what I think you should do: Last year you were the first to want to give, and you were the first who gave. [11]So now finish the work you started. Then your "doing" will be equal to your "wanting to do." Give from what you have. [12]If you want to give, your gift will be accepted. It will be judged by what you have, not by what you do not have. [13]We do not want you to have troubles while other people are at ease, but we want everything to be equal. [14]At this time you have plenty. What you have can help others who are in need. Then later, when they have plenty, they can help you when you are in need, and all will be equal. [15]As it is written in the Scriptures, "The person who gathered more did not have too much, nor did the person who gathered less have too little.'"

TITUS AND HIS COMPANIONS HELP

[16]I thank God because he gave Titus the same love for you that I have. [17]Titus accepted what we asked him to do. He wanted very much to go to you, and this was his own idea. [18]We are sending with him the brother who is praised by all the churches because of his service in preaching the Good News. [19]Also, this brother was chosen by the churches to go with us when we deliver this gift of money. We are doing this service to bring glory to the Lord and to show that we really want to help.

[20]We are being careful so that no one will criticize us for the way we are handling this large gift. [21]We are trying hard

8:15 "The person . . . little." Quotation from Exodus 16:18.

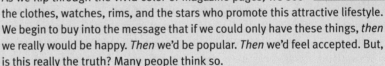

DEEP ISSUES

Money/Materialism

Money and materialism are both highly celebrated in our culture. If you click on a music channel or check out the latest issue of a hip-hop magazine, you'll quickly see wealth being flaunted everywhere. It begins to soak into our mentality. The TV screen gives images of cars, mansions, girls, and money. As we flip through the vivid color of magazine pages, we see the clothes, watches, rims, and the stars who promote this attractive lifestyle. We begin to buy into the message that if we could only have these things, *then* we really would be happy. *Then* we'd be popular. *Then* we'd feel accepted. But, is this really the truth? Many people think so.

Materialism almost destroyed one young life. Carlos grew up in the hood and didn't have much. As he got older, his outward appearance became very important to him. He loved to look good. Materialism sucked him in and quickly became his god. He began to do whatever it took to get material things, especially clothes. Carlos began to steal from his job. At first, he told himself he'd just take a few things to get his wardrobe up to par. Soon, he began to steal everything new that came into the store.

Carlos's closet was bulging, but his life was beginning to tear apart at the seams. He cheated in school, cheated on his girlfriend, stole from his job, and even lied to his family and his friends. In his selfish heart, life became all about Carlos. But he was never satisfied; his life was just a lie. Carlos's was self-destructing. He wandered from his faith, was caught in his sin, and ended up in the middle of a lot of drama. When he finally woke up and saw reality, he made some serious changes.

First Timothy 6:9-10 talks about this. It basically says that chasing these things ends in destruction. Don't fall for the world's lies. Don't hurt yourself and your people like Carlos did. Material things and money don't truly satisfy. There is nothing wrong with those things but, when we put them above our Creator, everything falls apart.

to do what the Lord accepts as right and also what people think is right.

[22]Also, we are sending with them our brother, who is always ready to help. He has proved this to us in many ways, and he wants to help even more now, because he has much faith in you.

[23]Now about Titus—he is my partner who is working with me to help you. And about the other brothers—they are sent from the churches, and they bring glory to Christ. [24]So show these men the proof of your love and the reason we are proud of you. Then all the churches can see it.

HELP FOR FELLOW CHRISTIANS

9 I really do not need to write you about this help for God's people. [2]I know you want to help. I have been bragging about this to the people in Macedonia, telling them that you in Southern Greece have been ready to give since last year. And your desire to give has made most of them ready to give also. [3]But I am sending the brothers to you so that our bragging about you in this will not be empty words. I want you to be ready, as I said you would be. [4]If any of the people from Macedonia come with me and find that you are not ready, we will be ashamed that we were so sure of you. (And you will be ashamed, too!) [5]So I thought I should ask these brothers to go to you before we do. They will finish getting in order the generous gift you promised so it will be ready when we come. And it will be a generous gift—not one that you did not want to give.

[6]Remember this: The person who plants a little will have a small harvest, but the person who plants a lot will have a big harvest. [7]Each of you should give as you have decided in your heart to give. You should not be sad when you give, and you should not give because you feel forced to give. God loves the person who gives happily. [8]And God can give you more blessings than you need. Then you will always have plenty of ev-

erything—enough to give to every good work. [9]It is written in the Scriptures:

"He gives freely to the poor.
The things he does are right and
will continue forever."

Psalm 112:9

[10]God is the One who gives seed to the farmer and bread for food. He will give you all the seed you need and make it grow so there will be a great harvest from your goodness. [11]He will make you rich in every way so that you can always give freely. And your giving through us will cause many to give thanks to God. [12]This service you do not only helps the needs of God's people, it also brings many more thanks to God. [13]It is a proof of your faith. Many people will praise God because you obey the Good News of Christ—the gospel you say you believe— and because you freely share with them and with all others. [14]And when they pray, they will wish they could be with you because of the great grace that God has given you. [15]Thanks be to God for his gift that is too wonderful for words.

> THANKS BE TO GOD FOR HIS GIFT THAT IS TOO WONDERFUL FOR WORDS.

PAUL DEFENDS HIS MINISTRY

10 I, Paul, am begging you with the gentleness and the kindness of Christ. Some people say that I am easy on you when I am with you and bold when I am away. [2]They think we live in a worldly way, and I plan to be very bold with them when I

come. I beg you that when I come I will not need to use that same boldness with you. [3]We do live in the world, but we do not fight in the same way the world fights. [4]We fight with weapons that are different from those the world uses. Our weapons have power from God that can destroy the enemy's strong places. We destroy people's arguments [5]and every proud thing that raises itself against the knowledge of God. We capture every thought and make it give up and obey Christ. [6]We are ready to punish anyone there who does not obey, but first we want you to obey fully.

[7]You must look at the facts before you. If you feel sure that you belong to Christ, you must remember that we belong to Christ just as you do. [8]It is true that we brag freely about the authority the Lord gave us. But this authority is to build you up, not to tear you down. So I will not be ashamed. [9]I do not want you to think I am trying to scare you with my letters. [10]Some people say, "Paul's letters are powerful and sound important, but when he is with us, he is weak. And his speaking is nothing." [11]They should know this: We are not there with you now, so we say these things in letters. But when we are there with you, we will show the same authority that we show in our letters.

[12]We do not dare to compare ourselves with those who think they are very important. They use themselves to measure themselves, and they judge themselves by what they themselves are. This shows that they know nothing. [13]But we will not brag about things outside the work that was given us to do. We will limit our bragging to the work that God gave us, and this includes our work with you. [14]We are not bragging too much, as we would be if we had not already come to you. But we have come to you with the Good News of Christ. [15]We limit our bragging to the work that is ours, not what others have done. We hope that as your faith continues to grow, you will help our work to grow much larger. [16]We

want to tell the Good News in the areas beyond your city. We do not want to brag about work that has already been done in another person's area. [17]But, "If people want to brag, they should brag only about the Lord."[n] [18]It is not those who say they are good who are accepted but those the Lord thinks are good.

PAUL AND THE FALSE APOSTLES

11 I wish you would be patient with me even when I am a little foolish, but you are already doing that. [2]I am jealous over you with a jealousy that comes from God. I promised to give you to Christ, as your only husband. I want to give you as his pure bride. [3]But I am afraid that your minds will be led away from your true and pure following of Christ just as Eve was tricked by the snake with his evil ways. [4]You are very patient with anyone who comes to you and preaches a different Jesus from the one we preached. You are very willing to accept a spirit or gospel that is different from the Spirit and Good News you received from us.

[5]I do not think that those "great apostles" are any better than I am. [6]I may not be a trained speaker, but I do have knowledge. We have shown this to you clearly in every way.

[7]I preached God's Good News to you without pay. I made myself unimportant to make you important. Do you think that was wrong? [8]I accepted pay from other churches, taking their money so I could serve you. [9]If I needed something when I was with you, I did not trouble any of you. The brothers who came from Macedonia gave me all that I needed. I did not allow myself to depend on you in any way, and I will never depend on you. [10]No one in Southern Greece will stop me from bragging about that. I say this with the truth of Christ in me. [11]And why do I not depend on you? Do you think it is because I do not love you? God knows that I love you.

[12]And I will continue doing what I am doing now, because I want to stop those people from having a reason to brag. They would like to say that the work they brag about is the same as ours. [13]Such men are not true apostles but are workers who lie. They change themselves to look like apostles of Christ. [14]This does not surprise us. Even Satan changes himself to look like an angel of light.[n] [15]So it does not surprise us if Satan's servants also make themselves look like servants who work for what is right. But in the end they will be punished for what they do.

> ## IF PEOPLE WANT TO BRAG, THEY SHOULD BRAG ONLY ABOUT THE LORD.

PAUL TELLS ABOUT HIS SUFFERINGS

[16]I tell you again: No one should think I am a fool. But if you think so, accept me as you would accept a fool. Then I can brag a little, too. [17]When I brag because I feel sure of myself, I am not talking as the Lord would talk but as a fool. [18]Many people are bragging about their lives in the world. So I will brag too. [19]You are wise, so you will gladly be patient with fools! [20]You are even patient with those who order you around, or use you, or trick you, or think they are better than you, or hit you in the face. [21]It is shameful to me to say this, but we were too "weak" to do those things to you!

But if anyone else is brave enough to brag, then I also will be brave and brag. (I am talking as a fool.) [22]Are they Hebrews?[n] So am I. Are they Israelites?

So am I. Are they from Abraham's family? So am I. [23]Are they serving Christ? I am serving him more. (I am crazy to talk like this.) I have worked much harder than they. I have been in prison more often. I have been hurt more in beatings. I have been near death many times. [24]Five times the Jews have given me their punishment of thirty-nine lashes with a whip. [25]Three different times I was beaten with rods. One time I was almost stoned to death. Three times I was in ships that wrecked, and one of those times I spent a night and a day in the sea. [26]I have gone on many travels and have been in danger from rivers, thieves, my own people, the Jews, and those who are not Jews. I have been in danger in cities, in places where no one lives, and on the sea. And I have been in danger with false Christians. [27]I have done hard and tiring work, and many times I did not sleep. I have been hungry and thirsty, and many times I have been without food. I have been cold and without clothes. [28]Besides all this, there is on me every day the load of my concern for all the churches. [29]I feel weak every time someone is weak, and I feel upset every time someone is led into sin.

[30]If I must brag, I will brag about the things that show I am weak. [31]God knows I am not lying. He is the God and Father of the Lord Jesus Christ, and he is to be praised forever. [32]When I was in Damascus, the governor under King Aretas wanted to arrest me, so he put guards around the city. [33]But my friends lowered me in a basket through a hole in the city wall. So I escaped from the governor.

A SPECIAL BLESSING IN PAUL'S LIFE

12 I must continue to brag. It will do no good, but I will talk now about visions and revelations[n] from the Lord. [2]I know a man

10:17 "If . . . Lord." Quotation from Jeremiah 9:24. **11:14 angel of light** Messenger from God. The devil fools people so that they think he is from God. **11:22 Hebrews** A name for the Jews that some Jews were very proud of. **12:1 revelations** Revelation is making known a truth that was hidden.

264

GOD UNIT ✠

COPING WITH HERPES

Seemed fun in college to be the playa. What girl didn't want to get with me? Though I had accepted the Lord back when I was in middle school, my actions did not show it. I knew I wasn't supposed to be having sex, but when it's thrown at you from several directions, it's hard to pass it up. The sex, the parties and women falling all over me was a fantasy-come-true for sure. The small amount of pleasure I had, however, wasn't worth the life-altering consequence. A burning sensation developed and a few days later I discovered red, oozing sores. After a visit to the doctor, I got the dreaded news. I had herpes, an STD with no cure.

All the strength I liked to show off to my many women deserted me and I broke down and cried like a baby. I couldn't believe I was scarred for life. I had no one to blame but myself. Reckless living had led me on a collision course with disaster. Worse, there was nothing I could do to erase my mistake. All I knew to do was pray. But even as I started, I felt I didn't deserve God's ear. How could he listen to such a sinner?

I was partly right, the Lord reminded me. I didn't deserve his grace. I had sinned and fallen so short. But reading a passage from a Bible I hadn't touched in years reminded me that God still loved me and would forgive me. Though I couldn't get rid of the disease, I could get rid of my sinful ways. I didn't have to stay on the path of sexual destruction. Now, during outbreaks, I feel very uncomfortable but the Lord is merciful enough to have provided medicine that controls what ails me. I am blessed that I did not catch something worse. God is more than good.

Romans 3:23—All have sinned and are not good enough for God's glory.

---

in Christ who was taken up to the third heaven fourteen years ago. I do not know whether the man was in his body or out of his body, but God knows. [3-4] And I know that this man was taken up to paradise.[n] I don't know if he was in his body or away from his body, but God knows. He heard things he is not able to explain, things that no human is allowed to tell. [5] I will brag about a man like that, but I will not brag about myself, except about my weaknesses. [6] But if I wanted to brag about myself, I would not be a fool, because I would be telling the truth. But I will not brag about myself. I do not want people to think more of me than what they see me do or hear me say.

[7] So that I would not become too proud of the wonderful things that were shown to me, a painful physical problem[n] was given to me. This problem was a messenger from Satan, sent to beat me and keep me from being too proud. [8] I begged the Lord three times to take this problem away from me. [9] But he said to me, "My grace is enough for you. When you are weak, my power is made perfect in you." So I am very happy to brag about my weaknesses. Then Christ's power can live in me. [10] For this reason I am happy when I have weaknesses, insults, hard times, sufferings, and all kinds of troubles for Christ. Because when I am weak, then I am truly strong.

PAUL'S LOVE FOR THE CHRISTIANS

[11] I have been talking like a fool, but you made me do it. You are the ones who should say good things about me. I am worth nothing, but those "great apostles" are not worth any more than I am!

[12] When I was with you, I patiently did the things that prove I am an apostle—signs, wonders, and miracles. [13] So you received everything that the other churches have received. Only one thing was different: I was not a burden to you. Forgive me for this!

[14] I am now ready to visit you the third time, and I will not be a burden to you. I want nothing from you, except you. Children should not have to save up to give

---

12:3-4 paradise Another word for heaven.   **12:7 painful physical problem** Literally, "thorn in the flesh."

to their parents. Parents should save to give to their children. [15]So I am happy to give everything I have for you, even myself. If I love you more, will you love me less?

[16]It is clear I was not a burden to you, but you think I was tricky and lied to catch you. [17]Did I cheat you by using any of the messengers I sent to you? No, you know I did not. [18]I asked Titus to go to you, and I sent our brother with him. Titus did not cheat you, did he? No, you know that Titus and I did the same thing and with the same spirit.

[19]Do you think we have been defending ourselves to you all this time? We have been speaking in Christ and before God. You are our dear friends, and everything we do is to make you stronger. [20]I am afraid that when I come, you will not be what I want you to be, and I will not be what you want me to be. I am afraid that among you there may be arguing, jealousy, anger, selfish fighting, evil talk, gossip, pride, and confusion. [21]I am afraid that when I come to you again, my God will make me ashamed before you. I may be saddened by many of those who have sinned because they have not changed their hearts or turned from their sexual sins and the shameful things they have done.

FINAL WARNINGS AND GREETINGS

13 I will come to you for the third time. "Every case must be proved by two or three witnesses."[n] [2]When I was with you the second time, I gave a warning to those who had sinned. Now I am away from you, and I give a warning to all the others. When I come to you again, I will not be easy with them. [3]You want proof that Christ is speaking through me. My proof is that he is not weak among you, but he

13:1 "Every . . . witnesses." Quotation from Deuteronomy 19:15.

HOW YA TRAVELIN'?

NO WHAT?

Just hear us out on this one . . .

You already know that the Bible says sex outside of marriage is wrong. It's as true for this generation as it ever was. Other than the obvious elimination of Sexually Transmitted Diseases (STD's, including AIDS) from your radarscope, the truth is that sex outside of marriage is not only using someone else for your pleasure but it is also misusing and harming your own body and soul.

Satan loves to mock and he mocks every time someone has sex outside of marriage. It's not "making love." It has nothing to do with love and everything to do with body lust. Love assigns value to another; lust uses them. Don't let anyone use your body. Instead, be somebody who says, "I am a prince of the King of kings and I am a blesser. To be out with me is a high privilege." If you value your partner and she values you, your bodies will not be used as mere sexual tools.

The more partners you have, sex becomes less special. That which was meant to be the greatest expression of love is reduced to nothing more than a vehicle for selfish, immediate gratification that ruins you and twists you into a *taker*. When the time comes and you really want to settle in with a spouse and family, it will be difficult to adapt to a *giving* relationship. No matter what the world says, the reality is that the satisfaction of the whole person (spirit, mind, and body) is found in commitment to another human in marriage.

THERE MUST BE NO SEXUAL SIN AMONG YOU – EPHESIANS 5:3

is powerful. ⁴It is true that he was weak when he was killed on the cross, but he lives now by God's power. It is true that we are weak in Christ, but for you we will be alive in Christ by God's power.

⁵Look closely at yourselves. Test yourselves to see if you are living in the faith. You know that Jesus Christ is in you—unless you fail the test. ⁶But I hope you will see that we ourselves have not failed the test. ⁷We pray to God that you will not do anything wrong. It is not important to see that we have passed the test, but it is important that you do what is right, even if it seems we have failed. ⁸We cannot do anything against the truth, but only for the truth. ⁹We are happy to be weak, if you are strong, and we pray that you will become complete. ¹⁰I am writing this while I am away from you so that when I come I will not have to be harsh in my use of authority. The Lord gave me this authority to build you up, not to tear you down.

¹¹Now, brothers and sisters, I say good-bye. Live in harmony. Do what I have asked you to do. Agree with each other, and live in peace. Then the God of love and peace will be with you.

¹²Greet each other with a holy kiss. ¹³All of God's holy people send greetings to you.

¹⁴The grace of the Lord Jesus Christ, the love of God, and the fellowship of the Holy Spirit be with you all.

HeartCry

Sex **Is sex a problem area in your life? Does waiting for marriage seem all but impossible? Let your heart cry . . .**

Lord, help me out! I'm struggling with sex. Everywhere I look, it's there. On billboards, tee-shirts, in stores, commercials, movies, and they even talk about it on the news. Everybody does it. I'm trying to hold out, but I'm slipping. I fight it off most of the time, but I just can't seem to make the thoughts go away. Give me the strength to wait. I want sex to be all you meant it to be, not just a way to spend time. Thanks for being there, God.

I never said you would not be tempted but I have promised to give you strength whenever you ask. Seek me and I will give you power to overcome all the lies of the world.
2 Corinthians 12:9, 10; John 16:33; 1 Corinthians 10:13

GALATIANS

FOLLOW THE SPIRIT'S LEADING

Paul's letter to the church in Galatia opposes religious legalism and breaks down his ministry to non-Jews (Gentiles). It was being taught by some that non-Jewish Christians needed to follow a laundry list of Jewish rules, regulations and religious practices to be righteous. Paul shut down these teachings as false and boldly taught that "a person is made right with God not by following the law, but by trusting in Jesus Christ."

If you've ever had unrealistic, heavy rules put around your neck by someone trying to "make you holy," you understand how destructive and enslaving religious legalism can be. Paul's answer is to make a quality choice to walk in the Spirit and not in the mess of the world. Following the Spirit's leading will bring you a good life, but giving in to the world's ways will mess you up for real.

1

From Paul, an apostle. I was not chosen to be an apostle by human beings, nor was I sent from human beings. I was made an apostle through Jesus Christ and God the Father who raised Jesus from the dead. [2]This letter is also from all those of God's family[n] who are with me.

To the churches in Galatia:[n]

[3]Grace and peace to you from God our Father and the Lord Jesus Christ. [4]Jesus gave himself for our sins to free us from this evil world we live in, as God the Father planned. [5]The glory belongs to God forever and ever. Amen.

THE ONLY GOOD NEWS

[6]God, by his grace through Christ, called you to become his people. So I am amazed that you are turning away so quickly and believing something different than the Good News. [7]Really, there is no other Good News. But some people are confusing you; they want to change the Good News of Christ. [8]We preached to you the Good News. So if we ourselves, or even an angel from heaven, should preach to you something different, we should be judged guilty! [9]I said

PAUL'S AUTHORITY IS FROM GOD

[11]Brothers and sisters, I want you to know that the Good News I preached to you was not made up by human beings. [12]I did not get it from humans, nor did anyone teach it to me, but Jesus Christ showed it to me.

[13]You have heard about my past life in the Jewish religion. I attacked the church of God and tried to destroy it. [14]I was becoming a leader in the Jewish religion, doing better than most other Jews of my age. I tried harder than anyone else to follow the teachings handed down by our ancestors.

[15]But God had special plans for me and set me apart for his work even before I was born. He called me through his grace [16]and showed his son to me so that I might tell the Good News about him to those who are not Jewish. When God called me, I did not get advice or help from any person. [17]I did not go to Jerusalem to see those who were apostles before I was. But, without waiting, I went away to Arabia and later went back to Damascus.

[18]After three years I went to Jerusalem to meet Peter and stayed with him

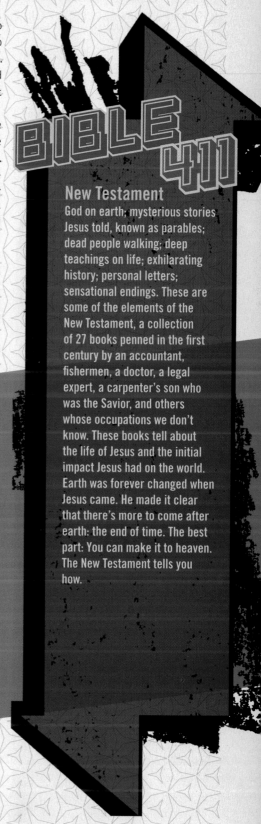

Bible 411

New Testament

God on earth; mysterious stories Jesus told, known as parables; dead people walking; deep teachings on life; exhilarating history; personal letters; sensational endings. These are some of the elements of the New Testament, a collection of 27 books penned in the first century by an accountant, fishermen, a doctor, a legal expert, a carpenter's son who was the Savior, and others whose occupations we don't know. These books tell about the life of Jesus and the initial impact Jesus had on the world. Earth was forever changed when Jesus came. He made it clear that there's more to come after earth: the end of time. The best part: You can make it to heaven. The New Testament tells you how.

THE WORLD'S WAYS WILL MESS YOU UP FOR REAL

this before, and now I say it again: You have already accepted the Good News. If anyone is preaching something different to you, let that person be judged guilty!

[10]Do you think I am trying to make people accept me? No, God is the One I am trying to please. Am I trying to please people? If I still wanted to please people, I would not be a servant of Christ.

for fifteen days. [19]I met no other apostles, except James, the brother of the Lord. [20]God knows that these things I write are not lies. [21]Later, I went to the areas of Syria and Cilicia. [22]In Judea the churches in Christ had never met me. [23]They had only heard it said, "This man who was attacking us is now preaching the same faith that he once tried to destroy." [24]And these believers praised God because of me.

 1:2 those . . . family The Greek text says "brothers." **1:2 Galatia** Probably the same country where Paul preached and began churches on his first missionary trip. Read the Book of Acts, chapters 13 and 14.

OTHER APOSTLES ACCEPTED PAUL

2 After fourteen years I went to Jerusalem again, this time with Barnabas. I also took Titus with me. ²I went because God showed me I should go. I met with the believers there, and in private I told their leaders the Good News that I preach to the non-Jewish people. I did not want my past work and the work I am now doing to be wasted. ³Titus was with me, but he was not forced to be circumcised, even though he was a Greek. ⁴We talked about this problem because some false believers had come into our group secretly. They came in like spies to overturn the freedom we have in Christ Jesus. They wanted to make us slaves. ⁵But we did not give in to those false believers for a minute. We wanted the truth of the Good News to continue for you.

⁶Those leaders who seemed to be important did not change the Good News that I preach. (It doesn't matter to me if they were "important" or not. To God everyone is the same.) ⁷But these leaders saw that I had been given the work of telling the Good News to those who are not Jewish, just as Peter had the work of telling the Jews. ⁸God gave Peter the power to work as an apostle for the Jewish people. But he also gave me the power to work as an apostle for those who are not Jews. ⁹James, Peter, and John, who seemed to be the leaders, understood that God had given me this special grace, so they accepted Barnabas and me. They agreed that they would go to the Jewish people and that we should go to those who are not Jewish. ¹⁰The only thing they asked us was to remember to help the poor—something I really wanted to do.

PAUL SHOWS THAT PETER WAS WRONG

¹¹When Peter came to Antioch, I challenged him to his face, because he was wrong. ¹²Peter ate with the non-Jewish people until some Jewish people sent from James came to Antioch. When they arrived, Peter stopped eating with those who weren't Jewish, and he separated himself from them. He was afraid of the Jews. ¹³So Peter was a hypocrite, as were the other Jewish believers who joined with him. Even Barnabas was influenced by what these Jewish believers did. ¹⁴When I saw they were not following the truth of the Good News, I spoke to Peter in front of them all. I said, "Peter, you are a Jew, but you are not living like a Jew. You are living like those who are not Jewish. So why do you now try to force those who are not Jewish to live like Jews?"

¹⁵We were not born as non-Jewish "sinners," but as Jews. ¹⁶Yet we know that a person is made right with God not by following the law, but by trusting in Jesus Christ. So we, too, have put our faith in Christ Jesus, that we might be made right with God because we trusted in Christ. It is not because we followed the law, because no one can be made right with God by following the law. ¹⁷We Jews came to Christ, trying to be made right with God, and it became clear that we are sinners, too. Does this mean that Christ encourages sin? No! ¹⁸But I would really be wrong to begin teaching again those things that I gave up. ¹⁹It was the law that put me to death, and I died to the law so that I can now live for God. ²⁰I was put to death on the cross with Christ, and I do not live anymore—it is Christ who lives in me. I still live in my body, but I live by faith in the Son of God who loved me and gave himself to save me. ²¹By saying these things I am not going against God's grace. Just the opposite, if the law could make us right with God, then Christ's death would be useless.

BLESSING COMES THROUGH FAITH

3 You people in Galatia were told very clearly about the death of Jesus Christ on the cross. But you were foolish; you let someone trick you. ²Tell me this one thing: How did you receive the Holy Spirit? Did you receive the Spirit by following the law? No, you received the Spirit because you heard the Good News and believed it. ³You began your life in Christ by the Spirit. Now are you trying to make it complete by your own power? That is foolish. ⁴Were

VIEWPOINT

WHAT GENRE OF MUSIC INSPIRES AND MOTIVATES YOU, AND WHY?

I'm a lover of various genres of music and cannot limit it to just one style. Music is an inspiration and the words of many songs motivate me for different reasons. Hip-hop music may inspire me to remain conscious about people growing up in the ghetto and the things they face on the daily. Gospel may motivate me to stay in tune with God. Neo-soul may remind me to let go and let love.

all your experiences wasted? I hope not! [5]Does God give you the Spirit and work miracles among you because you follow the law? No, he does these things because you heard the Good News and believed it.

[6]The Scriptures say the same thing about Abraham: "Abraham believed God, and God accepted Abraham's faith, and that faith made him right with God."[n] [7]So you should know that the true children of Abraham are those who have faith. [8]The Scriptures, telling what would happen in the future, said that God would make the non-Jewish people right through their faith. This Good News was told to Abraham beforehand, as the Scripture says: "All nations will be blessed through you."[n] [9]So all who believe as Abraham believed are blessed just as Abraham was. [10]But those who depend on following the law to make them right are under a curse, because the Scriptures say, "Anyone will be cursed who does not always obey what is written in the Book of the Law."[n] [11]Now it is clear that no one can be made right with God by the law, because the Scriptures say, "Those who are right with God will live by faith."[n] [12]The law is not based on faith. It says, "A person who obeys these things will live because of them."[n] [13]Christ took away the curse the law put on us. He changed places with us and put himself under that curse. It is written in the Scriptures, "Anyone whose body is displayed on a tree[n] is cursed." [14]Christ did this so that God's blessing promised to Abraham might come through Jesus Christ to those who are not Jews. Jesus died so that by our believing we could receive the Spirit that God promised.

THE LAW AND THE PROMISE

[15]Brothers and sisters, let us think in human terms: Even an agreement made between two persons is firm. After that agreement is accepted by both people, no one can stop it or add anything to it. [16]God made promises both to Abraham and to his descendant. God did not say, "and to your descendants." That would mean many people. But God said, "and to your descendant." That means only one person; that person is Christ. [17]This is what I mean: God had an agreement with Abraham and promised to keep it. The law, which came four hundred thirty years later, cannot change that agreement and so destroy God's promise to Abraham. [18]If the law could give us Abraham's blessing, then the promise would not be necessary. But that is not possible, because God freely gave his blessings to Abraham through the promise he had made.

[19]So what was the law for? It was given to show that the wrong things people do are against God's will. And it

IMPACT!

FLA.VOR Alliance

Crossover Community Church in Tampa, Florida specifically targets the hip-hop culture to spread the gospel. In addition to their regular Bible study and worship services, they offer talent development classes such as MC class, DJ and Production, and B-Boy class. A group of ministers from Crossover Community Church make up the FLA.VOR Alliance. This outreach group ministers to youth at Crossover weekly but is also involved with organizing concerts, producing CDs, and Flavor Fest, a hip-hop/urban ministry conference. To be down with the Alliance, you must be a member of the Crossover Community Church, but if you're not in the area, visit their Web site at www.flavoralliance.com to learn about upcoming events.

3:6 "Abraham . . . God." Quotation from Genesis 15:6. **3:8 "All . . . you."** Quotation from Genesis 12:3 and 18:18. **3:10 "Anyone . . . Law."** Quotation from Deuteronomy 7:26. **3:11 "Those . . . faith."** Quotation from Habakkuk 2:4. **3:12 "A person . . . them."** Quotation from Leviticus 18:5. **3:13 displayed on a tree** Deuteronomy 21:22-23 says that when a person was killed for doing wrong, the body was hung on a tree to show shame. Paul means that the cross of Jesus was like that.

continued until the special descendant, who had been promised, came. The law was given through angels who used Moses for a mediator[n] to give the law to people. [20]But a mediator is not needed when there is only one side, and God is only one.

THE PURPOSE OF THE LAW OF MOSES

[21]Does this mean that the law is against God's promises? Never! That would be true only if the law could make us right with God. But God did not give a law that can bring life. [22]Instead, the Scriptures showed that the whole world is bound by sin. This was so the promise would be given through faith to people who believe in Jesus Christ.

[23]Before this faith came, we were all held prisoners by the law. We had no freedom until God showed us the way of faith that was coming. [24]In other words, the law was our guardian leading us to Christ so that we could be made right with God through faith. [25]Now the way of faith has come, and we no longer live under a guardian.

[26-27]You were all baptized into Christ, and so you were all clothed with Christ. This means that you are all children of God through faith in Christ Jesus. [28]In Christ, there is no difference between Jew and Greek, slave and free person, male and female. You are all the same in Christ Jesus. [29]You belong to Christ, so you are Abraham's descendants. You will inherit all of God's blessings because of the promise God made to Abraham.

4 I want to tell you this: While those who will inherit their fathers' property are still children, they are no different from slaves. It does not matter that the children own everything. [2]While they are children, they must obey those who are chosen to care for them. But when the children reach the age set by their fathers, they are free. [3]It is the same for us. We were once like children, slaves to the useless rules of this world.

3:19 mediator A person who helps one person talk to or give something to another person.

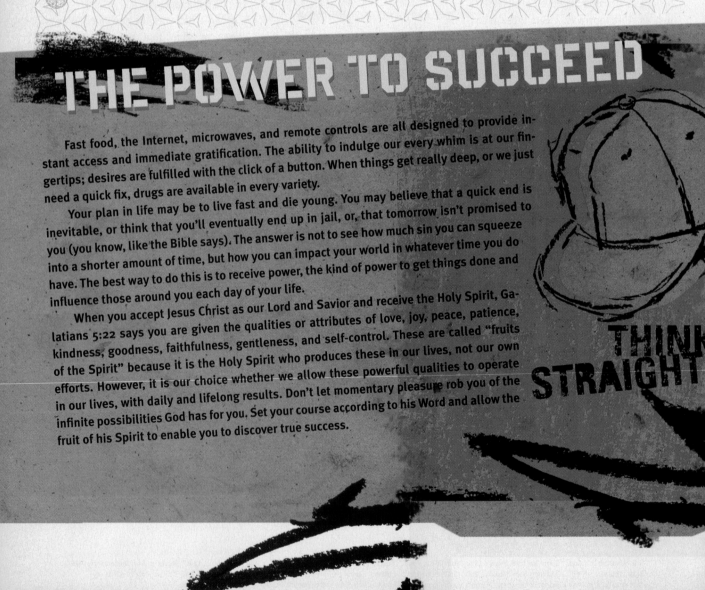

THE POWER TO SUCCEED

Fast food, the Internet, microwaves, and remote controls are all designed to provide instant access and immediate gratification. The ability to indulge our every whim is at our fingertips; desires are fulfilled with the click of a button. When things get really deep, or we just need a quick fix, drugs are available in every variety.

Your plan in life may be to live fast and die young. You may believe that a quick end is inevitable, or think that you'll eventually end up in jail, or, that tomorrow isn't promised to you (you know, like the Bible says). The answer is not to see how much sin you can squeeze into a shorter amount of time, but how you can impact your world in whatever time you do have. The best way to do this is to receive power, the kind of power to get things done and influence those around you each day of your life.

When you accept Jesus Christ as our Lord and Savior and receive the Holy Spirit, Galatians 5:22 says you are given the qualities or attributes of love, joy, peace, patience, kindness, goodness, faithfulness, gentleness, and self-control. These are called "fruits of the Spirit" because it is the Holy Spirit who produces these in our lives, not our own efforts. However, it is our choice whether we allow these powerful qualities to operate in our lives, with daily and lifelong results. Don't let momentary pleasure rob you of the infinite possibilities God has for you. Set your course according to his Word and allow the fruit of his Spirit to enable you to discover true success.

THINK STRAIGHT

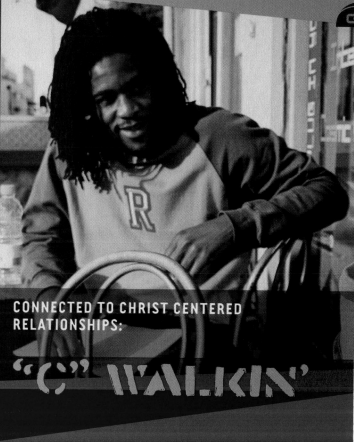

CONNECTED

CONNECTED TO CHRIST CENTERED RELATIONSHIPS:

"C" WALKIN'

Did Jesus really turn water to wine or were the partygoers so faded that they couldn't tell the difference? He did it because the Word of God says he did. But his mere presence would been enough to liven up the party. When Jesus walks into a place, things change from disastrous to hopeful. He made a paralyzed man walk (Matthew 9:2-8), a deaf man hear (Mark 7:31-37), and a dead man live again (John 11:43-44). He fed five thousand people with just two fish and five loaves of bread (Matthew 14:13-21). The wild thing about these situations is that every time Christ showed up, a monster change occurred.

When we accept Christ into our lives, we should expect change. The very nature of Christ's character creates a shift in our hearts that will cause us to line up to the will of God the Father. Even in your relationships, when Christ is at the center, big things will occur. Jesus has definitely got your back, but only if you make him Lord of all of your life and relationships.

From the jump off, Christ was a miracle (his mother was a virgin), all the way to the time he rose from the dead and ascended into heaven. Christ changed the entire world. His miracle birth and resurrection gave us hope by fulfilling prophecy and changing the route of death. He conquered death and his mere presence is guaranteed to bring new life. Keep Christ at the center of your life and watch the changes happen.

[4]But when the right time came, God sent his Son who was born of a woman and lived under the law. [5]God did this so he could buy freedom for those who were under the law and so we could become his children.

[6]Since you are God's children, God sent the Spirit of his Son into your hearts, and the Spirit cries out, "Father."[n] [7]So now you are not a slave; you are God's child, and God will give you the blessing he promised, because you are his child.

PAUL'S LOVE FOR THE CHRISTIANS

[8]In the past you did not know God. You were slaves to gods that were not real. [9]But now you know the true God. Really, it is God who knows you. So why do you turn back to those weak and useless rules you followed before? Do you want to be slaves to those things again? [10]You still follow teachings about special days, months, seasons, and years. [11]I am afraid for you, that my work for you has been wasted.

[12]Brothers and sisters, I became like you, so I beg you to become like me. You were very good to me before. [13]You remember that it was because of an illness that I came to you the first time, preaching the Good News. [14]Though my sickness was a trouble for you, you did not hate me or make me leave. But you welcomed me as an angel from God, as if I were Jesus Christ himself! [15]You were very happy then, but where is that joy now? I am ready to testify that you would have taken out your eyes and given them to me if that were possible. [16]Now am I your enemy because I tell you the truth?

[17]Those people[n] are working hard to persuade you, but this is not good for you. They want to persuade you to turn against us and follow only them. [18]It is good for people to show interest in you, but only if their purpose is good. This is always true, not just when I am with you. [19]My little children, again I feel the pain of childbirth for you until you truly become like Christ. [20]I wish I could be with

 4:6 "Father" Literally, "Abba, Father." Jewish children called their fathers "Abba." **4:17 Those people** They are the false teachers who were bothering the believers in Galatia (Galatians 1:7).

you now and could change the way I am talking to you, because I do not know what to think about you.

THE EXAMPLE OF HAGAR AND SARAH

²¹Some of you still want to be under the law. Tell me, do you know what the law says? ²²The Scriptures say that Abraham had two sons. The mother of one son was a slave woman, and the mother of the other son was a free woman. ²³Abraham's son from the slave woman was born in the normal human way. But the son from the free woman was born because of the promise God made to Abraham.

²⁴This story teaches something else: The two women are like the two agreements between God and his people. One agreement is the law that God made on Mount Sinai,ⁿ and the people who are under this agreement are like slaves. The mother named Hagar is like that agreement. ²⁵She is like Mount Sinai in Arabia and is a picture of the earthly city of Jerusalem. This city and its people are slaves to the law. ²⁶But the heavenly

He's got answers

What's wrong with watching porn? It doesn't hurt anyone.

Really? So is it okay if that was your sister or mother up there on the screen? Your little girl crawls up into your lap and says, "Daddy, what do you want me to be when I grow up?" Do you say, "Honey, I think you should be a porn star"? Deep inside you know it's wrong. You just may not know why.

Pornography is the big lie. There alone in your room with images of hundreds of unbelievably beautiful women willing to give themselves to you (and thousands of other men at the same time), it's easy to feel like a super-stud. But it's not real. It's all smoke and mirrors. It's ink and paper, videotape and celluloid. It is addictive and it is a trap. It can mess up your expectations when it comes to real-life sex with your real-life spouse and your ability to relate to a potential mate. And because porn is all about you, it can turn you into a selfish partner, which will inevitably end up hurting your relationship with your loved ones in the long run.

Read on: Matthew 5:28; 2 Timothy 2:22; 1 John 2:16

PEEP THIS:

The estimated Hispanic population of the United States as of July 1, 2003, is 39.9 million (not including Puerto Rico), making people of Hispanic origin the nation's largest race or ethnic minority, constituting 13.7 percent of the nation's total population.

Jerusalem, which is above, is like the free woman. She is our mother. ²⁷It is written in the Scriptures:

"Be happy, Jerusalem.
    You are like a woman who never gave birth to children.
Start singing and shout for joy.
    You never felt the pain of giving birth,
but you will have more children than the woman who has a husband."   *Isaiah 54:1*

²⁸My brothers and sisters, you are God's children because of his promise, as Isaac was then. ²⁹The son who was born in the normal way treated the other son badly. It is the same today. ³⁰But what does the Scripture say? "Throw out the slave woman and her son. The son of the slave woman should not inherit anything. The son of the free woman should receive it all."ⁿ ³¹So, my brothers and sisters, we are not children of the slave woman, but of the free woman.

KEEP YOUR FREEDOM

5 We have freedom now, because Christ made us free. So stand strong. Do not change and go back into the slavery of the law. ²Listen, I Paul tell you that if you go back to the law by being circumcised, Christ does you no good. ³Again, I warn every man: If you allow yourselves to be circumcised, you must follow all the law. ⁴If you try to be made right with God through the law, your life with Christ is

4:24 **Mount Sinai** Mountain in Arabia where God gave his Law to Moses (Exodus 19 and 20).   4:30 **"Throw . . . all."** Quotation from Genesis 21:10.

WORLD SAYS, WORD SAYS,

FRIENDS WITH BENEFITS

Sex is a part of life. Everyone needs it. It makes you feel loved and wanted, even if it's just for that moment. You're not hurting anybody, and you can sleep with as many people as you please. If you're not "giving it up," nobody will want to be with you. Sex is everywhere. It's what people do.

"So run away from sexual sin. Every other sin people do is outside their bodies, but those who sin sexually sin against their own bodies" (1 Corinthians 6:18).

"God wants you to be holy and to stay away from sexual sins" (1 Thessalonians 4:3).

"But run away from the evil young people like to do. Try hard to live right and to have faith, love, and peace, together with those who trust in the Lord from pure hearts" (2 Timothy 2:22).

over—you have left God's grace. [5]But we have the true hope that comes from being made right with God, and by the Spirit we wait eagerly for this hope. [6]When we are in Christ Jesus, it is not important if we are circumcised or not. The important thing is faith—the kind of faith that works through love.

[7]You were running a good race. Who stopped you from following the true way? [8]This change did not come from the One who chose you. [9]Be careful! "Just a little yeast makes the whole batch of dough rise." [10]But I trust in the Lord that you will not believe those different ideas. Whoever is confusing you with such ideas will be punished.

[11]My brothers and sisters, I do not teach that a man must be circumcised. If I teach circumcision, why am I still being attacked? If I still taught circumcision, my preaching about the cross would not be a problem. [12]I wish the people who are bothering you would castrate[n] themselves!

[13]My brothers and sisters, God called you to be free, but do not use your freedom as an excuse to do what pleases your sinful self. Serve each other with love. [14]The whole law is made complete in this one command: "Love your neighbor as you love yourself."[n] [15]If you go on hurting each other and tearing each

other apart, be careful, or you will completely destroy each other.

THE SPIRIT AND HUMAN NATURE

[16]So I tell you: Live by following the Spirit. Then you will not do what your sinful selves want. [17]Our sinful selves want what is against the Spirit, and the Spirit wants what is against our sinful selves. The two are against each other, so you cannot do just what you please. [18]But if the Spirit is leading you, you are not under the law.

[19]The wrong things the sinful self does are clear: being sexually unfaithful, not being pure, taking part in sexual sins, [20]worshiping gods, doing witchcraft, hating, making trouble, being jealous, being angry, being selfish, making people angry with each other, causing divisions among people, [21]feeling envy, being drunk, having wild and wasteful parties, and doing other things like these. I warn you now as I warned you before: Those who do these things will not inherit God's kingdom. [22]But the Spirit produces the fruit of love, joy, peace, patience, kindness, goodness, faithfulness, [23]gentleness, self-control. There is no law that says these things are wrong. [24]Those who belong to Christ Jesus have crucified their own sinful selves. They have given up their old selfish feelings

and the evil things they wanted to do. [25]We get our new life from the Spirit, so we should follow the Spirit. [26]We must not be proud or make trouble with each other or be jealous of each other.

HELP EACH OTHER

6 Brothers and sisters, if someone in your group does something wrong, you who are spiritual should go to that person and gently help make him right again. But be careful, because you might be tempted to sin, too. [2]By helping each other with your troubles, you truly obey the law of Christ. [3]If anyone thinks he is important when he really is not, he is only fooling himself. [4]Each person should judge his own actions and not compare himself with others. Then he can be proud for what he himself has done. [5]Each person must be responsible for himself.

[6]Anyone who is learning the teaching of God should share all the good things he has with his teacher.

LIFE IS LIKE PLANTING A FIELD

[7]Do not be fooled: You cannot cheat God. People harvest only what they plant. [8]If they plant to satisfy their sinful selves, their sinful selves will bring them ruin. But if they plant to please the

---

 5:12 castrate To cut off part of the male sex organ. Paul uses this word because it is similar to "circumcision." Paul wanted to show that he is very upset with the false teachers.
5:14 "Love . . . yourself." Quotation from Leviticus 19:18.

Spirit, they will receive eternal life from the Spirit. [9]We must not become tired of doing good. We will receive our harvest of eternal life at the right time if we do not give up. [10]When we have the opportunity to help anyone, we should do it. But we should give special attention to those who are in the family of believers.

PAUL ENDS HIS LETTER

[11]See what large letters I use to write this myself. [12]Some people are trying to force you to be circumcised so the Jews will accept them. They are afraid they will be attacked if they follow only the cross of Christ.[n] [13]Those who are circumcised do not obey the law themselves, but they want you to be circumcised so they can brag about what they forced you to do. [14]I hope I will never brag about things like that. The cross of our Lord Jesus Christ is my only reason for bragging. Through the cross of Jesus my world was crucified, and I died to the world. [15]It is not important if a man is circumcised or uncircumcised. The important thing is being the new people God has made. [16]Peace and mercy to those who follow this rule—and to all of God's people.

[17]So do not give me any more trouble. I have scars on my body that show[n] I belong to Christ Jesus.

[18]My brothers and sisters, the grace of our Lord Jesus Christ be with your spirit. Amen.

HeartCry

Temptation   **Are you struggling to resist doing the wrong things? Does it seem that you are nearly powerless to say no? Let your heart cry . . .**

God, it feels like a war is going on inside me. It's so hard to say no to things that part of me really wants to do. I feel bad that I want to do wrong things, things you don't want for me, but there it is. That's the truth of it. I feel like I am losing the war. I just don't feel strong enough to keep resisting. How do I find the power to continue saying no?

You are right to say there is a war. You have an enemy who wants you to make the wrong choices, who wants you to fall. You realize your strength is not enough, so call upon mine. Through my Holy Spirit I will give you all the strength you need to resist any temptation your enemy sends your way. **Ephesians 6:12-17; Romans 7:21-25**

6:12 cross of Christ Paul uses the cross as a picture of the Good News, the story of Christ's death and rising from the dead to pay for our sins. The cross, or Christ's death, was God's way to save us.   **6:17 that show** Many times Paul was beaten and whipped by people who were against him because he was teaching about Christ. The scars were from these beatings.

GOD USES SMALL THINGS TO DO IT BIG

Paul wrote this letter from behind bars where he had been put on lock down for preaching the message of Christ. But you'll quickly notice that his situation didn't hold him down. Even from prison, he still did his thing!

Paul hoped to stretch the thinking of the church in Ephesus. He wanted them to see the big picture of God's purpose and the big goals God had for the relatively small church. (That's exactly how God always does it. He uses small things to do it big!)

This letter sparks off with a lot of encouragement as Paul gives the people vision. He cleverly uses a metaphor comparing the fellowship of believers to the human body. He stresses how each believer is vitally important to make it happen. They might be a hand or an ear, but all are needed to help the body of Christ fully represent and fulfill its purpose. Paul recognized the mad diversity and talent in the crew and he acknowledged and celebrated it. He called for everyone to come together in unity and accomplish the vision. After he encouraged and instructed them, he advised them to get ready for spiritual battle. Even back then . . . the controversy in the streets was real!

1 From Paul, an apostle of Christ Jesus. I am an apostle because that is what God wanted.

To God's holy people living in Ephesus,[n] believers in Christ Jesus:

[2]Grace and peace to you from God our Father and the Lord Jesus Christ.

SPIRITUAL BLESSINGS IN CHRIST

[3]Praise be to the God and Father of our Lord Jesus Christ. In Christ, God has given us every spiritual blessing in the heavenly world. [4]That is, in Christ, he chose us before the world was made so that we would be his holy people—people without blame before him. [5]Because of his love, God had already decided to make us his own children through Jesus Christ. That was what he wanted and what pleased him, [6]and it brings praise to God because of his wonderful grace. God gave that grace to us freely, in Christ, the One he loves. [7]In Christ we are set free by the blood of his death, and so we have forgiveness of sins. How rich is God's grace, [8]which he has given to us so fully and freely. God, with full wisdom and understanding, [9]let us know his secret purpose. This was what God wanted, and he planned to do it through Christ.

chosen so that we would bring praise to God's glory. [13]So it is with you. When you heard the true teaching—the Good News about your salvation—you believed in Christ. And in Christ, God put his special mark of ownership on you by giving you the Holy Spirit that he had promised. [14]That Holy Spirit is the guarantee that we will receive what God promised for his people until God gives full freedom to those who are his—to bring praise to God's glory.

PAUL'S PRAYER

[15]That is why since I heard about your faith in the Lord Jesus and your love for all God's people, [16]I have not stopped giving thanks to God for you. I always remember you in my prayers, [17]asking the God of our Lord Jesus Christ, the glorious Father, to give you a spirit of wisdom and revelation so that you will know him better. [18]I pray also that you will have greater understanding in your heart so you will know the hope to which he has called us and that you will know how rich and glorious are the blessings God has promised his holy people. [19]And you will know that God's power is very great for us who believe. That power is

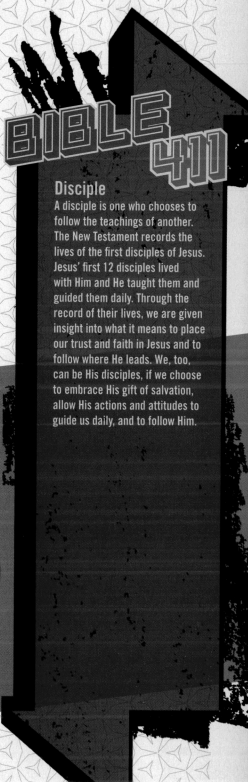

Disciple

A disciple is one who chooses to follow the teachings of another. The New Testament records the lives of the first disciples of Jesus. Jesus' first 12 disciples lived with Him and He taught them and guided them daily. Through the record of their lives, we are given insight into what it means to place our trust and faith in Jesus and to follow where He leads. We, too, can be His disciples, if we choose to embrace His gift of salvation, allow His actions and attitudes to guide us daily, and to follow Him.

COME TOGETHER IN UNITY AND ACCOMPLISH THE VISION

[10]His goal was to carry out his plan, when the right time came, that all things in heaven and on earth would be joined together in Christ as the head.

[11]In Christ we were chosen to be God's people, because from the very beginning God had decided this in keeping with his plan. And he is the One who makes everything agree with what he decides and wants. [12]We are the first people who hoped in Christ, and we were

the same as the great strength [20]God used to raise Christ from the dead and put him at his right side in the heavenly world. [21]God has put Christ over all rulers, authorities, powers, and kings, not only in this world but also in the next. [22]God put everything under his power and made him the head over everything for the church, [23]which is Christ's body. The church is filled with Christ, and Christ fills everything in every way.

1:1 in Ephesus Some Greek copies do not have this phrase.

WE NOW HAVE LIFE

2 In the past you were spiritually dead because of your sins and the things you did against God. [2] Yes, in the past you lived the way the world lives, following the ruler of the evil powers that are above the earth. That same spirit is now working in those who refuse to obey God. [3] In the past all of us lived like them, trying to please our sinful selves and doing all the things our bodies and minds wanted. We should have suffered God's anger because we were sinful by nature. We were the same as all other people.

[4] But God's mercy is great, and he loved us very much. [5] Though we were spiritually dead because of the things we did against God, he gave us new life with Christ. You have been saved by God's grace. [6] And he raised us up with Christ and gave us a seat with him in the heavens. He did this for those in Christ Jesus [7] so that for all future time he could show the very great riches of his grace by being kind to us in Christ Jesus. [8] I mean that you have been saved by grace through believing. You did not save yourselves; it was a gift from God. [9] It was not the result of your own efforts, so you cannot brag about it. [10] God has made us what we are. In Christ Jesus, God made us to do good works, which God planned in advance for us to live our lives doing.

ONE IN CHRIST

[11] You were not born Jewish. You are the people the Jews call "uncircumcised." Those who call you "uncircumcised" call themselves "circumcised." (Their circumcision is only something they themselves do on their bodies.) [12] Remember that in the past you were without Christ. You were not citizens of Israel, and you had no part in the agreements with the promise that God made to his people. You had no hope, and you did not know God. [13] But now in Christ Jesus, you who were far away from God are brought

2:11 **uncircumcised** People not having the mark of circumcision as the Jews had.   2:12 **agreements** The agreements that God gave to his people in the Old Testament.

PURPOSE AND DESTINY

Is there anything more futile than a life that lacks meaning and purpose? Within each one of us, there is a desire—our most basic need—to know why we exist; we all seek a purpose for being and a reason for living. Every soul cries out to know why it was created and what value it adds to the world.

Everyone dreams of possibilities. If you are honest with yourself, you will have to admit that you have a desire to conquer the unknown, to become someone, and to accomplish something significant. This image of possibility has nothing to do with acquiring things or amassing wealth, but everything to do with who you are at the very core of your being. Jeremiah 29:11 says that God has a plan for your life and will give you a future and a hope. Psalm 37 says that God will give you the desires of your heart if you turn your heart toward him. The key to finding true fulfillment is recognizing that God created you with purpose and destiny. Your purpose is to love and serve him and your destiny lies in courageously following your heart's truest desire. God placed this desire in you and he will lead you on the path toward making it a reality, if you will seek his guidance and listen to his leading.

Discovering your purpose and ultimate destiny is not as impossible as it may seem, but it requires determination and honesty. You must be willing to focus your energy beyond the distractions of your everyday life and direct your strength toward becoming the person you dream of being. You must make the choice to reach beyond where you are and work toward where you want to be. Above all, you must recognize that God is the creator of your heart and the author of your future. Your true destiny will be found only in him.

THINK STRAIGHT

ANGER UNLEASHED

When the cops pull you over for no reason, or your boss confronts you right in front of everyone, or someone does something to make you mad, you have every right to tell them where to go and how to get there. Get angry! Don't let people run over you. They did you wrong; now it's your turn to retaliate.

"A gentle answer will calm a person's anger, but an unkind answer will cause more anger" (Proverbs 15:1).

"Smart people are patient; they will be honored if they ignore insults" (Proverbs 19:11).

"When you are angry, do not sin, and be sure to stop being angry before the end of the day" (Ephesians 4:26).

near through the blood of Christ's death. [14]Christ himself is our peace. He made both Jewish people and those who are not Jews one people. They were separated as if there were a wall between them, but Christ broke down that wall of hate by giving his own body. [15]The Jewish law had many commands and rules, but Christ ended that law. His purpose was to make the two groups of people become one new people in him and in this way make peace. [16]It was also Christ's purpose to end the hatred between the two groups, to make them into one body, and to bring them back to God. Christ did all this with his death on the cross. [17]Christ came and preached peace to you who were far away from God, and to those who were near to God. [18]Yes, it is through Christ we all have the right to come to the Father in one Spirit.

[19]Now you who are not Jewish are not foreigners or strangers any longer, but are citizens together with God's holy people. You belong to God's family. [20]You are like a building that was built on the foundation of the apostles and prophets. Christ Jesus himself is the most important stone[n] in that building, [21]and that whole building is joined together in Christ. He makes it grow and become a holy temple in the Lord. [22]And in Christ you, too, are being built together with the Jews into a place where God lives through the Spirit.

PAUL'S WORK IN TELLING THE GOOD NEWS

3 So I, Paul, am a prisoner of Christ Jesus for you who are not Jews. [2]Surely you have heard that God gave me this work to tell you about his grace. [3]He let me know his secret by showing it to me. I have already written a little about this. [4]If you read what I wrote then, you can see that I truly understand the secret about the Christ. [5]People who lived in other times were not told that secret. But now, through the Spirit, God has shown that secret to his holy apostles and prophets. [6]This is that secret: that through the Good News those who are not Jews will share with the Jews in God's blessing. They belong to the same body, and they share together in the promise that God made in Christ Jesus.

[7]By God's special gift of grace given to me through his power, I became a servant to tell that Good News. [8]I am the least important of all God's people, but God gave me this gift—to tell those who are not Jews the Good News about the riches of Christ, which are too great to understand fully. [9]And God gave me the work of telling all people about the plan for his secret, which has been hidden in him since the beginning of time. He is the One who created everything. [10]His purpose was that through the church all the rulers and powers in the heavenly world will now know God's wisdom, which has so many forms. [11]This agrees with the purpose God had since the beginning of time, and he carried out his plan through Christ Jesus our Lord. [12]In Christ we can come before God with freedom and without fear. We can do this through faith in Christ. [13]So I ask you not to become discouraged because of the sufferings I am having for you. My sufferings are for your glory.

THE LOVE OF CHRIST

[14]So I bow in prayer before the Father [15]from whom every family in heaven and on earth gets its true name. [16]I ask the Father in his great glory to give you the power to be strong inwardly through his Spirit. [17]I pray that Christ will live in your hearts by faith and that your life will be strong in love and be built on love. [18]And I pray that you and all God's holy people will have the power to understand the greatness of Christ's love—how wide and how long and how high and how deep that love is. [19]Christ's love is greater than anyone can ever know, but I pray that you will be able to know that love. Then you can be filled with the fullness of God.

[20]With God's power working in us, God can do much, much more than any-

2:20 most important stone Literally, "cornerstone." The first and most important stone in a building.

AGAINST ALL ODDS

and one leg slightly shorter than the other. I also suffered from chronic muscle spasms as a result of that cruelty.

In my suffering, I cried out to God. I spoke to the Lord as my best friend. Even though I wasn't expected to live, I survived because God had a purpose for my life. I was a shy child with a speech impediment, but God gave me talents and strengths. Although I was abused and grew up with physical ailments, I thrived as God's child. He has done great things throughout my life.

Today I am a public speaker and a singer. The hole in my heart is so small that the doctors can hardly detect it. I counsel others and am an inspirational speaker, empowering others to stand up against abuse. I have become a living example of God's mercy, and grace. I am a walking, talking testimony to the power of God to heal, restore and bring purpose to life. Even when I look back on the trials, pain, and struggles, I am thankful for my past because it developed me into the person I am today.

Genesis 50:20 — You meant to hurt me, but God turned your evil into good to save the lives of many people, which is being done.

It seems as if hard times were my fate from before I was born. Just at the time when doctors told my mama that she had three months to live, she got pregnant with me. The doctors told her that both she and the baby would die, but she carried me longer than anyone expected. When she went into premature labor, the doctors asked my grandmother whose life should be saved, her daughter's or the baby's. My grandmother told the doctors to save my mother.

I should have been dead, but I made it, spending the first four months of my life in the hospital. I was very small, had a hole in my heart, a tongue that was stuck to the bottom of my mouth, and two ankles on one foot. As I grew, I began to have the necessary surgeries.

Life did not get much easier for me. At the age of eight, a family member beat me severely. I couldn't walk for a week and was left with a permanent curvature in my spine

---

thing we can ask or imagine. [21]To him be glory in the church and in Christ Jesus for all time, forever and ever. Amen.

THE UNITY OF THE BODY

4 I am in prison because I belong to the Lord. Therefore I urge you who have been chosen by God to live up to the life to which God called you. [2]Always be humble, gentle, and patient, accepting each other in love. [3]You are joined together with peace through the Spirit, so make every effort to con-

tinue together in this way. [4]There is one body and one Spirit, and God called you to have one hope. [5]There is one Lord, one faith, and one baptism. [6]There is one God and Father of everything. He rules everything and is everywhere and is in everything.

[7]Christ gave each one of us the special gift of grace, showing how generous he is. [8]That is why it says in the Scriptures,

"When he went up to the heights, he led a parade of captives, and he gave gifts to people."

Psalm 68:18

[9]When it says, "He went up," what does it mean? It means that he first came down to the earth. [10]So Jesus came down, and he is the same One who went up above all the heaven. Christ did that to fill everything with his presence. [11]And Christ gave gifts to people—he made some to be apostles, some to be prophets, some to go and tell the Good News, and some to have the work of caring for and teaching God's people. [12]Christ gave those gifts to prepare God's holy people for the work of serving, to make the body of Christ stron-

ger. [13]This work must continue until we are all joined together in the same faith and in the same knowledge of the Son of God. We must become like a mature person, growing until we become like Christ and have his perfection.

[14]Then we will no longer be babies. We will not be tossed about like a ship that the waves carry one way and then another. We will not be influenced by every new teaching we hear from people who are trying to fool us. They make plans and try any kind of trick to fool people into following the wrong path. [15]No! Speaking the truth with love, we will grow up in every way into Christ, who is the head. [16]The whole body depends on Christ, and all the parts of the body are joined and held together. Each part does its own work to make the whole body grow and be strong with love.

THE WAY YOU SHOULD LIVE

[17]In the Lord's name, I tell you this. Do not continue living like those who do not believe. Their thoughts are worth nothing. [18]They do not understand, and they know nothing, because they refuse to listen. So they cannot have the life that God gives. [19]They have lost all feeling of shame, and they use their lives for doing evil. They continually want to do all kinds of evil. [20]But what you learned in Christ was not like this. [21]I know that you heard about him, and you are in him, so you were taught the truth that is in Jesus. [22]You were taught to leave your old self—to stop living the evil way you lived before. That old self becomes worse, because people are fooled by the evil things they want to do. [23]But you were taught to be made new in your hearts, [24]to become a new person. That new person is made to be like God—made to be truly good and holy.

[25]So you must stop telling lies. Tell each other the truth, because we all belong to each other in the same body.[n] [26]When you are angry, do not sin, and be sure to stop being angry before the end of the day. [27]Do not give the devil a way to defeat you. [28]Those who are stealing must stop stealing and start working. They should earn an honest living for themselves. Then they will have something to share with those who are poor.

[29]When you talk, do not say harmful things, but say what people need—words that will help others become stronger. Then what you say will do good to those who listen to you. [30]And do not make the Holy Spirit sad. The Spirit is God's proof that you belong to him. God gave you the Spirit to show that God will make you free when the final day

IMPACT!

Fellowship of Christian Athletes

Coaches and athletes on all levels belong to the Fellowship of Christian Athletes (FCA) to demonstrate their love for Christ though their love of sports. FCA is the largest Christian sports ministry in the world. If you are an athlete, joining this group is as easy as signing the Competitor's Creed: professing your love for Christ and your desire to do his will. By joining the FCA, you can unite with other brothers and sisters in Christ. You even can get more involved by becoming a ministry leader. Applications and the Competitor's Creed are available on the Web site, www.fca.org or by calling toll free: 1-800-289-0909.

4:25 Tell . . . body. Quotation from Zechariah 8:16.

comes. ³¹Do not be bitter or angry or mad. Never shout angrily or say things to hurt others. Never do anything evil. ³²Be kind and loving to each other, and forgive each other just as God forgave you in Christ.

LIVING IN THE LIGHT

5 You are God's children whom he loves, so try to be like him. ²Live a life of love just as Christ loved us and gave himself for us as a sweet-smelling offering and sacrifice to God.

³But there must be no sexual sin among you, or any kind of evil or greed. Those things are not right for God's holy people. ⁴Also, there must be no evil talk among you, and you must not speak foolishly or tell evil jokes. These things are not right for you. Instead, you should be giving thanks to God. ⁵You can be sure of this: No one will have a place in the kingdom of Christ and of God who sins sexually, or does evil things, or is greedy. Anyone who is greedy is serving a false god.

⁶Do not let anyone fool you by telling you things that are not true, because these things will bring God's anger on those who do not obey him. ⁷So have nothing to do with them. ⁸In the past you were full of darkness, but now you are full of light in the Lord. So live like children who belong to the light. ⁹Light brings every kind of goodness, right living, and truth. ¹⁰Try to learn what pleases the Lord. ¹¹Have nothing to do with the things done in darkness, which are not worth anything. But show that they are wrong. ¹²It is shameful even to talk about what those people do in secret. ¹³But the light makes all things easy to see, ¹⁴and everything that is made easy to see can become light. This is why it is said:

DEEP ISSUES
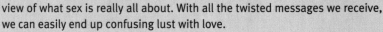

Sex

Sex sells. Just putting that three-letter word on paper turns heads. It probably got you looking right now. Sex gets people's attention. Almost everywhere we look, it's in our faces—on billboards, in magazines, at the movies, on TV shows, on the Internet. It has become a dominating force in hip-hop music lyrics and videos. As a result, we've developed a messed-up view of what sex is really all about. With all the twisted messages we receive, we can easily end up confusing lust with love.

But what does God say about sex? The Bible actually talks a lot about that three-letter buzzword. It's not something new. Many people think God is against sex. Wrong! God created sex to be a beautiful and very enjoyable act. Sex was meant to be an expression of love and commitment between a man and a woman in marriage.

We have all bought something and had to read the manufacturer's instruction manual to find out how it worked. Life is much the same. None of us have it all figured out and we need to check out the instruction manual written by our Creator. We may not always understand why things work the way they do, but God does. He knows our emotions and how we function. He knows what will hurt us and what will help us. Sex outside of its proper place is destructive! Look at all the broken families, sexual diseases, and unhappy people. We can see the pain firsthand. It's not worth it! Paul instructs readers in 1 Thessalonians 4:3-7 to stay away from sexual immorality and learn to control themselves. It may not be easy at times, but God is always there to give us the strength. If we can learn to follow our Creator's instructions and do it his way, we'll lead much happier lives as we fulfill his purposes.

REAL RHYMES.

REAL MAN

BY SPEC, SABE & REFLEX THE SON ©2005 FLAVOR ALLIANCE MUSIC

HE WAS A REAL MAN. HE HAD AN ILL PLAN.

I AWAIT THE LONG AWAITED AND THE SLEEPLESS NIGHTS TO
   DETERMINE WHAT IS RIGHT IN THE HEAT OF
   THE NIGHT
YOU CAN NEVER UNDERSTAND WHAT HE DID IN MY MIND, SON.
DON'T UNDERSTAND, ESTIMATE, 'CUZ HIS POWER'S DIVINE, ONE.
DEVOUR WHO OPPOSE STEPPIN' ILL IN MY SECTA. YOU THINK YOU
   GOT THE JUICE NOW YOU TASTE
   THE GOD NECTA.
DISSECT WITH COLD STEEL. I KNOW THAT YOU FEEL THIS. THE
   SCALPEL THEN INCISION, NOW YOU KNOW WHO
   THE REAL IS.
FOCUS ON THE SITUATION WAITIN' AT HAND. THIS BE GODLY OL'
   WISDOM NOT NO THEORIES FROM MAN.
IN ME THERE IS ONLY ONE I KING THAT HAS MY CARDIAC.
   DEFEATED THE DEVIL—LE NOT THE CADILLAC.
IMMA IST PETER 4:11 SPEAKING THROUGH GOD'S TONGUE.
   ANYTHING NOT OF HIM GET PUTS IN THE DEAD
   NUMB.
NO RUM CAN NEVER EVER ENTER THIS MAN. NO GUNS CAN
   NEVER EVER, EVER SURVIVE IN MY HANDS.
UNDERSTAND I SPEAK THE LIFE OF AN OLD HOOLIGAN. HIS WILL
   FOR ME TO GO ABOUT AND TRAVEL THIS LAND, AS I REST
   AND I WAIT UP IN THE PALM OF HIS HAND.
I SPEAK OF THE LIVING GOD—THE TRUE CHRIST—THE REAL MAN,
   HOLLA!

I, FIEND FOR THE GLORIOUS, THE RISEN GOD. I BEEN GONE FOR
   A MINUTE, NOW ITS BACKYARD.
WRESTLING MY FLESH WITHIN, SPITTIN' BLOOD, ONE LAMB VS. A
   SERPENT FOR ETERNAL LOVE.
SCRUB THE FLOORS, NOT AFRAID TO GET DIRTY. THROW ME A
   PEN PROTECTOR, I'M FEELIN' NERDY.
CALL ME A BOOKWORM. I KEPT MY HEAD UP IN THE PAGES.
SAVE MY LIFE STRAIGHT OUT THE GATES LEAVING LAS VEGAS.
I'M NICHOLAS CAGE, BUT I'M FIXED IN THE STRENGTH OF MY
   GOD'S WAYS.
I ESCAPE THROUGH THESE UNDERGROUND LAYERS LIKE
   ALCATRAZ. TAKE A QUIZ, DO THE MATH.

TAKE MY LIFE, MULTIPLY IT BY A TRILLION, MINUS GOD. YO—YOU
   STARIN' AT A VILLAIN.
MY LIFE AIN'T JACK WITHOUT CHRIST. I'M FLAT LIKE WILL HUNG,
   SINGING A SONG.
IT'S JUST WRONG LIKE PING—PONG. BACK AND FORTH, LIFE
   GOING IN A CIRCLE ON A ONE WAY COURSE.
NEVER JERK YOUR CHAIN. I'M SERIOUS. I'M DEDICATED TO THE
   SUN, NOT THE BURNING STAR.
I SPEAK ABOUT THE ONE BEATEN DOWN TO A BLOODY PULP,
   BUT GAVE US TREASURE BEYOND WEALTH.
TOOK US FROM ETERNAL HELL AND WHEN THE BELL RANG, HE
   KEPT US IN THE FIGHT.
DESPITE BEING FULL OF SIN, YO, HE MADE US RIGHT!

REFLEX THE SON, NOT JUST A NAME, 'CAUSE I'M NOT THE
   SAME SINCE MY ENCOUNTER WITH THE SON.
IT REFLECTS THE NAME CHANGE NEVER TO GAIN FAME, BUT TO
   ROCK THE SAME NAME THAT'S ON HIGH—LIKE THE
   SKY.
NEVER SINNED, BUT BECAME PAIN. SLAIN FOR HEALIN' THE LAME
   BUT HE REMAINED SANE TO MAKE KINGS AND QUEENS FROM
   JOHN DOE'S AND PLAIN JANE'S.
RULED THE SKY, CREATED THE EARTH, AND WHEN RAIN CAME,
   CREATED REBIRTH.
'CAUSE MAN HAD BECAME CAIN, MADE RAINBOWS A SIGNAL LIKE
   WHEN YOU'RE 'BOUT TO CHANGE LANES.
STILL MAN'S HEART WAS ILL AND NEVER BECAME TAMED.
   NEEDED TO RENEW AS IF YOU HAD TO CHANGE
   BRAINS.
IT'S INSANE TO EXPECT CHANGE WHEN YOU DOING THE SAME
   THINGS.
CHRIST CAME. CHANGED THE GAME THROUGH THE CROSS AND
   PAIN.
GAINED SOULS WERE LOST. THE COST WAS PAID, STAINED BY
   BLOOD DRAINED SACRIFICE.
IT WAS INHUMANE, BUT IT WAS JESUS THE CHRIST AND NOW
   HIS NAME REIGNS!
HE WAS A REAL MAN. HE HAD AN ILL PLAN. THREW HIMSELF ASIDE
   TO SAVE A DEAD LAND. I'M JUST A HUMAN, BUT I'M A NEW
   MAN. OUTSIDE OF CHRIST I'M JUST A WEAKLIN'.

DREAM Jobs for Women

10. Fashion designer

9. Teacher

8. Nurse

7. Athlete/ dancer

6. Writer

5. Housewife/ mother

4. Lawyer

3. Doctor

2. President of own company

1. Actress/singer

"Wake up, sleeper!
Rise from death,
and Christ will shine on you."
[15]So be very careful how you live. Do not live like those who are not wise, but live wisely. [16]Use every chance you have for doing good, because these are evil times. [17]So do not be foolish but learn what the Lord wants you to do. [18]Do not be drunk with wine, which will ruin you, but be filled with the Spirit. [19]Speak to each other with psalms, hymns, and spiritual songs, singing and making music in your hearts to the Lord. [20]Always give thanks to God the Father for everything, in the name of our Lord Jesus Christ.

WIVES AND HUSBANDS

[21]Yield to obey each other as you would to Christ.

[22]Wives, yield to your husbands, as you do to the Lord, [23]because the husband is the head of the wife, as Christ is the head of the church. And he is the Savior of the body, which is the church. [24]As the church yields to Christ, so you wives should yield to your husbands in everything.

[25]Husbands, love your wives as Christ loved the church and gave himself for it [26]to make it belong to God. Christ used the word to make the church clean by washing it with water. [27]He died so that he could give the church to himself like a bride in all her beauty. He died so that the church could be pure and without fault, with no evil or sin or any other wrong thing in it. [28]In the same way, husbands should love their wives as they love their own bodies. The man who loves his wife loves himself. [29]No one ever hates his own body, but feeds and takes care of it. And that is what Christ does for the church, [30]because we are parts of his body. [31]The Scripture says, "So a man will leave his father and mother and be united with his wife, and the two will become one body."[n] [32]That secret is very important—I am talking about Christ and the church. [33]But each one of you must love his wife as he loves

himself, and a wife must respect her husband.

CHILDREN AND PARENTS

6 Children, obey your parents as the Lord wants, because this is the right thing to do. [2]The command says, "Honor your father and mother."[n] This is the first command that has a promise with it— [3]"Then everything will be well with you, and you will have a long life on the earth."[n]

[4]Fathers, do not make your children angry, but raise them with the training and teaching of the Lord.

SLAVES AND MASTERS

[5]Slaves, obey your masters here on earth with fear and respect and from a sincere heart, just as you obey Christ. [6]You must do this not only while they are watching you, to please them. With all your heart you must do what God wants as people who are obeying Christ. [7]Do your work with enthusiasm. Work as if you were serving the Lord, not as if you were serving only men and women. [8]Remember that the Lord will give a reward to everyone, slave or free, for doing good.

[9]Masters, in the same way, be good to your slaves. Do not threaten them. Remember that the One who is your Master and their Master is in heaven, and he treats everyone alike.

WEAR THE FULL ARMOR OF GOD

[10]Finally, be strong in the Lord and in his great power. [11]Put on the full armor of God so that you can fight against the devil's evil tricks. [12]Our fight is not against people on earth but against the rulers and authorities and the powers of this world's darkness, against the spiritual powers of evil in the heavenly world. [13]That is why you need to put on God's full armor. Then on the day of evil you will be able to stand strong. And when you have finished the whole fight, you will still be standing. [14]So stand strong, with the belt of truth tied around your

5:31 "So . . . body." Quotation from Genesis 2:24. **6:2 "Honor . . . mother."** Quotation from Exodus 20:12; Deuteronomy 5:16. **6:3 "Then . . . earth."** Quotation from Exodus 20:12; Deuteronomy 5:16.

waist and the protection of right living on your chest. [15]On your feet wear the Good News of peace to help you stand strong. [16]And also use the shield of faith with which you can stop all the burning arrows of the Evil One. [17]Accept God's salvation as your helmet, and take the sword of the Spirit, which is the word of God. [18]Pray in the Spirit at all times with all kinds of prayers, asking for everything you need. To do this you must always be ready and never give up. Always pray for all God's people.

[19]Also pray for me that when I speak, God will give me words so that I can tell the secret of the Good News without fear. [20]I have been sent to preach this Good News, and I am doing that now, here in prison. Pray that when I preach the Good News I will speak without fear, as I should.

FINAL GREETINGS

[21]I am sending to you Tychicus, our brother whom we love and a faithful servant of the Lord's work. He will tell you everything that is happening with me. Then you will know how I am and what I am doing. [22]I am sending him to you for this reason—so that you will know how we are, and he can encourage you.

[23]Peace and love with faith to you brothers and sisters from God the Father and the Lord Jesus Christ. [24]Grace to all of you who love our Lord Jesus Christ with love that never ends.

HeartCry

Anger   Are people messing with you and getting in your face? Are you struggling to keep from losing control? Let your heart cry . . .

Hello, God. Man, do I need help. I feel like I'm going to explode. Seems like everyone is out to make me lose it. I'm scared, 'cause I'm afraid I will lose control and do something I'll regret. How do I keep from getting so angry? It's not like I decide to be this way. It just happens. I know you don't want me to be like this. Help me, please!

When you feel anger boiling up inside, look to me rather than the circumstance. I have promised you peace but you must choose to find it, and you will find it in me. Ephesians 4:31; James 1:20

SURFACE THINGS LEAVE US WANTING MORE

If we channel surf around in current culture it seems everyone is looking for happiness through some type of extreme makeover: their ride, their crib, their job and even their body. People get these things all hooked up on reality TV. But these surface things only bring satisfaction for a little while and then leave us wanting more.

As we pick up the remote and click on the channel of Philippians we see true happiness. Paul writes this letter from a Roman prison cell. We don't need a plasma screen in HD to picture Paul's rough life, yet his happiness and excitement flood the set. His circumstances have nothing to do with his state of mind. Most of us would be complaining and questioning God if we got locked up for speaking the truth, but not Paul. As we watch this drama unfold we see him using his situation to continue to tell others about Christ. He preaches to the guards and everyone who visits him. He tells people not to put their trust in their own accomplishments or their own strength, but only in Christ and the power of his resurrection. Paul reminds them not to get caught up in material things that only lead to selfishness.

Even though Paul could have acted like the man, he continually stayed humble and encouraged others to follow his example. Paul was not interested in big network ratings for himself; he speaks the real truth and gives all the props to Christ.

1

From Paul and Timothy, servants of Christ Jesus.

To all of God's holy people in Christ Jesus who live in Philippi, including your overseers and deacons:

[2]Grace and peace to you from God our Father and the Lord Jesus Christ.

PAUL'S PRAYER

[3]I thank my God every time I remember you, [4]always praying with joy for all of you. [5]I thank God for the help you gave me while I preached the Good News—help you gave from the first day you believed until now. [6]God began doing a good work in you, and I am sure he will continue it until it is finished when Jesus Christ comes again.

[7]And I know that I am right to think like this about all of you, because I have you in my heart. All of you share in God's grace with me while I am in prison and while I am defending and proving the truth of the Good News. [8]God knows that I want to see you very much, because I love all of you with the love of Christ Jesus.

[9]This is my prayer for you: that your love will grow more and more; that you

PAUL'S TROUBLES HELP THE WORK

[12]I want you brothers and sisters to know that what has happened to me has helped to spread the Good News. [13]All the palace guards and everyone else knows that I am in prison because I am a believer in Christ. [14]Because I am in prison, most of the believers have become more bold in Christ and are not afraid to speak the word of God.

[15]It is true that some preach about Christ because they are jealous and ambitious, but others preach about Christ because they want to help. [16]They preach because they have love, and they know that God gave me the work of defending the Good News. [17]But the others preach about Christ for selfish and wrong reasons, wanting to make trouble for me in prison.

[18]But it doesn't matter. The important thing is that in every way, whether for right or wrong reasons, they are preaching about Christ. So I am happy, and I will continue to be happy. [19]Because you are praying for me and the Spirit of Jesus Christ is helping me, I know this

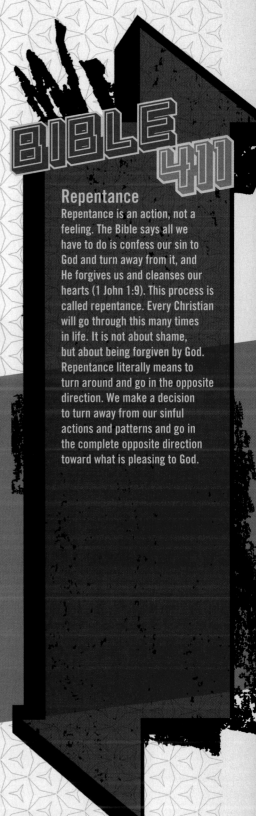

BIBLE 411

Repentance

Repentance is an action, not a feeling. The Bible says all we have to do is confess our sin to God and turn away from it, and He forgives us and cleanses our hearts (1 John 1:9). This process is called repentance. Every Christian will go through this many times in life. It is not about shame, but about being forgiven by God. Repentance literally means to turn around and go in the opposite direction. We make a decision to turn away from our sinful actions and patterns and go in the complete opposite direction toward what is pleasing to God.

TRUST IN CHRIST AND THE POWER OF HIS RESURRECTION

will have knowledge and understanding with your love; [10]that you will see the difference between good and bad and will choose the good; that you will be pure and without wrong for the coming of Christ; [11]that you will be filled with the good things produced in your life by Christ to bring glory and praise to God.

trouble will bring my freedom. [20]I expect and hope that I will not fail Christ in anything but that I will have the courage now, as always, to show the greatness of Christ in my life here on earth, whether I live or die. [21]To me the only important thing about living is Christ, and dying would be profit for me. [22]If I continue living in my body, I will be able to work for the Lord. I do not know what to choose—living or dying. ²³It is hard to choose between the two. I want to leave this life and be with Christ, which is much better, ²⁴but you need me here in my body. ²⁵Since I am sure of this, I know I will stay with you to help you grow and have joy in your faith. ²⁶You will be very happy in Christ Jesus when I am with you again.

²⁷Only one thing concerns me: Be sure that you live in a way that brings honor to the Good News of Christ. Then whether I come and visit you or am away from you, I will hear that you are standing strong with one purpose, that you work together as one for the faith of the Good News, ²⁸and that you are not afraid of those who are against you. All of this is proof that your enemies will be destroyed but that you will be saved by God. ²⁹God gave you the honor not only of believing in Christ but also of suffering for him, both of which bring glory to Christ. ³⁰When I was with you, you saw the struggles I had, and you hear about the struggles I am having now. You yourselves are having the same kind of struggles.

2 Does your life in Christ give you strength? Does his love comfort you? Do we share together in the spirit? Do you have mercy and kindness? ²If so, make me very happy by having the same thoughts, sharing the same love, and having one mind and purpose. ³When you do things, do not let selfishness or pride be your guide. Instead, be

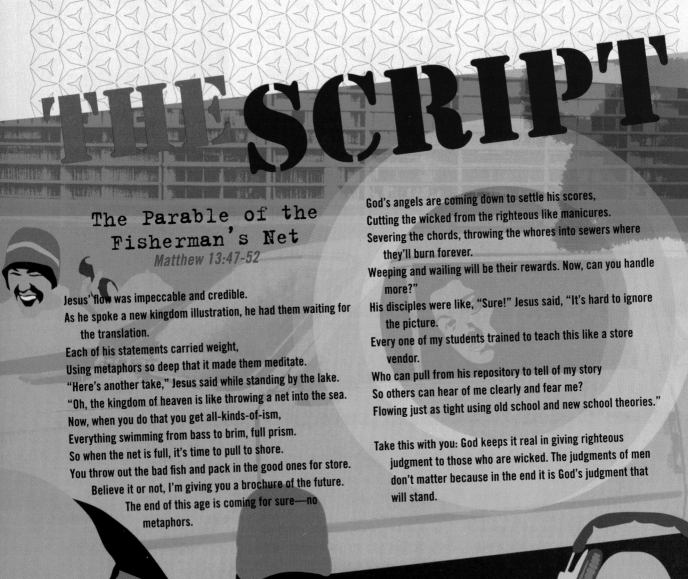

THE SCRIPT

The Parable of the Fisherman's Net
Matthew 13:47-52

Jesus' flow was impeccable and credible.
As he spoke a new kingdom illustration, he had them waiting for the translation.
Each of his statements carried weight,
Using metaphors so deep that it made them meditate.
"Here's another take," Jesus said while standing by the lake.
"Oh, the kingdom of heaven is like throwing a net into the sea.
Now, when you do that you get all-kinds-of-ism,
Everything swimming from bass to brim, full prism.
So when the net is full, it's time to pull to shore.
You throw out the bad fish and pack in the good ones for store.
Believe it or not, I'm giving you a brochure of the future.
The end of this age is coming for sure—no metaphors.

God's angels are coming down to settle his scores,
Cutting the wicked from the righteous like manicures.
Severing the chords, throwing the whores into sewers where they'll burn forever.
Weeping and wailing will be their rewards. Now, can you handle more?"
His disciples were like, "Sure!" Jesus said, "It's hard to ignore the picture.
Every one of my students trained to teach this like a store vendor.
Who can pull from his repository to tell of my story
So others can hear of me clearly and fear me?
Flowing just as tight using old school and new school theories."

Take this with you: God keeps it real in giving righteous judgment to those who are wicked. The judgments of men don't matter because in the end it is God's judgment that will stand.

humble and give more honor to others than to yourselves. [4]Do not be interested only in your own life, but be interested in the lives of others.

BE UNSELFISH LIKE CHRIST

[5]In your lives you must think and act like Christ Jesus.

[6]Christ himself was like God in
everything.
But he did not think that being
equal with God was something
to be used for his own benefit.
[7]But he gave up his place with God
and made himself nothing.
He was born as a man
and became like a servant.
[8]And when he was living as a man,
he humbled himself and was fully
obedient to God,
even when that caused his
death—death on a cross.
[9]So God raised him to the highest
place.
God made his name greater than
every other name
[10]so that every knee will bow to the
name of Jesus—
everyone in heaven, on earth, and
under the earth.
[11]And everyone will confess that Jesus
Christ is Lord
and bring glory to God the Father.

BE THE PEOPLE GOD WANTS YOU TO BE

[12]My dear friends, you have always obeyed God when I was with you. It is even more important that you obey now while I am away from you. Keep on working to complete your salvation with fear and trembling, [13]because God is working in you to help you want to do and be able to do what pleases him.

[14]Do everything without complaining or arguing. [15]Then you will be innocent and without any wrong. You will be God's children without fault. But you are living with crooked and mean people all around you, among whom you shine like stars in the dark world. [16]You offer the teaching that gives life. So when

Christ comes again, I can be happy because my work was not wasted. I ran the race and won.

[17]Your faith makes you offer your lives as a sacrifice in serving God. If I have to offer my own blood with your sacrifice, I will be happy and full of joy with all of you. [18]You also should be happy and full of joy with me.

> YOUR FAITH MAKES YOU OFFER YOUR LIVES AS A SACRIFICE IN SERVING GOD.

TIMOTHY AND EPAPHRODITUS

[19]I hope in the Lord Jesus to send Timothy to you soon. I will be happy to learn how you are. [20]I have no one else like Timothy, who truly cares for you. [21]Other people are interested only in their own lives, not in the work of Jesus Christ. [22]You know the kind of person Timothy is. You know he has served with me in telling the Good News, as a son serves his father. [23]I plan to send him to you quickly when I know what will happen to me. [24]I am sure that the Lord will help me to come to you soon.

[25]Epaphroditus, my brother in Christ, works and serves with me in the army of Christ. When I needed help, you sent him to me. I think now that I must send him back to you, [26]because he wants very much to see all of you. He is worried because you heard that he was sick. [27]Yes, he was sick, and nearly died, but God had mercy on him and me too so that I would not have more sadness. [28]I want very much to send him to you so that when you see him you can be happy, and I can stop worrying about you. [29]Wel-

come him in the Lord with much joy. Give honor to people like him, [30]because he almost died for the work of Christ. He risked his life to give me the help you could not give in your service to me.

THE IMPORTANCE OF CHRIST

3 My brothers and sisters, be full of joy in the Lord. It is no trouble for me to write the same things to you again, and it will help you to be more ready. [2]Watch out for those who do evil, who are like dogs, who demand to cut[n] the body. [3]We are the ones who are truly circumcised. We worship God through his Spirit, and our pride is in Christ Jesus. We do not put trust in ourselves or anything we can do, [4]although I might be able to put trust in myself. If anyone thinks he has a reason to trust in himself, he should know that I have greater reason for trusting in myself. [5]I was circumcised eight days after my birth. I am from the people of Israel and the tribe of Benjamin. I am a Hebrew, and my parents were Hebrews. I had a strict view of the law, which is why I became a Pharisee. [6]I was so enthusiastic I tried to hurt the church. No one could find fault with the way I obeyed the law of Moses. [7]Those things were important to me, but now I think they are worth nothing because of Christ. [8]Not only those things, but I think that all things are worth nothing compared with the greatness of knowing Christ Jesus my Lord. Because of him, I have lost all those things, and now I know they are worthless trash. This allows me to have Christ [9]and to belong to him. Now I am right with God, not because I followed the law, but because I believed in Christ. God uses my faith to make me right with him. [10]I want to know Christ and the power that raised him from the dead. I want to share in his sufferings and become like him in his death. [11]Then I have hope that I myself will be raised from the dead.

 3:2 cut The word in Greek is like the word "circumcise," but it means "to cut completely off."

365

1
2
3
4
5
6
7
8
9
10
11
12
13
14
15
16
17
18
19
20
21
22
23
24
25
26
27
28
29

Think outside
the box:
What can you do to spread
joy to others?

_____

"We may be suprised at the
people we find in heaven.
God has a soft spot for
sinners. His standards are
quite low."
– *Bishop Desmond Tutu*

_____

It's your birthday, Bishop Desmond Tutu!

Happy Birthday Marion Jones!

It's your birthday, Ashanti!

Happy Birthday Usher!

On This Day In History 1964—Dr. Martin Luther King, Jr. awarded the Nobel Peace Prize.

Phone a friend you haven't
spoken to in a while.

HOLIDAY—Columbus Day

It's your birthday, Monica!

On This Day In History 2002—Jason Mizell (aka Jam Master Jay) was shot and killed

MUSIC REVIEWS

ARTIST: DMX   ALBUM: FLESH OF MY FLESH, BLOOD OF MY BLOOD   CUT: "BRING YOUR WHOLE CREW"

DMX says in his lyrics, "I got blood on my hands and there's no remorse." There is only chaos in what he says. DMX believes that he is a minister of God. On every album, he prays after he has rapped some of the most vulgar lyrics known to the industry. He is covered in blood on his album cover. He claims to be the "Dark Man X," but some of his lyrics have been so catchy that preachers quote him in the pulpit! "Ya'll gonna make me lose my mind, up in here, up in here." But the rest of the song is talking about prison and even mentions using his "private part" to beat on an inmate! Before you quote a lyric, make sure the whole song is something you'd like people to identify you with.

"REJECTED"

CONTINUING TOWARD OUR GOAL

[12]I do not mean that I am already as God wants me to be. I have not yet reached that goal, but I continue trying to reach it and to make it mine. Christ wants me to do that, which is the reason he made me his. [13]Brothers and sisters, I know that I have not yet reached that goal, but there is one thing I always do. Forgetting the past and straining toward what is ahead, [14]I keep trying to reach the goal and get the prize for which God called me through Christ to the life above.

[15]All of us who are spiritually mature should think this way, too. And if there are things you do not agree with, God will make them clear to you. [16]But we should continue following the truth we already have.

[17]Brothers and sisters, all of you should try to follow my example and to copy those who live the way we showed you. [18]Many people live like enemies of the cross of Christ. I have often told you about them, and it makes me cry to tell you about them now. [19]In the end, they will be destroyed. They do whatever their bodies want, they are proud of their shameful acts, and they think only about earthly things. [20]But our homeland is in heaven, and we are waiting for our Savior, the Lord Jesus Christ, to come from heaven. [21]By his power to rule all things, he will change our humble bodies and make them like his own glorious body.

WHAT THE CHRISTIANS ARE TO DO

4 My dear brothers and sisters, I love you and want to see you. You bring me joy and make me proud of you, so stand strong in the Lord as I have told you.

[2]I ask Euodia and Syntyche to agree in the Lord. [3]And I ask you, my faithful friend, to help these women. They served with me in telling the Good News, together with Clement and others who worked with me, whose names are written in the book of life.[n]

[4]Be full of joy in the Lord always. I will say again, be full of joy.

[5]Let everyone see that you are gentle and kind. The Lord is coming soon. [6]Do not worry about anything, but pray and ask God for everything you need, always giving thanks. [7]And God's peace, which is so great we cannot understand it, will keep your hearts and minds in Christ Jesus.

[8]Brothers and sisters, think about the things that are good and worthy of praise. Think about the things that are true and honorable and right and pure and beautiful and respected. [9]Do what you learned and received from me, what I told you, and what you saw me do. And the God who gives peace will be with you.

PAUL THANKS THE CHRISTIANS

[10]I am very happy in the Lord that you have shown your care for me again. You continued to care about me, but there was no way for you to show it. [11]I am not telling you this because I need anything. I have learned to be satisfied with the things I have and with everything that happens. [12]I know how to live when I am poor, and I know how to live when

 4:3 book of life God's book that has the names of all God's chosen people (Revelation 3:5; 21:27).

I have plenty. I have learned the secret of being happy at any time in everything that happens, when I have enough to eat and when I go hungry, when I have more than I need and when I do not have enough. [13]I can do all things through Christ, because he gives me strength.

[14]But it was good that you helped me when I needed it. [15]You Philippians remember when I first preached the Good News there. When I left Macedonia, you were the only church that gave me help. [16]Several times you sent me things I needed when I was in Thessalonica. [17]Really, it is not that I want to receive gifts from you, but I want you to have the good that comes from giving. [18]And now I have everything, and more. I have all I need, because Epaphroditus brought your gift to me. It is like a sweet-smelling sacrifice offered to God, who accepts that sacrifice and is pleased with it. [19]My God will use his wonderful riches in Christ Jesus to give you everything you need. [20]Glory to our God and Father forever and ever! Amen.

[21]Greet each of God's people in Christ Jesus. Those who are with me send greetings to you. [22]All of God's people greet you, particularly those from the palace of Caesar.

[23]The grace of the Lord Jesus Christ be with you all.

HeartCry

Consequences   Have the choices you've made led you to a place you don't want to be? Does it seem like your life is out of control and there is nothing you can do to fix it? Let your heart cry . . .

What's up, Lord? I need to come real with you. I really messed up and now I'm paying the price. Please forgive me for doing what I knew was wrong. Is there a way you can fix all this? I didn't mean for this to happen and I need a way out. Are you listening, Lord? Please, get back to me.

You are forgiven and my love for you has not changed. Although the effect of your choices may not end tomorrow, I will be with you through it all. And you have my promise that sorrow will only last for a night and joy will come in the morning. Luke 15:11-24; Psalm 30:5

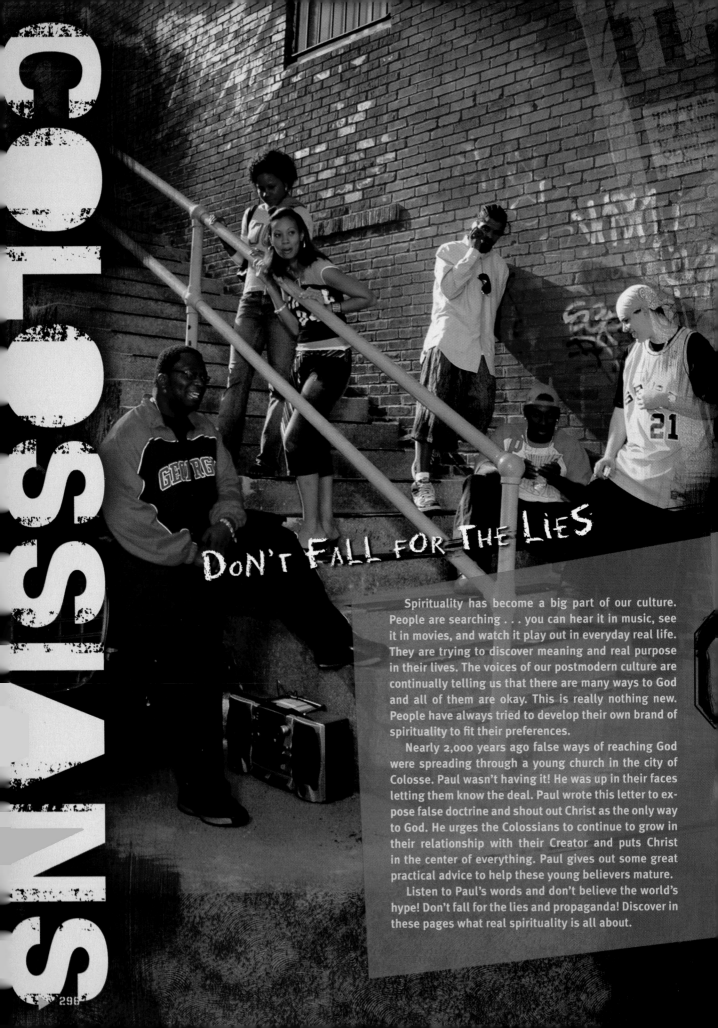

COLOSSIANS

Don't Fall for the Lies

Spirituality has become a big part of our culture. People are searching . . . you can hear it in music, see it in movies, and watch it play out in everyday real life. They are trying to discover meaning and real purpose in their lives. The voices of our postmodern culture are continually telling us that there are many ways to God and all of them are okay. This is really nothing new. People have always tried to develop their own brand of spirituality to fit their preferences.

Nearly 2,000 years ago false ways of reaching God were spreading through a young church in the city of Colosse. Paul wasn't having it! He was up in their faces letting them know the deal. Paul wrote this letter to expose false doctrine and shout out Christ as the only way to God. He urges the Colossians to continue to grow in their relationship with their Creator and puts Christ in the center of everything. Paul gives out some great practical advice to help these young believers mature.

Listen to Paul's words and don't believe the world's hype! Don't fall for the lies and propaganda! Discover in these pages what real spirituality is all about.

1 From Paul, an apostle of Christ Jesus. I am an apostle because that is what God wanted. Also from Timothy, our brother.

[2] To the holy and faithful brothers and sisters in Christ that live in Colossae:

Grace and peace to you from God our Father.[n]

[3] In our prayers for you we always thank God, the Father of our Lord Jesus Christ, [4] because we have heard about the faith you have in Christ Jesus and the love you have for all of God's people. [5] You have this faith and love because of your hope, and what you hope for is kept safe for you in heaven. You learned about this hope when you heard the message about the truth, the Good News [6] that was told to you. Everywhere in the world that Good News is bringing blessings and is growing. This has happened with you, too, since you heard the Good News and understood the truth about the grace of God. [7] You learned about God's grace from Epaphras, whom we love. He works together with us and is a faithful servant of Christ for us.[n] [8] He also told us about the love you have from the Holy Spirit.

[11] God will strengthen you with his own great power so that you will not give up when troubles come, but you will be patient. [12] And you will joyfully give thanks to the Father who has made you[n] able to have a share in all that he has prepared for his people in the kingdom of light. [13] God has freed us from the power of darkness, and he brought us into the kingdom of his dear Son. [14] The Son paid for our sins,[n] and in him we have forgiveness.

THE IMPORTANCE OF CHRIST

[15] No one can see God, but Jesus Christ is exactly like him. He ranks higher than everything that has been made. [16] Through his power all things were made—things in heaven and on earth, things seen and unseen, all powers, authorities, lords, and rulers. All things were made through Christ and for Christ. [17] He was there before anything was made, and all things continue because of him. [18] He is the head of the body, which is the church. Everything comes from him. He is the first one who was raised from the dead. So in all things Jesus has first place. [19] God was pleased for all of himself to live in Christ. [20] And

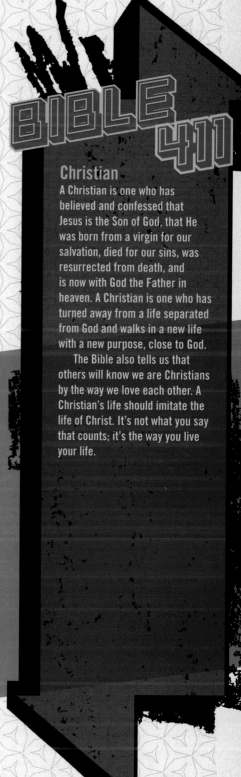

Christian

A Christian is one who has believed and confessed that Jesus is the Son of God, that He was born from a virgin for our salvation, died for our sins, was resurrected from death, and is now with God the Father in heaven. A Christian is one who has turned away from a life separated from God and walks in a new life with a new purpose, close to God.

The Bible also tells us that others will know we are Christians by the way we love each other. A Christian's life should imitate the life of Christ. It's not what you say that counts; it's the way you live your life.

CHRIST IS THE ONLY WAY TO GOD

[9] Because of this, since the day we heard about you, we have continued praying for you, asking God that you will know fully what he wants. We pray that you will also have great wisdom and understanding in spiritual things [10] so that you will live the kind of life that honors and pleases the Lord in every way. You will produce fruit in every good work and grow in the knowledge of God.

through Christ, God has brought all things back to himself again—things on earth and things in heaven. God made peace through the blood of Christ's death on the cross.

[21] At one time you were separated from God. You were his enemies in your minds, and the evil things you did were against God. [22] But now God has made you his friends again. He did this through Christ's

1:2 Father Some Greek copies continue, "and the Lord Jesus Christ." **1:7 for us** Some Greek copies read "for you." **1:12 you** Some Greek copies read "us." **1:14 sins** Some Greek copies continue, "with his blood."

death in the body so that he might bring you into God's presence as people who are holy, with no wrong, and with nothing of which God can judge you guilty. ²³This will happen if you continue strong and sure in your faith. You must not be moved away from the hope brought to you by the Good News that you heard. That same Good News has been told to everyone in the world, and I, Paul, help in preaching that Good News.

PAUL'S WORK FOR THE CHURCH

²⁴I am happy in my sufferings for you. There are things that Christ must still suffer through his body, the church. I am accepting, in my body, my part of these things that must be suffered. ²⁵I became a servant of the church because God gave me a special work to do that helps you, and that work is to tell fully the message of God. ²⁶This message is the secret that was hidden from everyone since the beginning of time, but now it is made known to God's holy people. ²⁷God decided to let his people know this rich and glorious secret which he has for all people. This secret is Christ himself, who is in you. He is our only hope for glory. ²⁸So we continue to preach Christ to each person, using all wisdom to warn and to teach everyone, in order

He's got answers

I know about Jesus and all, but I can't live like my mom and pop. If I become a Christian, do I have to act all holy?

You make the word holy sound bad. Anyone can act holy, but that doesn't make them holy. Sometimes those who pretend to be holy are only twisting what the word means.

Understanding holiness is pretty simple; holiness is what God is, just as being male is what a man is. God is holy because he is God. Jesus, God's Son, is holy. When someone becomes a Christian, God lives in them. The way they choose to live their lives will either reflect the holiness of God in them or hide it.

In the Bible, the temple leaders were supposed to be the best example of holy lives, yet there were many times when Jesus called them hypocrites. Most of these leaders cared about the outward appearance of holiness; they didn't really want to be holy. At the same time, there were people the temple, whom leaders thought were sinners, yet, Jesus praised these people because they decided to live changed lives.

If you become a Christian, if you truly love the Lord, then you won't have to act all holy, because it won't be an act.

Read on: Matthew 3:7-12, 8:11; Acts 2:28; Hebrews 12:10

PEEP THIS:

Seventy-seven percent of all Americans describe themselves as Christians; 3.7 percent belong to other religions.

to bring each one into God's presence as a mature person in Christ. ²⁹To do this, I work and struggle, using Christ's great strength that works so powerfully in me.

2 I want you to know how hard I work for you, those in Laodicea, and others who have never seen me. ²I want them to be strengthened and joined together with love so that they may be rich in their understanding. This leads to their knowing fully God's secret, that is, Christ himself. ³In him all the treasures of wisdom and knowledge are safely kept.

⁴I say this so that no one can fool you by arguments that seem good, but are false. ⁵Though I am absent from you in my body, my heart is with you, and I am happy to see your good lives and your strong faith in Christ.

CONTINUE TO LIVE IN CHRIST

⁶As you received Christ Jesus the Lord, so continue to live in him. ⁷Keep your roots deep in him and have your lives built on him. Be strong in the faith, just as you were taught, and always be thankful.

⁸Be sure that no one leads you away

with false and empty teaching that is only human, which comes from the ruling spirits of this world, and not from Christ. [9]All of God lives fully in Christ (even when Christ was on earth), [10]and you have a full and true life in Christ, who is ruler over all rulers and powers.

[11]Also in Christ you had a different kind of circumcision, a circumcision not done by hands. It was through Christ's circumcision, that is, his death, that you were made free from the power of your sinful self. [12]When you were baptized, you were buried with Christ, and you were raised up with him through your faith in God's power that was shown when he raised Christ from the dead. [13]When you were spiritually dead because of your sins and because you were not free from the power of your sinful self, God made you alive with Christ, and he forgave all our sins. [14]He canceled the debt, which listed all the rules we failed to follow. He took away that record with its rules and nailed it to the cross. [15]God stripped the spiritual rulers and powers of their authority. With the cross, he won the victory and showed the world that they were powerless.

DON'T FOLLOW PEOPLE'S RULES

[16]So do not let anyone make rules for you about eating and drinking or about a religious feast, a New Moon Festival, or a Sabbath day. [17]These things were like a shadow of what was to come. But what is true and real has come and is found in Christ. [18]Do not let anyone disqualify you by making you humiliate yourself and worship angels. Such people enter into visions, which fill them with foolish pride because of their human way of thinking. [19]They do not hold tightly to Christ, the head. It is from him that all the parts of the body are cared for and held together. So it grows in the way God wants it to grow.

[20]Since you died with Christ and were made free from the ruling spirits of the world, why do you act as if you still belong to this world by following rules like these: [21]"Don't handle this," "Don't taste that," "Don't even touch that thing"? [22]These rules refer to earthly things that are gone as soon as they are used. They are only human commands and teachings. [23]They seem to be wise,

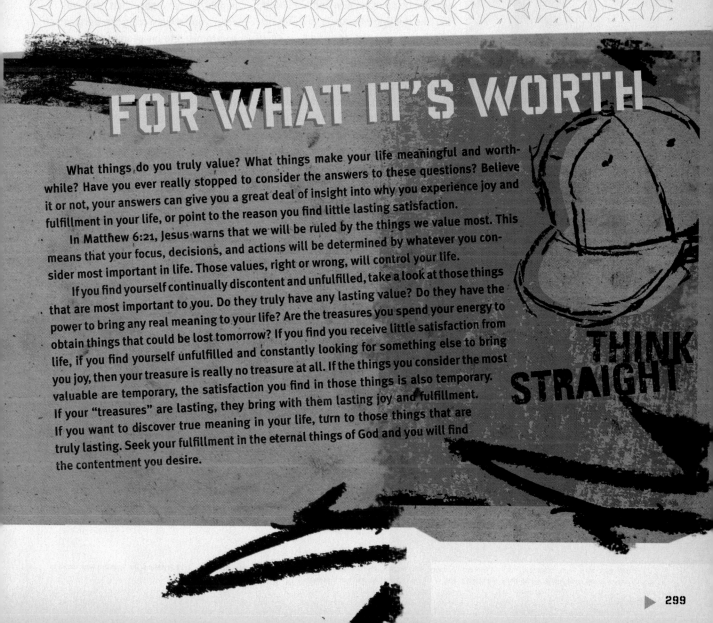

FOR WHAT IT'S WORTH

What things do you truly value? What things make your life meaningful and worthwhile? Have you ever really stopped to consider the answers to these questions? Believe it or not, your answers can give you a great deal of insight into why you experience joy and fulfillment in your life, or point to the reason you find little lasting satisfaction.

In Matthew 6:21, Jesus warns that we will be ruled by the things we value most. This means that your focus, decisions, and actions will be determined by whatever you consider most important in life. Those values, right or wrong, will control your life.

If you find yourself continually discontent and unfulfilled, take a look at those things that are most important to you. Do they truly have any lasting value? Do they have the power to bring any real meaning to your life? Are the treasures you spend your energy to obtain things that could be lost tomorrow? If you find you receive little satisfaction from life, if you find yourself unfulfilled and constantly looking for something else to bring you joy, then your treasure is really no treasure at all. If the things you consider the most valuable are temporary, the satisfaction you find in those things is also temporary. If your "treasures" are lasting, they bring with them lasting joy and fulfillment. If you want to discover true meaning in your life, turn to those things that are truly lasting. Seek your fulfillment in the eternal things of God and you will find the contentment you desire.

THINK STRAIGHT

VIEWPOINT

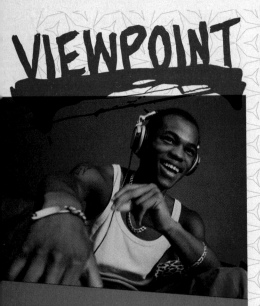

WHAT GENRE OF MUSIC INSPIRES AND MOTIVATES YOU, AND WHY?

I've learned to appreciate all kinds of music but I would have to say that praise and worship music, contemporary Christian music, and gospel music have inspired me the most. Growing up, gospel music was the only type of music that my sister and I were allowed to listen to. Now that I'm older I've grown to appreciate it because I have learned that it's this kind of music that can help a person get through bad times.

but they are only part of a human religion. They make people pretend not to be proud and make them punish their bodies, but they do not really control the evil desires of the sinful self.

YOUR NEW LIFE IN CHRIST

3 Since you were raised from the dead with Christ, aim at what is in heaven, where Christ is sitting at the right hand of God. [2]Think only about the things in heaven, not the things on earth. [3]Your old sinful self has died, and your new life is kept with Christ in God. [4]Christ is your[n] life, and when he comes again, you will share in his glory.

[5]So put all evil things out of your life: sexual sinning, doing evil, letting evil thoughts control you, wanting things that are evil, and greed. This is really serving a false god. [6]These things make God angry.[n] [7]In your past, evil life you also did these things.

[8]But now also put these things out of your life: anger, bad temper, doing or saying things to hurt others, and using evil words when you talk. [9]Do not lie to each other. You have left your old sinful life and the things you did before. [10]You have begun to live the new life, in which you are being made new and are becoming like the One who made you. This new life brings you the true knowledge of God. [11]In the new life there is no difference between Greeks and Jews, those who are circumcised and those who are not circumcised, or people who are foreigners, or Scythians.[n] There is no difference between slaves and free people. But Christ is in all believers, and Christ is all that is important.

[12]God has chosen you and made you his holy people. He loves you. So you should always clothe yourselves with mercy, kindness, humility, gentleness, and patience. [13]Bear with each other, and forgive each other. If someone does wrong to you, forgive that person because the Lord forgave you. [14]Even more than all this, clothe yourself in love. Love is what holds you all together in perfect unity. [15]Let the peace that Christ gives control your thinking, because you were all called together in one body[n] to have peace. Always be thankful. [16]Let the teaching of Christ live in you richly. Use all wisdom to teach and instruct each other by singing psalms, hymns, and spiritual songs with thankfulness in your hearts to God. [17]Everything you do or say should be done to obey Jesus your Lord. And in all you do, give thanks to God the Father through Jesus.

YOUR NEW LIFE WITH OTHER PEOPLE

[18]Wives, yield to the authority of your husbands, because this is the right thing to do in the Lord.

[19]Husbands, love your wives and be gentle with them.

[20]Children, obey your parents in all things, because this pleases the Lord.

[21]Fathers, do not nag your children. If you are too hard to please, they may want to stop trying.

[22]Slaves, obey your masters in all things. Do not obey just when they are watching you, to gain their favor, but serve them honestly, because you respect the Lord. [23]In all the work you are doing, work the best you can. Work as if you were doing it for the Lord, not for people. [24]Remember that you will receive your reward from the Lord, which he promised to his people. You are serving the Lord Christ. [25]But remember that anyone who does wrong will be punished for that wrong, and the Lord treats everyone the same.

4 Masters, give what is good and fair to your slaves. Remember that you have a Master in heaven.

WHAT THE CHRISTIANS ARE TO DO

[2]Continue praying, keeping alert, and always thanking God. [3]Also pray for us that God will give us an opportunity to tell people his message. Pray that we can preach the secret that God has made known about Christ. This is why I am in prison. [4]Pray that I can speak in a way that will make it clear, as I should.

[5]Be wise in the way you act with people who are not believers, making the most of every opportunity. [6]When you talk, you should always be kind and pleasant so you will be able to answer everyone in the way you should.

NEWS ABOUT THE PEOPLE WITH PAUL

[7]Tychicus is my dear brother in Christ and a faithful minister and servant with

---

 3:4 your Some Greek copies read "our." **3:6 These . . . angry** Some Greek copies continue, "against the people who do not obey God." **3:11 Scythians** The Scythians were known as very wild and cruel people. **3:15 body** The spiritual body of Christ, meaning the church or his people.

me in the Lord. He will tell you all the things that are happening to me. [8]This is why I am sending him: so you may know how we are[n] and he may encourage you. [9]I send him with Onesimus, a faithful and dear brother in Christ, and one of your group. They will tell you all that has happened here.

[10]Aristarchus, a prisoner with me, and Mark, the cousin of Barnabas, greet you. (I have already told you what to do about Mark. If he comes, welcome him.) [11]Jesus, who is called Justus, also greets you. These are the only Jewish believers who work with me for the kingdom of God, and they have been a comfort to me.

[12]Epaphras, a servant of Jesus Christ, from your group, also greets you. He always prays for you that you will grow to be spiritually mature and have everything God wants for you. [13]I know he has worked hard for you and the people in Laodicea and in Hierapolis. [14]Demas and our dear friend Luke, the doctor, greet you.

[15]Greet the brothers and sisters in Laodicea. And greet Nympha and the church that meets in her house. [16]After this letter is read to you, be sure it is also read to the church in Laodicea. And you read the letter that I wrote to Laodicea. [17]Tell Archippus, "Be sure to finish the work the Lord gave you."

[18]I, Paul, greet you and write this with my own hand. Remember me in prison. Grace be with you.

HeartCry

Which Way? **Are you hanging with a group that is leading you down a path going away from the Lord? Are you afraid you will end up alone if you don't follow them? Let your heart cry . . .**

Whats up, Lord? I wanted to give you a shout out about my friends. You know they are off the chain sometimes with their lifestyles, and they don't consider you in the things that they do and say. I love my peeps. We've been kicking it since we were kids. Don't worry. I don't want to go where they're going. I know who you are and I want to be in with you. But if I choose you, I may lose them and I don't want to end up alone. I am so confused and I don't know what to do.

I know it's not easy to follow me. But I did promise you would not be alone. I have sent the Holy Spirit to walk with you, to lead you, and to comfort you. Look for others who serve me to get encouragement. Remember, I have already chosen you. Ephesians 1:4; John 14:16

4:8 so . . . are Some Greek copies read "so he may know how you are."

Put Things into the Right Perspective

Hip-hop started in the streets of New York. There were a handful of DJ's and artists who pioneered the music that has now become a movement and culture and spread across the globe. My man Paul was also a pioneer, but of an even bigger movement. One that has swept the planet and its followers number in the billions. It goes much deeper than music or culture; it reaches into our spirit and provides forgiveness and a reconnection with our Creator. Paul was a pioneer in spreading the message of Christ to places it had never been heard.

Everywhere Paul went it seemed that people were always ready to get at him. He planted a new church in the city of Thessalonica, but it wasn't long before people there threatened his life and ran him out of town. Even though he had to dip he immediately wrote two letters to the Thessalonian church to give them instructions and teachings on how to grow in their new relationships with Christ. It was a young church full of issues and drama. Some of the members were so caught up with the return of Christ that they got lazy and put off their work, while others didn't even catch the hope that Christ was someday coming back for his people. Paul put things into the right perspective . . . Christ is coming back, but he has a lot for us to accomplish for him right here, right now. Paul lived what he talked and was a real pioneer.

1

From Paul, Silas, and Timothy.
To the church in Thessalonica, the church in God the Father and the Lord Jesus Christ:

Grace and peace to you.

THE FAITH OF THE THESSALONIANS

²We always thank God for all of you and mention you when we pray. ³We continually recall before God our Father the things you have done because of your faith and the work you have done because of your love. And we thank him that you continue to be strong because of your hope in our Lord Jesus Christ.

⁴Brothers and sisters, God loves you, and we know he has chosen you, ⁵because the Good News we brought to you came not only with words, but with power, with the Holy Spirit, and with sure knowledge that it is true. Also you know how we lived when we were with you in order to help you. ⁶And you became like us and like the Lord. You suffered much, but still you accepted the teaching with the joy that comes from the Holy Spirit.

⁷So you became an example to all the believers in Macedonia and Southern Greece. ⁸And the Lord's teaching spread from you not only into Macedonia and Southern Greece, but now your faith in God has become known everywhere. So we do not need to say anything about it. ⁹People everywhere are telling about the way you accepted us when we were there with you. They tell how you stopped worshiping idols and began serving the living

and true God. ¹⁰And you wait for God's Son, whom God raised from the dead, to come from heaven. He is Jesus, who saves us from God's angry judgment that is sure to come.

PAUL'S WORK IN THESSALONICA

2

Brothers and sisters, you know our visit to you was not a failure. ²Before we came to you, we suffered in Philippi. People there insulted us, as you know, and many people were against us. But our God helped us to be brave and to tell you his Good News. ³Our appeal does not come from lies or wrong reasons, nor were we trying to trick you. ⁴But we speak the Good News because God tested us and trusted us to do it. When we speak, we are not trying to please people, but God, who tests our hearts. ⁵You know that we never tried to influence you by saying nice things about you. We were not trying to get your money; we had no selfishness to hide from you. God knows that this is true. ⁶We were not looking for human praise, from you or anyone else, ⁷even though as apostles of Christ we could have used our authority over you.

But we were very gentle with you,ⁿ like a mother caring for her little children. ⁸Because we loved you, we were happy to share not only God's Good News with you, but even our own lives. You had become so dear to us! ⁹Brothers and sisters, I know you remember our hard work and difficulties. We worked night and day so

CATCH THE HOPE THAT CHRIST IS COMING BACK

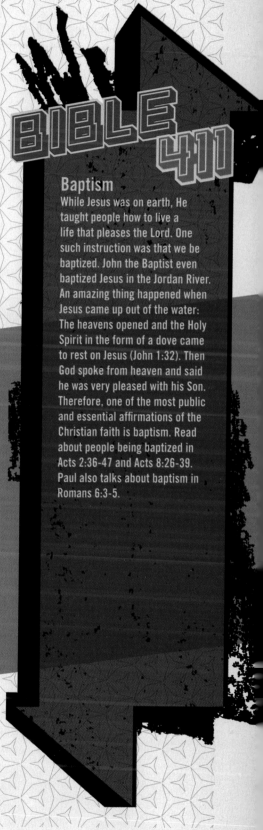

Baptism

While Jesus was on earth, He taught people how to live a life that pleases the Lord. One such instruction was that we be baptized. John the Baptist even baptized Jesus in the Jordan River. An amazing thing happened when Jesus came up out of the water: The heavens opened and the Holy Spirit in the form of a dove came to rest on Jesus (John 1:32). Then God spoke from heaven and said he was very pleased with his Son. Therefore, one of the most public and essential affirmations of the Christian faith is baptism. Read about people being baptized in Acts 2:36-47 and Acts 8:26-39. Paul also talks about baptism in Romans 6:3-5.

 2:7 But . . . you Some Greek copies read "But we were like infants among you."

we would not burden any of you while we preached God's Good News to you.

[10]When we were with you, we lived in a holy and honest way, without fault. You know this is true, and so does God. [11]You know that we treated each of you as a father treats his own children. [12]We encouraged you, we urged you, and we insisted that you live good lives for God, who calls you to his glorious kingdom.

[13]Also, we always thank God because when you heard his message from us, you accepted it as the word of God, not the words of humans. And it really is God's message which works in you who believe. [14]Brothers and sisters, your experiences have been like those of God's churches in Christ that are in Judea.[n] You suffered from the people of your own country, as they suffered from the Jews [15]who killed both the Lord Jesus and the prophets and forced us to leave that country. They do not please God and are against all people. [16]They try to stop us from teaching those who are not Jews so they may be saved. By doing this, they are increasing their sins to the limit. The anger of God has come to them at last.

PAUL WANTS TO VISIT THEM AGAIN

[17]Brothers and sisters, though we were separated from you for a short time, our thoughts were still with you. We wanted very much to see you and tried hard to do so. [18]We wanted to come to you. I, Paul, tried to come more than once, but Satan stopped us. [19]You are our hope, our joy, and the crown we will take pride in when our Lord Jesus Christ comes. [20]Truly you are our glory and our joy.

3 When we could not wait any longer, we decided it was best to stay in Athens alone [2]and send Timothy to you. Timothy, our brother, works with us for God and helps us tell people the Good News about Christ. We sent him to strengthen and

2:14 **Judea** The Jewish land where Jesus lived and taught and where the church first began.

HOW YA TRAVELIN'?

FEAR

Fear wants to destroy you. But where there is faith, there is no fear.

Fear strangles dreams, purposes, relationships, plans, and lives. It causes failure. For example, it is clear from King Saul's life that fear can and will destroy you unless you resist it: "I was afraid of the people, and I did what they said" (1 Samuel 15:24). If your life is full of fears and worries, it's because you have no assurance of anything. If you start a conflict with others because you think you are better than them, you are operating out of fear—not strength or authority.

"God did not give us a spirit that makes us afraid but a spirit of power and love and self-control" (2 Timothy 1:7). The key to triumphing over fear is to substitute faith for fear. While fear is irrational, stifling, and self-focused: "Oooh, I'm scared, too scared to step my foot out in front of my body," faith, on the other hand, is God-focused, confident, and expectant: "Dear Father, give me strength to walk in Your ways this day. In Jesus' name. Amen."

GOD DID NOT GIVE US A SPIRIT THAT MAKES US AFRAID – 2 TIMOTHY 1:7

DEALING WITH RACISM

Ⓜany people don't understand what it is to be an African-American male. Saved or not, tall, short, whatever, it has its own set of challenges. It seems there's always something to prove. Sure, every man has to deal with ego and the "dog-eat-dog" world, but don't tell me it's the same for all races. I'm not one to play the race card, but I've seen it played on me plenty of times. It's the collision of two worlds with two entirely different climates. When my parents grew up, there was no association with the "other" world. When I was coming up, there was always the thought that maybe there couldn't be a genuine friendship with someone of another race.

I got so tired of stepping onto elevators and seeing Caucasian women quickly grasp their handbags, or crossing the street and hearing the power locks of car doors. It happened so often that I started responding by grabbing my little brother's hand and moving to the corner of the elevator when a White woman got on. Or I'd lock my car door when an elderly White lady came my way, just so she would know what I felt like when they did it to me.

I prayed and asked God to take away the hurt I had experienced from racism. I was bitter and felt like a victim until God uncovered my own prejudices. I kept finding myself in situations that showed me that I refused to trust people of other races. I read the Scripture that says, "If God loved us that much we also should love each other." I was guilty. How could I say I loved God when I couldn't show love to those around me who were different from me? I didn't think that was what Jesus had in mind. The Bible showed me that no matter who we are, God loves us. Once I started considering myself his child, rather than just a Black man, I was able to love everyone, just as he does. God showed me my own issues with people and forced me to look to him for answers. Once I realized that God doesn't discriminate, I found out that love has no color.

encourage you in your faith ³so none of you would be upset by these troubles. You yourselves know that we must face these troubles. ⁴Even when we were with you, we told you we all would have to suffer, and you know it has happened. ⁵Because of this, when I could wait no longer, I sent Timothy to you so I could learn about your faith. I was afraid the devil had tempted you, and perhaps our hard work would have been wasted.

⁶But Timothy now has come back to us from you and has brought us good news about your faith and love. He told us that you always remember us in a good way and that you want to see us just as much as we want to see you. ⁷So, brothers and sisters, while we have much trouble and suffering, we are encouraged about you because of your faith. ⁸Our life is really full if you stand strong in the Lord. ⁹We have so much joy before our God because of you. We cannot thank him enough for all the joy we feel. ¹⁰Night and day we continue praying with all our heart that we can see you again and give you all the things you need to make your faith strong.

¹¹Now may our God and Father himself and our Lord Jesus prepare the way for us to come to you. ¹²May the Lord make your love grow more and multiply for each other and for all people so that you will love others as we love you. ¹³May your hearts be made strong so that you will be holy and without fault before our God and Father when our Lord Jesus comes with all his holy ones.

A LIFE THAT PLEASES GOD

4 Brothers and sisters, we taught you how to live in a way that will please God, and you are living that way. Now we ask and encourage you in the Lord Jesus to live that way even more. ²You know what we told you to do by the authority of the Lord Jesus. ³God wants you to be holy and to stay away from sexual sins. [4]He wants each of you to learn to control your own body[n] in a way that is holy and honorable. [5]Don't use your body for sexual sin like the people who do not know God. [6]Also, do not wrong or cheat another Christian in this way. The Lord will punish people who do those things as we have already told you and warned you. [7]God called us to be holy and does not want us to live in sin. [8]So the person who refuses to obey this teaching is disobeying God, not simply a human teaching. And God is the One who gives us his Holy Spirit.

[9]We do not need to write you about having love for your Christian family, because God has already taught you to love each other. [10]And truly you do love the Christians in all of Macedonia. Brothers and sisters, now we encourage you to love them even more.

[11]Do all you can to live a peaceful life. Take care of your own business, and do your own work as we have already told you. [12]If you do, then people who are not believers will respect you, and you will not have to depend on others for what you need.

THE LORD'S COMING

[13]Brothers and sisters, we want you to know about those Christians who have died so you will not be sad, as others who

He's got answers

I pray and nothing happens or things just get worse. Why? Isn't God listening or does he just not care?

For God to hear and answer our prayers, we must first have a relationship with him through Jesus Christ. He has no obligation to answer the prayers of those who reject his Son. While God is deeply concerned for our wants and desires, he is not some cosmic Santa Claus waiting to fulfill every item on our wish list. God is a heavenly Father, and, like any good Father, he wants only what is best for his children. Because God sees things from an eternal perspective, rather than from our limited, finite perspective, he knows that some things that we think are necessary for our happiness would really be harmful to us.

While there is nothing you can do to twist God's arm, there are some ways to make your prayers more effective. Pray on your own in secret. Pray in agreement with other believers. Pray with faith that God will answer according to his Word and will. Pray and persist in praying. Remember that prayer is not a magic spell. It is a conversation between you and God.

Read on: Matthew 6:5-8; 18:19; Luke 11:1-13; 1 Thessalonians 5:16-22

PEEP THIS:

Christianity is the largest religion in the world with 1.9 billion members or one-third of the world's population. It is followed by Islam with 1.1 billion members or one-fifth of the world's population.

have no hope. [14]We believe that Jesus died and that he rose again. So, because of him, God will raise with Jesus those who have died. [15]What we tell you now is the Lord's own message. We who are living when the Lord comes again will not go before those who have already died. [16]The Lord himself will come down from heaven with a loud command, with the voice of the archangel,[n] and with the trumpet call of God. And those who have died believing in Christ will rise first. [17]After that, we who are still alive will be gathered up with them in the clouds to meet the Lord in the air. And we will be with the Lord forever. [18]So encourage each other with these words.

BE READY FOR THE LORD'S COMING

5 Now, brothers and sisters, we do not need to write you about times and dates. [2]You know very well that the day the Lord comes again will be a surprise, like a thief that comes in the night. [3]While people are saying, "We have peace and we are

4:4 **learn . . . body** This might also mean "learn to live with your own wife." 4:16 **archangel** The leader among God's angels or messengers.

safe," they will be destroyed quickly. It is like pains that come quickly to a woman having a baby. Those people will not escape. [4]But you, brothers and sisters, are not living in darkness, and so that day will not surprise you like a thief. [5]You are all people who belong to the light and to the day. We do not belong to the night or to darkness. [6]So we should not be like other people who are sleeping, but we should be alert and have self-control. [7]Those who sleep, sleep at night. Those who get drunk, get drunk at night. [8]But we belong to the day, so we should control ourselves. We should wear faith and love to protect us, and the hope of salvation should be our helmet. [9]God did not choose us to suffer his anger but to have salvation through our Lord Jesus Christ. [10]Jesus died for us so that we can live together with him, whether we are alive or dead when he comes. [11]So encourage each other and give each other strength, just as you are doing now.

FINAL INSTRUCTIONS AND GREETINGS

[12]Now, brothers and sisters, we ask you to appreciate those who work hard among you, who lead you in the Lord and teach you. [13]Respect them with a very special love because of the work they do. Live in peace with each other. [14]We ask you, brothers and sisters, to warn those who do not work. Encourage the people who are afraid. Help those who are weak. Be patient with everyone. [15]Be sure that no one pays back wrong for wrong, but always try to do what is good for each other and for all people.

[16]Always be joyful. [17]Pray continually, [18]and give thanks whatever happens. That is what God wants for you in Christ Jesus.

[19]Do not hold back the work of the Holy Spirit. [20]Do not treat prophecy as if it were unimportant. [21]But test everything. Keep what is good, [22]and stay away from everything that is evil.

[23]Now may God himself, the God of peace, make you pure, belonging only to him. May your whole self—spirit, soul, and body—be kept safe and without

hot 10

NBA Teams

10. Bulls

9. Nets

8. Celtics

7. Mavericks

6. Knicks

5. Heat

4. Timberwolves

3. 76ers

2. Spurs

1. Lakers

fault when our Lord Jesus Christ comes. [24]You can trust the One who calls you to do that for you.

[25]Brothers and sisters, pray for us.

[26]Give each other a holy kiss when you meet. [27]I tell you by the authority of the Lord to read this letter to all the believers.

[28]The grace of our Lord Jesus Christ be with you.

2 THESSALONIANS

1

From Paul, Silas, and Timothy.

To the church in Thessalonica in God our Father and the Lord Jesus Christ:

[2]Grace and peace to you from God the Father and the Lord Jesus Christ.

PAUL TALKS ABOUT GOD'S JUDGMENT

[3]We must always thank God for you, brothers and sisters. This is only right, because your faith is growing more and more, and the love that every one of you has for each other is increasing. [4]So we brag about you to the other churches of God. We tell them about the way you continue to be strong and have faith even though you are being treated badly and are suffering many troubles.

[5]This is proof that God is right in his judgment. He wants you to be counted worthy of his kingdom for which you are suffering. [6]God will do what is right. He will give trouble to those who trouble you. [7]And he will give rest to you who are troubled and to us also when the Lord Jesus appears with burning fire from heaven with his powerful angels. [8]Then he will punish those who do not know God and who do not obey the Good News about our Lord Jesus Christ. [9]Those people will be punished with a destruction that continues forever. They will be kept away from the Lord and from his great power. [10]This will happen on the day when the Lord Jesus comes to receive glory because of his holy people. And all the people who have believed will be amazed at Jesus. You will be in that group, because you believed what we told you.

[11]That is why we always pray for you, asking our God to help you live the kind of life he called you to live. We pray that with his power God will help you do the good things you want and perform the works that come from your faith. [12]We pray all this so that the name of our Lord Jesus Christ will have glory in

you, and you will have glory in him. That glory comes from the grace of our God and the Lord Jesus Christ.

EVIL THINGS WILL HAPPEN

2 Brothers and sisters, we have something to say about the coming of our Lord Jesus Christ and the time when we will meet together with him. [2] Do not become easily upset in your thinking or afraid if you hear that the day of the Lord has already come. Someone may have said this in a prophecy or in a message or in a letter as if it came from us. [3] Do not let anyone fool you in any way. That day of the Lord will not come until the turning away[n] from God happens and the Man of Evil,[n] who is on his way to hell, appears. [4] He will be against and put himself above any so-called god or anything that people worship. And that Man of Evil will even go into God's Temple and sit there and say that he is God.

[5] I told you when I was with you that all this would happen. Do you not remember? [6] And now you know what is stopping that Man of Evil so he will appear at the right time. [7] The secret power of evil is already working in the world, but there is one who is stopping that power. And he will continue to stop it until he is taken out of the way. [8] Then that Man of Evil will appear, and the Lord Jesus will kill him with the breath that comes from his mouth and will destroy him with the glory of his coming. [9] The Man of Evil will come by the power of Satan. He will have great power, and he will do many different false miracles, signs, and wonders. [10] He will use every kind of evil to trick those who are lost. They will die, because they refused to love the truth. (If they loved the truth, they would be saved.) [11] For this reason God sends them something powerful that leads them away from the truth so they will believe a lie. [12] So all those will be judged guilty who did not believe the truth, but enjoyed doing evil.

YOU ARE CHOSEN FOR SALVATION

[13] Brothers and sisters, whom the Lord loves, God chose you from the beginning[n] to be saved. So we must always thank

2:3 turning away Or "the rebellion." **2:3 Man of Evil** Some Greek copies read "Man of Sin." **2:13 God . . . beginning** Some Greek copies read "God chose you as the firstfruits of the harvest."

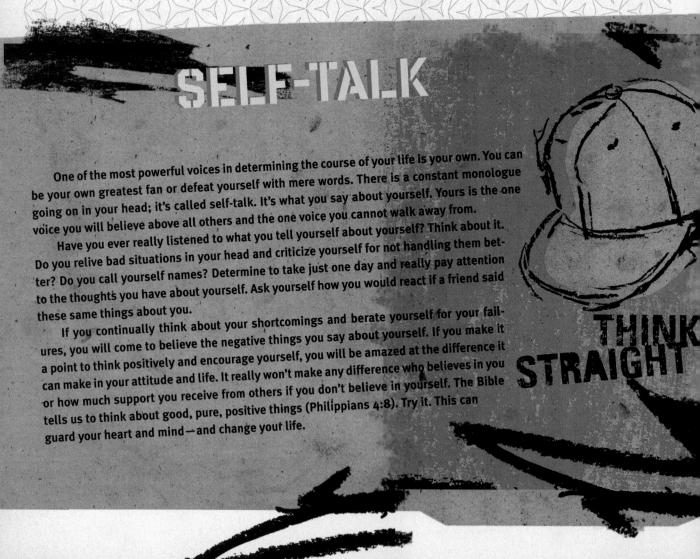

SELF-TALK

One of the most powerful voices in determining the course of your life is your own. You can be your own greatest fan or defeat yourself with mere words. There is a constant monologue going on in your head; it's called self-talk. It's what you say about yourself. Yours is the one voice you will believe above all others and the one voice you cannot walk away from.

Have you ever really listened to what you tell yourself about yourself? Think about it. Do you relive bad situations in your head and criticize yourself for not handling them better? Do you call yourself names? Determine to take just one day and really pay attention to the thoughts you have about yourself. Ask yourself how you would react if a friend said these same things about you.

If you continually think about your shortcomings and berate yourself for your failures, you will come to believe the negative things you say about yourself. If you make it a point to think positively and encourage yourself, you will be amazed at the difference it can make in your attitude and life. It really won't make any difference who believes in you or how much support you receive from others if you don't believe in yourself. The Bible tells us to think about good, pure, positive things (Philippians 4:8). Try it. This can guard your heart and mind—and change your life.

THINK STRAIGHT

God for you. You are saved by the Spirit that makes you holy and by your faith in the truth. ¹⁴God used the Good News that we preached to call you to be saved so you can share in the glory of our Lord Jesus Christ. ¹⁵So, brothers and sisters, stand strong and continue to believe the teachings we gave you in our speaking and in our letter.

¹⁶⁻¹⁷May our Lord Jesus Christ himself and God our Father encourage you and strengthen you in every good thing you do and say. God loved us, and through his grace he gave us a good hope and encouragement that continues forever.

PRAY FOR US

3 And now, brothers and sisters, pray for us that the Lord's teaching will continue to spread quickly and that people will give honor to that teaching, just as happened with you. ²And pray that we will be protected from stubborn and evil people, because not all people believe.

³But the Lord is faithful and will give you strength and will protect you from the Evil One. ⁴The Lord makes us feel sure that you are doing and will continue to do the things we told you. ⁵May the Lord lead your hearts into God's love and Christ's patience.

THE DUTY TO WORK

⁶Brothers and sisters, by the authority of our Lord Jesus Christ we command you to stay away from any believer who refuses to work and does not follow the teaching we gave you. ⁷You yourselves know that you should live as we live. We were not lazy when we were with you. ⁸And when we ate another person's food, we always paid for it. We worked very hard night and day so we would not be an expense to any of you. ⁹We had the right to ask you to help us, but we worked to take care of ourselves so we would be an example for you to follow. ¹⁰When we were with you, we gave you this rule: "Anyone who refuses to work should not eat."

HeartCry

Fear **Do you cringe at the thought of failure? Are you afraid to reach beyond where you are and step into the unknown? Is fear keeping you from stepping up and stepping out? Let your heart cry . . .**

False Evidence Appearing Real. That's what I struggle with, Lord. I'm blinded by the false realities of this world. Fear has taken away my courage and has watered down my boldness. You said I shouldn't be afraid of anything because you are in total control. Help me to overcome my fear by believing and accepting what you say. I don't want to be a faker or a hypocrite. But it's like fear rules my life. I'm afraid to do the things I really want to do, so I end up doing nothing. How do I get rid of this? Please answer back.

Do not seek courage, child. Seek me and allow yourself to trust me. I have overcome the world; you are safe in my hand. Trust in me will overcome all fear. John 16:33; 1 John 4:18; Isaiah 49:16

¹¹We hear that some people in your group refuse to work. They do nothing but busy themselves in other people's lives. ¹²We command those people and beg them in the Lord Jesus Christ to work quietly and earn their own food. ¹³But you, brothers and sisters, never become tired of doing good.

¹⁴If some people do not obey what we tell you in this letter, then take note of them. Have nothing to do with them so they will feel ashamed. ¹⁵But do not treat them as enemies. Warn them as fellow believers.

FINAL WORDS

¹⁶Now may the Lord of peace give you peace at all times and in every way. The Lord be with all of you.

¹⁷I, Paul, end this letter now in my own handwriting. All my letters have this to show they are from me. This is the way I write.

¹⁸The grace of our Lord Jesus Christ be with you all.

DON'T DOUBT THAT GOD CAN USE YOU

Most of us have had an adult take us under their wing at some point in our lives. It might have been a teacher, a parent, a grandparent, or even an older brother or sister. They were our mentor and probably offered us some good advice, even if we weren't always listening. This letter was written by Paul, Timothy's mentor. Although Timothy was very young, Paul saw great potential in him and invested a lot of time training him to be a leader. Tim listened carefully to every word Paul had to spit and had become the head of the church in Ephesus. Paul encouraged him to be a strong leader and not worry about his young age.

Many of us may have been looked down on because of our age. Maybe some folks didn't think they could trust us or may have questioned that we could actually follow through. If you take a good look at the disciples and the early church leaders, you'll see that most of them were pretty young. Even Jesus himself was only thirty when he began his short, three-year ministry. When we think of church leaders we usually think of older people and doubt that God can use us . . . well, think again. Check out Timothy who was very young and yet a *real* leader!

1

From Paul, an apostle of Christ Jesus, by the command of God our Savior and Christ Jesus our hope.

²To Timothy, a true child to me because you believe:

Grace, mercy, and peace from God the Father and Christ Jesus our Lord.

WARNING AGAINST FALSE TEACHING

³I asked you to stay longer in Ephesus when I went into Macedonia so you could command some people there to stop teaching false things. ⁴Tell them not to spend their time on stories that are not true and on long lists of names in family histories. These things only bring arguments; they do not help God's work, which is done in faith. ⁵The purpose of this command is for people to have love, a love that comes from a pure heart and a good conscience and a true faith. ⁶Some people have missed these things and turned to useless talk. ⁷They want to be teachers of the law, but they do not understand either what they are talking about or what they are sure about.

⁸But we know that the law is good if someone uses it lawfully. ⁹We also know that the law is not made for good people but for those who are against the law and for those who refuse to follow it. It is for people who are against God and are sinful, who are unholy and ungodly, who kill their fathers and mothers, who murder, ¹⁰who take part in sexual sins, who have sexual relations with people of the same sex, who sell slaves, who tell lies, who speak falsely, and who do anything against the true teaching of God. ¹¹That teaching is part of the Good News of the blessed God that he gave me to tell.

THANKS FOR GOD'S MERCY

¹²I thank Christ Jesus our Lord, who gave me strength, because he trusted me and gave me this work of serving him. ¹³In the past I spoke against Christ and persecuted him and did all kinds of things to hurt him. But God showed me mercy, because I did not know what I was doing. I did not believe. ¹⁴But the grace of our Lord was fully given to me, and with that grace came the faith and love that are in Christ Jesus.

¹⁵What I say is true, and you should fully accept it: Christ Jesus came into the world to save sinners, of whom I am the worst. ¹⁶But I was given mercy so that in me, the worst of all sinners, Christ Jesus could show that he has patience without limit. His patience with me made me an example for those who would believe in him and have life forever. ¹⁷To the King that rules forever, who will never die, who cannot be seen, the only God, be honor and glory forever and ever. Amen.

¹⁸Timothy, my child, I am giving you a command that agrees with the prophecies that were given about you in the past. I tell you this so you can follow them and fight the good fight. ¹⁹Continue to have faith and do what you know is right. Some people have rejected this, and their faith has been shipwrecked. ²⁰Hymenaeus and Alexander have done that, and I have given them to Satan so they will learn not to speak against God.

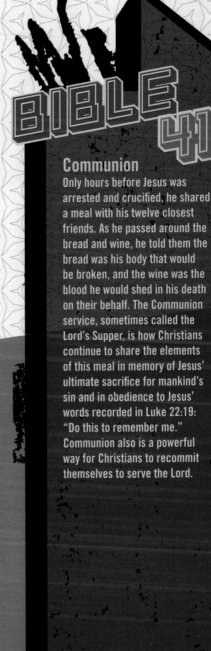

Communion

Only hours before Jesus was arrested and crucified, he shared a meal with his twelve closest friends. As he passed around the bread and wine, he told them the bread was his body that would be broken, and the wine was the blood he would shed in his death on their behalf. The Communion service, sometimes called the Lord's Supper, is how Christians continue to share the elements of this meal in memory of Jesus' ultimate sacrifice for mankind's sin and in obedience to Jesus' words recorded in Luke 22:19: "Do this to remember me." Communion also is a powerful way for Christians to recommit themselves to serve the Lord.

TIMOTHY WAS YOUNG AND A REAL LEADER

SOME RULES FOR MEN AND WOMEN

2 First, I tell you to pray for all people, asking God for what they need and being thankful to him. [2]Pray for rulers and for all who have authority so that we can have quiet and peaceful lives full of worship and respect for God. [3]This is good, and it pleases God our Savior, [4]who wants all people to be saved and to know the truth. [5]There is one God and one mediator so that human beings can reach God. That way is through Christ Jesus, who is himself human. [6]He gave himself as a payment to free all people. He is proof that came at the right time. [7]That is why I was chosen to tell the Good News and to be an apostle. (I am telling the truth; I am not lying.) I was chosen to teach those who are not Jews to believe and to know the truth.

[8]So, I want the men everywhere to pray, lifting up their hands in a holy manner, without anger and arguments.

[9]Also, women should wear proper clothes that show respect and self-control, not using braided hair or gold or pearls or expensive clothes. [10]Instead, they should do good deeds, which is right for women who say they worship God.

[11]Let a woman learn by listening quietly and being ready to cooperate in everything. [12]But I do not allow a woman to teach or to have authority over a man, but to listen quietly, [13]because Adam was formed first and then Eve. [14]And Adam was not tricked, but the woman was tricked and became a sinner. [15]But she will be saved through having children if she continues in faith, love, and holiness, with self-control.

ELDERS IN THE CHURCH

3 What I say is true: Anyone wanting to become an overseer desires a good work. [2]An overseer must not give people a reason to criticize him, and he must have only one wife. He must be self-controlled, wise, respected by others, ready to welcome guests, and able to teach. [3]He must not drink too much wine or like to fight, but rather be gentle and peaceable, not loving money. [4]He must be a good family leader, having children who cooperate with full respect. [5](If someone does not know how to lead the family, how can that person take care of God's church?) [6]But an elder must not be a new believer, or he might be too proud of himself and be judged guilty just as the devil was. [7]An elder must also have the respect of people who are not in the church so he will not be criticized by others and caught in the devil's trap.

DEACONS IN THE CHURCH

[8]In the same way, deacons must be respected by others, not saying things they do not mean. They must not drink too much wine or try to get rich by cheating others. [9]With a clear conscience they must follow the secret of the faith that God made known to us. [10]Test them first. Then let them serve as deacons if you find nothing wrong in them. [11]In the same way, women[n] must be respected by others. They must not speak evil of others. They must be self-controlled and trustworthy in everything. [12]Deacons must have only one wife and be good leaders of their children and their own families. [13]Those who serve well as deacons are making an honorable place for themselves, and they will be very bold in their faith in Christ Jesus.

THE SECRET OF OUR LIFE

[14]Although I hope I can come to you soon, I am writing these things to you now. [15]Then, even if I am delayed, you will know how to live in the family of God. That family is the church of the living God, the support and foundation of the truth. [16]Without doubt, the secret of our life of worship is great:

He[n] was shown to us in a human body,
   proved right in spirit,
   and seen by angels.
He was proclaimed to the nations,
   believed in by the world,
   and taken up in glory.

A WARNING ABOUT FALSE TEACHERS

4 Now the Holy Spirit clearly says that in the later times some people will stop believing the faith. They will follow spirits that lie and teachings of demons. [2]Such teachings come from the false words of liars whose consciences are destroyed as if by a hot iron. [3]They forbid people to marry and tell them not to eat certain foods which God created to be eaten with thanks by people who believe and know the truth. [4]Everything God made is good, and nothing should be refused if it is accepted with thanks, [5]because it is made holy by what God has said and by prayer.

BE A GOOD SERVANT OF CHRIST

[6]By telling these things to the brothers and sisters, you will be a good servant of Christ Jesus. You will be made strong by the words of the faith and the good teaching which you have been following. [7]But do not follow foolish stories that disagree with God's truth, but train yourself to serve God. [8]Training your body helps you in some ways, but serving God helps you in every way by bringing you blessings in this life and in the future life, too. [9]What I say is true, and you should fully accept it. [10]This is why we work and struggle:[n] We hope in the living God who is the Savior of all people, especially of those who believe.

[11]Command and teach these things. [12]Do not let anyone treat you as if you are unimportant because you are young. Instead, be an example to the believers with your words, your actions, your love, your faith, and your pure life. [13]Until I come, continue to read the Scriptures to the people, strengthen them, and teach them. [14]Use the gift you have, which was

3:11 women This might mean the wives of the deacons, or it might mean women who serve in the same way as deacons. **3:16 He** Some Greek copies read "God." **4:10 struggle** Some Greek copies read "suffer."

REAL RHYMES:

PERSEVERE (SONNET I)

BY JOHN F. DILWORTH II

THE WORLD HAS LOW EXPECTATIONS FOR ME, BUT INDEED I PERSEVERE.
THEY SAY I WON'T LIVE TO TELL MY STORY, BUT IN THE END MY VOICE WILL BE HEARD CLEAR.

AND WHEN I SHINE MY ETERNAL LIGHT, THEY WILL RECOGNIZE THE TRUTH.
HOW I STOOD STRONG IN THE DARKEST NIGHT AND THE TRIFLING DAYS OF MY YOUTH.

THEY SAY, "HE'S JUST ANOTHER BLACK BOY RAISED IN COLLEGE PARK AND THAT MAKES IT HARDER FOR HIM TO SUCCEED."
BUT I STAY VIGOROUS IN THESE TROUBLED WATERS, LIKE A SHARK AND I PERSEVERE INDEED.

I'VE TRAVELED THIS BUMPY ROAD OF LIFE, FACING THE OBSTACLES OF FEAR.
I DEFEAT THE ODDS WHEN THEY'RE AGAINST ME, AND INDEED I PERSEVERE.

VIEWPOINT

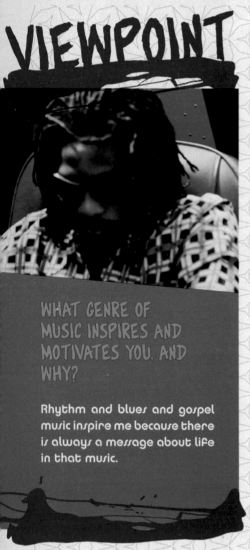

WHAT GENRE OF MUSIC INSPIRES AND MOTIVATES YOU, AND WHY?

Rhythm and blues and gospel music inspire me because there is always a message about life in that music.

given to you through prophecy when the group of elders laid their hands on[n] you. [15]Continue to do those things; give your life to doing them so your progress may be seen by everyone. [16]Be careful in your life and in your teaching. If you continue to live and teach rightly, you will save both yourself and those who listen to you.

RULES FOR LIVING WITH OTHERS

5 Do not speak angrily to an older man, but plead with him as if he were your father. Treat younger men like brothers, [2]older women like mothers, and younger women like sisters. Always treat them in a pure way.

[3]Take care of widows who are truly widows. [4]But if a widow has children or grandchildren, let them first learn to do their duty to their own family and to repay their parents or grandparents. That pleases God. [5]The true widow, who is all alone, puts her hope in God and continues to pray night and day for God's help. [6]But the widow who uses her life to please herself is really dead while she is alive. [7]Tell the believers to do these things so that no one can criticize them. [8]Whoever does not care for his own relatives, especially his own family members, has turned against the faith and is worse than someone who does not believe in God.

[9]To be on the list of widows, a woman must be at least sixty years old. She must have been faithful to her husband. [10]She must be known for her good works—works such as raising her children, welcoming strangers, washing the feet of God's people, helping those in trouble, and giving her life to do all kinds of good deeds.

[11]But do not put younger widows on that list. After they give themselves to Christ, they are pulled away from him by their physical desires, and then they want to marry again. [12]They will be judged for not doing what they first promised to do. [13]Besides that, they learn to waste their time, going from house to house. And they not only waste their time but also begin to gossip and busy themselves with other people's lives, saying things they should not say. [14]So I want the younger widows to marry, have children, and manage their homes. Then no enemy will have any reason to criticize them. [15]But some have already turned away to follow Satan.

[16]If any woman who is a believer has widows in her family, she should care for them herself. The church should not have to care for them. Then it will be able to take care of those who are truly widows.

[17]The elders who lead the church well should receive double honor, especially those who work hard by speaking and teaching, [18]because the Scripture says: "When an ox is working in the grain, do not cover its mouth to keep it from eating,"[n] and "A worker should be given his pay."[n]

[19]Do not listen to someone who accuses an elder, without two or three witnesses. [20]Tell those who continue sinning that they are wrong. Do this in front of the whole church so that the others will have a warning.

[21]Before God and Christ Jesus and the chosen angels, I command you to do these things without showing favor of any kind to anyone.

[22]Think carefully before you lay your hands on[n] anyone, and don't share in the sins of others. Keep yourself pure.

[23]Stop drinking only water, but drink a little wine to help your stomach and your frequent sicknesses.

[24]The sins of some people are easy to see even before they are judged, but the sins of others are seen only later. [25]So also good deeds are easy to see, but even those that are not easily seen cannot stay hidden.

6 All who are slaves under a yoke should show full respect to their masters so no one will speak against God's name and our teaching. [2]The slaves whose masters are believers should not show their masters any less respect because they are believers. They should serve their masters even better, because they are helping believers they love.

You must teach and preach these things.

FALSE TEACHING AND TRUE RICHES

[3]Anyone who has a different teaching does not agree with the true teaching of our Lord Jesus Christ and the teaching that shows the true way to serve God. [4]This person is full of pride and under-

---

4:14 laid their hands on The laying on of hands had many purposes, including the giving of a blessing, power, or authority.   **5:18 "When . . . eating."** Quotation from Deuteronomy 25:4.   **5:18 "A worker . . . pay."** Quotation from Luke 10:7.   **5:22 lay your hands on** The laying on of hands had many purposes, including the giving of a blessing, power, or authority.

WORLD SAYS, WORD SAYS,

THE LOVE OF MONEY

Do whatever it takes to make money. Don't let anyone or anything get in your way. Make as much as you can; everyone wants to be rich. Money makes life better. You'll be a happier person when you have all that cash in your pocket.

"Those who want to become rich bring temptation to themselves and are caught in a trap. They want many foolish and harmful things that ruin and destroy people. The love of money causes all kinds of evil. Some people have left the faith, because they wanted to get more money, but they have caused themselves much sorrow" (1 Timothy 6:9-10).

"Keep your lives free from the love of money, and be satisfied with what you have" (Hebrews 13:5).

stands nothing, but is sick with a love for arguing and fighting about words. This brings jealousy, fighting, speaking against others, evil mistrust, [5] and constant quarrels from those who have evil minds and have lost the truth. They think that serving God is a way to get rich.

[6] Serving God does make us very rich, if we are satisfied with what we have. [7] We brought nothing into the world, so we can take nothing out. [8] But, if we have food and clothes, we will be satisfied with that. [9] Those who want to become rich bring temptation to themselves and are caught in a trap. They want many foolish and harmful things that ruin and destroy people. [10] The love of money causes all kinds of evil. Some people have left the faith, because they wanted to get more money, but they have caused themselves much sorrow.

SOME THINGS TO REMEMBER

[11] But you, man of God, run away from all those things. Instead, live in the right way, serve God, have faith, love, patience, and gentleness. [12] Fight the good fight of faith, grabbing hold of the life that continues forever. You were called to have that life when you confessed the good confession before many witnesses. [13] In the sight of God, who gives life to everything, and of Christ Jesus, I give you a command. Christ Jesus made the good confession when he stood before Pontius Pilate. [14] Do what you were commanded to do without wrong or blame until our Lord Jesus Christ comes again. [15] God will make that happen at the right time. He is the blessed and only Ruler, the King of all kings and the Lord of all lords. [16] He is the only One who never dies. He lives in light so bright no one can go near

it. No one has ever seen God, or can see him. May honor and power belong to God forever. Amen.

[17] Command those who are rich with things of this world not to be proud. Tell them to hope in God, not in their uncertain riches. God richly gives us everything to enjoy. [18] Tell the rich people to do good, to be rich in doing good deeds, to be generous and ready to share. [19] By doing that, they will be saving a treasure for themselves as a strong foundation for the future. Then they will be able to have the life that is true life.

[20] Timothy, guard what God has trusted to you. Stay away from foolish, useless talk and from the arguments of what is falsely called "knowledge." [21] By saying they have that "knowledge," some have missed the true faith.

Grace be with you.

2 TIMOTHY

Always Be Prepared and Ready

This letter contains the final words of Paul. He tagged up his last letter from a cold cell in the dungeon of a Roman prison. In the past, many people had been there for him as he endured imprisonment, but as he neared the end of his life it seemed he had been abandoned by most of his crew. His work for Christ on this earth was coming to a close and you can hear his passion in these pages.

Paul really missed his spiritual son Timothy and wanted to leave him with some key things to help him in ministry. He starts out by encouraging Tim to not be afraid or timid and reminds him of his gifts, talents, and his calling. Paul teaches him about endurance, using the analogies of a soldier and an athlete: both must push through the difficulties if they wish to win. Soldiers must stay focused on the battle, and athletes must take their training seriously and always play by the rules of the game. Paul urged Timothy to focus on preaching God's message and always be prepared and ready for a spiritual battle.

Even though most of his crew had left and his final days were in a miserable place . . . Paul still represented and stayed *real* to the end.

1

From Paul, an apostle of Christ Jesus by the will of God. God sent me to tell about the promise of life that is in Christ Jesus.

[2] To Timothy, a dear child to me:

Grace, mercy, and peace to you from God the Father and Christ Jesus our Lord.

ENCOURAGEMENT FOR TIMOTHY

[3] I thank God as I always mention you in my prayers, day and night. I serve him, doing what I know is right as my ancestors did. [4] Remembering that you cried for me, I want very much to see you so I can be filled with joy. [5] I remember your true faith. That faith first lived in your grandmother Lois and in your mother Eunice, and I know you now have that same faith. [6] This is why I remind you to keep using the gift God gave you when I laid my hands on[n] you. Now let it grow, as a small flame grows into a fire. [7] God did not give us a spirit that makes us afraid but a spirit of power and love and self-control.

[8] So do not be ashamed to tell people about our Lord Jesus, and do not be ashamed of me, in prison for the Lord.

But suffer with me for the Good News. God, who gives us the strength to do that, [9] saved us and made us his holy people. That was not because of anything we did ourselves but because of God's purpose and grace. That grace was given to us through Christ Jesus before time began, [10] but it is now shown to us by the coming of our Savior Christ Jesus. He destroyed death, and through the Good News he showed us the way to have life that cannot be destroyed. [11] I was chosen to tell that Good News and to be an apostle and a teacher. [12] I am suffering now because I tell the Good News, but I am not ashamed, because I know Jesus, the One in whom I have believed. And I am sure he is able to protect what he has trusted me with until that day.[n] [13] Follow the pattern of true teachings that you heard from me in faith and love, which are in Christ Jesus. [14] Protect the truth that you were given; protect it with the help of the Holy Spirit who lives in us.

[15] You know that everyone in Asia has left me, even Phygelus and Hermogenes. [16] May the Lord show mercy to the family of Onesiphorus, who has often helped me and was not ashamed that I was in prison. [17] When he came to Rome, he looked eagerly for me until he found me. [18] May the Lord allow him to find mercy from the Lord on that day. You know how many ways he helped me in Ephesus.

SOLDIERS MUST STAY FOCUSED ON THE BATTLE

A LOYAL SOLDIER OF CHRIST JESUS

2

You then, Timothy, my child, be strong in the grace we have in Christ Jesus. [2] You should teach people whom you can trust the things you and many others have heard me say. Then they will be able to teach others.

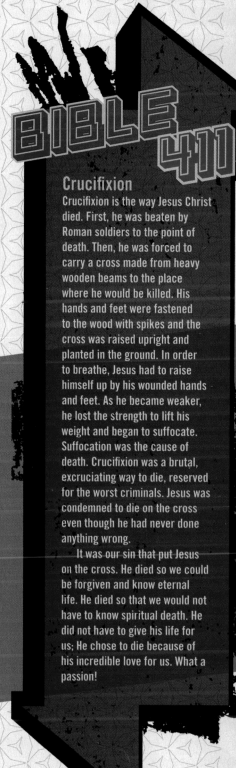

Crucifixion

Crucifixion is the way Jesus Christ died. First, he was beaten by Roman soldiers to the point of death. Then, he was forced to carry a cross made from heavy wooden beams to the place where he would be killed. His hands and feet were fastened to the wood with spikes and the cross was raised upright and planted in the ground. In order to breathe, Jesus had to raise himself up by his wounded hands and feet. As he became weaker, he lost the strength to lift his weight and began to suffocate. Suffocation was the cause of death. Crucifixion was a brutal, excruciating way to die, reserved for the worst criminals. Jesus was condemned to die on the cross even though he had never done anything wrong.

It was our sin that put Jesus on the cross. He died so we could be forgiven and know eternal life. He died so that we would not have to know spiritual death. He did not have to give his life for us; He chose to die because of his incredible love for us. What a passion!

 1:6 laid my hands on The laying on of hands had many purposes, including the giving of a blessing, power, or authority. **1:12 day** The day Christ will come to judge all people and take his people to live with him.

365

NOVEMBER

1 On This Day In History 1866—First Civil Rights Bill passed.

2 It's your birthday, Nelly!

3 Attend a health screening or have an annual health check-up.

4

5

6 On This Day In History 1936—First television
   sets debuted to the press.

7

8

9

10

11 On This Day In History 1831—Nat Turner hung
   for leading an insurrection.

12

13

14

15

16 Happy Birthday, Run (Run/DMC)!

17 HOLIDAY—Election Day

18

19

20

21 HOLIDAY—Thanksgiving

22 On This Day In History 1963—John F. Kennedy assassinated.

23 HOLIDAY—Veteran's Day

24

25

26

27

28

29

30

31

"I don't believe in luck.
I believe everything
happens for a reason."
–Nelly

Think outside
the box:
Do something special
for an elderly person
in your life.

Vote and make a difference.

Reflect on your blessings and
thank God for them.

MUSIC REVIEWS

ARTIST: BEYOND SKILLZ **ALBUM:** ESSENTIAL FUNDAMENTALS

The lyrical content in *Essential Fundamentals* by Beyond Skillz represents the issues we come up against every day. It's just plain life. The name of the album says it all. It's about the only essential fundamental. The lyrics tell God who you are, who he is to you, and how the things in the world are designed to get in the way of that relationship.

The CD blasts off right out of the box with getting the listeners hype, telling them to lift their hands. You know exactly what Beyond Skillz is there to do as they go into real issues and praise.

The sounds of the male/female rap duo are so full that it sounds like a bunch of folks. The group has a new spin on old-school rap that any rap listener can appreciate.

"ACCEPTED"

³Share in the troubles we have like a good soldier of Christ Jesus. ⁴A soldier wants to please the enlisting officer, so no one serving in the army wastes time with everyday matters. ⁵Also an athlete who takes part in a contest must obey all the rules in order to win. ⁶The farmer who works hard should be the first person to get some of the food that was grown. ⁷Think about what I am saying, because the Lord will give you the ability to understand everything.

⁸Remember Jesus Christ, who was raised from the dead, who is from the family of David. This is the Good News I preach, ⁹and I am suffering because of it to the point of being bound with chains like a criminal. But God's teaching is not in chains. ¹⁰So I patiently accept all these troubles so that those whom God has chosen can have the salvation that is in Christ Jesus. With that salvation comes glory that never ends.

¹¹This teaching is true:

If we died with him, we will also live with him.

¹²If we accept suffering, we will also rule with him.

If we say we don't know him, he will say he doesn't know us.

¹³If we are not faithful, he will still be faithful,

because he must be true to who he is.

A WORKER PLEASING TO GOD

¹⁴Continue teaching these things, warning people in God's presence not to argue about words. It does not help anyone, and it ruins those who listen. ¹⁵Make every effort to give yourself to God as the kind of person he will approve. Be a worker who is not ashamed and who uses the true teaching in the right way. ¹⁶Stay away from foolish, useless talk, because that will lead people further away from God. ¹⁷Their evil teaching will spread like a sickness inside the body. Hymenaeus and Philetus are like that. ¹⁸They have left the true teaching, saying that the rising from the dead has already taken place, and so they are destroying the faith of some people. ¹⁹But God's strong foundation continues to stand. These words are written on the seal: "The Lord knows those who belong to him,"ⁿ and "Everyone who wants to belong to the Lord must stop doing wrong."

²⁰In a large house there are not only things made of gold and silver, but also things made of wood and clay. Some things are used for special purposes, and others are made for ordinary jobs. ²¹All who make themselves clean from evil will be used for special purposes. They will be made holy, useful to the Master, ready to do any good work.

²²But run away from the evil desires of youth. Try hard to live right and to have faith, love, and peace, together with those who trust in the Lord from pure hearts. ²³Stay away from foolish and stupid arguments, because you know they grow into quarrels. ²⁴And a servant of the Lord must not quarrel but must be kind to everyone, a good teacher, and patient. ²⁵The Lord's servant must gently

2:19 "The Lord . . . him." Quotation from Numbers 16:5.

OVERCOMING

▶ IMPURITY

Giving it up before it's time is no small matter. The damage done by having sex outside of marriage is massive. It doesn't matter who you are. You just gave away a precious gift—you! God created you with a purpose and a plan for your life. For most people, part of that plan is to be joined to a mate who, through marriage, will compliment and complete you. Sex outside of marriage is giving to another what is really not yours to give.

But through the Lord, we can leave the past behind and look forward to a new and beautiful future. In 1 John 1:9 we have a promise from God that, "If we confess our sins, he will forgive our sins, because we can trust God to do what is right. He will cleanse us from all the wrongs we have done." Jesus died so our sins can be forgiven and we can be cleansed of the destructive effects. When you ask his forgiveness, he will begin to work on the inside of you. Yes, it's true you cannot go back and undo what has been done, but God can heal the damage. Your flesh may never be the same, but your soul can be totally renewed, just as if you had never sinned!

teach those who disagree. Then maybe God will let them change their minds so they can accept the truth. [26]And they may wake up and escape from the trap of the devil, who catches them to do what he wants.

THE LAST DAYS

3 Remember this! In the last days there will be many troubles, [2]because people will love themselves, love money, brag, and be proud. They will say evil things against others and will not obey their parents or be thankful or be the kind of people God wants. [3]They will not love others, will refuse to forgive, will gossip, and will not control themselves. They will be cruel, will hate what is good, [4]will turn against their friends, and will do foolish things without thinking. They will be conceited, will love pleasure instead of God, [5]and will act as if they serve God but will not have his power. Stay away from those people. [6]Some of them go into homes and get control of silly women who are full of sin and are led by many evil desires. [7]These women are always learning new teachings, but they are never able to understand the truth fully. [8]Just as Jannes and Jambres were against Moses, these people are against the truth. Their thinking has been ruined, and they have failed in trying to follow the faith. [9]But they will not be successful in what they do, because as with Jannes and Jambres, everyone will see that they are foolish.

OBEY THE TEACHINGS

[10]But you have followed what I teach, the way I live, my goal, faith, patience, and love. You know I never give up. [11]You know how I have been hurt and have suffered, as in Antioch, Iconium, and Lystra. I have suffered, but the Lord saved me from all those troubles. [12]Everyone who wants to live as God desires, in Christ Jesus, will be persecuted. [13]But people who are evil and cheat others will go from bad to worse. They will fool others, but they will also be fooling themselves.

[14]But you should continue following the teachings you learned. You know they are true, because you trust those who taught you. [15]Since you were a child you have known the Holy Scriptures which are able to make you wise. And that wisdom leads to salvation through faith in Christ Jesus. [16]All Scripture is inspired by God and is useful for teaching, for showing people what is wrong in their lives, for correcting faults, and for teaching how to live right. [17]Using the Scriptures, the person who serves God will be capable, having all that is needed to do every good work.

4 I give you a command in the presence of God and Christ Jesus, the One who will judge the living and the dead, and by his coming and his kingdom: [2]Preach the Good News. Be ready at all times, and tell people what they need to do. Tell them when they are wrong. Encourage them with great patience and careful teaching, [3]because the time will come when people will not listen to the true teaching but will find many more teachers who please them by saying the things they want to hear. [4]They will stop listening to the truth and will begin to follow false stories. [5]But you should control yourself

at all times, accept troubles, do the work of telling the Good News, and complete all the duties of a servant of God.

[6] My life is being given as an offering to God, and the time has come for me to leave this life. [7] I have fought the good fight, I have finished the race, I have kept the faith. [8] Now, a crown is being held for me—a crown for being right with God. The Lord, the judge who judges rightly, will give the crown to me on that day[n]—not only to me but to all those who have waited with love for him to come again.

PERSONAL WORDS

[9] Do your best to come to me as soon as you can, [10] because Demas, who loved this world, left me and went to Thessalonica. Crescens went to Galatia, and Titus went to Dalmatia. [11] Luke is the only one still with me. Get Mark and bring him with you when you come, because he can help me in my work here. [12] I sent Tychicus to Ephesus. [13] When I was in Troas, I left my coat there with Carpus. So when you come, bring it to me, along with my books, particularly the ones written on parchment.[n]

[14] Alexander the metalworker did many harmful things against me. The Lord will punish him for what he did. [15] You also should be careful that he does not hurt you, because he fought strongly against our teaching.

[16] The first time I defended myself, no one helped me; everyone left me. May they be forgiven. [17] But the Lord stayed with me and gave me strength so I could fully tell the Good News to all those who are not Jews. So I was saved from the lion's mouth. [18] The Lord will save me when anyone tries to hurt me, and he will bring me safely to his heavenly kingdom. Glory forever and ever be the Lord's. Amen.

FINAL GREETINGS

[19] Greet Priscilla and Aquila and the family of Onesiphorus. [20] Erastus stayed in Corinth, and I left Trophimus sick in Miletus. [21] Try as hard as you can to come to me before winter.

Eubulus sends greetings to you. Also Pudens, Linus, Claudia, and all the brothers and sisters in Christ greet you.

[22] The Lord be with your spirit. Grace be with you.

HeartCry

Doubt   **Are you really struggling to keep the faith? Do you sometimes wonder what's real? Are you having a hard time connecting with God and believing he cares? Let your heart cry . . .**

God, where are you? Why do you seem so far away? I am trying so hard to believe, but it's hard when my life is falling apart. If you are really there, if you really care, I need to know it. I need to find you, hear you, and feel you in my life. If you aren't there, life just makes no sense. If you are there, why can't I find you? I don't want to believe just because I was told; I want to believe because I know. Please find a way to be real to me. Help me find you. Help me find faith.

I do not move away from you, but I will not force you to remain close. I wait for you to choose to know me. I have given you my Word, the Bible, to learn of me; and I long to talk with you whenever you will seek me. Your faith will grow as you discover who I am.   Romans 10:17; Deuteronomy 4:29

 4:8 day The day Christ will come to judge all people and take his people to live with him.   **4:13 parchment** A writing paper made from the skins of sheep.

HELP!

SAVE ME!

By Bishop Kenneth Ulmer

"For whoever [whosoever] calls on the name of the Lord will be saved" (Romans 10:13).

The children's church choir had taken a trip to Fresno for the state convention. While there, they stayed at a large motel. After the morning sessions there was a break until the evening worship, and many of the members decided to go swimming. All seemed to be enjoying themselves listening to music and splish-splashing in the pool. Suddenly, a sharp, shrieking cry pierced the air. A prankster had pushed one of the girls into the deep end of the pool. Little did he know she could not swim. At first the kids laughed loudly at her flailing arms, garbled shouts, and panic-stricken face. Then her sister cried out, "She can't swim! She can't swim!"

"Help! Help! Save me!" she cried with eyes glazed as she began to bob up and down in the water. But all of the other kids seemed frozen and began to scream, "Somebody do something!"

One of the supervisors heard the shrieks and jumped into the pool in an attempt to rescue his young disciple. Unfortunately, he approached her from the front, only to be met with a death grip around his neck as she reached out choking and spitting water. In a few seconds, both of them began to go down. The would-be rescuer now shared the look of fear and panic that had gripped the drowning girl. Death seemed to be clawing at both of them. Then an older teen gathered his wits, dove into the water, and came up behind the girl. He pried her off the supervisor and pulled her to the side of the pool while the supervisor swam to safety.

In Romans 10:13 we read, "Anyone who [whosoever] calls on the Lord will be saved." Spiritual salvation is somewhat like a rescue. It is activated when we realize we are in danger of disaster, destruction, and spiritual death. It means someone is drowning in the waters of life and cannot save himself. The first response is to call out. But more important than the calling is the One to whom you call. Maybe in the frustration and discouragement of your life, you have called out for help. Maybe you called out to a friend. Maybe you called out to drugs. Maybe you called out to someone in the dark of a bedroom whose name you barely knew. In the end, you were just like the youth in the pool, the person you called could not help you, no matter how much you tried to hold on. There is no one, no name that you can call that can truly save you except the name of Jesus (*Acts 4:12*).

When you call on the Lord, his promise is that you will be saved. There is an old hymn that is still true. One of the lines says, "He will hear your faintest cry." Right now, you can call him in your spirit and he will hear you. You can call him where you are on you knees and he will hear you. You can call him even in the drowning waters of your frustrated life and he will hear you. And you shall be saved. "Whosoever." That means your crowd. That means your gang. Those are your homies. You are in the "whosoever" crowd. And as one of the whosoevers, you will be saved if you call on the name of Jesus!

Jesus told stories about "whosoever." He was a master storyteller, and the stories he told are called parables. (There is an old Sunday school definition of parable: A parable is an earthly story with a heavenly meaning; or a heavenly story with an earthly meaning.) But Jesus' parables did more than tell a story. They taught a principle, a truth, or a lesson about God, his kingdom and the human condition. They were stories about people (whosoevers) in their everyday life experiences. We can relate to them. Even if we have to translate them into our culture,

they speak to all of us. We are the whosoevers. You are a whosoever.

There are two important things to know about being a whosoever. First of all, God loves the whosoever. Second, God wants to save you. All you have to do is call on him. That's what Jesus meant when he spoke of himself and the love of his Father. "God loved the world so much . . . that whoever [whosoever] believes in him may not be lost, but have eternal life" (John 3:16). The world is made up of whosoevers. God loves you because you are a whosoever. Please don't hear that as being impersonal. In fact it is especially personal. Jesus is speaking to you. And you should know that God loves you just the way you are. That may shock you, because someone may have told you that God doesn't like you or that God hates you or that God doesn't care about you. Whenever you hear something like that, run quickly to John 3:16 and tell him or her, "That's a lie. I am a whosoever, and God says he loves me."

God loves you so much that he gave his only Son. You don't know anyone who loves you that much! You know some folk who may lend you some money, but they won't give you their only son. You know someone who may offer you a joint, but they won't give up their only son. You know someone who may give you their body, but you know they don't love you enough to give up their only child for you. Yet, that's what God did.

Now Ms. Whosoever, Mr. Whosoever, if you believe in Jesus, you will be saved. To believe in him means to believe that he is everything that he said he is. In Romans 10:10, we are told that if we confess with our mouth and believe in our hearts that Jesus is the Son of God, died for our sins, rose from death as Savior and King, we will be saved. To confess is a simple word, yet very deep. It means to make something known. So to believe and confess Jesus is to believe in your heart that he is exactly who he claimed to be and to speak out that you recognize and accept who he is and what he has done.

So go ahead and confess right now. You can say it verbally or in your heart. If you are by yourself or even in a room with other people, you can say it. Simply do what the Word says. Say to the Lord, "Lord, I believe. I put my trust in you to save me. I need to be rescued. I believe that you are everything you say you are. I believe you came to save me. I call on you now, Lord, to come into my life. Make me a child of God. Take control of my life and be my Savior and Lord. Teach me more and more about you. Thank you, Lord, for saving me. Amen" ★

TITUS

PAUL WAS LIKE A COACH

Paul was like a coach, training and instructing his team. He worked closely with his starting lineup, arming them with an arsenal of powerful plays that would keep them a step ahead of their opponents.

Although Titus isn't mentioned many times in Scripture, he served as Paul's point guard. He spent his career feeding the rock to key players in Crete, Corinth, and even Jerusalem. Titus was all about raising up new players and giving them some time in the game. In this letter, Paul instructs Titus in training up a new team of Christians on the island of Crete. Paul shares some incredible words of inspiration on how to turn them into true champions. Paul trained Titus as a coach would train a talented player, but for something much more important than a game. This was every day *real* life with real people's souls on the line.

From Paul, a servant of God and an apostle of Jesus Christ. I was sent to help the faith of God's chosen people and to help them know the truth that shows people how to serve God. ²That faith and that knowledge come from the hope for life forever, which God promised to us before time began. And God cannot lie. ³At the right time God let the world know about that life through preaching. He trusted me with that work, and I preached by the command of God our Savior.

⁴To Titus, my true child in the faith we share:

Grace and peace from God the Father and Christ Jesus our Savior.

TITUS' WORK IN CRETE

⁵I left you in Crete so you could finish doing the things that still needed to be done and so you could appoint elders in every town, as I directed you. ⁶An elder must not be guilty of doing wrong, must have only one wife, and must have believing children. They must not be known as children who are wild and do not cooperate. ⁷As God's managers, overseers must not be guilty of doing wrong, being selfish, or becoming angry quickly. They must not drink too much wine, like to fight, or try to get rich by cheating others. ⁸Overseers must be ready to welcome guests, love what is good, be wise, live right, and be holy and self-controlled. ⁹By holding on to the trustworthy word just as we teach it, overseers can help people by using true teaching, and they can show those who are against the true teaching that they are wrong.

¹⁰There are many people who refuse to cooperate, who talk about worthless things and lead others into the wrong way—mainly those who insist on circumcision to be saved. ¹¹These people must be stopped, because they are upsetting whole families by teaching things they should not teach, which they do to get rich by cheating people. ¹²Even one of their own prophets said, "Cretans are always liars, evil animals, and lazy people who do nothing but eat." ¹³The words that prophet said are true. So firmly tell those people they are wrong so they may become strong in the faith, ¹⁴not accepting Jewish false stories and the commands of people who reject the truth. ¹⁵To those who are pure, all things are pure, but to those who are full of sin and do not believe, nothing is pure. Both their minds and their consciences have been ruined. ¹⁶They say they know God, but their actions show they do not accept him. They are hateful people, they refuse to obey, and they are useless for doing anything good.

FOLLOWING THE TRUE TEACHING

But you must tell everyone what to do to follow the true teaching. ²Teach older men to be self-controlled, serious, wise, strong in faith, in love, and in patience.

REAL LIFE WITH REAL SOULS ON THE LINE

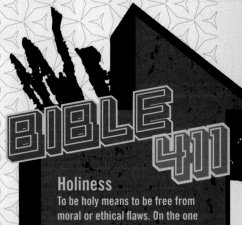

Holiness

To be holy means to be free from moral or ethical flaws. On the one hand, the Bible says everyone has sinned (Romans 3:23). On the other hand, it says that we are to be holy (2 Corinthians 7:1). How?

First, we are made holy in God's sight by the cleansing work of Christ on the cross. The blood of his sacrificial death is like a cleansing agent, washing away the stain of our sin (1 Corinthians 6:9-11). By receiving the gift of faith in Jesus, God applies Christ's holiness to us. But there's more!

Paul talks about clothing ourselves with Christ. That means we take upon ourselves the character of Christ, including his holiness. So, living the Christian life means putting on Christ, as if we were putting on a new suit of clothes. The great thing about this set of clothes is that it never gets dirty; it's always clean. When we clothe ourselves with Christ, we forget about satisfying our sinful selves. Now that's a change worth making.

Does this mean Christians never sin? No! But God's taken care of that too. When we come clean with God, he forgives us and cleanses us from our sins. So, while holiness may seem unrealistic, God shows us the way to be holy.

GOD UNIT

FINDING THE GOOD IN FAILURE

ig letter F. Failure. That was me. I was in my first year of college and involved in an ungodly sexual relationship. I met her and was intimate with her before I ever went to my first class. I was a campus leader in the academic and African-American Christian community, but I was stuck in a trap, and I didn't necessarily want out of it. I knew about God, but only based on what mama had said about him. I tried to act like a Christian, but when faced with temptation my weak love for God didn't stand a chance against the urges of my flesh. And what's worse, the young lady didn't know God, and my example surely wouldn't win her to Christ.

I was eighteen years old. I was a *grown man*. I could handle having God *and* sex. Each had a separate box; I could open and close either without the two ever meeting. I was getting good at leaving my casual girlfriend's dorm room and going straight to class, a football game, or

even the chapel for a campus service. But as I continued my escapades, the thrill wore off. I felt further away from God than I ever had at any point in my life. I had no peace and no self-respect. Was I addicted? The fellas were calling me "the man" and some of the ladies were acting as though I was a hot commodity, I loved being pursued by women but I knew God wasn't pleased. The truth is this: I needed God's help more than I needed any sexual relationship. I had to admit to myself and to my girlfriend that I could no longer do what I had been doing. I had to admit to God that I had absolutely no willpower to stop my destructive sexual behavior. When I did that, he stepped in. He ended the sexual addiction, but he had to do it by ending the relationship. The girl and I remained cordial, but soon we drifted apart. Little by little, God gave me the strength to say no. He taught me that, even when I was too weak to do the right thing on my own, I would be able to confront any challenge with him on my side . . . When I admitted I needed God, my life started making sense. I discovered what was really important to me and I've never been the same since. I'm free.

John 8:32—Then you will know the truth, and the truth will make you free.

---

[3] In the same way, teach older women to be holy in their behavior, not speaking against others or enslaved to too much wine, but teaching what is good. [4] Then they can teach the young women to love their husbands, to love their children, [5] to be wise and pure, to be good workers at home, to be kind, and to yield to their husbands. Then no one will be able to criticize the teaching God gave us.

[6] In the same way, encourage young men to be wise. [7] In every way be an example of doing good deeds. When you teach, do it with honesty and seriousness.

[8] Speak the truth so that you cannot be criticized. Then those who are against you will be ashamed because there is nothing bad to say about us.

[9] Slaves should yield to their own masters at all times, trying to please them and not arguing with them. [10] They should not steal from them but should show their masters they can be fully trusted so that in everything they do they will make the teaching of God our Savior attractive.

[11] That is the way we should live, because God's grace that can save every-

one has come. [12] It teaches us not to live against God nor to do the evil things the world wants to do. Instead, that grace teaches us to live in the present age in a wise and right way and in a way that shows we serve God. [13] We should live like that while we wait for our great hope and the coming of the glory of our great God and Savior Jesus Christ. [14] He gave himself for us so he might pay the price to free us from all evil and to make us pure people who belong only to him—people who are always wanting to do good deeds.

¹⁵Say these things and encourage the people and tell them what is wrong in their lives, with all authority. Do not let anyone treat you as if you were unimportant.

THE RIGHT WAY TO LIVE

3 Remind the believers to yield to the authority of rulers and government leaders, to obey them, to be ready to do good, ²to speak no evil about anyone, to live in peace, and to be gentle and polite to all people.

³In the past we also were foolish. We did not obey, we were wrong, and we were slaves to many things our bodies wanted and enjoyed. We spent our lives doing evil and being jealous. People hated us, and we hated each other. ⁴But when the kindness and love of God our Savior was shown, ⁵he saved us because of his mercy. It was not because of good deeds we did to be right with him. He saved us through the washing that made us new people through the Holy Spirit. ⁶God poured out richly upon us that Holy Spirit through Jesus Christ our Savior. ⁷Being made right with God by his grace, we could have the hope of receiving the life that never ends.

⁸This teaching is true, and I want you to be sure the people understand these things. Then those who believe in God will be careful to use their lives for doing good. These things are good and will help everyone.

⁹But stay away from those who have foolish arguments and talk about useless family histories and argue and quarrel about the law. Those things are worth nothing and will not help anyone. ¹⁰After a first and second warning, avoid someone who causes arguments. ¹¹You can know that such people are evil and sinful; their own sins prove them wrong.

SOME THINGS TO REMEMBER

¹²When I send Artemas or Tychicus to you, make every effort to come to me at Nicopolis, because I have decided to stay there this winter. ¹³Do all you can to help Zenas the lawyer and Apollos on their journey so that they have everything they need. ¹⁴Our people must learn to use their lives for doing good deeds to provide what is necessary so that their lives will not be useless.

¹⁵All who are with me greet you. Greet those who love us in the faith.

Grace be with you all.

HeartCry

Loss **Do you feel like life is just out to get you? Does it seem all the best things keep slipping through your fingers? Let your heart cry . . .**

Hey, Jesus. It's me again. Stuff down here is really messed up. I keep losing what I care about most until, sometimes, I feel like just giving up. This place has too many disappointments. Something bad is always happening. I keep hearing that you've got my back, but where are you in all this mess?

I am the only one who never changes and will never leave you. My love surrounds you even when you are not aware. Keep your eyes on me and the cares of this life will lose their power to defeat you. Isaiah 54:17; Philippians 3:8

PHILEMON

DRAMA CAN GET UGLY

We have all experienced conflict in relationships. More often than not, it results in confrontation that can lead to arguments, throwing blows, or even the end of a friendship. It's especially tough when you are forced to take sides between friends or you try to help patch things up. Both are difficult scenarios and sometimes the drama can get straight up ugly.

In this letter to Philemon, Paul was right in the middle of some serious drama. Philemon, a very close friend of Paul, had a servant named Onesimus who had run away. According to Roman law, a runaway servant could actually be killed. Onesimus had a true relationship with Christ and realized he needed to make things right with his master, but he was afraid he would be put to death if he returned. You can imagine that Philemon was mad angry! So, Paul carefully wrote this letter sharing how he had met Onesimus and led him to Christ. Paul put out an emotional plea to Philemon to accept Onesimus back, not as a slave, but now as a brother in Christ. This short book illustrates that a relationship with Christ can bring a *real* change to the way we view our world.

¹From Paul, a prisoner of Christ Jesus, and from Timothy, our brother.

To Philemon, our dear friend and worker with us; ²to Apphia, our sister; to Archippus, a worker with us; and to the church that meets in your home:

³Grace and peace to you from God our Father and the Lord Jesus Christ.

PHILEMON'S LOVE AND FAITH

⁴I always thank my God when I mention you in my prayers, ⁵because I hear about the love you have for all God's holy people and the faith you have in the Lord Jesus. ⁶I pray that the faith you share may make you understand every blessing we have in Christ. ⁷I have great joy and comfort, my brother, because the love you have shown to God's people has refreshed them.

ACCEPT ONESIMUS AS A BROTHER

⁸So, in Christ, I could be bold and order you to do what is right. ⁹But because I love you, I am pleading with you instead. I, Paul, an old man now and also a prisoner for Christ Jesus, ¹⁰am pleading with you for my child Onesimus, who became my child while I was in prison. ¹¹In the past he was useless to you, but now he has become useful for both you and me.

you first so that any good you do for me will be because you want to do it, not because I forced you. ¹⁵Maybe Onesimus was separated from you for a short time so you could have him back forever—¹⁶no longer as a slave, but better than a slave, as a loved brother. I love him very much, but you will love him even more, both as a person and as a believer in the Lord.

¹⁷So if you consider me your partner, welcome Onesimus as you would welcome me. ¹⁸If he has done anything wrong to you or if he owes you anything, charge that to me. ¹⁹I, Paul, am writing this with my own hand. I will pay it back, and I will say nothing about what you owe me for your own life. ²⁰So, my brother, I ask that you do this for me in the Lord: Refresh my heart in Christ. ²¹I write this letter, knowing that you will do what I ask you and even more.

²²One more thing—prepare a room for me in which to stay, because I hope God will answer your prayers and I will be able to come to you.

FINAL GREETINGS

²³Epaphras, a prisoner with me for Christ Jesus, sends greetings to you.

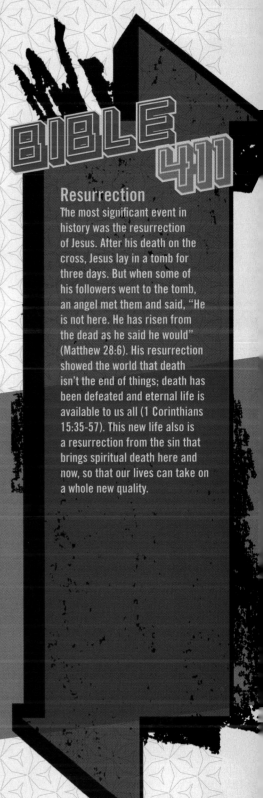

BIBLE 411

Resurrection

The most significant event in history was the resurrection of Jesus. After his death on the cross, Jesus lay in a tomb for three days. But when some of his followers went to the tomb, an angel met them and said, "He is not here. He has risen from the dead as he said he would" (Matthew 28:6). His resurrection showed the world that death isn't the end of things; death has been defeated and eternal life is available to us all (1 Corinthians 15:35-57). This new life also is a resurrection from the sin that brings spiritual death here and now, so that our lives can take on a whole new quality.

A RELATIONSHIP WITH CHRIST CAN BRING REAL CHANGE

¹²I am sending him back to you, and with him I am sending my own heart. ¹³I wanted to keep him with me so that in your place he might help me while I am in prison for the Good News. ¹⁴But I did not want to do anything without asking

²⁴And also Mark, Aristarchus, Demas, and Luke, workers together with me, send greetings.

²⁵The grace of our Lord Jesus Christ be with your spirit.

HEBREWS

A relationship with God is not about what we do; it's about who we know. This book is a letter written to a group of Jewish Christians in an effort to help them get that straight.

Back in the day, God taught the Jewish people about himself through a set of rules and ceremonies, all designed to help them keep it tight with him. He made a binding agreement, a blood oath, with the Jewish people. The sign of that agreement was the sacrifice of animals and the shedding of their blood. He promised that he would be there for them; their part was to obey his commands. But the people got it wrong and ended up more concerned about the rules than the relationship. Because the people lost sight of the reason for the rules, they ended up in bondage to them.

God sent Jesus to complete the intent of the old agreement with the Jewish people. Jesus made things clear and made things right, teaching the people about God and his love for them. He brought it back down to a relationship. He showed folks what living out the old agreement should look like. He lived his life according to the old agreement and then gave his life to begin a new agreement—a blood oath signed by the blood he shed on the cross. The rules and rituals of the old agreement hinted at what a relationship with God could be. Jesus provided a way to make that relationship a reality. The new agreement offers the way to God based on faith in Jesus and his final sacrifice.

This letter spells it out. God's love is real and he wants a real relationship with each of us.

GOD SPOKE THROUGH HIS SON

1 In the past God spoke to our ancestors through the prophets many times and in many different ways. [2]But now in these last days God has spoken to us through his Son. God has chosen his Son to own all things, and through him he made the world. [3]The Son reflects the glory of God and shows exactly what God is like. He holds everything together with his powerful word. When the Son made people clean from their sins, he sat down at the right side of God, the Great One in heaven. [4]The Son became much greater than the angels, and God gave him a name that is much greater than theirs.

[5]This is because God never said to any of the angels,

"You are my Son.
    Today I have become your
        Father." *Psalm 2:7*

Nor did God say of any angel,

"I will be his Father,
    and he will be my Son."
        2 Samuel 7:14

"God makes his angels become like
    winds.
He makes his servants become
    like flames of fire."
            Psalm 104:4

[8]But God said this about his Son:

"God, your throne will last forever
    and ever.
You will rule your kingdom with
    fairness.
[9]You love right and hate evil,
    so God has chosen you from
        among your friends;
he has set you apart with much
    joy." *Psalm 45:6-7*

[10]God also says,

"Lord, in the beginning you made
    the earth,
and your hands made the skies.
[11]They will be destroyed, but you will
    remain.
They will all wear out like clothes.
[12]You will fold them like a coat.
And, like clothes, you will change
    them.
But you never change,
    and your life will never end."
        Psalm 102:25-27

GOD WANTS A REAL RELATIONSHIP WITH EACH OF US

[6]And when God brings his firstborn Son into the world, he says,

"Let all God's angels worship
    him."[n]
        Psalm 97:7

[7]This is what God said about the angels:

[13]And God never said this to an angel:

"Sit by me at my right side
    until I put your enemies under
        your control."[n] *Psalm 110:1*

[14]All the angels are spirits who serve God and are sent to help those who will receive salvation.

Gospel

The first four books of the New Testament are called the gospels. They recount the life of Jesus coming from heaven and going back to heaven, and his 33 years of life on earth. But 85 of the 89 chapters of these four books deal with only three years of Jesus' life, meaning those three years are truly significant. The first three of the gospels, Matthew, Mark, and Luke, report many of the same events, but from different perspectives. John, the fourth gospel, singularly sees Jesus as the "Word," the "I Am," and the "door."

But the best part about "gospel" is what it means: Good News. It's good news because Jesus came to a world filled with lying, cheating, murders, gang banging, and drugs and said, "Hey, you can get free of all that! I've come to set you free." Jesus brings hope to the most desperate situation and power to overcome it. The Good News is for each one of us, custom-made for every situation. Take heart, the Gospel is yours.

 1:6 "Let . . . him." These words are found in Deuteronomy 32:43 in the Septuagint, the Greek version of the Old Testament, and in a Hebrew copy among the Dead Sea Scrolls.
1:13 until . . . control Literally, "until I make your enemies a footstool for your feet."

OUR SALVATION IS GREAT

2 So we must be more careful to follow what we were taught. Then we will not stray away from the truth. [2]The teaching God spoke through angels was shown to be true, and anyone who did not follow it or obey it received the punishment that was earned. [3]So surely we also will be punished if we ignore this great salvation. The Lord himself first told about this salvation, and those who heard him testified it was true. [4]God also testified to the truth of the message by using wonders, great signs, many kinds of miracles, and by giving people gifts through the Holy Spirit, just as he wanted.

CHRIST BECAME LIKE HUMANS

[5]God did not choose angels to be the rulers of the new world that was coming, which is what we have been talking about. [6]It is written in the Scriptures,

"Why are people even important
    to you?
Why do you take care of human
    beings?
[7]You made them a little lower than
    the angels
and crowned them with glory and
    honor.[n]
[8]You put all things under their
    control." *Psalm 8:4-6*

When God put everything under their control, there was nothing left that they did not rule. Still, we do not yet see them ruling over everything. [9]But we see Jesus, who for a short time was made lower than the angels. And now he is wearing a crown of glory and honor because he suffered and died. And by God's grace, he died for everyone.

[10]God is the One who made all things, and all things are for his glory. He wanted to have many children share his glory, so he made the One who leads people to salvation perfect through suffering.

[11]Jesus, who makes people holy, and those who are made holy are from the same family. So he is not ashamed to call them his brothers and sisters. [12]He says,

"Then, I will tell my brothers and
    sisters about you;
I will praise you in the public
    meeting." *Psalm 22:22*

[13]He also says,

"I will trust in God." *Isaiah 8:17*

And he also says,

"I am here, and with me are the
    children God has given me."
                    Isaiah 8:18

[14]Since these children are people with physical bodies, Jesus himself became like them. He did this so that, by dying, he could destroy the one who has the power of death—the devil— [15]and free those who were like slaves all their lives because of their fear of death. [16]Clearly, it is not angels that Jesus helps, but the people who are from Abraham.[n] [17]For this reason Jesus had to be made like his brothers and sisters in every way so he could be their merciful and faithful high priest in service to God. Then Jesus could die in their place to take away their sins. [18]And now he can help those who are tempted, because he himself suffered and was tempted.

JESUS IS GREATER THAN MOSES

3 So all of you holy brothers and sisters, who were called by God, think about Jesus, who was sent to us and is the high priest of our faith. [2]Jesus was faithful to God as Moses was in God's family. [3]Jesus has more honor than Moses, just as the builder of a house has more honor than the house itself. [4]Every house is built by someone, but the builder of everything is God himself. [5]Moses was faithful in God's family as a servant, and he told what God would say in the future. [6]But Christ is faithful as a Son over God's house. And we are God's house if we confidently maintain our hope.

WE MUST CONTINUE TO FOLLOW GOD

[7]So it is as the Holy Spirit says:

"Today listen to what he says.
[8]Do not be stubborn as in the past
    when you turned against God,
when you tested God in the desert.
[9]There your ancestors tried me and
    tested me
and saw the things I did for forty
    years.
[10]I was angry with them.
    I said, 'They are not loyal to me
    and have not understood my
    ways.'
[11]I was angry and made a promise,
    'They will never enter my rest.' "[n]
                    Psalm 95:7-11

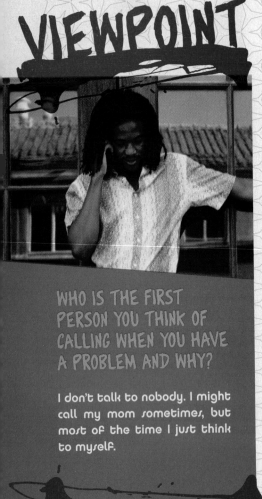

VIEWPOINT

WHO IS THE FIRST PERSON YOU THINK OF CALLING WHEN YOU HAVE A PROBLEM AND WHY?

I don't talk to nobody. I might call my mom sometimes, but most of the time I just think to myself.

2:7 You . . . honor. Some Greek copies continue, "You put them in charge of everything you made." See Psalm 8:6. **2:16 Abraham** Most respected ancestor of the Jews. Every Jew hoped to see Abraham. **3:11 rest** A place of rest God promised to give his people.

[12]So brothers and sisters, be careful that none of you has an evil, unbelieving heart that will turn you away from the living God. [13]But encourage each other every day while it is "today."[n] Help each other so none of you will become hardened because sin has tricked you. [14]We all share in Christ if we keep till the end the sure faith we had in the beginning. [15]This is what the Scripture says:

"Today listen to what he says.
Do not be stubborn as in the
    past
when you turned against God."

Psalm 95:7-8

[16]Who heard God's voice and was against him? It was all those people Moses led out of Egypt. [17]And with whom was God angry for forty years? He was angry with those who sinned, who died in the desert. [18]And to whom was God talking when he promised that they would never enter his rest? He was talking to those who did not obey him. [19]So we see they were not allowed to enter and have God's rest, because they did not believe.

4 Now, since God has left us the promise that we may enter his rest, let us be very careful so none of you will fail to enter. [2]The Good News was preached to us just as it was to them. But the teaching they heard did not help them, because they heard it but did not accept it with faith.[n] [3]We who have believed are able to enter and have God's rest. As God has said,

"I was angry and made a
    promise,
'They will never enter my rest.'"

Psalm 95:11

But God's work was finished from the time he made the world. [4]In the Scriptures he talked about the seventh day of the week: "And on the seventh day God rested from all his works."[n] [5]And again

---

3:13 "today" This word is taken from verse 7. It means that it is important to do these things now.   **4:2 because . . . faith** Some Greek copies read "because they did not share the faith of those who heard it."   **4:4 "And . . . works."** Quotation from Genesis 2:2.

HOW YA TRAVELIN'?

WISDOM

In Isaiah 11:1-9, Jesus is portrayed as the one on whom "the Spirit of the Lord" rested—that Spirit being one of wisdom and understanding. Being con-

Wisdom is the ability to understand truth and apply it to daily life. Proverbs 4:5 simply commands, "Get wisdom and understanding." God isn't making a mild

in the Scripture God said, "They will never enter my rest."

[6]It is still true that some people will enter God's rest, but those who first heard the way to be saved did not enter, because they did not obey. [7]So God planned another day, called "today." He spoke about that day through David a long time later in the same Scripture used before:

"Today listen to what he says.
Do not be stubborn." *Psalm 95:7-8*

[8]We know that Joshua[n] did not lead the people into that rest, because God spoke later about another day. [9]This shows that the rest[n] for God's people is still coming. [10]Anyone who enters God's rest will rest from his work as God did. [11]Let us try as hard as we can to enter God's rest so that no one will fail by following the example of those who refused to obey.

[12]God's word is alive and working and is sharper than a double-edged sword. It cuts all the way into us, where the soul and the spirit are joined, to the center of our joints and bones. And it judges the thoughts and feelings in our hearts. [13]Nothing in all the world can be hidden from God. Everything is clear and lies open before him, and to him we must explain the way we have lived.

JESUS IS OUR HIGH PRIEST

[14]Since we have a great high priest, Jesus the Son of God, who has gone into heaven, let us hold on to the faith we have. [15]For our high priest is able to understand our weaknesses. He was tempted in every way that we are, but he did not sin. [16]Let us, then, feel very sure that we can come before God's throne where there is grace. There we can receive mercy and grace to help us when we need it.

5 Every high priest is chosen from among other people. He is given the work of going before God for them to offer gifts and sacrifices for sins. [2]Since he himself is weak, he is able to be gentle with those who do not understand and who are doing wrong

hot10

NFL Teams

10. Minnesota Vikings

9. Dallas Cowboys

8. Philadelphia Eagles

7. Baltimore Ravens

6. Green Bay Packers

5. Washington Redskins

4. Kansas City Chiefs

3. Atlanta Falcons

2. Indianapolis Colts

1. New England Patriots

things. [3]Because he is weak, the high priest must offer sacrifices for his own sins and also for the sins of the people.

[4]To be a high priest is an honor, but no one chooses himself for this work. He must be called by God as Aaron[n] was. [5]So also Christ did not choose himself to have the honor of being a high priest, but God chose him. God said to him,

"You are my Son.
Today I have become your
Father." *Psalm 2:7*

[6]And in another Scripture God says,

"You are a priest forever,
a priest like Melchizedek.'"[n]
Psalm 110:4

[7]While Jesus lived on earth, he prayed to God and asked God for help. He prayed with loud cries and tears to the One who could save him from death, and his prayer was heard because he trusted God. [8]Even though Jesus was the Son of God, he learned obedience by what he suffered. [9]And because his obedience was perfect, he was able to give eternal salvation to all who obey him. [10]In this way God made Jesus a high priest, a priest like Melchizedek.

WARNING AGAINST FALLING AWAY

[11]We have much to say about this, but it is hard to explain because you are so slow to understand. [12]By now you should be teachers, but you need someone to teach you again the first lessons of God's message. You still need the teaching that is like milk. You are not ready for solid food. [13]Anyone who lives on milk is still a baby and knows nothing about right teaching. [14]But solid food is for those who are grown up. They are mature enough to know the difference between good and evil.

6 So let us go on to grown-up teaching. Let us not go back over the beginning lessons we learned about Christ. We should not again start teaching about faith in God and about turning away from those acts that lead to death. [2]We should not return to the teaching about baptisms,[n] about lay-

4:8 Joshua After Moses died, Joshua became leader of the Jewish people and led them into the land that God promised to give them. **4:9 rest** Literally, "sabbath rest," meaning a sharing in the rest that God began after he created the world. **5:4 Aaron** Moses' brother and the first Jewish high priest. **5:6 Melchizedek** A priest and king who lived in the time of Abraham. (Read Genesis 14:17-24.) **6:2 baptisms** The word here may refer to Christian baptism, or it may refer to the Jewish ceremonial washings.

ing on of hands,[n] about the raising of the dead and eternal judgment. [3]And we will go on to grown-up teaching if God allows.

[4]Some people cannot be brought back again to a changed life. They were once in God's light, and enjoyed heaven's gift, and shared in the Holy Spirit. [5]They found out how good God's word is, and they received the powers of his new world. [6]But they fell away from Christ. It is impossible to bring them back to a changed life again, because they are nailing the Son of God to a cross again and are shaming him in front of others.

[7]Some people are like land that gets plenty of rain. The land produces a good crop for those who work it, and it receives God's blessings. [8]Other people are like land that grows thorns and weeds and is worthless. It is about to be cursed by God and will be destroyed by fire.

[9]Dear friends, we are saying this to you, but we really expect better things from you that will lead to your salvation. [10]God is fair; he will not forget the work you did and the love you showed for him by helping his people. And he will remember that you are still helping them. [11]We want each of you to go on with the same hard work all your lives so you will surely get what you hope for. [12]We do not want you to become lazy. Be like those who through faith and patience will receive what God has promised.

[13]God made a promise to Abraham. And as there is no one greater than God, he used himself when he swore to Abraham, [14]saying, "I will surely bless you and give you many descendants."[n] [15]Abraham waited patiently for this to happen, and he received what God promised.

[16]People always use the name of someone greater than themselves when they swear. The oath proves that what they say is true, and this ends all arguing. [17]God wanted to prove that his promise was true to those who would get what he promised. And he wanted them to understand clearly that his purposes never change, so he made an oath. [18]These two

things cannot change: God cannot lie when he makes a promise, and he cannot lie when he makes an oath. These things encourage us who came to God for safety. They give us strength to hold on to the hope we have been given. [19]We have this hope as an anchor for the soul, sure and strong. It enters behind the curtain in the Most Holy Place in heaven, [20]where Jesus has gone ahead of us and for us. He has become the high priest forever, a priest like Melchizedek.[n]

> ## BE LIKE THOSE WHO THROUGH FAITH AND PATIENCE WILL RECEIVE WHAT GOD HAS PROMISED.

THE PRIEST MELCHIZEDEK

7 Melchizedek[n] was the king of Salem and a priest for God Most High. He met Abraham when Abraham was coming back after defeating the kings. When they met, Melchizedek blessed Abraham, [2]and Abraham gave him a tenth of everything he had brought back from the battle. First, Melchizedek's name means "king of goodness," and he is king of Salem, which means "king of peace." [3]No one knows who Melchizedek's father or mother was,[n] where he came from, when he was born, or when he died. Melchizedek is like the Son of God; he continues being a priest forever.

[4]You can see how great Melchizedek was. Abraham, the great father, gave him a tenth of everything that he won in battle. [5]Now the law says that those in the

tribe of Levi who become priests must collect a tenth from the people—their own people—even though the priests and the people are from the family of Abraham. [6]Melchizedek was not from the tribe of Levi, but he collected a tenth from Abraham. And he blessed Abraham, the man who had God's promises. [7]Now everyone knows that the more important person blesses the less important person. [8]Priests receive a tenth, even though they are only men who live and then die. But Melchizedek, who received a tenth from Abraham, continues living, as the Scripture says. [9]We might even say that Levi, who receives a tenth, also paid it when Abraham paid Melchizedek a tenth. [10]Levi was not yet born, but he was in the body of his ancestor when Melchizedek met Abraham.

[11]The people were given the law[n] concerning the system of priests from the tribe of Levi, but they could not be made perfect through that system. So there was a need for another priest to come, a priest like Melchizedek, not Aaron. [12]And when a different kind of priest comes, the law must be changed, too. [13]We are saying these things about Christ, who belonged to a different tribe. No one from that tribe ever served as a priest at the altar. [14]It is clear that our Lord came from the tribe of Judah, and Moses said nothing about priests belonging to that tribe.

JESUS IS LIKE MELCHIZEDEK

[15]And this becomes even more clear when we see that another priest comes who is like Melchizedek.[n] [16]He was not made a priest by human rules and laws but through the power of his life, which continues forever. [17]It is said about him,

> "You are a priest forever,
> a priest like Melchizedek."
>
> *Psalm 110:4*

[18]The old rule is now set aside, because it was weak and useless. [19]The law of Moses could not make anything perfect. But now a better hope has been given to us, and with this hope we can come near to God. [20]It is important that God did

---

6:2 laying on of hands The laying on of hands had many purposes, including the giving of a blessing, power, or authority. **6:14 "I . . . descendants."** Quotation from Genesis 22:17. **6:20; 7:1, 15 Melchizedek** A priest and king who lived in the time of Abraham. (Read Genesis 14:17-24.) **7:3 No . . . was** Literally, "Melchizedek was without father, without mother, without genealogy." **7:11 The . . . law** This refers to the people of Israel who were given the Law of Moses.

this with an oath. Others became priests without an oath, [21]but Christ became a priest with God's oath. God said:

"The Lord has made a promise
and will not change his mind.
'You are a priest forever.'"

Psalm 110:4

[22]This means that Jesus is the guarantee of a better agreement[n] from God to his people.

[23]When one of the other priests died, he could not continue being a priest. So there were many priests. [24]But because Jesus lives forever, he will never stop serving as priest. [25]So he is able always to save those who come to God through him because he always lives, asking God to help them.

[26]Jesus is the kind of high priest we need. He is holy, sinless, pure, not influenced by sinners, and he is raised above the heavens. [27]He is not like the other priests who had to offer sacrifices every day, first for their own sins, and then for the sins of the people. Christ offered his sacrifice only once and for all time when he offered himself. [28]The law chooses high priests who are people with weaknesses, but the word of God's oath came later than the law. It made God's Son to be the high priest, and that Son has been made perfect forever.

He's got answers

I keep hearing Christians complain about TV shows, movies, and video games. It's just entertainment, so what's wrong? I'm just watching, not doing.

There is an old computer saying: "Garbage in, garbage out." It means that the computer is only going to give you back what you put into it. If you put in garbage, you will get back garbage. Our minds work much the same way. If we regularly watch violent, coarse, and vulgar programming on television, movies, and video games, we become immune to it, or even begin to imitate it. Most Christians don't object to watching television, film, or video games in moderation. They are concerned about the effects the content has, particularly on younger audiences who may not be able to tell the difference between reality and make-believe.

By the way, Christians aren't the only ones who believe that what we see affects how we act. Why else would advertisers spend more than a million bucks for a thirty-second spot during the Super Bowl?

Read on: Philippians 4:8; Colossians 3:1-17; Titus 2:1-14

PEEP THIS:

Fifty-eight percent of people of Hispanic descent prefer to be called Hispanic; 12 percent prefer to be called "of Spanish origin"; 12 percent prefer Latino.

JESUS IS OUR HIGH PRIEST

8 Here is the point of what we are saying: We have a high priest who sits on the right side of God's throne in heaven. [2]Our high priest serves in the Most Holy Place, the true place of worship that was made by God, not by humans.

[3]Every high priest has the work of offering gifts and sacrifices to God. So our high priest must also offer something to God. [4]If our high priest were now living on earth, he would not be a priest, because there are already priests here who follow the law by offering gifts to God. [5]The work they do as priests is only a copy and a shadow of what is in heaven. This is why God warned Moses when he was ready to build the Holy Tent: "Be very careful to make everything by the plan I showed you on the mountain."[n] [6]But the priestly work that has been given to Jesus is much greater than the work that was given to the other priests. In the same way, the new agreement that Jesus brought from God to his people is much greater than the old one. And the

7:22 **agreement** God gives a contract or agreement to his people. For the Jews, this agreement was the Law of Moses. But now God has given a better agreement to his people through Christ. 8:5 **"Be . . . mountain."** Quotation from Exodus 25:40.

CONNECTED

DISCONNECTING FROM A RELATIONSHIP:

POP YA' COLLAR AND KEEP PUSHIN'

Joshua found himself in a dilemma. His leader, Moses, was dead. His will and determination to move forward diminished as the days passed. In ancient times, the law allowed people to mourn for only a specified time and then they were to keep it pushin'. Joshua's problem was that he did not have the will to move on and lead the children of Israel into the future God had for them.

In the death of intimate relationships, we often find ourselves bent over and mourning old flames. Whether a person has done a two-step on top of our heart or deceived us, it's still hard to deal with the death of a relationship that seemed to hold so much promise. Many times we are left wondering why things happened the way they did. We ask ourselves, "Why did he/she have to leave?" or "Why wasn't I good enough?"

The problem is not in taking time to reevaluate the things learned during the time spent in a relationship that has ended. The problem comes when that time is extended and thoughts about that situation take up every waking moment. Satan often uses this time to plant seeds of self-doubt, which causes stagnation. Joshua may have refused to move on forever if the Lord had not given him a shout out that caused him to keep it pushin'. God said, "Remember that I commanded you to be strong and brave. Don't be afraid, because the LORD your God will be with you everywhere you go" (Joshua 1:9).

God wants you to keep it pushin', too. It's foolish to keep thinking, crying, and tripping over a relationship or situation that is dead and not coming back—ever. Your destiny—who you are in Christ—does not stop at a failed relationship. It is the beginning of a new era, a new morning, and another chance to see new dimensions of God and your-self. So get up off your face, pop ya' collar and keep it pushin' into the new stage of your life that will bring God's promises and blessings.

---

new agreement is based on promises of better things.

7If there had been nothing wrong with the first agreement,[n] there would have been no need for a second agreement. 8But God found something wrong with his people. He says:[n]

"Look, the time is coming, says the Lord,
  when I will make a new
    agreement
  with the people of Israel
  and the people of Judah.
9It will not be like the agreement
  I made with their ancestors
  when I took them by the hand
  to bring them out of Egypt.
  But they broke that agreement,
  and I turned away from them,
    says the Lord.
10This is the agreement I will make
  with the people of Israel at that
    time, says the Lord.
  I will put my teachings in their
    minds
  and write them on their hearts.
  I will be their God,
  and they will be my people.
11People will no longer have to teach
    their neighbors and relatives
  to know the Lord,
  because all people will know me,
  from the least to the most
    important.
12I will forgive them for the wicked
    things they did,
  and I will not remember their sins
    anymore."   Jeremiah 31:31-34

13God called this a new agreement, so he has made the first agreement old. And anything that is old and worn out is ready to disappear.

THE OLD AGREEMENT

9 The first agreement[n] had rules for worship and a place on earth for worship. 2The Holy Tent was set up for this. The first area in the Tent was called the Holy Place.

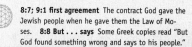

8:7; 9:1 **first agreement** The contract God gave the Jewish people when he gave them the Law of Moses. 8:8 **But . . . says** Some Greek copies read "But God found something wrong and says to his people."

TRUST

Trust no one! The only person you can trust is yourself. Don't let down your guard. You have to make sure no one is gonna get over on you. People will disappoint you if you let them in, so protect yourself.

"Trust the LORD with all your heart, and don't depend on your own understanding" (Proverbs 3:5).

"Those who trust in themselves are foolish, but those who live wisely will be kept safe" (Proverbs 28:26).

"So, trust the LORD always, because he is our Rock forever" (Isaiah 26:4).

"Do not put your trust in princes or other people, who cannot save you" (Psalm 146:3).

In it were the lamp and the table with the bread that was made holy for God. [3]Behind the second curtain was a room called the Most Holy Place. [4]In it was a golden altar for burning incense and the Ark covered with gold that held the old agreement. Inside this Ark was a golden jar of manna, Aaron's rod that once grew leaves, and the stone tablets of the old agreement. [5]Above the Ark were the creatures that showed God's glory, whose wings reached over the lid. But we cannot tell everything about these things now.

[6]When everything in the Tent was made ready in this way, the priests went into the first room every day to worship. [7]But only the high priest could go into the second room, and he did that only once a year. He could never enter the inner room without taking blood with him, which he offered to God for himself and for sins the people did without knowing they did them. [8]The Holy Spirit uses this to show that the way into the Most Holy Place was not open while the system of the old Holy Tent was still being used. [9]This is an example for the present time. It shows that the gifts and sacrifices offered cannot make the conscience of the worshiper perfect. [10]These gifts and sacrifices were only about food and drink and special washings. They were rules for the body, to be followed until the time of God's new way.

THE NEW AGREEMENT

[11]But when Christ came as the high priest of the good things we now have,[n] he entered the greater and more perfect tent. It is not made by humans and does not belong to this world. [12]Christ entered the Most Holy Place only once—and for all time. He did not take with him the blood of goats and calves. His sacrifice was his own blood, and by it he set us free from sin forever. [13]The blood of goats and bulls and the ashes of a cow are sprinkled on the people who are unclean, and this makes their bodies clean again. [14]How much more is done by the blood of Christ. He offered himself through the eternal Spirit[n] as a perfect sacrifice to God. His blood will make our consciences pure from useless acts so we may serve the living God.

[15]For this reason Christ brings a new agreement from God to his people. Those who are called by God can now receive the blessings he has promised, blessings that will last forever. They can have those things because Christ died so that the people who lived under the first agreement could be set free from sin.

[16]When there is a will,[n] it must be proven that the one who wrote that will is dead. [17]A will means nothing while the person is alive; it can be used only after the person dies. [18]This is why even the first agreement could not begin without blood to show death. [19]First, Moses told all the people every command in the law. Next he took the blood of calves and mixed it with water. Then he used red wool and a branch of the hyssop plant to sprinkle it on the book of the law and on all the people. [20]He said, "This is the blood that begins the Agreement that God commanded you to obey."[n] [21]In the same way, Moses sprinkled the blood on the Holy Tent and over all the things used in worship. [22]The law says that almost everything must be made clean by blood, and sins cannot be forgiven without blood to show death.

CHRIST'S DEATH TAKES AWAY SINS

[23]So the copies of the real things in heaven had to be made clean by animal sacrifices. But the real things in heaven need much better sacrifices. [24]Christ did not go into the Most Holy Place made by humans, which is only a copy of the real one. He went into heaven itself and is there now before God to help us. [25]The high priest enters the Most Holy Place once every year with blood that is not his own. But Christ did not offer himself many times. [26]Then he would have

9:11 good . . . have Some Greek copies read "good things that are to come." **9:14 Spirit** This refers to the Holy Spirit, to Christ's own spirit, or to the spiritual and eternal nature of his sacrifice. **9:16 will** A legal document that shows how a person's money and property are to be distributed at the time of death. This is the same word in Greek as "agreement" in verse 15. **9:20 "This . . . obey."** Quotation from Exodus 24:8.

had to suffer many times since the world was made. But Christ came only once and for all time at just the right time to take away all sin by sacrificing himself. [27]Just as everyone must die once and then be judged, [28]so Christ was offered as a sacrifice one time to take away the sins of many people. And he will come a second time, not to offer himself for sin, but to bring salvation to those who are waiting for him.

10 The law is only an unclear picture of the good things coming in the future; it is not the real thing. The people under the law offer the same sacrifices every year, but these sacrifices can never make perfect those who come near to worship God. [2]If the law could make them perfect, the sacrifices would have already stopped. The worshipers would be made clean, and they would no longer have a sense of sin. [3]But these sacrifices remind them of their sins every year, [4]because it is impossible for the blood of bulls and goats to take away sins.

[5]So when Christ came into the world, he said:

"You do not want sacrifices and offerings,
but you have prepared a body for me.
[6]You do not ask for burnt offerings and offerings to take away sins.
[7]Then I said, 'Look, I have come.
It is written about me in the book.
God, I have come to do what you want.'" *Psalm 40:6-8*

[8]In this Scripture he first said, "You do not want sacrifices and offerings. You do not ask for burnt offerings and offerings to take away sins." (These are all sacrifices that the law commands.) [9]Then he said, "Look, I have come to do what you want." God ends the first system of sacrifices so he can set up the new system. [10]And because of this, we are made holy through the sacrifice Christ made in his body once and for all time.

[11]Every day the priests stand and do their religious service, often offering the same sacrifices. Those sacrifices can never take away sins. [12]But after Christ

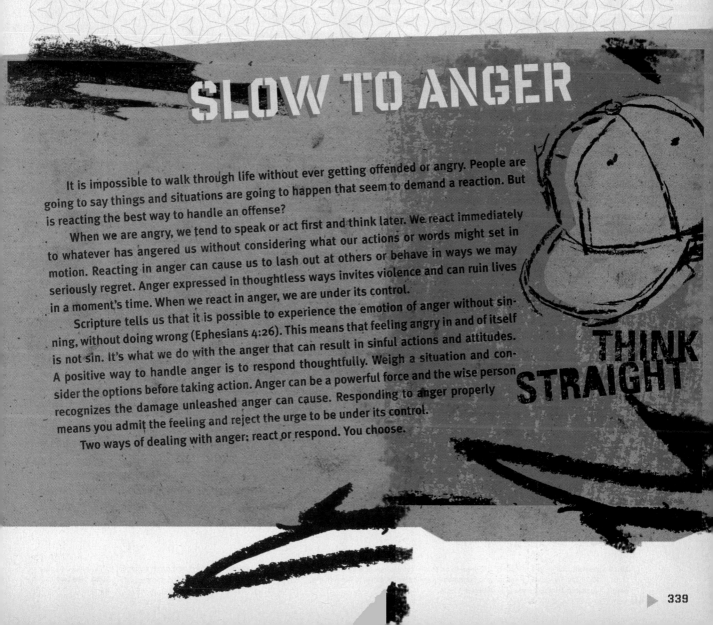

SLOW TO ANGER

It is impossible to walk through life without ever getting offended or angry. People are going to say things and situations are going to happen that seem to demand a reaction. But is reacting the best way to handle an offense?

When we are angry, we tend to speak or act first and think later. We react immediately to whatever has angered us without considering what our actions or words might set in motion. Reacting in anger can cause us to lash out at others or behave in ways we may seriously regret. Anger expressed in thoughtless ways invites violence and can ruin lives in a moment's time. When we react in anger, we are under its control.

Scripture tells us that it is possible to experience the emotion of anger without sinning, without doing wrong (Ephesians 4:26). This means that feeling angry in and of itself is not sin. It's what we do with the anger that can result in sinful actions and attitudes. A positive way to handle anger is to respond thoughtfully. Weigh a situation and consider the options before taking action. Anger can be a powerful force and the wise person recognizes the damage unleashed anger can cause. Responding to anger properly means you admit the feeling and reject the urge to be under its control.

Two ways of dealing with anger: react or respond. You choose.

THINK STRAIGHT

OVERCOMING

▶ DEPRESSION

Did you know the Bible talks about depression? In Psalm 6, David, the writer of the Psalm says, "LORD, have mercy on me because I am weak. Heal me, LORD, because my bones ache. I am very upset. LORD, how long will it be?" Sure sounds like depression to me. But David knew how to handle the funk he was in. By the time he wrote Psalm 8 he was enjoying all the beauty and wonder around him and speaking out the praises of God. He got outside himself long enough to remember all the wonderful things God had brought into his life.

Everyone experiences periods of sadness or times of just "being blue". It can be caused by loneliness, exhaustion, anger or even by nothing at all. Sometimes we are just down on life or ourselves. One in five people is affected by the growing epidemic of depression. Times of depression that last for a few hours or even a few days are normal and will pass when circumstances change. There are ways to deal with this that may shorten the gloomy times. First, don't isolate yourself. Get out and find someone to help. You'd be amazed how quickly depression ends when you start thinking about someone besides yourself. Secondly, remember all the gifts God has given you and thank him for them. Focusing on the positive will always cause the negative to fade.

If your depression last for weeks, you may need to seek professional help. Clinical depression is a disease that can be brought under control. If left untreated, it could begin to rule your life and devastate your future.

offered one sacrifice for sins, forever, he sat down at the right side of God. [13]And now Christ waits there for his enemies to be put under his power. [14]With one sacrifice he made perfect forever those who are being made holy.

[15]The Holy Spirit also tells us about this. First he says:

[16]"This is the agreement[n] I will
    make
    with them at that time, says the
    Lord.
I will put my teachings in their
    hearts
    and write them on their minds."

Jeremiah 31:33

[17]Then he says:

"Their sins and the evil things they
    do —
I will not remember anymore."

Jeremiah 31:34

[18]Now when these have been forgiven, there is no more need for a sacrifice for sins.

CONTINUE TO TRUST GOD

[19]So, brothers and sisters, we are completely free to enter the Most Holy Place without fear because of the blood of Jesus' death. [20]We can enter through a new and living way that Jesus opened for us. It leads through the curtain— Christ's body. [21]And since we have a great priest over God's house, [22]let us come near to God with a sincere heart and a sure faith, because we have been made free from a guilty conscience, and our bodies have been washed with pure water. [23]Let us hold firmly to the hope that we have confessed, because we can trust God to do what he promised.

[24]Let us think about each other and help each other to show love and do good deeds. [25]You should not stay away from the church meetings, as some are doing, but you should meet together and encourage each other. Do this even more as you see the day[n] coming.

[26]If we decide to go on sinning after we have learned the truth, there is no longer any sacrifice for sins. [27]There is nothing but fear in waiting for the judgment and the terrible fire that will destroy all those who live against God. [28]Anyone who refused to obey the law of Moses was found guilty from the proof given by two or three witnesses. He was put to death without mercy. [29]So what do you think should be done to those who do not respect the Son of God, who look at the blood of the agreement that made them holy as no different from others' blood, who insult the Spirit of God's grace? Surely they should have a much worse punishment. [30]We know that God said, "I will punish those who do wrong; I will repay them."[n] And he also said, "The Lord will judge his people."[n] [31]It is a terrible thing to fall into the hands of the living God.

[32]Remember those days in the past when you first learned the truth. You had a hard struggle with many sufferings, but you continued strong. [33]Sometimes you

10:16 agreement God gives a contract or agreement to his people. For the Jews, this agreement was the Law of Moses. But now God has given a better agreement to his people through Christ. **10:25 day** The day Christ will come to judge all people and take his people to live with him. **10:30 "I . . . them."** Quotation from Deuteronomy 32:35. **10:30 "The Lord . . . people."** Quotation from Deuteronomy 32:36; Psalm 135:14.

HOME SICKNESS

I grew up in a very dysfunctional home. My father just wasn't around and my mother was a drug addict. Mom was involved in very abusive relationships. Her relationships were so destructive that we ended up living in five different shelters for battered women, including one where we stayed twice in one year.

I had a very low self-image and was a very promiscuous teenager. I didn't understand what I was doing to my body or my soul. I just knew that my life was painful and I wanted an escape. I thought of committing suicide on several occasions but I was afraid that I would go to hell if I took my life. Instead, I began using drugs to dull my pain. I continued to sleep around and hide behind drugs well into my adult years. I finally landed a pretty good job but my wild life caused me to start messing up. My boss told me to either get help or be fired. My job was the only thing I had going for me so I agreed to see a counselor. The counselor my boss recommended was a Christian, and he told me that Jesus had come to die for all the sins in my life. I could give all of my hurt, pain, and doubts to God. It was the first time anyone had shown real concern for me so I was open to hearing what he had to say.

I started going to church and the minister explained to me from the Bible how Jesus had died for my sins. For the first time, I began to understand God's love. He sent his only Son Jesus to die *for me*! I began to see that God had been with me throughout my life, leading me to this place where I could give myself to him.

Difficult things still happen in my life, but instead of trying to escape through sex and drugs, I seek God. I know that Jesus is always there to give me a lift, a hand, a hug, a correction, or whatever I need in order to get through. Without Jesus I would be nothing!

Ephesians 2:10 — God has made us what we are.

---

were hurt and attacked before crowds of people, and sometimes you shared with those who were being treated that way. [34]You helped the prisoners. You even had joy when all that you owned was taken from you, because you knew you had something better and more lasting.

[35]So do not lose the courage you had in the past, which has a great reward. [36]You must hold on, so you can do what God wants and receive what he has promised. [37]For in a very short time,

"The One who is coming will come
    and will not be delayed.
[38]Those who are right with me
    will live by faith.

But if they turn back with fear,
    I will not be pleased with them."
                        Habakkuk 2:3-4

[39]But we are not those who turn back and are lost. We are people who have faith and are saved.

WHAT IS FAITH?

11 Faith means being sure of the things we hope for and knowing that something is real even if we do not see it. [2]Faith is the reason we remember great people who lived in the past.

[3]It is by faith we understand that the whole world was made by God's command so what we see was made by something that cannot be seen.

[4]It was by faith that Abel offered God a better sacrifice than Cain did. God said he was pleased with the gifts Abel offered and called Abel a good man because of his faith. Abel died, but through his faith he is still speaking.

[5]It was by faith that Enoch was taken to heaven so he would not die. He could not be found, because God had taken him away. Before he was taken, the Scripture says that he was a man who truly pleased God. [6]Without faith no one

can please God. Anyone who comes to God must believe that he is real and that he rewards those who truly want to find him.

[7]It was by faith that Noah heard God's warnings about things he could not yet see. He obeyed God and built a large boat to save his family. By his faith, Noah showed that the world was wrong, and he became one of those who are made right with God through faith.

[8]It was by faith Abraham obeyed God's call to go to another place God promised to give him. He left his own country, not knowing where he was to go. [9]It was by faith that he lived like a foreigner in the country God promised to give him. He lived in tents with Isaac and Jacob, who had received that same promise from God. [10]Abraham was waiting for the city[n] that has real foundations—the city planned and built by God.

[11]He was too old to have children, and Sarah could not have children. It was by faith that Abraham was made able to become a father, because he trusted God to do what he had promised.[n] [12]This man was so old he was almost dead, but from him came as many descendants as there are stars in the sky. Like the sand on the seashore, they could not be counted.

[13]All these great people died in faith. They did not get the things that God promised his people, but they saw them coming far in the future and were glad. They said they were like visitors and strangers on earth. [14]When people say such things, they show they are looking

11:10 city The spiritual "city" where God's people live with him. Also called "the heavenly Jerusalem." (See Hebrews 12:22.) **11:11 It . . . promised.** Some Greek copies refer to Sarah's faith, rather than Abraham's.

THE SCRIPT

The Betrayal
Matthew 26:36-50

Then Jesus and his disciples departed to a garden named Gethsemane.
The disciples, unaware of Judas's villainy, began to sense the Lord's intensity.
Now, with only eleven in his assembly, Jesus took three with him to pray.
He told the rest to stay while he picked out Peter, John, and James.
Jesus told them, "My heart is breaking but I must endure the strain.
It's killing me to face this, so please stay up and watch out while I pray."
After saying that, Jesus walked away a few paces, fell on his face and began his supplications:
"Father, if there's any way to change this situation,
I'm begging you, let this cup of the world's sins pass without my takin' it.
But at the same time I'm praying this, let me say this,
It's not about me, but about what your determination is."
Coming back to the place where he left Peter and them,
He saw that they dozed off and awakened them.
"Peter." He whispered, "You couldn't stay awake for one hour?
You've got to pray with your eyes open or your hopes can get devoured!
Your spirit is after the power, but your flesh is too weak to allow it!"
He walked away and prayed again, asking God to help him out of this pit:
"Father, if there's no other way but for me to take it,
Then pass the cup. I'll drink it, and fulfill your inclination."
Jesus came back to Peter, John, and James and saw them still sleeping,
But decided not to wake them. They were visibly drained and overtaken by fatigue.
Jesus went back for the third time and prayed the same prayer on his knees.

After praying, he came to the three and told them,
"Go on and slumber.
But the time is swiftly approaching where the Chosen One will get ambushed."
Then Jesus told them, "Stand up! The time is at hand, look! My betrayer has made it here."
Soon as he said that, Judas appeared and came near.
He rolled in with an entourage of temple guards armed with swords, sent from the synagogue.
Judas had already planned the scam to finger Jesus on the camouflage.
That way they could step in on the low and arrest the Lord.
It would be as simple as a petty street swindle.
"The one that I greet with a kiss is the one that you must get to,"
Said Judas, playing Satan's position, and he came to Jesus and kissed him.
Jesus said, "My friend, go on and complete your mission."
That's when the guards slipped in quick and laid their grips on Yeshua— Jesus—
Arrested him and prepared to hand him over to the evildoers.

Take this with you: Strength to face the hardest trials comes when we go to God and genuinely ask him to help us. God will either pull us out, or help us through. Either way, he'll always be with us.

for a country that will be their own. ¹⁵If they had been thinking about the country they had left, they could have gone back. ¹⁶But they were waiting for a better country—a heavenly country. So God is not ashamed to be called their God, because he has prepared a city for them.

¹⁷It was by faith that Abraham, when God tested him, offered his son Isaac as a sacrifice. God made the promises to Abraham, but Abraham was ready to offer his own son as a sacrifice. ¹⁸God had said, "The descendants I promised you will be from Isaac."ⁿ ¹⁹Abraham believed that God could raise the dead, and really, it was as if Abraham got Isaac back from death.

²⁰It was by faith that Isaac blessed the future of Jacob and Esau. ²¹It was by faith that Jacob, as he was dying, blessed each one of Joseph's sons. Then he worshiped as he leaned on the top of his walking stick.

²²It was by faith that Joseph, while he was dying, spoke about the Israelites leaving Egypt and gave instructions about what to do with his body.

²³It was by faith that Moses' parents hid him for three months after he was born. They saw that Moses was a beautiful baby, and they were not afraid to disobey the king's order.

²⁴It was by faith that Moses, when he grew up, refused to be called the son of the king of Egypt's daughter. ²⁵He chose to suffer with God's people instead of enjoying sin for a short time. ²⁶He thought it was better to suffer for the Christ than to have all the treasures of Egypt, because he was looking for God's reward. ²⁷It was by faith that Moses left Egypt and was not afraid of the king's anger. Moses continued strong as if he could see the God that no one can see. ²⁸It was by faith that Moses prepared the Passover and spread the blood on the doors so the one who brings death would not kill the firstborn sons of Israel.

²⁹It was by faith that the people crossed the Red Sea as if it were dry land. But when the Egyptians tried it, they were drowned.

³⁰It was by faith that the walls of Jericho fell after the people had marched around them for seven days.

³¹It was by faith that Rahab, the prostitute, welcomed the spies and was not killed with those who refused to obey God.

> [JESUS] HELD ON WHILE WICKED PEOPLE WERE DOING EVIL THINGS TO HIM. SO DO NOT GET TIRED AND STOP TRYING.

³²Do I need to give more examples? I do not have time to tell you about Gideon, Barak, Samson, Jephthah, David, Samuel, and the prophets. ³³Through their faith they defeated kingdoms. They did what was right, received God's promises, and shut the mouths of lions. ³⁴They stopped great fires and were saved from being killed with swords. They were weak, and yet were made strong. They were powerful in battle and defeated other armies. ³⁵Women received their dead relatives raised back to life. Others were tortured and refused to accept their freedom so they could be raised from the dead to a better life. ³⁶Some were laughed at and beaten. Others were put in chains and thrown into prison. ³⁷They were stoned to death, they were cut in half,ⁿ and they were killed with swords. Some wore the skins of sheep and goats. They were poor, abused, and treated badly. ³⁸The world was not good enough for them! They wandered in deserts and mountains, living in caves and holes in the earth.

³⁹All these people are known for their faith, but none of them received what God had promised. ⁴⁰God planned to give us something better so that they would be made perfect, but only together with us.

FOLLOW JESUS' EXAMPLE

12 We are surrounded by a great cloud of people whose lives tell us what faith means. So let us run the race that is before us and never give up. We should remove from our lives anything that would get in the way and the sin that so easily holds us back. ²Let us look only to Jesus, the One who began our faith and who makes it perfect. He suffered death on the cross. But he accepted the shame as if it were nothing because of the joy that God put before him. And now he is sitting at the right side of God's throne. ³Think about Jesus' example. He held on while wicked people were doing evil things to him. So do not get tired and stop trying.

GOD IS LIKE A FATHER

⁴You are struggling against sin, but your struggles have not yet caused you to be killed. ⁵You have forgotten the encouraging words that call you his children:

"My child, don't think the Lord's
    discipline is worth nothing,
and don't stop trying when he
    corrects you.
⁶The Lord disciplines those he loves,
    and he punishes everyone he
    accepts as his child."

Proverbs 3:11-12

⁷So hold on through your sufferings, because they are like a father's discipline. God is treating you as children. All children are disciplined by their fathers. ⁸If you are never disciplined (and every

 11:18 "The descendants . . . Isaac." Quotation from Genesis 21:12.   **11:37 they were cut in half** Some Greek copies also include, "they were tested."

child must be disciplined), you are not true children. [9]We have all had fathers here on earth who disciplined us, and we respected them. So it is even more important that we accept discipline from the Father of our spirits so we will have life. [10]Our fathers on earth disciplined us for a short time in the way they thought was best. But God disciplines us to help us, so we can become holy as he is. [11]We do not enjoy being disciplined. It is painful at the time, but later, after we have learned from it, we have peace, because we start living in the right way.

BE CAREFUL HOW YOU LIVE

[12]You have become weak, so make yourselves strong again. [13]Keep on the right path, so the weak will not stumble but rather be strengthened.

[14]Try to live in peace with all people, and try to live free from sin. Anyone whose life is not holy will never see the Lord. [15]Be careful that no one fails to receive God's grace and begins to cause trouble among you. A person like that can ruin many of you. [16]Be careful that no one takes part in sexual sin or is like Esau and never thinks about God. As the oldest son, Esau would have received everything from his father, but he sold all that for a single meal. [17]You remember that after Esau did this, he wanted to get his father's blessing, but his father refused. Esau could find no way to change what he had done, even though he wanted the blessing so much that he cried.

[18]You have not come to a mountain that can be touched and that is burning with fire. You have not come to darkness, sadness, and storms. [19]You have not come to the noise of a trumpet or to the sound of a voice like the one the people of Israel heard and begged not to hear another word. [20]They did not want to hear the command: "If anything, even an animal, touches the mountain, it must be put to death with stones."[n] [21]What they saw was so terrible that Moses said, "I am shaking with fear."[n]

[22]But you have come to Mount Zion,[n]

to the city of the living God, the heavenly Jerusalem. You have come to thousands of angels gathered together with joy. [23]You have come to the meeting of God's firstborn[n] children whose names are written in heaven. You have come to God, the judge of all people, and to the spirits of good people who have been made perfect. [24]You have come to Jesus, the One who brought the new agreement from God to his people, and you have come to the sprinkled blood[n] that has a better message than the blood of Abel.[n]

> I WILL NOT BE AFRAID, BECAUSE THE LORD IS MY HELPER. PEOPLE CAN'T DO ANYTHING TO ME.

[25]So be careful and do not refuse to listen when God speaks. Others refused to listen to him when he warned them on earth, and they did not escape. So it will be worse for us if we refuse to listen to God who warns us from heaven. [26]When he spoke before, his voice shook the earth, but now he has promised, "Once again I will shake not only the earth but also the heavens."[n] [27]The words "once again" clearly show us that everything that was made—things that can be shaken—will be destroyed. Only the things that cannot be shaken will remain.

[28]So let us be thankful, because we have a kingdom that cannot be shaken. We should worship God in a way that pleases him with respect and fear, [29]because our God is like a fire that burns things up.

13 Keep on loving each other as brothers and sisters. [2]Remember to welcome strangers, because some who have done this have welcomed angels without knowing it. [3]Remember those who are in prison as if you were in prison with them. Remember those who are suffering as if you were suffering with them.

[4]Marriage should be honored by everyone, and husband and wife should keep their marriage pure. God will judge as guilty those who take part in sexual sins. [5]Keep your lives free from the love of money, and be satisfied with what you have. God has said,

> "I will never leave you;
> I will never abandon you."
> *Deuteronomy 31:6*

[6]So we can be sure when we say,

> "I will not be afraid, because the
> Lord is my helper.
> People can't do anything to me."
> *Psalm 118:6*

[7]Remember your leaders who taught God's message to you. Remember how they lived and died, and copy their faith. [8]Jesus Christ is the same yesterday, today, and forever.

[9]Do not let all kinds of strange teachings lead you into the wrong way. Your hearts should be strengthened by God's grace, not by obeying rules about foods, which do not help those who obey them.

[10]We have a sacrifice, but the priests who serve in the Holy Tent cannot eat from it. [11]The high priest carries the blood of animals into the Most Holy Place where he offers this blood for sins. But the bodies of the animals are burned outside the camp. [12]So Jesus also suffered outside the city to make his people holy with his own blood. [13]So let us go to Jesus outside the camp, holding on as he did when we are abused.

[14]Here on earth we do not have a city that lasts forever, but we are looking for the city that we will have in the future.

12:20 "If . . . stones." Quotation from Exodus 19:12-13.   **12:21 "I . . . fear."** Quotation from Deuteronomy 9:19.   **12:22 Mount Zion** Another name for Jerusalem, here meaning the spiritual city of God's people.   **12:23 firstborn** The first son born in a Jewish family was given the most important place in the family and received special blessings. All of God's children are like that.   **12:24 sprinkled blood** The blood of Jesus' death.   **12:24 Abel** The son of Adam and Eve, who was killed by his brother Cain (Genesis 4:8).   **12:26 "Once . . . heavens."** Quotation from Haggai 2:6, 21.

¹⁵So through Jesus let us always offer to God our sacrifice of praise, coming from lips that speak his name. ¹⁶Do not forget to do good to others, and share with them, because such sacrifices please God.

¹⁷Obey your leaders and act under their authority. They are watching over you, because they are responsible for your souls. Obey them so that they will do this work with joy, not sadness. It will not help you to make their work hard.

¹⁸Pray for us. We are sure that we have a clear conscience, because we always want to do the right thing. ¹⁹I especially beg you to pray so that God will send me back to you soon.

²⁰⁻²¹I pray that the God of peace will give you every good thing you need so you can do what he wants. God raised from the dead our Lord Jesus, the Great Shepherd of the sheep, because of the blood of his death. His blood began the eternal agreement that God made with his people. I pray that God will do in us what pleases him, through Jesus Christ, and to him be glory forever and ever. Amen.

²²My brothers and sisters, I beg you to listen patiently to this message I have written to encourage you, because it is not very long. ²³I want you to know that our brother Timothy has been let out of prison. If he arrives soon, we will both come to see you.

²⁴Greet all your leaders and all of God's people. Those from Italy send greetings to you.

²⁵Grace be with you all.

HeartCry

Faithlessness Is it hard for you to stay committed to God? Are you constantly making promises to God that are hard for you to keep? Is it getting easier and easier for you to follow the world? If so, talk to God. Let your heart cry . . .

God, why am I so faithless? It seems like I'm messing up all the time. I keep selling out on you and choosing the world, but then I feel so empty. I get so caught up with the bling, but it's all poison to me. Help me to be more faithful to you and live what I believe. I know you don't want me running around on you with my fired-up attitude. But I can't seem to change. I just keep going back to the same old things. I'm messed up, Lord. I want to be different; please tell me how.

You must decide to follow me. It is a choice only you can make. Allow me to change your heart. I am a faithful God. I will teach you my ways if you will turn to me. Joshua 24:15; 1 Thessalonians 5:24; Ezekiel 11:19; Isaiah 2:3

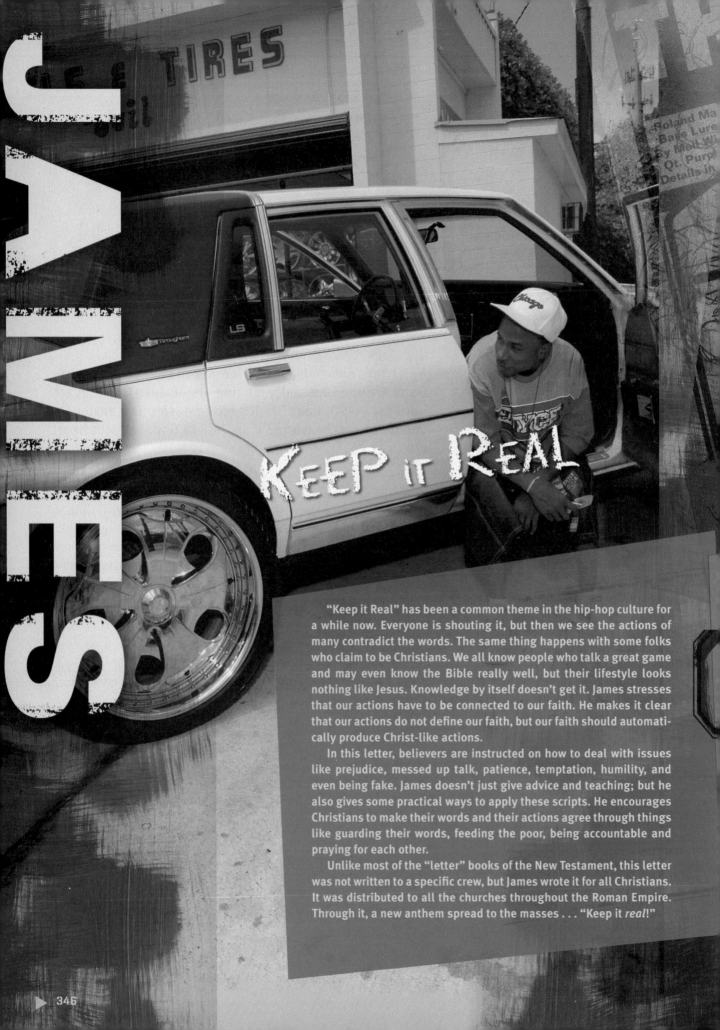

JAMES

Keep it Real

"Keep it Real" has been a common theme in the hip-hop culture for a while now. Everyone is shouting it, but then we see the actions of many contradict the words. The same thing happens with some folks who claim to be Christians. We all know people who talk a great game and may even know the Bible really well, but their lifestyle looks nothing like Jesus. Knowledge by itself doesn't get it. James stresses that our actions have to be connected to our faith. He makes it clear that our actions do not define our faith, but our faith should automatically produce Christ-like actions.

In this letter, believers are instructed on how to deal with issues like prejudice, messed up talk, patience, temptation, humility, and even being fake. James doesn't just give advice and teaching; but he also gives some practical ways to apply these scripts. He encourages Christians to make their words and their actions agree through things like guarding their words, feeding the poor, being accountable and praying for each other.

Unlike most of the "letter" books of the New Testament, this letter was not written to a specific crew, but James wrote it for all Christians. It was distributed to all the churches throughout the Roman Empire. Through it, a new anthem spread to the masses . . . "Keep it *real*!"

1

From James, a servant of God and of the Lord Jesus Christ.

To all of God's people who are scattered everywhere in the world:

Greetings.

FAITH AND WISDOM

[2]My brothers and sisters, when you have many kinds of troubles, you should be full of joy, [3]because you know that these troubles test your faith, and this will give you patience. [4]Let your patience show itself perfectly in what you do. Then you will be perfect and complete and will have everything you need. [5]But if any of you needs wisdom, you should ask God for it. He is generous to everyone and will give you wisdom without criticizing you. [6]But when you ask God, you must believe and not doubt. Anyone who doubts is like a wave in the sea, blown up and down by the wind. [7-8]Such doubters are thinking two different things at the same time, and they cannot decide about anything they do. They should not think they will receive anything from the Lord.

TRUE RICHES

[9]Believers who are poor should take pride that God has made them spiritually rich. [10]Those who are rich should take pride that God has shown them that they are spiritually poor. The rich will die like a wild flower in the grass. [11]The sun rises with burning heat and dries up the plants. The flower falls off, and its beauty is gone. In the same way the rich will die while they are still taking care of business.

TEMPTATION IS NOT FROM GOD

[12]When people are tempted and still continue strong, they should be happy. After they have proved their faith, God will reward them with life forever. God promised this to all those who love him. [13]When people are tempted, they should not say, "God is tempting me." Evil cannot tempt God, and God himself does not tempt anyone. [14]But people are tempted when their own evil desire leads them away and traps them. [15]This desire leads to sin, and then the sin grows and brings death.

[16]My dear brothers and sisters, do not be fooled about this. [17]Every good action and every perfect gift is from God. These good gifts come down from the Creator of the sun, moon, and stars, who does not change like their shifting shadows. [18]God decided to give us life through the word of truth so we might be the most important of all the things he made.

LISTENING AND OBEYING

[19]My dear brothers and sisters, always be willing to listen and slow to speak. Do not become angry easily, [20]because anger will not help you live the right kind of life God wants. [21]So put out of your life every evil thing and every kind of wrong. Then in gentleness accept God's

WE ALL KNOW PEOPLE WHO TALK A GOOD GAME

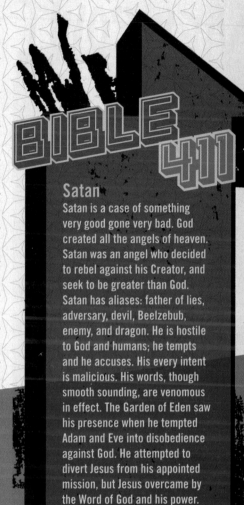

BIBLE 411

Satan

Satan is a case of something very good gone very bad. God created all the angels of heaven. Satan was an angel who decided to rebel against his Creator, and seek to be greater than God. Satan has aliases: father of lies, adversary, devil, Beelzebub, enemy, and dragon. He is hostile to God and humans; he tempts and he accuses. His every intent is malicious. His words, though smooth sounding, are venomous in effect. The Garden of Eden saw his presence when he tempted Adam and Eve into disobedience against God. He attempted to divert Jesus from his appointed mission, but Jesus overcame by the Word of God and his power. Peter describes him as a roaring lion roaming around looking for someone to eat (1 Peter 5:8). But Peter also says the devil can be resisted. "Refuse to give in to him, by standing strong in your faith." Though Satan is a formidable foe, Christ is more formidable when he fights for us against Satan. Through Christ alone, we can overcome Satan with God's Word and his power.

VIEWPOINT

WHO IS THE FIRST PERSON YOU THINK OF CALLING WHEN YOU HAVE A PROBLEM, AND WHY?

Anytime I have a problem the first persons I call are my parents. They always seem to know the right things to say to help me think the problem through and come up with a solution. Of course, I know they will give me an answer that they think will best benefit me, so I can trust whatever advice they give me.

teaching that is planted in your hearts, which can save you.

²²Do what God's teaching says; when you only listen and do nothing, you are fooling yourselves. ²³Those who hear God's teaching and do nothing are like people who look at themselves in a mirror. ²⁴They see their faces and then go away and quickly forget what they looked like. ²⁵But the truly happy people are those who carefully study God's perfect law that makes people free, and they continue to study it. They do not forget what they heard, but they obey what God's teaching says. Those who do this will be made happy.

THE TRUE WAY TO WORSHIP GOD

²⁶People who think they are religious but say things they should not say are just fooling themselves. Their "religion" is worth nothing. ²⁷Religion that God accepts as pure and without fault is this: caring for orphans or widows who need help, and keeping yourself free from the world's evil influence.

LOVE ALL PEOPLE

2 My dear brothers and sisters, as believers in our glorious Lord Jesus Christ, never think some people are more important than others. ²Suppose someone comes into your church meeting wearing nice clothes and a gold ring. At the same time a poor person comes in wearing old, dirty clothes. ³You show special attention to the one wearing nice clothes and say, "Please, sit here in this good seat." But you say to the poor person, "Stand over there," or, "Sit on the floor by my feet." ⁴What are you doing? You are making some people more important than others, and with evil thoughts you are deciding that one person is better.

⁵Listen, my dear brothers and sisters! God chose the poor in the world to be rich with faith and to receive the kingdom God promised to those who love him. ⁶But you show no respect to the poor. The rich are always trying to control your lives. They are the ones who take you to court. ⁷And they are the ones who speak against Jesus, who owns you.

⁸This royal law is found in the Scriptures: "Love your neighbor as you love yourself."ⁿ If you obey this law, you are doing right. ⁹But if you treat one person as being more important than another, you are sinning. You are guilty of break-ing God's law. ¹⁰A person who follows all of God's law but fails to obey even one command is guilty of breaking all the commands in that law. ¹¹The same God who said, "You must not be guilty of adultery,"ⁿ also said, "You must not murder anyone.'"ⁿ So if you do not take part in adultery but you murder someone, you are guilty of breaking all of God's law. ¹²In everything you say and do, remember that you will be judged by the law that makes people free. ¹³So you must show mercy to others, or God will not show mercy to you when he judges you. But the person who shows mercy can stand without fear at the judgment.

FAITH AND GOOD WORKS

¹⁴My brothers and sisters, if people say they have faith, but do nothing, their faith is worth nothing. Can faith like that save them? ¹⁵A brother or sister in Christ might need clothes or food. ¹⁶If you say to that person, "God be with you! I hope you stay warm and get plenty to eat," but you do not give what that person needs, your words are worth nothing. ¹⁷In the same way, faith by itself—that does nothing—is dead.

¹⁸Someone might say, "You have faith, but I have deeds." Show me your faith without doing anything, and I will show you my faith by what I do. ¹⁹You believe there is one God. Good! But the demons believe that, too, and they tremble with fear.

²⁰You foolish person! Must you be shown that faith that does nothing is worth nothing? ²¹Abraham, our ancestor, was made right with God by what he did when he offered his son Isaac on the altar. ²²So you see that Abraham's faith and the things he did worked together. His faith was made perfect by what he did. ²³This shows the full meaning of the Scripture that says: "Abraham believed God, and God accepted Abraham's faith, and that faith made him right with God."ⁿ And Abraham was called God's friend.ⁿ ²⁴So you see that people are made right with God by what they do, not by faith only.

2:8 "Love . . . yourself." Quotation from Leviticus 19:18. **2:11 "You . . . adultery."** Quotation from Exodus 20:14 and Deuteronomy 5:18. **2:11 "You . . . anyone."** Quotation from Exodus 20:13 and Deuteronomy 5:17. **2:23 "Abraham . . . God."** Quotation from Genesis 15:6. **2:23 God's friend** These words about Abraham are found in 2 Chronicles 20:7 and Isaiah 41:8.

DO WHATEVER IT TAKES

The end justifies the means. Decide what you want and then do whatever it takes to get it. So, you may hurt some people's feelings, or you may lose some friends, or you may have to do the boss some "favors." It doesn't matter; it's all about you reaching your goal no matter what it takes. You'll be better for it in the end.

"But people are tempted when their own evil desire leads them away and traps them. This desire leads to sin, and then the sin grows and brings death" (James 1:14-15).

"An evil person really earns nothing, but a good person will surely be rewarded" (Proverbs 11:18).

---

[25]Another example is Rahab, a prostitute, who was made right with God by something she did. She welcomed the spies into her home and helped them escape by a different road.

[26]Just as a person's body that does not have a spirit is dead, so faith that does nothing is dead!

CONTROLLING THE THINGS WE SAY

3 My brothers and sisters, not many of you should become teachers, because you know that we who teach will be judged more strictly. [2]We all make many mistakes. If people never said anything wrong, they would be perfect and able to control their entire selves, too. [3]When we put bits into the mouths of horses to make them obey us, we can control their whole bodies. [4]Also a ship is very big, and it is pushed by strong winds. But a very small rudder controls that big ship, making it go wherever the pilot wants. [5]It is the same with the tongue. It is a small part of the body, but it brags about great things.

A big forest fire can be started with only a little flame. [6]And the tongue is like a fire. It is a whole world of evil among the parts of our bodies. The tongue spreads its evil through the whole body. The tongue is set on fire by hell, and it starts a fire that influences all of life. [7]People can tame every kind of wild animal, bird, reptile, and fish, and they have tamed them, [8]but no one can tame the tongue. It is wild and evil and full of deadly poison. [9]We use our tongues to praise our Lord and Father, but then we curse people, whom God made like himself. [10]Praises and curses come from the same mouth! My brothers and sisters, this should not happen. [11]Do good and bad water flow from the same spring? [12]My brothers and sisters, can a fig tree make olives, or can a grapevine make figs? No! And a well full of salty water cannot give good water.

TRUE WISDOM

[13]Are there those among you who are truly wise and understanding? Then they should show it by living right and doing good things with a gentleness that comes from wisdom. [14]But if you are selfish and have bitter jealousy in your hearts, do not brag. Your bragging is a lie that hides the truth. [15]That kind of "wisdom" does not come from God but from the world. It is not spiritual; it is from the devil. [16]Where jealousy and selfishness are, there will be confusion and every kind of evil. [17]But the wisdom that comes from God is first of all pure, then peaceful, gentle, and easy to please. This wisdom is always ready to help those who are troubled and to do good for others. It is always fair and honest. [18]People who work for peace in a peaceful way plant a good crop of right-living.

GIVE YOURSELVES TO GOD

4 Do you know where your fights and arguments come from? They come from the selfish desires that war within you. [2]You want things, but you do not have them. So you are ready to kill and are jealous of other people, but you still cannot get what you want. So you argue and fight. You do not get what you want, because you do not ask God. [3]Or when you ask, you do not receive because the reason you ask is wrong. You want things so you can use them for your own pleasures.

[4]So, you are not loyal to God! You should know that loving the world is the same as hating God. Anyone who wants to be a friend of the world becomes God's enemy. [5]Do you think the Scripture means nothing that says, "The Spirit that God made to live in us wants us for himself alone"?[n] [6]But God gives us even more grace, as the Scripture says,

"God is against the proud,
but he gives grace to the humble."

Proverbs 3:34

 4:5 "The Spirit . . . alone." These words may be from Exodus 20:5.

365

DECEMBER

1   Create a handmade gift for someone you love.

2

3   On This Day In History 1847—North Star newspaper was founded
                                           by Frederick Douglass.

4   It's your birthday Tyra Banks!

5

6

7   On This Day In History 1941—Pearl Harbor
                         was attacked by the Japanese.

"Self-love has very little
to do with how you feel
about your outer-self.
It's about accepting
all of yourself."
–Tyra Banks

8

9

10

11

12   Collect toys for children in need.

13   Happy Birthday Jamie Foxx!

14

15

16   On This Day In History 1976—Andrew Young named U.S.
                              ambassador to the United Nations.

17

18   **Think** outside
19   the box:
20   Thinking back on this past
21   year, what would you have
22   done **differently?**

23

24

25   HOLIDAY—Christmas

26

27   Invite a **friend** to spend the
           holidays with you.

28

29

30   It's your birthday, LeBron James!

31

ARTIST: KRS-ONE ALBUM: KNOWLEDGE REIGNS SUPREME CUT: "ONLY BEGOTTEN SON"

KRS-One says in his lyrics that "reading of the Bible is irrelevant, you gotta look within yourself, not a scripture, KRS-One comes to rearrange the god picture." He believes that hip-hop is god and that knowledge of self is the creation.

This philosophy is in line with KRS-One's beliefs as a "Five Percenter," a segment of the hip-hop community that believes, according to KRS-One, that "there are no gods or goddesses. We are the gods and goddesses. We say to each other, 'peace god, peace goddess.' This concept has been lent to us by the 5 percent nation of gods and earths."

If you're down with the living God then you know that this rap artist does not give him glory. So why are you buying his albums?

"REJECTED"

[7]So give yourselves completely to God. Stand against the devil, and the devil will run from you. [8]Come near to God, and God will come near to you. You sinners, clean sin out of your lives. You who are trying to follow God and the world at the same time, make your thinking pure. [9]Be sad, cry, and weep! Change your laughter into crying and your joy into sadness. [10]Humble yourself in the Lord's presence, and he will honor you.

YOU ARE NOT THE JUDGE

[11]Brothers and sisters, do not tell evil lies about each other. If you speak against your fellow believers or judge them, you are judging and speaking against the law they follow. And when you are judging the law, you are no longer a follower of the law. You have become a judge. [12]God is the only Lawmaker and Judge. He is the only One who can save and destroy. So it is not right for you to judge your neighbor.

LET GOD PLAN YOUR LIFE

[13]Some of you say, "Today or tomorrow we will go to some city. We will stay there a year, do business, and make money." [14]But you do not know what will happen tomorrow! Your life is like a mist. You can see it for a short time, but then it goes away. [15]So you should say, "If the Lord wants, we will live and do this or that." [16]But now you are proud and you brag. All of this bragging is wrong. [17]Anyone who knows the right thing to do, but does not do it, is sinning.

A WARNING TO THE RICH

5You rich people, listen! Cry and be very sad because of the troubles that are coming to you. [2]Your riches have rotted, and your clothes have been eaten by moths. [3]Your gold and silver have rusted, and that rust will be a proof that you were wrong. It will eat your bodies like fire. You saved your treasure for the last days. [4]The pay you did not give the workers who mowed your fields cries out against you, and the cries of the workers have been heard by the Lord All-Powerful. [5]Your life on earth was full of rich living and pleasing yourselves with everything you wanted. You made yourselves fat, like an animal ready to be killed. [6]You have judged guilty and then murdered innocent people, who were not against you.

BE PATIENT

[7]Brothers and sisters, be patient until the Lord comes again. A farmer patiently waits for his valuable crop to grow from the earth and for it to receive the autumn and spring rains. [8]You, too, must be patient. Do not give up hope, because the Lord is coming soon. [9]Brothers and sisters, do not complain against each other or you will be judged guilty. And the Judge is ready to come! [10]Brothers and sisters, follow the example of the prophets who spoke for the Lord. They suffered many hard things, but they were patient. [11]We say they are happy because they did not give up. You have heard about Job's patience, and you know the Lord's purpose for him in the end. You know the Lord is full of mercy and is kind.

BE CAREFUL WHAT YOU SAY

[12] My brothers and sisters, above all, do not use an oath when you make a promise. Don't use the name of heaven, earth, or anything else to prove what you say. When you mean yes, say only yes, and when you mean no, say only no so you will not be judged guilty.

THE POWER OF PRAYER

[13] Anyone who is having troubles should pray. Anyone who is happy should sing praises. [14] Anyone who is sick should call the church's elders. They should pray for and pour oil on the person[n] in the name of the Lord. [15] And the prayer that is said with faith will make the sick person well; the Lord will heal that person. And if the person has sinned, the sins will be forgiven. [16] Confess your sins to each other and pray for each other so God can heal you. When a believing person prays, great things happen. [17] Elijah was a human being just like us. He prayed that it would not rain, and it did not rain on the land for three and a half years! [18] Then Elijah prayed again, and the rain came down from the sky, and the land produced crops again.

SAVING A SOUL

[19] My brothers and sisters, if one of you wanders away from the truth, and someone helps that person come back, [20] remember this: Anyone who brings a sinner back from the wrong way will save that sinner's soul from death and will cause many sins to be forgiven.

HeartCry

Conflict   **Is conflict getting to you? Do you feel pressured by folks to do or think what they want? Don't give in to the strife. Let your heart cry . . .**

God, I hate all this conflict! Why can't folks just back up off me? Always arguing and hating, everybody thinks they got it right. No one listens; they only try to make things happen their way. All these voices up in my face are making me crazy. Help me find a way to make it stop.

Be slow to anger and slow to speak. Take time to listen and really hear. A quiet voice, full of wisdom, will subdue an enemy. Ask me and I will give you the words through which my peace will flow. Galatians 5:16-18

5:14 pour oil on the person Oil was used in the name of the Lord as a sign that the person was now set apart for God's special attention and care.

FREE AT LAST BAIL BONDS

FREE AT LAST BAIL BONDS

I'LL RIDE WITH YOU UNTIL I DIE

"I'll ride with you till I die!" Peter made such a promise to Jesus only hours before Jesus was arrested. But before Jesus died, Peter had not only run out on him, he also had denied that he even knew Jesus.

In this book we find a much different Peter. We read the words of one who had denied Jesus and see how he had become the strong, steady leader of the early church. Peter had learned to stand up for his faith and wasn't ashamed to share with others about his wrong choices and God's faithfulness. Peter had accomplished much and touched many lives, but he gave all the props to Jesus.

Peter was eventually arrested, thrown in jail and murdered for refusing to deny Christ. History tells us that he actually requested to be crucified upside down because he did not consider himself worthy to die the same way that Jesus did.

Through the power of God's Spirit, Peter's life became a model for others to follow. But the change didn't happen overnight. It was a day-by-day process that turned a coward into a real man in Christ.

1

From Peter, an apostle of Jesus Christ.

To God's chosen people who are away from their homes and are scattered all around Pontus, Galatia, Cappadocia, Asia, and Bithynia. [2]God planned long ago to choose you by making you his holy people, which is the Spirit's work. God wanted you to obey him and to be made clean by the blood of the death of Jesus Christ.

Grace and peace be yours more and more.

WE HAVE A LIVING HOPE

[3]Praise be to the God and Father of our Lord Jesus Christ. In God's great mercy he has caused us to be born again into a living hope, because Jesus Christ rose from the dead. [4]Now we hope for the blessings God has for his children. These blessings, which cannot be destroyed or be spoiled or lose their beauty, are kept in heaven for you. [5]God's power protects you through your faith until salvation is shown to you at the end of time. [6]This makes you very happy, even though now for a short time different kinds of troubles may make you sad. [7]These troubles come to prove that your faith is pure. This purity of faith is worth more than gold, which can be proved to be pure by fire but will ruin. But the purity of your faith will bring you praise and glory and honor when Jesus Christ is shown to you. [8]You have not seen Christ, but still you love him. You cannot see him now, but you believe in him. So you are filled with a joy that cannot be explained, a joy full of glory. [9]And you are receiving the goal of your faith—the salvation of your souls.

[10]The prophets searched carefully and tried to learn about this salvation. They prophesied about the grace that was coming to you. [11]The Spirit of Christ was in the prophets, telling in advance about the sufferings of Christ and about the glory that would follow those sufferings. The prophets tried to learn about what the Spirit was showing them, when those things would happen, and what the world would be like at that time. [12]It was shown them that their service was not for themselves but for you, when they told about the truths you have now heard. Those who preached the Good News to you told you those things with the help of the Holy Spirit who was sent from heaven—things into which angels desire to look.

A CALL TO HOLY LIVING

[13]So prepare your minds for service and have self-control. All your hope should be for the gift of grace that will be yours when Jesus Christ is shown to you. [14]Now that you are obedient children of God do not live as you did in the past. You did not understand, so you did the evil things you wanted. [15]But be holy in all you do, just as God, the One who called you, is holy. [16]It is written in the Scriptures: "You must be holy, because I am holy."[n]

[17]You pray to God and call him Father, and he judges each person's work equally. So while you are here on earth, you should live with respect for God.

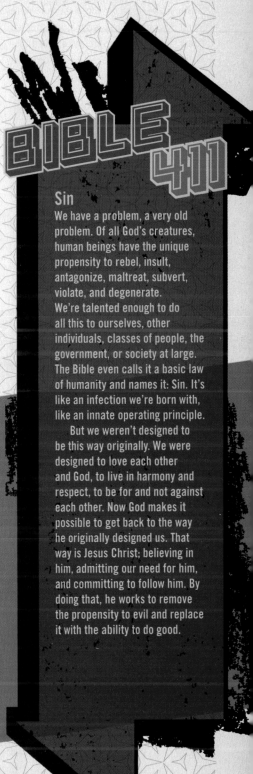

BIBLE 411

Sin

We have a problem, a very old problem. Of all God's creatures, human beings have the unique propensity to rebel, insult, antagonize, maltreat, subvert, violate, and degenerate. We're talented enough to do all this to ourselves, other individuals, classes of people, the government, or society at large. The Bible even calls it a basic law of humanity and names it: Sin. It's like an infection we're born with, like an innate operating principle.

But we weren't designed to be this way originally. We were designed to love each other and God, to live in harmony and respect, to be for and not against each other. Now God makes it possible to get back to the way he originally designed us. That way is Jesus Christ; believing in him, admitting our need for him, and committing to follow him. By doing that, he works to remove the propensity to evil and replace it with the ability to do good.

HE GAVE ALL THE PROPS TO JESUS

1:16 "You must be . . . holy." Quotation from Leviticus 11:45; 19:2; 20:7.

18You know that in the past you were living in a worthless way, a way passed down from the people who lived before you. But you were saved from that useless life. You were bought, not with something that ruins like gold or silver, 19but with the precious blood of Christ, who was like a pure and perfect lamb. 20Christ was chosen before the world was made, but he was shown to the world in these last times for your sake. 21Through Christ you believe in God, who raised Christ from the dead and gave him glory. So your faith and your hope are in God.

22Now that your obedience to the truth has purified your souls, you can have true love for your Christian brothers and sisters. So love each other deeply with all your heart." 23You have been born again, and this new life did not come from something that dies, but from something that cannot die. You were born again through God's living message that continues forever. 24The Scripture says,

"All people are like the grass,
    and all their glory is like the
    flowers of the field.
The grass dies and the flowers fall,

25   but the word of the Lord will live
    forever."   Isaiah 40:6-8
And this is the word that was preached to you.

JESUS IS THE LIVING STONE

2 So then, rid yourselves of all evil, all lying, hypocrisy, jealousy, and evil speech. 2As newborn babies want milk, you should want the pure and simple teaching. By it you can mature in your salvation, 3because you

1:22 with all your heart Some Greek copies read "with a pure heart."

HOW YA TRAVELIN?

MARRIAGE

Let's be real. A lot of married couples are living out a disaster. So how do you avoid creating a disaster of your own? First, you need to realize what marriage is meant to be. In Genesis 2:18, the Lord says, "It is not good for the man to be alone. I will make a helper who is right for him." Ephesians 5:22-33 tells us that marriage, as God intended it, is a powerful bond of love and commitment. It is a relationship with such importance that the Bible uses it as a picture of what your relationship with Jesus can and should be. Malachi 2:15 says, "God made husbands and wives to become one body and one spirit for his purpose . . ." So be careful, and do not break your promise to the wife you married when you were young." When a husband and wife are actually one in Christ, they will have the greatest earthly satisfaction and fulfillment of spirit, soul, and body. No one person can meet all of another person's needs. We can't have that expectation of a mate. We need to understand that only Jesus can meet our soul's deepest needs. Marriage can be wonderful when Christ is in it and both partners look to him for fulfillment, and not to each other.

MARRIAGE SHOULD BE HONORED – HEBREWS 13:4

have already examined and seen how good the Lord is.

[4]Come to the Lord Jesus, the "stone"[n] that lives. The people of the world did not want this stone, but he was the stone God chose, and he was precious. [5]You also are like living stones, so let yourselves be used to build a spiritual temple—to be holy priests who offer spiritual sacrifices to God. He will accept those sacrifices through Jesus Christ. [6]The Scripture says:

"I will put a stone in the ground in
    Jerusalem.
Everything will be built on this
    important and precious rock.
Anyone who trusts in him
    will never be disappointed."

Isaiah 28:16

[7]This stone is worth much to you who believe. But to the people who do not believe,

"the stone that the builders rejected
    has become the cornerstone."

Psalm 118:22

[8]Also, he is

"a stone that causes people to
    stumble,
a rock that makes them fall."

Isaiah 8:14

They stumble because they do not obey what God says, which is what God planned to happen to them.

[9]But you are a chosen people, royal priests, a holy nation, a people for God's own possession. You were chosen to tell about the wonderful acts of God, who called you out of darkness into his wonderful light. [10]At one time you were not a people, but now you are God's people. In the past you had never received mercy, but now you have received God's mercy.

LIVE FOR GOD

[11]Dear friends, you are like foreigners and strangers in this world. I beg you to avoid the evil things your bodies want to do that fight against your soul. [12]People who do not believe are living all around you, and might say that you are doing wrong. Live such good lives that they will see the good things you do and will give glory to God on the day when Christ comes again.

YIELD TO EVERY HUMAN AUTHORITY

[13]For the Lord's sake, yield to the people who have authority in this world: the king, who is the highest authority, [14]and the leaders who are sent by him to punish those who do wrong and to praise those who do right. [15]It is God's desire that by doing good you should stop foolish people from saying stupid things about you. [16]Live as free people, but do not use your freedom as an excuse to do evil. Live as servants of God. [17]Show respect for all people: Love the brothers and sisters of God's family, respect God, honor the king.

FOLLOW CHRIST'S EXAMPLE

[18]Slaves, yield to the authority of your masters with all respect, not only those who are good and kind, but also those who are dishonest. [19]A person might have to suffer even when it is unfair, but if he thinks of God and can stand the pain, God is pleased. [20]If you are beaten for doing wrong, there is no reason to praise you for being patient in your punishment. But if you suffer for doing good, and you are patient, then God is pleased. [21]This is what you were called to do, because Christ suffered for you and gave you an example to follow. So you should do as he did.

[22]"He had never sinned,
    and he had never lied." *Isaiah 53:9*

[23]People insulted Christ, but he did not insult them in return. Christ suffered, but he did not threaten. He let God, the One who judges rightly, take care of him. [24]Christ carried our sins in his body on the cross so we would stop living for sin and start living for what is right. And you are healed because of his wounds. [25]You were like sheep that wandered away, but now you have come back to the Shepherd and Overseer of your souls.

WIVES AND HUSBANDS

3 In the same way, you wives should yield to your husbands. Then, if some husbands do not obey God's teaching, they will be persuaded to believe without anyone's saying a word to them. They will be persuaded by the way their wives live. [2]Your husbands will see the pure lives you live with your respect for God. [3]It is not fancy hair, gold jewelry, or fine clothes that should make you beautiful. [4]No, your beauty should come from within you—the beauty of a gentle and quiet spirit that will never be destroyed and is very precious to God. [5]In this same way the holy women who lived long ago and followed God made themselves beautiful, yielding to their own husbands. [6]Sarah obeyed Abraham, her husband, and called him her master. And you women are true children of Sarah if you always do what is right and are not afraid.

[7]In the same way, you husbands should live with your wives in an understanding way, since they are weaker than you. But show them respect, because God gives them the same blessing he gives you—the grace that gives true life. Do this so that nothing will stop your prayers.

SUFFERING FOR DOING RIGHT

[8]Finally, all of you should be in agreement, understanding each other, loving each other as family, being kind and humble. [9]Do not do wrong to repay a wrong, and do not insult to repay an insult. But repay with a blessing, because you yourselves were called to do this so that you might receive a blessing. [10]The Scripture says,

"A person must do these things
    to enjoy life and have many happy
        days.
He must not say evil things,
    and he must not tell lies.
[11]He must stop doing evil and do good.
    He must look for peace and work
        for it.

 2:4 "stone" The most important stone in God's spiritual temple or house (his people).

VIEWPOINT

WHO IS THE FIRST PERSON YOU THINK OF CALLING WHEN YOU HAVE A PROBLEM. AND WHY?

I used to call friends and family members when I encountered difficulties or when I needed someone to talk to. However, I rapidly realized that people will fail me, but God promised to be with me always. I found that it is best to get on my knees in prayer and call my heavenly Father whenever I am faced with a dilemma. It is God who grants wisdom and understanding, not people.

12The Lord sees the good people
and listens to their prayers.
But the Lord is against
those who do evil." *Psalm 34:12-16*
13If you are trying hard to do good, no one can really hurt you. 14But even if you suffer for doing right, you are blessed.

"Don't be afraid of what they fear;
do not dread those things."

Isaiah 8:12–13

15But respect Christ as the holy Lord in your hearts. Always be ready to answer everyone who asks you to explain about the hope you have, 16but answer in a gentle way and with respect. Keep a clear conscience so that those who speak evil of your good life in Christ will be made ashamed. 17It is better to suffer for doing good than for doing wrong if that is what God wants. 18Christ himself suffered for sins once. He was not guilty, but he suffered for those who are guilty to bring you to God. His body was killed, but he was made alive in the spirit. 19And in the spirit he went and preached to the spirits in prison 20who refused to obey God long ago in the time of Noah. God was waiting patiently for them while Noah was building the boat. Only a few people—eight in all—were saved by water. 21And that water is like baptism that now saves you—not the washing of dirt from the body, but the promise made to God from a good conscience. And this is because Jesus Christ was raised from the dead. 22Now Jesus has gone into heaven and is at God's right side ruling over angels, authorities, and powers.

CHANGE YOUR LIVES

4 Since Christ suffered while he was in his body, strengthen yourselves with the same way of thinking Christ had. The person who has suffered in the body is finished with sin. 2Strengthen yourselves so that you will live here on earth doing what God wants, not the evil things people want. 3In the past you wasted too much time doing what nonbelievers enjoy. You were guilty of sexual sins, evil desires, drunkenness, wild and drunken parties, and hateful idol worship. 4Nonbelievers think it is strange that you do not do the many wild and wasteful things they do, so they in-

sult you. 5But they will have to explain this to God, who is ready to judge the living and the dead. 6For this reason the Good News was preached to those who are now dead. Even though they were judged like all people, the Good News was preached to them so they could live in the spirit as God lives.

USE GOD'S GIFTS WISELY

7The time is near when all things will end. So think clearly and control yourselves so you will be able to pray. 8Most importantly, love each other deeply, because love will cause people to forgive each other for many sins. 9Open your homes to each other, without complaining. 10Each of you has received a gift to use to serve others. Be good servants of God's various gifts of grace. 11Anyone who speaks should speak words from God. Anyone who serves should serve with the strength God gives so that in everything God will be praised through Jesus Christ. Power and glory belong to him forever and ever. Amen.

SUFFERING AS A CHRISTIAN

12My friends, do not be surprised at the terrible trouble which now comes to test you. Do not think that something strange is happening to you. 13But be happy that you are sharing in Christ's sufferings so that you will be happy and full of joy when Christ comes again in glory. 14When people insult you because you follow Christ, you are blessed, because the glorious Spirit, the Spirit of God, is with you. 15Do not suffer for murder, theft, or any other crime, nor because you trouble other people. 16But if you suffer because you are a Christian, do not be ashamed. Praise God because you wear that name. 17It is time for judgment to begin with God's family. And if that judging begins with us, what will happen to those people who do not obey the Good News of God?
18"If it is very hard for a good person
to be saved,
the wicked person and the sinner
will surely be lost!"

 4:18 "If . . . lost!" Quotation from Proverbs 11:31 in the Septuagint, the Greek version of the Old Testament.

[19]So those who suffer as God wants should trust their souls to the faithful Creator as they continue to do what is right.

THE FLOCK OF GOD

5 Now I have something to say to the elders in your group. I also am an elder. I have seen Christ's sufferings, and I will share in the glory that will be shown to us. I beg you to [2]shepherd God's flock, for whom you are responsible. Watch over them because you want to, not because you are forced. That is how God wants it. Do it because you are happy to serve, not because you want money. [3]Do not be like a ruler over people you are responsible for, but be good examples to them. [4]Then when Christ, the Chief Shepherd, comes, you will get a glorious crown that will never lose its beauty.

[5]In the same way, younger people should be willing to be under older people. And all of you should be very humble with each other.

"God is against the proud,
   but he gives grace to the humble."
Proverbs 3:34

[6]Be humble under God's powerful hand so he will lift you up when the right time comes. [7]Give all your worries to him, because he cares about you.

[8]Control yourselves and be careful! The devil, your enemy, goes around like a roaring lion looking for someone to eat. [9]Refuse to give in to him, by standing strong in your faith. You know that your Christian family all over the world is having the same kinds of suffering.

[10]And after you suffer for a short time, God, who gives all grace, will make everything right. He will make you strong and support you and keep you from falling. He

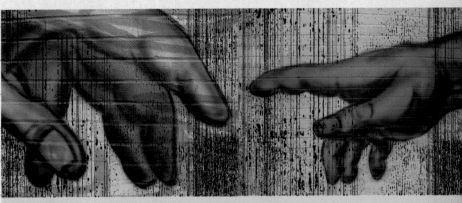

HeartCry

Abuse **Abuse can destroy your life and crush your very soul. Hate for your attacker and anger at yourself can fill your heart and control your mind. Let your heart cry...**

Help! Help! Help! Lord, I need some help! I'm being abused and I can't take it anymore. I'm so filled with anger and hate because it just keeps happening over and over again. Sometimes I just want to scrap so he will leave me alone, but it's hard to turn on someone who's such a huge part of my life. I've been struggling with this for so long, and it's killing me. I feel worthless and used. I need the strength to tell someone and end this nightmare. Help me find the right person to talk to, the one who can really help. Give me wisdom to know what's right and the strength to make this mess end. I need to know someone really cares. Please, holla back.

My child, there is no pain you experience that I do not feel, no tears you shed that do not also fall from my eyes. It breaks my heart that you are willing to accept cruelty at the hands of another in the name of love. I have sent you my word. Read the 13th chapter of 1 Corinthians and you will find a picture of love as it was meant to be. This is the love I offer and the love I long for you to find in your life. I will walk alongside you and lend you my strength, but you must be the one to decide to walk away from hatred and abuse. Even then, I will walk with you. **Hebrews 13:5-6**

called you to share in his glory in Christ, a glory that will continue forever. [11]All power is his forever and ever. Amen.

FINAL GREETINGS

[12]I wrote this short letter with the help of Silas, who I know is a faithful brother in Christ. I wrote to encourage you and to tell you that this is the true grace of God. Stand strong in that grace.

[13]The church in Babylon, who was chosen like you, sends you greetings. Mark, my son in Christ, also greets you. [14]Give each other a kiss of Christian love when you meet.

Peace to all of you who are in Christ.

CONTINUE TO REPRESENT FOR JESUS

Peter wrote this letter near the end of his life. He spit some great words to warn Christians to be cautious and wise.

More and more believers were accepting Christ and new churches were popping up everywhere. But false teachings were creeping into these young communities. People were misrepresenting and adding their own ideas to the message of Jesus. Peter warns people to watch out for these false teachers with their smooth talk. Peter closes the letter by reminding everyone that God is going to return for his people and how important it is to continue to represent for Jesus.

There is still a lot of false teaching being spread today. We need to know what the Word of God says so we can recognize truth. We should not listen to anyone who does not come correct about the real message of Jesus.

GOD UNIT

DEALING WITH MY DAD

They informed me that my father had suffered a massive stroke and I was his oldest surviving relative. I told the doctor that I couldn't remember my dad and wouldn't know him if I saw him. I was instructed to come anyway. I brought my mom with me to identify him. We got to the hospital and she said, "Yes, that's your father."

The first time I saw my dad he was being kept alive by a ventilator! My mother encouraged me not to give up. Taking a deep breath, I said, "I'm glad to meet you, Dad. I've been praying to meet you. Let me pray for you." And I did, asking God to heal his body and soul. After I had said, "Amen," I leaned close to his ear, "If you can hear me, dad, squeeze my hand." He sort of lifted his finger, and the room filled with joy. I told him that I didn't hold anything against him and asked him to talk to Jesus if he could. Tears fell from his eyes as he opened them and looked at me. Although he never spoke, I believe he heard me and understood me. The doctor said it was just a reflex; I knew better.

God answered my prayers. My dad died two months later, but I can live knowing that I met him and was able to talk to him and pray for him. For that I am thankful!

1 John 5:14–15—And this is the boldness we have in God's presence: that if we ask God for anything that agrees with what he wants, he hears us. If we know he hears us every time we ask him, we know we have what we ask from him.

I had never seen my dad. But as far back as I could remember, I had prayed that God would let me find him. My parents had separated when I was three. Mom raised me in the church. Every Sunday, I would look around at all of the men and think, *I wonder what my dad looks like?* When a man would come to visit our church, I would wonder if he could be my father. I was embarrassed that I didn't have a dad. But I kept praying that God would bring my father into my life.

Years later, I met a guy who turned out to be my cousin, my father's nephew. We exchanged phone numbers and I asked him about my dad. He had met my dad years before and thought he might be able to track him down. Some time later, he gave me a call with a possible address. I decided to write to my father but I wasn't sure what to say to him. When I got up the courage, I simply wrote to my father that I wanted to meet him. I mailed the letter and waited weeks for a reply. None came. I decided that I had the wrong address or my dad didn't want me bugging him.

A few months later, a hospital two hours away called.

---

1 From Simon Peter, a servant and apostle of Jesus Christ.

To you who have received a faith as valuable as ours, because our God and Savior Jesus Christ does what is right.

[2] Grace and peace be given to you more and more, because you truly know God and Jesus our Lord.

GOD HAS GIVEN US BLESSINGS

[3] Jesus has the power of God, by which he has given us everything we need to live and to serve God. We have these things because we know him. Jesus called us by his glory and goodness. [4] Through these he gave us the very great and precious promises. With these gifts you can share in God's nature, and the world will not ruin you with its evil desires.

[5] Because you have these blessings, do your best to add these things to your lives: to your faith, add goodness; and to your goodness, add knowledge; [6] and to your knowledge, add self-control; and to your self-control, add patience; and to your patience, add service for God; [7] and to your service for God, add kindness for your brothers and sisters in Christ; and to this kindness, add love. [8] If all these things are in you and are growing, they will help you to be useful and productive in your knowledge of our Lord Jesus Christ. [9] But anyone who does not have these things cannot see clearly. He is blind and has forgotten that he was made clean from his past sins.

VIEWPOINT

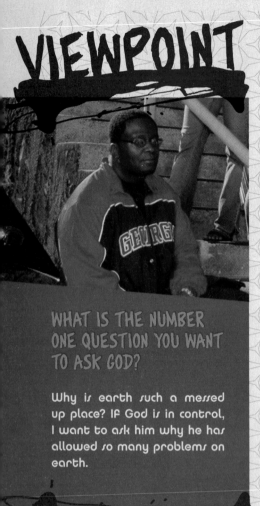

WHAT IS THE NUMBER ONE QUESTION YOU WANT TO ASK GOD?

Why is earth such a messed up place? If God is in control, I want to ask him why he has allowed so many problems on earth.

[10] My brothers and sisters, try hard to be certain that you really are called and chosen by God. If you do all these things, you will never fall. [11] And you will be given a very great welcome into the eternal kingdom of our Lord and Savior Jesus Christ.

[12] You know these things, and you are very strong in the truth, but I will always help you remember them. [13] I think it is right for me to help you remember as long as I am in this body. [14] I know I must soon leave this body, as our Lord Jesus Christ has shown me. [15] I will try my best so that you may be able to remember these things even after I am gone.

WE SAW CHRIST'S GLORY

[16] When we told you about the powerful coming of our Lord Jesus Christ, we were not telling just clever stories that someone invented. But we saw the greatness of Jesus with our own eyes. [17] Jesus heard the voice of God, the Greatest Glory, when he received honor and glory from God the Father. The voice said, "This is my Son, whom I love, and I am very pleased with him." [18] We heard that voice from heaven while we were with Jesus on the holy mountain.

[19] This makes us more sure about the message the prophets gave. It is good for you to follow closely what they said as you would follow a light shining in a dark place, until the day begins and the morning star rises in your hearts. [20] Most of all, you must understand this: No prophecy in the Scriptures ever comes from the prophet's own interpretation. [21] No prophecy ever came from what a person wanted to say, but people led by the Holy Spirit spoke words from God.

FALSE TEACHERS

2 There used to be false prophets among God's people, just as you will have some false teachers in your group. They will secretly teach things that are wrong—teachings that will cause people to be lost. They will even refuse to accept the Master, Jesus, who bought their freedom. So they will bring quick ruin on themselves. [2] Many will follow their evil ways and say evil things about the way of truth. [3] Those false teachers only want your money, so they will use you by telling you lies. Their judgment spoken against them long ago is still coming, and their ruin is certain.

[4] When angels sinned, God did not let them go free without punishment. He sent them to hell and put them in caves[n] of darkness where they are being held for judgment. [5] And God punished the world long ago when he brought a flood to the world that was full of people who were against him. But God saved Noah, who preached about being right with God, and seven other people with him. [6] And God also destroyed the evil cities of Sodom and Gomorrah[n] by burning them until they were ashes. He made those cities an example of what will happen to those who are against God. [7] But he saved Lot from those cities. Lot, a good man, was troubled because of the filthy lives of evil people. [8] (Lot was a good man, but because he lived with evil people every day, his good heart was hurt by the evil things he saw and heard.) [9] So the Lord knows how to save those who serve him when troubles come. He will hold evil people and punish them, while waiting for the Judgment Day. [10] That punishment is especially for those who live by doing the evil things their sinful selves want and who hate authority.

These false teachers are bold and do anything they want. They are not afraid to speak against the angels. [11] But even the angels, who are much stronger and more powerful than false teachers, do not accuse them with insults before[n] the Lord. [12] But these people speak against things they do not understand. They are like animals that act without thinking, animals born to be caught and killed. And, like animals, these false teachers will be destroyed. [13] They have caused many people to suffer, so they themselves will suffer. That is their pay for what they have done. They take pleasure in openly doing evil, so they are like dirty spots and stains among you. They delight in deceiving you while eating meals with you. [14] Every time they look at a woman they want her, and their desire for sin is never satisfied. They lead weak people into the trap of sin, and they have taught their hearts to be greedy. God will punish them! [15] These false teachers left the right road and lost their way, following the way Balaam went. Balaam was the son of Beor, who loved being paid for doing wrong. [16] But a donkey, which cannot talk, told Balaam he was sinning. It

2:4 caves Some Greek copies read "chains." **2:6 Sodom and Gomorrah** Two cities God destroyed because the people were so evil. **2:11 before** Some Greek copies read "from."

REAL RHYMES:

NO ESCAPE

BY JOANNA ROBINSON

YOU CAN RUN, YOU CAN HIDE, BUT YOU'LL BE RUNNING IN VAIN IF YOU DON'T CHANGE YOUR LIFESTYLE.
KEEP YOUR HEAD UP AND FIGHT THE GOOD FIGHT. STRUGGLE ON. LOOK STRAIGHT, HOLDING YOUR OWN FAITH.
LOOKING AT THE DEVIL OR LOOKING AT GOD, THE TIME HAS COME. JUST PLAY THE RIGHT CARD.
DON'T WORRY 'BOUT YOUR TROUBLES, THOUGH I KNOW IT'S HARD 'CAUSE YOU KNOW WHAT?
WITHOUT HIM THERE'S NO ESCAPE.

SAY WHAT YOU SAY, BUT THERE IS NO ESCAPE. LOOK AROUND 'BOUT THE PLACE, DOORS CLOSED IN YOUR FACE.
NOW WHATCHA GOIN' DO WID THE STRESS YOU GOIN' THROUGH?
THE STRIFE AND THE PAIN MAN IT'S ALL UP TO YOU. CRAZY ENOUGH THAT YOU LIVIN' LIKE YOU DO.
SITUATIONS GOT YOU SCRAPIN', TOO HOT TO HANDLE. DON'T YOU GIVE IN TO ALL THE SCANDAL?
GO TO GOD 'CAUSE YOU KNOW WITHOUT HIM THERE'S NO ESCAPE.

NO ESCAPE, NO ESCAPE. YOU CAN SAY WHAT YOU SAY BUT THERE IS NO ESCAPE.
NO ESCAPE, NO ESCAPE. YOU CAN RUN 'BOUT THE PLACE BUT THERE'LL BE NO ESCAPE.
NO ESCAPE, NO ESCAPE. YOU CAN SAY WHAT YOU SAY BUT THERE IS NO ESCAPE.
NO ESCAPE, NO ESCAPE. YOU CAN RUN YOU CAN HIDE BUT THERE'LL BE NO ESCAPE.

SEE, I KNOW WHERE I CAME FROM, WHERE I'M GOING. WILL YOU COME WITH ME TOO?
THIS PLACE IS OPEN TO ANYONE WHO WANTS TO COME IN. TRUST IN GOD, HE'LL SEE YOU THROUGH.

spoke with a man's voice and stopped the prophet's crazy thinking.

[17] Those false teachers are like springs without water and clouds blown by a storm. A place in the blackest darkness has been kept for them. [18] They brag with words that mean nothing. By their evil desires they lead people into the trap of sin—people who are just beginning to escape from others who live in error. [19] They promise them freedom, but they themselves are not free. They are slaves of things that will be destroyed. For people are slaves of anything that controls them. [20] They were made free from the evil in the world by knowing our Lord and Savior Jesus Christ. But if they return to evil things and those things control them, then it is worse for them than it was before. [21] Yes, it would be better for them to have never known the right way than to know it and to turn away from the holy teaching that was given to them. [22] What they did is like this true saying: "A dog goes back to what it has thrown up,"[n] and, "After a pig is washed, it goes back and rolls in the mud."

2:22 "A dog . . . up." Quotation from Proverbs 26:11.

JESUS WILL COME AGAIN

3 My friends, this is the second letter I have written you to help your honest minds remember. [2] I want you to think about the words the holy prophets spoke in the past, and remember the command our Lord and Savior gave us through your apostles. [3] It is most important for you to understand what will happen in the

DEEP ISSUES

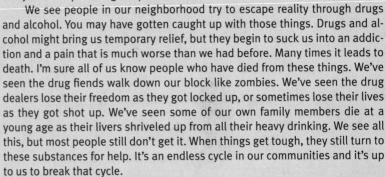

Substance Abuse

Sometimes we want to escape from an ugly reality. There are a lot of ill things that many of us living in urban environments have to face—from family problems, to money issues, to violence, to school, to relationships . . . the list could go on and on. We've all been through some drama and experienced some serious pain. At those times, we look for something to ease the pain. Many people look for relief in the wrong places and just end up making the pain even worse.

We see people in our neighborhood try to escape reality through drugs and alcohol. You may have gotten caught up with those things. Drugs and alcohol might bring us temporary relief, but they begin to suck us into an addiction and a pain that is much worse than we had before. Many times it leads to death. I'm sure all of us know people who have died from these things. We've seen the drug fiends walk down our block like zombies. We've seen the drug dealers lose their freedom as they got locked up, or sometimes lose their lives as they got shot up. We've seen some of our own family members die at a young age as their livers shriveled up from all their heavy drinking. We see all this, but most people still don't get it. When things get tough, they still turn to these substances for help. It's an endless cycle in our communities and it's up to us to break that cycle.

Jesus offers us relief from the pain of our reality. Check out Matthew 11:28-30. In these verses Jesus promises to give us rest. He also tells us to accept the load that he gives us. Some versions of the Bible say that he gives us his "yoke." Have you ever wondered what a yoke is? Back in the days before machines, people would get two big oxen to plow the farming fields. The oxen would be connected across the shoulders with a piece of wood so they could work as a team. This piece of wood was called the yoke. It yoked the animals together. Jesus said to take his yoke. He tells us that "The load I give you to carry is light." We need to get connected with Jesus. We must give him our heavy burdens because he says he'll carry them. Our problem is that we want to handle our problems on our own. We'll hold it down. Many times the weight is too much, and we end up turning to the wrong things to ease the pressure. All along, the real solution is right there in front of us. Jesus is right there saying, "Come to me, all of you who are tired and have heavy loads, and I will give you rest."

last days. People will laugh at you. They will live doing the evil things they want to do. [4]They will say, "Jesus promised to come again. Where is he? Our fathers have died, but the world continues the way it has been since it was made." [5]But they do not want to remember what happened long ago. By the word of God heaven was made, and the earth was made from water and with water. [6]Then the world was flooded and destroyed with water. [7]And that same word of God is keeping heaven and earth that we now have in order to be destroyed by fire. They are being kept for the Judgment Day and the destruction of all who are against God.

[8]But do not forget this one thing, dear friends: To the Lord one day is as a thousand years, and a thousand years is as one day. [9]The Lord is not slow in doing what he promised—the way some people understand slowness. But God is being patient with you. He does not want anyone to be lost, but he wants all people to change their hearts and lives.

[10]But the day of the Lord will come like a thief. The skies will disappear with a loud noise. Everything in them will be destroyed by fire, and the earth and everything in it will be exposed.[n] [11]In that way everything will be destroyed. So what kind of people should you be? You should live holy lives and serve God, [12]as you wait for and look forward to the coming of the day of God. When that day comes, the skies will be destroyed with fire, and everything in them will melt with heat. [13]But God made a promise to us, and we are waiting for a new heaven and a new earth where goodness lives.

[14]Dear friends, since you are waiting for this to happen, do your best to be without sin and without fault. Try to be at peace with God. [15]Remember that we are saved because our Lord is patient. Our dear brother Paul told you the same thing when

HeartCry

Death **Have you lost someone close to you? Are you struggling to cope with the loss? Does it seem impossible to grasp the reality of death? Let your heart cry . . .**

Father, I really need to talk. My heart hurts from the loss and I just can't cope with someone I love being suddenly gone from my life. Death scares me and confuses me. It's so final and seems so hopeless. What happens to folks when they die? Will I see them again? I can't deal with death without you. Help me understand. Help me deal with the pain. I really need you to answer back.

Death is not an end, but a beginning. For those who know me it is only a transition, from physical life to a life outside of time. Allow my love to be a healing balm. I will soothe your pain and hold you close as you learn to smile again. John 3:16; Romans 2:7; 1 Peter 1:5-7

he wrote to you with the wisdom that God gave him. [16]He writes about this in all his letters. Some things in Paul's letters are hard to understand, and people who are ignorant and weak in faith explain these things falsely. They also falsely explain the other Scriptures, but they are destroying themselves by doing this.

[17]Dear friends, since you already know about this, be careful. Do not let those evil people lead you away by the wrong they do. Be careful so you will not fall from your strong faith. [18]But grow in the grace and knowledge of our Lord and Savior Jesus Christ. Glory be to him now and forever! Amen.

3:10 and . . . exposed Some Greek copies read "and everything in it will be burned up."

1-3 JOHN

TRUE LOVE COMES FROM GOD

If you search out the word "love" on the Internet you'll get over 294 million hits. Even with all of this information at our fingertips, it is obvious that our culture is pretty confused about the meaning of this word. John's letters give us some real answers about love: what it means and what it looks like.

John had been one of Jesus' closest friends. He sparked off his time with Jesus as one selfish dude, always trying to get over on others so he could get ahead and get his props. All that changed as he traveled with Jesus, heard his teachings and saw his love in action.

In these pages, John tells us that true love comes from God. He tells us what God's love looks like. The human kind of love is conditional. It is based on emotions and "What's in it for me?" Not with God. He doesn't love us based on how he feels or stop loving us if we mess up. He loves us unconditionally. He doesn't love our sin, but he truly loves us!

As Jesus hung on the cross taking his last few breaths, he told John to take care of his mother. Jesus knew that John had learned the meaning of love. John stayed true and cared for Jesus' mom until her death. He had learned his lessons well. He not only understood love; he also lived it.

Do you want to know real love? Then get to know the author of it—God. He doesn't just have love; he is love.

1

We write you now about what has always existed, which we have heard, we have seen with our own eyes, we have looked at, and we have touched with our hands. We write to you about the Word[n] that gives life. [2]He who gives life was shown to us. We saw him and can give proof about it. And now we announce to you that he has life that continues forever. He was with God the Father and was shown to us. [3]We announce to you what we have seen and heard, because we want you also to have fellowship with us. Our fellowship is with God the Father and with his Son, Jesus Christ. [4]We write this to you so we may be full of joy.[n]

GOD FORGIVES OUR SINS

[5]Here is the message we have heard from Christ and now announce to you: God is light,[n] and in him there is no darkness at all. [6]So if we say we have fellowship with God, but we continue living in darkness, we are liars and do not follow the truth. [7]But if we live in the light, as God is in the light, we can share fellowship with each other. Then the blood of Jesus, God's Son, cleanses us from every sin.

[8]If we say we have no sin, we are fooling ourselves, and the truth is not in us. [9]But if we confess our sins, he will forgive our sins, because we can trust God to do what is right. He will cleanse us from all the wrongs we have done. [10]If we say we have not sinned, we make God a liar, and we do not accept God's teaching.

JESUS IS OUR HELPER

2

My dear children, I write this letter to you so you will not sin. But if anyone does sin, we have a helper in the presence of the Father—Jesus Christ, the One who does what is right. [2]He died in our place to take away our sins, and not only our sins but the sins of all people.

[3]We can be sure that we know God if we obey his commands. [4]Anyone who says, "I know God," but does not obey God's commands is a liar, and the truth is not in that person. [5]But if someone obeys God's teaching, then in that person God's love has truly reached its goal. This is how we can be sure we are living in God: [6]Whoever says that he lives in God must live as Jesus lived.

THE COMMAND TO LOVE OTHERS

[7]My dear friends, I am not writing a new command to you but an old command you have had from the beginning. It is the teaching you have already heard. [8]But also I am writing a new command to you, and you can see its truth in Jesus and in you, because the darkness is passing away, and the true light is already shining.

[9]Anyone who says, "I am in the light,"[n] but hates a brother or sister, is still in the darkness. [10]Whoever loves a brother or sister lives in the light and will not cause anyone to stumble in his faith. [11]But whoever hates a brother or sister is in darkness, lives in darkness, and does not know where to go, because the darkness has made that person blind.

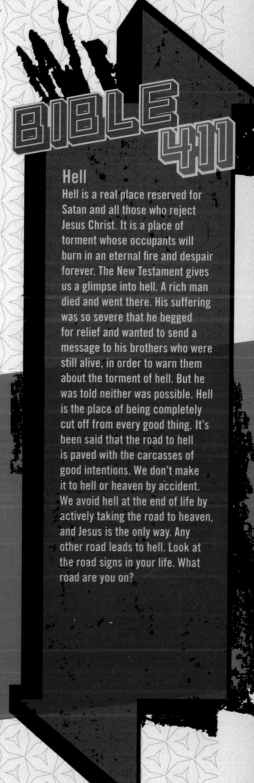

Hell

Hell is a real place reserved for Satan and all those who reject Jesus Christ. It is a place of torment whose occupants will burn in an eternal fire and despair forever. The New Testament gives us a glimpse into hell. A rich man died and went there. His suffering was so severe that he begged for relief and wanted to send a message to his brothers who were still alive, in order to warn them about the torment of hell. But he was told neither was possible. Hell is the place of being completely cut off from every good thing. It's been said that the road to hell is paved with the carcasses of good intentions. We don't make it to hell or heaven by accident. We avoid hell at the end of life by actively taking the road to heaven, and Jesus is the only way. Any other road leads to hell. Look at the road signs in your life. What road are you on?

GOD DOESN'T JUST HAVE LOVE; HE is LOVE

1:1 Word The Greek word is "logos," meaning any kind of communication. Here, it means Christ, who was the way God told people about himself. **1:4 so . . . joy** Some Greek copies read "so you may be full of joy." **1:5; 2:9 light** Here, it is used as a symbol of God's goodness or truth.

¹²I write to you, dear children,
   because your sins are forgiven
      through Christ.
¹³I write to you, fathers,
   because you know the One who
      existed from the beginning.
I write to you, young people,
   because you have defeated the
      Evil One.
¹⁴I write to you, children,
   because you know the Father.
I write to you, fathers,
   because you know the One who
      existed from the beginning.
I write to you, young people,
   because you are strong;
      the teaching of God lives in you,
      and you have defeated the Evil One.
¹⁵Do not love the world or the things
in the world. If you love the world, the
love of the Father is not in you. ¹⁶These
are the ways of the world: wanting to
please our sinful selves, wanting the sinful things we see, and being too proud
of what we have. None of these come
from the Father, but all of them come
from the world. ¹⁷The world and everything that people want in it are passing
away, but the person who does what God
wants lives forever.

REJECT THE ENEMIES OF CHRIST

¹⁸My dear children, these are the last
days. You have heard that the enemy of
Christ is coming, and now many enemies
of Christ are already here. This is how
we know that these are the last days.
¹⁹These enemies of Christ were in our
fellowship, but they left us. They never
really belonged to us; if they had been a
part of us, they would have stayed with
us. But they left, and this shows that
none of them really belonged to us.

²⁰You have the gift ⁿ that the Holy One
gave you, so you all know the truth.ⁿ ²¹I
do not write to you because you do not
know the truth but because you do know
the truth. And you know that no lie
comes from the truth.
²²Who is the liar? It is the person who
does not accept Jesus as the Christ. This
is the enemy of Christ: the person who
does not accept the Father and his Son.
²³Whoever does not accept the Son does
not have the Father. But whoever confesses the Son has the Father, too.
²⁴Be sure you continue to follow the
teaching you heard from the beginning.
If you continue to follow what you heard
from the beginning, you will stay in the
Son and in the Father. ²⁵And this is what
the Son promised to us—life forever.
²⁶I am writing this letter about those
people who are trying to lead you the
wrong way. ²⁷Christ gave you a special
gift that is still in you, so you do not
need any other teacher. His gift teaches
you about everything, and it is true, not
false. So continue to live in Christ, as his
gift taught you.

IMPACT!

The Cross Movement

Cross Movement Ministries, Inc. trains others to use their talents for the purpose of evangelism. The purpose is to encourage Christians who are a part of the hip-hop community to counter the secular philosophies of hip-hop with biblical ones. The independent record label and brother of the ministry is Cross Movement Records. They recently signed a deal with a major distributor to make sure the gospel is available in retail outlets throughout the U.S. Details on the ministry are available on their Web site www.crossmovement.com and info about the record label can be found on www.crossmovementrecords.com. There you can learn about the artists involved in the movement, view their concert schedule, listen to the latest tracks, or get info about how to submit a demo.

2:20 gift This might mean the Holy Spirit, or it might mean teaching or truth as in verse 24.   2:20 you . . . truth Some Greek copies read "so you know all things."

28Yes, my dear children, live in him so that when Christ comes back, we can be without fear and not be ashamed in his presence. 29Since you know that Christ is righteous, you know that all who do right are God's children.

WE ARE GOD'S CHILDREN

3 The Father has loved us so much that we are called children of God. And we really are his children. The reason the people in the world do not know us is that they have not known him. 2Dear friends, now we are children of God, and we have not yet been shown what we will be in the future. But we know that when Christ comes again, we will be like him, because we will see him as he really is. 3Christ is pure, and all who have this hope in Christ keep themselves pure like Christ.

4The person who sins breaks God's law. Yes, sin is living against God's law. 5You know that Christ came to take away sins and that there is no sin in Christ. 6So anyone who lives in Christ does not go on sinning. Anyone who goes on sinning has never really understood Christ and has never known him.

7Dear children, do not let anyone lead you the wrong way. Christ is righteous. So to be like Christ a person must do what is right. 8The devil has been sinning since the beginning, so anyone who continues to sin belongs to the devil. The Son of God came for this purpose: to destroy the devil's work.

9Those who are God's children do not continue sinning, because the new life from God remains in them. They are not

THE SCRIPT

The Crucifixion
Matthew 27:32-61

Now it was still early when the chief priest and elders met together to plot out Jesus' fate.
They tied him up like a slave, took him out on parade for statement's sake.
Led him before Pilate who was Pontius, a racist ruler with little conscience.
"Tell me, what are the charges?" Pilate argued.
The religious leaders said Jesus was guilty of civil dissidence,
And Satan was fully into playin' the script; didn't know that the script was already writ,
So Pilate bit. Pontius brought Jesus before him and wanted to know:
"Are you the Jewish King?" Pilate questioned and Jesus asked, "Who do you think you're addressing?"
The Jews and others started yelling, things quickly were getting messy.
Yet Jesus stood unmoved by the commotion they were expressing.
Pilate tripped out how Jesus showed no emotion.
"His own people sold him out, and he still refused to speak up and oppose them."
Then Pilate had a notion: In fact it was his own custom during the Jews' Passover Feast
To release a prisoner, someone the crowd had chosen.
So Pilate brought out a well-known captive named Barabbas,
Stood him next to Jesus like the two were in a balance.
Then he left it to the masses. Whoever they chose to condemn would catch it.
Persuaded by the elders (and the devil), the masses asked to release Barabbas.
"And what about Jesus of Nazareth?" Pilate asked again.
The crowd was in full frenzy, and cried out, "Crucify him!"
There was no denying them. So Pilate washed his hands of it.
Next, the Roman soldiers took hold of Jesus, leading him to the Praetorian:
It was brutal when they stripped him down; robed him in red and platted a crown of thorns and then
Placed the thorns on his skull and forced them in! Of course, it was just the beginning of their distorted sport.

They tied him up and whipped him till his back was raw
And all you saw was mangled carnage of the grossest sort.
Far from over, the soldiers beat him, till he could no longer stand, then placed the cross upon his shoulders.
Jesus couldn't hold it, in fact, he fell under the weight. So they found a Cyrene named Simon
And forced him to carry the heavy, wooden stake. They made it to the place called Golgotha.
While the angels and demons watched the unfolding, Creation nailed the Creator to a cross and propped him
Up for history to see: from B.C. to A.D. Jesus cried in agony even though he knew
And accepted his fate and agreed to go through it.
He could have come down from that cross, calling on angels by the legions.
But Jesus gave up his life with full knowledge of the reason.
"Father, father, why have you forsaken me! *Eli, Eli lama sabachthani!*
Asphyxiation through crucifixion. Jesus' destiny was to die for all men, women, and children's sin.
It was God's will when Jesus, fully yielding, releasing his last breath, obedience killed him.

Take this with you: Whenever this life's journey pulls you from your path and you feel lost, remember that up on the cross, God found you.

able to go on sinning, because they have become children of God. [10]So we can see who God's children are and who the devil's children are: Those who do not do what is right are not God's children, and those who do not love their brothers and sisters are not God's children.

WE MUST LOVE EACH OTHER

[11]This is the teaching you have heard from the beginning: We must love each other. [12]Do not be like Cain who belonged to the Evil One and killed his brother. And why did he kill him? Because the things Cain did were evil, and the things his brother did were good.

[13]Brothers and sisters, do not be surprised when the people of the world hate you. [14]We know we have left death and have come into life because we love each other. Whoever does not love is still dead. [15]Everyone who hates a brother or sister is a murderer,[n] and you know that no murderers have eternal life in them. [16]This is how we know what real love is: Jesus gave his life for us. So we should give our lives for our brothers and sisters. [17]Suppose someone has enough to live and sees a brother or sister in need, but does not help. Then God's love is not living in that person. [18]My children, we should love people not only with words and talk, but by our actions and true caring.

[19-20]This is the way we know that we belong to the way of truth. When our hearts make us feel guilty, we can still have peace before God. God is greater than our hearts, and he knows everything. [21]My dear friends, if our hearts do not make us feel guilty, we can come without fear into God's presence. [22]And God gives us what we ask for because we obey God's commands and do what pleases him. [23]This is what God commands: that we believe in his Son, Jesus Christ, and that we love each other, just as he commanded. [24]The people who obey God's commands live in God, and God lives in them. We know that God lives in us because of the Spirit God gave us.

He's got answers

I don't like the direction my life is going, but I don't know how to do anything else. Will becoming a Christian fix my life?

When you become a Christian, you become a whole new person. In God's eyes, everything in your past is gone. Sometimes God will totally redirect your life and make everything great. But, most of the time, the changes are more gradual. God may not "fix" your life immediately, but he will definitely give you the tools you need in order to change.

The most important tool he gives is his Holy Spirit. Jesus called him "the Comforter," and that is a great description. His job is to change us into the image of Christ. He teaches us to live a righteous life. He helps us to understand the Bible, which can be a pretty tough book to understand. He even prays for us when we don't know how to pray for ourselves.

Becoming a Christian doesn't guarantee everything will be perfect, but you will be headed in the right direction spiritually and things will most definitely start getting better.

Read on: John 14:16-27; Romans 8; 2 Corinthians 5:5-17

WARNING AGAINST FALSE TEACHERS

 My dear friends, many false prophets have gone out into the world. So do not believe every spirit, but test the spirits to see if they are from God. [2]This is how you can know God's Spirit: Every spirit who confesses that Jesus Christ came to earth as a human is from God. [3]And every spirit who refuses to say this about Jesus is not from God. It is the spirit of the enemy of Christ, which you have heard is coming, and now he is already in the world.

[4]My dear children, you belong to God and have defeated them; because God's Spirit, who is in you, is greater than the devil, who is in the world. [5]And they belong to the world, so what they say is from the world, and the world listens to them. [6]But we belong to God, and those who know God listen to us. But those who are not from God do not listen to us. That is how we know the Spirit that is true and the spirit that is false.

LOVE COMES FROM GOD

[7]Dear friends, we should love each other, because love comes from God. Everyone who loves has become God's child and knows God. [8]Whoever does not love does not know God, because God is love. [9]This is how God showed his love to us: He sent his one and only Son into the world so that we could have life through him. [10]This is what real love is: It is not

---

 3:15 Everyone . . . murderer If one person hates a brother or sister, then in the heart that person has killed that brother or sister. Jesus taught about this sin to his followers (Matthew 5:21-26).

our love for God; it is God's love for us. He sent his Son to die in our place to take away our sins.

[11]Dear friends, if God loved us that much we also should love each other. [12]No one has ever seen God, but if we love each other, God lives in us, and his love is made perfect in us.

[13]We know that we live in God and he lives in us, because he gave us his Spirit. [14]We have seen and can testify that the Father sent his Son to be the Savior of the world. [15]Whoever confesses that Jesus is the Son of God has God living inside, and that person lives in God. [16]And so we know the love that God has for us, and we trust that love.

God is love. Those who live in love live in God, and God lives in them. [17]This is how love is made perfect in us: that we can be without fear on the day God judges us, because in this world we are like him. [18]Where God's love is, there is no fear, because God's perfect love drives out fear. It is punishment that makes a person fear, so love is not made perfect in the person who fears.

[19]We love because God first loved us. [20]If people say, "I love God," but hate their brothers or sisters, they are liars. Those who do not love their brothers and sisters, whom they have seen, cannot love God, whom they have never seen. [21]And God gave us this command: Those who love God must also love their brothers and sisters.

FAITH IN THE SON OF GOD

5 Everyone who believes that Jesus is the Christ is God's child, and whoever loves the Father also loves the Father's children. [2]This is how we know we love God's children: when we love God and obey his commands. [3]Loving God means obeying his commands. And God's commands are not too hard for us, [4]because everyone who is a child of God conquers the world.

And this is the victory that conquers the world—our faith. [5]So the one who conquers the world is the person who believes that Jesus is the Son of God.

[6]Jesus Christ is the One who came by water[n] and blood.[n] He did not come by water only, but by water and blood. And the Spirit says that this is true, because the Spirit is the truth. [7]So there are three witnesses:[n] [8]the Spirit, the water, and the blood; and these three witnesses agree. [9]We believe people when they say something is true. But what God says is more important, and he has told us the truth about his own Son. [10]Anyone who believes in the Son of God has the truth that God told us. Anyone who does not believe makes God a liar, because that person does not believe what God told us about his Son. [11]This is what God told us: God has given us eternal life, and this life is in his Son. [12]Whoever has the Son has life, but whoever does not have the Son of God does not have life.

WE HAVE ETERNAL LIFE NOW

[13]I write this letter to you who believe in the Son of God so you will know you have eternal life. [14]And this is the boldness we have in God's presence: that if we ask God for anything that agrees with what he wants, he hears us. [15]If we know he hears us every time we ask him, we know we have what we ask from him.

[16]If anyone sees a brother or sister sinning (sin that does not lead to eternal death), that person should pray, and God will give the sinner life. I am talking about people whose sin does not lead to eternal death. There is sin that leads to death. I do not mean that a person should pray about that sin. [17]Doing wrong is always sin, but there is sin that does not lead to eternal death.

[18]We know that those who are God's children do not continue to sin. The Son of God keeps them safe, and the Evil One cannot touch them. [19]We know that we belong to God, but the Evil One controls

VIEWPOINT

WHAT HAS BEEN THE GREATEST SOURCE OF PAIN IN YOUR LIFE AND HOW HAS IT HELPED YOU TO GROW?

The times I stepped away from God are the most painful times of my past. Being separated from God was not only heart-breaking, but tormenting as well. The loneliness and need for connection to the Lord was a terrible experience.

the whole world. [20]We also know that the Son of God has come and has given us understanding so that we can know the True One. And our lives are in the True One and in his Son, Jesus Christ. He is the true God and the eternal life.

[21]So, dear children, keep yourselves away from false gods.

 5:6 water This probably means the water of Jesus' baptism.   **5:6 blood** This probably means the blood of Jesus' death.   **5:7–8 So . . . witnesses** A few very late Greek copies and the Latin Vulgate continue, "in heaven: the Father, the Word, and the Holy Spirit, and these three witnesses agree. [8]And there are three witnesses on earth:"

2 JOHN

[1]From the Elder.[n]

To the chosen lady[n] and her children:

I love all of you in the truth,[n] and all those who know the truth love you. [2]We love you because of the truth that lives in us and will be with us forever.

[3]Grace, mercy, and peace from God the Father and his Son, Jesus Christ, will be with us in truth and love.

[4]I was very happy to learn that some of your children are following the way of truth, as the Father commanded us. [5]And now, dear lady, this is not a new command but is the same command we have had from the beginning. I ask you that we all love each other. [6]And love means living the way God commanded us to live. As you have heard from the beginning, his command is this: Live a life of love.

[7]Many false teachers are in the world now who do not confess that Jesus Christ came to earth as a human. Anyone who does not confess this is a false teacher and an enemy of Christ. [8]Be careful yourselves that you do not lose everything you[n] have worked for, but that you receive your full reward.

[9]Anyone who goes beyond Christ's teaching and does not continue to follow only his teaching does not have God. But whoever continues to follow the teaching of Christ has both the Father and the Son. [10]If someone comes to you and does not bring this teaching, do not welcome or accept that person into your house. [11]If you welcome such a person, you share in the evil work.

[12]I have many things to write to you, but I do not want to use paper and ink. Instead, I hope to come to you and talk face to face so we can be full of joy. [13]The children of your chosen sister[n] greet you.

3 JOHN

[1]From the Elder.[n]

To my dear friend Gaius, whom I love in the truth:[n]

[2]My dear friend, I know your soul is doing fine, and I pray that you are doing well in every way and that your health is good. [3]I was very happy when some brothers and sisters came and told me about the

---

1 Elder "Elder" means an older person. It can also mean a special leader in the church (as in Titus 1:5).   **1 lady** This might mean a woman, or in this letter it might mean a church. If it is a church, then "her children" would be the people of the church.   **1 truth** The truth or "Good News" about Jesus Christ that joins all believers together.   **8 you** Some Greek copies read "we."   **13 sister** Sister of the "lady" in verse 1. This might be another woman or another church.
1 Elder "Elder" means an older person. It can also mean a special leader in the church (as in Titus 1:5).   **1 truth** The truth or "Good News" about Jesus Christ that joins all believers together.

DEEP ISSUES

Single Parenting

No matter how it happened, being a single parent is hard work. It can be stressful, frustrating, intense, hectic, and it takes all you have just to go from day to day. It's a lonely place, and for some, even a frightening place. The responsibility of another life is totally on your shoulders. You're right if you're feeling as though you can't do it on your own. Ideally, being a parent was never meant to be a solo job. Without a partner, raising a child is a daunting task; but you can do it with God's help.

It is very important that you maintain your relationship with God. This will give you the strength, focus, and patience you need to raise strong, well-adjusted children. Matthew 6:33 says, "The thing you should want most is God's kingdom and doing what God wants. Then all these other things you need will be given to you." By keeping your mind on the things of God, you will be better able to focus on the values and strengths you want to instill in your child. Remember, you have the awesome privilege and responsibility of shaping this young life. Much of what you do can pave the way for a happy fulfilling future, or set in motion events that could cause lifelong struggle and insecurity. Above all, the most important thing any parent can give their child is total, unconditional love. By and large, if you truly love your children and determine to make sure they know, you are well on your way to successful parenthood.

truth in your life and how you are following the way of truth. [4]Nothing gives me greater joy than to hear that my children are following the way of truth.

[5]My dear friend, it is good that you help the brothers and sisters, even those you do not know. [6]They told the church about your love. Please help them to continue their trip in a way worthy of God. [7]They started out in service to Christ, and they have been accepting nothing from nonbelievers. [8]So we should help such people; when we do, we share in their work for the truth.

[9]I wrote something to the church, but Diotrephes, who loves to be their leader, will not listen to us. [10]So if I come, I will talk about what Diotrephes is doing, about how he lies and says evil things about us. But more than that, he refuses to accept the other brothers and sisters; he even stops those who do want to accept them and puts them out of the church.

[11]My dear friend, do not follow what is bad; follow what is good. The one who does good belongs to God. But the one who does evil has never known God.

[12]Everyone says good things about Demetrius, and the truth agrees with what they say. We also speak well of him, and you know what we say is true.

[13]I have many things I want to write you, but I do not want to use pen and ink. [14]I hope to see you soon and talk face to face. [15]Peace to you. The friends here greet you. Please greet each friend there by name.

HeartCry

Love **Does real love sometimes seem an alien concept? Have you ever known true love or wondered exactly what it is? Would you like to? Let your heart cry . . .**

Hello, God. I know the Bible says that you are love, but what does that mean? What is love? Folks talk about loving their cars and their houses. Men say they love their wives and then beat them. Mothers are supposed to love their children, but just look how many kids end up on the streets 'cause no one really cares. God, I really don't know what love looks like, so I guess I don't know what you look like either. Can you give me a little help here? Can you tell me something to help me get you?

Love is all that is good and holy put into action. Love is constant. It does not end when disappointment comes. Love is sacrificing, always putting the needs of another first. If you wish to see me, look at my Son. If you wish to see love, look at Jesus. Song of Solomon; 1 Corinthians 13:4

STAND UP FOR THE REAL FAITH

JUDE

Jude is a letter written to an unknown church as a faith builder and a heads-up warning that undercover preachers were running game on folks. Jude told this church to stand up for the real faith. He gave them clues that would expose the false preachers: sexual immorality, rebelliousness, self-serving attitude, complaining, greed and straight-up mess. Jude didn't want anybody to walk away from God or bump the church because of these messed up men.

The only way to make sure you don't fall for lies is to be sure of the truth. It is important that you seek God and make every effort to know him. Then, when the con has your ear, God knows your heart and will keep you straight, even when it's hard to tell who's real and who's fake.

¹From Jude, a servant of Jesus Christ and a brother of James.

To all who have been called by God. God the Father loves you, and you have been kept safe in Jesus Christ:

²Mercy, peace, and love be yours richly.

GOD WILL PUNISH SINNERS

³Dear friends, I wanted very much to write you about the salvation we all share. But I felt the need to write you about something else: I want to encourage you to fight hard for the faith that was given the holy people of God once and for all time. ⁴Some people have secretly entered your group. Long ago the prophets wrote about these people who will be judged guilty. They are against God and have changed the grace of our God into a reason for sexual sin. They also refuse to accept Jesus Christ, our only Master and Lord.

⁵I want to remind you of some things you already know: Remember that the Lord[n] saved his people by bringing them out of the land of Egypt. But later he destroyed all those who did not believe. ⁶And remember the angels who did not keep their place of power but left their proper home. The Lord has kept these angels in darkness, bound with everlasting chains, to be judged on the great day. ⁷Also remember the cities of Sodom and Gomorrah[n] and the other towns around them. In the same way they were full of sexual sin and people who desired sexual relations that God does not allow. They suffer the punishment of eternal fire, as an example for all to see.

⁸It is the same with these people who have entered your group. They are guided by dreams and make themselves filthy with sin. They reject God's authority and speak against the angels. ⁹Not even the archangel[n] Michael, when he argued with the devil about who would have the body of Moses, dared to judge the devil guilty. Instead, he said, "The Lord punish you." ¹⁰But these people speak against things they do not understand. And what they do know, by feeling, as dumb animals know things, are the very things that destroy them. ¹¹It will be terrible for them. They have followed the way of Cain, and for money they have given themselves to doing the wrong that Balaam did. They have fought against God as Korah did, and like Korah, they surely will be destroyed. ¹²They are like dirty spots in your special Christian meals you share. They eat with you and have no fear, caring only for themselves. They are clouds without rain, which the wind blows around. They are autumn trees without fruit that are pulled out of the ground. So they are twice dead. ¹³They are like wild waves of the sea, tossing up their own shameful actions like foam. They are like stars that wander in the sky. A place in the blackest darkness has been kept for them forever.

¹⁴Enoch, the seventh descendant from Adam, said about these people: "Look, the Lord is coming with many thousands of his holy angels to ¹⁵judge every person. He is coming to punish all who are against God for all the evil they have done against him. And he will punish the sinners who are against God for all the evil they have said against him."

¹⁶These people complain and blame others, doing the evil things they want to do. They brag about themselves, and they flatter others to get what they want.

A WARNING AND THINGS TO DO

¹⁷Dear friends, remember what the apostles of our Lord Jesus Christ said before. ¹⁸They said to you, "In the last times there will be people who laugh about God, following their own evil desires which are against God." ¹⁹These are the people who divide you, people whose thoughts are only of this world, who do not have the Spirit.

²⁰But dear friends, use your most holy faith to build yourselves up, praying in the Holy Spirit. ²¹Keep yourselves in God's love as you wait for the Lord Jesus Christ with his mercy to give you life forever.

²²Show mercy to some people who have doubts. ²³Take others out of the fire, and save them. Show mercy mixed with fear to others, hating even their clothes which are dirty from sin.

PRAISE GOD

²⁴God is strong and can help you not to fall. He can bring you before his glory without any wrong in you and can give you great joy. ²⁵He is the only God, the One who saves us. To him be glory, greatness, power, and authority through Jesus Christ our Lord for all time past, now, and forever. Amen.

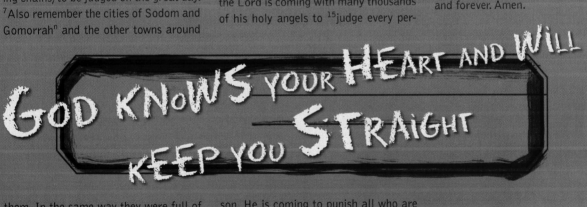

GOD KNOWS YOUR HEART AND WILL KEEP YOU STRAIGHT

5 the Lord Some Greek copies read "Jesus." **7 Sodom and Gomorrah** Two cities God destroyed because they were so evil. **9 archangel** The leader among God's angels or messengers.

REVELATION

HE'S COMING BACK BEFORE YOU KNOW IT

The Revelation is an "off the chain" end time vision experienced and written by the Apostle John. Revelation breaks down the crazy chain of events leading up to Jesus' ultimate battle against Satan and his demonic crew. It reveals the fate of all those who do not belong to Jesus Christ. God will put the fire on those in the earth who got so caught up doing their dirt that they refused God's free gift of eternal life. In the end, it's all good for those who are down with Christ. The "saints" made righteous by Jesus' blood sacrifice will be from every street corner, hood, state, country and continent. Heaven will be a melting pot of nations, colors, and creeds. Whites, Blacks, Latinos, and Asians, all in complete unity with one love for Jesus.

The end of the book rolls out a picture of heaven made of nothing but pure gold, platinum, and ice, the eternal hang out for the saints. There will be no more Death, Drama, or Pain. At the end of this book God invites those who are dying of spiritual thirst to get full on the living water. He's coming back before you know it. Are you down with the King? Peace.

1 This is the revelation[n] of Jesus Christ, which God gave to him, to show his servants what must soon happen. And Jesus sent his angel to show it to his servant John, ²who has told everything he has seen. It is the word of God; it is the message from Jesus Christ. ³Blessed is the one who reads the words of God's message, and blessed are the people who hear this message and do what is written in it. The time is near when all of this will happen.

JESUS' MESSAGE TO THE CHURCHES

⁴From John.

To the seven churches in Asia:

Grace and peace to you from the One who is and was and is coming, and from the seven spirits before his throne, ⁵and from Jesus Christ. Jesus is the faithful witness, the first among those raised from the dead. He is the ruler of the kings of the earth.

He is the One who loves us, who made us free from our sins with the blood of his death. ⁶He made us to be a kingdom of priests who serve God his Father. To Jesus Christ be glory and power forever and ever! Amen.

⁷Look, Jesus is coming with the clouds, and everyone will see him, even those who stabbed him. And all peoples of the earth will cry loudly because of him. Yes, this will happen! Amen.

⁸The Lord God says, "I am the Alpha and the Omega.[n] I am the One who is and was and is coming. I am the Almighty."

⁹I, John, am your brother. All of us share with Christ in suffering, in the kingdom, and in patience to continue. I was on the island of Patmos,[n] because I had preached the word of God and the message about Jesus. ¹⁰On the Lord's day I was in the Spirit, and I heard a loud voice behind me that sounded like a trumpet. ¹¹The voice said, "Write what you see in a book and send it to the seven churches: to Ephesus, Smyrna, Pergamum, Thyatira, Sardis, Philadelphia, and Laodicea."

¹²I turned to see who was talking to me. When I turned, I saw seven golden lampstands ¹³and someone among the lampstands who was "like a Son of Man."[n] He was dressed in a long robe and had a gold band around his chest. ¹⁴His head and hair were white like wool, as white as snow, and his eyes were like flames of fire. ¹⁵His feet were like bronze that glows hot in a furnace, and his voice was like the noise of flooding water. ¹⁶He held seven stars in his right hand, and a sharp double-edged sword came out of his mouth. He looked like the sun shining at its brightest time.

¹⁷When I saw him, I fell down at his feet like a dead man. He put his right hand on me and said, "Do not be afraid. I am the First and the Last. ¹⁸I am the One who lives; I was dead, but look, I am alive forever and ever! And I hold the keys to death and to the place of the dead. ¹⁹So write the things you see, what is now and what will happen later. ²⁰Here is the secret of the seven stars that you saw in my right hand and the seven golden lampstands: The seven lampstands are the seven churches, and the seven stars are the angels of the seven churches.

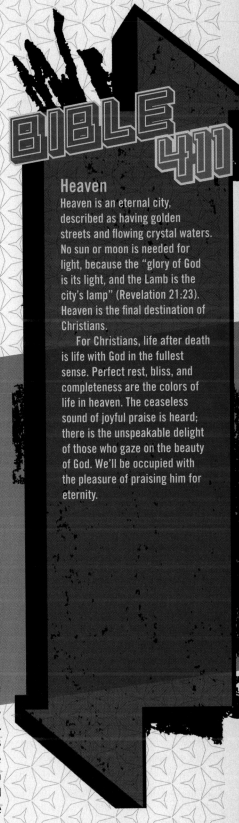

Heaven

Heaven is an eternal city, described as having golden streets and flowing crystal waters. No sun or moon is needed for light, because the "glory of God is its light, and the Lamb is the city's lamp" (Revelation 21:23). Heaven is the final destination of Christians.

For Christians, life after death is life with God in the fullest sense. Perfect rest, bliss, and completeness are the colors of life in heaven. The ceaseless sound of joyful praise is heard; there is the unspeakable delight of those who gaze on the beauty of God. We'll be occupied with the pleasure of praising him for eternity.

 1:1 revelation Making known truth that has been hidden. **1:8 Alpha and the Omega** The first and last letters of the Greek alphabet. This means "the beginning and the end." **1:9 Patmos** A small island in the Aegean Sea, near the coast of Asia Minor (modern Turkey). **1:13 "like . . . Man"** "Son of Man" is a name Jesus called himself.

TO THE CHURCH IN EPHESUS

2 "Write this to the angel of the church in Ephesus:

"The One who holds the seven stars in his right hand and walks among the seven golden lampstands says this: [2]I know what you do, how you work hard and never give up. I know you do not put up with the false teachings of evil people. You have tested those who say they are apostles but really are not, and you found they are liars. [3]You have patience and have suffered troubles for my name and have not given up.

[4]"But I have this against you: You have left the love you had in the beginning. [5]So remember where you were before you fell. Change your hearts and do what you did at first. If you do not change, I will come to you and will take away your lampstand from its place. [6]But there is something you do that is right: You hate what the Nicolaitans[n] do, as much as I.

[7]"Every person who has ears should listen to what the Spirit says to the churches. To those who win the victory I will give the right to eat the fruit from the tree of life, which is in the garden of God.

TO THE CHURCH IN SMYRNA

[8]"Write this to the angel of the church in Smyrna:

"The One who is the First and the Last, who died and came to life again, says this: [9]I know your troubles and that you are poor, but really you are rich! I know the bad things some people say about you. They say they are Jews, but they are not true Jews. They are a synagogue that belongs to Satan. [10]Do not be afraid of what you are about to suffer. I tell you, the devil will put some of you in prison to test you, and you will suffer for ten days. But be faithful, even if you have to die, and I will give you the crown of life.

[11]"Everyone who has ears should listen to what the Spirit says to the churches. Those who win the victory will not be hurt by the second death.

He's got answers

What does a Christian look like? What are the characteristics of a Christian?

Christians look like everyone and anyone. In heaven we will look around and see every "nation, tongue, and tribe" represented. God has not excluded anyone from having the free gift of salvation. It's there for each of us to accept or reject. Once we become Christians, the Lord begins to transform us as we allow him to mold us. To the degree that we are open to the work of the Lord in our lives, we begin to look more and more like Jesus in our attitudes and our actions. The transforming power of God begins on the inside and change appears on the outside in the form of fruit: love, joy, peace, patience, kindness, goodness, faithfulness, gentleness, and self-control.

Read on: Matthew 7:15-23; 25:31-46; Romans 8:9-14, 29; Colossians 3:12-17; Galatians 5:16-25; James 1:26-27

TO THE CHURCH IN PERGAMUM

[12]"Write this to the angel of the church in Pergamum:

"The One who has the sharp, double-edged sword says this: [13]I know where you live. It is where Satan has his throne. But you are true to me. You did not refuse to tell about your faith in me even during the time of Antipas, my faithful witness who was killed in your city, where Satan lives.

[14]"But I have a few things against you: You have some there who follow the teaching of Balaam. He taught Balak how to cause the people of Israel to sin by eating food offered to idols and by taking part in sexual sins. [15]You also have some who follow the teaching of the Nicolaitans.[n] [16]So change your hearts and lives. If you do not, I will come to you quickly and fight against them with the sword that comes out of my mouth.

[17]"Everyone who has ears should listen to what the Spirit says to the churches.

"I will give some of the hidden manna to everyone who wins the victory. I will also give to each one who wins the victory a white stone with a new name written on it. No one knows this new name except the one who receives it.

TO THE CHURCH IN THYATIRA

[18]"Write this to the angel of the church in Thyatira:

"The Son of God, who has eyes that blaze like fire and feet like shining bronze, says this: [19]I know what you do. I know about your love, your faith, your service, and your patience. I know that you are doing more now than you did at first.

 2:6, 15 Nicolaitans This is the name of a religious group that followed false beliefs and ideas.

[20]"But I have this against you: You let that woman Jezebel spread false teachings. She says she is a prophetess, but by her teaching she leads my people to take part in sexual sins and to eat food that is offered to idols. [21]I have given her time to change her heart and turn away from her sin, but she does not want to change. [22]So I will throw her on a bed of suffering. And all those who take part in adultery with her will suffer greatly if they do not turn away from the wrongs she does. [23]I will also kill her followers. Then all the churches will know I am the One who searches hearts and minds, and I will repay each of you for what you have done.

[24]"But others of you in Thyatira have not followed her teaching and have not learned what some call Satan's deep secrets. I say to you that I will not put any other load on you. [25]Only continue in your loyalty until I come.

[26]"I will give power over the nations to everyone who wins the victory and continues to be obedient to me until the end.
[27] 'You will rule over them with an
     iron rod,
   as when pottery is broken into
     pieces.'   *Psalm 2:9*
[28]This is the same power I received from my Father. I will also give him the morning star. [29]Everyone who has ears should listen to what the Spirit says to the churches.

TO THE CHURCH IN SARDIS

3 "Write this to the angel of the church in Sardis:

"The One who has the seven spirits and the seven stars says this: I know what you do. People say that you are alive, but really you are dead. [2]Wake up! Strengthen what you have left before it dies completely. I have found that what you are doing is less than what my God wants. [3]So do not forget what you have received and heard. Obey it, and change your hearts and lives. So you must wake up, or I will come like a thief, and you will not know when I will come to you. [4]But you have a few there in Sardis who have kept their clothes unstained, so they will walk with me and will wear white clothes, because they are worthy. [5]Those who win the victory will be dressed in white clothes like them. And I will not erase their names from the book of life, but I will say they belong to me before my Father and before his angels. [6]Everyone who has ears should listen to what the Spirit says to the churches.

TO THE CHURCH IN PHILADELPHIA

[7]"Write this to the angel of the church in Philadelphia:

"This is what the One who is holy and true, who holds the key of David, says. When he opens a door, no one can close it. And when he closes it, no one can open it. [8]I know what you do. I have put an open door before you, which no one can close. I know you have little strength, but you have obeyed my teaching and were not afraid to speak my name. [9]Those in the synagogue that belongs to Satan say they are Jews, but they are not true Jews; they are liars. I will make them come before you and bow at your feet, and they will know that I have loved you. [10]You have obeyed my teaching about not giving up your faith. So I will keep you from the time of trouble that will come to the whole world to test those who live on earth.

[11]"I am coming soon. Continue strong in your faith so no one will take away your crown. [12]I will make those who win the victory pillars in the temple of my God, and they will never have to leave it. I will write on them the name of my God and the name of the city of my God, the new Jerusalem,[n] that comes down out of heaven from my God. I will also write on them my new name. [13]Everyone who has ears should listen to what the Spirit says to the churches.

TO THE CHURCH IN LAODICEA

[14]"Write this to the angel of the church in Laodicea:

"The Amen,[n] the faithful and true witness, the ruler of all God has made, says this: [15]I know what you do, that you are not hot or cold. I wish that you were hot or cold! [16]But because you are lukewarm—neither hot, nor cold—I am ready to spit you out of my mouth. [17]You say, 'I am rich, and I have become wealthy and do not need anything.' But you do not know that you are really miserable, pitiful, poor, blind, and naked. [18]I advise you to buy from me gold made pure in fire so you can be truly rich. Buy from me white clothes so you can be clothed and so you can cover your shameful nakedness. Buy from me medicine to put on your eyes so you can truly see.

[19]"I correct and punish those whom I love. So be eager to do right, and change your hearts and lives. [20]Here I am! I stand at the door and knock. If you hear my voice and open the door, I will come in and eat with you, and you will eat with me.

[21]"Those who win the victory will sit with me on my throne in the same way that I won the victory and sat down with my Father on his throne. [22]Everyone who has ears should listen to what the Spirit says to the churches."

JOHN SEES HEAVEN

4 After the vision of these things I looked, and there before me was an open door in heaven. And the same voice that spoke to me before, that sounded like a trumpet, said, "Come up here, and I will show you what must happen after this." [2]Immediately I was in the Spirit, and before me was a throne in heaven, and someone was sitting on it. [3]The One who sat on the throne looked like precious stones, like jasper and carnelian. All around the throne was a rainbow the color of an emerald. [4]Around the throne there were twenty-four other thrones with twenty-four elders sitting on them. They were dressed in white and had golden crowns

---

3:12 Jerusalem This name is used to mean the spiritual city God built for his people. See Revelation 21–22. **3:14 Amen** Used here as a name for Jesus; it means to agree fully that something is true.

on their heads. [5]Lightning flashes and noises and thunder came from the throne. Before the throne seven lamps were burning, which are the seven spirits of God. [6]Also before the throne there was something that looked like a sea of glass, clear like crystal.

In the center and around the throne were four living creatures with eyes all over them, in front and in back. [7]The first living creature was like a lion. The second was like a calf. The third had a face like a man. The fourth was like a flying eagle. [8]Each of these four living creatures had six wings and was covered all over with eyes, inside and out. Day and night they never stop saying:

"Holy, holy, holy is the Lord God Almighty.

He was, he is, and he is coming."

[9]These living creatures give glory, honor, and thanks to the One who sits on the throne, who lives forever and ever. [10]Then the twenty-four elders bow down before the One who sits on the throne, and they worship him who lives forever and ever. They put their crowns down before the throne and say:

[11]"You are worthy, our Lord and God, to receive glory and honor and power,

because you made all things.

Everything existed and was made, because you wanted it."

5 Then I saw a scroll in the right hand of the One sitting on the throne. The scroll had writing on both sides and was kept closed with seven seals. [2]And I saw a powerful angel calling in a loud voice, "Who is worthy to break the seals and open the scroll?" [3]But there was no one in heaven or on earth or under the earth who could open the scroll or look inside it. [4]I cried bitterly because there was no one who was worthy to open the scroll or look inside. [5]But one of the elders said to me, "Do not cry! The Lion[n] from the tribe of Judah, David's descendant, has won the victory so that he is able to open the scroll and its seven seals."

[6]Then I saw a Lamb standing in the center of the throne and in the middle of the four living creatures and the elders. The Lamb looked as if he had been killed. He had seven horns and seven eyes, which are the seven spirits of God that were sent into all the world. [7]The Lamb came and took the scroll from the right hand of the One sitting on the throne. [8]When he took the scroll, the four living creatures and the twenty-four elders bowed down before the Lamb. Each one of them had a harp and golden bowls full of incense, which are the prayers of God's holy people. [9]And they all sang a new song to the Lamb:

"You are worthy to take the scroll and to open its seals,

because you were killed,

and with the blood of your death you bought people for God

from every tribe, language, people, and nation.

[10]You made them to be a kingdom of priests for our God,

and they will rule on the earth."

[11]Then I looked, and I heard the voices of many angels around the throne, and the four living creatures, and the elders. There were thousands and thousands of angels, [12]saying in a loud voice:

"The Lamb who was killed is worthy to receive power, wealth, wisdom, and strength,

honor, glory, and praise!"

[13]Then I heard all creatures in heaven and on earth and under the earth and in the sea saying:

"To the One who sits on the throne and to the Lamb

be praise and honor and glory and power

forever and ever."

[14]The four living creatures said, "Amen," and the elders bowed down and worshiped.

6 Then I watched while the Lamb opened the first of the seven seals. I heard one of the four living creatures say with a voice like thun-

der, "Come!" [2]I looked, and there before me was a white horse. The rider on the horse held a bow, and he was given a crown, and he rode out, determined to win the victory.

[3]When the Lamb opened the second seal, I heard the second living creature say, "Come!" [4]Then another horse came out, a red one. Its rider was given power to take away peace from the earth and to make people kill each other, and he was given a big sword.

[5]When the Lamb opened the third seal, I heard the third living creature say, "Come!" I looked, and there before me was a black horse, and its rider held a pair of scales in his hand. [6]Then I heard something that sounded like a voice coming from the middle of the four living creatures. The voice said, "A quart of wheat for a day's pay, and three quarts of barley for a day's pay, and do not damage the olive oil and wine!"

[7]When the Lamb opened the fourth seal, I heard the voice of the fourth living creature say, "Come!" [8]I looked, and there before me was a pale horse. Its rider was named death, and Hades[n] was following close behind him. They were given power over a fourth of the earth to kill people by war, by starvation, by disease, and by the wild animals of the earth.

[9]When the Lamb opened the fifth seal, I saw under the altar the souls of those who had been killed because they were faithful to the word of God and to the message they had received. [10]These souls shouted in a loud voice, "Holy and true Lord, how long until you judge the people of the earth and punish them for killing us?" [11]Then each one of them was given a white robe and was told to wait a short time longer. There were still some of their fellow servants and brothers and sisters in the service of Christ who must be killed as they were. They had to wait until all of this was finished.

[12]Then I watched while the Lamb opened the sixth seal, and there was a great earthquake. The sun became black

---

5:5 Lion Here refers to Christ. **6:8 Hades** The unseen world of the dead.

CONNECTED TO RIGHT RELATIONSHIPS:

LOOK DEEPER

It's true that we are made in God's image (Genesis 1:26). The ability to make our own choices is part of this legacy. The right to choose can bring us pain and suffering as well as joy and happiness. It all depends on the choices we make on the road to our destiny.

Adam was given dominion over all that God laid before him. God also made it clear that Adam could eat from any tree in the garden, except one. Every choice set before him was a right choice—except one. The choice Adam made by eating from the forbidden tree affected more than just his destiny. It affected the entire world for all time and severed his relationship with God. One bad choice altered Adam's future and the future of all people for all time.

Few things in life hold the power of relationships to affect our future and us. Many times, we are faced with choosing relationships with people that will maintain and enhance our relationship with God, or linking ourselves with those who will wreck and dismantle it. Like Adam, God will show us, through circumstance or revelation, the one choice that is best. Unfortunately, that same sinful nature that rose out of Adam often rises out of us. It can cause us to make choices that drag us away from God's divine plan for our lives and create deep emotional scars.

If the opportunity to date a Christian comes along, take it. A relationship with a Christian will enhance your chances of finding someone who really knows what it means to love and commit. You will find how fulfilling it can be to have a relationship that is pleasing to God.

like rough black cloth, and the whole moon became red like blood. ¹³And the stars in the sky fell to the earth like figs falling from a fig tree when the wind blows. ¹⁴The sky disappeared as a scroll when it is rolled up, and every mountain and island was moved from its place.

¹⁵Then the kings of the earth, the rulers, the generals, the rich people, the powerful people, the slaves, and the free people hid themselves in caves and in the rocks on the mountains. ¹⁶They called to the mountains and the rocks, "Fall on us. Hide us from the face of the One who sits on the throne and from the anger of the Lamb! ¹⁷The great day for their anger has come, and who can stand against it?"

THE 144,000 PEOPLE OF ISRAEL

7 After the vision of these things I saw four angels standing at the four corners of the earth. The angels were holding the four winds of the earth to keep them from blowing on the land or on the sea or on any tree. ²Then I saw another angel coming up from the east who had the seal of the living God. And he called out in a loud voice to the four angels to whom God had given power to harm the earth and the sea. ³He said to them, "Do not harm the land or the sea or the trees until we mark with a sign the foreheads of the people who serve our God." ⁴Then I heard how many people were marked with the sign. There were one hundred forty-four thousand from every tribe of the people of Israel.

⁵From the tribe of Judah twelve thousand were marked with the sign,
from the tribe of Reuben twelve thousand,
from the tribe of Gad twelve thousand,
⁶from the tribe of Asher twelve thousand,
from the tribe of Naphtali twelve thousand,

from the tribe of Manasseh twelve thousand,

[7]from the tribe of Simeon twelve thousand,

from the tribe of Levi twelve thousand,

from the tribe of Issachar twelve thousand,

[8]from the tribe of Zebulun twelve thousand,

from the tribe of Joseph twelve thousand,

and from the tribe of Benjamin twelve thousand were marked with the sign.

THE GREAT CROWD WORSHIPS GOD

[9]After the vision of these things I looked, and there was a great number of people, so many that no one could count them. They were from every nation, tribe, people, and language of the earth. They were all standing before the throne and before the Lamb, wearing white robes and holding palm branches in their hands. [10]They were shouting in a loud voice, "Salvation belongs to our God, who sits on the throne, and to the Lamb." [11]All the angels were standing around the throne and the elders and the four living creatures. They all bowed down on their faces before the throne and worshiped God, [12]saying, "Amen! Praise, glory, wisdom, thanks, honor, power, and strength belong to our God forever and ever. Amen!"

[13]Then one of the elders asked me, "Who are these people dressed in white robes? Where did they come from?"

[14]I answered, "You know, sir."

And the elder said to me, "These are the people who have come out of the great distress. They have washed their robes[n] and made them white in the blood of the Lamb. [15]Because of this, they are before the throne of God. They worship him day and night in his temple. And the One who sits on the throne will be present with them. [16]Those people will never be hungry again, and they will never be thirsty again. The sun will not hurt them, and no heat will burn them, [17]because the Lamb at the center of the throne will be their shepherd. He will lead them to springs of water that give life. And God will wipe away every tear from their eyes."

THE SEVENTH SEAL

8 When the Lamb opened the seventh seal, there was silence in heaven for about half an hour. [2]And I saw the seven angels who stand before God and to whom were given seven trumpets.

IMPACT!

Operation Hope

Economic Education and Digital Empowerment are the major programmatic areas of Operation Hope, an organization founded to help revitalize America's inner cities. Their goal is to move people from being renters to homeowners, from being check-cashing customers to bank account holders, and from being minimum-wage earners to living-wage earners. They also help people empower themselves through small-business ownership. They have other useful services including an Emergency Financial First Aid Kit that helps Americans minimize the financial impact of a natural disaster or national emergency. You can download the kit or get other information right from the Operation Hope Web site, www.operationhope.org. To speak with an Operation Hope case management worker, volunteer your time, or make an in-kind or monetary donation, call 1-323-290-2410.

 7:14 washed their robes This means they believed in Jesus so that their sins could be forgiven by Christ's blood.

³Another angel came and stood at the altar, holding a golden pan for incense. He was given much incense to offer with the prayers of all God's holy people. The angel put this offering on the golden altar before the throne. ⁴The smoke from the incense went up from the angel's hand to God with the prayers of God's people. ⁵Then the angel filled the incense pan with fire from the altar and threw it on the earth, and there were flashes of lightning, thunder and loud noises, and an earthquake.

THE SEVEN ANGELS AND TRUMPETS

⁶Then the seven angels who had the seven trumpets prepared to blow them.

⁷The first angel blew his trumpet, and hail and fire mixed with blood were poured down on the earth. And a third of the earth, and all the green grass, and a third of the trees were burned up.

⁸Then the second angel blew his trumpet, and something that looked like a big mountain, burning with fire, was thrown into the sea. And a third of the sea became blood, ⁹a third of the living things in the sea died, and a third of the ships were destroyed.

¹⁰Then the third angel blew his trumpet, and a large star, burning like a torch, fell from the sky. It fell on a third of the rivers and on the springs of water. ¹¹The name of the star is Wormwood.ⁿ And a third of all the water became bitter, and many people died from drinking the water that was bitter.

¹²Then the fourth angel blew his trumpet, and a third of the sun, and a third of the moon, and a third of the stars were struck. So a third of them became dark, and a third of the day was without light, and also the night.

¹³While I watched, I heard an eagle that was flying high in the air cry out in a loud voice, "Trouble! Trouble! Trouble for those who live on the earth because of the remaining sounds of the trumpets that the other three angels are about to blow!"

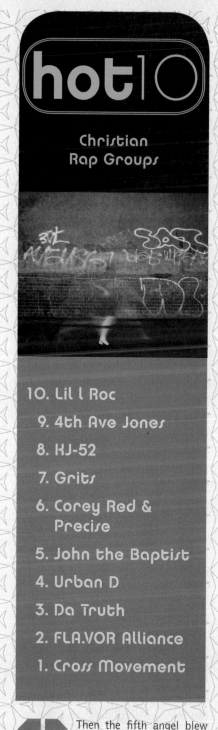

hot 10
Christian Rap Groups

10. Lil l Roc
9. 4th Ave Jones
8. KJ-52
7. Grits
6. Corey Red & Precise
5. John the Baptist
4. Urban D
3. Da Truth
2. FLA.VOR Alliance
1. Cross Movement

9 Then the fifth angel blew his trumpet, and I saw a star fall from the sky to the earth. The star was given the key to the deep hole that leads to the bottomless pit. ²Then it opened up the hole that leads to the bottomless pit, and smoke came up from the hole like smoke from a big furnace. Then the sun and sky became dark because of the smoke from the hole. ³Then locusts came down to the earth out of the smoke, and they were given the power to sting like scorpions.ⁿ ⁴They were told not to harm the grass on the earth or any plant or tree. They could harm only the people who did not have the sign of God on their foreheads. ⁵These locusts were not given the power to kill anyone, but to cause pain to the people for five months. And the pain they felt was like the pain a scorpion gives when it stings someone. ⁶During those days people will look for a way to die, but they will not find it. They will want to die, but death will run away from them.

⁷The locusts looked like horses prepared for battle. On their heads they wore what looked like crowns of gold, and their faces looked like human faces. ⁸Their hair was like women's hair, and their teeth were like lions' teeth. ⁹Their chests looked like iron breastplates, and the sound of their wings was like the noise of many horses and chariots hurrying into battle. ¹⁰The locusts had tails with stingers like scorpions, and in their tails was their power to hurt people for five months. ¹¹The locusts had a king who was the angel of the bottomless pit. His name in the Hebrew language is Abaddon and in the Greek language is Apollyon.ⁿ

¹²The first trouble is past; there are still two other troubles that will come.

¹³Then the sixth angel blew his trumpet, and I heard a voice coming from the horns on the golden altar that is before God. ¹⁴The voice said to the sixth angel who had the trumpet, "Free the four angels who are tied at the great river Euphrates." ¹⁵And they let loose the four angels who had been kept ready for this hour and day and month and year so they could kill a third of all people on the earth. ¹⁶I heard how many troops on horses were in their army—two hundred million.

¹⁷The horses and their riders I saw

 8:11 Wormwood Name of a very bitter plant; used here to give the idea of bitter sorrow. **9:3 scorpions** A scorpion is an insect that stings with a bad poison. **9:11 Abaddon, Apollyon** Both names mean "Destroyer."

in the vision looked like this: They had breastplates that were fiery red, dark blue, and yellow like sulfur. The heads of the horses looked like heads of lions, with fire, smoke, and sulfur coming out of their mouths. [18]A third of all the people on earth were killed by these three terrible disasters coming out of the horses' mouths: the fire, the smoke, and the sulfur. [19]The horses' power was in their mouths and in their tails; their tails were like snakes with heads, and with them they hurt people.

[20]The other people who were not killed by these terrible disasters still did not change their hearts and turn away from what they had made with their own hands. They did not stop worshiping demons and idols made of gold, silver, bronze, stone, and wood—things that cannot see or hear or walk. [21]These people did not change their hearts and turn away from murder or evil magic, from their sexual sins or stealing.

THE ANGEL AND THE SMALL SCROLL

10 Then I saw another powerful angel coming down from heaven dressed in a cloud with a rainbow over his head. His face was like the sun, and his legs were like pillars of fire. [2]The angel was holding a small scroll open in his hand. He put his right foot on the sea and his left foot on the land. [3]Then he shouted loudly like the roaring of a lion. And when he shouted, the voices of seven thunders spoke. [4]When the seven thunders spoke, I started to write. But I heard a voice from heaven say, "Keep hidden what the seven thunders said, and do not write them down."

[5]Then the angel I saw standing on the sea and on the land raised his right hand to heaven, [6]and he made a promise by the power of the One who lives forever and ever. He is the One who made the skies and all that is in them, the earth and all that is in it, and the sea and all that is in it. The angel promised, "There will be no more waiting! [7]In the days when the seventh angel is ready to blow his trumpet, God's secret will be finished. This secret is the Good News God told to his servants, the prophets."

[8]Then I heard the same voice from heaven again, saying to me: "Go and take the open scroll that is in the hand of the angel that is standing on the sea and on the land."

[9]So I went to the angel and told him to give me the small scroll. And he said to me, "Take the scroll and eat it. It will be sour in your stomach, but in your mouth it will be sweet as honey." [10]So I took the small scroll from the angel's hand and ate it. In my mouth it tasted sweet as honey, but after I ate it, it was sour in my stomach. [11]Then I was told, "You must prophesy again about many peoples, nations, languages, and kings."

THE TWO WITNESSES

11 I was given a measuring stick like a rod, and I was told, "Go and measure the temple of God and the altar, and count the people worshiping there. [2]But do not measure the yard outside the temple. Leave it alone, because it has been given to those who are not God's people. And they will trample on the holy city for forty-two months. [3]And I will give power to my two witnesses to prophesy for one thousand two hundred sixty days, and they will be dressed in rough cloth to show their sadness."

[4]These two witnesses are the two olive trees and the two lampstands that stand before the Lord of the earth. [5]And if anyone tries to hurt them, fire comes from their mouths and kills their enemies. And if anyone tries to hurt them in whatever way, in that same way that person will die. [6]These witnesses have the power to stop the sky from raining during the time they are prophesying. And they have power to make the waters become blood, and they have power to send every kind of trouble to the earth as many times as they want.

[7]When the two witnesses have finished telling their message, the beast that comes up from the bottomless pit will fight a war against them. He will defeat them and kill them. [8]The bodies of the two witnesses will lie in the street of the great city where the Lord was killed. This city is named Sodom[n] and Egypt, which has a spiritual meaning. [9]Those from every race of people, tribe, language, and nation will look at the bodies of the two witnesses for three and one-half days, and they will refuse to bury them. [10]People who live on the earth will rejoice and be happy because these two are dead. They will send each other gifts, because these two prophets brought much suffering to those who live on the earth.

[11]But after three and one-half days, God put the breath of life into the two prophets again. They stood on their feet, and everyone who saw them became very afraid. [12]Then the two prophets heard a loud voice from heaven saying, "Come up here!" And they went up into heaven in a cloud as their enemies watched.

[13]In the same hour there was a great earthquake, and a tenth of the city was destroyed. Seven thousand people were killed in the earthquake, and those who did not die were very afraid and gave glory to the God of heaven.

[14]The second trouble is finished. Pay attention: The third trouble is coming soon.

THE SEVENTH TRUMPET

[15]Then the seventh angel blew his trumpet. And there were loud voices in heaven, saying:

"The power to rule the world now

11:8 Sodom City that God destroyed because the people were so evil.

STEPPING UP

Though I was saved at age fourteen, went to church with my parents every week, and did my best to follow the Lord, my Christian values went out the window when I got older. I started doing what I wanted to do or what felt good at the time. My "relationship" with God was just a front for my friends at church and my parents. Eventually, I moved away from my parents, my church, and everything I knew. I went from living where people knew me and would hold me accountable to living in a major urban area where nobody knew my name. I realized that with all this new freedom, I could go buck wild. I was glad when I met a group of churchgoers. With them, church was the place to be on Sunday, and Jesus was everyone's homeboy. I was excited to finally get my act together and live right with Christ. I was also excited to have friends around me who would support that. I should have known Satan wasn't going to let me off that easy.

Slowly, I began to notice that some of those enthusiastic churchgoers were the ones who were getting drunk three times a week, hitting up every club on the weekend, and sleeping around. Then I would see them at church on Sunday praising the Lord. It was all too hypocritical to me. I realized that I didn't like the way these people were acting because it was two-faced. These churchgoers didn't last. As quickly as they came into my life they were gone, usually leaving some mess behind. But as they started to fall to my left and to my right, I turned to God. I returned to the faith I had learned as a child. God didn't fail me. He sat me down to look in the mirror. What those so-called friends had done was not much different than the holy front I had put on for my parents and friends back home. God is teaching me how to really live what I believe. I was one of those "Sunday Christians," a hypocrite. Don't be a half-way Christian: Go all out and seek God in everything you do.

James 1:6—Anyone who doubts is like a wave in the sea, blown up and down by the wind.

---

belongs to our Lord and his
  Christ,
  and he will rule forever and ever."
[16] Then the twenty-four elders, who sit on their thrones before God, bowed down on their faces and worshiped God. [17] They said:
  "We give thanks to you, Lord God
    Almighty,
  who is and who was,
  because you have used your great
    power
  and have begun to rule!
[18] The people of the world were angry, but your anger has come.
The time has come to judge the
    dead,
  and to reward your servants the
    prophets
  and your holy people,
  all who respect you, great and
    small.
The time has come to destroy those
  who destroy the earth!"
[19] Then God's temple in heaven was opened. The Ark that holds the agreement God gave to his people could be seen in his temple. Then there were flashes of lightning, noises, thunder, an earthquake, and a great hailstorm.

THE WOMAN AND THE DRAGON

12 And then a great wonder appeared in heaven: A woman was clothed with the sun, and the moon was under her feet, and a crown of twelve stars was on her head. [2] She was pregnant and cried out with pain, because she was about to give birth. [3] Then another wonder appeared in heaven: There was a giant red dragon with seven heads and seven crowns on each head. He also had ten horns. ⁴His tail swept a third of the stars out of the sky and threw them down to the earth. He stood in front of the woman who was ready to give birth so he could eat her baby as soon as it was born. ⁵Then the woman gave birth to a son who will rule all the nations with an iron rod. And her child was taken up to God and to his throne. ⁶The woman ran away into the desert to a place God prepared for her where she would be taken care of for one thousand two hundred sixty days.

⁷Then there was a war in heaven. Michael[n] and his angels fought against the dragon, and the dragon and his angels fought back. ⁸But the dragon was not strong enough, and he and his angels lost their place in heaven. ⁹The giant dragon was thrown down out of heaven. (He is that old snake called the devil or Satan, who tricks the whole world.) The dragon with his angels was thrown down to the earth.

He's got answers

Everyone gossips a little. What's the harm?

For some people, gossip is like an addiction. They can't seem to get through the day unless they dish dirt about someone. Gossiping hurts people. It makes light of the situations in someone's life and treats them like nothing more than a source of entertainment. Gossipers pass judgments on lives without knowing the facts, never giving the subject of their gossiping tongues a chance to defend themselves. The Bible groups gossipers in with the untrustworthy, the unloving, and the unrighteous—including murderers. Gossip is a sin and God hates sin.

Read on: Proverbs 11:13; Romans 1:28-32

PEEP THIS:

Many hip-hop leaders call themselves "Five Percenters," also known as "Nation of Gods and Earths." That phrase refers to one of the basic tenets of the Five Percent movement: Blacks are gods and women are earths. "Five Percent" refers to the belief that only five percent of all people knows and teaches the truth. These beliefs are not consistent with Christianity.

¹⁰Then I heard a loud voice in heaven saying:

"The salvation and the power and
    the kingdom of our God
and the authority of his Christ
    have now come.
The accuser of our brothers and sisters,
    who accused them day and night
    before our God,
    has been thrown down.
¹¹And our brothers and sisters
    defeated him
by the blood of the Lamb's death
    and by the message they
    preached.
They did not love their lives so much
    that they were afraid of death.
¹²So rejoice, you heavens
    and all who live there!
But it will be terrible for the earth
    and the sea,
because the devil has come down
    to you!
He is filled with anger,
    because he knows he does not
    have much time."

¹³When the dragon saw he had been thrown down to the earth, he hunted for the woman who had given birth to the son. ¹⁴But the woman was given the two wings of a great eagle so she could fly to the place prepared for her in the desert. There she would be taken care of for three and one-half years, away from the snake. ¹⁵Then the snake poured water out of its mouth like a river toward the woman so the flood would carry her away. ¹⁶But the earth helped the woman by opening its mouth and swallowing the river that came from the mouth of the dragon. ¹⁷Then the dragon was very angry at the woman, and he went off

12:7 Michael The archangel—leader among God's angels or messengers (Jude 9).

to make war against all her other children—those who obey God's commands and who have the message Jesus taught. [18]And the dragon[n] stood on the seashore.

THE TWO BEASTS

13 Then I saw a beast coming up out of the sea. It had ten horns and seven heads, and there was a crown on each horn. A name against God was written on each head. [2]This beast looked like a leopard, with feet like a bear's feet and a mouth like a lion's mouth. And the dragon gave the beast all of his power and his throne and great authority. [3]One of the heads of the beast looked as if it had been killed by a wound, but this death wound was healed. Then the whole world was amazed and followed the beast. [4]People worshiped the dragon because he had given his power to the beast. And they also worshiped the beast, asking, "Who is like the beast? Who can make war against it?"

[5]The beast was allowed to say proud words and words against God, and it was allowed to use its power for forty-two months. [6]It used its mouth to speak against God, against God's name, against the place where God lives, and against all those who live in heaven. [7]It was given power to make war against God's holy people and to defeat them. It was given power over every tribe, people, language, and nation. [8]And all who live on earth will worship the beast—all the people since the beginning of the world whose names are not written in the Lamb's book of life. The Lamb is the One who was killed.

[9]Anyone who has ears should listen:

[10]If you are to be a prisoner,
    then you will be a prisoner.
If you are to be killed with the
        sword,
    then you will be killed with the
        sword.

This means that God's holy people must have patience and faith.

[11]Then I saw another beast coming up out of the earth. It had two horns like a lamb, but it spoke like a dragon. [12]This beast stands before the first beast and uses the same power the first beast has. By this power it makes everyone living on earth worship the first beast, who had the death wound that was healed. [13]And the second beast does great miracles so that it even makes fire come down from heaven to earth while people are watching. [14]It fools those who live on earth by the miracles it has been given the power to do. It does these miracles to serve the first beast. The second beast orders people to make an idol to honor the first beast, the one that was wounded by the deadly sword but sprang to life again. [15]The second beast was given power to give life to the idol of the first one so that the idol could speak. And the second beast was given power to command all who will not worship the image of the beast to be killed. [16]The second beast also forced all people, small and great, rich and poor, free and slave, to have a mark on their right hand or on their forehead. [17]No one could buy or sell without this mark, which is the name of the beast or the number of its name. [18]This takes wisdom. Let the one who has understanding find the meaning of the number, which is the number of a person. Its number is 666.[n]

THE SONG OF THE SAVED

14 Then I looked, and there before me was the Lamb standing on Mount Zion.[n] With him were one hundred forty-four thousand people who had his name and his Father's name written on their foreheads. [2]And I heard a sound from heaven like the noise of flooding water and like the sound of loud thunder. The sound I heard was like people playing harps.

[3]And they sang a new song before the throne and before the four living creatures and the elders. No one could learn the new song except the one hundred forty-four thousand who had been bought from the earth. [4]These are the ones who did not do sinful things with women, because they kept themselves pure. They follow the Lamb every place he goes. These one hundred forty-four thousand were bought from among the people of the earth as people to be offered to God and the Lamb. [5]They were not guilty of telling lies; they are without fault.

THE THREE ANGELS

[6]Then I saw another angel flying high in the air. He had the eternal Good News to preach to those who live on earth—to every nation, tribe, language, and people. [7]He preached in a loud voice, "Fear God and give him praise, because the time has come for God to judge all people. So worship God who made the heavens, and the earth, and the sea, and the springs of water."

[8]Then the second angel followed the first angel and said, "Ruined, ruined is the great city of Babylon! She made all the nations drink the wine of the anger of her adultery."

[9]Then a third angel followed the first two angels, saying in a loud voice: "If anyone worships the beast and his idol and gets the beast's mark on the forehead or on the hand, [10]that one also will drink the wine of God's anger, which is prepared with all its strength in the cup of his anger. And that person will be put in pain with burning sulfur before the holy angels and the Lamb. [11]And the smoke from their burning pain will rise forever and ever. There will be no rest, day or night, for those who worship the beast and his idol or who get the mark of his name." [12]This means God's holy people must be patient. They must obey God's commands and keep their faith in Jesus.

[13]Then I heard a voice from heaven saying, "Write this: Blessed are the dead who die from now on in the Lord."

 12:18 the dragon Some Greek copies read "I." **13:18 666** Some Greek copies read "616." **14:1 Mount Zion** Another name for Jerusalem; here meaning the spiritual city of God's people.

The Spirit says, "Yes, they will rest from their hard work, and the reward of all they have done stays with them."

THE EARTH IS HARVESTED

[14] Then I looked, and there before me was a white cloud, and sitting on the white cloud was One who looked like a Son of Man.[n] He had a gold crown on his head and a sharp sickle[n] in his hand. [15] Then another angel came out of the temple and called out in a loud voice to the One who was sitting on the cloud, "Take your sickle and harvest from the earth, because the time to harvest has come, and the fruit of the earth is ripe." [16] So the One who was sitting on the cloud swung his sickle over the earth, and the earth was harvested.

[17] Then another angel came out of the temple in heaven, and he also had a sharp sickle. [18] And then another angel, who has power over the fire, came from the altar. This angel called to the angel with the sharp sickle, saying, "Take your sharp sickle and gather the bunches of grapes from the earth's vine, because its grapes are ripe." [19] Then the angel swung his sickle over the earth. He gathered the earth's grapes and threw them into the great winepress of God's anger. [20] They were trampled in the winepress outside the city, and blood flowed out of the winepress as high as horses' bridles for a distance of about one hundred eighty miles.

THE LAST TROUBLES

15 Then I saw another wonder in heaven that was great and amazing. There were seven angels bringing seven disasters. These are the last disasters, because after them, God's anger is finished.

[2] I saw what looked like a sea of glass mixed with fire. All of those who had won the victory over the beast and his idol and over the number of his name were standing by the sea of glass. They had harps that God had given them. [3] They sang the song of Moses, the servant of God, and the song of the Lamb:

"You do great and wonderful things,
　　　　　　　　　　　Psalm 111:2
Lord God Almighty. 　*Amos 3:13*
Everything the Lord does is right
　and true, 　　　　*Psalm 145:17*
King of the nations.[n]
[4] Everyone will respect you, Lord,
　　　　　　　　　　　Jeremiah 10:7
　and will honor you.
Only you are holy.
All the nations will come
　and worship you, 　*Psalm 86:9-10*
because the right things you have
　done
are now made known."
　　　　　　　　Deuteronomy 32:4

[5] After this I saw that the temple (the Tent of the Agreement) in heaven was opened. [6] And the seven angels bringing the seven disasters came out of the temple. They were dressed in clean, shining linen and wore golden bands tied around their chests. [7] Then one of the four living creatures gave to the seven angels seven golden bowls filled with the anger of God, who lives forever and ever. [8] The temple was filled with smoke from the glory and the power of God, and no one could enter the temple until the seven disasters of the seven angels were finished.

THE BOWLS OF GOD'S ANGER

16 Then I heard a loud voice from the temple saying to the seven angels, "Go and pour out the seven bowls of God's anger on the earth."

[2] The first angel left and poured out his bowl on the land. Then ugly and painful sores came upon all those who had the mark of the beast and who worshiped his idol.

[3] The second angel poured out his bowl on the sea, and it became blood like that of a dead man, and every living thing in the sea died.

[4] The third angel poured out his bowl on the rivers and the springs of water, and they became blood. [5] Then I heard the angel of the waters saying:

"Holy One, you are the One who is
　and who was.
You are right to decide to punish
　these evil people.
[6] They have poured out the blood
　of your holy people and your
　prophets.
So now you have given them blood
　to drink as they deserve."
[7] And I heard a voice coming from the altar saying:

"Yes, Lord God Almighty,
　the way you punish evil people is
　right and fair."

[8] The fourth angel poured out his bowl on the sun, and he was given power to burn the people with fire. [9] They were burned by the great heat, and they cursed the name of God, who had control over these disasters. But the people refused to change their hearts and lives and give glory to God.

[10] The fifth angel poured out his bowl on the throne of the beast, and darkness covered its kingdom. People gnawed their tongues because of the pain. [11] They also cursed the God of heaven because of their pain and the sores they had, but they refused to change their hearts and turn away from the evil things they did.

[12] The sixth angel poured out his bowl on the great river Euphrates so that the water in the river was dried up to prepare the way for the kings from the east to come. [13] Then I saw three evil spirits that looked like frogs coming out of the mouth of the dragon, out of the mouth of the beast, and out of the mouth of the false prophet. [14] These evil spirits are the spirits of demons, which have power to do miracles. They go out to the kings of the whole world to gather them together for the battle on the great day of God Almighty.

[15] "Listen! I will come as a thief comes! Blessed are those who stay

---

14:14 Son of Man "Son of Man" is a name Jesus called himself. **14:14 sickle** A farming tool with a curved blade. It was used to harvest grain. **15:3 King . . . nations** Some Greek copies read "King of the ages."

WORLD SAYS, WORD SAYS.

ORAL SEX

It's okay for a guy or girl to place their mouths and hands all over your body. It's your body, and you aren't hurting anybody. Go ahead, feel good, relax, and jump into that groove. You are technically not having sex, so it's safe.

"You should know that your body is a temple for the Holy Spirit who is in you. You have received the Holy Spirit from God. So you do not belong to yourselves" (1 Corinthians 6:19).

"Keep what is good, and stay away from everything that is evil" (1 Thessalonians 5:21-22).

"But there must be no sexual sin among you, or any kind of evil or greed. Those things are not right for God's holy people" (Ephesians 5:3).

---

awake and keep their clothes on so that they will not walk around naked and have people see their shame."

[16]Then the evil spirits gathered the kings together to the place that is called Armageddon in the Hebrew language.

[17]The seventh angel poured out his bowl into the air. Then a loud voice came out of the temple from the throne, saying, "It is finished!" [18]Then there were flashes of lightning, noises, thunder, and a big earthquake—the worst earthquake that has ever happened since people have been on earth. [19]The great city split into three parts, and the cities of the nations were destroyed. And God remembered the sins of Babylon the Great, so he gave that city the cup filled with the wine of his terrible anger. [20]Then every island ran away, and mountains disappeared. [21]Giant hailstones, each weighing about a hundred pounds, fell from the sky upon people. People cursed God for the disaster of the hail, because this disaster was so terrible.

THE WOMAN ON THE ANIMAL

17 Then one of the seven angels who had the seven bowls came and spoke to me. He said, "Come, and I will show you the punishment that will be given to the great prostitute, the one sitting over many waters. [2]The kings of the earth sinned sexually with her, and the people of the earth became drunk from the wine of her sexual sin."

[3]Then the angel carried me away by the Spirit to the desert. There I saw a woman sitting on a red beast. It was covered with names against God written on it, and it had seven heads and ten horns. [4]The woman was dressed in purple and red and was shining with the gold, precious jewels, and pearls she was wearing. She had a golden cup in her hand, a cup filled with evil things and the uncleanness of her sexual sin. [5]On her forehead a title was written that was secret. This is what was written:

THE GREAT BABYLON
MOTHER OF PROSTITUTES
AND OF THE EVIL THINGS OF THE EARTH

[6]Then I saw that the woman was drunk with the blood of God's holy people and with the blood of those who were killed because of their faith in Jesus.

When I saw the woman, I was very amazed. [7]Then the angel said to me, "Why are you amazed? I will tell you the secret of this woman and the beast she rides—the one with seven heads and ten horns. [8]The beast you saw was once alive but is not alive now. But soon it will come up out of the bottomless pit and go away to be destroyed. There are people who live on earth whose names have not been written in the book of life since the beginning of the world. They will be amazed when they see the beast, because he was once alive, is not alive now, but will come again.

[9]"You need a wise mind to understand this. The seven heads on the beast are seven mountains where the woman sits. [10]And they are seven kings. Five of the kings have already been destroyed, one of the kings lives now, and another has not yet come. When he comes, he must stay a short time. [11]The beast that was once alive, but is not alive now, is also an eighth king. He belongs to the first seven kings, and he will go away to be destroyed.

[12]"The ten horns you saw are ten kings who have not yet begun to rule, but they will receive power to rule with the beast for one hour. [13]All ten of these kings have the same purpose, and they will give their power and authority to the beast. [14]They will make war against the Lamb, but the Lamb will defeat them, because he is Lord of lords and King of kings. He will defeat them with his called, chosen, and faithful followers."

15Then the angel said to me, "The waters that you saw, where the prostitute sits, are peoples, races, nations, and languages. 16The ten horns and the beast you saw will hate the prostitute. They will take everything she has and leave her naked. They will eat her body and burn her with fire. 17God made the ten horns want to carry out his purpose by agreeing to give the beast their power to rule, until what God has said comes about. 18The woman you saw is the great city that rules over the kings of the earth."

BABYLON IS DESTROYED

18 After the vision of these things, I saw another angel coming down from heaven. This angel had great power, and his glory made the earth bright. 2He shouted in a powerful voice:

"Ruined, ruined is the great city of Babylon!
She has become a home for demons
and a prison for every evil spirit,
and a prison for every unclean bird and unclean beast.
3She has been ruined, because all the peoples of the earth
have drunk the wine of the desire of her sexual sin.
She has been ruined also because the kings of the earth
have sinned sexually with her,
and the merchants of the earth have grown rich from the great wealth of her luxury."

THE SCRIPT

The Resurrection
John 20:1-6

Mary Magdalene got up early Monday mornin', yawning.
Coming to the tomb and saw that the stone was gone, "Oh man!"
So she ran to Simon Peter and John (loved by Jesus) to greet them, speaking,
"They've taken the body of Jesus away from the tomb, and we don't know where they've moved him."
Before you knew it, that disciple Jesus loved and Pete were movin',
Running to the tomb site, they both took flight. But that other disciple, John, outran Peter, outright,
And got to the tomb first. Then stooping down, looked in, expecting the worst.
But didn't burst in, 'cause all he saw was Jesus' linen clothing folded up there laying.
But Peter was bold and so he went in, and checked out the clothes
And the handkerchief used to cover Jesus face and nose, folded up by itself, neatly.
Then the other disciple, John, repeated Peter's bold step and came in the tomb and he believed, see!
Although no one understood, the Scriptures decreed that Jesus had to rise from the dead.
Even the disciples had missed what the script had said!
So the two disciples went to the rest to try to figure out what they had been witnesses of,
But Mary was sick with confusion, remorse, missing the Lord whom she loved.
She couldn't hold it in and broke down at the site.
Bent over like she was in labor with tears in her eyes, she looked inside

And saw two angels sitting, clothed in white, positioned at the slab where had lain the Lord's remains.
They asked her, "Woman, why are you crying with pain?"
She spoke through her tears, "Because they've taken my Lord's body away."
Then she turned around to see somebody else at the grave site.
It was the Lord! But she couldn't recognize that it was Christ, even in daylight.
So Jesus said, "Woman, why are you crying and who are you looking for?"
Mary thought this was a gardener, so she said, "I'm sorry, sir,
But if you've taken his corpse away, let me know and I'll retrieve it."
Jesus spoke her name, "Mary," and she turned toward him, could she believe it?
It was really Jesus! Standing there before her eyes, alive!
Overcome with surprise, she cried out, "Rabbi!"

Take this with you: God's word holds promises that are forever true. We can trust that God will always keep his word, his promises are sure.

⁴Then I heard another voice from heaven saying:

"Come out of that city, my people,
so that you will not share in her sins,
so that you will not receive the disasters that will come to her.
⁵Her sins have piled up as high as the sky,
and God has not forgotten the wrongs she has done.
⁶Give that city the same as she gave to others.
Pay her back twice as much as she did.
Prepare wine for her that is twice as strong
as the wine she prepared for others.
⁷She gave herself much glory and rich living.
Give her that much suffering and sadness.
She says to herself, 'I am a queen sitting on my throne.
I am not a widow; I will never be sad.'
⁸So these disasters will come to her in one day:
death, and crying, and great hunger,
and she will be destroyed by fire, because the Lord God who judges her is powerful."

⁹The kings of the earth who sinned sexually with her and shared her wealth will see the smoke from her burning. Then they will cry and be sad because of her death. ¹⁰They will be afraid of her suffering and stand far away and say:

"Terrible! How terrible for you, great city,
powerful city of Babylon,
because your punishment has come in one hour!"

¹¹And the merchants of the earth will cry and be sad about her, because now there is no one to buy their cargoes— ¹²cargoes of gold, silver, jewels, pearls, fine linen, purple cloth, silk, red cloth; all kinds of citron wood and all kinds of things made from ivory, expensive wood, bronze, iron, and marble; ¹³cinnamon,

spice, incense, myrrh, frankincense, wine, olive oil, fine flour, wheat, cattle, sheep, horses, carriages, slaves, and human lives.

¹⁴The merchants will say,

"Babylon, the good things you wanted are gone from you.
All your rich and fancy things have disappeared.
You will never have them again."

¹⁵The merchants who became rich from selling to her will be afraid of her suffering and will stand far away. They will cry and be sad ¹⁶and say:

"Terrible! How terrible for the great city!
She was dressed in fine linen, purple and red cloth,
and she was shining with gold, precious jewels, and pearls!
¹⁷All these riches have been destroyed in one hour!"

Every sea captain, every passenger, the sailors, and all those who earn their living from the sea stood far away from Babylon. ¹⁸As they saw the smoke from her burning, they cried out loudly, "There was never a city like this great city!" ¹⁹And they threw dust on their heads and cried out, weeping and being sad. They said:

"Terrible! How terrible for the great city!
All the people who had ships on the sea
became rich because of her wealth!
But she has been destroyed in one hour!
²⁰Be happy because of this, heaven!
Be happy, God's holy people and apostles and prophets!
God has punished her because of what she did to you."

²¹Then a powerful angel picked up a large stone, like one used for grinding grain, and threw it into the sea. He said:

"In the same way, the great city of Babylon will be thrown down,
and it will never be found again.
²²The music of people playing harps and other instruments, flutes, and trumpets,

will never be heard in you again.
No workman doing any job
will ever be found in you again.
The sound of grinding grain
will never be heard in you again.
²³The light of a lamp
will never shine in you again,
and the voices of a bridegroom and bride
will never be heard in you again.
Your merchants were the world's great people,
and all the nations were tricked by your magic.
²⁴You are guilty of the death of the prophets and God's holy people
and all who have been killed on earth."

PEOPLE IN HEAVEN PRAISE GOD

19 After this vision and announcement I heard what sounded like a great many people in heaven saying:

"Hallelujah!
Salvation, glory, and power belong to our God,
²because his judgments are true and right.
He has punished the prostitute
who made the earth evil with her sexual sin.
He has paid her back for the death of his servants."

³Again they said:

"Hallelujah!
She is burning, and her smoke will rise forever and ever."

⁴Then the twenty-four elders and the four living creatures bowed down and worshiped God, who sits on the throne. They said:

"Amen, Hallelujah!"

⁵Then a voice came from the throne, saying:

"Praise our God, all you who serve him
and all you who honor him, both small and great!"

 19:1 Hallelujah This means "praise God!"

[6]Then I heard what sounded like a great many people, like the noise of flooding water, and like the noise of loud thunder. The people were saying:

"Hallelujah!
Our Lord God, the Almighty,
rules.
[7]Let us rejoice and be happy
and give God glory,
because the wedding of the Lamb
has come,
and the Lamb's bride has made
herself ready.
[8]Fine linen, bright and clean, was
given to her to wear."

(The fine linen means the good things done by God's holy people.)

[9]And the angel said to me, "Write this: Blessed are those who have been invited to the wedding meal of the Lamb!" And the angel said, "These are the true words of God."

[10]Then I bowed down at the angel's feet to worship him, but he said to me, "Do not worship me! I am a servant like you and your brothers and sisters who have the message of Jesus. Worship God, because the message about Jesus is the spirit that gives all prophecy."

THE RIDER ON THE WHITE HORSE

[11]Then I saw heaven opened, and there before me was a white horse. The rider on the horse is called Faithful and True, and he is right when he judges and makes war. [12]His eyes are like burning fire, and on his head are many crowns. He has a name written on him, which no one but himself knows. [13]He is dressed in a robe dipped in blood, and his name is the Word of God. [14]The armies of heaven, dressed in fine linen, white and clean, were following him on white horses. [15]Out of the rider's mouth comes a sharp sword that he will use to defeat the nations, and he will rule them with a rod of iron. He will crush out the wine in the winepress of the terrible anger of God the Almighty. [16]On his robe and on his upper leg was written this name: KING OF KINGS AND LORD OF LORDS.

[17]Then I saw an angel standing in the sun, and he called with a loud voice to all the birds flying in the sky: "Come and gather together for the great feast of God [18]so that you can eat the bodies of kings, generals, mighty people, horses and their riders, and the bodies of all people—free, slave, small, and great."

[19]Then I saw the beast and the kings of the earth. Their armies were gathered together to make war against the rider on the horse and his army. [20]But the beast was captured and with him the false prophet who did the miracles for the beast. The false prophet had used these miracles to trick those who had the mark of the beast and worshiped his idol. The false prophet and the beast were thrown alive into the lake of fire that burns with sulfur. [21]And their armies were killed with the sword that came out of the mouth of the rider on the horse, and all the birds ate the bodies until they were full.

THE THOUSAND YEARS

20 I saw an angel coming down from heaven. He had the key to the bottomless pit and a large chain in his hand. [2]The angel grabbed the dragon, that old snake who is the devil and Satan, and tied him up for a thousand years. [3]Then he threw him into the bottomless pit, closed it, and locked it over him. The angel did this so he could not trick the people of the earth anymore until the thousand years were ended. After a thousand years he must be set free for a short time.

[4]Then I saw some thrones and people sitting on them who had been given the power to judge. And I saw the souls of those who had been killed because they were faithful to the message of Jesus and the message from God. They had not worshiped the beast or his idol, and they had not received the mark of the beast on their foreheads or on their hands. They came back to life and ruled with Christ for a thousand years. [5](The others that were dead did not live again until the thousand years were ended.) This is the first raising of the dead. [6]Blessed and holy are those who share in this first raising of the dead. The second death has no power over them. They will be priests for God and for Christ and will rule with him for a thousand years.

[7]When the thousand years are over, Satan will be set free from his prison. [8]Then he will go out to trick the nations in all the earth—Gog and Magog—to gather them for battle. There are so many people they will be like sand on the seashore. [9]And Satan's army marched across the earth and gathered around the camp of God's people and the city God loves. But fire came down from heaven and burned them up. [10]And Satan, who tricked them, was thrown into the lake of burning sulfur with the beast and the false prophet. There they will be punished day and night forever and ever.

PEOPLE OF THE WORLD ARE JUDGED

[11]Then I saw a great white throne and the One who was sitting on it. Earth and sky ran away from him and disappeared. [12]And I saw the dead, great and small, standing before the throne. Then books were opened, and the book of life was opened. The dead were judged by what they had done, which was written in the books. [13]The sea gave up the dead who were in it, and Death and Hades[n] gave up the dead who were in them. Each person was judged by what he had done. [14]And Death and Hades were thrown into the lake of fire. The lake of fire is the second death. [15]And anyone whose name was not found written in the book of life was thrown into the lake of fire.

THE NEW JERUSALEM

21 Then I saw a new heaven and a new earth. The first heaven and the first earth had disappeared, and there was no sea any-

---

20:13 Hades The place of the dead.

more. [2]And I saw the holy city, the new Jerusalem,[n] coming down out of heaven from God. It was prepared like a bride dressed for her husband. [3]And I heard a loud voice from the throne, saying, "Now God's presence is with people, and he will live with them, and they will be his people. God himself will be with them and will be their God."[n] [4]He will wipe away every tear from their eyes, and there will be no more death, sadness, crying, or pain, because all the old ways are gone."

[5]The One who was sitting on the throne said, "Look! I am making everything new!" Then he said, "Write this, because these words are true and can be trusted."

[6]The One on the throne said to me, "It is finished. I am the Alpha and the Omega,[n] the Beginning and the End. I will give free water from the spring of the water of life to anyone who is thirsty. [7]Those who win the victory will receive this, and I will be their God, and they will be my children. [8]But cowards, those who refuse to believe, who do evil things, who kill, who sin sexually, who do evil magic, who worship idols, and who tell lies—all these will have a place in the lake of burning sulfur. This is the second death."

[9]Then one of the seven angels who had the seven bowls full of the seven last troubles came to me, saying, "Come with me, and I will show you the bride, the wife of the Lamb." [10]And the angel carried me away by the Spirit to a very large and high mountain. He showed me the holy city, Jerusalem, coming down out of heaven from God. [11]It was shining with the glory of God and was bright like a very expensive jewel, like a jasper, clear as crystal. [12]The city had a great high wall with twelve gates with twelve angels at the gates, and on each gate was written the name of one of the twelve tribes of Israel. [13]There were three gates on the east, three on the north, three on the south, and three on the west. [14]The walls of the city were built on twelve foundation stones, and on the stones were written the names of the twelve apostles of the Lamb.

[15]The angel who talked with me had a measuring rod made of gold to measure the city, its gates, and its wall. [16]The city was built in a square, and its length was equal to its width. The angel measured

21:2 new Jerusalem The spiritual city where God's people live with him.   **21:3 and . . . God** Some Greek copies do not have this phrase.   **21:6 Alpha and the Omega** The first and last letters of the Greek alphabet. This means "the beginning and the end."

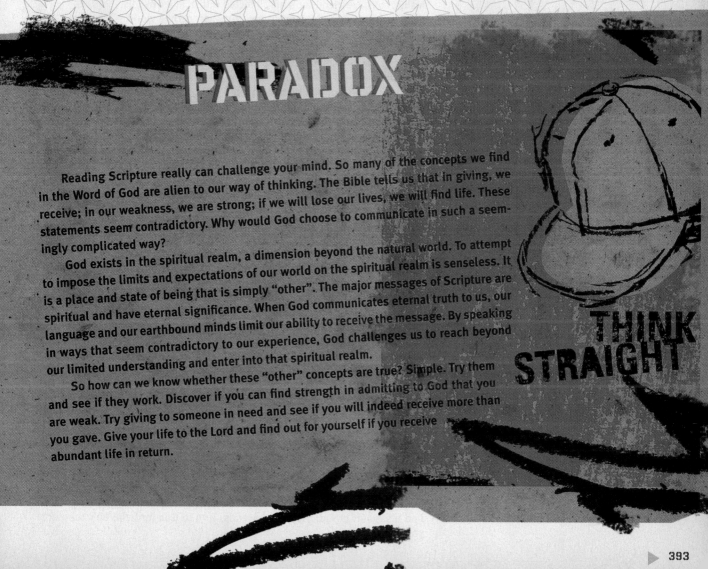

PARADOX

Reading Scripture really can challenge your mind. So many of the concepts we find in the Word of God are alien to our way of thinking. The Bible tells us that in giving, we receive; in our weakness, we are strong; if we will lose our lives, we will find life. These statements seem contradictory. Why would God choose to communicate in such a seemingly complicated way?

God exists in the spiritual realm, a dimension beyond the natural world. To attempt to impose the limits and expectations of our world on the spiritual realm is senseless. It is a place and state of being that is simply "other". The major messages of Scripture are spiritual and have eternal significance. When God communicates eternal truth to us, our language and our earthbound minds limit our ability to receive the message. By speaking in ways that seem contradictory to our experience, God challenges us to reach beyond our limited understanding and enter into that spiritual realm.

So how can we know whether these "other" concepts are true? Simple. Try them and see if they work. Discover if you can find strength in admitting to God that you are weak. Try giving to someone in need and see if you will indeed receive more than you gave. Give your life to the Lord and find out for yourself if you receive abundant life in return.

THINK STRAIGHT

the city with the rod. The city was 1,500 miles long, 1,500 miles wide, and 1,500 miles high. [17]The angel also measured the wall. It was 216 feet high, by human measurements, which the angel was using. [18]The wall was made of jasper, and the city was made of pure gold, as pure as glass. [19]The foundation stones of the city walls were decorated with every kind of jewel. The first foundation was jasper, the second was sapphire, the third was chalcedony, the fourth was emerald, [20]the fifth was onyx, the sixth was carnelian, the seventh was chrysolite, the eighth was beryl, the ninth was topaz, the tenth was chrysoprase, the eleventh was jacinth, and the twelfth was amethyst. [21]The twelve gates were twelve pearls, each gate having been made from a single pearl. And the street of the city was made of pure gold as clear as glass.

[22]I did not see a temple in the city, because the Lord God Almighty and the Lamb are the city's temple. [23]The city does not need the sun or the moon to shine on it, because the glory of God is its light, and the Lamb is the city's lamp. [24]By its light the people of the world will walk, and the kings of the earth will bring their glory into it. [25]The city's gates will never be shut on any day, because there is no night there. [26]The glory and the honor of the nations will be brought into it. [27]Nothing unclean and no one who does shameful things or tells lies will ever go into it. Only those whose names are written in the Lamb's book of life will enter the city.

22

Then the angel showed me the river of the water of life. It was shining like crystal

DEEP ISSUES

HIV/AIDS

HIV/AIDS is very real to most of us in urban communities. Many of us have friends or family infected with or killed by this deadly virus. Currently, more than 42 million people worldwide are infected with HIV. More than 23 million have died from AIDS since the disease broke out over 20 years ago. Estimates show that as many as 70 million more may die within the next 20 years if a cure is not found. In the year 2004, North America saw 44,000 adults and children newly infected with HIV and 16,000 die of AIDS. In the United States, HIV/AIDS is the number one cause of death in both Black males and females ages 22-45. Of the 25 US cities with the highest incidence of HIV infection, 18 are in the South.

HIV is spreading fastest in third world countries. In more developed countries its progress has slowed, but it still thrives in the minority population of the urban communities. The HIV virus infects people of all ages, genders, races, religions, and nationalities. It doesn't discriminate. Whether gay, straight, a drug user or not, all are at risk from this epidemic.

Some will tell you that HIV/AIDS is a punishment from God for homosexual activity. Don't buy that. HIV is evidence of a much larger issue than one's sexual behavior. All diseases, whether cancer, HIV, MS, Parkinson's, glaucoma, or a hundred other diseases, are evidence of a world broken by sin. The first man and woman disobeyed God in Eden. That act sent a perfect world into a downward spin and began a heritage of sin for all of us. Read Genesis 3. Their action had cosmic effects on a previously perfect creation and the result was sickness, disease, and death for all of us.

Understand this. Some diseases are inherited. Some are just common among people and happen to us, regardless of what we do or don't do. Some, like STDs, can be avoided. Want to greatly decrease the chances of HIV? Then:

- Keep sex to within marriage and with an HIV-free spouse.
- Stay free of drugs.
- Get blood transfusions only from HIV-free donors.
- If you're in a high-risk group, get tested for HIV. Early treatment can help.

Someone you know have AIDS or just discover they're HIV-positive? Show them you don't reject them because of their disease. Support them, encourage them, pray for them, be there for them when they want to talk. Help them find a support group; they need friends. Turn to God for help; he's there for you and your friend.

and was flowing from the throne of God and of the Lamb ²down the middle of the street of the city. The tree of life was on each side of the river. It produces fruit twelve times a year, once each month. The leaves of the tree are for the healing of all the nations. ³Nothing that God judges guilty will be in that city. The throne of God and of the Lamb will be there, and God's servants will worship him. ⁴They will see his face, and his name will be written on their foreheads. ⁵There will never be night again. They will not need the light of a lamp or the light of the sun, because the Lord God will give them light. And they will rule as kings forever and ever.

⁶The angel said to me, "These words can be trusted and are true." The Lord, the God of the spirits of the prophets, sent his angel to show his servants the things that must happen soon.

⁷"Listen! I am coming soon! Blessed is the one who obeys the words of prophecy in this book."

⁸I, John, am the one who heard and saw these things. When I heard and saw them, I bowed down to worship at the feet of the angel who showed these things to me. ⁹But the angel said to me, "Do not worship me! I am a servant like you, your brothers the prophets, and all those who obey the words in this book. Worship God!"

¹⁰Then the angel told me, "Do not keep secret the words of prophecy in this book, because the time is near for all this to happen. ¹¹Let whoever is doing evil continue to do evil. Let whoever is unclean continue to be unclean. Let whoever is doing right continue to do right. Let whoever is holy continue to be holy."

¹²"Listen! I am coming soon! I will bring my reward with me, and I will repay each one of you for what you have done. ¹³I am the Alpha and the Omega,ⁿ the First and the Last, the Beginning and the End.

¹⁴"Blessed are those who wash their robesⁿ so that they will receive the right

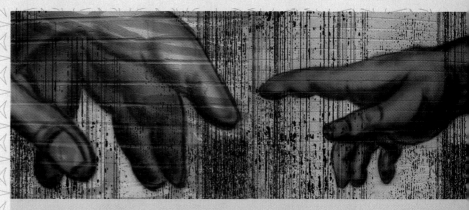

HeartCry

New Life **Do you want to meet Jesus? Do you want to know him as your Savior and accept him as your Lord? Let your heart cry . . .**

Father, I realize now that I have chosen sin instead of you. I don't want that life anymore. I want to know you and be your child. I know you sent your only Son, Jesus, to die in my place. I thank you that you raised him from the dead so I can know a new life. I accept Jesus' sacrifice on my behalf. Jesus, please come live in my heart and rule as my Lord and King. I give you my heart and my life.

You are my child. Nothing can ever separate you from my love. I will be your refuge, your strength, and your deliverer. One day you will be with me where I am. I will return for you. Surely I am coming soon. Stand firm in the salvation of your God. **Ephesians 1:13; Romans 8:3**

to eat the fruit from the tree of life and may go through the gates into the city. ¹⁵Outside the city are the evil people, those who do evil magic, who sin sexually, who murder, who worship idols, and who love lies and tell lies.

¹⁶"I, Jesus, have sent my angel to tell you these things for the churches. I am the descendant from the family of David, and I am the bright morning star."

¹⁷The Spirit and the bride say, "Come!" Let the one who hears this say, "Come!" Let whoever is thirsty come; whoever wishes may have the water of life as a free gift.

¹⁸I warn everyone who hears the words of the prophecy of this book: If anyone adds anything to these words, God will add to that person the disasters written about in this book. ¹⁹And if anyone takes away from the words of this book of prophecy, God will take away that one's share of the tree of life and of the holy city, which are written about in this book.

²⁰Jesus, the One who says these things are true, says, "Yes, I am coming soon."

Amen. Come, Lord Jesus!

²¹The grace of the Lord Jesus be with all. Amen.

 22:13 Alpha and the Omega The first and last letters of the Greek alphabet. This means "the beginning and the end." **22:14 wash their robes** This means they believed and obeyed Jesus so that their sins could be forgiven by Christ's blood. The "washing" may refer to baptism (Acts 22:16).

Urban trilogy

WHAT *Makes* A MAN

BY KENDRA

Hunter Woods shook his head knowingly as he heard the familiar rhythmic drumming at the door to his new apartment.

"East Siiide!" Tyson Brown said, showing off his best Omega stance as his fraternity brother opened the door.

"Now that I'm 'bout done moving everything in myself, you here to help?" Hunter asked.

"I told you I was coming, man. Ain't nobody tell you to start without a brotha."

"You said noon, Tyson," Hunter reminded him. "It's four o'clock."

The two twenty-five-year-olds had been friends since their rival Atlanta high school track teams met in the state finals seven years before. With controversy surrounding the fraction of a second that separated Hunter's first-place finish from Tyson's second, the resulting friendship surprised most of their teammates. Though they shared some common interests, their personalities were as different as night and day.

"I like your pad, man," Tyson said with a mouth full of potato chips he'd just taken from the kitchen cabinet. "It's a little cramped and all, but one bedroom is all you need for you and the honeys."

Ignoring his friend's last remark, Hunter stood back and examined the dull white wall he'd just brought to life with an oil painting he'd purchased for his new home.

"You already late, Tyson. Prove to me you're not totally worthless by putting the dishes in that box into the cabinet."

"What? You mad now? C'mon Hunter, man, you know I'm just messing with you. If you don't want no honey, that just leaves more for me, and you know I ain't got a problem with that."

Hunter had been down this road too many times. Tyson had had more than his share of women. Hunter knew Tyson found it hard to accept his vow of celibacy, hard to accept the fact that they could no longer compare "last night" stories. Hunter had completely changed his outlook on relationships after giving his life to Christ two years ago.

Tyson continued, "All I'm saying is that people gonna start drawing their own conclusions if you don't get out more. You know what I mean?" He opened a nearby box.

"Who is 'people,' Tyson? You?" Hunter's challenge was laced with irritation. "All I care about is what God thinks of me. When the time is right, I'll find the right girl and the right relationship. Until then, I'm cool. The woman who sleeps in my bed will be my wife. Her sharing my space will mean something."

"It means something when a woman shares my space, too," Tyson said with a laugh.

"Can you just drop it?"

Tyson threw both hands in the air in surrender. "Aiight, dog. You ain't got to get all defensive. But let me just say this. You can't expect to just pray and think God's gonna drop some chick at your front door."

"Why not?"

"Okay. Let's try it your way, man," Tyson said as he put the plate he'd just retrieved from the box onto the countertop. He dropped to his knees.

Sighing, Hunter shook his head and turned away to continue his task.

"Oh, Lawd!" Tyson dragged out his words in musical fashion and pounded on the floor like an old church deacon. "Please send Hunter a woman! Oh, Lawd! Drop her from the windows of heaven so he can get some before it's everlastingly too late. Oh, Lawd!"

"Okay, Tyson, that's enough," Hunter warned.

A faint knock ended the brief silence that followed. Stepping over boxes, Hunter made his way to the door. When he opened it, he found himself looking into the face of an attractive woman with bright eyes and a kind face. At six feet, Hunter towered over her by a full foot.

"Hi." She seemed a bit uneasy. "I'm sorry to disturb you, but I just moved out of this unit a few days ago and I think I left something here."

It took a few seconds for Hunter to speak through his stare. "A curling iron?" Hunter had seen it in the bathroom closet earlier.

"Yes."

"Come on in," he offered, and wondered how he could find out more about her. "I'll get it for you."

Without completely entering the apartment, the woman stood in the doorway and waited as Hunter maneuvered his way around the boxes and into the bedroom.

"Girl, I know you tired, 'cause you were running around in my dreams all last night!" Tyson remarked.

Hunter overheard his friend's played-out line just as he entered his bedroom. When he returned, he found Tyson propped against the doorframe writing down information about a woman who had been there for less than three minutes.

"Here you go," Hunter said, throwing his friend a brief look of disapproval, as he handed his visitor the curling iron.

"Thank you," she said.

"Later, shawty," Tyson called behind her as he watched her walk away.

"You are unbelievable," Hunter said over his friend's lustful moans, although he had to admit that part of his

But, throughout all of their discussions and disagreements, their bond remained strong. As foolish as Tyson's reasoning might be, Hunter knew that, at the core of it all, his friend really did want what was best for him. They just had two different definitions of what that was. When it got right down to it, Hunter knew Tyson had his back and, as hopeless as it seemed now, he also knew he'd one day be instrumental in leading Tyson to Christ.

Hunger was getting the best of Hunter and he slipped on a sweat suit and tennis shoes and polished up on his running skills as he jogged his way to the grocery store that was less than a mile from his home. He wandered around the store and, as he rounded the corner to the cereal aisle, a familiar face caught his eye.

"Felicity?"

She didn't look in his direction, but Hunter was certain it was her. He stepped closer.

"Felicity Cole?"

Slowly, as if not sure who he was talking to, she

Sometimes Hunter wondered how their friendship had remained tight over the last two years.

irritation was that he hadn't had more time to talk to the young lady.

"That's aiight, fool," Tyson laughed. "I know everything I need to know about her and this ain't even my crib. Man, you need to learn how to handle your business. You let a fine woman like that slip through your fingers."

"Well, if she went for you, then she wasn't my type anyway," Hunter replied, hiding his disappointment that the woman he'd been attracted to preferred Tyson. "Any woman who would give a man all her information within a few seconds of meeting him—I don't know what to call her."

"Mine; that's what I call her," Tyson bragged. "Yep, me and Felicity Cole will be making some memories by Friday. You can believe that. I got the name, the address, and the digits. By nightfall, Hunter's apartment had begun to look like a home. All he needed was some food for his kitchen so he could stop munching on the few chips Tyson had left behind when he made his quick exit just an hour before. Sometimes Hunter wondered how their friendship had remained tight over the last two years. Tyson was always making jokes about Hunter's lifestyle, and Hunter didn't agree with most of Tyson's choices, either.

turned and looked in his direction. She immediately recognized him. Smiling, she walked toward Hunter and accepted his extended hand.

"Hunter Woods," he introduced himself. "I don't know if you remember me, but we . . ."

"Of course, I remember you. I don't think we were properly introduced before, though. I'm sorry. I didn't know you were talking to me just now."

"How many women besides you have the name Felicity?" Hunter remarked with a laugh.

"That's just it. My name is Tara Gordon."

"Huh?"

It was Tara's turn to laugh as she watched a look of utter confusion replace his grin.

"I guess Felicity is the name I gave your friend today," she explained. "I don't even remember what I told him. I just made something up so he'd leave me alone. I don't mean to talk about your boy, but he was kind of freaking me out."

"Yeah, well he can be a bit overbearing," Hunter admitted. "What about the address and phone number?"

"I made those up, too. As I said, he was freaking me out."

Feeling good that Tyson had gotten exactly what he deserved and that Tara wasn't attracted to the shallow type, Hunter laughed with her. He couldn't wait to see the look on Tyson's face tomorrow after he'd tried unsuccessfully to contact the woman who had beaten him at his own game.

"Well, it was good seeing you," Tara said abruptly, as if she were in a hurry.

He tried to think of something that would prolong their conversation, but all he did was wave and say, "Catch ya, later."

In the days that followed, Tara Gordon stayed on Hunter's mind. His attraction to her went beyond the physical. She was cute, and had a warm smile. But there was something about her, something he couldn't see or understand. Her appeal was magnetic.

"Nothing, man. I gotta go. I'm coming by to pick you up for church tomorrow, so be ready."

Before Tyson could respond, Hunter ended the call and motioned for Tara to enter. She seemed apprehensive, but slowly stepped inside so he could close his door.

"It's late and I'm sorry," she said, "but I locked myself out of my place."

A cloud of suspicion immediately loomed over Hunter's head. "Why would you drive all the way over here to tell me that? Surely you have people you know better than me."

Instantly, Hunter could tell she'd taken offense to his insinuation. "I didn't drive over here. Believe me, walking here was not what I wanted to do." She reached for the doorknob as she explained, "I was in my apartment, which by the way is only three blocks away. Anyway, I was home

I CHOOSE TO LIVE MY LIFE THE WAY GOD WANTS ME TO.

Tyson's meaningless attraction to her faded after he complained to Hunter that "that woman, Felicity," had dissed him. But while Tyson's interest went away, Hunter's fascination grew. He visited the grocery store for three consecutive days, hoping to catch a glimpse of her—maybe even to ask her out. But she was never there.

By Saturday night, Hunter's apartment was finally complete. Home alone, Hunter struggled to divide his attention between the movie he was watching and his friend's voice on the other end of the telephone.

"Man, it's the weekend," Tyson was saying. "You act like you twelve or something. What kinda single man sits home on a Saturday night? You need to come on over here to Dugan's with us. It's off the heezie fo'sheezie! The Georgia peaches are up in here, and they are ripe for the picking."

Between the television and the telephone, Hunter barely heard the knock at his door. Not expecting company, he peered through the peephole before answering. It was Tara.

"You hear me, Hunter?" Tyson said. "I ain't got nothing against a decent sistah and all, but you find one who can match up to these and I'll start going to church so I can meet me one or two."

"I just did," Hunter replied.

"What?"

and had to throw some trash into the dumpster. When I went back to my apartment, my door was locked. My keys are inside my apartment." She took a breath as if she was trying to keep tears away. "I came here because you're the only person I thought I knew in this neighborhood. Apparently, I was wrong," she said, swinging open the door.

"Wait, Tara, my bad," Hunter apologized as he closed the door and stood in front of it, blocking her from leaving. "I didn't know you lived around here. I just—I'm sorry. What do you need for me to do? Do I need to take you somewhere? You want to use the phone to call somebody?"

She wasn't doing a good job fighting her tears, and the fact that he had caused them brought a pain to the pit of his stomach.

"I'm sorry," he repeated, restraining a desire to hold her. Inviting her to have a seat on his couch, Hunter went to the kitchen to get her a glass of juice and then sat next to her, leaving enough space so she wouldn't feel uncomfortable.

"The manager of my building wasn't in his apartment," she said, as if she was beginning to get nervous. "I don't have family here. It was getting dark, and I didn't know what else to do."

Hunter saw the anguish on her face. He knew her

coming to him wasn't an easy decision, but knowing she trusted him enough to chance it felt good.

"No problem," he said. "You can stay here tonight."

"I gotta go." Tara stood and rushed to the door.

"Wait," Hunter quickly said. "Hear me out. My sister lives only a few blocks away. I'll go stay with her and since this used to be your apartment, I don't mind you crashing here for the night."

"Are you sure?" She looked at him as if she couldn't believe his offer. "I mean, you don't really know me."

He nodded. "I know enough."

She smiled. "Well, I don't really know you. How do I know you won't come sneaking back here tonight."

He laughed. "Do you think I would go through all of this trouble for that?"

"I guess not." She laughed with him.

"There are lots of reasons why I wouldn't do that, but the number one being . . . I'm celibate. Tara, If that doesn't make you feel safe, nothing will."

"You're celibate?"

It didn't make him feel great that he was explaining himself again, but he said, "I choose to live my life the way I feel God wants me to until I'm married. So yes," Hunter nodded, "I'm celibate."

Returning to the couch, Tara flashed her star-quality smile.

"You can laugh if you like," he told her. "It's okay. I'm used to my manhood being questioned."

"I don't think it's funny, Hunter. I think it's wonderful," she told him. "You know, I knew there was something different about you the first day we met. I guess I felt a kindred spirit because, in essence, we have the same Father. Tyson kind of threw me off a little bit and made me think the vibes I got from you were wrong. But I see I was right."

Hunter didn't respond. His mind traveled back to the day of Tyson's antics. The prayer he'd prayed in mockery and the timing of Tara's visit suddenly didn't seem coincidental.

"What makes a man a man isn't who he lays down with, but who he stands up for," she added. "Your manhood is not in question."

He grinned. He should have known she was a woman who knew the Lord. That was the "something" about her that had attracted him.

Hunter grabbed a bag and tucked a change of clothes inside. He called his sister, and then turned to Tara. "Well, the apartment is yours." He jotted a number down on a piece of paper and handed it to her. "Call me if you need anything."

She shook her head as she looked at the number. "You're a good man, Hunter." She stood on her toes and kissed his cheek. "Thank you, again."

At two o'clock in the morning, sleep still escaped Hunter as he lay awake on the couch in his sister's living room. He thought about Tara, resting in his bed and he recalled the words he had said to his best friend just days earlier.

"The woman who sleeps in my bed will be my wife. Her sharing my space will mean something."

He wondered if this was a sign that God was answering his prayers. Tara was the first woman to share his space since he'd given his life to the Lord. It had to mean something.

Finally, Hunter closed his eyes. "Thank you, Lord," he said. And then, he slept. ★

THE LAST MAN STANDING

BY TERRANCE JOHNSON

"That's all I can stand, and you can't stand no more," Vince the Prince utters from my blind side as he steps in my path and flashes the sign of the Royal Gangsta Disciples in my face. Four of his foot soldiers surround me. While Vince has to look up at me—like most men (I stand six feet five inches)—the four henchmen measure up to me and can look me level in the eye. And they are linebacker-thick compared to my slim track-runner's frame.

"Popeye the Slaya, it's your birthday, playa." Vince's mockery has a ring of truth to it, seeing that I was baptized just five hours ago.

Still, I throw back, "My birthday's actually next month."

"Okay, sailor man." Vince's dark-rimmed grin spreads as he pulls his shirt back to reveal the gat in his waistband.

"Gimme one reason why I shouldn't sink your ship right here, right now, and I'll give you three reasons why I'm gonna bury you on this spot."

My fear is real. His threat ain't no bluff. After all, according to Royal doctrines and covenants, he owes me big time for smokin' one of his boys back in the day: King Roy. That is the rule, and I had expected it to be enforced a long time ago. Vince had an added incentive to take me out right now: King Roy had not only been his fellow and

leading Royal, but also his blood brother. Even if I hadn't been defending myself (and the choice had been either shoot or be shot), I had felt a blood lust for my foes, so King Roy had to go. I happened to fire with accuracy to his heart before he could even draw his Glock. King Roy was my first kill in the bitter war that my set—the East Side Pirates—had with the Royals, along with the many other gangs in the area.

My silent prayer, "Help me, Lord," is answered right away.

"For one, when One Time hears the shot," I finally say, answering his question and nodding at what's just coming up behind him, "he'll have a reason to send you to hell or take you to jail."

They all peer behind Vince at the squad car that has just pulled up on the corner.

"By the way, Popeye the Slayer . . . is dead, and I go by my given name, Perry Wright."

Vince chuckles, "Are you sayin' you're a ghost? Well, call me a ghost-busting priest, 'cause I'm gonna exorcise you from this hood!" Making a last-rites sign across his head and chest, Vince warns, "Believe that, 'cause I been watchin' you and I know when, where, why, and how you, your wife, and three kids come and go." Then, he and his foot soldiers retreat into the darkness of the night, leaving me in the light of the love of God.

I dash back up the stairs to the 79th Street apartment that I had just left on my way to my night job. "Get dressed, pack some things, we're out," I declare, startling my wife, Cherish, who's nursing my newborn son, Sir Trent. I waste no time packing the suitcases.

"What's going on?" Cherish springs up and follows me to the bedroom.

"My past is back with a vengeance," I say as I glance at her.

She stops in her tracks and, aware of our son, she calmly lays Sir Trent in his cradle. As I frantically toss clothing and other necessities around, Cherish walks toward me and gently places her hand on my tense shoulder. "Let's pray," she resigns.

I'm jolted still. Theoretically, prayer is all well and good, but in this case, it's good to get away . . . quickly.

But I submit to her suggestion, take a deep breath, set the clothes down, and lower myself to my knees, saying "Awright." Cherish has been saved a little longer than me, and she's the more seasoned Christian.

We clasp our hands together and bow our heads as I utter the petition to God. "Lord . . ." I start, not knowing what to say, so I tell the truth. "I'm scared and I wanna take Vince the Prince out before he takes me out, not so much for my safety, but for my wife and my babies. I could run or gun. That's what I know; that's who . . . I used to be," I declare, reflecting on my past; now erased by the blood of the Lamb, Jesus. I meditate on how he rescued me.

Jail or hell—every life on the street comes to that crossroad. Hustlers, ballers, and shot callers are rarely granted the privilege to pick their end. Detours are not an option, and the trip is fast and the destination inevitable. When it's all said and done, that is justice and I had deserved to die a very ugly, violent death. I didn't deserve rest and peace, but to burn in hell. But I was one of the privileged few, blessed to get out. Looking back, it had been a long, hard time coming; it was like three the hard way.

From the beginning, life had been a struggle. Mama only cared so much. Dad (a broke hustler) was unknown to me and probably in jail or dead. Mama was fifteen when she had me; she put herself in a position of responsibility when she was still trying to figure life out. Needless to say, the discipline in my life had been weak. I had taken my beatings when I got on her nerves, but she didn't have the know-how or resources to keep me occupied with beneficial distractions that would have kept me from the negative influences and elements.

The South Shore area where I grew up had a mixture of affluent, middle-class, and poverty-stricken black folk. There were success stories and tales of failure from each social class: folks who rose from generations of poverty to prosperity and people who sank from riches to rags. We were closer to the have-nots than to the prosperous, but there was food and shelter, thanks to Mama struggling with two jobs, public assistance, and the benevolence of my grandmother, Big Momma. But that's not how I wanted to live.

School certainly had not been interesting, and furthering my education had been the last thing on my mind. I had found my kindred spirits among the many other have-nots and had started getting into trouble when I was only eight, with stuff like petty stealing and fighting. By the time I had reached high school, I had graduated to hustling for and rolling with the East Side Pirates. At that point, I was out of school.

My name became known around town and every set knew my reputation for being crazy, even if they hadn't had the displeasure of crossing paths with me. I had carried a 9 mm and used it whenever my trigger finger itched. My pockets were fat and I had street cred. I had convinced myself that I was on top of the world, but I knew at any moment that I could and would fall. I thought that was part of the excitement. It didn't take long for me to start falling.

The eye that had flashed the glare of death at others was lost. It took losing an eye to see Christ.

I had delivered drugs here and there, collecting the cash and just using my feet to keep the flow going for my crew. It wasn't a covert operation. I was bold enough to do it on the corner of 79th and Essex during the day shift. So when One Time swooped in on me, I knew I would catch a case. Whether it was surveillance or an undercover cop as their witness, I was guilty as sin. But they had to catch me first, because I wasn't going willingly.

When the narc had pulled up, smelling like bacon and trying to purchase, I had taken off just as the other squad cars stormed the corner. With reefer smoke all in my lungs, I shot through alleys, gangways, houses, and yards—eluding two of Chicago's finest and fastest for four blocks. Finally, they caught me after chasing me up the stairs of an apartment on Kingston, causing me to leap from the second floor. Landing awkwardly and breaking my leg, I couldn't run anymore. But being caught had given me a sense of relief mixed with dread.

Somehow, some way beyond my own luck and merit, I was out of jail and on my feet less than a year later. But my step was a little hesitant; not slower, but just a little more reluctant to run to do evil. That was just the beginning, the beginning of the end.

Six months after being released from jail, I was back on the streets and enforcing a debt violation. I was about to set fire to a no-name hype just for the sadistic pleasure of it (a simple bullet to the head would've sufficed) when I was distracted by a super-rat in the alley. Instead of igniting the junkie, my right gun hand caught fire from the excess kerosene. I suffered third-degree burns and was once again out of commission. The hand that I used to smoke folks with had been partially paralyzed for a while.

I banked on my reputation and bluffed with a former gang rival, who in turn shot my right eye out. That's when I started thinking seriously about my mortality. It happened when Slick Victor the Dictator, formerly of the Gangster Disciples Deck of Cards, fired a .357 Magnum at point-blank range at my head. He hit the target, and I knew without a doubt that I should've been killed on the spot. The eye that had flashed the glare of death at others was lost. It took losing an eye to see Christ.

Now, kneeling beside the bed next to my wife, my prayer continues, "You have kept me through many death-defying events and gotten me out of dire situations before. And you saved me from my enemies, from hell, and from myself. . . ."

Several months after losing my eye, I had had an encounter with a dude from my hood. I was depressed, drunk, and high, not wanting to live or die. We had exchanged nasty words and I pulled my gun on him. He hadn't backed down, but instead boldly told me that God was gracious to me. Cooler heads prevailed and we had ended up discussing this, that, and God over a hamburger.

When it was all over, I had acknowledged that I was a sinner and deserved the worst type of death, that I couldn't get myself right or save myself—that only God could save me. It was then that I realized God's love for me is real and evident in Jesus dying on the cross for my sins. I believed and declared that Jesus died and that God raised him from the dead for me. That day, I called on the name of Jesus, even though I didn't officially join a church and get baptized until ten years later. While I was used to preying on souls, this was the first time I prayed for my own soul. I considered myself under a new jurisdiction, new management, and a new authority.

That wasn't going to set well with Captain Hook and the Pirates. The only way out was to walk the plank, which in essence meant committing a merciless killing. As it stands, the Captain of my Salvation already had worked out my release. That following weekend, a bounty was placed on Hook's head by not only our rivals, but by every denomination of the Gang. So, Hook relocated to another town and hasn't been seen or heard from since. Consequently, the Pirates sank into oblivion and I was freed and cleared to move to another neighborhood and to a new life. Until now.

"So Lord, protect my family and help me to stand in your will. Amen," I rise slowly from my prayer with Cherish—more calm but still unsure.

Cherish embraces me and encourages, "It's going to be all right." My wife retrieves the Bible from the nightstand and opens it to Romans, chapter 8. We park on the bed and read it out loud. With a peace embracing me, I dial my job and inform them that I'll be late.

* * *

Work is hard—always is—but I am at peace. My mind isn't on the lingering threat, but my focus is on the opportunity to lend my musical talents to the church, in honor of God. Before I know it, I'm punching out and reading the sports section of the Chicago Defender on the 79th Street bus, riding on a cloud of joy.

When I exit on Ashland, my cloud disintegrates as a surge of anxiety fills my being. I gaze at the front door to my apartment building, knowing that my nemesis knows where I live and could possibly be waiting to ambush me. But if there's anything that I've learned at this point in my life, it's that not only can God protect me, but even if I am killed—which is a real possibility—I will live in heaven forever. That blessed assurance gives me the boldness to press on.

When I make it upstairs, Cherish is putting the finishing touches on her makeup as she prepares to head off to work as a receptionist for a law firm downtown. The morning news plays, and I make my way into the bathroom and peer at her peaceful, brown face. "Hey love," I greet her, embracing her and kissing her cheek.

Cherish smiles and returns a kiss to my lips. "How was work?"

I close my eyes, responding, "Productive and peaceful."

"Good," she says, nodding. "The kids have been fed, so all you have to do is drop them off in an hour at the daycare center." The thought of walking the streets with someone after me and my family doesn't enter my mind, as I see the latest news story being shown on the TV screen.

The news anchor announces breaking news: A drug gang had been busted up the night before—just two blocks from where I live with my wife and kids. An image appears of Vince, his four soldiers, and several cohorts being loaded into a paddy wagon. The anchor names Vince and states that he's in custody. I almost float toward the center of the living room, intently listening to the report. Silently, I speak to my God, "Thank you, for allowing me to stand in the face of a major test." And I pray that somehow, in the same way that God saved me, he will save Vince and the rest of the hustlers caught up in the game. ★

NOT ALONE WITH HIM

BY VICTORIA CHRISTOPHER MURRAY

Another Saturday night she would spend alone. Rachel looked into the mirror. The black knit dress she wore clung to her curves. Her hair was in place and the light foundation that covered her buttery smooth skin was perfect. She was ready to go. But like last week, and the week before, and all the weeks she could remember, Jay-T had swaggered out the door, leaving her alone.

The tears welled in her eyes, but then she heard the front door open. Rachel dried her tears and rushed into the living room. Jay-T stood with a grin as wide as the ocean. But the joy left his face when he saw her.

"What are you doing?" His face twisted as if it was painful for him to look at her.

"You came back for . . ."

"Not for you! I came back for my cell phone." He moved around their apartment, searching. "Where is it?" he asked as if he were speaking to a child. "You didn't move it, did you?"

Rachel shook her head.

"I told you not to touch it." His voice rose with each word.

She stood frozen. She knew the rules. She didn't touch his cell. Couldn't answer it. Couldn't even look at it to see who was calling. His rules—and she knew his reasons. He gave his number to women all the time, and took all their calls, even while he was with her.

"Where is my cell phone?" he screamed.

Rachel jumped. "I . . . didn't touch it." She wanted him to believe her because if he did, he might take her with him.

"Oh, here it is." He dusted off the cell phone as if it was a valuable block of gold. Then, he looked at her again. "What are you doing in those clothes? I told you to stay home."

She was shaking, but still, she stepped to him with a smile that was meant to be seductive. "Jay-T, I was hoping you'd changed your mind. I wanna go with you."

He leaned back and laughed. "You think I'm goin' to take you with me?" His laughter stopped. "Look at you. You're fat; you're ugly. I don't want anyone to know that I'm with you."

His words made her step backward. But as she moved, he moved. "I don't want you with me," he spat in her face.

"I'm going out and when I get back, you'd better be here."

He glared at her and then sauntered through the door. She heard him singing, some song about "honeys in the club."

His words had bolted Rachel in place. She couldn't remember when he'd started talking to her that way. But then, she couldn't remember a time when he hadn't. It hadn't been this way in the beginning.

She had met Jay-T six years before, at her prom. He wasn't even her date. Jay-T came with her best friend, Leah. From the moment Jay-T and Leah arrived in the limo, Rachel wanted him. All evening long, Jay-T and Rachel eyed each other and she had been beyond impressed.

She'd never met anyone so smooth. While all the high school guys wore the standard tuxedos, Jay-T was in a red tuxedo-style jacket with jeans. He even wore sneakers! Excitement and danger oozed from him—the way he talked, the way he walked, the way all the girls swarmed around him as if he were a star. When he looked at her, she felt like a woman.

Thoughts of Jay-T stayed with her for weeks after the prom. All during that summer, she asked Leah about him. But Leah wasn't interested.

"I didn't like him much," Leah told her one day.

How could you not like him? Rachel thought. But she said, "He seemed nice."

"Don't let him fool you. He may look good, but he's nothin' but a dog. Did you see the way he collected all of those phone numbers at the prom?"

That made Rachel a bit sad. He hadn't asked for her number.

Leah said, "Anyway, his mom was just doing my mom a favor by getting him to take me to the prom."

Rachel was sure she'd never see Jay-T again.

Then one day as she was waiting for the bus, a shiny black BMW 645 stopped in front of her. And he called her name.

One month later, Rachel moved from her parent's home and in with Jay-T. Even though her mother cried and her father screamed, Rachel refused to listen to their pleas.

"We're in love," she tried to explain.

"If he loved you, he'd marry you," her father said.

But she didn't need to be married. She just needed

But she knew why. Jay-T took care of her. He paid all the bills, bought her new clothes, and even purchased her a car. She didn't know if she could do any of those things without him.

The ringing phone drew her away from her thoughts. "Hey, Rachel."

She was glad to hear Leah's voice. Although they didn't see each other much because Jay-T couldn't stand Leah, her friend stayed in touch.

Leah said, "So what are you doing?"

"Nothing."

"Great, then come with me to church."

Rachel groaned. "Girl, you know, I don't like church." Her words weren't actually true. She missed the time she'd spent in church with her parents and friends. She missed the relationship she'd had with God since she was a little girl and had accepted Christ into her heart. But Jay-T told her to stay away.

"You don't need to be going to nobody's church," he had snarled. "Those preachers don't want nothin' but your money."

"You can be anything God enables you to be. You can do anything God enables you to do."

to be with Jay-T. No matter what she did, she couldn't get anyone to understand. Not even Leah.

"Jay-T is not good for you," Leah said. "You're worth a whole lot more."

"But, he loves me."

"Okay, but you don't have to live with him. That's not the kind of life God wants for you. You can see him and just stay with your parents. Maybe you and I can get an apartment together."

But Rachel just shook her head and closed her ears.

Now, six years later, she wished she'd listened. Almost from the moment she'd moved in, Jay-T had changed. According to him, she couldn't cook, she couldn't clean, she couldn't satisfy him. He even criticized the way she walked and talked. In the last year, it had gotten worse. He didn't spend any time with her. All he did was work and go out with his boys. And on the weekends, when he didn't come home until five or six in the morning, she didn't even want to imagine what he'd been doing.

Rachel sighed and returned to the bedroom. Why do I stay? She'd asked herself that question so many times.

Leah stopped Rachel's thoughts. "Please, Rachel. We're having a guest speaker tonight, and Franklin can't go because it's for women only. I don't want to go by myself."

Rachel knew Leah had other friends she could call. But there was something in the way her friend asked, something that pulled her, even though Jay-T had told her to stay home.

"Okay." Rachel jotted down the address and promised to meet Leah in front of Hope Chapel in thirty minutes. She didn't give any thought to Jay-T as she walked from the apartment to her car and drove to meet her friend. She'd never seen Leah happier than when they met in the parking lot.

"You're going to love this," Leah said as she took her friend's arm and directed her inside.

Rachel wasn't sure why she'd come. It had been so long. But as soon as the speaker began, Rachel leaned forward in her chair wondering how this woman knew her life.

The speaker talked about women being used by men because they didn't feel worthy of better treatment.

"You can't measure your worthiness by anyone except God. As women, our self-esteem is attacked daily, but the only way to have a feeling of self-worth is by having a right relationship with the Lord.

"You may not think you're valuable, but you are. God paid a high price for you, the highest price ever—the blood of his Son. So, you can't let men trample over you like you're nothing, because you are everything to God."

Rachel sat for the next hour listening to the points the speaker made about how she was worthy, how she had value, how she couldn't find her significance inside a relationship. But the most important words she heard were ones she already knew. The speaker reminded her that she was loved by God.

"You can be anything God enables you to be. You can do anything God enables you to do."

At the end, Rachel stood on her feet and cheered with the other women in the church. It was only then that she noticed the tears streaming down her face. She had her answers. She'd been putting her faith in Jay-T instead of putting her faith in God.

Before they left the church, Rachel said a quick prayer. God moved her heart and she knew what she had to do.

"Leah, can I stay with you for just a week or two? Until I find my own apartment?"

Leah hugged her friend, knowing what that meant. "Do you want me to go home with you and help you pack?"

Rachel shook her head. "I won't be taking much. Jay-T bought most of my clothes and I plan on leaving them. I'm just going to take the bare necessities."

Leah nodded. "Just remember you can do anything God enables you to do."

By the time Jay-T staggered home, Rachel had her suitcase packed.

"What are you doing?" he slurred as he stumbled into the bedroom.

Rachel could smell the alcohol on his breath. She wondered what she had seen in him. How had she let her life get so far away that she put more value on him than she did on herself? She had even let him become more important than God.

For the second time that night, Rachel said another quick prayer, grateful that she had never married Jay-T.

She pulled her key from her chain and dropped it onto the dresser. "I'm leaving, Jay-T."

He laughed. "Where you gonna go? Who's gonna take you in now? Your parents? Your friends? You don't have anyone but me."

She realized then that this had been his plan all along—to keep her away from everyone she loved. But it wasn't going to work anymore. She remembered what she'd heard tonight. God had paid a high price for her. God wanted more for her than being with Jay-T.

Rachel reached for the suitcase, but he grabbed it before she could. "You're not taking anything out of here," he bellowed. "You wanna go? Go, but everything you have I gave you."

Rachel looked down at her dress and shoes and sweater and realized that was all she had. But she smiled, knowing she had much more.

She walked toward the door. "Okay, good-bye, Jay-T."

"You'll be back," he screamed as she stepped into the hallway. "You don't have anyone. You'll be back."

Rachel smiled. Jay-T thought he knew everything. But his words proved he didn't know the most important thing. She did have someone. She had all she needed. She had God. ★

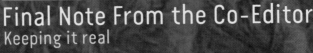

Final Note From the Co-Editor
Keeping it real

Let me be real. Working on this BibleZine was a very tough blessing. Honestly, I'd successfully edited several Bibles before, so going into this one I probably had the big head. I knew what I was doing. I knew what I needed to say in the piece. If left to do my job, I could create a dynamic product that would bless many. But very quickly I learned that this project was God's. In order for me to help and not hinder the project, I had to talk to God through prayer, spend time with God in his word, and let the Holy Spirit in my heart lead the way. Quickly, I found I couldn't do jack on my own.

Ironically, I now hope that in reading Real you also now know that things are only possible through God. See no matter what life throws at you and no matter how hard things get, our Father in Heaven has the answers. This BibleZine was created to meet you where you were, but bring you closer to the Lord. If you want more for your life, he has everything you'll ever need. If you want happiness, spending time with him gives you joy. If you want wisdom, only God has the answers.

Whether you read all the pages or only one, the Word was written to comfort, strengthen and guide you. In addition to the NCV version of the New Testament, many features in Real are good tools to help you become a stronger believer once you've accepted Christ. The book intros and the Bible 411 sections are there to help explain what the bible is about. The Script section is a unique way of telling biblical accounts. Deep Issues, Overcoming, Connected and God Unit are features that deal with combating tough subjects, with biblical solutions.

I know life can be cruel, but I'm also happy I know the one that can make it more rewarding than a big paycheck, a fat promotion, or possessing the sweetest material goods. God can help you ward off temptations, forgive those that have wronged you, and give you peace that passes all understanding. I along with my partner, the contributors, and the folks at Nelson Bible put our hearts into making this BibleZine, so that you could feel God's word was written for you. Well, we've done our part. Now you've got to read it, re-read it, and live it. Being connected to God's word is the only way you can truly Keep It Real.

Blessings to ya,

Stephanie Perry Moore
Co-Editor

Contributors' Bios

Josh Alston – Christian rap artist and songwriter.

Daven Baptiste – Graduate of San Diego State, Executive Producer/Composer of the Film "Matchups" (2003), and Director/Writer/Editor of the Film "A Night in Compton" (2004).

Winnie Sarah Clark-Jenkins – Student, Howard University School of Communications in Journalism and contributor to "The Woman of Color Devotional Bible" and "The Grace and Wisdom Devotional Bible."

John F. Dilworth II – Christian rap artist and songwriter.

Deljah Dickson – Author of "Freshman 101," a survival guide and journal for the first year of college.

Donna I. Douglas – Multi-platinum award-winning songwriter, speaker/author of "God Stories" and "Winks From God" and producer/ writer of the nationally syndicated TV series, "Two Lane Traveller."

John Fichtner – Senior Pastor, Liberty Church, Marietta, Georgia.

Quisa Foster – PR consultant in public and media relations with expertise in higher education, corporate relations, and arts and entertainment.

Derwin L. Gray, M. Div. A. – Candidate, Founder and President of One Heart At A Time Ministries.

Rachelle Guillory – Inspirational speaker, author of the books "The Known Stranger," "Her Daily Sword," "Rachelle's Expressions of Soul" and "Articles of Inspiration" and playwright of "Lord, I Want A Man...Can I Get An Amen" and a contributor to various publications.

S. James Guitard – Popular Christian author of the national bestsellers Mocha Love and Chocolate Thoughts as well as a contributing author to the national bestseller Blessed Assurance: Inspirational Short Stories Full of Hope and Strength for Life's Journey.

Dean Heath – Graduate of Oral Roberts University and President and co-owner of Reconcile Entertainment, a Christian rap music production company.

Keren Heath – Graduate of Oral Roberts University and co- owner of Reconcile Entertainment, a Christian rap music production company.

Phil Jackson – Senior Pastor of The House (www.thahouse.org), Chicago's first all youth and young adult hip-hop church and Evangelical Covenant Church and Lawndale Community Church plant.

Michele Clark Jenkins – Entertainment attorney and media business consultant. Formerly General Manager of the Estate of Dr. Martin Luther King, Jr., President of United Image Entertainment and Director of Business Affairs: Programming for HBO. Contributor to "The Women of Color Devotional Bible" and "The Grace and Wisdom Devotional Bible" and Writer/Editor of "The Children of Color Storybook Bible."

Terrance Johnson – Publisher and author of the novels Shades of Black, Eyes of Faith, and Baptism of Fire, and contributor in the best-selling Christian fiction short story anthology, Blessed Assurance: Inspirational Short Stories Full of Hope and Strength for Life's Journey.

Tommy Kyllonen – Lead Pastor of Crossover Community Church in Tampa, Fla. also has recorded 5 national hip-hop albums as Urban D.

G. Craige Lewis – Founder and Visionary of EX Ministries (www.exministries.com) and a producer/songwriter for Group 3 Productions.

Fred Lynch – Author of The Epic: an artistic translation of the book of John in rap (www.gettheepic.com).

Markesha McWilliams – Director of Communications for the Southern Intercollegiate Athletic Conference.

Derrick Moore – Former NFL player, Motivational speaker, author of "The Great Adventure," and the FCA chaplain for the Georgia Tech Yellow Jackets football team.

Stephanie Perry Moore – President of Soul Publishing, Inc. Editorial Director of the "Women of Color Devotional Bible" and other World/Nia Publishing products, and trailblazing Christian author of the "Payton Skky" Series, "Laurel Shadrach" Series, "Carmen Browne" Series, "Flame" and "A Lova' Like No Otha'."

John W. Moorer (aka John the Baptist) – Christian rap recording artist and songwriter.

Victoria Christopher Murray – Author of popular Christian books, "Temptation," "Joy," "Truth Be Told," "Grown Folks Business" and contributor to the anthology "Blessed Assurance: Inspirational Short Stories Full of Hope and Strength for Life's Journey.

Kendra Norman-Bellamy – Author of "A Love So Strong" and "For Love And Grace" (www.knb-publications.com).

Cedric Perry – Assistant Pastor, Parklane Baptist Church, Baltimore, Maryland.

Joannna Robinson – Student, Georgia State University; and Christian musical artist and songwriter.

Naomi Shedd – Author of "Pictures With A Purpose," creator of Faithbooking, and co-owner of www.Walkingwithwisdom.com which provides Christian tapes and materials.

Catina Slade – Contributor, "Chicken Soup for the African-American Soul."

Platinum Souls – Richardo Flo and Ty Scott, Christian Rap recording artists and songwriters.

Kenneth C. Ulmer, D.Min., Ph.D. – Senior Pastor, Faithful Central Bible Church, Los Angeles and Trustee, The King's College and Seminary.

Michael Woodard – High School History teacher and founder and CEO of Alpha Educational Consultants, Inc., the parent company of the Alpha Learning and Tutoring Center. (www.alphalearningandtutoring.com)

"Real" by John The Baptist
Written by John Moorer
2004 © John Moorer
Produced by Tommy Stevenson
for Reconcile Entertainment/Forerunna Music
Purchase information: www.cdbaby.com (keyword: John the Baptist) or www.johnnybap.com
Booking Information: 800-852-0921

"My Love" by Platinum Souls
written by Platinum Souls: R.Valentine (For Lord Only Publishing/ASCAP), T. Scott (Tiffany Scott Publishing/BMI)
© 2004 Platinum Souls, Inc. Records
Produced by Big Ran
From the "Created 2 Rule" CD project, Platinum Souls, Inc. Records
Purchase information: www.platinumsoulsinc.com
Booking Information: 678-698-3860

"American Dream" by Urban D., featuring Corey Red and Precise
Written by T. Kyllonen, C. Sullivan, R. Young
2005 © Fla.vor Alliance
Producer by Element for Tabernacle Musik
Taken from Urban D.'s "The Immigrant V.2"
Contact Urban D. at www.flavoralliance.com

"Pre-Paid" by Verbs, featuring Grits and Nirva Dorsaint
Written by Michael Boyer, Ric Robbins, Otto Price, Stacy Jones, Teron Carter
Produced by Incorporated Elements
© 2003 Gotee Music/Phullon Empty Music/Five E Music/COF Music (BMI) – Administered by EMI CMG Publishing. Twelve Eighteen
Music/Butter Hits Music (BMI)
Taken from Verbs "Unlocked"

Grits and Nirva Dorsaint appear courtesy of Gotee Records

"One Time" by Liquid
Written by Victor Oquendo, Stefan Moss
© 2005 Emack Music/Rita's Song Music (ASCAP). Administered by EMI CMG Publishing. Fun Attic Music (ASCAP).
Taken from Liquid's "The Badlands"

"Where Are You Going" by Grits
Written by Teron Carter, Stacy Jones, Otto Price, Dwayne Petty
© 2004 Gotee Music/Five E Music/COF Music (BMI). Administered by EMI CMG Publishing (BMI). Twelve Eighteen Music/Pettiville
Music (BMI)
Taken from Grits' "Dichotomy A"

"The Ringleader" by DJ Maj
Written by Michael Allen, Lisa Kimmey, Dave Wyatt
Produced by:
© 2003 Gotee Music/Big Shoe Music (BMI)/Paper Girl Music/Emack Music (ASCAP). Administered by EMI CMG Publishing (BMI),
Emack Music/Papergirl Music – Admin. By EMI CMG Publishing. Giddy Up Music (ASCAP).